HIGHER EDUCATION IN INDIA

About the Author

Moonis Raza, a scholar of international repute is currently Professor Emeritus of the Jawaharlal Nehru University, Naik National Fellow of the Indian Council of Social Science Research, Honorary Director of the Centre of South Asian Studies, President of the National Association of Geographers, India and President of the Indian Council of Educational Planners and Administrators. He was, until recently the Vice-Chancellor of the University of Delhi. He was earlier Professor of Geography, Centre for the Study of Regional Development, Jawaharlal Nehru University. He was also a member of the faculty of Aligarh Muslim University, and Professor and the Principal at the Regional Engineering College, Srinagar. He has been a Visiting Professor at the Cornell University. Among the distinguished posts he has held are that of the Founder Chairman of the Centre for the Study of Regional Development and Rector of the Jawaharlal Nehru University, Director of the National Institute of Educational Planning and Administration, member of the Executive Board of the Commonwealth Council of Educational Administration. He was twice the National Lecturer in Geography. He has singly and in collaboration authored and edited twenty books and contributed to numerous others besides having published a large number of research papers.

Nirmal Malhotra is the Librarian of the National Institute of Educational Planning and Administration, New Delhi. She was trained in Library and Information Science at Laughborough University of Technology U.K.

HIGHER EDUCATION IN INDIA

A COMPREHENSIVE BIBLIOGRAPHY

MOONIS RAZA
NIRMAL MALHOTRA

CONCEPT PUBLISHING COMPANY PVT. LTD.
NEW DELHI-110059

ISBN-13: 978-81-7022-346-7

Edition 2016

Published and Printed by

Concept Since 1974

Concept Publishing Company Pvt. Ltd.
A/15-16, Commercial Block, Mohan Garden
New Delhi-110059 (India)
T: 25351460, 25351794, *F*: 091-11-25357109
E: publishing@conceptpub.com, W: www.conceptpub.com
Editorial Office: H-13, Bali Nagar, New Delhi-110 015, India.

Cataloging in Publication Data--Courtesy: D.K. Agencies (P) Ltd. <docinfo@dkagencies.com>

Raza, Moonis, author.
Higher education in India : a comprehensive bibliography / Moonis Raza, Nirmal Malhotra.
pages cm
Includes indexes.
ISBN 9788170223467

1. Education, Higher--India--Bibliography. I. Malhotra, Nirmal, author. II. Title.

Z5815.I4R39 2016 DDC 016.370954 23

to
the kothari commission

. . . and there are promises to keep!

PREFACE

This is the first comprehensive bibliography of Higher Education in India. The purpose of this volume is to provide a useful resource to scholars, planners, administrators, policy makers, government officials and others concerned with higher education in India.

The bibliography is arranged alphabetically according to theme and within that theme alphabetically according to author. Entries under each theme are classified under four types of material: Books, Articles, Committee/ Commission Reports and Research Studies. The four types of material mentioned above are assigned specific alphabets throughout the bibliography as follows:

Books	A
Articles	B
Committee/Commission Reports	C
Research Studies	D

What makes this work distinctive is the fact that the Committee/Commission Reports have been annotated so that the scholars, using this work, may be able to get a general idea about the coverage and the main recommendations of the Committee/ Commission referred to.

How to locate an entry in the bibliography with the aid of these notations?

Let us take the example of a book : *Educational Planning: A Long Term Perspective*, edited by Moonis Raza, published by Concept Publishing Company of New Delhi in 1986. Since it is a book, it would acquire the alphabet A; since it deals with planning, it would acquire the number 31, allotted to planning; and its entry number is 16. Its composite indentificatory number — which is specifically its own and which it does not share with any other entry is, therefore, A-31-16.

Let us take the example of an article: Functions of Teachers in Higher Education by Moonis Raza and Marjorie Fernandes published in *Journal of Higher Education*, New Delhi and appearing in Volume 13 No. 1-3, 1987-88. p. 3-27. Since it is an article, it would acquire the alphabet B; since it deals with Teachers it would acquire the number 47 allotted to Teachers' Role and Responsibility; and its entry number is 21. Its composite indentificatory number would therefore be B-47-21.

Let us take the example of a committee/Commission Report: *Report of the Education Commission* also known as the Kothari Commission published by the Government of India in 1966. Since it is a Report, it would acquire the alphabet C; since it deals with the general aspects of higher education as a whole it would acquire the number 1 allotted to the whole spectrum; and its entry number is 016. Its composite indentificatory number would therefore be C-1-016.

Let us take the example of a Research Study: "Unfair means in university examinations: A study, conducted under the auspices of the Association of Indian Universities in 1989; the Project team consisting of V. Natarajan and Asha Arora. Since it is a Research Study, it would acquire the alphabet D; since it deals with Examinations, it would acquire the number 23, allotted to examination; and its entry number is 01. Its composite indentificatory number would therefore be D-23-01.

The following Indices are appended to facilitate researchers in their endeavour:

Author index,
Regional index, and
University Index.

A table with number of works listed under each type of material and a User's Guide to entries is appended.

As has been stated earlier this is a pioneering work — the first of its kind on Indian higher education. It is bound to have, and it has many limitations, infirmities and shortcomings. It is quite possible that some significant works have been missed and some trivial material has slipped in. We can only say in our defence that we have worked quite hard to make this volume as less incomplete as possible. But omissions are still bound to be there — may be, even some important ones. Though assessment has been kept to the minimum, no work of scholarship can claim strict "neutrality" or being entirely "value free". We can, however, claim that if some "erroneous" or "debatable" value judgments — or even some that appear to be so — have crept in, it is entirely inadvertent and in spite of our best efforts to avoid them. We requests that the inadequacies of this work may please be brought to our notice so that they may be removed in the next up-date edition which is under preparation.

We wish to state towards the end of this opening statement that the preparation of this volume has generated in us an uneasy feeling — a sense of dis-satisfaction about the imbalance in the thematic spread of studies on Indian Higher Education as well as about the preponderance of "imported" structures of thought and high clustering of "invertebrate" studies without an analytical backbone. We are, however, happy to note that the vitality of the Indian intellect and its ability to generate generalisations and distill higher order formulations from empirical reality is asserting itself. We look to the future with hope but these are miles to go!

Delhi,
1991

MOONIS RAZA
NIRMAL MALHOTRA

ACKNOWLEDGEMENT

The contribution of the following is gratefully acknowledged :-

- The Association of Indian Universities for making it possible for this volume to reach Executive Heads of Commonwealth Universities
- UNESCO, ROEAP, Bangkok: this volume being the final end product of a project originally sponsored by them
- Professor M.B. Buch and Dr. P.L. Malhotra for permitting and, infact, encouraging us to incorporate entries about research studies from *Survey of Research in Education*
- Professor Satya Bhushan, Director, National Institute of Educational Planning and Administration for his guidance and support
- Dr. G.D. Sharma for advice
- Shri Onkar Singh and B.D. Joshi for their assistance
- Shri Naurang Rai and Alok Mittal of the Concept Publishing Company for the meticulous care with which the volume has been brought out
- Library Staff of the NIEPA for their cooperation and assistance
- Mr. Satinder Singh, Librarian of the Association of Indian Universities and his colleagues for advice and support

CONTENTS

Contd.

xiv

Contd.

Number of works listed under each type of material

Theme No.	Theme	Books	Articles	Committee/ Commission Reports	Research Studies
1.	General	168	360	84	52
2.	Administration	27	76	5	9
3.	Admission	1	10	—	—
4.	Affiliated Colleges	4	12	—	7
5.	Agricultural Universities	8	15	1	2
6.	Association of Indian Universities	3	4	—	—
7.	Autonomous Colleges	7	38	1	1
8.	Autonomy	4	24	—	—
9.	Buildings	1	—	3	—
10.	Centre State Relations	4	9	—	—
11.	Community Participation	1	11	—	—
12.	Continuing Education	3	6	1	—
13.	Curriculum	3	20	25	—
14.	Distance Education	12	45	1	—
15.	Dropouts	3	5	—	2
16.	Economic Aspects	26	32	—	15
17.	Educational Psychology	3	2	—	39
18.	Educational Sociology	3	15	1	24
19.	Educational Technology	7	15	1	—
20.	Employment	58	32	1	5
21.	Enrolment	2	5	—	1
22.	Evaluation	2	30	—	—
23.	Examination Reform	21	104	14	—
24.	Finance	41	52	3	12
25.	Future	2	2	—	—
26.	Law	3	10	—	1
27.	Management	12	47	—	1
28.	Manpower Planning	10	8	—	—

Contd.

Contd.

Theme No.	Theme	Books	Articles	Committee/ Commission Reports	Research Studies
29.	National Development	6	39	—	—
30.	National Integration	3	5	2	—
31.	Planning	18	39	—	—
32.	Policy	5	24	—	—
33.	Political Aspects	11	21	—	5
34.	Private Colleges	2	5	—	—
35.	Quality and Quantity	—	7	—	—
36.	Reform	4	20	—	2
37.	Research	13	27	—	3
38.	Rural Education	8	12	1	1
39.	Scheduled Castes and Scheduled Tribes	38	20	—	15
40.	Semester System	4	8	—	4
41.	Staff Development	4	28	1	—
42.	Statistics	6	—	—	—
43.	Students	4	19	2	24
44.	Students Unrest	32	50	3	13
45.	Teacher Evaluation	1	14	—	3
46.	Teachers: Role and Responsibility	10	16	—	6
47.	Teachers: Service Conditions	8	30	2	—
48.	Teaching	7	35	—	9
49.	University Grant Commission	3	18	1	—
50.	Women	3	17	1	3
	Total	629	1443	154	259

USER'S GUIDE

BOOKS

A-31-16

- Type of Material: A
- Theme: 31
- Entry No.: 16

Moonis Raza, Education Planning: A Long Term Perspective

- Author: Moonis Raza
- Title: Education Planning: A Long Term Perspective

New Delhi, Concept

- Place: New Delhi
- Publisher: Concept

1986, 488 p.

- Year of Publication: 1986
- Pages: 488 p.

ARTICLES

B-47-21

- Type of Material: B
- Theme: 47
- Entry No.: 21

Moonis Raza and Marjorie Fernandes Functions of Teachers in Higher Education

- Author: Moonis Raza and Marjorie Fernandes
- Title: Functions of Teachers in Higher Education

Journal of Higher Education 13 (1-3) (1987-88)

- Name of the Journal: Journal of Higher Education
- Volume: 13
- Issue No: (1-3)
- Year: (1987-88)

3-27p.

- Pages: 3-27p.

COMMITTEE/COMMISSION REPORTS

Theme — Type of Material — Entry No.

C-1-016

Title

Education Commission

Year of Appointment — Place

1964, Report. Delhi,

Year

1966

Chairman

Prof. D.S. Kothari

RESEARCH STUDIES

Theme — Type of Material — Entry No.

D-23-01

Researcher — Title

V. Natrajan and Asha Arora Unfair means in University Examinations: A Study

Name of the Institution

Association of Indian Universities

Year

1989

PROLOGUE

Compiling and annotating a bibliography has been till recently considered to be a highly individualistic exercise – each scholar searching the foot–prints of his predecessors in his own way. The bibliographic notes of a scholar bore the deep imprint of his personality, carried, so to say, his signature. With the emergence of the research industry in the new world and the sprouting of Information Sciences in the old, the situation has been basically transformed. Research cards, data sets, press cuttings, computer software and bibliographies can now be purchased in a departmental store across the counter. Research has spilled over from the private and personal domain of the scholar's own intellection to the public domain of the market place. This transition may be evaluated as a mixed blessing, with both positive and negative features. It is positive if and only to the extent the researcher is able to secure research tools corresponding to rigorous specifications laid down by him with a view to facilitate his intellection and not to purchase substitute end-products in terms of market specifications as in the case of shoes or underwears. Research activity, particularly in the soft sciences, is essentially personal, and the less intrusions there are from others in the sacred realm, the better it is.

A bibliography in this sense is, at best, a sketch map depicting the trails of early explorers through the thick forests, wherein carnivores prowl, towards the ever-receding boundaries of the *terra incognita*. The trails have been laid by the footsteps of others engrossed in their own wanderings. One may like to avoid the beaten tracks in search of one's own holy grail; take a short cut, for one is tired and breathless; or make a detour to look at the sunset from a far off commanding height. Too much dependence on a published bibliography sometimes tends to push the scholar in directions of others' choosing and quite often imposes premature closure on ideas, particularly those rare ones which are specifically ones own.

Compiling a bibliography on higher education is particular hazardous. As one moves from the relatively exact nature of the hard sciences towards the ephimeral "data sets" of the humanities, from information towards knowledge and further from knowledge towards wisdom, from the once to the thrice-distilled, the subject matter of a book or a paper goes on becoming more and more rarified and elusive so that docketing and labelling it goes on becoming more and more difficult. Classificatory schemes break down; and one continues to search the black cat in a closed room on a dark night, the cat which is perhaps not there at all or perhaps is!

The compilation of a partly annotated comprehensive bibliography of Higher Education in India, like the present work, is a particularly complex and arduous task. Its complexity is a function of the chronological depth, spatial spread, structural diversity and the size of the tertiary level of education in a country of sub-continental dimensions. The difficulties have been further compounded by the unfortunate fact that unlike Narcissus who constantly gazed at himself, the universities, the world over and the Indian universities in particular have consistently shown a contradictory tendency – focussing their attention on everything else in the universe except themselves. Centres of advanced studies in Economics have refused to touch the economics of higher education with a pair of tongs. Universities with good law schools have their own statutes and ordinances in a pitiable condition. Prestigious faculties of management manage their own affairs in the style of the late 19th century. While many flourishing departments of education go on producing a plethora of studies in the much researched area of pedagogy, they generally show a complete lack of interest in the analysis of the educational sector as a sub-system of the social system, linked with the latter with every fibre of its being. While education has been marginalized in the social sciences, socio-economic analysis has been marginalized in education. Both have paid a heavy price for their complementary inadequacies.

It may, therefore, be said both with confidence and in sorrow that while the coverage of the bibliography is fairly comprehensive, the material so covered is unfortunately only good in parts. Arranging the available material in a system called for classification at two levels – at the lower level in terms of identificatory categories as well as themes and at the higher level in terms of contending issues in the debate that have been raging both within the cloisters of the academia and the corridors of power during the last four decades.

The first of these tasks in classification, which has provided the skeletal structure of the present volume, was shouldered by developing a matrix with the four type of texts in the columns and 50 themes in the rows, getting 200 cells, with 2,485 entries, quite a few of the cells being empty.

The second of these two tasks - i.e. developing a system of classification in terms of the issues of the raging debate was far more difficult. It called for value judgements on quite complex questions and became particularly hazardous because the senior member of our team of two was a participant observor in the debate and cannot (and does not!) claim to be "objective", "neutral" or "non-partisan". It is, however, obvious that such a discussion, though crucially important in the context of higher education, is beyond the purview of an introduction to a bibliography and has, therefore, to be undertaken elsewhere. It is enough in the present context to note that the nature of such a debate can be properly understood if the model used is one of contending poles of the good rather than of the good against the bad, of the progressive against the retrogressive or of the positive against the negative. Quantity and quality, equity and efficiency, utility and value, integration and differentiation, learning and teaching, transmission and generation, specialists and generalists, concentration and dispersal, autonomy and accountability, evaluation and accredition and above all "pure" academics and "involved" teachers have been contending against each other, correcting the excesses of the other and keeping the ship of higher education on even keel in the stormy seas of resurgent India.

Some of the crucial problems being faced by Indian higher education today are a function of the persistence of the chronic malady injected in the system by the colonial power and the inability of the ruling elite of independent India to uproot the poisonous weeds from academic pastures. The transformation of an essentially dysfunctional system inherited from the colonial past into a live, vibrant and multi-faceted support system for the continuing social revolution in the crucial sphere of the intellect and ideology was a highly complex process. In the long journey on the tortuous path of contemporary history, the Indian academia continued to be haunted by indigeneous ghosts of historical fears and deep-rooted prejudices, and misdirected by mirages of spurious objectives transplanted from accros the seas. The middle classes, nurtured in the amorphous work-ethic of colonial India wherein the tertiary sector had almost no links with production, demanded their pound of flesh in independent India and contributed in so small measures to the quicksands of the marshy regions in Indian academia. Fortunately, the social situation produced opposite and countervailing forces. The demands of self-reliance and import substitution in the sphere of the intellect led to the emergence and strengthening of corrective trends. What appears as directionless meanderings of educational policy in independent India should be appreciated as the operationalisation of compensatory mechanisms generated by the turbulence of the transition from under-development to development.

But there are many promises still to keep!

MOONIS RAZA
NIRMAL MALHOTRA

1. GENERAL

A BOOKS

001 Adiseshiah, Malcolm S. *Backdrop to the learning society: The development of education in Tamil Nadu*, 1976-86. Madras, Institute of Development Studies, 1978.

002 ——. *Remoulding Indian higher education*. New Delhi, India International Centre 1982, 13p.

003 ——. *University in 1975*. Madras, Avvai Achukkoodam, 1976, 36p.

004 Aggarwal, J.C. *National Commission on Teacher I — School Teachers and the National Commission on Teachers II — Higher Education, 1983-1985: Major Recommendations*. Delhi, Doaba House, 1988. 64p.

005 Airan, J.W. *Climbing a wall of glass: Aspects of educational reform in India*. Bombay, Manaktala, 1965. 176p.

006 ——. *Educational reform of India* by J.W. Airan, J. Barnhas and A.B. Shah. Ajmer, Sachin, 1979, 176p.

007 ——. ed. *College education in India*. Ajmer, Sachin, 1979. 226p.

008 Aiyer, C.P.R. *Indian universities: Retrospect and prospects*. Annamalai, Annamalai University, 1964.

009 Altbach, P.G. "Higher education in India". In Barbara Burn et al., *Higher education in nine countries*. New York. McGraw-Hill, 1971, pp.317-344.

010 ——. "India and the world university crisis". *In* P. Altbach, ed. *Student revolution: A global analysis*. Bombay, Lalvani, 1970. pp.1-26.

011 ——. *University in transition: An Indian case study*. Cambridge, Sachenkman, 1972. 136p.

012 Amrik Singh, ed. *Higher learning in India*. Delhi, Vikas, 1974. 415p.

013 ——, Sharma, G.D. eds. *Higher education in India: Institutional context*. Delhi, Konark, 1989. 364p.

014 Amrik Singh, Sharma, G.D., eds. *Higher education in India: The social context*. Delhi, Konark, 1988. 339p.

015 Amrik Singh, *Redeeming higher education: Essays in educational policy*. Delhi, Ajanta, 1985. 299p.

016 Anderson, George. *Christian higher education in India*. London, Macmillan, 1932.

017 Apte, D.C. *Universities in ancient India*. Baroda, Faculty of Education and Psychology, Maharaja Sayajirao University of Baroda, 1917.

018 Ashby, E. *Universities: British, Indian, African – A study in the ecology of higher education*. London, Nicolson and Weidenfield, 1966. 558p.

019 *AIU Handbook*. New Delhi. AIU, 1986. 81p.

020 Association of Indian Universities (AIU). *Higher education and development*, 1975.

021 ——. *Preparations made by universities to receive 10+2+3*. New Delhi. A.I.U., 1979. 104p.

022 ——. *Three aspects of university education*. New Delhi, A.I.U., n.d. 206p.

023 Banerjee, P.N., ed. *Hundreds years of the University of Calcutta*. Calcutta, Calcutta University, 1957.

024 Barnabas, Thomas. *Profile of a ·ollege: A self study of Ahmednager College. Bombay,* Nachiketa Pub., 1972. 247p.

025 Basu, A. *Growth of education and political development in India, 1989-1920*. New Delhi, Oxford University Press, 1974. 258p.

026 Basu, A.N. *University education in India: Past and present*. Calcutta, Book Emporium, 1944.

027 Bhandarkar, S.S. *Association of Indian Universities: A short history, 1925-75*. New Delhi, A.I.U., 1975. 227p.

028 ——. *Association of Indian Universities 1925-85*. New Delhi, A.I.U., 1985. 258p.

029 Bhatnagar, S.K. *History of the M.A.O. College, Aligarh*. Aligarh, Asia Publishing House, 1969. 372p.

030 Bose, Anima. *Higher education in India in the 19th century: The American involvement, 1883-1893*. Calcutta, Punthi Pustak, 1978. 411p.

031 Bose, P.K. *Calcutta university: Some problems and their remedies*. Calcutta, University of Calcutta, 1973. 113p.

032 Bose, P.K. *Higher education at cross roads*. Calcutta, World Press, 1977. 109p.

033 ——. *Role of universities in post-experience higher education: A case study of Calcutta University.* Calcutta, Calcutta University, 1975. 40p.

034 ——. *Working conditions of colleges affiliated to the university of Calcutta during 1962-63: An educational survey* by P.K. Bose, P.K. Banerjee and S.P. Mukherjee. Calcutta, Department of Statistics, Calcutta University, n.d. 43p.

035 Butler, L. *Survival depends on higher education.* New Delhi, Indian Council for Cultural Relations, 1971. 42p.

036 *Burdwan University: A review of the progress of the University, 1960-61 to 1973-74.* Burdwan, Burdwan University, n.d. 284p. (Mimeographed).

037 Chandola, A.C. "Challenge to higher education in India". *In* F. Robert Paulsen, ed. *Changing dimension in international education.* Tucson, University of Arzona Press, 1969. pp.121-36.

038 Chatterji, G.C. *et al. My idea of a university: A symposium.* Delhi, Manager of Publications, 1957.

039 Chaube, S.P. *Survey of educational problems and experiment in India.* Allahabad, Kitab Mahal, 1965.

040 Chitnis, Suma, ed. *Indian academic profession* ed. by Suma Chitnis and Philip G. Altbach. Delhi, Macmillan, 1979. 192p.

041 *Christian College in India.* London, Oxford University Press, 1931.

042 Cormack, Margaret L. *She who rides a peacock: Indian students and social change — a research analysis.* Bombay, Asia Publishing House, 1961. 264p.

043 Dar, S.L. *Banaras Hindu University agitation of 1958.* Banaras, University Press, 1958. 149p.

044 Das, Sisir Kumar. *Sahibs and munshis: An account of the college of Fort William.* Calcutta, Orion Pub., 1978. 192p.

045 Dash, S.C. *Problems of higher education.* Cuttack, Santosh Pub., 1976. 59p.

046 Desai, D.M. *Some critical issues of higher education in India.* Bombay, A.R. Sheth, 1970.

047 Desai, D.M. and Saraswati, S.P. *Growth and development of Maharaja Sayajirao University of Baroda, 1949-1967.* Baroda, Department of Educational Administration, Maharaja Sayajirao University of Baroda, 1968.

048 Deshmukh, C.D. *In the portals of Indian universities.* New Delhi, University Grants Commission, 1959. 336p.

049 ——. *On the threshold of India's citizenhood.* New Delhi, University Grants Commission, 1962. 392p.

050 DiBona, Joseph. *Change and conflict in the Indian university.* Bombay, Lalvani, 1972.

051 ——. "Modernization and parochialization in Indian higher education: The role of the university in facilitating rural-urban mobility". *In* R. Fox, ed. *Urban India: Society, space, and image.* Durham, North Carolina, Dunke University program in Comparative studies on Southern Asia, 1970. pp.77-90.

052 Dickinson, R.D.N. *Christian college in developing India: A sociological inquiry.* Madras, Oxford University Press, 1971. 370p.

053 Dongerkery, S.R. *History of the university of Bombay, 1857-1957.* Bombay, University of Bombay, 1957. 313p.

054 ——. *Memories of two universities.* Bombay, Manaktalas, 1966. 276p.

055 ——. *Thoughts on university education.* Bombay, Popular Book Depot, 1955.

056 ——. *Universities and national life.* Bombay, Hind Kitabs, 1950.

057 ——. *Universities and their problems.* Bombay, Hind Kitab, 1948.

058 ——. "Universities of India". *In Commonwealth universities yearbook, 1969.* London, Association of Commonwealth Universities, 1969. pp.1635-1661.

059 ——. *University education in India.* Bombay. Manaktalas, 1967.

060 Gandhi, Kishore. *Issues and choices in higher education: A sociological analysis.* Delhi, B.R. Pub., 1977. 195p.

061 Gandhi, M.K. *My view on education* by Anand T. Hingorani. Bombay, Bharatiya Vidya Bhavan, 1970.

062 Gaudino, Robert L. *Indian university.* Bombay. Popular Prakashan, 1965. 268p.

063 Gautam, G.S. *Crisis in the temples of learning.* New Delhi, S. Chand, 1972. 136p.

064 Ghosh, D.K. *University system in India.* Jabalpur, Rahul Pub., 1983. 474p.

065 Ghosh, J. *Higher education in Bengal under British rule.* Calcutta, The Book Co., 1926.

066 Ghosh, Suresh Chandra ed. *Development of university education, 1916-1920.* New Delhi, Zakir Husain Centre for Educational Studies, J.N.U., 1977. 394p. (Selections from Educational Records, Vol. 2).

067 Gokak, Vinayak Krishna. *Indian higher education*. Bangalore, IBH, 1981. 191p.

068 Gopinath, P.R. and Ajit D. *Parallel Colleges in Kerala: A case study of their structure in terms of enrolment costs and employment*. Trivendarum, Centre for Development Studies, 1983. 38p. (Working paper, 156).

069 Gore, M.S. "Crisis in university education". *In* T.K.N. Unnithan, *et al. Towards a sociology of culture in India*. New Delhi. Prentice-Hall of India, 1965. pp.339-51.

070 Govind, Vijal. *Higher education in India: Bibliography*. New Delhi, Ess Ess, 1978. 229p.

071 Grimshaw, Allen D. "National goals, planned social change, and higher education: The Indian case". *In* Feldmesser, R.A. and Sobel, B.Z. eds. *Education and social change: A comparative view*. New York, Wiley, n.d.

072 Gupta, S.S. *A.M.U., the national context*. Aligarh, Viveka Publications, 1980. 168p.

073 Hart, H.C. *Campus India: An appraisal of American College programs in India*. Michigan, University Press, 1961. 217p.

074 Haggerty, W. *Higher and professional education in India*. Washington, D.C., U.S. Department of Health Education, and Welfare, 1969.

075 *Higher Education in South India, University of Madras, 1857-1957*. Madras, University of Madras 1957.

076 Hudson, Y. *Profile of a college*. Bombay, Nachiketa, 1972.

077 Husain, Zakir, *Dynamic university*. Bombay, Asia Publishing House, 1965. 119p.

078 India, Bureau of Education. *Education in universities in India*. Delhi, Manager of Publications, 1948.

079 Iyengar, K.R.S. *Mainly academic: Talks to students and teachers*. Bombay, Asia Publishing House, 1968. 304p.

080 ——. New deal for our universities. Calcutta, Longmans, 1951.

081 James, H.R. *Problems of higher education in India*. Bombay, Longmans, 1916.

082 Jayaram, N. *Higher education and status retention*. Delhi, Mittal, 1987. 193p.

083 John, V.V. *Great classroom hoax and other reflections on India's education*. New Delhi, Vikas, 1978. 229p.

084 ——. *Misadventures in higher education*. New Delhi, Young Asia, 1973. 253p.

085 Joshi, K.L. *Higher education: Historical and other problems.* Bombay, Popular, 1981. 143p.

086 ——. *Notes on university education.* Bombay, Popular Book Depot, 1941.

087 ——. *Problems of higher education in India.* Bombay, Popular, 1977. 312p.

088 Joshi, Navin Chandra. *Perspectives on higher education: Critical issues analysed.* New Delhi, Ashish, 1978. 110p.

089 Kamalavijayan, D. *Problems of higher education in India: An annotated bibliography of source material.* New Delhi, Indian Documentation Service, 1979. xxii, 116p.

090 Kanvinde, A. and Miller, H.J. *Campus design in India: Experience of a developing nation.* Topeka, Kansas, Fostens/American Yearbook Company, 1969.

091 Kapur, J.N. *Current issues in higher education in India.* New Delhi, S. Chand, 1975. viii, 248p.

092 Kaul, J.N. *Higher education in India, 1951-71.* Simla, Indian Institute of Advanced Study, 1974. 203p.

093 ——. *Higher education, social change, and national development.* Simla, Indian Institute of Advanced Study, 1975. 232p.

094 Kopf, D. *British orientation and the Bengal renaissance.* Berkeley, University of California Press, 1969.

095 Kothari, D.S. *Education on surges: Teaching linked to need.* New Delhi, U.G.C., 1968.

096 ——. *Education, science, and national development.* London, Asian Publishing House, 1970.

097 ——. *Science and Universities.* New Delhi, U.G.C., 1965.

098 ——. *Some aspects of university education: Report of vice-chancellors' conference, 1962.* New Delhi, University Grants Commission, 1962.

099 Lelvyveld, David. *Aligarh's first generation.* New Delhi, Oxford, 1978. 380p.

100 Lulla, B.P. and Murty, S.K. *Essential problems of Indian Education.* Agra, Lakshmi Narain Agarwal, 1971.

101 McCully, B.T. *English education and the origin of Indian nationalism.* New York, Columbia University Press, 1940.

102 Madan Mohan. *Problems of university education in India: A memoir.* Meerut, Meenakshi, 1972. 187p.

103 Magal, Ramachandra. *Structure of higher education in India.* New Delhi, USEFI, 1974. 30p.

104 Mahajani, G.S. *My six years in University: University of Rajasthan.* Jaipur, Rajasthan University, 1982.

105 Mansukhani, G.S., ed. *Crisis in Indian universities.* New Delhi, Oxford, 1972. 211p.

106 Mathai, S. *Indian universities.* New Delhi, Ministry of Education, 1956.

107 ——. "Universities of India." *In Commonwealth Universities Yearbook, 1973.* London, Association of Commonwealth Universities, 1973. p. 1171-178.

108 Mathur, M.V. *Task of universities in India.* New Delhi, Asian Institute of Educational Planning and Administration, 1971. 30p.

109 Mayhew, A. *Education of India: A study of British educational policy in India, 1835-1920.* 2nd ed. London, Faber & Gurier, 1928.

110 Menon, K.R. *Higher education in India.* Geneva, World University Service, 1950.

111 Misra, D.K., ed. *Youth university and community.* New Delhi, S. Chand & Co., 1976.

112 Mukherjee, H. and Mukerjee, U. *Origins of the national education movement, 1905-1910.* Calcutta, Jadavpur University, 1957.

113 Mukerjee, K.C. *Comparative study of some educational problems.* Bombay, Lalvani, 1972.

114 ——. "Indian universities." *In* B. Holmes and D. Scanlon, eds. *Higher education in a changing world.* New York, HarCourt Brace Jovanovich, 1971 pp. 367-83.

115 Murty, K.S. *General education reconsidered.* New York, Asia Publishing House, 1963. 132p.

116 Murthy, V. Rama. *Restructuring the university.* New Delhi, Sterling, 1977. 90p.

117 Naik, J.P. *Access, structure and quality in higher education: Some suggestions for reorganization.* Prasarnagar. University of Mysore. 1972. iii, 30p. (Princess Lilavathi Memorial Lectures).

118 ——. *Development of university education, 1860-87.* Delhi, Manager of Publications, 1963.

119 Nair, K.R.R. *Emerging spectrum essays on Indian higher education.* Bombay, Himalaya, 1986. 115p.

120 National *Council of Educational Research and Training Educational investigations in Indian universities,* 1939-61. New Delhi, 1966. 286p.

121 Padmavathi, P., Comp. *Directory of Indian higher educational institutions*. Hyderabad, Panchayat Publishers, 1970.

122 Parikh, G.D. *General education and Indian universities*. London, Asia Pub., 1959. 203p.

123 Raghavaiah, Y. *Contemporary issues in higher education*. Hyderabad, Osmania, 1979. 156p.

124 Raj, K.N. *Crisis of higher education in India*. New Delhi, Publications, 1971. (Patel Memorial Lectures, 1970). 12p.

125 Rajasthan. Directorate of College Education. *Higher education in Rajasthan, 1976-77*. Jaipur, the author, 1976. 34p.

126 Ramachandran, C.M. *Problems of higher education in India: A case study*. Delhi, Mittal, 1987. 263p.

127 Rao, K. *Higher education in India and abroad*. Guntur, K. Narshimha Rao, 1974.

128 Raza, Moonis, Aggarwal, Y.P. and Hasan, M. *Higher Education in India — A survey*. New Delhi, National Institute of Educational Planning and Administration, 1984: 154p. (Research Studies NCT-II).

129 Raza, Moonis. *Higher education in India: The regional dimension*. New Delhi, NIEPA, 1984. 52p. (NIEPA Occasional paper-7).

130 Reddy, D.J. *Challenges in higher education*. Tirupati, Sri Venkateswara University, 1972.

131 ——. *Issues in higher education*. Madras, Seshachalam, 1973.

132 Roy, B. *U.S. infiltration in Indian education*. New Delhi, Perspective Publications, 1973.

133 Saiyidain, K.G. and Gupta, H.C. *Access to higher education in India*. New Delhi, UNESCO, 1962.

134 Saiyidain, K.G. *Facets of Indian education*. New Delhi, National Council of Educational Research and Training, 1970.

135 ——. *Indian universities and higher education*. Bombay, Asia Publishing House, 1967, 109p.

136 —— and Dawood, A.R. "Relationship between secondary schools and universities–India". *In* G. Bereday and J. Lauwerys, eds. *Yearbook of Education, 1959*. London, Evans, 1959. pp.489-93.

137 ——. *Universities and the life of the mind*. Bombay, Asia Publishing House, 1965. 236p.

138 Sankalia, H.D. *University of Nalanda*. Delhi, Oriental, 1972. 297p.

139 Sarkar, Jagdish Narayan. *History of the Patna College, 1863-1963*. Patna, Patna College, 1963. 182p.

140 Saxena, Shakuntala. *Education as an academic study*. Bombay, Asia, 1971. 121p.
141 Seshadri, P. *Universities of India*. London, Humphery Milford, 1935.
142 Sethi, J.D. *Crisis and collapse of higher education in India*. New Delhi, Vikas, 1983. 255p.
143 Sethi, R.R. and Mehta, J.L. *History of the Panjab University, Chandigarh, 1947-67*. Chandigarh, Panjab University, 1968. 441p.
144 Shah, A.B., ed. *Education, scientific policy and developing societies*. Bombay, Manaktalas, 1967. 506p.
145 ——. *Higher education in India*. Bombay, Lalvani Publishing House, 1967. 237p.
146 Sharma, G.D. *Elite in the making*. New Delhi, A.I.U. 1986. 163p.
147 Sharma, R.M., ed. *First decade, 1970-80*. Haryana Agriculture University. Hissar. Haryana Agricultural University, 1980. 184p.
148 Sharma, S.L. *Modernizing effects of university education*. New Delhi, Allied, 1979. 236p.
149 Shils, E. "Modernization and higher education". *In* Myron Weiner, ed. *Modernization*. New York, Basic Books, 1966. pp.81-97.
150 Shukla, S. *University in Indian society*. Delhi, Central Institute of Education, 1960.
151 Singh, R.K. *Our universities and our vice-chancellors*. Agra, The Educational Press, 1950. 160p.
152 Sinha, P.R.R., ed. *Studies in extension education*. Hyderabad, National Institute of Community Development, 1972.
153 Srinivasa Iyengar, K. *New deal for our universities*. Calcutta, Orient Longmans, 1951.
154 Srivastava, Anand P. *Pathology of higher education*. Kanpur, Reprint Pub., 1979. 294p.
155 Sundaram, V.A., ed. *Banaras Hindu University, 1905 to 1935*. Banaras, Tara Printing Work, 1936.
156 Suri, M. Shahnaz. *American influence on higher education in India*. New Delhi, Sterling, 1979. 88p.
157 Thomas, T.M. *Indian educational reform in cultural perspective*. Delhi, S. Chand, 1970. 312p.
158 Tickoo, Champa, *Indian universities: A historical comparative perspective*. Bombay, Orient, 1980. 197p.
159 University Grants Commission. *Development programmes*. New Delhi, U.G.C., 1964. 31p.

160 ——. *Handbook of information on college of humanities and social sciences improvement programme (COHSSIP)*, New Delhi, U.G.C., 1983. 11p.

161 ——. *List of degrees specified for purposes of section 22 of the University Grants Commission Act, 1956*. New Delhi, U.G.C. 1989. 15p.

162 ——. *Report on general education*. New Delhi, UGC., 1961.

163 University of Calcutta. *Hundred years of the University of Calcutta: A history of the university*. Calcutta, University of Calcutta, 1957. 539p.

164 Vaidyanathan, P.S. *University of Madras: A record of twenty-five years, 1942-1967*. Madras, The Central Art Press, n.d. 71p.

165 Vaidyanathan, R. *Development of universities in India. 1857-1970*. Toronto, Ryerson Polytechnical Institute, 1972.

166 Veera Raghavan, J. *Higher education in the eighties: Opportunities and objectives*. Delhi, Lancer International, 1985. 286p.

167 Veera Raghavan, J. "Higher education and development" *In Higher educational development*. Association of Indian university, 1975.

168 Wilson College, Bombay. *Problems that challenge us: Our perspectives on Indian higher education*. Bombay, Popular Book Depot, 1963.

B ARTICLES

001 Abdul Kareem, S. Excellence and relevance in education. *University News*. 26 (16), 1988. p.1-4, 9.

002 Abraham, A.S. Government sets out to reorganize universities. *Times Higher Education Supplement*. 9 May, 1980. p.8.

003 ——. India prepares for student increase. *Times Higher Education Supplement*. 6 June, 1980, p.6.

004 ——. A stimulant for India's intellectuals. *Times Higher Education Supplement*. 11, February, 1983. p.8.

005 Abraham, Kashy. Higher education in the State of Kerala. *New Frontiers in Educatiton*. 1 (1), May, 1971. p. 78-81.

006 Abraham, Ninan, Our 'peripheral' universities. *University News*.19(3), 1981. p.72-73.

007 Adiseshiah, Malcolm S. University to be a university. *University News*. 25(50) 1987. p.3-5, 46.

008 Ahmed, Rais, Perspectives in higher education. *University News*. 15 June, 1981. p.345-350.

009 ——. Universities: Perspectives and problems. *Journal of Higher Education.* 7 (3), 1982.

010 Alavi, S.M. Ziauddin. Our universities today. *Education India.* 41(5), 1974. p.105-107.

011 Ali, Asgher. Trouble at Aligarh Muslim University: A report. *Economic and Political Weekly.* 15 August, 1981. p. 1340-42.

012 Ali, Syed Mahmood. Baftling task of educational reconstruction in India. *University News.* 9(11), 1971. p.12-15.

013 Altbach. P.G. Bombay colleges. *Minerva.* 8, October, 1970 p. 520-41.

014 ——. Permanent crisis of Indian higher education. *Quest.* January-March, 1969. p.28-43.

015 ——. Problems of university reform in India. *Comparative Education Review.* 16 June, 1972. p.252-66.

016 ——. University crisis in India. *Change.* (6), April, 1974. p.20-21.

017 Amrik Singh. Baby sitting years. *Seminar.* (296) 1984. p.29-33.

018 ——. Education commission and after. *Asian Survey.* 9, October, 1969. p.734-741.

019 ——. Higher Education. Andhra experiment. *Hindustan Times.* 16.5.89. p.11.

020 ——. Higher education in India. Problems and perspectives. *University News.* 10 (12), 1972. p.22-28.

021 ——. Higher education in the seventies. *Quest.* (72), September-October, 1971. p.71-81.

022 ——. Industry growth and the role of universities. *Journal of University Education.* 3 December, 1964. p.95-104.

023 ——. Parliament versus universities. *University News.* 20 (22), 1982. p.690-691.

024 ——. Problems of post-graduate education. *University News.* 13 (11), 1975. p.7-10.

025 ——. Problems of small colleges in Punjab. *University News.* 15 (16), 1977 p. 431 and 433.

026 ——. The mess that is education. *University News.* 15 (20), 1977. p.547-550.

027 Anand, Mulk Raj. Plea for higher education. *Quest.* (57), April-June, 1968. p.30-40.

028 Apparow, M.R. New pattern of education: A case for four year integrated under-graduate and post-graduate courses. *University News.* 14 (15), 1976. p.4 and 30.

029 ——. Role of higher education in the process of development and change. *University News.* 17 (9), 1979. p.238.

030 Apte, B.P. Colleges and post-graduate teaching. *University News.* 10 (3), 1972. p.16-17.

031 Attack on higher education. Editorial. *Educational Review.* Vol. 56 (9), September 1950. p.185.

032 Azad, J.L. Higher education in India: A dimensional Analysis. *University Administration.* (1), June-July, 1974. p.1-22.

033 Bahadur, R.P. Indian universities in welfare state. *Indian Journal of Economics.* 36, April, 1956. p.387-408.

034 Balachander, K.K. Higher education in India: The shifting perspectives — I, II, III. *University News.* 26 (12-14), 1988. pp.1-4, 1-5, 5-9.

035 ——. Information base of higher education in India. *University News.* 24 (30), 1986. p.1-5.

036 Balan, K.R. Meaningful guidance to students. *University News.* 17 (17), 1979. p.455.

037 Banerjee, Syamelendu, Crisis in university education. *Capital.* (Annual volume), 1974. p.109-113.

038 Bandopadhyay, R. Linking universities with environment: Issues relating to internal management and structure. *University News.* 17 (10), 1979. p.263-43.

039 Banerji, S.K. What ails centres of higher learning. *University News.* 20 (2), 1982. p.42-43.

040 Basanna, H. Role of private managements in higher education in Karnataka. *Southern Economist.* 20 (13), 1981. p. 35-36.

041 Bhagwati, N.H. Some problems of university education. *Education India.* 17 (3), September, 1950. p.81-86.

042 Bhalerao, C.N. Some major tasks. *University News.* 13(2), 1975. p.5-6.

043 Bhanadarkar, S.S. University bodies and their role, *University News.* 7(4), 1968. p.18-20.

044 ——. The colleges of tomorrow. *University News.* 5 (4), 1967. p.3-5.

045 Bharati, Jai Prakash. Concept of a children's university: An academic innovation. *University News.* 25 (45), 1987. p.7-8.

046 Bhatia, L.D. Higher education: The problem of number. *University News.* 16 (8), 1978. p.879 and 899.

047 Bhatt, S.S. Need for improvement in university education. *University News.* 8 (12), 1970. p.16-17.

048 Bhatnagar, K.N. The University of Allahabad : A perspective. *University News*. 227 (9), 1989. p. 4-8.

049 Bhattacharyya, Nirmal Chandra. University education in India. *Journal of Education*. 4 (1), September-November, 1956. p.17-30.

050 Bhiday, M.R. Integration of higher education for effective vocational training. *Journal of Higher Education*. 5 (3), Spring, 1980. p.371-379.

051 Bhogle, A.D. Challenge to Indian science. *University News*. 7 (1), 1969. p.3-5.

052 Biswas, Dalip K. Maladies and remedies in college education. *Journal of Education*. 4 (3-4), March-August, 1957. p.131-36.

053 Bullayya, L. Is the junior college an anomaly? *University News*. 9 (12), 1971. p.15-18.

054 Board discusses. Problems of urgent academic importance. *University News*. 7 (2), 1969. p.14.

055 Carrier, Herve. Role of the university in the new society. *New Frontiers in Education*. 5 (1), January-March, 1975. p.1-12.

056 Chacko, P.C. Kerala Private colleges' crisis: The compromise and after. *New Frontiers in Education*. 2, December, 1972. p. 90-94.

057 Chaitanya. Outlook for the seventies: Relevance of higher education in India. *Education Quarterly*. 22 (3), October, 1970. p.31-34.

058 Chitra, M.N. Higher education and society in Mysore under British rule. *Sociological Bulletin*. 21, September, 1972. p. 91-102.

059 Chakrabarty, Mohindra Mohan. Higher education in times of crisis. *Journal of Education*. 10 (2), December, 1962 — February, 1963. p.39-44.

060 Chaudhari, U.S. University and imagination. *University News*. 21 (23), 1983. p.833-837.

061 Chandi, P.T. Christian higher education in India. *Christian Scholar*. 41, Autumn, 1958. p.246-53.

062 Changing university. *Education Quarterly*. 14 December, 1962. p.214-30.

063 Chari, M.S.V. Higher education. *Educational India*. 39(10), April, 1973. p.274-275.

064 ——. Some problems of education. *Education*. 42(9), September, 1963. p.5-7.

065 Christian College in India: A consultation. *University News*. 15(2), 1967. p.1-2.

066 Chitnis, S. Urban Concentration of higher education. *Economic and Political Weekly.* 4, July, 1969.

067 Closure of Banaras University. Editorial. *Educational India.* 25 (5), Novermber, 1958. p. 163-65.

068 College teaching in India. *University News.* 17(24), 1979. p.635-637.

069 Colleges to award degress : Move in Delhi varsity. *University News.* 4 (8), 1966 p. 1-2.

070 Collegiate education. *Educational India.* 37(3), September, 1970. p.96-97.

071 Collegiate education in Andhra Pradesh. *Educational India.* September, 1970. p. 96-97.

072 Consultation on higher education and social justice. *New Frontiers in Education.* 4(3), July-September, 1974. p.89-99.

073 Damle, P.R. Problem of higher education in western India. *Progress of Education.* 40 (3), October, 1965. p. 92-97.

074 Das, Mamota, Higher education for all. *University News.* 27 (37), 1989. p.1-3 and 9.

075 Dasgupta, A.K. On higher education in India. *Economic and Political Weekly.* 2-9 June, 1984. p.888.

076 Datta, Bhabatosh. Presidency college, Calcutta. *Journal of Higher Education.* 4 (2), Autumn, 1978. p. 145-56.

077 De, Barun. The heritage of our educational framework. *Journal of Higher Education.* 14(1-3), 1988-89. p.1-17.

078 Delhi varsity development schemes. *University News.* 8 (6), 1970.

079 Deshmukh, C.D. Students, values and the world of tomorrow. *University News.* 4(12), 1966. p.3-5.

080 Desai, D.A. Whither higher education? *Mainstream.* 23(22), 1985. pp.27-29.

081 Desai, Dhanwant M. Study of some aspects of standards of university education in the Gujarat State. *Education and Psychology Reviews.* 7 (2), April, 1967. p. 79-85.

082 Development plan of Mithila University. *University News.* 12 (11), 1974. pp. 12-14.

083 Dinesh Mohan, Travails of higher education: More graduates not the answer. *University News.* 22(44), 1984. p.4-5.

084 Disturbance at the Banaras Hindu University. *Minerva.* 4, Spring. 1966. p. 429-33.

085 Dubey, S.M. Problems of higher education : Role of hill university. *University News.* 12 (4), 1974. p. 8-10.

086 Dutt, Kalyannath. Higher education in West Bengal. *New Quest.* January-February, 1981. p. 48-50.

087 Flathee, Paul, Challenge that was not met. *The Times Higher Education Supplement.* 29-1-1988. p.v.

088 Flather, Paul. Dangers of elitism in 'the sahibs' college. *Times Higher Education Supplement.* 6 March, 1981. p. 8.

089 Ghanchi, D.A. Conflict in higher education: The Indian scenario. *University News.* 27(25), 1989. p.1-5.

090 ——. Perstroika in Indian higher education. *University News.* 36 (30), 1988. p.3-4, 8.

091 ——. The soft state of Indian higher education. *University News.* 27(14), 1989. p.1-4.

092 ——. Three myths of Indian higher education. *University News.* 27 (14), 1989. pp.1-5.

093 Ghodkc, N.B. Corrective measures in the field of higher education. *University News.* 22 (46), 1984. p.41.

094 Ghose, Sisir Kumar. Higher education. What's wrong with it? *Statesman.* 1 July, 1977. p.6.

095 Ghosh, A.K. University Education in Bihar. *University News.* 26 (26), 1988. p. 1-5.

096 Ghosh, D.K. Changing character of universities in India. *University News.* 12 (9), 1974. p.10-11.

097 ——. Coordinating the varsities. *University News.* 13(7), 1975. p.1, 11.

098 Ghosh, Mriganka Nath. Universalising the university. *Indian Education.* 3(3), February, 1964. p.27-30.

099 Giles, M. Higher education in the states : Mysore. *New Frontiers in Education.* I, August, 1971. p. 182-96.

100 Giri, V.V. University students and their responsibilities. *Educational Forum.* 13(1), January, 1968. p.1-7.

101 Goel, B.S. Changing functional character and organisation of Indian university. 1905-29. *Paedagogica Historica.* 14 (1), 1974. p.34-63.

102 Goel, S.C. Issues and options in higher education. *University News.* 19(18), 1981. p.501-504 and 506.

103 Gogoi, D.K. Students and mass education. *University News.* 25 (38), 1987. p.6-7.

104 Gokak, V.K. universities and the individual. *Journal of University Education.* 1(1), September, 1962. p.26-32.

105 Gore, M.S. Obstacles to creativity in higher education. *University News*. 23(10), 1985. p.5-8.

106 ——. The education explosion. *University News*. 23 (28), 1985. p.9-14.

107 Grimshaw, Allen D. University education in India: A trans-Atlantic view. *Journal of University Education*. 2(1), September, 1963. p.7-18.

108 Gupta, L.N. University education in India. *Educational Review*. 70(11), November, 1964. p.261-264.

109 Gupta, S.K. Distance education – problems of co-ordination, Cooperation and functional autonomy. *Journal of Higher Education*. 7(3), 1982, 1982. p.237-242.

110 Gupta, S.P. Conceptualizing higher education as a system. *Progress of Education*. 59(12), 1985. p.260-65+.

111 Harper, A. Edwin. Education for what? *Journal of University Education*. 5(1), September, 1966. p.7-12.

112 Hartog, P.J. Work of the Calcutta University Commission. *Asiatic Review*. Vol. 16, October, 1920. p. 597-608.

113 Heredia, Rudolf C. Modernity, rationality and higher education. *Economic and Political Weekly*. 15(20), May, 1980. p.885-886.

114 ——. Structure and performance of college education in India: An organisational analysis of arts and science colleges in Bombay. *New Frontiers in Education*. 10(2), April-June, 1980. p.20-33.

115 Higher education and the new context. *Journal of Higher Education*. 3(1), 1977. p.1-3.

116 Higher education in India. *Bulletin of the Unesco Regional Office for Education in Asia*. 7, September, 1972. p.46-63.

117 Higher education in Parliament. *University News*. 3(2), 1965. p.12.

118 ——. *University News*. 4(4), 1966. 12.

119 ——. *University News*. 4(5), 1966. p.12.

120 ——. *University News*. 4(6), 1966. p.14.

121 ——. *University News*. 4(9), 1966. p.12-13.

122 ——. *University News*. 4(10), 1966. p.14-15.

123 ——. *University News*. 4(12), 1966. p.12-13

124 ——. *University News*. 5(7), 1967. p.6-7.

125 Higher education: Objectives and improvement: Report of Education Commission 1966. *University News*. 6(7), pp.I-XVI.

126 Higher education today. *Educational India*. 16(7), p.192-95.

127 Hingorani, D.K. Higher education in India: Recent development. *Higher Education*. II, February, 1955. p.77-85.

128 Hogie, H. Exportation of ideas, men and materials : The case of Baroda, India. *Viewpoints*. 47, Sptember, 1971. p. 153-90.

129 Hooja, G.B.K. Mobility of teachers an students in the university system. *University News*. 26 (28), 1988. p.6-7.

130 ——. Population education and the Indian university system. *University News*. 26 (36).

131 Hua, Z.Y. Some steps on the reform in higher education. *University News*. 1985. 23 (15), p.4-5.

132 Indian university reform. Higher education: Objectives and improvement. *Minerva*. 5, Autumn, 1966. p.47-81.

133 Indian University reform IV: Science education and research. *Minerva*. 6, Autumn, 1967. p.48-80.

134 India's crisis and challenge. *Times Higher Education Supplement*. 27 February, 1981. p.31.

135 Intellectual aspects of higher education. 6 (9), 1968. p.14-17.

136 Israney, S.M. Pricing higher education. *University News*. 27(8), 1989. p.1-3.

137 ——. Participation in higher education. *University News*. 26 (31), 1988. p.21-23.

138 Issues in higher education: What students, parents and teachers say. *University News*. 5 (6), 1967. p.1-2.

139 Iyengar, R. Srinivasa. General education in college. *Educational India*. 21 (2), August, 1954. p.44-46.

140 ——. Pre-university course. *Educational Review*. 61 (10), October, 1955. p.197.

141 Jacob, Plamthogthil S. Remedial approach in college education. *New Frontiers in Education*. II (14), October-December, 1981. p.15-27.

142 ——. Learning through participation. *New Frontiers in Education*. 1, May, 1971. p.29-46.

143 Jan Mohamad. Higher education and its future. *University News*. 21 (16), August, 1983. p.511-14.

144 Jesdenwala, Z. Educational aspects of development. *New Frontiers in Education*. 1, May, 1971. p.24-28.

145 John, E.J. Priorities in higher learning. *The Hindu*. 26-4-88. p.19.

146 John. V.V. and Dastur, A.J. AMU once again. *New Quest*. March-April. 1980. p. 97-99.

147 John, V.V. Crisis of higher education - Some problems and solutions. *University News*. 19 (16), 1981, p.442-445.

148 ——. Higher education in the seventies : Crisis and hope. New Frontiers in Education. 3 (1), 1973. p.1-10.

149 ——. Rising by degrees. *Sunday Standard.* 25 September, 1977. p.11.

150 ——. Towards a meaningful first degree. *Journal of Higher Education.* 1 (1), 1975. p.51-60.

151 John, V.V. University for Goa. *University News.* 16 (2), 1978. p. 707-08.

152 Joshi, Dinesh Chandra. Role of an academic in higher education. *University News.* 22 (34), 1984. p.2-4 and 6.

153 Joshi, K.L. The junior college : Its place in the educational structure. *University News.* 19 (12), 1971. p.10-14.

154 Joshi, Navin Chander, New direction for higher education. *Teacher Education.* 20 (30-31), 1985. p.33-36.

155 Kabir, H. On Indian universities. *Education Quarterly.* 3, (December), 1951. p.218-25.

156 Kalra, R.M. Should higher education be value-oriented? *University News.* 20 (2), 1982. p.41 and 43.

157 Kalyankar, V.G. Status of higher education in Developing Countries with special reference to India. *University News.* 27 (21), 1989. p.3-6.

158 Kamat, A.R. Higher education : Kothari Commission and after. *Journal of Higher Education.* 8 (2), 1982. p.141-153.

159 Kannappan, S. Some Problems in the development of advanced education and research capability in India. *Asian Survey.* 9, October, 1969. p.752-57.

160 Kapur, J.N. Excellence in higher education. *University News.* 23 (44), 1985. p.9-

161 Karve, D.D. On the improvement of the Indian Universities. *Minerva.* 3, (Winter), 1965. p. 159-172.

162 ——. Universities and the public in India. *Minerva.* 1, (Spring), 1963. p.263-84.

163 Kaul, J.N. Development of Indian higher education. *Economic and Political Weekly.* August 1972. (Special Issue). p.1645-1652.

164 Khader, M.A. and Singhal, Sushila. Institutional quality student input and output : Analysis of six Indian universities. *Journal of Higher Education.* 9 (1), 1983. p.167-182.

165 Khan, Q.S. Higher education in India-some issues. *Journal of Higher Education.* 5 (2), (Autumn), 1979. p.167-182.

166 Khanna, S.K. Development of higher education in India. *University News*. 27 (28), 1989. p.1-4.
167 Kolhatkar, M. Higher education in India – some issues. *Journal of Higher Education*. Vol.5 (2), 1979. p.167-182.
168 Koshy, T.K. Restructuring the university system. *University News*. 14 (9), 1976. p.4-5 and 18.
169 Kothari, D.S. Higher education and national development : Second Das Gupta Memorial lecture. *Library Herald*. 11 April-July, 1969. p.18-31.
170 Kothari, V.N. and others. Access to higher education and equalization of educational opportunities through freeships : A case study. *Journal of Higher Education*. 8 (1), 1982. p.74-79.
171 ——. Disguised dimensions of problems in higher education in India. *Conspectus*. 3 (2), 1967. p.47-55.
172 Krishan Kumar, K. Revitalizing colleges. *University News*. 26 (30), 1988. p.5-8.
173 Kurrien, John. Salvaging higher education : Limiting the importance of degrees. *Journal of Higher Education*. 9 (2), 1985. p.207-16.
174 Laha, P.N. University education in India : Past and present. *University News*. 18 (14), 1980. p.382-85.
175 Lakshmanna, C. Educational reforms : Myths and reality. *University Administration*. 5 (1), 1976. p.1-7.
176 Lingamurty, V. New look at higher education in India. *Education India*. 41 (4), October, 1974. p.85-88.
177 Lulla, B.P. Problems of post graduate studies in India. *University News*. 7, (3), 1969. p.13-14.
178 Macphail, J.R. Christian colleges in India today. *International Review of Missions*. 53, April, p.162-168.
179 Madtha, W. Concientization: The aim of university education. *Journal of Higher Education*. 2 (3), 1977. p.309-315.
180 Mahadevan, T.R. Approach to the study of Gandhi. *Gandhi Marg*. 13, January, 1969. p. 29-45.
181 Mahajan, J.M. College teachers and professional preparation. *Educational India*. 34 (2), August, 1967. p.51-53.
182 Mahajani, G.S. An alternative to the proposal regarding major universities. 4 (10), 1966. P.3-4.
183 ——. Language policy in education. *University News*. 2 (2), 1964. p.15-17.

184 ——. New education structure : A viewpoint. *University News.* 14 (8), 1976. p.7-8.

185 ——. Some issues in higher education. *University News.* 15 (16), 1977. p.432-433.

186 ——. 10+2+3 pattern of education. *University News.* 13 (1), 1975. p.1, 13.

187 Maiancheruvil, George. Shift system in Kerala colleges. *New Frontiers in Education.* 9 (4), October-December, 1979. p. 57-62.

188 Malhotra, Nirmal, dissenting academics and their libraries. *Journal of Higher Education.* 13 (1-3), 1987. p.134-138.

189 Maria, Elias and Shirur, Rajani. Syndicate studies - A teaching learning technique in higher education. *University News.* 18 (8), 1980. p. 195-196.

190 Marshall, M.W. Universities in the hinterland; at Nagpur and Saugur. *Journal of Higher Education.* 32, February 1961. p. 77-83.

191 Marshall, M.W. Week at Annamalai University : The experience of two fulbright professors. *Journal of Higher Education.* 30, December, 1959. p. 480-88.

192 Mathai, Samuel. Co-ordination of university education in India. *Education Quarterly.* 4, September, 1952. p.157-161.

193 ——. Higher education and the university. *University News.* 18 (17), 1980. p.470-474 and 485.

194 ——. Patterns and problems of higher education. *New Frontiers in Education.* April-June, 1981. p.37-72.

195 Mathias, T.A. Kerala colleges in turmoil. *Quest.* (78) September-October, 1972. p. 17-36.

196 Mathur, P.N. Banasthali Vidyapith : Origin, growth and present position. *University News.* 26 (20), 1988. pp. 4, 9.

197 Mathur, V.S. Raising standards in college education. *University News.* 20 (3), 1982. p.84-86.

198 Mehra, O.P. Need for improvement in quality of higher education. *University News.* 19 (24), 1981. p.683-686.

199 Mehrotra, R.C. Development of higher education - Issues and perspectives. *Administrative Change.* 11 (2), 1984. p. 197-205.

200 Memorandum on the UGC scheme and the present situation. *Journal of Education.* 9 (1), September-November, 1961. p.21-29.

201 Minault, G. and Lelyveld, D. Campaign for a Muslim university, 1898-1920. *Modern Asian Studies.* 8, April, 1974. p. 145-89.

202 Mishra, R.S. Limits to higher education. *University News*. 23 (35), 1985. p. 11-13.

203 Misra, R.G. Problems of linkage between +2 and +3 levels. *University News*. 15 (15), 1977. p. 406-408.

204 Misra, V.N. Higher education - Quality and Qualification. *University News*. 18 (19), 1980. p. 539-540.

205 Misri, M.L. Some dimensions. *Seminar*. (166), June, 1973. p. 29-31.

206 Mitra, C.R. Indian University system : A call to action. *University News*. 27 (10), 1989. p. 3-8.

207 Mitra, Shib K. Let us have more universities. *University News*. 18 (6), 1980. p. 133-134 & 152.

208 Mohan Lal. Restricting university education. *Educational India*. 23 (4), October, 1961. p. 116-18.

209 Mohan, Ramesh. Basic goals of a university education in the light of general social development. *University News*. 20 (118), 1982. p. 574-578.

210 Mujeeb, M. Fifty years of Jamia Millia. *University News*. 8 (11), 1970. p. 12-13.

211 Mujeeb, M. Dr. Zakir Hussain and the Jamia Millia. *University News*. 7 (6), 1969. p. 3-4, *contd*. 23.

212 Mujib, A. Education as a university discipline : Some aspects of teaching – training and research. *Journal of University Education*. 2, December, 1963. p. 85-106.

213 Mukherjee, Kartick C. Some implications of the Robbins report for higher education in India. *International Review of Education*. 12, 1966. p.47-60.

214 Mukherjee, L. Present crisis in higher education. *Progress of Education*. 37(7), February, 1962.

215 Murty, A.G.K. Crisis of higher education. *University News*. 13 (2), 1975. p. 13, 15.

216 Nag Chaudhuri, B.D. Science and technology in the future of India. *University News*. 16 (1), 1978. p. 675-677 and 686.

217 Nagarajan, B.S. Linking extension with university education. *Economic Times*. 25 October, 1983. p. 4.

218 Nagarkar, D.D. Genesis and development of higher learning. *Progress of Education*. 47 (10), May, 1973. p. 345-47.

219 Naik, J.P. Higher education in India : Some suggestions for reorganisation. *New Frontiers in Education*. April-July, 1972. p. 27.

220 Nair, K.R. Ramachandran. Discipline and authority in higher education. *University News.* 15, October, 1980. p. 565-566 and 569.
221 Nath, T. Why don't they go to the college? *Journal of Education and Psychology*. 22 (2), July, 1964. p. 49-99.
222 Navathe, D.V. Indian university then and now. *Education Quarterly*. 14 (56), December, 1962. p. 236-239.
223 Nayar, D.P. Gandhiji and universities. *University News.* 7 (10), 1969. p. 7-cont.19.
224 Nigam, Raghuvir, Sahay. Four faults in university education. *Educational India*. 29 (5), November, 1962. p. 160-161.
225 Nigam, Raghuvir Sahay. M.P. Shiksha Anudan Ayog. *University News*. 12 (7), 1974. p. 9-10.
226 — —. Universities have failed. *Educational India*. 35 (3), September, 1968. p. 66-100.
227 Objectives of higher education. Editorial. *Educational India.* 26 (4), October, 1959. p. 123-25.
228 Oomen, T.K. Higher learning in an affluent society. *Journal of University Education*. 3 (3), March, 1965. p. 223-232.
229 Our universities : A symposium on how to orient higher education to the needs of a growing industrial society. *Seminar*. (7), March, 1960. p. 10-44.
230 Padmanabhan, C.B. Expansion of higher education in the context of recent trends in development strategy. *New Frontiers in Education*. 7 (1), 1977. p. 82-92.
231 ——. Recurrent education as a means of regulating expansion of higher education in India. *New Frontiers in Education*. 4 (1), January-March, 1974. p. 53-58.
232 Palsane, M.N. Expansion of university education. *Journal of Education and Psychology*. 19 (1), April, 1961. p. 39-40.
233 Panandikar, S. Some problems of university education. *Progress of Education*. 31 (9), April, 1957. p. 301-304.
234 Panchamukhi, P.R. Devaluation of education : A quantitative analysis. *Journal of Higher Education*. 1 (1), April, 1975. p. 15-30.
235 Pandit, H.N. Trends in higher education in India. *University News*. 12 (6), 1974. p. 6-7.
236 Paralysed universities. *Seminar*. (166), June, 1973. p. 10-44.
237 Parikh, Ramlal. Imperative need for value-based higher education.

238 Parikh, G.D. University government and society : The Indian experience. *Quest.* (88), May-June, 1974. p. 35-40.
239 Parthasarthi, A. Universities and nation building. *Quest.* (52), Winter, 1967. p. 19-26.
240 Parthasarathy, R.T. Decline in standards in universities. *University News.* 13 (9), 1975. p. 25-26.
241 Patel, I.J. Mahatma Gandhi : An Embodiment of education potential. *University News.* 7 (10), 1969. p. 3-4.
242 Pathusha, K.M. College development wing : An appraisal. *University News.* 23 (1), 1985. p. 5-6 and 8.
243 Pattanayak, D.P. Crisis in higher education in India. *Journal of Higher Education.* 6 (1-3), 1980-81. p. 51-55.
244 Penderson, Paul, Bilingual alternative for higher education. *University News.* 13 (7), 1975. p. 9-11.
245 Pillai, C.R. Making the system work. *University News.* 27 (51), 1989. p. 7-10.
246 Pillai, N.P. Report on junior colleges in Kerala. *University News.* 4 (4), 1966. p. 17-36.
247 Prasad, K.N. Maintenance of academic standards in Indian Universities. *University News.* 18 (7), 1980. p. 163-164 cont. 167.
248 Problems of our universities. *University News.* 22 (24), 1984. p. 1-2.
249 Rabindranathan M.R. Regional imbalance in the growth of higher education in India. *Journal of Higher Education.* 4 (1), Monsoon, 1978. p. 33-40.
250 Raghaviah, Y. The midget bureaucratic phenomenon-reflection of system transformation in universities. *Journal of Higher Education.* 9 (2), 1988. p. 157-175.
251 Rahman, A. Social attitudes and scientific outlook. *University News.* 8 (1), 1970. p. 23-25.
252 Rais Ahmad. Perspectives in higher education. *University News.* 19 (12), 1981. p. 345-359.
253 ——. Universities : Perspectives and Problems. *Journal of Higher Education.* 7 (3), 1982. p. 177-187.
254 Raja, K.C.K.E. Changing universities. *Education Quarterly.* 14 (56), December, 1962. p. 217-24.
255 Rajan, B. Now days are dragon-ridden. *American Scholar.* (32), Summer, 1963. p. 407-14.
256 Rajaraman, R. Higher education : To set the house in order. *Economic and Political Weekly.* 4 March, 1972. p. 554-56.

257 Ramakrishna, G. Higher education : A perspective from the periphery. *Journal of Higher Education*. 7 (1-2), 1981. p. 51-58.
258 Ramamurthy, M.S. The North-Eastern Region and the University. *University News*. 23 (8), 1985. p. 5-6.
259 Rana, K.P.S. Uneconomic expansion of higher educational institutions. *University News*. 20 (9), 1982. p. 306-307 and 311.
260 Rao, Ramachandra B. Role of scientific and engineering societies in national development. *University News*. 19 (21), 1981. p. 589-593.
261 Rao, N.V.R.L.N. Development of higher education in India. *University News*. 13 (6), 1975. p. 6-7.
262 ——. Universities. *University News*. 16(19), 1978. p. 1183-84.
263 Rao, Tirupati U. Toning up of higher education in India. *Educational Review*. 91 (12), 1985. p. 211-14.
264 Rao, V.K.R.V. Our universities. *Education Quarterly*. 9 (34), June, 1957. p. 112-114.
265 Rao, Venkateswara V. and Sastri, A.G.R. Sai. Collegiate education in Andhra. *University News*. 12 (12), 1974. p. 7-9.
266 Rastogi, S. Need for an academic community. *University News*. 25 (49), 1987. p. 1-2, 7.
267 Rathi, G.K. Extension services in degree and post-graduate colleges. *University News*. 15 (4), 1977. p. 85.
268 Ray, Anil Baran. Parochialism vs. cosmopolitanism in India higher education. *Journal of Higher Education*. 3 (1), Monsoon, 1977. p. 55-63.
269 Raychaudhuri, T. Standards of university education in India: Some neglected questions. *Conspectus*. 2 (1), 1966. p. 13-24.
270 Raza, Moonis and Aggarwal, Y.P. Higher education: Regional Dimension. *Journal of Higher Education*. 11 (1-2), 1985-86. p. 1-38.
271 Regional imbalances in the development of higher education. *Bulletin of Higher Education*. 5 (3) 1981. p. 2-8.
272 Reddy, K.S.V. Basivi. Students freedom of association. *University News*. 8 (2), 1970. p. 13-14.
273 Report of the committee on colleges. *University News*. 5 (9), 1967. p. 12-13.
274 Roy, Ramani Mohan. Some problems of higher education. *Indian Education*. 4 (3), February, 1965. p. 26-44.
275 Rozario, A.J. Parallel colleges in Kerala. *New Frontiers in Education*. 13 (1), January-March, 1983. p. 37-41.

276 Rudrappa, Y.P. University of Mysore : Prabhava project. *University News.* 25 (26), 1987. p. 1-2, 10.
277 Ruhela, Satya Pal. Education in human values. *University News.* 25 (45), 1989. p. 3-8.
278 Saha, A.K. Indian science congress has come to age. *University News.* 8 (1), 1970. p. 5-6.
279 Sahay, S. Some problems of higher education. *Indian Education.* 3 (2), January, 1964. p. 16-23.
280 Sailabala Debi. Higher education in Orissa. *University News.* 22 (19), 1984. p. 4-5.
281 Salamatullah. Thoughts on a national system of education. *Journal of University Education.* 3 (3), March, 1965. p. 215-221.
282 Salunkhe, D.K. Our universities need national policy. *University News.* 15 July, 1982. p. 457-58.
283 Sambalpur university : A profile. *University News.* 26 (45). p. 15-17, 21.
284 Santosh Kumar. Restriction of varsity education. *Educational India.* 30(4), October, 1963. p. 113-16.
285 Sarkar, S.C. Crisis of Visvabharati and the ailing university system. *Modern Review.* 127, August, 1970
286 Saraf, S.N. Education for all : Dimensions and dilemmas. *University News.* 23(21), 1985. p. 2-5.
287 Satish Chandra. Higher Education in India : A review and a look ahead. *Mainstream.* March. 23, 1985. p. 15-21.
288 ——. Higher education in India – Plans and prospects. *Journal of Higher Education.* 1(1), 1975. p. 5-13.
289 Schenkman, A. Universities in India : Their yesterday and their today. *University Quarterly.* (6) November 1953. p. 55-62, and (8), February, 1954. p. 170-77.
290 Seminarist. Search for purpose. *Seminar.* (148), December, 1971. p. 28-29.
291 Sen, Triguna. Higher education through mother-tongue media. *University News.* 5 (8) 1967. p. 7-8.
292 Shah, A.B. Aligarh once again. *New Quest.* May-June, 1978. p. 143-44.
293 Shah, A.B. Higher education : The bottomless pit. *New Quest.* March-April, 1978. p. 129-131.
294 ——. Universities in crisis. *New Quest.* May-June, 1980. p. 125-36.
295 Shah, A.K. Structuring basic university functions : An alternate model. *University News.* 26 (11), 1988. p. 1-6.

296 Shah, K.J. Many facts. *Seminar*. (148), December, 1971. p. 23-27.

297 Shah, Madhuri, R. Equity, Excellence and efficiency in higher education. *University News*. 23 (41), 1985. p. 2-5.

298 ——. Future of university education. *University News*. 19 (20), 1981. p. 561-562 and 569.

299 ——. Some facets of higher education in India. *University News*. 21 (2), 1983. p. 55-56.

300 Shahare, M.L. and Ramasami, T. Examination of union public service commission *vis-a-vis* higher education in India. *Journal of Higher Education*. 7 (1-2), 1981. p. 45-50.

301 Shamsuddin. Higher education in new Madhya Pradesh, 1956-64. *Education Quarterly*. 29 (4), January, 1978. p. 36-40.

302 Shanker Narayan D. Higher education in India. *Bulletin of UNESCO Regional Office for Education in Asia*. 7 (1), 1972. p. 46-63.

303 Shanmugasundaram, V. Human values in higher education. *University News*. 22 (47), 1984. p. 5-7.

304 Sharma, B.D. A centre of excellence in North East – NEHU. *University News*. 23 (8), 1985. p. 2-4.

305 Sharma, G.D. Education : Needs, fulfilments and alternatives. *Journal of Higher Education*. 3 (6) March, 1978. p. 31-36.

306 ——. 10+2+3 New pattern of education : Window dressing. *Mainstream*. 15 (47), 1977. p. 24-26.

307 Sharma, S.L. University education & modernity orientation. *University News*. 15 (18), 1977. p. 490-492.

308 Sharp, H. Development of Indian universities. *Journal of Royal Society of Arts*. (73), 1925. p. 513-35.

309 Shiek Ali, B. Universities of tomorrow. *University News*. 26 (10), 1988. p. 1-4.

310 Shenoy, G.L. Is higher education spurious? *University News*. 10 (5), 1972. p. 18-20.

311 Shenoy, B.R. National university for India. *Quest*. (40), Winter, 1964. p. 39-45.

312 Shinde, A.B. Some experiments in higher education. *University News*. 14 (3), 1976. p. 5-6.

313 Shukla, S. Two campuses. *Seminar*. (148), December, 1971. p. 36-39.

314 ——. University academic. *Journal of University Courses*. 33 (2), 1964. p. 113-22.

315 ——. University in the Indian society. *Journal of University Education.* 2 (3), March, 1964. p. 171-79.

316 Siddiqui, Zakia A. Comparison of students' performance under the semester and non-semester system of education in the Aligarh Muslim University. *Journal of Higher Education.* 3 (3), Spring, 1979. p. 369-80.

317 Simons, Hans. General education in Indian universities. *Journal of Education and Psychology.* 22 (4), January, 1965. p. 179-84.

318 Singh Abhimanyu. Computerizing large systems : Lessons from an application. *University News.* 27 (7), 1989. p. 5-13.

319 Singh, M. Higher education in India - Some problems. *Indian Journal of Public Administration.* (17), January-March, 1971. p. 117-35.

320 Singh, Nand K. University and social change. *University News.* 18 (1), 1980. p. 3.

321 Singh, R.K. Adding years to education. *University News.* 20 (22), 1982. p. 692-695.

322 Singh, S.N. Higher education and contemporary Indian society. *University News.* 15 (23), 1977. p. 627-30 and 633.

323 Singhal, Sushila. Organisation and functioning of universities in India. *Journal of Higher Education.* 1 (2), 1975. p. 223-240.

324 Sinha, Uma. Some facts and figures about higher education in India. *Indian Educational Review.* 5 (1), January, 1970. p. 155-58.

325 Sivia, G.S. Sports in society and higher education. *University News.* 26 (20), 1988. p. 1-3.

326 Sivayya, K.V. Students, participation in varsity affairs. *Univesity News.* 8 (7), 1970. p. 15 and 16.

327 Some aspects of the growth and development of the Maharaja Sayajirao University of Baroda. *Education and Psychology Review.* 9, January, 1969. p. 5-15.

328 Sri, Padmavati Mahila Visvavidyalayam : A profile. *University News.* 27 (32), 1989. p. 1-4.

329 Srivastava, Akhileshwar Lal. Type of education and modernization among university students. *NIE Journal.* (4), November, 1969. p. 40-46.

330 Srivastava, Anand P. Three decades of higher education. *University News.* 17 (4), 1979. p. 89-91.

331 Subramanyan, N.S. College education. *Patriot.* 25 November, 1979. p. 1.

332 Sundram, P.S. Plea for acceptance of major universities concept. *Conspectus*. 2 (4), 1966. p. 39-44.

333 Suraj Bhan. Crisis of values in universities. *University News*. 6 (5), 1968. p. 9-11.

334 Swaminathan, M.S. Higher education into the 21st century. *Journal of Higher Education*. 7 (1), 1981. p 23-30.

335 Sweeney, L.J. Evaluation of Indian higher education. *Colleges and University*. (44), Summer, 1969. p. 356-70.

336 Symposium on higher education in India's Asian Drammma. *Asian Survey*. 9, October, 1969. p. 723-95.

337 Takawala, Ram. Progress of higher education in Maharashtra. *Progress of Education*. 59 (10-11), 1985. p. 218-23.

338 Taneja, G.R. University in Delhi. *Quest*. (94), March-April, 1975. p. 9-15.

339 Thapar, R. Cultural traditions and the university of India. *Science and Freedom*. (13), November, 1959. p. 64-71.

340 The concept of "major" universities : A redefinition. *University News*. 4 (12), 1966. p. 1-2.

341 Thomas, P.C. Fear of fall in standards in Kerala's higher education. *University News*. 10(8), 1972, p. 15 and 17-18.

342 Three-year degree course. Editional. *Educational India*. 30 (11-12), May-June, 1964. p. 410-63.

343 Tope, T.K. Higher education for development. *University News*. 21 (4), 1983. p. 106-09.

344 Tulsyan, S.L. Higher education in India : Problems and Perceptions. *University News*. 21 (15), 1983. p. 487-88.

345 Unnithan, T.K.N. Education in human values. *University News*. 26 (49), Dec. 5, 1988. p. 21-31.

346 Value orientation in higher education. *University News*. 25 (35), 1987. p. 10.

347 Varma, R.S. Some observations on college education. *Modern Review*. (124), July, 1969. p. 225-51.

348 Vasuder, T. Student Teacher relationship. *University News*. 22 (14), 1984. p. 1-2, 5.

349 Varghese, Vijay K. Great brain robbery. *Illustrated Weekly of India*. 23 March, 1980. p. 31-32.

350 Verma, D.P. Apathy in our universities. *University News*. 22 (28), 1984. p. 2-5.

351 Verma, D.P. Indian university : A tragedy of small mind. *University News*. 16 (15), 1978. p. 1071-72 and 1086.

352 Verstraction, A. College as an academic community. *New Frontiers in Education.* (5), January-March, 1975. p. 52-67.

353 ——. Higher education in India : A survey of teacher opinion. *New Frontiers in Education.* 8 (2), April-June, 1978. p. 37-47.

354 Vinayak, J.P. Crisis in higher education. *University News.* 16 (4), 1978. p. 767 and 780.

355 Wood, H.B. Higher education in India. *Teachers College Record.* (55), May, 1954. p. 418-424.

356 Wrago, M. Recent developments in higher education in India. *Comparative Education.* (5), June, 1969. p. 167-76.

357 Wright, R.C. Freedom's impact on higher education in India. *Journal of Higher Education.* (23), April, 1952, p. 198-208.

358 Yadav, Gorelal. Higher education in Bihar. *University News.* 16 (13), 1978. p. 1019 and 1038.

359 Yadav, R.K. Far from the main campus. *Journal of Higher Education.* 1 (1), 1975. p. 99-102.

360 Yagnik, K.S. Major problems of higher education in India. *Journal of Education and Psychology.* 27 (1), April, 1969. p. 91-95.

C COMMITTEES/COMMISSIONS/REPORTS

001 Indian University Commission, 1902. Report. Simla, Government of India, 1902. 95p. President : T. Releigh.

Lord Curzon appointed the commission in 1902 to inquire into the conditions and prospects of the universities established in British India; to consider and report upon any proposals which have been or may be made for improving their constitution and working; and to recommend to the Governor General-in-Council such measures as may tend to elevate the standard of university teaching and to promote the advancement of learning.

The recommendations of the commission can be put as under:

(i) The reorganisation of administration of universities and the territorial jurisdiction of each university to be defined;

(ii) a much more strict and systematic supervision of the affiliated colleges by the university and the imposition of more exacting conditions of affiliation;

(iii) a much closer attention to the conditions under which students live and work, provision of adequate library facilities etc.;

(iv) substantial changes in curricula, and in the methods of examination; and

(v) the assumption of teaching functions by the university within defined limits.

002 Review of the Growth of Education in British India, 1928. Report. Calcutta, Government of India, 1929. 401p. Chairman: Sir Philip Hortog.

This report presents an exhaustive account of the growth of education in British India till 1928. Though the secondary and the university education have been discussed at some length, the major focus has been the mass (primary) education as, in the view of the commission, the condition of the latter is far less satisfactory than that of the former. The report also gives a good account of the state of education of women; of Muhammadan and other religious communities such as the Sikhs; the Anglo-Indian, the Parsees; and the Christians. Investigation has also been made to assess the extent to which the education systems in India are designed to promote a reasonable degree of uniformity among different sections of people. The organisation of education; the causes of the acceleration or retardation of growth of education in the immediate past; their likely ways of operation in the near future; and the ways to promote healthy growth of education, are the other issues under discussion in this report.

003 Christian Higher Education in India: An enquiry into the place of the Christian college in modern India, 1929. Report. London, Oxford University Press, 1931. Chairman : A.D. Lindsay.

This commission on Christian higher education in India and Burma, was constituted by the International Missionary Council at its meeting at Willamstown, Massachusetts, in 1929. The terms of reference of the commission are:

(a) To review the field of service open to the Christian colleges under present conditions in India and to suggest ways in which the available resources of the church can be more effectively used for this purpose;

(b) to suggest where the local conditions make it advisable such co-operation as may prevent unnecessary duplication and may make possible a higher standard of education and missionary efficiency and to make definite recommendations; and

(c) to consider how the needs of the Christian colleges for men and funds can best be presented in Britain and America.

004 Sargent Report or the Report on the Post-war Educational Development, 1944.

In 1944, while, in England, Butlers' White paper on education was passing into an act, the Central Advisory Board of Education in India published a comprehensive report on the Post-war educational development of the country. This was a first systematic and national level attempt at tackling the problems of education as a whole. The report summarises its recommendations on university education in the following world:

"Indian universities, as they exist to-day, despite many admirable features do not fully satisfy the requirements of a national system of education. In order to raise standards all round, the conditions of admission must be revised with the subject of ensuring that all students are capable of taking full advantage of a university course. The proposed reorganisation of the high school system will facilitate this. Adequate financial assistance must be provided for poor students. The present intermediate course should be covered in the high school, but as an immediate step, the first year of the course should be transferred to high school and second to universities. The minimum length of a university course should be three years (in certain subjects, longer). The tutorial system should be widely extended and closer personal contacts be established between teachers and students. The importance of establishing a high standard in post-graduate studies and particularly, in pure and applied research, should be emphasised. Steps should be taken to improve the conditions of service, including remuneration of university and college teachers where those now in operation are not attracting men and women of the requisite calibre".

005 Committee on Development of Higher Technical Institutions in India, 1948. Report. New Delhi, Manager of Publications, 1948. Chairman: N.R. Sarkar.

The report contains development of higher technical institutions in India. The committee suggested that it is necessary to establish four institutions, i.e. one in North, one in East, one in West, and one in South to satisfy the post-war requirements. The recommendations have also been made, (see page 2 of the report).

006 University Education Commission, 1948 Report. Delhi, Manager of Publications, 1949. 1356p. Charts. 2 Vols. Chairman: Dr. S. Radhakrishnan.

The commission was appointed under a resolution of the Government of India, Ministry of Education to report on Indian university education and to suggest improvements and extension that may be desirable to suit the present and the future requirements of the country. The commission was asked to consider and make recommendations in regard to: (1) the aim and objectives of university education and research in India; (2) the changes considered necessary and desirable in the constitution, control, function and jurisdiction of universities in India and their relations with governments, central and provincial; (3) the finance of the university; (4) the maintenance of the higher standards of teaching and examination; (5) the standards of admission to university; (6) the medium of instruction; (7) the need for more universities; (8) the organisation of advanced research; (9) religious instruction in the universities; (10) the special problems of Banaras Hindu University, Aligarh Muslim University, Delhi University and other institutions of an all-India character; (11) the qualifications, conditions of service, salaries, privileges and functions of teachers and the encouragement of original research by teachers; and (12) the discipline of students hostels and organisations of tutorial word and any other matter which is essential to a comprehensive enquiry into all aspects of university education and adv[illegible]ced research in India.

007 Experts Committee Appointed to Consider the Establishment of New Universities, 1953. Report. New Delhi, Ministry of Education, 1953. Chairman: Mr. Humayun Kabir.

The committee was appointed to consider the minimum number of students and of educational institutions at various levels necessary for the establishment of a new university. The committee suggested that a new university may be established for Madhya Bharat. Recommendations have been made on page 4 of the report.

008 General Education Study Team, 1955. Report. New Delhi, Ministry of Education, 1957. 97p. Chairman : Dr. S. Bhagavantam.

The study team was appointed to study general education courses in U.S.A. and U.K. in order to find out what approaches to the problem have proved most effective suggest suitable approaches, which may be tried out in our country; to formulate illustrative syllabuses and courses of lectures which may be introduced in our universities; to work out the approximate financial implications; and to suggest suitable methods for preparing reading material.

009 Three-year Degree Course Estimates Committee, 1956. Report. New Delhi, Ministry of Education, 1958. 23p. Chairman : C.D. Deshmukh.

The Education Ministers' Conference held on 2nd-3rd September, 1956, gave further impetus to the reform by recommending the appointment of a Committee to work out the estimates of expenditure to be incurred on introducing this reform, making it possible for all universities to change over to the new pattern. In accordance with the above recommendation a Three-Year Degree Course Estimates Committee was set up on 1st October, 1956. Terms of reference are:

1. To make recommendations regarding the best manner in which three-year degree course could be introduced in the affiliated colleges and universities in the country and the arrangements which would be made during the interim period for admission of students to the reorganised Arts and Science Colleges and the professional colleges as constituted at present till the new pattern is fully introduced.
2. To frame the estimates of expenditure involved in the reorganisation of collegiate education implicit in the introduction of Three-Year Degree Course in Universities and affiliated colleges.
3. To suggest the proportions in which the expenditure may be shared between the Central Government and the State Governments for

introducing the Three-Year Degree Course.

4. To recommend the best manner in which interim grants form Central Government may be made to the State Governments for the, year 1956-57 in case formulation of schemes by the State Governments is delayed.
5. To consider and examine the future of the Intermediate colleges and such other problems as may be ancillary to the main question of introducing Three-Year Degree Course.
6. To consider any other issues which may be relevant to the question of introducing a 3-Year Degree Course in the Universities and the affiliated colleges.

The main recommendations or conclusions of the Committee may be summarized as follows:

1. The Three-Year Degree Course should be introduced in as many Universities as possible during the Second Five-Year Plan period. On an average; one Intermediate college should be upgraded for every two Degree colleges assisted to introduce the Course. No new Intermediate colleges should be permitted to be started.
2. The Unit of reorganisation should be a University and not a college, so that no University will give two types of degrees for the same courses except for those students who fail to qualify for the four-year degree in the first attempt.
3. During the transitional period, students passing the Intermediate Examination should be admitted to the Second year of the three-year degree course.
4. The total amount which would be required to introduce the reform including recurring expenditure for four years, will be about Rs. 2 crores.
5. The expenditure involved in introducing the reform should be shared between the Central and State Governments in equal proportion.
6. During the Second Five-Year Plan period, the Central Government should give Rs. $7^1/_2$ crores, including Rs. $2^1/_2$ crores to be made available by the University Grants Commission. A similar amount should be found by the State Governments including contributions from Private Managements. The total amount available will thus be Rs. 15 crores which will be sufficient for upgrading 180 Intermediate Colleges and reorganising 300 Degree Colleges which should be taken as the targets for the Second Five-Year Plan.
7. The basis for allocating recurring grants should be additional cost per pupil, and that for non-recurring grants the additional cost per institution. The only exception to the latter rule will be the colleges which have an enrolment of over 1000 but which were actually built only for that number. For such colleges it would be fairer to pay the non-recurring grant also on a *per capita* basis.
8. The share of the Central Government/University Grants Commission should be paid only when a University has taken a decision to introduce the Three-Year Degree Course and either the State Government concerned is prepared to pay its share to the University/College from its own resources or private resources are

available to match the cost.

9. There should be a public examination at the end of the pre-University class.
10. Professional colleges should either conduct their own admission tests or select candidates for pre-professional courses on the basis of Higher Secondary/Pre-University examination, both of which will be public examinations.
11. The number of students should be restricted to 800-1000 per colleges. Colleges with larger enrolment but with no suitable accommodation should stabilize as a ceiling the present number of students and should prepare a scheme of gradually diminishing their enrolment so that the desired limit is reached by 1961. The University Grants Commission should prepare a brochure for the guidance of such colleges indicating how this may be done without undue hardship to students or the colleges.
12. While the Three-Year Degree Course is introduced, steps should be taken to improve the quality of collegiate education in general. For this purpose from the grants available, it is necessary to revise syllabuses, introduce General Education Courses, reduce over-crowding in colleges, improve the teacher-pupil ratio, strengthen laboratories, replenish libraries and, wherever possible, institute tutorial system.
13. The State of U.P. will present a special problem because of the entirely system operating in that State. This problem should be further studied by the Ministry of Education, and the statements of estimated expenditure prepared by the State Government in this behalf should also be examined. Of the 250 Intermediate Colleges to be upgraded, 100 should be selected from U.P.

010 Committee on General Education, 1958. Report. New Delhi, University Grants Commission, 1961. 89p. Chairman: S. Govindarajulu.

To assess the needs of additional staff, financial assistance and other facilities for the general education, this committee was asked to go into the whole question of general education in Indian universities.

011 Review Committee on Education, 1960. Report. New Delhi, University Grants Commission, 1966. 94p. Chairman: Prof. N.K. Sidhanta (died) and Prof. K.G. Saiyidain took over as Chairman.

The committee was asked to go into the details of different types of courses which should be offered by the universities; recommend to the universities the schemes of papers for each course with a view to providing specialisation; recommend teaching methods; lay down entrance qualificrtions for students for the various courses; recommend the duration of course; and indicate any other steps that may be necessary to achieve a uniform and high standard in education.

012 Committee on 'Model Act for Universities', 1961. Report. New Delhi, Ministry of Education, 1964. Chairman: Dr. D.S. Kothari.

The committee submitted a comprehensive report in which the position of President, Governor and Vice-Chancellor in universities has been discussed. The term of office of a Vice-chancellor should be five years. He should not normally be appointed for more than two terms in the same university, subject to any retiring age that may be fixed. The position of Pro-Vice Chancellor, the Registrar and the composition of the Courts has also been enumerated. The committee further suggested that the increasing demand for admission should not be met by expanding the size of existing colleges but by other measures such as evening and correspondence courses and other types of education besides arts and science courses. The work of the Dean of students has been described. The conditions of service and salary of the teachers in the affiliated colleges and university departments have also been enumerated. Recommendations have been made on pages 32 to 34 of the report.

013 Committee on Standards of University Education, 1961. Report. New Delhi, University Grants Commission, 1965. 268p. Charts. Chairman: Prof. N.K. Sidhanta.

The standards committee was appointed to make a systematic and objective assessment of standards of university education and to suggest various measures of improvement.

014 Committee on Members of Parliament on Higher Education, 1963. Report. New Delhi, Ministry of Education, 1964. 65p. Chairman: P.N. Sapru.

This committee was. appointed to examine the provision of the constitution regarding the responsibility of the Central Government in the field of higher education with a view to finding out the extent to which the centre could assume greater responsibility in this field, and to suggest appropriate steps to be taken for this purpose. Major recommendations are: University and higher education should be transferred from the State List to the Concurrent List, retaining intact Entry 65 in the union list; U.G.C. should have 15 members, of whom at least five should be full time members; condition of the grants should be liberalised; affiliated colleges should adopt the pay scales of the commission; professional education cannot be completely divorced from general education; increase in the efficiency of secondary education; scholarships should be increased; scholarship for women should be increased; State governments should consult the commission before setting up a new university; inter-university board should be made more effective; common policy with regard to the admission; and morning, evening and correspondence courses should be established.

015 Committee on Colleges, 1964. Report. New Delhi, University Grants Commission, 1967. 44p. Chairman: Dr. G.S. Mahajani.

This committee was constituted to suggest measures to improve collegiate education in the field of arts, science, commerce and education; and to suggest any steps in this regard for the fourth plan.

016 Education Commission, 1964. Report. Delhi, Manager of Publications, 1966. 692+xiiip. Chairman: Prof. D.S. Kothari.

The committee was appointed to advise government on the national pattern of education and on the general principles and policies for the development of education at all stages and in all aspects. Chapters XI, XII and XIII deal with problems of higher education which include, amongst others, the establishment of major universities, programmes of qualitative improvement, enrolment and university governance. Recommendations have been made on pages 645 to 656 of the report.

017 Committee on the Indian School of International Studies, 1968. Report. New Delhi, Ministry of Education, 1968. 25+15p. Chairman: P.C. Reddly (Mimeograph).

This report deals mainly with the findings of the committee with regards to the maintenance grants to be given by the Government of India to the School. Other issues discussed in the report are those related to the autonomy and all-India character of the school; its expansion in area studies; re-organisation of departments; fellowships; admissions; the strength of teaching and research staff; abolition of the posts of special instructors for languages, Research Assistant and Editor of publications; and reduction of administrative staff etc.

018 Advisory Committee of Vice-Chancellors (Sources—University Grants Commission Report for the Year 1970-71, presented to the Government of India in Compliance with section 13 of the University Grants Commission Act, 1956, New Delhi, 1971).

An advisory committee of vice-chancellors was set up to advise the commission on matters relating to the development of higher education in the country. The committee normally meets two or three times a years. Some of the important recommendations made by the committee at its meetings, held on 2 July and 3 December, 1970 are as follows:

1. It would be desirable to make provision for the appointment of pro-vice chancellors/rectors in the universities;
2. each university may appoint a group to assess the needs and priorities as regards amenities for students;
3. a committee may be appointed to examine the facilities required for the teaching staff in colleges to enables them to improve their competence and effectiveness;
4. working groups may be appointed to examine the role and functions of the advisory committee of the vice-chancellors and the visiting committees that are constituted by the commission for the assessment of the development programmes of the universities;

5. if a college on temporary affiliation has functioned well for five years and has fulfilled the basic requirements, it should normally be given permanent affiliation. For details, see pages 30 and 31 of the report.

019 Review Committee on the University Grants Commission, 1974. Report. New Delhi, Ministry of Education and Social Welfare, 1977. 155p. Chairman: Dr. V.S. Jha.

The committee was asked to review the functioning of the University Grants Commission, with particular reference to coordination and determination of standard of higher education, and to make recommendations conducive to more effective discharge of its responsibilities. The other topics discussed in detail are those related to grants; research, planning and evaluation; organisation and structure; and constitutional and legal aspects. The recommendations have been presented at the end of the chapters.

020 Postgraduate Review Committee, 1978. Report. Delhi, Manager of Publications, 1980. Chairman: Prof. Y. Nayudamma.

The committee was appointed by the Government of India in June 1978 to review the progress so far made by the country in the area of postgraduate education and research in engineering and technology, and to report on all aspects of their further development. In order to fulfil the task assigned, almost all institutions offering postgraduate programmes held extensive discussions with the students, the teachers, the academicians, the industrialists, the researchers, the administrators etc. In various parts of India, a large number of documents and reports were consulted and trends and practices in other parts of the world were looked into while bringing in force the major issues and problems. The committee made several far-reaching recommendations regarding the reorganization and development of postgraduate education and research in engineering and technology. For recommendations, see pages 36 and 37 of the report.

021 Committee to Enquire into the Working of the Central Universities, 1982. Report, New Delhi, University Grants Commission, 1984. 177p. Chairperson: Madhuri R. Shah.

The committee was appointed to examine whether the central universities are fulfilling the objectives set for them in their Acts and Statutes; to examine the general state of indiscipline in the central universities; causes of periodic disturbances in the campuses and remedial action therefore; to examine the adequacy of the machinery in the central universities to deal with the grievances of the students, the teachers and the administrative staff and suggest measures for strengthening corporate life in these universities; to examine the desirability of evolving a code of conduct for political parties and to set limits to their involvement in the university affairs; and to suggest such other measures of reforms as are necessary for the efficient functioning of central universities and promoting an academic atmosphere conducive to study and scholarship on the campuses.

022 National Commission on Teachers in Higher Education 1983. Report. New Delhi, Ministry of Education and Culture, 1985. Chairman: Rais Ahmed.

The terms of reference of this commission are as follows:

(a) lay down clear objectives for the teaching profession with reference to the search for excellence, breadth of vision and cultivation of values in keeping with the country's heritage and ideals of democracy, secularism and social justice;
(b) identify steps to be taken to give an appropriate status to members of the profession;
(c) suggest measures for fostering dynamism in the profession and responsiveness to developments elsewhere in the world;
(d) recommend measures needed for attracting and retaining talented persons in the teaching profession and widening the base for recruitment, particularly of women;
(e) review the existing arrangements for pre-service and in-service training/orientation for teachers and to recommend improvements;
(f) review and recommend th application of improved methods and technology for teaching;
(g) recommend measures to enhance the role of teachers in facilitating, motivating and inspiring students in the acquisition of knowledge, skills and values, and promoting through them, the spread of the scientific temper, secular outlook, environmental consciousness and civic responsibility;
(h) identify the role of teachers in integrating education with development work in the community and at home;
(i) study the special requirements of teachers in the field of non-formal and continuing education and to suggest ways and means by which these requirements can be met;
(j) identify the role of teachers' organisations in professional growth and professional consciousness;
(k) look into the feasibility of evolving an acceptable and operational code of conduct for teachers; and
(l) assess the adequacy of arrangements for promotion of teachers' welfare with special reference to the National Foundation of wherever necessary.

Main recommendations of the Committee are regarding:- (1) Support to National Policy on Education; (2) Pursuit of excellence an relevance: curricula; (3) Enforcement of minimum standards; (4) Autonomy and major support to selected colleges; (5) Distance learning and Audio-visual software in libraries; (6) Linkage with community and development; (7) Resources of education; (8) Management of institutions; (9) Living and working conditions; (10) Work environment;

(11) Professional excellence.

023 **Committee for Framing Regulations under UGC Act for charging fees by colleges, 1984. Report. New Delhi, University Grants Commission, 1986. 88p. Convener: Jagdish Narain.**

In 1984 UGC constituted a Committee to draft regulations in respect of fees that may be charged and the scales of fee in accordance with which fees be charged by the colleges for various courses of study.

The commission makes the following recommendations:

1. Charging of capitation fee or donations in any from is unethical, as it prevents more meritorious candidates, who cannot afford to pay such charges, from securing admission to such courses of study.
2. Private institutions also have a role to play in imparting higher education. Due to financial constraints, all non-aided colleges cannot be brought on the 'grant-in-aid' list of the Government. The fees charges by the non-aided/self-supporting private colleges should be reasonable, and it should be ensured that such institutions do not degenerate into a commercial venture, aimed at making profits.
3. The Committee confined its deliberations to the study of fee-structure in the colleges providing first degree course in Engineering and Technology, Architecture and Pharmacy only. The Committee suggests that the fees to be charged from the students should be worked out on the basis of operational cost of running these courses in the colleges on self-supporting basis and may cover the following items:
   (a) Tuition fee to cover establishment charges. viz. expenditure on salary and allowances of teaching and non-teaching staff, including contribution towards Provident Fund and other statutory liabilities;
   (b) contingent charges to cover expenditure on light, water, electricity, municipal rates and taxes, consumables and raw materials;
   (c) development fund @1% per annum of total cost of building (at the time of construction), library and workshop equipment;
   (d) Expenditure towards maintenance and repairs of building @3% p.a. of the cost of building (at the time of construction); and
   (e) Depreciation fund for furniture, equipment, fixtures, books and periodicals @7.5% p.a. of the value of furniture, equipment, fixtures, books and periodicals.
4. The University Grants Commission should fix the maximum rates of fees, taking into account the items of para 3 above. The fees charged from the students by any college should be calculated on the basis of average cost per student per year, and should in no case exceed the maximum limit to be fixed by notification by the UGC. In view of the frequent escalation of operational cost, the UGC may have to review and revise the maximum limit, from time to time, by notifying the same.
5. The fee to be charged from the students per year by a college for pursuing a first degree course in Engineering and Technology, Architecture and Pharmacy should not presently exceed Rs. 8,000

p.a. This limit includes tuition fee, laboratory fee, library fee, gymkhana, students activity fee etc. It does not include caution fee and security.

6. Draft regulations prepared by the committee are enclosed. The University Grants Commission may also consult the Vice-Chancellor of the Universities before these regulations are notified, as required under Section 12A of the UGC Act.
7. Admission to all courses of study should be made strictly by merit, determined on the basis of a competitive test to be conducted by the Government for admission to all such colleges. The merit list should be publicly declared.
8. Scholarships and financial support in any other form may be provided by the Government and/or any other organisation to ensure that no meritorious candidate is denied facilities for pursuing his studies due to lack of financial resources.
9. The norms and standards laid down by the All-India Council for Technical Education should be strictly enforced in these institutions.

024 Committee on setting up State Council of Higher Education 1986. Report. New Delhi, University Grants Commission, 1988, 8p.

The Committee was constituted to make the recommendations regarding setting up the State Council of Higher Education, as per National Policy on Education, 1986 and the Programme of Action in this regard. The guidelines formulated by sub-committee contains objectives, composition terms and condition of services, staff, temporary association of a person, Meeting, Power and functions, Planning and Coordination, Academic functions, Advisory functions, Administrative functions, Payment to the council, Budget and Annual Report.

025 Review Committee on the Scheme of University Level Book Production in Indian Languages, 1987. Report. New Delhi, Ministry of Human Resource Development, 1987. 98p. Chairman: Suresh Dalal.

The Review Committee for reviewing the scheme of production of University level books in Indian languages, appointed by the Ministry of Human Resource Development, Government of India, vide their letter No. F.7-3/86-D.III(L), dated the 17th March, 1987 having completed their deliberations, present this Report.

Terms of Reference of the Review Committee

(i) A critical and factual assessment of the scheme of production of university-level books in Indian languages, in terms of their effective absorption in the university system, as the most manifest element of the adoption of Indian languages as the media of instruction in the level of higher education.

(ii) A report on the question whether Central assistance provided to the 15 participating States has been actually and properly utilized for the declared purpose, namely, the production of university-level books in Indian languages.

(iii) A study of whether, and in what manner, the concerned State agencies have built up the revolving fund (out of the sale proceeds) for the continued implementation of the programme by the State themselves, without further Central assistance, in view of the fact that a majority of the participating States have already lifted central assistance to the committed extent.

(iv) A study of the operational arrangements adopted by the State agencies for the preparation, production, sale and off-take of the books produced.

(v) A specific study of the linkages between the State agencies and the Universities in the respective States in regard to the Scheme.

(vi) Stock position of books produced, the value of books held in stock, actual reasons for the accumulation of unsold stock, and the action being taken by the State Governments and the State agencies to dispose of the stock.

(vii) Preparation of a tabulated tally of the decisions taken by the universities all over the country for :

(a) The introduction of Indian languages as the media for the various university courses; and

(b) adoption of these books for these courses.

After collection of factual data on these lines, the Committee would also be expected to make specific recommendations on the 'Directions for the future' in respect of the programme of production of ULB in Indian languages. These 'Directions' may include:

(i) The pre-requisite considerations for selection, preparation and production of the titles.

(ii) The administrative infrastructure required. (The Committee could also usefully consider the exclusion of the BHU and the Haryana Agricultural University from the Programme, since their performance in this respect has not been very material. Besides, the implementation of the programme has been somewhat dispersed among different universities both in Karnataka and in Assam. A recommendation for unification of the implementation process in these two States could also be useful.)

(iii) The State Agencies are also discharging other functions assigned to them by the State Governments in addition to the ULB programme. Therefore, there could be a recommendation for maintaining the distinct identity of the State agencies *vis-a-vis* the ULB programme.

(iv) Suggestions for modifications in the scheme, on the basis of the past experience, and on the present findings of the Committee.

(v) Specific recommendations on the question whether the scheme is at all viable, and if so, whether it should be continued with or without central assistance and for how long.

Following are the recommendations of the Committee:

The Scheme should be continued at least till the end of the 8th plan period. The programme should, however remain restricted to university level books in Indian languages.

The Central assistance due under the on going rupees one crore scheme should be released and the Central Government should consider providing further assistance of rupees three crores to each State till the end of the 8th plan period.

The State governments should assume full responsibility for the Academies/Boards by providing them with adequate finances, necessary manpower, autonomous identity.

The Central assistance should no longer be provided direct to any university or its sub-formation under the scheme.

Payment to authors may be made either on royalty basis or partly on royalty and partly on lump sum basis. The rate of honorarium to authors should be uniform among all States and prescribed by the commission for scientific and technical terminology.

A list of core-books in all subjects should be prepared on priority basis.

Academies/Boards should adopt the service conditions, recruitment rules and other benefits for their staff at par with State government employees.

Each State Academies/Board must have an Academic cell for continuous evaluation and for monitoring the standard of books published both in their contents and get-up.

There should be a separate cell in the University Grants Commission with adequate representation from Commission for scientific and technical terminology for monitoring co-ordination and promoting the policy of Indian languages as media of instruction at university level.

Zonal co-ordination committees should be set up for co-ordinating the programme of book production and terminology in Indian languages.

Andhra Pradesh

026 Andhra University Enquiry Commission, 1966. Report by Justice K.V.G. Nair. Waltair, Andhra University, 1966. 95p.

This report contains the findings of the commission appointed to probe into the truth and validity of the allegations levelled against the university administration. The focus is primarily on the irregularities observed in the appointment of the teaching and non-teaching staff; in admissions to the research activities; in the conduct of examinations; and in floating the tenders for contract. Besides, it investigates into certain allegations made against the vice-chancellor.

Assam

027 Assam University Enquiry, 1935. Report by J.R. Cunningham. Shillong, Assam Government Press, 1936.

This is a general survey about the establishment of a university in the province of Assam. Apart from the basic questions of the aims and purposes of the university, its style, the territorial scope and academic range, the other principal issues discussed in this report relate to the relationship of Assam to the University of Calcutta; Assamese-Bengali question; education and employment; affiliation of the colleges; and the provision of finance etc.

028 Gauhati University Enquiry Commission, 1962. Report. Shillong, Gauhati University, 1962. 74p. Chairman: D.C. Pavte.

It is a detailed report of the findings of the commission which was asked to probe into the affairs of the university with particular reference to (i) causes and the nature of the incident of 16th August, 1961 which led to the resignation of three Administrative Officers and the Dean of the Faculty; (ii) general state of discipline in the university; (iii) the finance and financial transactions of the university from 1955-56, as well as the account of the University Development Committee from the beginning to date and the audit objection relating to the accounts of the past years; (iv) the recruitment, appointment, promotions and commendations of service of teachers and all other employees of the university and also the general conditions of residence and buildings; and (v) general administration of the university.

Bihar

029 Bihar University Affairs, 1962. Report by K.S.V. Raman. Muzzaffarpur, University of Bihar, 1964. 145p.

This report deals with the following issues: (i) The affairs of Rajendra college, Chapra with particular reference to the causes for the unrest and disturbances; (ii) alleged mismanagement of the college and its finances; (iii) the system at present adopted by the university in getting printed the question papers the causes for their leakage, and the persons responsible therefor; (iv) the general unrest in the university and the causes of the last strike; and (v) the inspection into the accounts of the university for the year 1960.

030 Bihar University Enquiry Commission, 1964. Report by K.S.V. Raman. Patna, Government of Bihar, 1965. 81p.

The present report deals with (a) the affairs of the Rajendra College, Chapra with particular reference to the causes and remedies for the unrest and disturbances; (b) the alleged mismanagement of the college and its finances; (c) the system adopted by the university in getting the question paper printed and the causes for their leakage; (d) the general unrest in the university with special reference to the disturbances caused at the convocation; and (e) miscellaneous matters covering the misuse of construction material meant for the university building and the irregularities said to have been observed in the case of the study leave.

031 University Enquiry Commission on the Working of Patna University, 1966. Report. Patna, Government of Bihar, 1967. 116p. Chairman: S.P. Singh.

Like other reports of the enquiry commission on the functioning of the universities in Bihar, the subject-matter of this report on Patna University is also more or less identical it deals with (a) the working of the senate, the syndicate, the academic council and the examination board; (b) the irregularities on the part of the officers of the university in the disposal of their official work; (c) the working of the affiliated colleges; and (d) the financial conditions of the university. Besides, the report also covers the Patna University Act, 1961, and has suggested certain amendments to suit the changing requirements of the university.

032 University Enquiry Commission on the Working of the Magadh University, Gaya, 1966. Report. Patna, Government of Bihar, 1968. 68p. Chairman: S.P. Singh.

This report contains the findings of the commission with regard to the alleged irregularities, administrative or otherwise said to have been omitted by the vice-chancellors and the registrar; the allegations against the working of the senate, the syndicate, the academic council and the examination board. The other subjects dealt with in this report are those related to the financial administration and the functioning of the affiliated colleges.

033 University Enquiry Commission on the Working of the Ranchi University, 1966. Report. Patna, Government of Bihar, 1968. 109 p. Chairman: S.P. Singh.

This report, which deals with the functioning of the Ranchi University, covers the following subjects: The university office and the officers of the university; the senate and the syndicate; the academic council and the examination board; the finance and the financial administration; and the constitutent and the affiliated colleges; It also contains certain recommendations with regard to the better functioning of the university.

034 University Enquiry Commission on the Working of the Bhagalpur University, 1966. Report. Patna, Government of Bihar, 1969. 156 p. Chairman: S.P. Singh.

The present report contains the findings of the commission with regard to the general functioning of the Bhagalpur University; the charges made against the appointment and the promotion of teaching and non-teaching staff; misappropriation of university funds; leakage of question papers; misuse of power; and the irregularities observed in the functioning of the affiliated colleges etc. The report also carries a number of recommendations made in this regard.

035 Gaya College Affairs Inquiry, 1969. Report by K. Abraham. Gaya, Magadh University, 1970. 55 p.

This report contains the finding of the one man commission appointed to enquire into the incident of firing within the campus of the Gaya College on 29th September, 1969 and to report the mismanagement of the affairs of the said college. The report deals with the following aspects: (i) the causes of the incident; (ii) the question of whether the authorities of the Gaya college and the university could have had any advance information about the possibility of this incident, and if so, what measures were taken by them to avoid it; (iii) the measures which were taken by the college and the university authorities to check the development of the incident after it actually took place and (iv) whether the administration of the Gaya College suffers from mismanagement.

036 Committee on University Reforms, 1973. Report. Patna, Government of Bihar, 1978. 103 p. Chairman: Shri Zawar Hussain.

The committee was constituted with an objective of studying the existing structure of the universities of Bihar and in the light of the experience of their working, to suggest a suitably reformed structure to ensure better working. The committee after reviewing the role and the functions of the various components of the universities in Bihar, has made a number of recommendations so that the university becomes the real centre of learning and knowledge. For recommendations, see pages 84-93 of the report.

Delhi

037 Delhi University Shyamlal College Affairs, 1973. Report by R.K. Baweja. Delhi, Delhi University, 1974. 45 p.

This report deals with the findings of the enquiry committee set up to investigate into the happenings of the Shyamlal College on or after 2nd of November, 1973. The focus of the document is primarily on the following issues: Inter-group rivalry of teachers' associations; neglect of classes by the teachers; misbehaviour with the students by the teachers; students indiscipline; and outside interference in the internal matters of the college. The report also contains certain perceptive suggestions in this regard.

Goa

038 Goa University Committee, 1966. Report. Panaji, Government of Goa, Daman and Diu, 1969. 68 p. Chairman: G.D. Parikh.

The committee was appointed to consider and recommend to the government the steps required to be taken for the establishment of a university in Goa through the progressive development of the post-graduate centre established by the university of Bombay; the type of university to be set up, its location, powers, composition etc.; and measures to be taken for overall development of higher education in that union territory. Some of the important recommendations of the committee are: Post-graduate centre be developed under the administration of board to be set up by the Government of Goa with the cooperation of Bombay university; the board of centre will have administrative power and academic control will be with the Bombay university; the Lt. Governor will be chancellor of the university; the authorities of the new university should be the senate, the syndicate, the faculties, and the boards of studies; the power of affiliation and disaffiliation of colleges should be with the university. The vice-chancellor should be full time salaried officer nominated by the chancellor and a special programme of scholarships for Goa, Daman and Diu students should be established.

Gujarat

039 Baroda University Commission, 1926. Report. Baroda, Maharaja Gaekwad, 1927. Chairman: A.G. Widgrey.

The commission was appointed to consider the possibility of establishing a university in Baroda. General education, examination, medium of instruction have been enumerated. Indian language and English have also been discussed. The recommendations have been given at pages 88-101 of the report.

040 Baroda University Committee, 1947. Report. Baroda, Baroda State, 1948. 63 p. Chairman: Mr. K.M. Munshi.

This report deals with the establishment of a university at Baroda. The scope and the type of the university to be established, its site and location, the medium of instruction, the constitution and the finance etc., are the principal topics of discussion of this report.

041 Gujarat University Committee, 1947. Report. Bombay, Government of Bombay, 1949. 174 p. Chairman: Justice M.C. Chagla.

This report deals with the establishment of a regional university for the province of Gujarat. The terms of reference of this committee are: (a) To make recommendations as to the scope, the form the constitution and the jurisdiction of a University for Gujarat, including the question of granting affiliation to the institutions outside the limits of Bombay province; (b) to report on the case of the establishment and the maintenance of the university and to make proposals for raising the necessary funds; and (c) to make any other recommendations germane to the subject.

042 Commission on Modernization of University Acts, 1970. Report. Gandhinagar Gujarat Education and Labour Department, 1971. 200 p. Chairman: Shri S.R. Dongerkery.

The commission was asked to examine and report on the difficulties experienced in the way of furthering the objects of the universities and how far the present pattern of the constitution of various authorities of the universities in the State as well as the terms and the conditions for appointment of the officers of these universities have contributed towards the same; to suggest changes in the constitutions of the various authorities of the universities in the State and the terms and the conditions of appointment of the officers of the universities which would be in the best interest of the university education; and to suggest, if necessary, a readjustment or extension of powers and duties of the various authorities.

043 Review Committee on the State of Higher Education in Gujarat, 1973. Report. Gandhinagar, Government of Gujarat, 1976. 67 p. Chairman: V.V. John.

This report contains the findings of the committee set up to examine the following aspects of higher education: (i) To review the state of higher education and assess the need for institutions for higher education in Gujarat over the next decade; (ii) to consider changes in the areas of the universities, including the establishment of new universities, so as to enable them to discharge their functions and meet their obligations effectively and adequately; and (iii) to indicate the financial implications of its recommendations.

Karnataka

044 Fact Finding Committee into the Affairs of the National Institute of Social Sciences, Bangalore, 1972. Report. Bangalore, Association of Schools of Social Work in India and Indian Association of Trained Social Workers, 1974. 8 p. Convener: Rev. Father Francis Sales.

It is an account of the nature of the crisis the institute is facing as a consequence of the demotion and subsequent dismissal of its director Dr. Sridharan, by the board of management. To end the impasse, the committee has suggested the immediate reinstatement of Dr. Sridharan and the integration of the institute with Bangalore university.

045 Lakkappa, K. Untold tale of the Bangalore University: Comments on Prof. Mathai's report. Bangalore, Eswar Printers, 1973. 144 p.

This document makes a critical assessment of the report of Prof. Samuel Mathai who headed the one man commission to enquire into certain charges levelled against the university administration related to the subjects like, the communal domination; promotions; the construction of new buildings; revision of pay scale; the appointment of the examiner; publication of the results; the functioning of certain departments; and the advertisement of posts etc. The author has concluded that the report is "one-sided and tutored", and "is a supreme example of what an inquiry should not be like".

046 Commission for Establishment of New Universities: Gulbarga and Mangalore, 1979. Report. Karnataka, Education and Youth Services Department, 1980. Chairman : D.V. Urs.

Government of Karnataka vide their order No. ED 30 UNÍ 79 Bangalore, dated 27th July, 1979 constituted a one man committee with following terms of references:

(i) To take necessary action towards the establishment of universities at Gulburga and Mangalore in all its aspects in the light of the proposals received by the Government and to suggest to what extent the personnel employed at present in the Karnataka and Mysore Universities could be utilised in the new universities; what additional posts to the minimum extent in each category require to be created for the functioning of the two new universities. It shall also take necessary steps to ensure maximum assistance possible from the University Grants Commission.

(ii) To examine, in all aspects, whether a Technical University be established in the State and if so, to suggest the set-up of such university with its financial implications. It shall also take necessary steps to ensure maximum assistance from the University Grants Commission.

(iii) To go into the question of imparting education through radio transmission referred to in the preamble and to work out full details thereof — both administrative and financial.

Commission while making its recommendations pointed that at the moment there are three Universities viz., Mysore, Karnataka and Bangalore, with their own traditions, under the Karnataka Universities Act, 1976. In creating Gulbarga and Mangalore Universities, the jurisdiction of the Karnataka and Mysore universities will necessarily be reduced. The Commission strongly feels that the post-graduate centre is Simoga which caters to the districts of Chickmagalur, Chitradurga and Simoga and has about 40 colleges, be simultaneously, like Gulbarga and Mangalore, established as an university.

It is the view of the commission that any future development in the governance and management of higher education in Karnataka State should be in the direction of creating autonomous colleges and institutions of higher learning and not starting of new universities. The commission recommends State University Commission to evaluate continuously the functioning of such institutions.

Commission made detailed recommendation regarding, legislative, financial, administrative and academic needs for the establishment of these universities.

047 Karnataka Universities Review Commission, 1979. Report. Bangalore, 1980. 206 p. Chairman : K.N. Roy.

Commission was appointed in January 1979 in exercise of the powers conferred on the chancellor by sub-sections (1), (2) and (3) of section 61 of the Karnataka Universities Act, 1976.

According to the terms of reference of the Commission, it was to:

(a) review the past working of the three universities of the State in all aspects, academic (including teaching, research and extension) as well as administrative;

(b) make recommendations for the future working and progress of these universities in all aspects, academic as well as administrative, and to suggest the broad outlines of the priorities for their future development;

(c) suggest where necessary changes or improvements to the Karnataka State University Act, 1976, to enable various officers, authorities and other functionaries of these universities to function effectively to realise the objectives enunciated in section 4;

(d) advise on measures to be adopted for meeting the various requirements for all round development of students, including provision for their curricular and extra-curricular activities, vocational guidance, hostel accommodation, health and welfare measures etc., as well as for maintenance of discipline among teachers and employees of the universities, keeping in view the need for co-operation and co-ordination between them and among the faculties and departments for successful implementation of interdisciplinary programmes; and

(f) make any other recommendations, incidental or ancillary to the above, which the Commission may consider important.

For effective greater decentralisation in the governance of the universities the commission recommends that in each university the senate should be fully empowered to pass status, the syndicate to make ordinances, and the Academic council to frame regulations.

For co-ordination and development of higher education the Commission recommends a State Commission for Higher Education be set up immediately. Departmental council and committee of management should be set up. The commission supports the proposal made by the Education Commission earlier for setting up autonomous colleges within the framework of universities.

The Commission makes some recommendations for improving the procedure for selection and appointment of teachers in the universities and colleges; they are mainly to ensure that the selection committee have enough members with the necessary background and expertise and the selection process is reasonably expeditious.

After reviewing the policies followed by the State government in regard of financing of colleges under private management, the commission makes number of recommendations. They are: private colleges may be allowed to retain the standard fee collected; the proposed state Commission should make available funds for the development of undergraduate colleges. The Commission strongly recommends that levying of capitation fees should be totally disallowed in all colleges.

The main thrust of the recommendations made in regard to undergraduate programmes is to introduce a measure of flexibility in the structure as well as the content of the courses. The recommended examination system attempts to incorporate the good features of internal or college level examination and external or university examination. The commission also made recommendations for strengthening post-graduate teaching and evaluation.

The commission also recommended for setting up of centres of advanced study and Sstate Commission for Higher Education would be given the responsibility of identifying and building up such centres.

The Commission also made recommendation for engineering, medical and teacher education while making recommendation about non-formal and library development, the Commission recommended for linking them with a wider network of public libraries.

The Commission is of the view that student welfare should be an integral part of the education programme. The Commission believes that discipline among student is best developed by improving student-teacher relationships.

The Committee also recommended better service conditions for teaching and non-teaching staff.

Kerala

048 University Committee, Travancore, 1923, Report. Trivandrum, Government of Travancore, 1925. 466 p. President: Rao Bahadur K.A.K. Aiyangar.

This report deals with the question of setting up a university in the State of Travancore by itself or in association with the adjacent areas. Apart from the location, the other major points discussed are as follows: (a) The ways and the means to coordinate the resources, so as to create teaching and residential centres, providing facilities for higher work and research; (b) the departments in which the instructions should be offered, the facilities to be organised and the examinations to be provided in the university with a clear indication of the order of priority; (c) the additions that must be made for the residential accommodation available at present in possible university centres both immediate and for some years to come; (d) the immediate and proximate requirements of the university with regard to the buildings, the equipment and the staff, both for itself and for its constituent institutions; (e) the relations of the university to the secondary and the intermediate education; (f) special provision for facilities for university education of women, the advancement of the oriental studies and the university publication; (g) the type of relationship to be established between the university and the colleges or the halls or residence or hostels; (h) safe guards to be devised to prevent any improper lowering of the standard of examination, the diplomas and the degrees; (i) the constitution of the chief constituent bodies such as the senate, the academic body etc., including specific proposals for their composition; and (j) the estimate of probable initial and recurring costs of the university to be established.

049 Commission of Enquiry, 1970. Report by S. Padma Kumar. Trivandrum, Government of Kerala, 1970. 135 p.

This report contains the findings of the commission with regard to the following matters: (a) The proper role of the State government, the university, the parents and the private college managements in financing higher education in the State, within the ambit of the relevant university Act, the Constitution of India and the grant-in-aid code for private colleges (both under the directorate of collegiate education and the director of technical education) and polytechnics, including the direct payment of the salaries of the staff by the government; (b) the amendments to be made in the grant-in-aid code applicable for (i) arts, science and training colleges in the private sector and (ii) engineering colleges and polytechnics in the private sector; and (c) the question of implementing a uniform rate of fee for the different courses in all the colleges in the state.

050 Commission of Inquiry on the University of Kerala, 1970. Report by G.K. Pillai. Trivandrum, Government of Kerala, 1971. 253+xxix p.

The commission was appointed to enquire into certain allegations levelled against the university administration. The commission covers the following aspects: (a) Whether there is any truth in the allegation that the syndicate of the Kerala University did not care to place the second and the subsequent ordinances before the senate; (b) whether there is sufficient ground to conclude that the syndicate had taken upon itself the powers of the senate to institute teaching posts; (c) whether the creation of the post of Controller of examinations did conform to the various requirements of the University Act, 1957; (d) whether there is any substance in the allegations that the vice-chancellor overlooked the legitimate claim of other qualified persons for the post of reader in marine biology; and (e) whether there was deliberate postponement of filling up of the vacancy of a reader in the department of politics.

051 General Inspection Commission, 1971. Report. Trivandrum, Sri Venkateswara University, 1971. 310 p. Chairman: Dr. D.J. Reddy.

This report highlights the general working conditions of as many as 44 colleges of Sri Venkateswara Uuniversity. The affiliated colleges and the medical colleges have been dealt with separately. For the former, the primary focus of the report has been on the assessment of (i) the growth and the development of the institution; (ii) the physical facilities, the lab-equipment, the library books and the utilization of grants; (iii) the adequacy of staff strength; (iv) the areas of expansion; and (v) the possibility of opening of post-graduate courses, whereas for the latter, the objective of the inspection has been (i) to review the existing conditions of the colleges; (ii) to carryout a detailed assessment of the available facilities such as the buildings, the equipment and the staff in accordance with the recommendations of the medical council of India; (iii) to intimate as to where the existing facilities for the undergraduate and the post-graduate training are sufficient; and (iv) to suggest the guidelines for the future development of the colleges for teaching as well as for the patient care.

052 Review Committee on Sri Venkateswara University College, Tirupati and Sri Venkateswara Post-Graduate Centre, Anantpur, 1972. Report Tirupati, Sri Venkateswara University, 1972. 189 p. Chairman: Prof, B.K. Seshachar.

It is an account of the committee constituted to assess and evaluate the current academic and research programmes being conducted at Sri Venkateswara university college and at the post-graduate centre. The subjects covered in this report include Zoology, English, Telugu, Hindi, Political Science, Philosophy, Psychology, Economics and Commerce, History, Anthropology and Sociology, Mathematics, Physics, Chemistry, Botany, Homescience, Statistics, and Geology.

Lahore

053 Panjab University Enquiry Committee, 1932-33. Report. Lahore, Superintendent of Publications, 1933. Chairman: Sir Geoga Anderson.

The Punjab University enquiry committee assembled in Lahore on 18th October, 1932 under the chairmanship of Sir Geoga Anderson. It is a detailed report on education in the province. The committee suggested to increase industrial and the craft schools in the province. The recommendations have been given at pages 301-356 of the report.

Punjab University, Lahore is a predecessor University of Panjab Uuniversity, Chandigarh).

Madhya Pradesh

054 Inquiry Commission on University of Jabalpur, 1968. Report by G.K. Shinde. Indore Education Department of Government of Madhya Pradesh, 1968. 61 p.

This report highlights the findings of the commission with regard to: (i) The propriety of appointments made in the university during the period commencing from 1st July, 1956 to first July 1968; (ii) the financial conditions of the university and the propriety of the creation and the filling of new posts during the year 1967; (iii) the irregularities committed by the university regarding the promotion of teaching staff etc.; (iv) the cause of the general dissatisfaction prevailing in the university in the matter of appointments, the conduct of examination and the declaration of results during the period under reference; and (vi) the inspection of records, the equipment and the laboratories of the university.

Maharashtra

055 Committee on University Reform, 1924. Report. Bombay, Government of Bombay, 1925. 266+vi p. Chairman: Sri C.H. Setalvad.

This report contains the findings of the committee which was constituted to examine the following issues regarding the university of Bombay. These are: (a) the constitution and the function of the Bombay University with a view to broaden and liberalize its constitution; (b) the relations between the university and its affiliated colleges both in Bombay city and in the Mofussil, and the feasibility to institute other universities at Mofussil centres; (c) the relations which exist between the university and the government; and (d) the question of bringing the university into closer relation with the commercial and the industrial interest and the public bodies in the city of Bombay.

056 Maharashtra University Committee, 1942. Report. Bombay, Bombay University, 1943. Chairman: Dr. M.R. Jayakar.

The committee was appointed by the Governor of Bombay. Chapter III of the report deals with the courses of study, including science, arts, language and literature. The committee also refers to the different faculties of arts, science, technology, law and medicine. The departments of studies relating to fine arts and music have also been enumerated. The recommendations have been given at pages 79-85 of the report.

057 Bombay University Reorganisation Committee, 1950. Report. Bombay, Government of Bombay, 1951. 253 p. Chairman: N.H. Bhagwati.

The committee was appointed to consider the effect of the establishment of the regional universities of the Bombay University, including its relationship with the affiliated colleges and the institutions and to make recommendations regarding its future structure and the functions; to consider the ways and the means for co-ordinating the activities of the various universities in the State and to make proposals for the settlement of the problems affecting more than one university; to recommend a revised constitution for the university; and to make any other recommendations germane to the subject.

058 Summary of Main Recommendations of the Bombay University Re-Organisation Committee and Draft Bill for the Bombay University Act. 1951. Bombay, University of Bombay, 1952. 42 p.

As the title suggests, this volume provides chapter-wise summary of the main recommendations of the committee. Draft bill for the University Act is, however, presented in detail.

059 Committee on Shri Chhatrapati Shivaji University, 1961. Report. Bombay, Government of Maharashtra, 1962. 109 p. Chairman: SRTRS Shahupuri.

This report is about the establishment of a university at Kolhapur. It deals with (i) the form, the scope, the constitution and the jurisdiction of the university to be established for the southern parts of the Maharashtra state keeping in view the area under the jurisdiction of Poona University and the facilities for higher education available in the same; and (ii) the cost of establishment and the maintenance of the university.

060 Work Study of the University of Poona, 1964. Report Prepared by Kirloskar Consultant Ltd., Poona. Maharashtra State, 1964. 55+88 p.

This report by a consultant house deals with the following matters: (a) Reorganisation of the university administration, job evaluation, cost control, budgetary control, laying down communication systems and manuals with simplification and methods improvements, including elimination of the duplicate and unnecessary operations, introducing office aids wherever feasible and eliminating bottlenecks; (b) examination of the accounts procedures followed by the university with a view to introducing such procedural improvements as may seem necessary which would make the work more simple without loss of efficiency; (c) assessment of staff requirements at different levels; and (d) providing the management with rational basis for altering staff strength with varying volumes of work.

061 Committee on Dr. Syed Mehdi Ali, 1972. Report. Poona, Marathwada University, 1973. 204+25 p. Chairman: S.R. Dongerkery.

This report contains in detail the findings of the committee appointed to enquire into certain acts alleged to have been committed and certain statements alleged to have been made by Dr. Syed Mehdi Ali, Head of the Department of Zoology of Marathwada University which were derogatory to the dignity of the university and in particular, to the person of the vice-chancellor.

062 Marathwada University Enquiry Committee, 1974. Report. Marathwada University, 1974. 123+49p. Chairman: P.G. Ghate.

This report contains the findings of the committee set up to investigate into the facts behind the two articles regarding the university affairs, published in The Maharashtra Times, a Marathi daily of Bombay, in its issues of 9th and 10th January, 1974. Allegations which the committee has inquired into, pertain to the misbehaviour of the students with vice-chancellor; political groupism; misuse of university funds; unfair appointments and promotions; irregularities in the conduct of examinations and admission, caste groupism; and deterioration in the standard of education in the colleges affiliated to the university etc.

North-Eastern Region

063 Committee on Setting up a University for the North-Eastern Region of India 1963. Report. New Delhi, University Grants Commission, 1965. 50 p. Chairman: Prof. A.R. Wadia.

This committee was set up jointly by the U.G.C. and the Ministry of Education to assess the present facilities for higher education in the north-eastern areas of India (Nagaland, NEFA, Manipur and hill areas of Assam); to consider the pattern and the development of higher education best suited to the needs of these areas; and to examine whether it would be desirable to set up a university in the region or an autonomous institution 'deemed to be a university' under the U.G.C. Act of 1956.

Orissa

064 The State Universities Committee, 1962, Report. Cuttack, Orissa Government Press, 1963. 60 p. Chairman: Dr. P. Parija.

The committee was appointed to examine the need for more universities in Orissa and the nature, the structure and the constitution of such universities. The steps to be taken to streamline the existing provisions of the Utkal university Act and the need to turn out the maximum number of graduates in various subjects, including technology, are the other topics of current importance dealt with in this report.

065 Committee on Establishment of New Colleges in Orissa from 1978-79 to 1982-83. Report. Bhubaneswar, Education and Youth Services Department. Orissa, 1979. 169+xxx p. Chairman : Bama Charan Das.

In order to determine the policy that should be adopted for development of higher education and to ensure a planned development, the Government of Orissa in the Education and Youth Services Department, in their Resolution No. 31932 dated 24th Sept., 1977 set up a Committee to carry out a State-wide survey to assess the need for establishing new colleges in the state during 1978-1983.

The terms of reference of the committee are as follows:

1. To make a State-wide survey to assess the number of additional

colleges required to be set up in each district over the period of next five years and to indicate the financial implications thereof.

2. To suggest the annual phasing of the programme for setting up of colleges as would be recommenued for being established by the committee during the next five years.

A summary of the main recommendations is given bellow:

1. In preparing the priority list of applicants for admission of students to colleges on the basis of marks obtained in the qualifying examinations a weightage ranging from 5 to 10 per cent in lieu of reservation of seats be given to students belonging to (a) Scheduled Caste (b) Scheduled Tribes and (c) first generation learners (3.71).
2. Provision should be made for vertical mobility from the Vocationalised Spectrum to the General Education Spectrum on the basis of achievement in examination at the end of the Intermediate stage, and not *vice versa* (3.72).
3. (a) High priority should be given to making education a medium of socio-economic transformation as no marked progress has so far been made in this direction.
   (b) Improvement of the existing institutions and removing physical deficiencies in them should receive high priority.
   (c) Provision of part-time education, continuing education and correspondence courses should be made for those who will not be able to make the grade for being considered eligible for admission to full-time institutions, but will have the desire to continue their studies.
   (d) Those of the socially under-privileged group, who will qualify for admission but are unable to continue on financial grounds should be provided with scholarships or bursaries.
   (e) Admission to degree classes should be restrictive and selective to avoid wastage of efforts.
   (f) Greatest priority should be given to the scheme of vocationalisation at the Intermediate stage.
   (g) Middle-level jobs should be delinked from degree and linked to job-training at the (Higher Secondary) Intermediate level, so that there may not be undue and unreasonable rush of indifferent students to the degree classes (3.9).
4. For increase of enrolment in colleges (a) Steps should be taken to boost up the outturn of matriculates and for greater provision of facilities for collegiate education in districts where it is very low. (b) The Courses of study in colleges should be restructured and redesigned so as to be related to socio-economic developmental plans in the State and the country. (c) confidence among the students regarding wage-employment and self-employment possibilities on completion of courses of higher education is to be created (4.5).
5. (a) Since Orissa (2.6% enrolment in colleges) is far behind India (4.9% enrolment in colleges) in the matter of development of Higher Education, every effort should be made during the Sixth Plan to increase enrolment in colleges so that the difference may be narrowed. (b) For achieving this, it is necessary not only (i) to

rapidly increase facilities for admission to colleges, but also, (ii) to take bold steps for rapid increase in the number of students passing the qualifying examinations for entrance to universities (4.6).

6. Consolidation of existing colleges so as to make them viable should be given priority over increase of enrolment and admission facilities. The Planning Commission and U.G.C. should be approached to give sufficient out-right grants to achieve this by a phased programme (5.13).
7. (a) Only those students who are of proved merit and are likely to take studies seriously should be admitted to colleges;
   (b) Steps should be taken to motivate students for serious applications to study;
   (c) The content of courses should be suitably increased wherever necessary, so that students are kept under pressure of work throughout the session;
   (d) Periodical tests should be held to keep the students on their tiptoe with sufficient safeguards to make them reliable;
   (e) The basic physical facilities should be provided by each institution and the spirit of self-study should be inculcated;
   (f) Students securing less than 300 marks (37.5%) at the H.S.C. or equivalent examination should be considered ineligible for collegiate education. In order to give a second chance to those who have accidentally secured less than 300 marks to improve their grades, such students and even all students who are placed in the 3rd division in the H.S.C. Examination may be permitted to appear again at the H.S.C. Examination if they so desire;
   (g) The students passing the Second Examinations at any stage should take admission in higher classes in the next session, unless separate sessions commencing in January are started for them in some colleges (5.35).
8. (i) Facilities for continuation of education at the higher level should not ordinarily be increased in the Faculty of Arts.
   (ii) Whenever seats are required to be increased in the existing co-educational colleges in the process of consolidation, they should be increased in the Faculties of Science and Commerce.
   (iii) No new college should be ordinarily allowed to take students in the Faculty of Arts, until the present tendency of rapid increase of unemployed in this faculty is reversed.
   (iv) Highest priority should be given to vocationalisation at the Intermediate level immediately. Vocationalisation at the First degree level should be taken up subsequently.
   (v) Contents and courses of studies in higher education should be reoriented to meet the socio-economic and developmental needs of the people.
   (vi) P.G. Courses in Arts Departments should not ordinarily be allowed to open (5.45).
9. In the post-matric stage vocational courses of work and study be introduced in Junior Functional Colleges to equip at least 50 per cent

of those who go in for higher education, with skills and entrepreneurship necessary to meet the present day challenges at the middle level as well as the socio-economic needs of the people (5.55).

10. A separate Intermediate Board be formed to manage the schemes of Vocational and General streams of education at the Intermediate level. All Higher Secondary and Intermediate classes may be academically controlled by the Board (5.55/5.56).
11. Out of the 56 (or 54 if Government do not give permission to Jamsuli and Aul) Proposed Intermediate Colleges to be started during the Sixth Plan, 40 should be Junior Functional Colleges (5.71).
12. There should be one Women's College in the headquarters of each district by 1982 provided sufficient number of women students are likely to take admission in such colleges (5.73).
13. There should be one Junior College in every Subdivision by the end of the Sixth Plan (5.74).
14. The Tutorial Colleges or coaching classes should not be considered for being given permission by Government or affiliation by a University. They should be left alone by the Government and Universities to find their own means to coach students desirous of appearing at University examinations as non-collegiate candidates. Such institutions do exist in large numbers elsewhere in India and outside it (5.81).
15. Colleges should not be started with a hope to develop an area. On the other hand, returns from the developed land should be available before a college is started (5.82).
16. Admission to degree classes both Pass and Hons. should be selective and restrictive. In case the three year Hons. degree course is introduced, this course should be confined to selected institutions of high standard and students of proved merit (5.9).
17. Every effort should be made to reduce Inter-District and Intra-District disparities in the first place at the school level and at the college level (6.52).
18. The following variation scale of percentage for districtwise provision of facilities for admission to colleges calculated on the total number of students anticipated to pass the qualifying examinations in 1982 be adopted:
    - I Puri, Cuttack and Balasore — 65%
    - II Sundargarh and Sambalpur — 70%
    - III Ganjam, Mayurbhanj and Dhenkanal — 75%
    - IV Keonjhar and Bolangir — 80%
    - V Koraput, Phulbani and Kalahandi — 85% (6.72).
19. Universities should not consider any application for affiliation, unless it is accompanied by Government permission. The Government should fix a last date for receiving applications for opening of new colleges in the next session and after due consideration either give permission or refuse to give permission in good time for the organisers of the college to submit an application

to the concerned University by 30th November of the year, just preceding the year in which the college is proposed to be started (7.26).

20. (a) Government and the Universities should take into consideration the realities of the situation and grant permission and affiliation only after all the conditions required in the statutes are fulfilled on the grounds of academic necessity, viability and the needs of development.
(b) The Universities should not grant provisional affiliation to colleges with the hope of conditions being fulfilled in near future, nor should Government give permission before essential conditions are actually satisfied.
(c) The concerned University should complete the process laid down in the statutes and come to a final decision in the matter of granting or refusing affiliation in the annual meeting of the Senate held in the month of March of the year in which students are expected to be admitted to the newly affiliated college.
(d) Neither the Government nor the Universities should vacillate on the question of granting or refusing to grant affiliation or further affiliation by postponing decisions, however unpleasant they may be, to later dates, thus necessitating at times violations of the provisions in the Acts, Statutes or Regulations.
(e) The sponsors of a proposed college should provide the infrastructure of the college, the minimum standard of which has been suggested by the Committee before Government permission or University affiliation is given. In no case should there be any relaxation of this minimum standard.
(f) The Government shall take the responsibility of selecting persons for appointment as teachers in aided colleges. If at any stage appointment of teachers on *ad hoc* basis is necessary, lecturers should be selected from a list prepared by the Department.
(g) The Government shall pay in full the expenditure to be incurred for payment of salaries of teachers from the beginning i.e., from the session for which affiliation is granted.
(h) The Government shall take the responsibility of selecting persons for appointment as teachers in aided colleges.
(i) Students will be admitted to colleges only after the concerned University gives affiliation and permission to admit students.
(j) Even if the initial investment is made by the sponsors of a proposed college or even if adequate funds are available for running a college from the interest of a trust, Government should control the location of colleges on a rational basis in the interest of the State as a whole (7.7).

21. In order to help reduce the gap between Orissa and other States of India in the matter of general and higher education, the allocation of the State Government and the percentage of expenditure on education and training to the total revenue expenditure should increase. Government of India should be approached for special

grants in this regard (Ch. VIII).

22. The present scheme for Central assistance which has been in operation since 1977, for the diversification of education at the Higher Secondary (Intermediate) stage and other Central schemes if any, should be fully utilised (Ch. VIII).
23. The existing institutions should be made viable so as to avail themselves of the U.G.C. assistance to the fullest extent (Ch. VIII).
24. The existing fee structure in colleges may be enhanced (8.59).
25. The organisers and the public in a locality wherever the location of a college is found suitable should use their resources.
    (i) to build up infrastructure for the college,
    (ii) to build up permanent assets for the college and
    (iii) to have a built-in income for maintenance and repair of the buildings and for augmenting the permanent assets (8.6).
26. Government should frame rules in respect of
    (i) collections made from the public by organisers of new colleges and
    (ii) accountability of expenditure (8.6).
27. Government should form a Committee consisting of educationists and experts in agriculture, industry etc. to recommend to Government the particular elective subjects teaching of which should be provided in each of the Junior Functional Colleges recommended by the Committee. This matter should not be left to the organisers of proposed colleges, as the planned development of the State is likely to be hampered that way.
28. New Colleges recommended by the Committee:

The following Junior Traditional and Functional Colleges are recommended to be started phasewise:

Year & phase	Sl. No.	Traditional Colleges	Sl. No.	Functional Colleges
1979-80	1.	Boudh, Phulbani	1.	Ispat College, Steel Town, Rourkela
	2.	Uditnagar, Rourkela		
1980-81	1.	Athmallik, Dhenkanal	1.	Choudwar, Cuttack
	2.	Second College in Berhampur Town	2.	Dharmasala, Cuttack
	3.	Nuapada, Kalahandi		
1981-82	1.	Hindol, Dhenkanal	1.	Niali, Cuttack
	2.	Women's College, Sundargarh	2.	Buguda, Ganjam
			3.	Kendupadar, Ganjam
			4.	Dharmgarh, Kalahandi
			5.	Ekamra, Bhubaneswar, Puri
			6.	Daspalla College, Puri
1982-83	1.	Nilagiri, Balasore	1.	Avana-Bishnupur-Gopalpur, Balasore
	2.	Women's College, Kalahandi	2.	Rampur, Bolangir
	3.	Women's College, Keonjhar	3.	Mahakalpara, Cuttack
			4.	Balikuda, Cuttack

	4. Women's College, Koraput in Cuttack	5. Kandarpur, Cuttack 6. Sahaspur-Mahanga area
		7. Joranda, Dhenkanal
		8. Bhismagiri, Ganjam
		9. Gatagaon, Keonjhar
		10. Makangiri, Koraput
		11. Simanta College, Mayurbhanj
		12. Jashipur, Mayurbhanj
		13. Baliguda, Phulbani
		14. Rajsunakhala, Puri
		15. Brajarajnagar, Sambalpur
		16. Biramitrapur, Sundargarh
		17. Pallahara, Dhenkanal
		18. Baranga, Puri
Total	11	27 = 38

066 Committee on Concurrence to new colleges in Orissa, 1981-85. Report. Bhubaneswar, Education and Youth Services, 1981. 52p. Chairman: Sadasiv Misra.

Government of Orissa in the Education and Youth Services Department in its Resolution No. 20730-EYS dated 25th April, 1981 appointed a committee to assess the need for establishing new colleges.

The terms of reference included assessment of the need for establishing new colleges and the possibility of extending accommodation in the existing colleges, in relation to the increase demand for higher education in the State. The committee was required to indicate the principles to be adopted for considering the grant of concurrence by Government to new colleges. It was further required to suggest how best the opening of new colleges could be linked with the impending introduction of the plus two course of higher secondary education. The other item included consideration of the system of grants-in-aid and the general purpose of according Government concurrence.

Recommendations are:

The Committee considered the issues referred to it in the terms of reference within the framework of the National Policy on Education, 1968, the new 10+2+3 pattern of Education, vocationalisation of the Secondary Course and the guidelines enunciated in the Sixth Five Year Plan. Accordingly, at the beginning of the report, broad objectives have been analysed to guide the nature, quantum and quality of development of higher education in the State (Chapter II).

Then follows an exercise, projected up to the year 1985, estimating the demand for higher education and provision of facilities for the purpose. The exercise has been made on the assumption that the number of candidates qualifying at the H.S.C. Examination would increase at the rate of 10 per cent. a year and 70 per cent would seek admission to the higher stage of general education. In 1985, their number will be 71,000.

At present (1981), the number of seats available in the 1st year class of the 187 colleges is 45,600. The plus two course of Secondary Educaticn will be introduced in 1983. The committee recommends the establishment by Government of 15 Junior Colleges to provide model vocationalised Secondary Education and at least 50 High Schools should be upgraded to Higher Secondary stage. Additional accommodation will be available in the existing colleges by improved utilisation and feasible extension within the optimum level. The total number of seats in 1983 will be 30,600. The Committee therefore recommends that there is no need or justification for granting recognition to any new college, up to the year 1985 (Chapter III).

Government concurrence is an effective instrument of planning, direction and control of higher education of the State. During recent years, many spurious and substandard colleges have come into existence. Grant of concurrence has not always been effective and has in many cases been affected by non-academic considerations. To make the issue of concurrence systematic and effective, the Committee makes the following recommendations:

A. Applications for concurrence are to be considered only after assessing the over-all need for expansion of higher education in the State at the time and optimum utilisation of the existing college.

B. If after such assessment, there is over-all need for expansion, the following conditions should be adhered to for according concurrence to any proposed college–

(i) application for concurrence must be received atleast one year ahead of the commencement of the academic year in which it is proposed to admit students.

(ii) fixed deposits of rupees one lakh and one lakh twenty five thousand for I.A. and I. Sc. classes and similar amounts for B.A. and B.Sc. classes shall be pledged to the University.

(iii) college classes shall not be started in any school, excepting upgradation of a High School to Higher Secondary level.

(iv) financial stability of Rs. 60,000 for annual recurring expenditure Rs. three lakhs for undertaking construction of building is ensured.

(v) atleast 10 acres of land in rural areas and 3 acres in urban areas must have been obtained.

(vi) the teaching staff shall be appointed on the recommendation of a Selection Board appointed by Government.

(vii) temporary independent working structure of building must be available before students are admitted.

(viii) atleast 64 students must be admitted in every faculty to start with and the number should rise to 128 in three years.

(ix) basic facilities prescribed by the University are provided before students are admitted.

(x) fulfilment of immediate requirements are reported before students are admitted.

(xi) no application shall be entertained for opening the first degree course until three batches have appeared at the Intermediate final examination.

The committee further recommends that technical and professional colleges, post-graduate classes and control of capitation fees should be brought under the purview of concurrence (Chapter IV).

The Committee offers specific recommendations for the plus two course of secondary education. Vocationalised higher secondary education is very different from vocational craft or technical training. Vocationalised secondary education is general education. It has core subjects such as language and general studies, common with academic streams; it has further core subject in language sciences, management etc. relevant to the vocations selected along with practical vocations.

The Committee recommends that Government should start atleast 15 Junior Colleges in 1983 to provide model plus two courses of Higher Secondary Education. Since this will eventually be the terminal stage of education for 50 per cent of the students, linking man-power requirement with this education, plus two courses should steadily be expanded on the model of the Government Junior Colleges (Chapter V).

For giving effect to the 10+2+3 pattern, two classes in the High Schools were amalgamated in 1980 to constitute class VIII. In 1983, this class will appear at the High School Certificate Examination. This year will be a hump year when double the usual number of candidates will seek admission in the Intermediate (or +2) class. It is a colossal task to provide accommodation to (58,000×2) 1,16,000 students. This is a passing phase; the hump will move upwards, normalcy will prevail in 1984. Temporary and make shift arrangements have to be made for 1983-84 which will be passed on to the second year in 1984-85.

There will be some excess capacity available in 1983, as has been estimated in the over-all expansion of higher education in the State. The Committee recommends that *ad hoc* shifts should be arranged in the existing colleges and 50 more high schools should be upgraded to the Higher Secondary level. This will provide necessary accommodation to the excessive number seeking admission in 1983. In 1985, the *ad hoc* shifts in the colleges should be withdrawn and the 50 higher secondary schools will cater to the normal growth (Chapter VI).

The existing grants-in-aid may be modified so that one-half should be paid at the end of five years and the full amount at the end of seven years. The Committee does not recommend any Foundation Fund to be given by Government.

Punjab

067 Punjabi University Commission, 1960. Report. Punjab Government, 1961. 64p. Chairman: Sir Yadavindra Singh.

The commission was asked to examine and propose the scope and the functions of the university; to examine and propose the steps necessary for the development of the Punjabi language and literature on scientific lines, including its development as a medium of instruction for university education; to propose the location and jurisdiction of the university; and to examine the financial implications of the establishment of the university.

068 Punjab Education Reforms Commission 1982. Report: Frame-work for implementation of educational reforms in Punjab. Punjab, Governor of Punjab, 1985. 5 vols. Chairman : R.N. Dogra.

Punjab Education Reforms Commission was set up by the Governor of Punjab vide *Punjab Government Gazette* (Extraordinary) Notification No. 19/2/82-3-Edu-(3)641 dated the 20th Febuary, 1982.

The Commission's terms of reference are:

(i) To critically assess the functioning of the present education system and to pin-point its inadequacies.

(ii) To suggest specific changes in the structure and content of education at all levels and incorporate in it ideals of democracy, secularism and national integration.

(iii) To suggest concrete steps to give education a vocational bias with the objective of reducing the incidence of unemployment among the educated persons.

(iv) To suggest specific changes in the administration of educational system with particular reference to qualifications, conduct, pre- and in-service training and re-orientation programme of teachers.

(v) To review the syllabus at all levels of Primary, Middle, High/Higher Secondary Schools and also suggest course content for encouraging values of national integration, democracy, secularism, socialism and development of universal humanitarian values.

(vi) To examine availability of essential facilities to the schools such as seating arrangements, drinking water, sanitary conditions, text-books and stationery items at controlled rates within the premises of educational institutions.

(vii) To suggest measures for inculcating respect for manual labour with particular emphasis on self-employment.

(viii) To suggest schemes for providing incentives for children of the weaker section.

(ix) To suggest special schemes to encourage girls' education.

(x) To review teaching methods, their evaluation and examination methods.

(xi) To suggest measures for improving social control over education in Punjab.

Regarding university education commission makes following recommendations:

The major task before the universities is to expand and explore new horizons of knowledge relevant to our social needs and purposes. The technological revolution requires the creation of a reservoir of highly skilled workers, planners, inventors and managers. Without financial autonomy university autonomy has no meaning. To ensure financial autonomy block grants should be provided to a university with an in-built mechanism for meeting its normal needs. For effective participation in the decision-making adequate representation should be provided to different sections of the academic community.

Academic council should deal with broad matters of academic policies and provide appropriate direction to the university in the pursuit of its academic programmes.

There should be two boards of studies in each subject one for under-graduate courses and the other for post-graduate courses, with an in-built mechanism for adequate coordination between the two sets of boards in a subject.

The teaching departments should be provided with a competent and efficient leadership.

The University Act should provide for broad supervision by Chancellor. The acts of the university should include provisions for the statutory bodies : senate, syndicate, Academic Council, Finance Committee, Planning Board, College Development Council. Students Advisory Committees should also be set up. Commission also recommend for the constitution of statutory bodies : (a) Admission Committee; (b) Examination Committee; (c) Grievances Committee; (d) Joint Consultative Committee; and (e) Campus Committee.

It has been recommended that the vice-chancellor should he appointed only for one term of five years, and that be should not normally be older than 65 years. Each university may have four Rectors, one each for administration, academic affairs, fed affiliated colleges and student's welfare. Commission is not in favour of the post of pro-vice-chancellor.

Deans of Faculties should be appointed from amongst university professors by rotation for a period of two years. The principal function of the Registrar should be to ensure coordination in the implementation of the policies framed and decision taken by the various university bodies.

Universities should devise their own rules, procedures and norms of functioning, which should help in the promotion of a flexible approach to the various problems which arise from time to time. A separate cell should be created in the university for critical examination of the various provisions in the statues, rules and regulations of universities from time to time.

Provision should be made in the Acts for constituting certain well established colleges in Punjab and Chandigarh as autonomous colleges.

City university should be set up to act as a catalyst for setting and improving standards in most tertiary level institutions.

The university system should provide for a three-tier mechanism to deal with problems and grievances of students, teachers and members of the administrative and supportive staff.

The committee recommends that recruitment procedure given in report should be followed.

Examination reform and also the reorganisation of courses on a modular basis, should be introduced at the university level as early as possible.

Rajasthan

069 Committee to Suggest Amendments in the Acts of the Universities in Rajasthan, 1968, Report. Jaipur, Rajasthan Government, 1971. Chairman : Mohan Sinha Mehta.

The Government of Rajasthan appointed committee on 23rd Dec., 1968 for suggesting amendments in the Acts under which the universities have been established and functioning in the State of the Rajasthan.

The committee recommended that the constitution of the universities of the State may be identical in respect of policies and principles but not rigidly uniform. Committee also made recommendations regarding, university autonomy, role of teacher, language issue, teaching and research, reforms in examinations, job-oriented education and development of university committee recommended certain changes.

While making recommendations regarding university bodies the committee recommended that the Act should be brief and simple containing mainly the basic principles of university organization. The university bodies should be much smaller in size than at present.

Committee also made recommendation regarding the university officers : Chancellor, Vice-chancellor and Pro-vice-chancellor.

The system of block grants should be introduced and its quantum should be settled every five years by mutual consultations. Block grant should also include provision for construction of hostel for 100 students and 10 staff quarters.

Committee also made recommendation regarding autonomous colleges, admission policy, student unrest, political aspects, teachers, affiliated colleges and remuneration for examination work.

070 Committee for Reorganisation of Universities in the State, 1979. Report. Jaipur, Government of Rajasthan, 1980. Chairman : M.V. Mathur.

The Government of Rajasthan set up a committee vide order No. 7(4)Ar/G.5/79, dated 30th Jan., 1979 to review the development of higher education in the State and suggest changes in the organisation of its three universities.

The terms of reference of the committee are :

1. Delinking of the Degree Colleges situated at Jaipur from the University of Rajasthan, Jaipur and placing them under the control of the Directorate of College Education, Rajasthan, Jaipur.
2. Reorganisation of the University of Udaipur in the light of recommendations made by the Justice S.D. Singh Commission.
3. Distribution of the affiliated colleges in the State in the three regions.
4. Limiting the responsibility of three State Universities to postgraduate teaching and research, and shifting the responsibility of affiliation to and conduction of examination by one university.

Recommendations of the Committee are:

1. As far as the issue of delinking of the constituent colleges of the University of Rajasthan, Jaipur and placing them under the Directorate of College Education is concerned, the Committee is of opinion that it does not appear to be a practical proposition. The Committee, however, emphasizes that the effort has go to be made to ensure that these constituent colleges be run in such a manner that the interests of undergraduate students are duly protected. These colleges should be run on collegiate pattern with full time Principals and as far as possible the staff should not be placed under two masters, i.e., the University Head of the Department and the Principals of these colleges, for, the dual control tends to bread irresponsibility and lacks of accountability.
2. In order to bring about qualitative improvement in higher education the ceiling should be imposed on enrolment of university departments and that of constituent colleges and also on the enrolment of the affiliated colleges in the State. To meet the requirements of growing numbers more affiliated colleges should be opened by the Government. In a word, the process of consolidation should go on simultaneous by with that of expansion. It is, therefore, suggested that the university departments should not admit more than a section strength in each of the departments. Likewise the strength of the Degree level constituent/affiliated colleges should, ideally, be between 750-1,000 but not beyond 2,000.
3. Keeping in view the educational needs of the State, the Committee recommends the setting up of two new Universities in the State; (i) a full-fledged Agricultural University; and (ii) an innovative affiliating University. The former is needed to meet the growing agricultural requirements of the State and the latter as more rational response to the requirements of colleges and qualitative academic growth of higher education in universities. This model of now innovative affiliating university has been envisaged as one which incorporates in its set-up appropriate academic inputs of all the three State Universities while providing majority representation in its bodies to affiliated colleges. Over a period of 18 years, Rajasthan has shown tremendous restraint by not setting up new Universities. If one studies the pace of growth of the universities in the neighbouring States of Rajasthan, one gathers that while in the Union Territory of Delhi there is 100 per cent increase, in Haryana and Madhya Pradesh each the increase is by 200 per cent in Gujarat the increase is 167 per cent and in Punjab and U.P. each the increase is 100 per cent in Rajasthan the growth has remained static. In view of this it appears imperative to have two new Universities to ensure qualitative and quantitative growth and development of higher education in the State.
4. With a view to promoting better and more purposeful higher education in the State and to encourage a spirit of innovation and experiment the Committee recommends the establishment of a few Faculty improvement and Resource Centres in the State. The main

functions of these centres should be to provide well-designed continuing faculty improvement programmes and to undertake and superwise research in specialised areas preferably linked to the development of the region. The libraries at these centres, should function as 'resource centres' for all the affiliated colleges. Both the U.G.C. and the State Government should provide adequate financial support to these centres.

5. The Committee is of the opinion that the University of Jodhpur should retain its unitary character by limiting its responsibility to the Municipal limits of Jodhpur town only. As the establishment of a separate university exclusively for Engineering and Technology is a highly expensive business, the only possible and also desirable step in view of the present state of affairs within the university is that the Faculty of Engineering and Technology of the University of Jodhpur should be made completely autonomous as far as its academic, administrative and financial controls are concerned. Regarding the posting of staff in the University managed K.N. Hall for Women College, the Committee recommends the same measures as it has suggested about the four constituent colleges of the Rajasthan University.
6. The committee is not in favour of distribution of affiliated colleges in the State in the three regions; for, it would mean not so much as solving the problems as for distributing them among all the three universities. The Rajasthan University may receive some relief from the unmanageably heavy load of responsibilities but other universities most likely would suffer the same fate in course of time.
7. As far as the limiting of the responsibility of the three State Universities to postgraduate teaching and research is concerned, by and large, it would become gradually acceptable if the Government approves, in the first place, the idea of an innovative affiliating University with its 'Faculty Improvement and Resource Centres,' and in the second place, a full-fledged Agricultural University for Rajasthan.
8. With a view to bringing about more effective coordination of the University education in the State, the Committee recommends that the Inter-University Coordination Committee which exists at present be strengthened and suitably staffed.

Tamil Nadu

071 General Inspection Commission, 1955. Report. Madras, University of Madras, 1959. Chairman: A.L. Mudaliar.

It is a detailed report about the progress of the university. Chapter VII of the report has been devoted to the courses of study and the women education. Physical instruction, games and sports have also been enumerated. The suggestions made by the commission have been given at pages 6-66. See also Appendices II and III of the report.

Uttar Pradesh

072 Allahabad University Enquiry Committee, 1951. Report. Allahabad, University of Allahabad, 1953. 267 p. Chairman: Justice O.H. Mootham.

This report contains the findings of the committee with regard to the following aspects: (i) the building, the laboratories, the workshops and the equipment of the university; (ii) the constitution and the working of important committees and other bodies; (iii) the existing relationship of the university with the State government, the Chancellor and that of the university authorities and the Vice-chancellor; (iv) the style of the functioning of the university with regard to the academic activities; (v) the adequacy of financial resources; (vi) recruitment to the teaching and the non-teaching staff; (vii) service conditions of the teachers; (viii) performance of the teachers with regard to the teaching and the research activities; (ix) the admission, the examination, and the logging and the living conditions of the students; and any other defects pertaining to the university administration. The report also carries detailed recommendations in this regard so as to enable the university to become better fitted for the fulfilment of its various aims and tasks.

073 Banaras Hindu University Enquiry Committee, 1957. Report. Delhi, Manager of Publications, 1958. 44 p. Chairman: Dr. A.D. Mudaliar.

The memoranda received by the committee dealt with the reports of occurrences in the university, particularly with the incidents that took place in recent years; the complaints regarding the manner in which the university was being administered; the complaints regarding certain principals and professors of the university; the complaints regarding the method of recruitment of the teaching staff and appointment of the examiners and the method of advertisement for such posts; the complaints regarding the elections to the university bodies; the complaints regarding the attitude of certain teachers toward the students indiscipline; and the complaints about the injustice done to the individual members of the staff.

074 Enquiry Committee on Aligarh Muslim University, 1960. Report. Aligarh, Aligarh Muslim University, 1961. 134 p. Chairman : Prof. G.L. Chatterji.

The committee was appointed to enquire into (i) the financial transaction of the university since 1951-52, with special reference to the audit objections relating to the accounts of these years and the steps taken by the university to meet these objections; (ii) to enquire into the recruitment, the appointment and the promotion of the teaching and the administrative staff of the university and the admission of the students to the university since 1951-52; and (iii) to suggest suitable measures of reform necessary for the efficient functioning of the university.

075 U.P. Universities Commission, 1960. Report. Allahabad, Government of Uttar Pradesh, 1964. 275+103 p. Chairman: Harish Chandra.

The committee was appointed to enquire into: (i) the conduct of the financial administration of the universities of Allahabad, Lucknow, Agra, Gorakhpur and V.S.V. Vidyalaya, Varanasi; (ii) the procedure followed with respect to the appointments of the teachers; (iii) implementation of the recommendations of the Mootham enquiry committee by Allahabad University, and the magnitude of the improvement of the standard of higher education after the introduction of two grade system; (iv) the pattern on which the university of Gorakhpur be developed; (v) the work done by the institute of Hindi studies and the institute of social sciences of the Agra University; and (vi) the steps necessary, for the establishment of autonomous and working men colleges as envisaged in the Agra University Act. The other topics dealt with in the report are those related to the causes of indiscipline among the students; the removal of congestion in the universities; enactment of legislation to provide adequate security in service to the teachers in degree colleges; and essential minimum requirement for opening a new degree college.

076 Remarks of the Sub-Committee on the Report of the Enquiry Committee on Aligarh Muslim University, 1961. Report. Aligarh, Aligarh Muslim University, 1961. 92p.

This report deals with the comments of the sub-committee on the findings and the recommendations of the enquiry committee with regard to the financial affairs of the university; the recruitment,the appointment and the promotion of the teaching and the administrative staff; the admission of the students to the university; and general considerations and reforms.

077 Banaras Hindu University Inquiry Committee, 1968. Report. New Delhi, Ministry of Education and Youth Services, 1969. 238p. Chairman: Dr. P.B. Gajendra-gadkar.

The terms of reference of the committee are as under: (i) to inquire into the recent state of unrest and the agitation in the university, and (ii) to make such recommendations as may be considered necessary to expedite for remedying the situation and for improving the general tone of discipline and law and order in the university.

078 Lucknow University Enquiry Commission, 1970. Report by S.D. Singh. Allabahad, Government of Uttar Pradesh, 1974. 535p.

This report is an exhaustive account of the inspection of the buildings, the laboratories, the libraries and other institutions forming part of the

Lucknow University, and to hold an inquiry into the state of unrest and the agitation in the university with particular reference to the following: (i) incidents of indiscipline occuring in the university during the past 2 years; (ii) existence of groupism; (iii) irregularities in the admissions to the courses, the examination system, the financial expenditure and in making appointments; and (iv) general breakdown of the machinery of the university administration.

079 Inquiry Committee. Report. Varanasi, Banaras Hindu University, 1971. 34 p. Chairman : M.C. Desai.

Consequent to the closure of the Banaras Hindu University on 13th Sept., 1971, a high powered one-man enquiry committee was appointed to enquire into the conduct of 39 students who were guilty of various acts of indiscipline and who were duly charge-sheeted. Committee examined more than 50 witnesses and an opportunity was given to the delinquent students not only to cross-examine these witnesses but to lead whatever defence evidence they wished.

On the recommendation of committee the university withdrew the suspension order of 10 students. In case of 29 students, committee found them guilty, a few of all the charges and remaining of some of the charges. After carefully considering the report of enquiry committee delinquents have been punished.

West Bengal

080 Calcutta University Commission or the Sadler Commission, 1917. Report. Government of India, 1919. Chairman: Dr. M.E. Sadler.

The Sadler commission was appointed to enquire into the condition and the prospects of the University of Calcutta and to consider the question of a constructive policy in relation to the question it presents. Important recommendations of the commission are as follows: (i) intermediate classes should be separated from universities and a curriculum spreading over three years should be prescribed for the degree of B.A., and the stage of admission to the university should be intermediate and not matriculation examination; (ii) intermediate colleges should be established for the sake of completing the first stage and these colleges should conduct teaching in Arts, Science, Medicine, Engineering, Education, Agriculture, and Commerce; and (iii) a separate High school and Intermediate Board should be formed in every province, consisting of representatives of the government, the universities, the high schools and the intermediate colleges for the sake of managing the secondary education.

081 Calcutta University Enquiry Committee, 1950. Report. Calcutta, Government of West Bengal, 1951. 3 volumes. 281 p. Chairman: B.L. Miller.

This report contains the findings of the committee whose terms of reference were as follows: (i) to enquire into the complaints and the allegations of abuses and malpractices relating to the departments of the Controller of examination, the accounts and audit and the press; (ii) to suggest remedies to prevent the recurrence of any abuses and irregularities that may be found; and (iii) to make recommendations generally for improving the administration.

082 Kalyani University Inquiry Committee, 1968. Report. Calcutta, Department of Education, Government of West Bengal, 1968. 108 p. Chairman: B.K. Guha.

This report contains details of the findings of the commission set up to enquire into the performance of the University of Kalyani with respect to the following aspects: (a) staff pattern for the different departments of the university and the policy followed in making the appointment; (b) financial management and the utilization of grants; and (c) the building programmes, specifically the academic buildings, the laboratories, the hostels, the staff quarters and other students amenities.

083 Committee on Calcutta University, 1970. Report. Calcutta, University of Calcutta, 1974. 91 p. Chairman: Prof. M.M. Ghani.

This committee was asked to assess broadly the needs for higher education and research which the university would be expected to meet over the next ten years or so, and in particular to examine the developmental needs of the university departments; to examine the question of conferring the status of autonomous colleges on selected institutions on the lines recommended by the Education Commission (1964-66), and to consider the relationship between the university and its colleges; to recommend such changes into the structure and the organisation of the university as would enable it to fulfil its role and obligations effectively and adequately; and to indicate the financial implication of its recommendations. The committee has made certain recommendations with regard to the size, the jurisdiction, the organisation and the structure, the autonomous colleges, the vocational courses and the finance etc.

084 Committee on Visva-Bharati, 1974. Report. New Delhi, Ministry of Education and Social Welfare, 1975. 91 p. Chairman: Justice S.A. Masud.

This committee was set up to provide guidelines on which Visva-Bharati be developed, keeping in view the educational ideas of Rabindranath Tagore; and how the academic programmes of the institutions of the university be reorganised. The committee also gave suggestions for the amendment of Visva-Bharati Act.

D RESEARCH STUDIES

001 Ahmed, Shakti R. and Luthra, S.N. *Work ethos.* New Delhi, National Institute of Educational Planning and Administration, 1984. 180p.

This paper examines the following aspects. Number of working days and number of days that the institution remained closed in the past three years; nature and quantum of work done by teachers in teaching, research, para-academic work and administration; and average size of the class and pupil-teacher ratio.

002 Amrik Singh, *Recruitment: Base and procedures.* New Delhi, National Institute of Educational Planning and Administration, 1984. 29+36p.

The focus of this paper is on the following: (i) Base criteria for the recruitment of teachers such as academic, regional, urban/rural, language, age, sex and SC/ST; (ii) selection criteria such as academic qualifications, personality variables such as motivation and aptitude for teaching, adaptability with students and fellow teachers; and (iii) various aspects of the procedures of recruitment such as, declaration of vacancy, advertisement, constitution of selection committee, selection, issue of appointment order etc.

003 Arora, P.N. *Students' perception of some problems and issues in higher education*, Deptt. of Measurement and Evaluation, NCERT, 1979.

The major objectives of the study were: (i) to ascertain the reasons which prompted students to enter higher education, (ii) to identify students perception of the occupational world, and (iii) to find out the extent of their involvement in studies.

The sample comprised 313 students studying in the first year of college out of whom 131 had taken up social sciences and humanities courses, 89 physical sciences and 93 commerce courses. These students were from seven colleges of Delhi. A specially prepared questionnaire was used to collect data. The statistical techniques used for analysing the data were percentage and chi-square.

The major findings of the study were: (i) Sixty-eight per cent students belonged to white-collar families. Of these, 12 per cent belonged to professional and semiprofessional groups and 56 per cent to the service group. About 23 per cent were from business families. (ii) There was real association between the occupation of the father and the academic achievement of the student. (iii) There was significant association between the economic status of the parents and the academic achievement of the student (iv) There was strong association between the level of education of the father and the level of academic achievement of the student. (v) Predominantly academic reasons were mentioned by the majority of the students as the most important consideration for entering higher education. (vi) About 26 per cent students aspired to enter service and most of them were from social sciences and commerce groups. About 25 per cent desired entry into medical profession. (vii) The students of first year were found to devote, on an average, 2.55 hours per day to home study. The girls devoted less time (2.50 hours) to their studies than the boys (3.06 hours).

004 Banerji, Anita, and Pylee, M.V. *Grievances and their redressal.* New Delhi, National Institute of Educational Planning and Administration, 1984, 78p.

The study provides an analysis of the nature, the types and the causes of grievances of teachers in higher education. It focuses attention on the grievances of teachers with respect to academic and administrative areas.

005 Benal, B.I., *A critical study of development of higher education in the State of Karnataka during Six Five Year Plans (1950-1980) with special reference to Karnatak University*, Ph.D. Edu., Karnatak University, 1987.

The objectives of the investigation were: (i) to study the development of higher education in Karnatak University, (ii) to study the qualitative development through institutional materials, (iii) to study the improvement of quality of teachers, (iv) to study the problems of examinations and evaluation, (v) to critically evaluate the nature and extent to development with respect to the trends in developed States in the country and (vi) to suggest steps for improvement of higher education.

The hypotheses of the study were: (1) There is no increase in the growth and expansion of higher education in the Karnatak University region. (a) There is no increase in the enrolment in higher education at degree level during the plan period. (b) There is no increase in the enrolment in higher education at postgraduate and at research level. (c) There is no improvement in the service conditions of the teacher during the plan period. (2) There is no improvement in the quality of higher education during the plan periods. (3) There is no improvement in the efficiency of the teacher of higher education during the plan period. (4) There is no improvement in the examination system during the plan period. (5) There is no improvement in the system of evaluation during the plan period.

Data were collected from the annual reports of the Karnatak University right from 1949 to 1985 which covered six five-year plans. A questionnaire was prepared with the help of experts in order to collect certain other information required for the study in addition to the annual reports. The entire population of the study was 190 covering fifty-four university departments and 136 constituent and affiliated colleges of higher education, but the researcher could finally get only 120 filled in questionnaires.

The findings of the study were: (1) There was considerable increase in the quantitative growth of institutions, namely, the affiliated, the constituent colleges and the university postgraduate departments during the plan period. (2) It was also seen that the receipts and expenditures had significantly increased due to the developmental programmes initiated and implemented. Similarly it was seen that the sources of income had increased to the best advantage of the educational institutions. (3) The library of the Karnatak University had expanded considerably and it was supposed to be the second biggest in Asia. (4) With regard to modernization of science, departments of physics, chemistry and geology had greatly expanded and were offering leadership courses in their disciplines in the country. (5) For the student facilities, financial efforts had not been made to the extent expected. (6) Qualitative improvement at the affiliated colleges and also at the university was not very significant. No effort had been made for reorientating the inservice training providing up to date knowledge to the teachers recruited at the affiliated colleges and at the university level. The authorities of the university had not made any attempt in looking to the academic problems of the teachers. (7) There had not been any consistent effort made by the university authorities to evolve new techniques and devices in evaluating the students progress at the examination.

006 Bose, Anima. *American missionaries' involvement in higher education in India in the nineteenth century*. University of Kansas, 1971.

007 Bose, P.K., *Calcutta University: Some problems and their remedies*, Calcutta University, 1983. (UGC and MOE financed).

The objectives of the project were: (i) to assess broadly the needs for higher education and research and to examine, in particular, the developmental needs of the university departments; (ii) to examine the question of conferring the status of autonomous colleges on selected institutions; (iii) to suggest organisational and structural changes in the university; and (iv) to indicate the financial implications of the recommendations.

The study was done with regard to Calcutta University. The problems of the university were identified in terms of undergraduate education and postgraduate education as well as the academic administration of the university. Case studies were made on undergraduate students in Calcutta as to how they lived and worked, and on seven big colleges in Calcutta pertaining to their academic, administrative and financial affairs. The main sources of information were: (i) interviews with the senior administrative officers, and (ii) statements, reports and comments made by different individuals and institutions.

Some of the major findings were as follows: (i) The problems of the university as detected were the increase in number of the institutions, students and examinees irrespective of the constant remaining resources at the disposal of the university, shortcomings in the administrative arrangements, overconsciousness among students and employees about their rights and privileges, paucity of funds, paucity of space, recurring deficits, problems related to opening of new departments and starting new courses, developing university press, maintenance and repair of buildings, starting hostels, providing students with satisfactory welfare services, holding examinations, maintaining adequate and able staff (teachers and administrative officers), financial position of some affiliated colleges, the demand for more teachers, and improvements in the library and laboratory facilities. (ii) As regards the undergraduate education, the percentages of passes were less than forty in the university examinations in a large number of private colleges, the main causes being inadequate number of working days, poor college libraries, ill-equipped laboratories, disproportionate teacher-student ratio and lack of motivation on the part of teachers and students. The per capita expenditure of the affiliated colleges was less than the government sponsored colleges. Some of the important remedial suggestions with regard to the affiliated colleges, were to provide more inputs in the nature of grants, equipments and books, formation of undergraduate college boards responsible for introducing new types of examinations, teaching methods and admission policies. (iii) Almost all the colleges had financial difficulties except two or three. Every college had common problems of library, laboratory, building and furniture. However, the emoluments of teachers did not differ remarkably. The enrolment in commerce stream was found to be higher. Conclusively, student explosion and the extreme paucity of funds were the two main factors which hindered the functioning of the university efficiently.

008 Bose P.K. Banerjee, P.R. and Mukherjee, S.P., *Case study of seven big colleges in Calcutta: Their academic, administrative and financial affairs*, Deptt. of Statistics, Calcutta University, 1973.

The main aim of the study was to examine academic and financial aspects as well as administrative arrangements of the seven big colleges in Calcutta since these and financial issues were interelated.

Academic, administrative and financial aspects of seven big colleges in Calcutta, viz., Asutosh, Bangabasi, Charuchandra, City, Maharaja Manindra Chandra, Surendranath, and Vidyasagar College, which came under the phased reduction scheme in different years following 1959-60 were examined. Six of these colleges were managed by trusts or societies and the remaining one was a privately managed institution.

The study revealed that the colleges spent more than their income on maintenance of teaching and non-teaching staff alone; the colleges were obliged to spend very little on maintenance of building, furniture, library and laboratories. Recurring expenses on stores, consumables and specimens in laboratories were also inadequate. Capital grants from government for development of buildings, library and laboratories were major sources from which development expenses were usually incurred. The government's contributions towards maintenance and development expenses in these seven big colleges were quite considerable. Percentage contribution by the government towards total salary costs of teachers, including all allowances, exceeded 50 per cent in Bangabasi, City and Surendranath Colleges and was slightly less in Asutosh, Charuchandra and Vidyasagar Colleges. Corresponding figures for non-teachings staff varied around thirty. The colleges had outstanding liabilities as well as unpaid loans. In a few colleges, the staff benevolent fund, the sports ground fund, etc., had been created out of revenue income. Running expenses on science laboratory in some colleges were not adequate. Purchase of library books from the college fund was inadequate. Average number of lectures delivered by a teacher in a particular subject per teachering day was quite small – in some cases less than one. The problem of coordination between the colleges for use and maintenance of common facilities requiring usually common services of several employees was felt. The basic pay of the non-teaching employees in affiliated non-government colleges was inadequate. The college teachers should get provident fund benefits on the entire basic pay as admissible in the new integrated scale of pay and not merely on the college share of such pay.

009 Chattopadhayay, Sikha. *Besant Malaviya, the Maharaja of Darbhanga and the emergence of the Banaras Hindu University: The first denominational university in India*. New Delhi, Jawaharlal Nehru University, 1982.

010 Doctor, T.H. *Progress of university education in Gujarat state after independence*, Ph.D. Edu., Gujarat University, 1979.

This study starts with the position of university education in Gujarat from the year 1950-51 and stretches it up to the year 1974-75. There were only two universities in 1950-51 while in 1974-75, there were five academic and two professional universities. The study was done in blocks of four years and traced the growth of all the five universities in the matter of enrolment, faculty-wise number of colleges, strength of faculty members, postgraduate centres, enrolment of postgraduate students, amount of research work done, addition of books in the library, number of readers of the library books, external examinations, income and expenditure of the university, students' welfare activities and such other aspects. The growth study of each university was done separately for each block of four years and for the whole period under study.

At the end of the thesis the progress of university education for the whole of Gujarat was also studied. The trends of development were crystallized and suggestions were made for improvement.

011 Dube, S.C. and Swarup, Hemlata. *Professional values*. New Delhi, National Institute of Educational Planning and Administration, 1984. 52+xxip.

This study examines the academic, social and moral values which the profession cherishes and needs to cherish in keeping with the country's heritage and ideals of democracy, socialism, secularism, and the scientific temper, as well as with the concept of academic excellence; actions repugnant to the teaching profession; and teachers' accountability to the profession and to the society.

012 Dwivedi, M., *A study of the attitudes of students, parents and teachers towards the current system of higher education*, Ph.D. Edu., Gorakhpur University, 1970.

The investigation aimed to study the attitudes of students, parents and teachers towards the present system of higher education and also to study the differences in their attitudes. These differences were also studied on the basis of subject combination, educational status and sex and their interaction.

For the study, students of undergraduate classes of the affiliated colleges in the Varanasi region, their parents and their teachers were taken up. To obtain precise unbiased samples, the random sampling technique was adopted and the size of the sample was kept considerably large – students 500, parents 200 and teachers 300, with a total of 1,000. The attitude scale was constructed by the researcher. A questionnaire was also used for getting information about the present system of higher education.

In the present study, strongly favourable or strongly unfavourable attitudes were not shown by any group. Almost all the groups had shown a neutral attitude. The students were found to be quite higher on the attribute continuum than the parents and the teachers. The parents seemed to make an objective assessment of the system. The teachers were at the lowest point on the attitude continuum because their judgement was ever more objective than that of the parents. Amongst the students, no significant difference was found between the attitudes of arts students and science students, but quite a significant difference was observed between the attitudes of boys and girls. Among the different groups of parents non-matriculates were on the highest point on the attitude continuum. Among the teachers, the female arts teachers were highest on the attitude continuum. Next to them in order were male science teachers and male arts teachers.

013 Ghosh, A. *American influence on postwar educational development in India*. University of Sheffield, 1969.

014 Gogate, S.B., *A comprehensive study of junior colleges in Marathwada*, project undertaken by IIE, Pune, in collaboration with Swami Ramanand Teerth Research Institute, Aurangabad, 1981.

The objectives of the investigation were: (i) to assess the availability of physical and academic facilities in junior colleges in Marathwada in regard to library, laboratory, staff, co-curricular activities, teaching aids, finances of institutions conducting junior colleges (XI and XII) and their examination results, (ii) to study the causes of poor results of Higher Secondary Certificate (HSC) Examination in Marathwada, (iii) to find out whether malpractices took place during the HSC Examinations, and if so, to study the factors contributing to these malpractices, (iv) to assess the relationship between the heads of junior colleges and the staff and to study the educational climate in these institutions in this regard, (v) to undertake a comprehensive evaluation of junior colleges in Marathwada, (vi) to study whether the teachers, parents and members of the management were aware of educational objectives, and (vii) to identify individuals and institutions who were willing to volunteer for educational improvement in Marathwada and to plan activities to change the educational climate in the institutions.

The study was undertaken with the help of questionnaires for the heads to junior colleges, teachers, members of management, parents and student. By and large, personal information, attitudes towards education, facilities available in junior colleges, the use of libraries and laboratories were the items which figures in the questionnaires. Responses from sixty-three heads of junior colleges, 646 teachers, 116 members of management, 422 parents and 3,597 students were obtained.

The major findings of the investigation were: (i) The junior colleges in Marathwada did not have good libraries. Reading arrangements were not adequate in the libraries. Very few institutions had night libraries. Students were happy about laboratory facilities. Teachers teaching at the +2 stage lacked in knowledge of content as also in methodology of teaching. All junior colleges did not have minimum co-curricular activities. Teaching aids were not used adequately. The junior colleges attached to schools did not have sufficient funds to spend on libraries and laboratories. The results of HSC (XII) in Marathwada were poor in relation to the rest of Maharashtra. (ii) The causes of poor results were: students felt that teachers were not regular; colleges did not provide sufficient facilities; teachers brought outside politics in the college; teachers felt that students were not able to cope with the heavy syllabus and were not able to do hard work; parents felt that political leaders and students were responsible for poor results; they also felt that colleges should begin their session in time and function regularly, and that there should be coaching classes for retarded students; students felt that they should be given orientation in methods of study and that the teachers should come to classes well prepared. (iii) Regarding malpractices at the time of examinations, the teachers felt that they were due to the fact that students wanted to achieve results without putting any efforts and that officials did not take decisions on time and connived at malpractices and educational climate was spoiled and political leaders interfered. (iv) There appeared to be a lot of misunderstanding among the members of the management, principals and teachers.

015 Gopalakrishnan, M. *Higher education in post-independent India. (1947-1970): A critical evaluation in terms of selected criteria of effectiveness*. Montana State University, 1973.

016 Goyal, M., *Student perceptions of the university environment as related to their satisfaction in the Northern Indian university*, Ph.D. Edu., Kurukshetra University, 1981.

The major objectives of the investigation were: (i) to explore the question of individual-environment interaction in northern Indian universities, (ii) to find out the relationship between the self and various aspects of the university environment and dissatisfaction, (iii) to study whether students of different universities perceived their university environment differently, (iv) to study the trends in the perception of various dimensions of the northern Indian university environment by the university students, and (v) to assess the sources of conflicts and strain within the university environment.

The sample consisted of 2,151 final year students of 14 Indian universities of the northern region. The sample students were administered the Transactional Analysis of Personality and Environment (TAPE) and the University Environment Inventory (UEI).

The findings of the investigation were: (i) There were large discrepancies between the way the students saw themselves and the various parts of the university, viz., students, faculty, administration, etc. (ii) The students viewed their university environment not very positively although they viewed their university environment slightly above average with respect to academic interest and enthusiasm, teacher scholarship and academic attitudes and work facilities and student discipline. (iii) There were more than 20 per cent university students who perceived the university environment as 'a little' or 'not at all' as 'highly developed' or does not give opportunity for co-curricular activities', as not 'flexible' or 'paying' and as 'men-making' or 'challenging'. (iv) Most of the students felt out of place while in the university, felt uncomfortable with other students of the university, had the feeling that their values were not similar to those of the faculty and were in disagreement with the administrative rules and regulations. (v) Students of different universities tended to differ in their satisfaction with the different dimensions of the university environment. They were dissatisfied with respect to breadth of interest, student scholarship, academic achievement and clarity of instruction.

017 Gupta, N.P. *Participation in decision-making*, New Delhi, National Institute of Educational Planning and Administration, 1984. 41+Lp.

The focus of this study is on the participation of teachers in decision-making within the institutions, regarding academic, para-academic and institutional administration matters; and outside the institutions in State and Central legislatures, development boards and commissions at district, State and national levels.

018 Gupta, S., *A study of the attitudes of teachers of Agra University towards higher education*. Ph.D. Soc., Agra University, 1979.

The study was designed to investigate the attitudes of the teachers of

Agra University towards higher education, taking four aspects, viz., university autonomy, admission on the basis of selection, importance assigned to research and the importance assigned to higher education (at the postgraduate level). The attitudes were measured on scales based on the method of equal appearing interval. The sample included 300 teachers selected on the basis of systematic sampling.

The study yielded the following conclusions: (i) The majority of the teachers of the university and colleges had a positive view towards higher education. (ii) The male and the female teachers showed significant difference in their attitudes. (iii) As age increased, the attitudes tended to become negative. (iv) The teachers differed significantly in their attitude towards the trade-technical groups and the non-trade and non-technical courses of study. (v) Those teachers who had teaching experience had negative attitudes while those who had short experience should positive attitudes. (vi) The standard of teaching influenced the attitude. (vii) Those teachers whose attainments were high showed negative attitude as compared to those whose attainments were low. (viii) The teachers' attitudes were affected by their satisfaction in the family life. (ix) Those teachers who had experiences of failure, had negative attitudes while those who had experiences of success, showed favourable attitudes. (x) The political condition of the country, the economic status and the working conditions affected teachers' attitudes. (xi) The teachers' attainments were positively related with the evaluation of students. (xii) The satisfaction/dissatisfaction of the teachers in respect of modern higher education affected the evaluation of students. (xiii) Teaching experience and evaluation of students were interrelated. (xiv) The teaching experiences, scholastic attainments, satisfaction with modern higher education affected the attitudes towards students' cooperation and welfare. (xv) The teaching experience and attainments affected their thoughts about the vice-chancellor's qualities. (xvi) Higher educational attainments and teaching experiences affected their thinking towards the role of the University Grants Commission in education.

019 Indian Institute of Education, *Development of colleges in Marathwada University -- 1980-1900*, Pune, 1980.

This project was undertaken to study the status of arts, science and commerce colleges in Marathwada University and also their projected plan of development during the decade 1980-1990. The project covered all the five districts, viz., Aurangabad, Beed, Nanded, Osmanabad and Parbhani. The tool used was an exhaustive questionnaire sent to all the sixty-seven colleges of the region.

The major findings of the project were: (i) There were sixty-seven colleges of which two were government managed and sixty-five privately managed; only one was a women's college and sixty-six were mixed colleges, (ii) Thirty-two colleges had arts, science and commerce faculties, thirty-two had arts and commerce faculties, one college had arts and science faculties, six had only science, two only commerce and two only arts faculties, (iii) The media of instruction were English and

Marathi at the undergraduate level for arts and commerce and English for science. (iv) The total strength of students from Class XI to postgraduate and diploma classes on 1 October 1979 was 14,775 (3,005 women) for arts, 12,505 (1,928 women) for science and 20,752 (2,337 women) for commerce. The women students numbered 7270 out of 48,032 in all the colleges. According to information received from some colleges, it was seen that of 30,405 students, Scheduled Caste students accounted for 7,674, Scheduled Tribe students were 588, students from denotified and nomadic tribes were 2,148, from other backward classes were 3876 and from advanced communities were 16,119. (v) Forty-six colleges paid rent to their management. (vi) Forty-one colleges had a common-room for men, fifty-three had a common-room for women, thirty-six had auditorium, twelve had gymkhana and fifteen had cooperative stores. (vii) Out of sixty-seven colleges, fifty-one had hostel facilities. Forty-three colleges together had seats in hostels for 4,571 boys and 403 girls. (viii) While about thirty-two colleges offered courses in physics, chemistry, botany and zoology, only two colleges offered microbiology, eight offered biochemistry and one college offered geology. Thirty colleges had laboratories for physics, chemistry, botany and zoology. Twenty-one colleges had one of five laboratory assistants, eight had five to 10, two had 10 to 15 and three had 15 to 20. (ix) Between fifty-nine colleges, there were 2,674 teachers of whom 197 were women. One hundred and thirty-two teachers had Ph.D. degree. Sixty-one colleges had trained librarians. (x) Many colleges had fewer than ten students in many subjects at the undergraduate stage. In English and Marathi, the colleges did not have more than ten students at the postgraduate level. (xi) The total income per students on an average in the Marathwada University was Rs.1,328 against an expenditure of Rs.1,475. (xii) It was seen that three colleges had fewer than fifty students twenty-seven colleges had between 50 to 100, thirty-one colleges had 101 to 200 and five colleges had between 301 and 500. (xiii) The colleges, on the whole, suffered due to low student strength and the position was not likely to improve during the next five years.

020 Jindal. S.K. *Student perceptions of the college environment as related to their satisfaction in the colleges of Haryana*, Ph.D. Edu., Kurukshetra University, 1977.

The study was conducted with the main objective to find the relationship between perceived discrepancies between the self and various aspects of college environment and the sources of conflicts or strain within the college environment.

A sample of 1850 students was selected from the different colleges of Haryana. They were administered TAPE (Transitional Analysis of Personality and Environment) test which was based on the semantic differential technique and asked the students to rate a number of concepts on bipolar adjective scales. The data were analysed on the two bases — (i) intra- and inter-institutional comparisons, and (ii) student *versus* college interactions.

It was found that there were large discrepancies between the way the students saw themselves and the various aspects of college environment. The sources of strain were in the functioning of the college. The student *versus* college interaction suggested that the students were dissatisfied with the other students in the college, faculty and the administration of the college. The largest variability was however found on student and administration concept.

021 Joseph, T.M., *Progress and problems of higher education in Maharashtra since independence (1947-1982)*, Ph.D. Edu., Bombay University, 1987.

The main objectives of the research study were: (i) to study the progress of higher education in Maharashtra as evidenced by qualitative and quantitative measures, (ii) to study the innovative schemes launched by the universities, (iii) to identify the problems in higher education, (iv) to study the extent, causes, consequences and effects of these problems on higher education in Maharashtra, and (v) to suggest alternatives and changes in the pattern of higher education.

The method of purposive random sampling was used for the selection of the sample. The data were collected from six non-agricultural universities in Maharashtra State. Tools used for data collection were: (i) reports of commissions and committees, periodicals, journals and newspaper articles on education, (ii) annual reports of the University Grants Commission and of the Bombay, Nagpur, SNDT, Poona, Marathwada and Shivaji universities, occasional publications of universities, university acts and related literature, (iii) a questionnaire for principals, professors, administrators and educationists, (iv) an interview schedule for the vice-chancellors, registrars, officers on special duty (Exam.), principals of the colleges and senior professors. The data were analysed with the help of statistical techniques.

The study revealed: 1. There had been a tremendous increase in student enrolment since independence. 2. The enrolment of women had gone up and Maharashtra State had the largest number of students from scheduled castes as compared to other States. 3. There had been noticeable increase in women's enrolment in the Marathwada University area. 4. The curriculum and syllabi for the various courses had been along traditional lines with little attempt to adopt to local needs and resources. 5. Shivaji University had a 'Work and Earn' scheme for needy students with facilities for students to engage themselves in farming and conducting a canteen on cooperative basis. 6. Poona University had started a programme of distance education with the preparation of audio-visual material in the University's television studio. 7. Every university performed its academic role in the traditional pattern with very little change. Syllabi framed by the boards of studies in the universities and colleges had no scope for experimentation and innovation. 8. Many university posts had been filled because funds were not forthcoming. Practically all the universities had deficit budgets that were carried forward year by year. 9. There was a marked decline in the attitude of teachers to their work as a vocation. A fairly significant number of college teachers gave tuitions and took up additional jobs. The existence of junior and senior college sections in the same college, with teachers having different salary scales, workload and service conditions created discontent. 10. The introduction of the 10+2+3 system had resulted in declining enrolments at the +3 stage in all universities. 11. No university had any special scheme for remedial courses for first generation learners. 12. There was acute lack of hostels for women students belonging to these groups in almost all universities. 13. No university had initiated any exercise in long term perspective planning. The main concern of the universities was to perform routine functions in which also efficiency was lacking due to absence of modern management techniques. 14. There was little coordination among the universities, State, Central governments and the UGC.

022 Kale, S.S., *A diagnostic study of incoming crisis in higher educational system in Maharashtra — A system analysis of higher educational system in the State, 1960-1970*, B.M. College of Commerce, Poona, 1972. (Government of Maharashtra financed).

The major objectives of the investigation were: (i) to study the growth of higher education in Maharashtra during 1960-1970; and (ii) to study the various aspects of the existing system of higher education in the State in order to provide a sound basis of educational planning for the State in future.

The study was conducted on all the then existing six universities in Maharashtra. The data were collected mainly through interview and discussion, and record analysis. Interviews and discussions were held with the Education Minister, the Under Secretary, the Director of Higher Education, the Director of the State Institute of Education, Vice-Chancellors and Registrars of the universities in Maharashtra, and a few eminent educationists. The records were available mainly from the Directorate of Education, and the universities of Maharashtra. The data were quantified and analysed.

The study provided a broader framework of higher education as the human capital forming industry imbibing input, processes and output aspects in it. This issue was further evaluated in terms of the significance of higher education in the process of socio-economic revolution in the country. The study revealed that during the period under study the higher education grew phenomenally in the State in terms of enrolment, number of institutions, and expenditure. The need for higher education was well recognised and a clearly defined policy on higher education was formulated. Some progress was made in terms of equalisation of educational opportunity. Nevertheless, serious discrepancies were also existing between the quantitative and qualitative growth in higher education, and scarcity and abundance of educated manpower between the sectors. The existing higher education system failed to adapt to the changing need of the community. The present situation revealed the unsatisfactory output both social — family membership, citizenship and productive labour, and individual — intellectual, attitudinal and motivational. The factors responsible for the present situation were absence of objectives and planned growth of higher education, deficiency of the competent staff, absence of adequate understanding of the social expectations before the system, dearth of effective leadership, absence of integrative planning of social, economic and (higher) educational sectors, organisational deficiencies, scarcity of resources, and underdeveloped information system. The future trends in terms of rising social demand for education, explosion of knowledge, resource scarcity, rising cost, further discrepancy between higher education and life needs and social aspirations, growing graduate unemployment and youth discontent indicated the probable deepening of the crisis in higher education. State level planned action strategies seemed imminent in order to overcome this crisis.

023 Koshy, S.N. *Role of higher education in India since independence*, The Catholic University of America, 1971.

024 Kumari, S., *Students' perceptions of the college environment as related to their satisfaction in the colleges of Haryana*, Ph.D. Edu., Kurukshetra University, 1977.

The objectives of the study were: (i) to explore the question of individual environment interaction in the colleges, (ii) to find out the relationship between the perceived discrepancies between the self and the various aspects of college environment and dissatisfaction, and (iii) to assess the sources of conflicts or strains within the college environment. The sample comprised 1,850 students of third degree class — part II and part III — from nineteen colleges of Haryana. The tool used to describe college environment and assess campus climates, as well as students' satisfaction was Transitional Analysis of Personality and Environment (TAPE) by Lawrence A. Pervin and Doueld B. Rubin, adapted to Indian conditions.

The major findings of the study were: (i) There were large discrepancies between the way students saw themselves and the various parts of the college environment, namely, students, faculty and administration, etc. (ii) The students were greatly dissatisfied with other students and the administration. Every student considered himself an ideal student and the college and other aspects of college environment far from his ideal self. (iii) Most of the students felt out of place while in the college. They felt uncomfortable with other students in the college. They did not find their value similar to their faculty and they did not agree to the rules and regulations of their college administration. (iv) Most of the students perceived their principal as very strict and staff members very partial. (v) Most of the students demanded jobs rather than degrees. They were not satisfied with learning which was theoretical and which had little relationship with their future careers.

025 McGreal, S.R. *History of Mayo College*, Ajmer, India. 1875-1971. University of Cincinnati, 1971.

026 Marr, E., Singh, L.C., Arora, K. and Gupta, S.P. *An intensive study of three colleges of education in Punjab*. New Delhi, National Council of Educational Research and Training, 1969.

027 Mathew, A., *Protestant missionary attitudes towards higher education and nationalism in Madras Presidency, 1872-1930*, Ph.D. Edu., Jawaharlal Nehru University, 1984.

The purposes of the investigation were: (i) to examine the protestant missionary efforts to bring about the conversion of India between 1872 and 1930, (ii) to discern and analyse the major attitudes and approaches which occurred over these six decades, (iii) to examine two clearly demarcated themes and approaches to the evangelisation of India through education and intelligentsia, adopted and adhered to between 1872 and 1910, and (iv) the evangelisation of the masses between 1910 and 1930.

The scope of this study was restricted to the Madras Presidency in general and the Tamil areas in particular. The main sources used in this study were the missionary literature, mainly contemporary, much of which were printed records and collected from a number of church/mission archives and libraries.

The findings of the study were: 1. It was in 1872 that a new perspective was advocated for christian education by changing its purpose and role from conversion to evangelic preparation through diffusion of christian principles. 2. When the object of educational mission was changed from conversion to evangelic preparations, it was conceived as the first part of the evangelisation of the Indian higher classes and castes outside educational institutions. 3. When it became clear by 1880's that the diffusion accomplished by educational missions failed to set in christian direction, two steps were suggested. One was to strengthen the evangelic preparatory role of educational missions and other to set up a special agency to deal with the religious outlook of educated Indians. 4. They adopted a sympathetic attitude towards Indian religious awakening and an approach of presenting christianity not as an exclusive religion but as one in which all the divine truths found in other religions could be seen in their fullness. 5. The disenhancement with intelligentsia besides a host of other factors, was responsible for rejecting the doctrine of evangelisation through education and intelligentsia. The thrust of the protestant missionaries activities after 1910 shifted in favour of the evangelisation of masses, and this resulted in the formation of the missionary councils at provincial and national levels. 6. The impact of nationalism on Indian christians witnessed their demand for home rule within Indian church, Indianization of the church hierarchy, including control over policy, and indigenisation of the forms of expression and worship. 7. The new outlook of the missions and

Indian christians known as the Social Gospel outlook, became evident from the spirit of types of activities undertaken after 1923. 8. The outlook and the activities of the councils between 1924-28 appeared to create an impression that what was agreed to in 1923, namely transfer of leadership of the church hierarchy and evangelic task into the hands of Indian christians and a change of outlook from mass conversion to Social Gospel were becoming a reality.

028 Mathew, E.T. and Nair, P.R.G., *Demand for higher education: A socio-economic profile of evening college students in Kerala*, Deptt. of Economic, Kerala University, 1979 (UGC-financed).

The purpose of the investigation was to understand the phenomenon of the rising demand for higher education in Kerala by studying the evening colleges which were started in Kerala in the year 1965-66.

Data for the study were obtained by conducting a survey on 439 evening college students (33 per cent of total population) enrolled for the B.A., B.Sc, and B.Com. courses. The data collected included details of demographical, environmental and academic factors of students as well as the main reasons for the discontinuance of studies, enrolment in evening college and suggestions for improving the evening college course organization. Frequency tabulation was done and wherever possible relevant sub-groups were compared.

The findings of the study were: (i) The total number of subjects for the three courses was eight in all the five centres taken together. (ii) Courses in languages and philosophy were not popular. (iii) Economics had the highest enrolment (33.26 per cent). (iv) The past academic record of the students was poor with 1.14 per cent first class and 7.06 per cent second class at the qualifying examination. (v) The year of passing the qualifying examination went back to 1962. (vi) The percentage of enrolment for the B.Com course was low (7.98) but B.Com. was not offered in all centres. (vii) The small number of subjects limited the choice of students. (viii) Forward castes had the highest enrolment (58.5 per cent), backward castes came next with 36.45 per cent and the last came scheduled castes and tribes with 2.73 per cent. (ix) The proportion of employed students was 58.6 per cent. (x) Occupational distribution of students showed high clustering for teachers, clerks and typists (86 per cent). (xi) Lower class occupations like agricultural and industrial workers, were also represented (9 per cent). (xii) The age range of the sample was between twenty-three and forty years. (xiii) The majority of the parents were literate (fathers 93 per cent, mothers 85 per cent). (xiv) The income of employed students was average. (xv) The major source of finance for employed students was their own income. (xvi) The main reasons for discontinuance were financial difficulties and entry into job. (xvii) The main reasons for enrolment in evening colleges were leisure-time diversion, prestige and indisciplined in day colleges.

029 Menon, Anila Bhatt. *University structure and reform in India: A field study and case analysis*. University of Wisconsin, 1969.

030 Nair, R.J. *A statistical portrait of the Kerala University*, Deptt. of Statistics, Kerala University, 1981 (UGC-financed).

The study intended to provide an account of the growth and development of higher education in the University of Kerala and in the affiliated colleges. It (i) reviewed the origin and growth of higher education, (ii) described the socio-cultural demand for higher education, and (iii) assessed the quantitative progress of enrolment in general education and professional education.

The major source of data for the study consisted of Form B. Statistics of Universities in India, budget estimates of the University of Kerala, the annual reports of the University of Kerala and census reports. Percentages were calculated for purpose of comparison and to assess growth. Coefficients of equality were calculated to compare the enrolment of Scheduled Caste and Scheduled Tribe pupils with the pupils of other communities.

The main conclusions of the study were: (i) Sex differences in enrolment which were significant up to 1977-78 were insignificant for 1978-79. (ii) The proportion of women entering higher education to those who passed the entrance requirement, the SSLC Examination, was significantly lower than the corresponding figure for men. (iii) Gradual expansion in the number of institutions was evident for general education and for professional education. (iv) The increase in the number of students saw a phenomenal increase during the period under study, with the percentage enrolled in the postgraduate courses also increasing. (v) In professional education the increase in enrolment was gradual in all faculties, with Commerce showing highest enrolment. (vi) Although the enrolment of Scheduled Castes/Scheduled Tribes showed overall improvement, the proportion to total enrolment was low (7.8 for Scheduled Caste and 0.54 for Scheduled Tribes). (vii) The coefficients of equality showed increasing values but the values showed that greater efforts needed to be made to make their proportion equal to that of the students of other communities. (viii) In professional education, the percentage of enrolment of Scheduled Castes was only 5 and of Scheduled Tribes 28 while their percentages of reservation were higher. (ix) The coefficient of equality for Scheduled Castes and Tribes calculated for professional education showed higher values for Scheduled Tribes when compared to general education. (x) The number of teachers in higher education, both general and professional, showed increase but the teacher-taught ratio appeared to be almost the same. (xi) The average annual growth of expenditure in higher education decreased from 15.2 per cent for the period 1957-58 to 1967-68 to 4.2 per cent for the period 1968-69 to 1976-77. (xii) The increase in expenditure showed amount of parity with the increase in enrolment. (xiii) The average cost of educating a student was lower in general education than in professional education. (xiv) The number of students who passed different examinations was shown to vary in different years. (xv) The interaction between sex and division was significant at the pre-degree level alone. (xvi) The student amenities provided by the University covered a number of areas.

031 Naqvi, K.A., Chopra, K. and Kapur, Aasha. *Mobility and inbreeding*. New Delhi, National Institute of Educational Planning and Administration, 1984. 128p.

This paper examines the following aspects of the teaching profession: (i) the factors which help or hamper the retention of teachers in the profession such as service, working and living conditions, and opportunities for professional development; (ii) opportunities for mobility with in teaching profession, to and from research organisation, industry, commercial houses and other private organisations, and leave arrangements; and (iii) various aspects of inbreeding, including its effects on teaching-learning process, assignments of student, and organisational climate.

032 Osmania University, *The report of the syndicate sub-committee on academic reforms — undergraduate studies*, Hyderabad, 1975.

Out of the need for a fresh look at the system of instruction and evaluation both at the undergraduate and postgraduate levels, the present study was undertaken. The main objectives were at follows: (i) to examine the revival or otherwise of the yearwise examination scheme for B.A., B.Sc., and B.Com. degree course; (ii) to revise the existing syllabus of the undergraduate and postgraduate course in all the faculties; (iii) to look into total academic improvement, standards, evaluation, teaching techniques and methods in the principles of modern educational concepts; and (iv) to study the content, direction and pace within the existing pattern and evolve a concensus among the principal constituents of educational system, namely, the teachers and the students.

The present investigation is an opinion survey. Data were collected by a questionnaire containing all the aspects of the existing system of education with an option to make suggestions and additional comments. Respondents were all the university students, teachers, the members of the Senate, Academic Council and Syndicate and a few administrators. As many as 1790 students and 1244 teachers responded. Suggestions were made by sixty-seven students, fiftytwo teachers and seven others. To supplement and cross-validate the questionnaire data, discussions were held with a representative cross-section of the academic community and leaders of the known teacher organisations of the university. Data were analysed and percentage of agreement or disagreement indicated the trend of opinion. The suggestions made by different respondents served as a backdrop to the questionnaire responses and revealed the complex causes that contributed to the erossive trends in the existing system of university education.

The following were some of the significant findings of the study: (i) For admission to B.A., B.Com., and B.Sc. courses, an entrance test was a necessity. (ii) Student orientation programme was not organised well and in proper time. (iii) Lecture schedules were not scientifically planned. There was little scope for the revision of the courses, seminar classes and for the tests to be conducted. Students had hardly any idea about the content and structure of the lecture they came to attend. (iv) Library and reading room facilities were utterly inadequate. (v) Textbook lending library was badly needed. (vi) Programme for remedial instruction to below average students was needed. (vii) Home assignment as a learning device was not regularly practised by the majority of teachers. (viii) There was scope for organising extension lectures to supplement the classroom teaching, and using all the available audio-visual aids to make teaching more effective. (ix) In selection of university lecturers more rigorous ways of judging their abilities in teaching were needed. (x) Functions of a university teacher in terms of teaching techniques adopted, seminars held, project work or fieldwork undertaken by the teacher, were not regularly and consistently carried out. (xi) A large majority of the respondents held that student evaluation of the teacher might from an essential part of an academic improvement programme as a feedback mechanism for the teacher to improve his teaching. (xii) All the departments of the university needed well planned and well coordinated action for their development. (xiii) Teaching schedules and workloads remained to be recasted on a more scientific and efficient basis. (xiv) Yearwise examination could be introduced at the undergraduate level with twenty per cent of marks in each paper for internal assessment through periodical test. (xv) Organising workshops for training the teachers in the preparation of better questions was an urgent necessity. (xvi) There was a general consensus for making the present syllabi up to date and relevant to life and also for job-oriented and/or application-oriented courses as a part of the undergraduate programme. (xvii) Greater administrative flexibility, more sympathetic approach to problems of the students, and more coordinated and all out efforts of all the university departments to follow through their programmes, were some of the keynotes, as opined by many of the respondents, for implementing academic reforms in the university.

033 Pande, R.C., *A study of the dimensionality and the differences in the college environment of Garhwal University*, Ph.D. Edu., Garhwal University, 1980.

The specific objectives of the study were: (i) to construct college environment scale (one each on the five dimensions as defined by Pace) and a sub-scale on campus morale, (ii) to make a comprehensive analysis of the institutional scores on the different scales, sub-scales and factors, (iii) to interpret the institutional scores on each dimension and on each factor and develop an environment profile for each college, and (v) to provide valid and reliable college environment scales.

The sample of the study consisted of 2,200 students, randomly selected from the ten affiliated and three constituent colleges of Garhwal University, having a minimum experience of one session on the campus. Tools were self-designed college environment scale, a sub-scale on campus morale and ten additional items related to the burning problems. F test an t-test were used for analysing the data.

The important findings of the study were: (i) Campus morale was dominant in eight colleges while, among the dimensions, propriety ranked highest in the government as well as other types of colleges. (ii) Scholarship with regard to top position in any two colleges was poor. (iii) The colleges significantly differed from one another on the basis of their environment. (iv) The female students were significantly well disposed towards their college than their male counterparts. (v) The low achievers showed a significantly better image of their college environment than the other two categories of achievers. (vi) The geographical location of a college was not a distinguishing feature of the environment. (vii) The university-managed colleges were able to provide a better educational environment than the government and privately managed.

034 Pandey, B., *A study of the problem of universities in U.P. and remedial measures adopted since 1947*, Ph.D. Edu., Gorakhpur University, 1982.

The study was primarily concerned with sorting out the problems of university education in Uttar Pradesh since Independence and finding out remedial measures that were taken by the administration for the improvement of worsening conditions.

The reports of various Commissions set up by the Central and State Governments were studied for having a general view of the main problem areas. The data regarding the number of colleges and universities in U.P., enrolment of students, funds provided to the institutions established before and after 1947 were taken from the government agencies and the universities. The phenomenal rise in the enrolment of students in the institutes of higher education after Independence, the increment in the number of institutions in the context of population growth, and fund granted to the institutions were analysed statistically.

The study revealed that every aspect of tertiary education in U.P. was problem-ridden. Difficulty in the formulation of aims, choosing the medium of instruction, inadequate research and accommodation facilities, lack of adequate funds and difficulty in following the rules for the affiliation of colleges emerged as the main problems. The remedial measures taken by the government and universities proved to be inadequate.

035 Patel, I.U., *A comparative study of the patterns of university education of UK, USA, and USSR with special reference to the university education in India*, Ph.D. Edu., Sardar Patel University, 1975.

The objectives of the study were: (i) to study, understand and describe the existing university education in UK, USA, USSR and India with special reference to the structure and organisation, philosophy and the patterns of curriculum, and the assessment of university education; (ii) to bring out the significant features of the different patterns of higher education in the countries under study; and (iii) to study and compare the typical problems of university education in the countries abroad with those of India and seek adequate cues for bettering content, organisation and such other aspects of university education of this country.

The present comparative historical study is a piece of library research. Data were collected through primary and secondary sources. Some of the main observations were as follows: (a) UK has a long tradition of education. The university administration in UK is a self governing business, the relation with the government being maintained through the UGC. The British universities have various courses of studies and the evaluation system in the field of higher education mainly includes written test, internal work and *viva voce*. Open university is an innovative experiment there. The Indian UGC is modelled after the corresponding British organisation, and India is also trying to implement the idea of open university. As regards the federal, residential and teaching universities, it seems that India has adopted more of the European models. (b) The American universities are geared to achieving the goal of highest academic standard of research, teaching and service. Financially the American institutes of higher learning are fairly well placed compared with the Indian counterparts. The load of tuition fee is rather quite high in India than most of the western countries. The universities in USA are mostly of unitary and teaching type, whereas the bulk of Indian universities are of affiliating and teaching type. Constitutionally education is a state responsibility both in USA and India, but the American universities enjoy greater autonomy than the Indian universities. Otherwise, the administrative structure of the universities in both the countries are of comparable similar patterns. (c) Due to difference of ideology and social pattern, the system of education in general and higher education in particular in USSR differ from that of India. Education in USSR is a central responsibility and is thoroughly controlled by the central government, while in case of India it is a matter of partnership between the state and the central authorities in the field of higher education. In USSR there are no fees from students. The Soviet examination system is predominantly based on a year round regular internal assessment. As regards the admission policy and curriculum for higher education in USSR, one might say that it is determined by the state economic plan. Russian students of higher learning are free from financial worries as most of them get scholarships. The Indian government also provides UGC scholarships, national scholarships and scholarships or economically backward students; but the amount and the number of scholarships do not seem to be adequate enough to attract the bright and scholarly students for higher education.

036 Pimpalkhare, M., *A study of arts, science and commerce colleges in Maharashtra (1971-72)*, Ph.D. Edu., Poona University, 1976.

The purpose of the investigation was to conduct a status study of the non-government arts, science and commerce colleges in Maharashtra in the year 1971-72, with a view to finding out the growth of these types of colleges during the period 1966 to 1972, studying the pattern of enrolment in the year 1971-72, the teaching and the non-teaching staff, the physical facilities and the financial position of the colleges, and teaching subjects under the faculties of arts, science and commerce.

Out of the 329 colleges teaching arts, science, and commerce in Maharashtra in 1971-72, as many as 303 colleges responded to the study. The data were collected through a mailed questionnaire. Visits to some of these colleges were also made. Reports of various commissions and committees, both Indian and foreign, dealing with higher education were also used.

There were 95 arts, science and commerce colleges in 1960 when the Maharashtra State came into being. The number of such colleges increased to 189 in 1965-66 and further to 329 in 1971-72. The figures of enrolment for 1966-67 and 1971-72 were 1,38,765 and 2,71,584 respectively. During the period 1966-70 the maximum enrolment was in the arts faculty followed by science and commerce. In 1966-67 the average enrolment per college was 806 and it increased to 896 in 1971-72. Nearly 7.27 per cent of the total seats available were lying vacant in 1971-72. In the same year, out of the total enrolment, girls formed 23.24 per cent. The percentage of girls varied from university to university, the maximum being 36.67 in Bombay and 7.23 in the colleges affiliated to the Marathwada University. About 4.23 per cent of the teachers had to their credit the Ph.D. degree. The pay scales of the non-teaching staff varied from the jurisdiction of each university and even among colleges affiliated to the same university. Compared to the norms of physical facilities laid down by the Committee on Improvement of Standards of University Education appointed by the UGC, a number of colleges fell below the expected norms. The state government incurred an expenditure of Rs. 22.10 lakhs in 1960-61 for payment of grant-in-aid to non-government colleges. It increased to Rs. 74.21 lakhs in 1966-67 and to Rs. 257.47 lakhs in 1971-72. Nearly 44.30 per cent of the students availed themselves of the facility of concession available to the economically backward classes.

037 Rath, R., *Attitudes of university students towards some politico-economic issues*, Deptt. of Psychology, Utkal University, 1955.

The present study aimed at measuring the attitudes of the university students of Orissa towards some politico-economic issues. Besides this, an attempt was also made to see if the distribution and intensity of attitudes scores had anything to do with the family occupation and the economic status of the subjects. The hypotheses tested in the present investigation were: (i) the student population have favourable attitudes regarding some political and economic issues; (ii) attitudes have definite relationship with the family occupation of the subjects; and (iii) attitudes have statistically significant relationship with the family economic status of the subjects belonging to different strata.

The sample consisted of 800 college students irrespective of their class and subjects from Orissa. For constructing an attitude test a set of five statements graded from most favourable to most unfavourable attitudes towards a particular issue was formulated. The test finally contained thirty important issues concerning social, political, economic and cultural problems. Besides this, the students were asked to give the details regarding their family occupation, annual income, land in acres and its approximate value, immovable property and other assets of their families. Data were analysed by computing percentages and using statistical technique of chi-square test.

The study revealed that (i) the distribution of attitude scores of all the subjects showed clear trends for three groups of politico-economic issues; (ii) the chi-square values obtained for Russian influence, Russia's responsibility for another war and communism were highly significant, yet compared to other chi-square values these were quite low; (iii) chi-square value for nationalisation of industries, etc., was the highest, (iv) none of the chi-square values for three occupational and three economic groups was significant at one per cent level; there were only two trends in economic group which were significant at five per cent level in regard to the pre sent day administration and nationalisation of the industries; and (v) the present sample represented the true population in regard to six out of eight attitudes studied; the chi-square values for the socialists and Marxism were significant at one per cent level.

038 Raza, Moonis and Fernandes, Marjorie. *Professional and career development.* New Delhi, National Institute of Educational Planning Administration, 1984. 126p.

The focus of this study is on the following aspects of the career development of teachers in higher education: (i) Minimum period of academic and professional preparation needed for entering the profession/fresh appointment/length of previous professional experience; (ii) promotion from temporary to permanent and from one cadre to the next higher cadre; and (iii) additional qualifications acquired such as M.Phil, Ph.D., D.Litt., research guidance, books/articles published, seminar/conferences and training programmes attended, the duration of visiting assignments, and the number of times and period the study leave availed during the career.

039 Raza, Moonis and Sharma, G.D. *Research design.* New Delhi, National Institute of Educational Planning and Administration, 1984. iv.

For conducting research studies keeping in view the terms of reference of the National Commission on Teachers in Higher Education, a proper research design was developed. The design included the following distinctive steps: (a) development of questionnaires; (b) canvassing of questionnaires; (c) verification and processing of data; and (d) analysis and report writing.

040 Raza, Moonis, Aggrawal, Y.P. and Hasan, M. *Higher Education in India: A Survey.* New Delhi, National Institute of Educational Planning and Administration, 1984. 154p.

This paper is a survey of higher education right from the British period to the modern period. It gives the development of higher education since independence keeping in view the enrolment, finance, manpower planning and inequalities. Regional dimensions of higher education are discussed in Chapter Three. Contradictory pulls in Indian higher education are discussed in Chapter Four. They system and sub-system is discussed in Chapter Five. It also provides tables, maps, and bibliography.

041 Shah, R.S., *College campus life in perspective*, Ph.D. Edu., Maharaja Sayajirao University of Baroda, 1975.

The major objectives of the investigation were: (i) to develop a profile of colleges in central Gujarat, including sociology of student and teacher community, physical facilities and qualitative status; (ii) to study some major trends and issues of higher education, namely, perception of academic life, and student unrest; and (iii) to identify desirable reforms in areas like curriculum, teaching, textbooks, and examination.

The study was confined to twentyeight out of thirtyfour colleges in Kheda and Panchmahal districts. A total of twentysix principals, 100 teachers (12.3 per cent of the total population) and 1,112 students (5.34 per cent of the population) were selected for the study on stratified randomisation basis. For the evaluation of the colleges, fifteen research tools were used. Out of these, fourteen were in the form of questionnaires, opinionnaires, rating scales, data-sheets and these were developed separately for principals, teachers and the students. The other tool included was the Organisational Climate Description Questionnaire developed by Halpin and Croft. The data were analysed using chi-square test and the contingency coefficient.

The important findings were: (i) students who secured first class marks in the qualifying examination joined the science courses; (ii) wards of highly educated parents tended to join the science courses, while the wards of less educated parents mostly joined arts courses; (iii) students who belonged to low socio-economic status selected arts courses, while students belonging to middle and high socio-economic status selected science courses; (iv) the students showed their maximum dissatisfaction towards students' welfare services, curriculum, examination, discipline, and interpersonal relationships; (v) strict admissions, compulsory attendance, small size of classes were supported by postgraduate students; (vi) sixty per cent teachers fully endorsed the selective admissions, small size classes consisting of fifty students and co-education classes; (vii) principals (sixty per cent) felt that there should be at least one college in each district located in rural and open air setting, admissions should be selective, and junior teachers should be given short-term inservice courses; (viii) teachers and principals observed that one final university examination should have less weightage and internal assessment should be adopted; (ix) students, teachers, and principals were divided on the issue of causes of student unrest; (x) students' satisfaction was higher when the management was committed to serve the cause of higher education, constructed best possible college buildings, etc.; and (xi) organisational climate of the college was significantly related to the principals', teachers' and students' perception of the causes and remedial measures of students' unrest.

042 Shah, S.Y., *Politicization of higher education in British India: A case study of the establishment of Aligarh Muslim University (1875-1920)*, Ph.D. Edu. Jawahar Lal Nehru University, 1981.

The inquiry aimed at studying the various aspects of the politicization of higher education in British India by making a case study of establishment of the Aligarh Muslim University, 1875-1920. In this process it attempted to (i) trace the evolution of the historic character of the university, its different dimensions and significance, (ii) analyse the Muslim educational thought of the Muslim intellectuals and British statesmen, (iii) throw light on the colonial policy towards Muslim higher education with particular reference to Aligarh Muslim University during 1875 and 1920, (iv) examine the extent to which the emergence of the other educational institutions, especially the Islamia colleges, Shia college and Banaras Hindu University, affected the process of the establishment of the AMU, and (v) study the attitude of the press and the public towards the proposed university at Aligarh.

The study adopted the historical method. It made use of a variety of unpublished and published primary and secondary sources available at the National Archives of India, U.P. State Archives, Nehru Museum Library, Jamia Millia Islamia, Sir Syed Archives and Central Secretariat Library. Some of the primary sources, viz., the papers of Syed Hossein Bilgrami, Raja of Mahmudabad, oral transcript of Dr. Syed Mahmud, proceedings of the U.P. Educational Department, were made use of for the first time. A good deal of untapped materials pertaining to Aligarh was also collected from the papers of Northbrook, Elgin, Chelmsford, Curzon, Hewett, Minto, Morley, Butler, James Meston, Badruddin Tyabji, Abdul Majid Khwaja, Syed Mahmud and the Ali brothers, a number of official and unofficial publications, contemporary newspapers, gazettes and unpublished doctoral dissertations.

The study showed that the politicization of higher education in British India was an extremely complex process. It manifested at various levels and in varying degrees with regard to the establishment of the AMU. The motives with which the founder of the Aligarh Muslim University, Sir Syed Ahmed Khan, his colleagues and the followers as well as the officials perceived and pursued the idea of the University, all had political overtones. By emphasizing the education of the elite and loyalty to the rulers and by seeking cooperation of the British to further the educational programme, Sir Syed gave political orientation to his educational endeavours. As a result he furthered an important objective of the colonial rulers, of producing loyal elite through education.

In this task Sir Syed was to a great extent aided by the British through honorary titles and grant-in-aid to his institution. Though inspired by the social reform activities of a Bengali intellectual, Nawab Abdul Lateef, and at the same time moved by the declining socio-economic condition of his community, Sir Syed decided to initiate various educational measures in the late 1860s. It was his visit to England in 1869 and the favourable policy of the British towards the Muslims in the early 1870s that enabled him to lay the foundation of the AMU in the form of M.A.O. College in 1875. In spite of his intense desire to raise it to the status of a full-fledged university and the constant support from the British, Sir Syed could not succeed due to a variety of reasons till his death in 1898. The idea of the university was kept alive by the friends and followers of the founder. There were two groups—the moderates and the liberals who took active interest in the implementation of the scheme. But the main motive of the majority was to emerge as the leaders of the community by championing the cause of the university. However, they differed with regard to their perception of the character of the contemplated university. The press was also divided. The Muslim community was not united in its demand for the university as observed by certain scholars.

The lack of consensus among the promoters of the scheme of the AMU and their intermittent involvement with the various political activities and association discouraged the British from granting the university. The Aligarhians continued to pursue the idea of the university even through the political platform of the Muslim League. Their growing influence forced the British to give encouragement to the Islamia colleges so as to minimize the dependence of distant Muslims on Aligarh and in this way the British policy towards Muslim education was to a certain extent moulded by the Aligarhians. Moreover, by persuading the Hindus to accept the Banaras Hindu University or official terms in 1915, the British tried to isolate the demand of the liberal Aligarhians for an autonomous affiliating university. The Lucknow Pact (1916), the growing Hindu-Muslim unity, Pan-Islamic activities of the liberal Aligarhians and their association with the Khilafat Movement and Gandhiji made the British realize the urgency of granting the university. At the same time they were cautious enough to grant the university with sufficient powers of control to the Government. So they started negotiations with the pro-British moderate Aligarhians and finalized the AMU Bill which was not acceptable to the liberals who, in protest, broke away from Aligarh and established an independent national university (Jamia Millia Islamia) in December 1920, when the AMU Act came into existence. Thus, the official interest in Aligarh was directly proportional to the degree of the involvement of the Aligarhians with various political factors and the political motives of the founder, his associates and the British, were mainly responsible for the establishment of the AMU. It was a unitary residential education in the Islamic atmosphere.

043 Shahnaz, Mushtar, *A critical study of American influences on post-independence higher education in India*, Ph.D. Edu., Aligarh Muslim University, 1975.

The study aimed at exploring American interest in Indian education and critically assessing American influence on the development of higher education in India, mainly its theory and practice, during the post-independence period. The study also tried to take into account the attitudes and opinions of those Indian scholars who had studied in the U.S.A. and other European countries and were now associated with various Indian institutions of higher learning.

A critical and evaluative study was made of the available relevant literature pertaining to the assistance in the shape of money and materials provided by the American government and private agencies for the development of education in India since independence. The efforts made by American personnel or American trained Indian personnel associated with higher education in India were also studied. A questionnaire was prepared and was sent to about 600 teachers engaged in teaching and research in various universities of India. The total number of questionnaires received back duly completed was 286. Statistical measures of critical ratio and chi-square test were used for analysing the data.

The findings of the study were: (i) American assistance to India came at a time when the nation possessed insufficient schools, too few textbooks, and an outmoded system of education. (ii) The U.S. aid was provided in such programmes as Marshal Plan, Point Four programmes, PL-480 programme, Mutuai Security Act, TCM, USAID and Fulbright, etc. (iii) The total financial assistance for the development of higher education in India through U.S. governmental agencies came to about Rs. 719.85 crores. During the same period, the assistance from Rockfeller and Ford Foundations came to about Rs. 261.7 crores. Apart from this, the equipments, apparatus and thousands of books were given as gifts and donations from the American government and various private publishers, organizations, etc. (iv) From 1951 to 1970, under the Fulbright programme 1151 and under USAID programme 3000 American specialists served as teachers and consultants in India. (v) The total number of Indian specialists who visited U.S.A. was 2449 under Fulbright scheme and 5778 under USAID scheme. Moreover, till 1969, about 68000 Indians studied in U.S.A. In the year 1969 alone, 8000 Indian students, 3000 Indian medical doctors, 4000 Indian university faculty members were in the U.S.A. studying for various degrees or engaged in research work.

044 Sharma, G.D. *Economic status*. New Delhi, National Institute of Educational Planning and Administration, 1984. 163p.

The focus of this study is on the following aspects of the teachers: (i) service conditions like salary scales, allowances, benefits etc.; (ii) working conditions; (iii) living conditions and standard of living; (iv) service and working conditions of persons in other professions such as

IAS, defence, banks, industry and medical professions; and (v) relative position of teaching in relation to other professions in developed and developing countries and in India.

045 Sharma, S.L., *Modernizing effects of university education*, Deptt. of Sociology, Panjab University, 1979 (ICSSR-financed).

The major objectives of the study were: (i) to examine the modernizing effects of higher education, independent of other factors, (ii) to determine the contribution of select components of higher education such as course content, teacher factor, co-curricular activities, and hostel context, (iii) to explore the interaction effect of some relevant predictors of student modernity, and (iv) to devise a measure of psycho-social modernity for assaying the attitudinal modernity in India.

The sample of the study comprised 770 students (515 males, 255 females), in the age-range of 16 to 26 years, based on the faculty (field of study) and the level of education (undergraduate and postgraduate classes), chosen from thirty-four teaching departments of Panjab University, Chandigarh, during the academic year 1973-74, using the stratified random sampling technique. Besides the student sample, 241 full-time faculty members constituted a complementary study group. The tools used for collecting data were developed by the investigator and his associates. They were Attitudinal Modernity Scale, Interview Schedule (Students) and Interview Schedule (Teachers). For analysing the data the statistical techniques used were analysis of variance. Kruskal-Wallis one-way analysis of variance, chi-square, coefficient of contingency, Guttman's coefficient of predictability, Goodman and Kruskal's Y, coefficient of correlation, and multiple and partial correlations. Besides the above, the data were subjected to Automatic Interaction Detection (AID) programme.

The major findings of the study were: (i) The level of higher education was inversely related to the students modernity. The level of education held a significant negative association with modernity in the faculties of professional courses, natural sciences, and the humanities. In social sciences, a trend of positive, though not significant, relationship between the two variables was observed. (ii) There was the lowest percentage of moderns in the humanities, followed by social sciences and professionals. The highest percentage of moderns was in the science faculty, lending support to the hypothesis that the science students were likely to be more modern than the students in other faculties. (iii) The male students were more modern than the female, and the high-status students were more modern than the low-status students. (iv) Faculties differed in respect of their sex composition; the faculties of the humanities and social sciences were male preponderant. (v) Holding sex constant, the original gross faculty differences with respect to modernity were diminished; similarly it altered the picture of paired faculty differences; originally science students appeared to be more modern but on controlling for sex, the social science males turned out to be more modern. (vi) On controlling the socio-economic status (SES), faculty failed to differentiate between the modernity levels of students. Initially the humanities faculty was found to be overpopulated with the high-status students. (vii) There was limited evidence of teacher effect on student modernity. (viii) Extra-academic component, though positively related to student modernity, had restricted relevance due to the fact that a very small minority of the students participated actively in these activities. (ix) The caste, family type, parental modernity and early residential background were not significantly related to student modernity although the variables of age, SES of family and duration of urban dwelling were weakly related to modernity. (x) The results of AID programme indicated that convent/public education affected more strongly than any previous or subsequent educational experience, the level of one's attitudinal modernity, which was due to both their better family background and the within-school factors. (xi) Differences in the institutional quality seemed to be related to significant differences in modernity.

046 Shejwal, B.R., *Investigation into study habits of college students*, Deptt. of Expt. Psychology, Poona University, 1980.

The major objectives of the investigation were: (i) to identify the good and poor study habits of students, and (ii) to find out the difference, if any, between the study habits of boys and girls.

The sample comprised fifty boys and fifty girls residing in a hostel exclusively meant for the economically backward students from rural areas. The sample was drawn randomly out of the 360 boys and girls of the hostel. There were twelve boys and twelve girls studying in Class XII, thirteen boys and thirteen girls in the first year degree class, twelve boys and twelve girls in the second year degree class and thirteen boys and thirteen girls studying in the third year degree class. The tool used was Palsane's Study Habits Inventory. Means, standard deviations and t-test were the statistical techniques used for data analysis.

The major findings of the investigation were: (i) The mean score for boys was 61.16 and that for girls 56.94. The difference was significant at 0.05 level. The boys were found to have better study habits than the girls. (ii) There were sex differences in different aspects of study habits. (iii) About 91.0 per cent girls lacked the habit of preparing the topic in advance whereas about 81.0 per cent boys lacked this habit. (iv) The habit of note-taking was absent among 50 per cent to 80 per cent students. (v) Learning and memory skills were absent among more than 60 per cent students. (vi) The students had problems in planning their time for study, developing good reading habits and taking examinations.

047 Shishak, T.A., *Higher education for Nagaland: A proposal for curriculum, organisation and coordination.* Buffalo State University of New York, 1973.

048 Sinha, D.N. *Social status,* New Delhi, National Institute of Educational Planning and Administration, 1984. 56p.

This paper examines the following aspects: (a) Teachers' status as perceived by teachers themselves, the students and the community, and its changes over the past three decades; (b) service and working conditions of persons in other professions such as IAS, defence, banks, industry and medical professions; (c) a comparison between relative position of teachers with other professions in developed and developing countries and in India; and (d) the factors responsible for the deterioration of status of the teachers. The qualities of a good teacher and the factors which determine the high status of a teacher, ar the other topics dealt with in this study.

049 Sirirassamee, T., *A comparative study of the higher education system in Thailand and India*, Ph.D. Edu., Bombay University, 1980.

The main objectives of the study were: (i) to describe the historical development of higher education in India and Thailand, (ii) to analyse the similarity and difference in the teaching and learning community in the two countries, and (iii) to describe the innovative programmes in higher education in the two countries.

Data were collected through questionnaires and an interview schedule and analysed through the statistical techniques of chi-square and contingency coefficient. The sampling was stratified and purposive and two universities were selected for study from each country.

The major findings of the study were: (i) Higher education in India and Thailand was influenced by the West. (ii) The long period of change and development in Indian universities had created complex problems of higher education, which was not the case in Thailand where higher education had expanded only recently. (iii) In India many education commissions had been appointed; however, no such commission had been appointed in Thailand. (iv) The administration of higher education in India was more complex than in Thailand. (v) Thai universities were only unitary, teaching and residential whereas Indian universities were federal, affiliating, teaching, unitary and residential. (vi) Private colleges in Thailand were fewer in number than in India. (vii) There were fewer male teachers in Thailand than in India. (viii) Indian teachers had higher qualifications than teachers in Thailand. (ix) Indian teachers had more teaching experience than their counterparts. (x) The teaching load of Thai teachers was less than that of Indian teachers. (xi) Teachers in both the countries were dissatisfied with the curriculum they taught. (xii) More Thai teachers believed in the validity of the examination than teachers in India. (xiii) Less than half the teachers in both the countries did research work. (xiv) Most teachers in both the countries used the lecture method. (xv) There was a significant difference in the composition of Thai and Indian students

050 Sreenivasan, S., *Foreign influence on higher education in India*, Ph.D. Soc., Bombay University, 1978.

The main objectives of the study were: (i) to examine foreign influence, through aid, on higher education in India, (ii) to delineate the qualitative difference of western influence over time and (iii) to historically relate the educational aid to the total aid programme.

The analysis of foreign influence through aid was confined to one branch of education, namely, technical education, and to one period, the post-Independence period. The study singled out one group of recipient institutions, namely, Indian Institutes of Technology, for intensive study. The methodology of the study was historical. The aim and objectives of foreign aid as a whole were analysed within the framework of foreign policy of the donor countries, especially the U.S.A. Statistical data on the distribution of educational aid were tabulated for easy reference.

The main findings of the study were: (i) Foreign influence on Indian education was not an exclusively modern phenomenon. (ii) The reasons for the offer of assistance were found embedded in the strategy of the developed countries to forge upon the underdeveloped countries a network of relations designed to perpetuate their economic order and political power. (iii) The declared objectives of the aid did not favour total development. (iv) Allocation-wise, educational aid hardly comprised 10 per cent of the total aid-flow to India. (v) There was a lopsided concentration of aid in the higher sector, and the near-total negligence of the primary and secondary sectors. (vi) Within the higher sector, the distribution of the aid was skewed, with institutions which has been the recipients of bulky UGC aid also recipients of foreign aid. (vii) Foreign aid appeared to promote the elitist nature of the existing education system. (viii) Foreign aid did not give importance to the development of agricultural education which got only 3 per cent of the total educational aid in the higher sector. (ix) The bulk of the aid, 34 per cent, was diverted to the field of technological education, with Education being the next biggest recipient. (x) Scholarships, fellowships and travel grants as forms of aid actively facilitated the process of brain-drain. (xi) Foreign aid promoted a unilateral direction in the trend of higher technical education, pointing towards the developed countries, thereby rendering it academically irrelevant to the developmental needs of the country. (xii) The socialist donor, the U.S.S.R., had also not fostered a qualitatively better education. (xiii) None of the donors had been instrumental in developing a type of technological education that would be best suited to India and its development.

051 Tickoo, C., *Critical study of the history and development of university education in modern India*. University of London, 1968.

052 Ushadevi, M.D. A study of the motivational pattern of evening students studying in Bangalore University and its constituent colleges, Institute for Social and Economic Change, Bangalore, 1981.

The objective of the study was to identify the major or overriding motives in the evening college students of Bangalore City for taking up evening courses. The study also aimed at studying the characteristic background of evening students.

The sample consisted of 385 evening students drawn from different undergraduate and postgraduate evening courses of Bangalore University. A questionnaire was developed to tap the different motives in an individual for taking up evening courses. The broad categories of motives included knowledge, economic, self-esteem, political, social and personal areas. Data were analysed using percentages.

The following were the major findings of the study: (i) The number of students in the undergraduate evening courses was more than that of postgraduate evening courses particularly B.Com. and B.A. (ii) Men availed themselves of evening courses in greater number than women. (iii) A large number of Hindus utilized this opportunity than the other religious groups: Brahmins, particularly, were found availing themselves of this opportunity more than the socially or economically deprived communities. (iv) Over 70 per cent of the evening students were employed, the majority of whom were in private organizations and held clerical jobs. (v) The majority of the evening students came from families with low income, low occupation and low education. (vi) The knowledge motive was overriding the other categories of motives for taking up evening courses. But when specific motives were considered in different categories, the motive of fulfilling the desire of becoming a graduate or a postgraduate was found to be the uppermost motive for taking up evening courses.

2. ADMINISTRATION

A BOOK

01 Airan, J.W. *College administration: A proposal*. Bombay, Asia Publishing, 1965. 57p.

02 Amrik Singh. *Asking for trouble: What it means to be a vice-chancellor today*. New Delhi, Vikas, 1984. 269p.

03 Bhatnagar, R.P. and Verma, I.B. *Educational administration: Planning and Supervision*. Meerut, International, 1986. 252p.

04 Chaturvedi, R.N. *Administration of higher education in India*. Jaipur, Printwell, 1989. 202p.

05 Goswami, D.H. *University administration in North-East India*. Calcutta, Naya Prakashan, 1982. 409p.

06 Gupta, L.D. *Educational administration at college level*. New Delhi, Oxford, 1983. 427p.

07 Indian Institute of Public Administration, Vallabh Vidyanagar. *Issues in University administration*. Vallabh Vidyanagar, I.I.P.A., 1974. 105p.

08 Khusro, A.M. *Survey of living and working conditions at university of Delhi. Bombay*, Asia Publishing House, 1967.

09 Madan, P.J. *Symposium on university administration*. Baroda, The Maharaja Sayajirao University, 1968. 135p.

10 Malik, S.C. ed. *Management and organisation of Indian universities*. Simla, Indian Institute of Advance Study, 1971. 283p.

11 Mehendiratta, Pradeep R. *University administration in India and U.S.A.: Approaches, issues and implications: A comparative study*. New Delhi, Oxford, 1984. 374p.

12 Ministry of Education. *University administration*. Delhi, Manager of Publications, 1958.

13 Ruhela, Satya Pal. *Sociology of college administration: A self assessment*. Alwar, Raj Rishi College, 1966. 53p.

14 Samuel, N. Koshy. *Organization and administration of higher education in India since independence*. Lanham, University Press of America, 1983. 199p.

15 Sharma, J.C. *Comparative study of policies and practices in the administration of higher education since World War II*. U.K., U.S.A. and India. London, University of London; Institute of Education, 1970.

16 Singh, R.K. *Our university and our vice-chancellors*. Agra, The Educational Press, 1950.

17 Sinha, Niraj. *University administration in India*. Patna, Janaki Prakashan 1979. 331p.

18 Sinha, V.K. College administration and academic freedom. *In* Shah, A.B., ed. *Higher education in India*. Bombay, Lalvani, 1968, p. 88-100.

19 Somaiah, Malathi. *Governance of Universities*. Bangalore, Indian Institute of Management. n.d. 181p.

20 Srivastava, Ramesh Chandra. *College administration*. New Delhi, Metropolitan Book Co., 1980. 308p.

21 *Study of improvement in management of university administration, Lucknow University. Organisation analysis, systems and procedures, training needs*. Hyderabad, Administrative Staff College, Consulting and Applied Research Division, 1979.

22 *Study of improvement of management in university administration, University of Poona. Organization, analysis, systems and procedure*. Hyderabad, Administrative Staff College, Consulting and Applied Research Division, 1979.

23 Subramaniam, M.K. *Challenges in higher education administration: Readings and cases*. New Delhi, Ford Foundation, nd. Vol. 1: Readings 673p.

24 ——. Seminar of registrars and administrative officers; Fifth administrative development programme, August 21-31, 1978: Background reading material. Hyderabad, Administrative Staff College, 1978. 94p.

25 Symposium on University administration, Baroda, April 1967. Report. Baroda, M.S. University of Baroda, 1968. 135p.

26 Trivedi, R.S. and Pathak, M.T., eds. *Issues in university administration*. New Delhi, Indian Institute of Public Administration, 1974.

27 Willey, M.M. *Self-study manual for Indian universities and colleges*. New Delhi, Ford Foundation, 1968. 79p.

B ARTICLES

01 Ahluwalia, Sartaj S. Students participation in university administration. *Students Services Review*. 7 (1), 1972. p.23-25.

02 Aiyar, S.P. Students participation in university administration. *University Administration*. 1 (1), 1974. p.1-10.

03 Amrik Singh. Problems of small colleges in Punjab. *University News*. 15 (16), August, 1977. p.431-433.

04 ——. Relations between the Teaching and the administrative staff. *University News*. 9 (3), 1971. p.14-17.

05 ——. University governance : Academic versus non-academics. *University Administration*. 4 (1-2), 1077. p.1-5.

06 ——. The Unquiet campus travails of men at the top. *University News*. 20 (2), 1982. p.39-40.

07 ——. Who should run the universities. *University News*. 19 (16), 1981. p.441 and 445.

08 Anand Surup. National apex body and state councils of Higher Education. *University News*. 26 (10), 1988. p.5-6 and 10.

09 Azad, J.L. Academic and financial management of higher education. *University News*. July 1, 1977. p.344-347.

10 Balasubramanian, V. Problems in Indian college/university hostels: Some suggestions for remedial measures. *Student Services Review*. 6 (2), 1972. p.26.

11 Baker, D. and Ford, B. How much student participation? *Universities Quarterly*, 22 (4), 1968. p.385-388.

12 Bannerji, R.C. Use of part time teachers in colleges. *Progress of Education* 40 (5), December, 1956.

13 Basargekar, S.K. Action against dismissal of university and college employees. *University Administration*. 3 (2), 1976. p.33-36.

14 Bhattacharya, Swapan K. and Manobendranath Pal. Management information system in university administration. *Journal of Higher Education*. 2 (2), 1976. p.913-999.

15 Bhattacharya, S.K. Managerial issues in university administration. *Bulletin of Centre for Educational Policy and Management*. July, 1976. p.46-59.

16 Bhirud, G.L. Participation of students in administration. *Process of Education*. 44, (October), p. 82-86, (November), p.136-40, (December), 1969. p.170-73.

17 Chaitanya. Democratisation of higher education: A plea for student participation. *Education Quarterly*. 22(4), January, 1971. p. 29-32.

18 Chandi, P.T. Concept of educational administration and institutional planning. *New Frontiers in Education.* 1, August, 1971. p.122-129

19 ——. Role of the management in building up the college as an Academic community. *New Frontiers in Education.* 6 (2), April-June, 1976. p.49-59.

20 Chatterjee, Sibranjan. Role of the governors as university Chancellor. *Modern Review.* 133 (5), 1973. p.336-340.

21 Collegiate administration. *University News.* 9 (5), 1971. p.1.

22 Collegiate administration programme. *University News.* 9 (8), 1971. p.5 and 23.

23 Desai, Uday. Vice Chancellor : A man for all seasons. *New Frontiers in Education.* 13 (3), 1983. p.1-20.

24 Doss, L.S. Gandhi. Student participation in varsity set-up. *University News.* 17 (18), 1979. p.477.

25 Ghosh, D.K. Administration in the university system. *University Administration.* 3 (2), 1976. p.1-7.

26 Ghosh, D.K. Rejuvenating the university administration. University Administration. *University News.* 15 (16), 1977. p.234-235.

27 Govil, K.P. Administrative reforms in varsities : Some suggestions. *University News.* 6 (12), 1968. p.17-19.

28 Govil, K.P. Non-academic personnel in universities. *University News.* 6 (8), 1968. p.19-20.

29 Guruge, A.W.P. Human relations in college administration. *New Frontiers in Education.* 1, August, 1971. p.101-21.

30 Inamdar, N.R. Decentralisation in university administration. *Indian Journal of Public Administration.* 24 (3), July-September, 1978. p.852-85.

31 Indian University Reform III. Higher Education : The governance of universities. *Minerva.* 5, Spring, 1967. p.391-412.

32 Jafri, H.A.S. University administration in India : An overview. *University News.* 25 (47), 1987. p.7-11.

33 Jain, M.C. The governor as Chancellor. *University News.* 27 (15), 1989. p.1.

34 Jain, Vinay; Jain, Promila. Campus reconstruction. *University News.* 21 (22), 1983. p.796-797.

35 John, V.V. Legend of timid men : Good old days that were no good. *Times of India.* 19 May, 1977. p.4.

36 Joshi, A.W. What ails the Indian university. *Journal of Higher Education.* 4 (2), 1978. p.280-285.

37 Joshi, D.C. The role of layman in university administration. *University Administration.* 4 (1-2), 1977. p.33-38.

38 Kapur, J.N. Privileges and responsibilities of a college principal. *University News.* 26 (33), 1988. p.1-2 and 7.

39 Kaptan, Sanjay Shankar. Introducing quality circles in university administration. *University News.* 28 (2), 1990. p.6-8.

40 Khan, Y.D. University administration. *Indian Educational Review.* (4), July, 1969. p.7-16.

41 Kiranmayi, Y.S. Restructuring organisational structure of universities in India. *University News.* 27 (40), 1989. p.23-38.

42 Kurien, C.T. Open and participatory college administration. *Journal of Higher Education.* 2 (2), 1976. p.203-212.

43 Mathias, T.A. Governing bodies in non-government colleges. *New Frontiers in Education.* 5 (1), 1975. p.i-vii.

44 Mathur, Gautam. Participation of non-teachers in university administration. *University Administration.* 4 (1-2), 1977. p.6-11.

45 Mathur, Kuldeep. Leadership and organizational structure in a university. *Journal of Higher Education.* 2 (2), 1976. p.233-242.

46 Mehta, Usha. Some reflections on university administration. *University Administration.* 1 (1), 1974. p.17-23.

47 Muthukumaran, S. Selecting a Vice-Chancellor. *University News.* 25 (45), 1987. p.1-6.

48 Narayanaswami, Srinivasa. Democratising the governance of universities and colleges. *University News.* 23 (43), 1989. p.1-3.

49 On administrative reforms. *University News.* 4 (8), 1966. p.3-5.

50 Puri, R.P. Evaluation of performance *vs* our universities. *University News.* 18 (11), June, 10, 1980. p.296-297.

51 Pylee, M.V. Application of management principles in college administration. *New Frontiers in Education.* 1, August, 1971. p.149-65.

52 Raghaviah, Y. and Srinivasan, K.V. University governance in India : A case for lay-governing boards. *University Administration.* 4 (1-2), 1977. p.41-36.

53 Rai, H. and Jha, R.N. The governor as chancellor : The Bihar experience. *Indian Journal of Political Science.* 32 (April-June), 1971. p. 125-144.

54 Rajagopal, M.V. Role of a registrar. *University News.* 18 (2), 1980. p.27-29.

55 Recommendations of the committee on support for the establishment of college development councils in the universities. *Bulletin of Higher Education.* 4 (1, 2-3), August, 1979. p.43-46.

56 Reddy, G. Ram. Problems of Indian universities. *Higher Education Policy.* 1 (3), 1988. p.49-50.

57 ——. University administration in India - Some critical issues. *Indian Journal of Public Administration* Vol. 26(3), 1980. p. 1-14.

58 Rao, M.R. and Raju, V.B. Administration of university affiliated college systems. New frontiers of Education. 5(1), 1975. p.13-25.

59 Rao, M.R. and Raju, V.B. University past graduate centres : A case for decentralisation of university administration. *New Frontiers in Education.* 6 (1), 1976. p.23-28.

60 Rao, S.V. Faculty and administration in Indian University. *Philippine Journal of Public Administration.* 16 (3), 1972. p.259-381.

61 Ruddar Datt. College administration. *University Affairs.* January, 1974. p.10-12.

62 Rudolph, Lloyd and Susanne. Standards in democratised higher education : An analysis of the Indian experience. *Economic and Political Weekly.* 5, January, 1970. p.209-218.

63 Satish Chandra. Organisational pattern of university departments. *University News.* 6 (7), 1968. p.12 & 20.

64 Singhal, Sushila. Organisation of functioning of university in India. *Journal of Higher Education.* 1 (2), 1975. p.223-240.

65 Sinha, Dharni P. State education administration in Andhra Pradesh : A review and analysis 1956-1976. *University Administration.* 3 (1), 1976. p.1-15.

66 Srinivasan Iyengar, K.R. Student participation in university administration. *Education Quarterly.* 21, July, 1969. p.8-11 & 14.

67 Subramaniam, N.K. Seminar of Registrars and Administrative officers. *University Administration.* 3 (1), 1976. p.87-91.

68 Suraj Bhan. Some aspects of university administration. *University News.* 1 (5), 1963. p.12-13.

69 Taylor, H.J. University Administration. *University News.* 1 (5), 1963. p.10-11.

70 Through teachers eyes. *Economic and Political Weekly.* 14 (41), October, 1979. p.1707-1708.

71 Tikkiwal, B.D. Governance of universities. *University News.* 16 (2), 1978, p.709-711.

72 Vaish, L.P. Concept of college development council in an affiliating university. *University News.* 16 (21), 1978. p.1238-1239 and 1253.

73 Verma, D.P. Agitations in the universities. *University News*. 20 (24), 1982. p.743-744.

74 Walsh, W. University problems : The university in India. *Twentieth Century*. 168, August, 1960. p.154-60.

75 Who should run the universities? Views expressed by members and ex-members of the AIU regarding management of universities. *University News*. 19 (17), 1981, p.478-480.

76 Workshop of principals. *University News*. 4 (6), 1966. p.1-2.

C COMMITTEE/COMMISSION/REPORTS

01 Committees on Some Problems of University Administration, 1964. Report. New Delhi, University Grants Commission, 1967. 22p. Chairman: Shri D.C. Pavate. (This committee was appointed by the U.G.C. following the report of the Santhanam Committee on prevention of corruption).

The University Grants Commission at its meeting held on August 5, 1964 considered the observation made by the committee of prevention of corruption set up by the Government of India. The commission after consideration of the above observation appointed this committee to examine the extent of malpractices prevalent, if any, in the universities.

02 Committee on Governance of Universities, 1969. Report. New Delhi, University Grants Commission, 1971. Part I. Governance of universities. 96p. Chairman: Dr. P.B. Gajendragadkar.

The committee on governance of universities was constituted to consider the following issues: Acts, statutes, ordinances and regulations; the visitor and the universities; authorities of the universities; other university bodies; organisations of teaching departments; university administrators; student participation; autonomous colleges/departments; grants committee in the states, collegiate education committee; annual report, audited account; delegation of powers; and administrative/financial procedure.

03 Committee on Governance of Universities and Colleges, 1969. Report. New Delhi, University Grants Commission, 1973. Part II: Teachers: Conditions of service, emoluments, responsibility and other matters relating to university and college teachers. 20p. Chairman: S.N. Sen.

The committee considered the issues relating to the following: the need to attract the best talents; the need to improve the functions and professional competence of teachers, pay scales and their rationale; university teachers, college teacher; evaluation of teachers; principals of colleges; tutors and demonstrators; basis of fixation of pay; scale of pay of library staff and physical instructor; the need for a national wage policy;

recruitment of teachers in affiliated colleges; conditions of service; and code of conduct.

04 Committee on Administrative Structure of the Universities, 1978. Report. Andhra Pradesh, Education Department, 1979. 98p. Chairman : G. Ram Reddy.

The Government of Andhra Pradesh appointed the Committee on Administrative Structures of the Universities. The terms of reference of the Committee outlined in G.O.Ms. No.1001 Education, dated 20th October, 1978 are :-

To look into the administrative structures of the universities and to suggest suitable changes in the pattern of university administration and the establishment of the university and college service commission.

The committee recommended :

The existing system, wherein the Governor is the Chancellor of all the universities may be continued. All levels of teachers, students and non-teaching staff should be represented on the university bodies. Besides ex-officio members of the university and Government, four persons from the Academic council, two from the principals/professors/deans and one professor from sister university should be elected from the syndicate. Similarly for senate officers of the university, Government officials, Principals of colleges, teachers and students should be nominated.

Apart from the usual membership of the Academic Council Chancellor should nominated teachers, principals and students.

For the appointment of vice-chancellor there should be search committee. The rectors should be appointed from among the teachers of university. The recruitment of suitable persons as a registrar should be left to the university authorities.

Reorganising the inter-disciplinary role of the faculty, the heterogeneous, new prevalent, university colleges should be regrouped into schools. The dean should be appointed by the university for a term of three years. The Board of studies, should be divided into to distinct units – one to cater to post-graduate and other to under-graduate courses.

The department committee and development council should be constituted for sound academic decision-making.

The head of the department should be appointed by the university on the recommendation of the committee of the syndicate for three years.

The existing system of selection of university teachers should be strengthened and broad based. It is recommended that a separate cell be created under a senior officer of the university to prepare and to execute welfare programmes for the staff.

Committee strongly recommend the U.G.C. Scheme of subbatical leave. Two standing committees for inter-university co-ordination should be constituted to provide the working structure for the meetings of the vice-chancellors. Rapport between the functionaries of the Government and the universities could be improved further by regular and frequent meetings. The committee recommends a two-tier system to look after the matters concerning student welfare.

05 Committee of Elders, 1988. Draft report. New Delhi, AIU, 1988. Chairman : R.C. Paul.

The AIU constituted a Committee of Elders on September 6, 1988.

The terms of reference of the Committee (as enlarged by the resolutions of AIU bodies) are:

(i) to enquire into the circumstances leading to the dismissals or so-called resignations in the Universities in Bihar:
Prof. Ekbal Bahadur Singh, VC, Bhagalpur University;
Prof. Shakeelur Rehman, VC, L.N. Mithila University;
Dr. R.D. Munda, VC Ranchi University;
Dr. S.N. Das, VC, Patna University;
Prof. (Mrs) Lalita Sinha, VC, Bihar University;
Prof. Mangal Dubey, VC, Magadh University;
Dr. B.S. Kumar, VC, Kameshwara Singh Darbhanga Sanskrit University.

(ii) to enquire into the circumstances leading to the resignation of Dr. P.D. Hajela, Vice-Chancellor, Dr. Hari Singh Gour Vishwavidyalaya, Sagar;

(iii) to suggest appropriate provisions for the appointment of Vice-Chancellors;

(iv) to suggest measures to ensure that the Governor when acting as Chancellor acts independently and not on the aid and advice of the Council of Ministers;

(v) to suggest legal modalities for ensuring the security of tenure of Vice-Chancellors, and in this context to examine the provisions of university enactments providing for the supersession of university bodies and authorities and/or for the removal of Vice-Chancellors, and to suggest viable alternatives;

(vi) to review the provisions of the Orissa Universities Act, 1989 (which replaced the Orissa Universities Ordinance of 1988).

The Committee of Elders met on September 21, 1988, October 27, 1988 and February 13, 1989. After detailed deliberations the Committee finalised the following report:

The Report is being presented in the following order: *Section I*: Dismissal and so-called Resignations of Vice-Chancellors in Bihar Universities in 1988: (A) Background : Funding of Universities and Constituent Colleges in Bihar. (B) Dismissal and so-called Resignations of Vice-Chancellors in Bihar. *Section II*: So-called Resignation of Dr. P.D. Hajela, Vice-Chancellor, Dr. H.S. Gour University, Sagar. *Section III*: Appointment of Vice-Chancellors and some related issues: (A) Appointment of Vice-Chancellors and Pro-Vice-Chancellors; (B) Governor to act as Chancellor in his individual capacity; (C) should Chancellor be a person other than the Governor? *Section IV*: Security of tenure of Vice-Chancellors. *Section V*: Some comments on the Orissa

Universities Act, 1989. *Section VI*: Summary of Findings and Recommendations. Section VII: Concluding Remarks.

The committee found that removal of vice-chancellors in all cases was completely arbitrary, illegal and politically motivated.

In the opinion of the committee, sections 14 and 52 of the M.P. Vishwavidyalyas Adhiniyam 1973 (as amended) Section 11 and the amended section 10(3) incorporating the pleasure cause and S.14 of the Bihar University Act, S.31 of Orissa University Act, 1989 or parallel provisions elsewhere should be deleted from the respective university enactments.

The vice-chancellor should be selected out of a panel of at least three names. The panel should be proposed by a committee consisting of (1) a nominee of the Executive Council of the university, being a person not connected with the university or its colleges : (ii) the chairman of the UGC or his nominee and (iii) a nominee of the chancellor in his personal capacity. The pro-vice-chancellor. The term of office of the vice-chancellor should be five years and it should be renewable. The vice-chancellor must retire at the age of 65, under any conditions.

The committee has recommended that the Governor should continue to be the chancellor of the state universities.

The removal of a vice-chancellor should be contemplated only in case he has been charged with an offence involving moral turpitude and has been found guilty after proper enquiry by a sitting of retired judge of a High Court or Supreme Court, after having been given an opportunity of being heard in accordance with the principles of natural justice.

The Finance Officer/Comptroller of Finance of the university should be a person appointed by the university itself through open advertisement.

Section 31 of the Act, providing for supersession of the senate and other authorities including the vice-chancellor and handling over management to an administrator, is highly undesirable and should be deleted.

The committee recommended that the provisions introduced through amendments in the university enactment should also be periodically examined and the modifications of deletion of the same insisted upon by the UGC.

AIU should advise the vice-chancellors not to tender their resignation if they are not inclined to do so on their own. AIU should be vigilant in the admission of new member.

The committee feels and suggests that a central legislation overriding the universities in the country is absolutely necessary and should be framed, passed and implemented without any loss of time to save the universities from further deterioration.

D RESEARCH STUDIES

01 Desai, U.C., University Vice-chancellor – Profile of leadership, Administrative Staff College of India, Hyderabad, 1979 (ICSSR-financed).

The objectives of the study were: (i) to acquire basic information on the social economic and educational background of vice-chancellors, their parents and grandparents, (ii) to analyse career patterns of vice chancellors, and (iii) to find out the attitudes of the vice-chancellors towards university and their own role.

The sample consisted of 112 vice-chancellors. Of these, forty-seven were present vice-chancellors and sixty-five former vice-chancellors. A questionnaire was designed to collect the necessary information. In a pilot study, a draft questionnaire was filled out by eight present vice-chancellors. On the basis of comments and suggestions, the instrument was modified and finalized. The final questionnaire was divided into five sections. The first three sections were designed to collect information on personal background, education, and career. The fourth section included questions about the family background, and the fifth section contained questions, both structured and open-ended, concerning vice-chancellors' views on university matters. Percentage and frequency distribution were used to analyse the data.

The findings of the study were: (i) The typical vice-chancellor was a middle-aged married man. He was born and brought up in a town or a city. He came from a middle class family. He typically went to a government or private school. He rarely attended public or convent schools. He had at least a postgraduate degree. He mostly studied science or humanities. Predominantly, he was a high caste Hindu; and least likely a Muslim or a low caste Hindu. He was not very different from a typical higher civil servant (IAS, IFS) or an Indian manager. He was a little more likely than a higher civil servant to be from lower middle class and rural area. He was seen to have more higher education than the higher civil servant or manager, but the class obtained by him was found lower than that of the higher civil servant. (ii) The vice-chancellor was typically an academic bureaucrat. He typically started his career in a college or university as a teacher or researcher. He moved to administrative positions in government or academic set up as his career progressed. He typically occupied an academic administrative or government bureaucratic position just prior to becoming vice-chancellor. He rarely ever worked in a private enterprise. Typically, the only other career he ever considered was that of a government bureaucrat. He was dedicated to public service. He was university organization as a combination of bureaucratic, judicial and consensus systems. His views on university organization and leadership were conventionally Indian. He valued consensus and impartiality above everything else. (iii) He was parochial. He did not see himself as a member of a small, well-knit national educational elite. He did not know much about the work or performance of other vice-chancellors. His information network was local. He viewed vice-chancellorship in grandiose but essentially empty cliches. A vice-chancellor, according to him, should be paragon of virtue and efficiency and everything good, and should know everything desirable. He saw unruly students, uncooperative, unmotivated and lazy faculty and staff, meddlesome and unsupportive politicians and bureaucrats as the major sources of difficulty for the university administration and the vice-chancellor.

02 Heredia, R.C., *Structure and performance of college education – An organizational analysis of arts and science colleges in Bombay*, Social Science Centre, St. Xavier's College, Bombay, 1981.

The major objective of the study was to examine the internal organizational structure of selected arts and science colleges affiliated to Bombay University, with special reference to organization, principles of bureaucracy and professionalism, teaching-research dilemma, institutional innovation and external examination system. The basic research problem focused on the functional efficiency of the affiliating university in a changing social situation and rising expectations it must meet within the constricting limitations.

The study used quantitative methodology for the organizational analysis. The tools used for data collection were records on file, closed-ended questionnaires and open-ended interviews. The sample was drawn from twenty-two colleges out of the twenty-three colleges affiliated to Bombay University. It included 440 respondents spread through different departments of the colleges selected by using the technique of stratified sampling. The data analysis was done at the level of the individual, the department and the college. The statistical techniques used were descriptive statistics, correlational analysis and regression analysis.

Some of the major findings to the study were: (i) The recurring expenditure per student was Rs.680 to Rs.638, of which 54.63 per cent came from the student, 40.84 per cent from government grants and scholarships and 4.55 per cent from the management. All colleges were affected by serve financial stress. (ii) The average score or entering an arts college was 49.512 per cent and that for entering a science college 57.47 per cent. (iii) The average faculty strength for arts and science colleges was 32.5 and 18.5, respectively. (iv) The student-faculty ratio for art colleges was 45.126 whereas the same for science colleges was 54.317. The average class size for the first and second years was 132.818 and the same for the third and fourth years was 72.636. (v) About 52 per cent of the time of a college teacher was used up in preparation, teaching, correction, etc., and only 19 per cent of the time was left for study and research. Senior teachers had fewer a courses to teach, a smaller teaching load and more time or study and search. (vi) The profile of a college teacher as seen from the study did not categorize the teacher as a professional but rather placed him in the category of a salaried employee constrained by his pedagogic burden. (vii) The principals influence was seen clearly as dominant in all areas of college organization but only a few enjoyed freedom from the management and support of colleagues to exercise a strong and creative leadership. The departmental head had a great say in appointments in his department but the faculty's share in institutional authority was small. Administrative and academic policy and institutional finance were controlled by the principal and the management. (viii) The colleges had a high degree of paternalism and bureaucratization and low professionalization. Paternalism was positively affected by a high student-faculty proportion but negatively by institutional complexity.

Bureaucratization was positively affected by institutional complexity and negatively by institutional age. Professionalization was positively affected by a well qualified faculty and institutional specialization.

03 Hommadi, A.H., The application of modern scientific management principles to the development of the university administration in developing Countries, Ph.D. Com., Rajasthan University, 1978.

The investigation aimed at studying the application of modern scientific management principles to the development of the university administration in development countries. It attempted to offer some conceptual outlines of how a university of a developing country might transform itself and become one of the more active agents for 'world's transformation'. It also concentrated on stating the problems in higher education and what general directions should be taken to solve them.

A major portion of the reference work done during the past ten years in Iraq, Europe, U.S.A., Egypt and Libya was taken into consideration. Books and journals of academic institutions of the above countries were referred to. A major portion of the study was about analysing and drafting the functioning of higher education in Afghanistan, Pakistan, India and Bangladesh. The investigator also observed the administrative mechanics, operations and interviewing relevant people in all universities and other institutions of higher learning of the above countries. The investigator tried to understand the view-points of students, professors, administrators and staff, but he based his analysis and judgement on his experience in the field and factual observations and evidence obtained through interviews.

The investigation yielded the following findings: (i) Population explosion, rapid advance and expansion of new areas of knowledge, increased reliance of social institutions on faculty, talent to aid in solution of social and scientific problems, and the resultant increased interest of all high school graduates in college and university degrees – all contributed to the shaping of the university responsibilities and goals. (ii) Despite considerable educational planning activities over the years, educational administration in general and university administration in particular, until very recently, was totally neglected by educators and planners alike. (iii) The impetus of the current attention to university administration in the developed countries came primarily from the development of elaborate management principles and techniques and methods. Several professions were concerned with university administration and management in one way or another. (iv) University administration field had always been a team work in which several types of expertise were called upon to cooperate in solving a complicated case or studying a new administrative sub-system or system. (v) Written objectives of the university administration system should be implemented by a set of the system performance requirements which characterized the desired system output. University administration performance evaluation should be for the purpose of determining the extent to which actual performance fulfilled specified performance requirements. (vi) University administration performance evaluation criteria should be of different kinds including recorded observations, checklists, performance test, critical incidents, rating scales, comparison systems, timing, quantity and quality of output which should be free from causes or effects of other systems or subsystems, relevant or reliable. (vii) Positions in the university organization systems should be designed with certain principles in mind, so that the positions are appropriately structured and built or shaped. For option in human gratifications in university administration, the activities should demand the use of human skill, should be meaningful, should provide clear functions, should provide responsibility, should provide opportunity for natural self-satisfactions and should be compatible with cultural and social value of the society and nation.

04 Kaushik, S.P., A study of the dimensions of administrative leadership in relation to group acceptance and some other educational aspects in the colleges of Meerut University. Ph.D. Edu., Meerut University, 1979.

The objectives of the investigation were: (i) to describe the administrative leadership of college principals in terms of significant patterns of real administrative behaviours, (ii) to ascertain their administrative behaviour as it ought to be in the view of the staff members, (iii) to analyse the relationship that might be existing between the real administrative behaviour and the ideal administrative behaviour of principals, (iv) to study the significant patterns of administrative behaviour of college principals with regard to educational factors such as subject faculties, age and role status, (v) to study the significant patterns of administrative behaviours of rural-urban and male-female college principals, (vi) to analyse the relationship between real administrative behaviour, ideal administrative behaviour, real-ideal discrepancy and acceptance of the principal by the group of staff members, (vii) to identify factors that lay at the back of the emerging patterns of the administrative behaviour of principals, and (viii) to analyse the significant patterns of administrative behaviour of the most acceptable and the least acceptable college principals.

The hypotheses formulated were: (i) The administrative behaviour of college principals might be described in terms of certain significant trends of behaviours and that these unitary critical behaviours might be combined into broad categories yielding certain reasonably well defined the independent dimensions. (ii) These behavioural patterns might be determined by certain background factors operating in or outside colleges. (iii) The real administrative behaviours might not conform to the ideal administrative behaviour of college principals. (iv) The acceptance of a principal as leader in a group of college teachers may be a function of certain characteristic dimensions of his educational leadership. (v) The coincidence of real and ideal administrative behaviours was related to the acceptance of the principal by the group. The sample consisted of fifty-nine colleges affiliated to Meerut University. The study used Principal's Behaviour Description Questionnaire (PBDQ), Background Factors Description Questionnaire (BFDQ) and Leadership Acceptance

Questionnaire (LAQ). The study applied t-test and chi-square test for data analysis.

The findings of the investigation were: (i) The principals were highly ego-centric, interactive, flexible and achievement-oriented. (ii) In the opinion of the teachers, college principals should be less ego-centric, authoritarian and inertia-prone, and more extra-centric, interactive, democratic, progressive, flexible, achievement-oriented and moderately tolerant. (iii) The patterns of real and ideal administrative behaviour were quite different from each other. (iv) On extra-centric, interactive, democratic, progressive flexible, achievement-oriented and tolerant dimension, the teachers wished the administrative leadership to attain a higher level than the level they exhibited currently. (v) The teachers of different faculties viewed their principals uniformly highly ego-centric. (vi) The administrative behaviour of urban principals on interactive, progressive and achievement-oriented dimensions was rated higher than that of their rural counterparts. (vii) Ideal administrative behaviours on extra-centric, interactive, democratic, inertia-prone, progressive, achievement-oriented and tolerant dimensions were independent of group acceptance. (viii) Group acceptance west contrary to real administrative behaviours on ego-centric, inertia-prone and authoritarian dimensions, and went with extra-centric, interactive, democratic, progressive, flexible, achievement-oriented and tolerant dimensions. (ix) Real-ideal discrepancy was negatively related to group acceptance for the all dimensions. (x) Acceptance of the administrative leadership by the teachers might be a function of administrative behaviour on extra-centric, interactive, democratic progressive, flexible, achievement-oriented and tolerant dimensions. (xi) Pressure groups among teachers, maintenance of law and order in the college, one's own concept of administration, and prevailing general atmosphere in society, were some of the important background factors affecting the administrative behaviour of the principal.

05 Kumar, D., A study of some identifying college characteristics and teachers' personality needs in relation to organizational climates of colleges of Haryana State, Ph.D. Edu., Meerut University, 1978.

The objectives of the study were: (i) to find out whether the colleges of Haryana differed among themselves with regard to their organizational climates, (ii) to identify the colleges with open and closed climate, (iii) to find out on what aspects of teachers' behaviour and principals' behaviour these colleges differed significantly from one another, (iv) to find out how the location, sex size and type of management of a college were related to the organizational climate, (v) to investigate the relationship between the personality needs of the teachers and the organizational climate, (vi) to find out if any difference existed in the organizational climate between men and women, urban and rural, big and small, and private and government colleges, and (vii) to find out the relationship between the organizational climates of the colleges and pupils' achievement.

The hypotheses formulated were: (i) There was no single pattern of organizational climate in the colleges of the state of Haryana. (ii) The location of colleges was not related to their organizational climate. (iii)

The faculty size of the colleges was not related to their organizational climate. (iv) There was no relationship between the sex of the faculty members and the organizational climate of colleges. (v) The types of management and the organizational climate of colleges were not related. (vi) The climate profiles of the colleges having the same climate did not have one to one congruence with regard to the dimensions of the organizational climate. (vii) The faculty members of rural colleges significantly differed from the faculty members of urban colleges with regard to their perception of teachers' behaviour and principal's behaviour. (viii) There was no agreement between the faculty members of big colleges and those of small colleges with regard to perception of teachers' behaviour and principal's behaviour. (ix) Statistically significant different existed between the perception of the faculty members of government colleges and those of private colleges regarding the leadership behaviour of the principal and teacher's behaviours. (x) The faculty members of male colleges and those of women colleges perceived the leadership behaviour of the principal and teachers' behaviours differently. (xi) Personality needs of the teachers were not related to the organizational climate of a college. (xii) Achievement indices of colleges were not related to their organizational climates. (xiii) Correlation between the achievement index and the organizational climate was not influenced by sex and size of the faculty members. The study was conducted on 300 teachers.

The findings of the study were: (1) The colleges of Haryana differed among themselves with regard to their organizational climate. (2) The rural colleges had more open-type climate than the urban colleges. (3) The faculty size of a college did not affect the organizational climate. (4) The private colleges had more open-type of organizational climate than the government colleges. (5) Sex did not affect the organizational climate. (6) Irrespective of the location, size and sex of the faculty members and the type of management of colleges, the teachers group behaviour were uniform and so were the principals' leadership behaviours. (7) All the dimensions of the organizational climate were positively related to the students achievement index.

06 Portia, D.R., The structure and functioning of the academic departments of an Indian University – A case study, Ph.D. Edu., Andhra University, 1979.

The objective of the study was to test the following hypotheses: (1) Neither the present university structure nor the academic departmental structure facilitates changing objectives of the university. (2) Organisation of academic departments which is based on the bureaucratic principles of hierarchy in causing tension in human relations of the members of academic department. (3) There is a conflict between the academic and administrative functions of the heads of the departments. (4) The overlapping of functions of key persons of the university, namely, dean of the faculty and the principal of the college is due to the fact that their functions are not defined in clear terms. (5) There are anomalies involved in the university structure due to the outmoded practices of statutory bodies like academic council and board of studies. (6) Interdepartmental collaboration in the university is not because of academic reasons but because of nonacademic reasons.

The study was exploratory as well as empirical. It was exploratory in the sense that various documents concerning university functioning were studied. These documents included reports of various education commissions, Andhra University Acts and Statutes. It was empirical in the sense that data were collected from heads of the department, lecturers, readers, professors and principals of colleges with the help of a questionnaire about the goals and functions of the university.

The findings of the study were: (1) There was general agreement among the respondents that there was disjunction between the university structure and the functions that the university was expected to perform. (2) Majority of the faculty members were aware that the academic departmental structure was not suitable for the changing objectives of the university. (3) The younger faculty members particularly from science faculties felt that they were not involved in decision-making in the university. (4) The heads of the departments felt that all faculty members could be consulted in academic matters but not in administrative matters. (5) The heads of the departments felt that they were subjected to strict accountability within the rigid framework of rules which permitted little individual discretion. (6) Majority of faculty members expressed that heads of departments spend more of their time in administrative work and neglected academic work. (7) The heads of the departments expressed that they had difficulty in reconciling administrative duties with academic interests and invariably it was academic work which suffered. (8) The respondents agreed that there was overlapping of the functions of deans of faculties and the principals of colleges. (9) Majority of the heads of departments felt that the existing practice of getting all academic issues pertaining to individual discipline ratified in the academic council after they were approved in the board of studies was not necessary. (10) There was no interdepartmental collaboration in using the resources, both physical and human. The major constraints identified were fear of loosing departmental autonomy, fear of cutting into the resources of the department, and fear of being criticised by other departments.

07 Ramasehan, B., and Shenoy, M., Study of improvement of measurement in the university administration of Poona University, Administrative Staff College of India, Hyderabad. 1979 (Poona University-financed).

The aims of the study were: (i) to examine the organization of the Poona University administration and evolve a systematic and harmonious arrangement of work to enable the university administration to meet its desired objectives, (ii) to examine the existing systems and procedures for important transactions in the university administration from the point of view of work simplification and smooth and timely disposal of work and (iii) to provide guidelines for academic self-evaluation.

Discussions were held with various officers and supervisory staff and details regarding their duties and responsibilities were compiled and analysed. Discussions were also held with the heads of the teaching departments and the principals of the affiliated colleges to identify areas where the university administration had interface with these institutions, the staff, the public and students and outline the procedure by which the administration could provide effective service to these agencies. With regard to academic evaluation, relevant information was obtained from the teachers, principals of colleges, and students with the help of structured questionnaires, followed by detailed discussions.

Following were the recommendations made to enable the university administration function effectively in fulfilling its desired objectives: (i) A section for performing the important function of public relations and information should be created in the university administration. (ii) A legal branch headed by a law officer of the rank of Assistant Registrar reporting directly to the Registrar be created to attend to (a) court cases arising out of disputes between the administration on the one hand, and the employees, students and society, on the other, (b) setting draft statutes, ordinances, rules and regulations and the amendments thereof, and (c) offering legal opinion, wherever necessary. (iii) An organization and methods unit should be created with a view to undertaking (a) periodic analysis of the prevailing systems and procedures and suggest modifications as a means of developing and applying easier and more effective methods, (b) systematic forms analysis and bringing improvements in the design and handling of forms, and (c) objective assessment of manpower requirements and development of rational work norms through work measurement. (iv) A cell headed by an officer of the rank of Deputy Registrar or above, reporting directly to the Vice-Chancellor, should be created as early as possible to deal with the activities pertaining to examination reforms. (v) The Vice-Chancellor's office should be strengthened by providing an Executive Assistant to the Vice-Chancellor. The post of Executive Assistant should, as far as possible, be not below the rank of a Deputy Registrar. (vi) The work of registration of external students, viz., receiving applications for registration, determining the eligibility and intimating the concerned students of their registration to the particular courses/subjects and all other correspondence with these students currently with the Examination Branch, should be attached to the Academic Branch. (vii) The entire preparatory work done up to the appointment of all university teachers currently being carried out by the Assistant Registrar (Academic) should be integrated with the Administration Branch. (viii) The entire work of granting affiliations to colleges, in extension of affiliations, forming inspection committees, etc., which is currently with the Development Branch should be integrated with the Academic Branch.

08 Sharma, M.P., Organizational structure and climate in universities of Rajasthan, Ph.D. Edu., Mohanlal Sukhadia University, 1985.

The objectives of the study were: (i) to study organizational structure of universities in terms of developmental personality, departmental organization and committee structure i.e. authorities and officers, communication channels and autonomy and academic freedom in functioning, and (ii) to study organizational climate in universities in terms of general social climate and inter-personal relationship between heads of departments and teachers and between teachers and teachers. The ultimate aim of the research was to suggest ways and means of improvements in the organizational structure and climate in universities of Rajasthan.

The necessary data were collected from all the three universities located in the state. To study the organizational structure and climate of these universities, descriptive survey method alongwith case study approach was used. For studying organizational climate of the university departments, adapted version of OCDQ (Organizational Climate Description Questionnaire) developed by Halpin & Croff, was used. Besides, an interview schedule and an opinionnaire were developed to collect necessary data regarding structure and climate. A General Atmosphere Recording Form (GARF) was also developed and used as a subsidiary tool. University Acts, reports and minutes were also consulted to collect necessary data.

Main findings of the research were: (1) University education in Rajasthan was of recent origin. It came into being in post-independence era. (2) Number of universities in the the state was quite small looking to the actual need of the state. There was only one university in the state which was of an affiliating nature. It had become unmanagable. (3) Distribution of universities in the state was also not proper and called for recognization on regional basis. (4) All the universities in the state had identical traditional structure, i.e., administrator and administration-oriented structure, unconducive to autonomy and academic freedom. (5) There appeared to be a tendency of centralization in the entire structure of the universities. (6) University departments had mainly 'closed' or 'intermediate' type at climate except a very few with 'open' type climate. (7) The morale of the teachers was found to be low.

09 Sinha, N., University administration in Bihar, Ph.D. Soc., Patna University, 1975.

The main purpose of the study was to analyse the present administrative structure of universities in Bihar and suggest some sort of planning in university administered manner.

This survey type study was confined to the universities in Bihar. The sources of information utilised were – books, journals, periodicals, reports of various committees and commissions on university education and administration, both at the national and state levels. Besides, some eminent administrators and teachers of Patna University were interviewed in a structured manner.

The major findings of the study were as follows: (i) The evils, such as, casteism, petty politics, low level of morality resulting from mass illiteracy, were reflected in the universities. (ii) The authoritarian traits of the society too were reflected in the universities, e.g., rigid hierarchy, emphasis on compliance, and resistance towards innovation and experimentation. The power of decision-making concentrated in the hands of a few. (iii) Principles of democracy, election for example, whenever or wherever introduced, failed mainly due to social factors, lack of training and half-hearted efforts. Democracy was prevalent in the form of 'casteocracy'. (iv) Channels of communication between the different components of the universities were restricted, and the junior teachers and students were prevented from taking active part in the affairs of the universities. This frustrated the sense of belongingness to the universities and resulted in problems of discipline and lower level of academic output. (v) The universities, on the whole, were not performing their role as the main producer of knowledge and intellect or trained personnel. They were, thus, unable to become agents of social change.

3. ADMISSION

A BOOK

01. Saiyidain, K.G. *Access to higher education in India : A depth study of university admission procedures.* New Delhi, International Association of Universities, 1962. 101p.

B ARTICLE

01 Airan, J.W. A note on admission to colleges. *University News* 4(2), 1966. p.12-13.

02 Deshmukh, C.D. Selective admission : The crucial issue in India higher education. *Asian Survey.* 1, July, 1961. p.3-8.

03 D'Souza, Victor S. Restrictions on admission to higher education : The criterion of selection. *Sociological Bulletin.* 10 (March), 1961. p.82-91.

04 Dongerkery, S.R. Admission and selection of students. *University Quarterly.* 9, February, 1955. p.186-91.

05 Hooja, G.B.K. What ails the university system-numbers. *University News.* 20(16), 1982. p.517-18.

06 Kogekar, N.V. Admission and education of students in colleges. *Progress of Education.* 40(4), November 1965. p.127-32.

07 Kothari, V.N. Why cut engineering admission? *Economic and Political Weekly.* 3(23), 8 June, 1968. p.867-68.

08 Misra, V.S. An Investigation into admission criteria. *University News.* 7(2), 1969. p.18-19.

09 Nagappa, S. Admission to higher education : Some policy implications. *Education India.* 41(9), 1975. p.196-208.

10 Narayan, Shanti, Resources and numbers : A few thoughts. *University News.* 4(9), 1966. p.3-4.

4. AFFILIATED COLLEGES

A BOOKS

01 Bhatnagar, P.L. *Problems of an affiliated university: A case study of university of Rajasthan*. Jaipur, Rajasthan University Press, 1969.

02 Bose, P.K., Banerjee, P.K. and Mukherjee. *Working conditions of colleges affiliated to the University of Calcutta during 1962-63: An educational survey*. Calcutta, Department of Statistics, Calcutta University, 1966. 43p.

03 Gujarat, *Government of Grant-in-aid to affiliated colleges in the State of Gujarat*. Ahmedabad, Govt. of Gujarat, 1977. 60p.

04 University Grants Commission. UGC Guidelines on terms and conditions of affiliation of colleges by a University. New Delhi, UGC, 1989. 19p.

B ARTICLES

01 Azad, J.L. Problems of affiliated colleges. *University Administration*. 3 (2), 1976. p.8-11.

02 Azad, J.L. Problems of affiliated colleges. *University News*. 15 (24), 1977. p.651-52.

03 Ghanchi, D.A. Interactive relationship in the affiliating system. *University News*. 26 (45), 1988. p.4-7.

04 Guidelines in the implementation of faculty improvement programmes pertaining to teachers in affiliated colleges. *Journal of Higher Education*. 1 (2), August, 1975. p. 273-275.

05 Joshi, Umashankar. On affiliation of colleges. *University News*. 5 (7), 1967. p.8-9.

06 Kapur, J.N. Post-graduate Teaching in affiliated colleges. *University News*. 9 (12), 1971. p.5-6.

07 Pawar, A.G. Affiliation and disaffiliation. *University News*. 10 (1), 1972. p.21.

08 Rajagopalan, K.R., Venkataraman, G.R. Research in affiliated colleges. *University News*. 25 (1), 1977. p.14.

09 Ramakrishnan, G. Weakness of affiliating university. *University News.* 19 (24), 1981. p.677-78.

10 Rao, M.R. and Raju, V.B. Administration of universities affiliated college systems. *New Frontiers in Education.* (5), January-March, 1975. p.13-24.

11 Teachers in affiliated colleges. *Educational India.* 22 (7), January, 1956. p.234-36.

12 Vaish, L.P. Concept of college development council in an affiliating university. *University News.* 16(21), 1978. p.1238-39 and 1253.

C RESEARECH STUDIES

01 Awasthi, J.N., *Administrative problems of principals of affiliated colleges of Avadh University*, Faizabad, Ph.D. Edu., Avadh University, 1981.

The study was designed to find out the characteristics of teachers and principals of colleges affiliated to Avadh University, Faizabad, and aimed at highlighting the problems faced by the principals in dealing with the management, university office, the state government, teachers, office staff, students and their guardians.

A questionnaire concerning different types of administrative problem was prepared and data were collected from twenty-four degree colleges affiliated to Avadh University. The data so collected were supplemented through personal visits to the colleges and through observations during these visits.

The findings of the study were: (i) More than half of the principals had only master's degrees whereas quite a few of the teachers working under them possessed doctorate degrees. (ii) It was reported by the principals that the Executive Council of the University and the Examination Committee met regularly but the decisions taken by the Examination Committee were very often not implemented. (iii) The principals were, in general, satisfied with the role of the state government. (iv) Most of the principals were not happy with the functioning of the managing committees. They felt that the managing committees interfered with the day-to-day functioning of the colleges. At the time of appointment of teachers the managements were guided by feelings of caste and kinship. The management showed favours to certain teachers and this created groupism among the staff. (v) The principals were not very happy with the functioning of the teachers. They felt that the teachers did not take their invigilation work seriously. They showed special favours to girl students. (vi) In general, the principals were satisfied with the working of their office staff, which was generally hard-working and obedient. (vii) It was felt that the rush of admission was difficult to control and it resulted in overcrowding in the classrooms. Adequate finances were not available for the expansion of buildings and provision of adequate library and laboratory facilities. It was not possible to establish closer contact with the students, which led to increase in indiscipline among them. (viii) The principals were critical of the attitude of parents also. They felt that instead of cooperating, a majority of the parents interfered with the working of the colleges and were at times rude to them and to the teachers.

02 Bose, P.K., Banerjee, P.K., and Mukherjee, S.P., *Working conditions of colleges affiliated to the University of Calcutta during 1962-63*, Deptt. of Stat., Calcutta University, 1966.

The study aimed at determining the extent of facilities currently available in the constituent and affiliated colleges of the University of Calcutta during 1962-63.

The sample consisted of ninetyeight affiliated colleges and two constituent ones as existing in the year 1964. The questionnaire technique was used for the collection of data. Attempts were also made to obtain the desired information by interviewing the principal/vice-principal or some other responsible members of the teaching staff and by consulting college records.

The study revealed the following: (i) Fiftytwo of the 100 colleges investigated were situated in Calcutta, thirtyeight of them being managed by private bodies. Of the remaining fourteen, six were managed and eight were sponsored by the state government. (ii) During the session 1962-63 only twenty (out of 100) colleges imparted instructions in all the three branches, viz., arts, science and commerce. Teaching in science subjects was provided by sixtyfive colleges, of which twentynine were located within Calcutta. (iii) The overall percentage of colleges where the annual total number of working days went below 150 was as high as 41.4. The average number of working days was 163 in government colleges, 157 in sponsored and 154 in private colleges. (iv) It was found that students in about fortyfive per cent of the respondent colleges had to pay tuition fees of Rs. 10 or Rs. 11 for study in arts classes. Government colleges charged less fees from their pupils than privately managed colleges. (v) It was felt that the financial position of some colleges was not bright. The largest percentage of total income received in the form of fees was shown by private colleges and the smallest figures applied to government colleges. In fortytwo per cent of the colleges more than half of the total income was derived in the form of fees. (vi) In 31.5 per cent of colleges the expenditure involved per student did not exceed Rs. 200, while in 23.7 per cent of colleges the amount was higher than Rs. 500 (vii) Results were somewhat less satisfactory in government sponsored colleges, where the percentage of passes was less than fifty in twenty per cent of the institutions. Performance of students from privately managed colleges was worse. More than sixty per cent of examinees appearing from 13.5 per cent of such institutions failed in the university examinations.

03 Gogate, S.B., *Development programme of arts, science and commerce colleges affiliated to the Marathwada University, 1980-1990*, Marathwada University, Aurangabad, and the Indian Institute of Education, Pune, 1980.

As a result of the introduction of 10+2+3 pattern of education in

Maharashtra in July 1975, arts, science and commerce colleges in the state, particularly in its rural areas, faced a problem of inadequate student strength from June 1977. The problem became acute in the years 1979-80 and 1980-81. The colleges were worried about their future. At the same time the colleges in Marathwada region felt many inadequacies, insufficiencies and lack of funds. It was, therefore, decided, as a first step, to undertake a comprehensive survey of the colleges and then to assess the situation as would develop during the decade 1980-90.

The tool employed for collecting information was an exhaustive questionnaire which included (i) general information regarding the type of colleges, faculties, medium, students as on 1 October 1979, etc., (ii) college building and accommodation, (iii) college laboratories, (vi) college staff, teaching and non-teaching, (v) subjects taught at the undergraduate and postgraduate levels, (vi) available teaching aids, (vii) details of college library and library services, (viii) co-curricular activities, (ix) finance, (x) management, (xi) gymkhana activities, (xii) targets of enrolment for 1980-90, (xiii) courses and subjects the college proposed to introduce in 1980-90, (xiv) proposed additions to physical facilities, (xv) proposed additions to library books and science equipment, (xiv) proposed additional co-curricular, gymkhana, extension activities, (xvii) proposed changes in the pattern of administration, (xviii) developmental projects the college proposed to undertake during the period 1980-90, (xix) resources necessary for development, (xx) the manner in which college proposed to raise the resources, (xxi) expectation of the college regarding the role of the state government and the university in this development, and (xxii) the direction in which the college expected the Marathwada University to develop during the period 1980-90. All the 66 arts, science and commerce colleges responded to the questionnaire.

The major findings of the study were: (i) Out of the 66 colleges, three colleges had a student strength below 50 in all the classes leading to the first degree, 27 colleges had students between 51 and 100, 31 colleges between 101 and 300 and five colleges between 301 and 500. (ii) All the 66 colleges together had 5,235 students (781 women and 4,454 men) in First Year classes, 3,882 (705 women and 3,177 men) in Second Year classes, 2,945 (524 women and 2,421 men) in Third Year classes and 2,200 (238 women and 1,962 men) in postgraduate classes. (iii) Enrolment in commerce faculty was maximum. This was followed by arts faculty. Science faculty had the minimum strength. (iv) The colleges in Marathwada suffered in student strength mainly due to poor results at SSC(X) and HSC(XII), which were in the range of 30 and 40 per cent. (v) A large number of students, around 40 per cent, did not pursue academic courses beyond SSC(X). (vi) Fifty-one colleges had hostel facilities. (vii) Out of sixty-six colleges only twenty colleges had separate staff room for women teachers, thirty colleges had toilet facilities for women teachers, fifty colleges had toilet facilities for boys and forty-nine colleges had toilet facilities for girls. Thirty-one colleges had a college canteen. (viii) Out of around 2,800 staff members 192 teachers belonging to junior colleges and 124 teachers belonging to senior colleges did not have adequate qualifications as per University/Government rules. (ix) Unit cost of education in Marathwada was Rs. 1,300 out of which Rs. 979 was expenditure on salary to teachers. This unit cost was lower as compared to Maharashtra. It was also lower due to the fact that major part of expenditure was shared by junior colleges which were financially separate entities. (x) The normal rise of student strength expected during 1980 and 1990 was 5 per cent per year. (xi) The colleges in Marathwada needed a development fund on the basis of which they could undertake additional activities during the next ten years. (xii) Teachers both in junior and senior colleges needed orientation in content and methodology. (xiii) Better and effective college-school complexes were necessary to improve results at SSC(X).

04 Goyal, J.C. and Ajit Singh. *Non-enforcement of conditions of affiliation in colleges of education — A study of reasons*, NCERT, New Delhi, 1981.

The major objectives of the study were: (i) to inquire into the conditions of affiliations laid down by different universities, (ii) to identify the conditions which were not enforced properly by the universities, (iii) to investigate the reasons for non-enforcement of conditions of affiliation, and (iv) to make recommendations for proper enforcement of conditions of affiliation.

The sample consisted of nine colleges selected from nine universities of four states selected on a random basis. The tools used in the enquiry were a questionnaire and an interview schedule.

The main findings of the study were: (i) The conditions of affiliation laid down by most universities were not comprehensive and specific. It appeared to be one of the reasons for their non-enforcement. (ii) Most of the universities did not have adequate machinery for proper enforcement of conditions. Only some universities had provision for the posts of inspectors of colleges, who, however, were not very effective because of involvement in other activities. (iii) Some universities had the practice of granting temporary affiliation to newly started colleges on condition that the colleges would comply with the requirements of affiliation but there was no strict enforcement of conditions later on. (iv) Autonomy granted to some types of institutions also came in the way of enforcing the conditions of affiliation. (v) Having B.Ed. course as a part of the arts/science college also contributed to non-enforcement. (vi) Inadequate and ineffective inspection, lack of interest on the part of management, social and political pressures were the additional factors responsible for the non-enforcement of conditions.

05 Jaganmohan, M., *An investigation into the existing conditions and development problems of affiliated colleges in Andhra University area*, Ph. D. Edu., Andhra University, 1983.

The objectives of the investigation were: (i) to examine the background information, staff qualifications, physical structure and facilities available in some of the affiliated colleges in rural and urban areas managed by private and government authorities under the Andhra University, (ii) to compare the enrolment at the intermediate level in private *vs.* government and rural *vs.* urban colleges over a period of ten years, (iii) to compare the enrolment at the degree level (B.A., B.Sc., B.Com.) in private *vs.* government and rural *vs.* urban colleges, over a period of ten years, (iv) to compare the total expenditure of the colleges in government and private, and rural and urban colleges over a period of ten years and also to study the sources of income, (v) to compare the scholarship granted at the intermediate and degree levels in government and private and rural and urban colleges over a period of ten years, (vi) to study the future plans in introducing new courses in affiliated colleges and modifications of the existing courses and to study the types of problem related to the financial, administrative and academic matters in the affiliated colleges.

The existing colleges in Andhra university area were classified into private/government on the basis of the type of management and rural/urban on the basis of location. The courses considered were Intermediate, B.A., B.Sc. and B.Com. Both Telugu and English medium colleges were included in the sample. For these institutions a schedule was sent for collecting data covering a period of ten years.

The findings of the study were: (i) There were eighty-four affiliated degree colleges in Andhra University area. Out of them, fifty-seven were private colleges and twenty-seven were government colleges. A majority of the affiliated colleges were in urban area (67 colleges) and women's colleges were only ten in number and colleges with postgraduate courses were only nine in number. (ii) The enrolment of commerce graduates was more (18,240) than that of B.Sc. students 10,724, B.A. students 9,394 and postgraduate students 1,585. (iii) The enrolment of boys was more (2,961) than the enrolment of girls (8,698). (iv) The student-teacher ratio was 12 : 1. The students hostel-residents ratio was 4 : 1. (v) The major problems of affiliated colleges were related to teaching staff and staff appointments. (vi) The rural private colleges wanted to merge into government colleges; lack of teaching aids and of opportunities to improve their qualifications were the problems of the teachers. (vii) Financial problems could be considered from two angles, namely, the scarcity of funds even to pay salaries and scarcity of funds for developmental purposes including funds for the construction of buildings, and for meeting library and laboratory expenditure. (viii) Union elections were giving scope for local political parties and communal elements to exploit the student community for their selfish ends. (ix) Rural colleges mentioned that they did not have permanent building, library, playground, etc.

06. Krishnraj, R. *Organization structure, leadership behaviour and decision-making in autonomous and affiliated colleges.* University of Madras, 1987.

The main objectives of the study are:

1. To find out the existing organization structure, leadership behaviour and principal decision-making styles in autonomous and affiliated colleges, and

2. To compare the organization structure, leadership behaviour and dimensions of decision-making styles of principals of autonomous colleges with those of affiliated colleges.

The study is based on survey data collected from the colleges of three universities of Tamil Nadu state. The sample included nine colleges in Madras University region, five in Bharthiyar University region, and five in Bharathidhasan University region.

The findings the analysis of organization structure in affiliated and autonomous colleges reveals the following results :

In the two types of college, teacher are assigned more specialized activities. But there is more specialization in autonomous colleges than in affiliated colleges. The two types of college are highly formalized than affiliated colleges. But affiliated colleges experience more breach of rules and regulations when compared to autonomous colleges. Breach of procedures and rules are only minimal in autonomous colleges. The two types of colleges are centralized organizations. But when compared to affiliated colleges, autonomous colleges are less centralized. Consulting the lower levels of hierarchy is at a higher level and more frequent in autonomous colleges than in affiliated colleges. The departments of both autonomous and affiliated colleges are well integrated to achieve common objectives. The departments of affiliated colleges are more integrated than the departments of autonomous colleges. The departments of both affiliated and autonomous colleges are autonomous. But the departments of affiliated colleges are more autonomous than the departments of autonomous colleges.

There is no significant difference between autonomous and affiliated colleges in leadership behaviour. Out of the 15 dimensions of leadership behaviour, only in 2, dimensions namely representation and integration, the two types of colleges very. The principals of affiliated colleges take more steps in speaking and acting as representatives of the members of organization when compared to principals of autonomous colleges. Moreover, principals of affiliated colleges take more efforts in maintaining a well-knit organization by resolving inter-member conflicts than principals of autonomous colleges.

In decision-making dimensions, principals of autonomous and affiliated colleges differ in four dimensions out of 15 dimensions. They are (i) request/advice, (ii) receptivity to advice, (iii) independence of judgement, and (iv) explicitness of method.

07 Singh, N., *A study of administrative problems of affiliated colleges*, Ph.D. Edu. Maharaja Sayajirao University of Baroda, 1981.

The objectives of the investigation were: (i) to study the college plant and physical facilities provided in the colleges and problems arising out of them, (ii) to study the administrative problems with respect to management board of colleges, affiliating university, etc., (iii) to determine leadership behaviour patterns of the principals of the colleges, (iv) to determine the organizational climate prevalent in the colleges, and (v) to find out the relationship of the administrative problems with leadership pattern and organizational climate of the colleges.

The sample was drawn from among the affiliated colleges of the Gujarat University and Gorakhpur University. A stratified random sampling method was used to select the sample for the study. Data were collected by using College Data Sheet, Checklist for Administrative Problems, Leadership Behaviour Description Questionnaire and Organizational Climate Description Questionnaire. The collected data were analysed by using percentages, frequency distribution and t-test.

The major findings of the investigation were: (i) All the colleges were haying playgrounds with adequate facilities for outdoor games and indoor games. (ii) In organizing co-curricular activities, lack of interest among the students and financial stringency were the major problems. (iii) There was HH pattern of leadership behaviour in the Gujarat University and LL pattern in the Gorakhpur University. (iv) Twenty per cent of the colleges belonged to open climate and 30 per cent to closed climate. (v) The colleges of open climate had lower score for problems and the colleges of closed climate had higher mean score for problems.

5. AGRICULTURAL UNIVERSITIES

A BOOKS

01 *Association of Indian Universities Handbook of agricultural education.* New Delhi, A.I.U., 1983. 140p.

02 Gupta, Mohan Prakash, *Education systems analysis and reforms with special reference to agricultural education.* New Delhi, Agricole Publishing Academy, 1984. 161p.

03 Mathai, Ravi John. *Management processes in universities: A study of decision-making and organizational health in two agricultural universities.* Ahmedabad, Indian Institute of Management, 1978. v p.

04 Mukerji, S.K. *Financing agricultural education in India:* Paper presented at AIU-ICSSR National Seminar on University and College Finance, New Delhi, 10-12 March, 1978.

05 Naik, K.C. and Sankaran, A. *History of agricultural universities.* New Delhi, Oxford & IBH, 1972. 296p.

06 Rangaswami, G. *Trimester system of teaching in agricultural universities in India.* Coimbatore, Tamil Nadu Agricultural University, 1971. 117p.

07 Thapar, Ashok. Agricultural universities: Pilits of rural change. *In* Amrik Singh and P.G. Altbach, eds. *The higher learning in India Delhi,* Vikas, 1974. p.397-408.

08 Willey, M.M. *Some notes and observations relating to U.P.* Agricultural University, Pantnagar, 1967. 29p.

B ARTICLES

01 Adiseshiah, Malcolm S. Some thoughts on agriculture in the seventh plan. *University News.* 23 (17), 1985. p.2-6.

02 Amrik Singh. On agricultural scientists. *University News.* 8 (7), 1970. p.3.

03 Kachwe, S.T. Administration in Indian agricultural universities. *University News.* 26 (17), 1988. p.6-7 and 26.

04 Pande, S.P. Role of agricultural universities in integrated rural development. *University News.* 15 (2), 1977. p.31 and 47.
05 Randhawa, M.S. Agricultural universities in India – Progress and problems. *University News.* 7 (1), 1969. p.16-17 and 21.
06 ——. Assam agricultural university and the agricultural scenario of the North East. *University News.* 27 (41), 1989. p.15-19.
07 Rangaswami, G. Educational reforms in the agricultural Universities. *University News.* 14(1). 1976. p.14-15.
08 ——. Emergence of a new educational pattern in agricultural sciences in India. *University News.* 8 (4), 1970. p.5-7.
09 Reasons behind the continuing crisis of Pantnagar — An introspective resolution of the Academic Council, 8th, March, 1982. *University News.* 20 (11 and 12), 1982. p.368-70 and 396-98.
10 Report of the Review Committee on Agricultural Universities. *University News.* 16 (13), 1978. p.1020-23.
11 Singh, Kirti. Role of agricultural universities in India. *University News.* 28 (5), 1990. p.1-6.
12 Stevenson, R.A.P. Role of agricultural universities in India. *Journal of University Education.* 3 (3), 1965. p.205-14.
13 Swaminathan, M.S. I.A.R.I. acts as catalyst in farm transformation. *University News.* 8 (1), 1970. p.15-16.
14 ——. Role in agricultural and rural development. *University News.* 13 (5), 1975. p.4-7.
15 ——. Social and educational requirements of new technology. *University News.* 12 (1), 1974. p.13-16.

C COMMITTEE/COMMISSION/REPORTS

01 *Review Committee on Agricultural Universities*, 1977 Report. New Delhi, Indian Council of Agricultural Research, 1978. Chairman: M.S. Randhawa.

The Ministry of Agriculture and Irrigation, Government of India and the president of ICAR decided to set up a Review Committee on Agricultural universities to critically assess the growth and development of agricultural universities in India.

The terms of reference of the committee are:

"To assess how far agricultural universities are meeting the needs of trained manpower at different levels and producing non-elite graduates with motivation for self-employment in agriculture, with competence to identify and resolve practical problems and with an attitude to demonstrate to farmers even by working on farms. In this context, the committee would assess the quality of educational programmes, adequacy of opportunities for work experience, international efficiency and relevance of research programmes of the university, particular attention being given to orientation of home science education to suit Indian conditions more particularly rural India."

The committee recommended that there should be complete transfer of research responsibility and the related facilities from the state governments to the concerned universities. The ICAR should not deviate from the policy of each state having only one agricultural university. Agricultural universities should not have affiliated colleges. The vice-chancellor should be a highly competent person with the requisite scientific and management experience.

The acts of agricultural universities may be suitably amended to ensure that the supreme body is the Board of Management and not the court/general council of boards of council. The minimum term of appointment of vice-chancellor should be five years with eligibility for reappointment for only one more term.

New educational programmes should be started after ensuring the demand for trained manpower in that subject and after ensuring the availability of competent faculty, reasonable research base and practical training facilities. While several areas offer potential scope for self-employment, a multi-pronged effort is required on the part of the various agencies, both of central and state levels, to make self-employment of agricultural graduates a practical proposition. Each university should clearly define and identify the target groups in rural areas which the home science college should aim to serve.

Staff selection committee should consist of professional experts and its recommendation should not be subject to change by the Board of Management. The revised UGC scales of pay should be introduced in all agricultural universities. A time-bound programme of staff development should be drawn up by each university.

The state governments should give liberal grants both for development and maintenance for the proper growth of agricultural universities. The ICAR should draw up a model university development plan. It should also prescribe norms and develop modules for construction of laboratories, colleges, libraries, classroom, etc. A small wing/unit should be set up at each university for planning and evaluation on a continuing basis. On the basis of observation on individual universities the committee made certain observations.

D RESEARCH STUDIES

01 Makhija, V.K., *Evaluating training adequacy of agricultural undergraduates against critical requirements of practical agricultural graduates*, Ph.D. Extn., Edu. Haryana Agricultural University, 1976.

The main objectives of the study were to determine the critical requirements of practical agricultural graduates and on the basis of these requirements develop an adequacy scale to evaluate the training adequacy of outgoing students of Haryana Agricultural University.

The study was conducted in Haryana State. As a prerequisite, the existing training programmes in the country were surveyed from a sample of thirtynine institutions to provide details of the special training programmes being followed in the institution in addition to the routine practicals in the respective courses. Flanagan's critical incident technique was used to determine the critical requirements of a practical agricultural graduate. A total of 568 nonpractical and 551 practical incidents were studied. On the basis of critical requirements, an adequacy scale consisting of sixtyone items developed to estimate the confidence level of students completing their graduation in the year 1974-75 in Haryana Agricultural University by their expressed confidence on each item given in the scale. The data through the scale was obtained from 125 students.

It was found that (i) the confidence level of the class as a whole was in the middle of the adequacy scale, i.e. 'somewhat confident': and (ii) the background variables of the students had no effect on their level of confidence.

02 Singh, Y.P., Pareek, U., and Arora, D.R., *Adoption of social sciences in higher agricultural education*, Haryana Agricultural University, 1974. (ICSSR and UGC financed).

The objectives of the study were: (i) to deal with the entry and development of social sciences in agricultural education system; (ii) to identify the various routes of entry of the programme into agricultural education system and its post entry progress through the years; (iii) to give the information on year-wise growth of Master and Ph.D. theses; and (iv) to find out the contribution of different institutions, the geographical locale of studies, nature of respondents, subject area covered and research tools and techniques used in these studies.

To collect information for this study, depth interviews of selected personnel in the institutions concerned were held.

The important findings were: (i) The entry of social sciences into higher agricultural education was facilitated through different routes of combinations of any of these, namely, the enthusiastic insiders, external change agents, student pressures, suggestions of visiting teams, special Government of India schemes, and highly motivated power figures. (ii) In the initial stage some problems related to the availability of staff, finance, clear-cut job opportunities and clear-cut teaching methods were encountered. (iii) The number of these submitted in 1957 was eleven which rose to 197 in 1968. (iv) U.P. Institute of Agricultural Sciences, Kanpur and I.A.R.I. accepted 119 theses, the number being followed by R.B.S. College, Agra and Bihar Agricultural College, Bhagalpur. (v) In terms of subject area, ninetyfive per cent of these pertained to rural people. Three studies covered agricultural labour while studies on rural women and tribal population were very few. As many as 970 studies were of survey, 105 of descriptive, 94 of evaluatory, 104 of experimental, 30 of case study and 4 of action research types. (vi) Ninetyfour per cent studies used interview schedule as the tool for investigation. (vii) Questionnaires, attitude scales, projective tools, teacher made tests and score cards were also made use of. (viii) Percentage was the most frequently used technique of analysis, followed by coefficient of correlation technique.

6. ASSOCIATION OF INDIAN UNIVERSITIES

A BOOKS

01 *AIU handbook.* New Delhi, AIU, 1986. 81p.
02 Bhandarkar, S.S. *Association of Indian Universities: A short history 1925-75*. New Delhi, A.I.U. 1975. 227p.
03 ——. *Association of Indian universities: A short history 1925-85*. New Delhi, A.I.U., 1985. 269p.

B ARTICLES

01 Adiseshiah, Malcolm. S. Some thoughts on the role of AIU in higher education education. *University News*. 23 (44), 1985. p.5-7.
02 Joshi, K.L. Coordinating agencies in higher education and the IUB. *University News*. 9 (5), 1971. p.14-16.
03 Rao, V.K.R.V. Inter-University board and higher education. *University News*. 5 (1), 1967. p.3.
04 Shah, Madhuri R. Role of AIU in higher education. *University News*. 23 (4), 1985. p.2-4.

7. AUTONOMOUS COLLEGES

A BOOKS

01 John, V.V. *Freedom to learn: The challenge of the autonomous colleges*. Delhi, Vikas, 1976. 108p.

02 *National Institute of Educational Planning and Administration. Autonomy and accountability: A report of study visit to autonomous colleges*. New Delhi, NIEPA, 1987, 135p.

03 National Institute of Educational Planning and Administration. *Critical issues in planning and management of autonomous colleges*. New Delhi, NIEPA, 1989. 30p.

04 *Task Force on Autonomous Colleges and Departments. Report*. New Delhi, AIU, 1988. 121p.

05 University Grants Commission. *Criteria, guidelines and pattern of assistance to autonomous colleges*. New Delhi, U.G.C., 1973. 4p.

06 University Grants Commission. *Revised guidelines on the scheme of autonomous colleges*. New Delhi, U.G.C., 1986. 90 p.

07 Verma, D.P. *Autonomous colleges: A study in the context of their working in Madras*. Chandigarh, Siddarth, 1984.

B ARTICLES

01 Abel, M. College autonomy: Its impact on higher education and national life. *New Frontiers in Education*. 10 (1), 1980. p.35-39.

02 Adiseshiah, Malcolm. Objectives of an autonomous college. *New Frontiers in Education*. 4 (2), 1974. p.58-64.

03 Amrik Singh. Autonomous colleges. The problems of governance. *New Frontiers in Education*. 4 (2), 1974. p.65-71.

04 Autonomous colleges: An assessment. *Hindu*. 20-10-1987. p.8.

05 Bajaj, K.K. Autonomous colleges: A debatable option. *University News*. 28 (2), 1990. p.1-3.

06 ——. Autonomous colleges in quest of quality education. *University News*. 26 (34), 1988. p.5-7.

07 Bajaj, K.K. University autonomous colleges interaction. *University News*. 27 (31), 1989. p.6-7.

08 Bhatia, B.M. Autonomous colleges: Prospects and potentialities. *University News*. 5 (6), 1967. p.3-5.

09 DeSouza, A. Autonomous college: The quest for quality. *Social Action*. 19, (January-March), 1969. p.28-35.

10 Devanesan, D.S. Autonomous colleges experiment. *University News*. 17 (20), 1979. p.529.

11 Devanesan, Chandran, Motivation and curriculum relevance in the context of college autonomy. *New Frontiers in Education*. 10 (2), 1980. p.44-51.

12 Filella, J. Autonomous colleges: Chips of the old block? *New Frontiers in Education*. 10 (1), 1980. p.14-27.

13 Hooja, G.B.K. Autonomous colleges. *University News*. 25 (16), 1987. p.1.

14 Idea of an autonomous college. *COHSSIP News Letter*. 3 (1), 1979. p.9-16.

15 Immanuel, S. Prabakar. Autonomy in action: Holy cross college, Tiruchirapalli. *University News*. 27 (1), 1989. p.9-10.

16 John, V.V. Freedom to teach: The idea of the autonomous college. *New Frontiers in Education*. 4 (2), 1974. p.42-57.

17 Kapur, J.N. Autonomous colleges: Role of teachers and principals. *University News*. 27 (8), 1989. p.6-7.

18 Mathias, T.A. Financial aspect of college autonomy. *New Frontiers in Education*. 10 (1), 1980. p.40-43.

19 Mathai, Samuel. Financing the autonomous college. *New Frontiers in Education*. 4 (2), 1974. p.72-74.

20 Mehta, Jeevan, Autonomous college, the idea and its significance. *Naya Shikshak*. 17 (3), 1975. p.40-46.

21 Mohan, A.L. Autonomy in action: SDS autonomous college, Shreeramangar. *University News*. 27 (14), 1989. p.5-6.

22 Naik, J.P., Adiseshiah, Malcolm S., Shah, A.B., Mansukhani, G.S. Idea of an autonomous college: A discussion. *New Frontiers of Education*. 3 (1), 1973. p.36-51.

23 Om, Prakash, Twenty point programme on autonomous college — University relationship. *University News*. 27 (43), 1989. p.4-6.

24 Pasupathinathan, K. Autonomous colleges: Will they lead to improvement in higher education? *Education Quarterly*. 27 (4), 1976. p.24-27.

25 Pereira, L. Autonomous colleges: A social nec sity. *Social Action.* 24, (July-September), 1974. p.213-22.
26 Pownraja, A. Autonomy in action: Ayya Naar Janaki Ammal College, Sivakasi. *University News.* 27 (21), 1989. p.10-12.
27 Raman, Anantanarayanan. Autonomy in action: Curriculum in the autonomous Loyola college, background, development process and reflection. *University News.* 27 (18), 1989. p.6-7.
28 Raman, A. and Casimir Raj, N. Autonomous loyola college: An analysis of its administrative structure. *New Frontiers in Education.* 17 (3), 1987. p.70-78.
29 Raman, Anantanarayan. Planning and implementation of college autonomy. *New Frontiers in Education.* 19 (3), 1989. p.361-64.
30 Riesz, R.P. Dimensions of the teaching — Learning process in the tertiary level of Education — Implications for autonomous colleges. *Educational Review.* 94 (11), 1988. p.184-187.
31 Riesz, R.P. and Venkitaraman, A.R. Implementation of college autonomy. *New Frontiers in Education.* 10 (1), 1980. p.28-34.
32 Report of the expert committee on autonomous colleges. *New Frontiers in Education.* 17 (2), 1987. p.68-99.
33 Rao, M.R. Autonomy in action: Autonomous colleges in Andhra Pradesh: A critical review. *University News.* 27 (29), 1989. p.3-5.
34 ——. Restructuring of courses in the autonomous colleges of Andhra University. *University News.* 27 (50), 1989. p.3-7.
35 Shankar Narayan, D. Towards a university with autonomous colleges. *New Frontiers in Education.* 4 (2), 1974. p.36-41.
36 Soundararaj, Francie. Restructuration of undergraduate courses in autonomous colleges. *University News.* 27 (48), 1989. p.1-6.
37 Thangaraj, M.A. Autonomous colleges. *University News.* 19 (15), 1981. p.416-19.
38 ——. Preparing a college for autonomy. *New Frontiers in Education.* 10 (2), 1980. p.34-43.

C COMMITTEE/COMMISSION/REPORTS

01 Expert Committee on Autonomous Colleges, 1984. Report. Government of Kerala, 1985. Chairman: K. Gopalan.

The Government of Kerala, Higher Education Department constituted an expert committee on autonomous colleges with the following terms of reference:

"to study the various aspects of the proposal to have autonomous colleges in the state and make recommendations to Government".

The committee recommends that autonomy for a college means and implies only that the college and its teachers assume full responsibility and accountability for the academic programmes they provide for the contents and quality of their teaching and for the admission and assessment of their students. The parent university will provide general guidelines, monitor programmes to ensure overall standards to and confer degrees upon the successful candidates accepting the evaluation done by and mentioning the name of the autonomous colleges.

Keeping in view some fears expressed about autonomous colleges, it is recommended that the Government of Kerala may take a policy decision to establish autonomous colleges in the state and move the State Legislature to amend the Acts of the concerned universities. However, establishment of autonomous colleges should be after taking into account the various issues raised and presented in this report, and also by observing all the cautions that have been given. [3.4, 3.5 and 5.0].

Autonomous colleges will need extra funds and also extra infrasturctural facilities particularly by way of administrative and supporting staff to take care of the additional work and added responsibilities. These will have to be provided based on actual requirements [3.4, 3.5 and 6.2].

For a variety of reasons, it is imperative that the +2 stage of education should be delinked from the colleges if they are to be considered for autonomy. In 1980, Tamil Nadu did this delinking successfully and with commendable swiftness. How this is to be achieved in Kerala is a matter of detail to be considered by the State government. One way is possibly to have separate junior colleges to take care of the +2 stage of education and delink them completely from the degree colleges [2.5 and 5.7].

Autonomous colleges — irrespective of whether they belong to unitary management, corporate management or government — should have independent Governing Bodies/Boards of Management as suggested in this report. Corporate managements and the government will have to look at and treat autonomous colleges under their control differently. It should be clearly understood that autonomy is earned and maintained by the individual institution and not by the corporate management/government to which the particular college belongs [5.8].

It is imperative that adequate preparation should precede actual conferment of autonomy. The mechanics of implementing the proposal and the details of actual governance of autonomous colleges have been indicated in Chapter 6 of this report for guidance [6.0].

On the basis of the evidence placed before the Committee, it is suggested that to begin with some of the well-established professional colleges and some of the well-established arts and science colleges may be considered for conferment of autonomous status. [2.8].

D RESEARCH STUDIES

01 Krishnraj, R. *Organization structure, leadership behaviour and decision-making in autonomous and affiliated colleges.* University of Madras, 1987.

The main objectives of the study are:

1. To find out the existing organization structure, leadership behaviour and principal decision-making styles in autonomous and affiliated colleges; and
2. to compare the organization structure, leadership behaviour and dimensions of decision-making styles of principals of autonomous colleges with those of affiliated colleges.

   The study is based on survey data collected from the colleges of three universities of Tamil Nadu state. The sample included 9 colleges in Madras university region, 5 in Bharthiyar university region, and 5 in Bharathidhasan university region.

The findings of the analysis of organization structure in affiliated and autonomous colleges reveals the following results:

In the two types of college, teacher are assigned more specialized activities. But there is more specialization in autonomous colleges than in affiliated colleges. The two types of college are highly formalized than affiliated colleges. But affiliated colleges experience more breach of rules and regulations when compared to autonomous colleges. Breach of procedures and rules are only minimal in autonomous colleges. The two types of college are centralized organization. But when compared to affiliated colleges, autonomous colleges are less centralized. Consulting the lower levels of hierarchy is at a higher level and more frequent in autonomous colleges than in affiliated colleges. The departments of both autonomous and affiliated colleges are well integrated to achieve common objectives. The departments of affiliated colleges are more integrated than the departments of autonomous colleges. The departments of both affiliated and autonomous colleges are autonomous. But the departments of affiliated colleges are more autonomous than the departments of autonomous colleges.

There is no significant difference between autonomous and affiliated colleges in leadership behaviour. Out of the 15 dimensions of leadership behaviour, only in 2, dimensions namely representation and integration, the two types of colleges vary. The principals of affiliated colleges take more steps in speaking and acting as representatives of the members of organization when compared to principals of autonomous colleges. Moreover, principals of affiliated colleges take more efforts in maintaining a well-knit organization by resolving inter-member conflicts than principals of autonomous colleges.

In decision-making dimensions, principals of autonomous and affiliated colleges differ in four dimensions out of 15 dimensions. They are (i) request/advice, (ii) receptivity to advice, (iii) independence of judgement, and (iv) explicitness of method.

8. AUTONOMY

A BOOKS

01 Dongerkery, S.R. *University autonomy in India.* Bombay Lalvani, 1967. 128p.

02 Lady Doak college, Madurai. *Autonomy — Another dimension.* Madurai, Lady Doak College, 1980. 61p.

03 National Institute of Educational Planning and Administration. *Autonomy and accountability: A report of study visits to autonomous colleges.* New Delhi, NIEPA, 1987. 135p.

04 Shrimali K.L. *Myth of university autonomy and other essays.* New Delhi, Kalamkar, 1979. 102p.

B ARTICLES

01 Abel, M. College Autonomy: Its impact on higher education and national life. *New Frontiers in Education.* 10(1), 1980. p.35-39.

02 Arun Kumar. Accountability and autonomy in higher education: Needed internal democracy. *Economic and Political Weekly.* 22(44), 1987. p. 1858-1861.

03 Anand Sarup, University autonomy and accountability. *University News.* 27 (51), 1989. p.1-6.

04 Azhieode, Sukumar. University autonomy — A jaded concept. *University News.* 18 (24), 1980. p.683.

05 DeSouza, A. Academic freedom in an environment of security. *Social Action.* 19 (July-Dec.), 1969. p.236-246.

06 Elsemou, T.O. Autonomy and authority in an Indian university: A study of the university of Bombay. *Compare.* 14 (1), 1984. p.59-67.

07 Erosion of university autonomy by Prema Nandakumar. *Hindu.* 9 June, 1979. p.3.

08 Ghosh, A.K. Crisis of academic authority. *University News.* 27 (47), 1989. p.1-3.

09 Ghose, A.M. Universities and their autonomy. *University News.* 6 (6), 1968. p.8-11 and 15.

10 Kamat, R.V. Case for autonomy. *Journal of Higher Education.* Vol. 1 (1), 1975, p.91-97.
11 Kumar, D. Must universities be autonomous? *Quest.* (57), April-June, 1968. p.52-57.
12 Lal, Man Mohan, Mathematics of accountability. *University News.* 27 (4), 1989. p.6-8.
13 Mathur, G. Autonomous universities in a democratic community. *Conspectus.* 2 (4), 1966. p.9-20.
14 Mathur, S.S. Autonomy of Indian universities at ideational and functional levels. *University News.* 12 (1), 1974. p.5-9.
15 Mazumdar, Shaswati. Autonomy is a victim of the new education policy. *Times of India.* 5-4-88. p.3.
16 Memorandum to the Prime Minister. *University News.* 4 (4), 1966. p.1-2.
17 Naik, J.A. Do our universities deserve autonomy? *Illustrated Weekly.* 22-28 January, 1978. p.28-29.
18 Pereira, Lancy. Plea for autonomy. *Illustrated Weekly.* 23 March, 1980. p.16-17.
19 Raturi, A.S. National educational Policy and university autonomy. *University News.* 7 (12), 1969. p.13-16.
20 Sancheti, Neelu. Institutional autonomy and intra and international networks in Indian management education. *Journal of Higher Education.* 13 (1-3), 1987-88. p.87-99.
21 Sarma, Ramesh Chandra. University autonomy — An analysis and proposal. *University Administration.* 5 (2), 1978. p.20-31.
22 States urged to restore autonomy of varsities by K.N. Malik. *Times of India.* 16 September, 1977. p.1.
23 Vithal, B.P.R. University autonomy and internal democracy. *Journal of University Education.* 1 (2), December, 1962. p.83-91.
24 Winifred, M. One year of autonomy. *University News.* 26 (46), 1988. p.5-7.

9. BUILDINGS

A BOOKS

01 Central Building Research Institute, Roorkee, *University hostels: Planning consideration, Roorkee,* The author, 1969. 22p.

C COMMITTEES/COMMISSIONS/REPORTS

01 Building Advisory Committee on Teachers' Hostels, 1964. Report. New Delhi, University Grants Commission, 1964. 8p.

Committee was asked to lay down the norms in general for the provision of various facilities in the teachers hostel for the guidance of the university.

02 Committee on Residential Accommodation for students and teachers, 1962. Report. New Delhi, University Grants Commission, 1965. 25p. Chairman: Dr. M.S. Mehta.

For enlarging and improving facilities for residential accommodation in the university and to study the problems in all aspects and prepare a broad outline plan for consideration of the commission, this committee was asked to give recommendations.

03 Panel on University Buildings – Hostels, 1960. Report. New Delhi, University Grants Commission, 1960. 31p. Charts. Chairman: Shri Bhailal Bhai Patel.

Members of the panel gave their recommendations with regard to the planning of hostel buildings, size of hostels, service space, drinking water facilities, common facilities, provision of hostel staff, provision for utility shops, circulation space, efficiency of planning, design and structural considerations, structural arrangement, design consideration, expansion joints, foundations, specifications and costs, joinery, flooring, terracing, finishing, services, furniture, execution of work, ceiling on cost, and the financial effects of recommendations.

10. CENTRE-STATE RELATIONS

A BOOKS

01 Amrik Singh. *Universities and the government. In* Shah, A.B. ed. Higher education in India. Bombay, Lalvani, 1968. p. 66-75.

02 Jain, M.P. *Centre-state jurisdiction in higher education in India.* New Delhi, Vikas, 1964.

03 Jayaraman, T.R. *Higher education and state government. In* Amrik Singh and P.G. Altbach, eds. *The higher learning in India.* Delhi, Vikas, 1974. p. 38-47.

04 Ramamurthy, M.S. *Constitutional framework. In* Amrik Singh, and P.G. Altbach, eds. *The higher learning in India.* Delhi, Vikas, 1974. p. 3-24.

B ARTICLES

01 Amrik Singh. Education tangle: UGC Vs State. *University News.* 25(52), 1987. p. 7-9.

02 ——. Right of affiliation: State versus Universities. *University News.* 5(7), 1967. p. 1.

03 Anand Sarup. National apex body and State Council of Higher Education. *University News.* 26(10), 1988. p. 5-6 and 10.

04 Joshi K.L. A central ministry for higher education. *University News.* 10(6), 1972. p. 16-19.

05 Kaushik, Shyam Lal. Education and state control. *NIE Journal.* 7(1), 1972. p. 25-30.

06 Mahajani, G.S. Universities and the state. *University News.* 6(7), 1966. p. 3-5.

07 Rao, Navaneeth. State council of higher education. *University News.* 25(52), 1987. p. 10-13.

08 Shils, Edward. Government and universities – I, II and III. *New Quest.* 1981, Jan.-Feb., p. 5-13. March-April, p. 93-103, May-June, p. 152-161.

09 State and the universities. *University News.* 4(3), 1966. p. 1-2.

11. COMMUNITY PARTICIPATION

A BOOKS

01 Devendra Kumar. *University and the community : Outline of a new response.* Tamil Nadu, Gandhigram Rural Institute, 1989. 63p.

B ARTICLES

01 Dakshinamurthi, V. College and Community. *University News.* 17(2), 1979. p.551-54.

02 Jacob, Plamthodathil S. College and community: A case study of Ahmednagar College. *New Frontiers in Education.* 13(1), 1983. p.24-30.

03 Joshi, K.L. Vocationalization and the need for community junior colleges. *University News.* 25(35), 1987. p.2-6.

04 Kamal, K.L. Linking the university with the community Prasar. 2(1), 1974. p.11-19.

05 Kolte, S.B. The college and the community : The Paragon experiment. *New Frontiers in Education.* 5(3), 1975. p. 72-76.

06 Mathias, T.A. College and the community. *New Frontiers in education.* 8(1), 1978. p.1-13.

07 Mehrotra, S.N. College and the community. *New Frontiers in Education.* 1, August, 1971. p.140-58.

08 Nair, K.R.R. Where is the need for community participation? *Hindu.* 10 April, 1984. p.19.

09 Rangpal, David L. College-community relations – The case of Baring college. *New Frontiers in Education.* 9(4), 1979. p.37-40.

10 University and the community in India. *Process of Education.* 26(8), 1952. p.240-44.

11 Yadav, M.S. and Roy, S. Integrating education with development : Role of University teacher. *New Frontiers in Education.* 14(2), 1987. p.43-51.

12. CONTINUING EDUCATION

A BOOKS

01 University Grants Commission. *New guidelines on adult and continuing education and extension programmes in universities and colleges, 1988.* New Delhi, U.G.C., 1988. 81p.

02 ——. *Report of the seminar on continuing education,* University of Poona. New Delhi, U.G.C., 1976. 47p.

03 University of Rajasthan. *Continuing education at the university : A plan.* Jaipur, The author, 1965. 141p.

B ARTICLES

01 Department of adult and continuing education, University of Rajasthan. *University News.* 22(46), 1984. p.9.

02 Eyford, Glen A. Universities, adult education and dinosaurs. *University News.* 5(9), 1967. p.5-6 and 13.

03 Santanagopalan, S. New concept of continuing education. *University News.* 18(2), 1980. p.31 and 40.

04 Srivastava, P.N. Continuing education with special reference to science and technology. *University News.* 26(22), 1988. p.1-2 and 7.

05 Venkataiah, N. and Naidu, Jayachandrama K. Extension and continuing education in universities. *University News.* 20(24), 1982. p.741-742.

06 Venkataiah N. and Adinarayana, P. Significance of adult, continuing education and extension programme in Universities. *University News.* 22(1), 1984. p.17-19.

C COMMITTEES/COMMISSIONS/REPORTS

01 Review Committee on Adult and Continuing Education, 1985. Report : University System and extension as the third dimension. New Delhi, University Grants Commission, 1986. 386p. Chairman: Ramlal Parikh.

To review the eradication of illiteracy programme run by university from Oct., 1983 up to 31st March, 1985, U.G.C. constituted committee in 1985. The terms of reference of the committee are:

Review of the current programme of adult education undertaken by the universities and colleges with a view to identify their short falls, problems, achievements and so on.

To make recommendation for greater and more effective involvement of universities/colleges in the programmes of adult education so as to fulfil aims and goals of the Government of India.

The Committee recommended:

1. Transforming Adult/Continuing Education movement into a life-centred life-long learning process.
2. The extension as a third dimension should permeate all disciplines of studies at all levels.
3. An area-based non-sectarian community approach envisaged in door-step of people.
4. Developing Adult/Continuing Education Departments/Centres as a separate inter-disciplinary faculty of Non-formal Education.
5. Encouraging students to opt for a semester, to work in adult Education programmes for preparing a project report in lieu of one of the optional papers in every subject.
6. Mass campaign by involving the entire student community along with their teachers through special literacy camps of 15 days for creating an environmental support and awareness among the people.
7. Use of new audio-visual technologies for rapid spread of new knowledge in every sphere of life particularly of new knowledge in Science and Technology with a view to inculcating scientific temper.

13. CURRICULUM

A BOOKS

01 Association of Indian Universities. *Monograph on syllabus analysis and restructuring*. New Delhi, A.I.U., 1982. 132p.

02 University Grants Commission. *Revised guidelines for restructuring of courses of first degree level in the faculties of arts, social sciences and science in universities and colleges*. New Delhi, U.G.C., 1983. 22p.

03 Uttar Pradesh. State Planning Manpower Planning Division. *Integration of Garhwal University courses with job opportunity in the Garhwal region*. Lucknow, The author, 1975. 184p. (Mimeographed).

B ARTICLES

01 Ediger, Marlow. Criteria in the higher education curriculum. *New Frontiers in Education*. 14(4), 1984. p.34-39.

02 Ghose, A.M. Modernisation of our courses and syllabi in the Humanities and the social sciences. *Journal of Higher Education*. 4(1), Monsoon, 1978.

03 Gosavi, S.S. Restructured courses at undergraduate level : A model and experience of implementation at university of Poona. *University News*. 28(5), 1990. p.7-18.

04 Guidelines for the re-organisation of courses at the plus three stage. *Bulletin of Higher Education*. 4(1-3), 1979. p.2-6.

05 Jayaraman, J. A strategy for reorientation of post-graduate courses in life sciences. *New Frontiers in Education*. 5(4), 1975. p.79-81.

06 John, V.V. Undergraduate curriculum and teaching : A symposium towards a meaningful first degree. *Journal of Higher Education*. 1(1), 1975. p.51-60.

07 Kapur, J.N. Undergraduate curriculum and teaching : A symposium; innovations in undergraduate education. *Journal of Higher Education*. 1(1), 1975. p.103-10.

08 Mathias, T.A. Modernising the curriculum. *New Frontiers in Education*. 2, April-July, 1972. p.28-39.

09 Mathur, M.L. National pattern of education and restructuring of courses. *University News*. 27(52), 1989. p.1-6.

10 Natarajan V. College science improvement project. *University News*. 16(23), 1978. p.1283 and 1288.

11 Nayudu, M.V. Some proposals to attune university courses for better education. *University News*. 9(10), 1971. p.11-14.

12 Portia, D.R. Curriculum development in higher education. *University Administration*. 3(1), 1976. p.48-53.

13 Quraishi, Z.M. On curriculum and teaching in higher education. *Journal of Higher Education*. 1(3), Spring, 1976. p.403-07.

14 Raj, K.N. Revision of courses in Delhi University. *University News*. 4(1), 1966. p.3-4.

15 Rao, M.R. Restructuring of courses in the autonomous colleges of Andhra University. *University News*. 27(50), 1989. p.3-7.

16 Restructuring education at the plus 3 level. *University News*. 15(13), 1977. p.351-57.

17 Shastri, Diwakar. Further reorganisation of first degree courses at Banasthali. *University News*. 27(35), 1989. p.3-10.

18 Soundararaj, Francis. Restructuration of undergraduate courses in autonomous colleges. *University News*. 27(48), 1989. p.1-6.

19 Tandon, S.L. Reorganisation of teaching in biological sciences at university level. *University News*. 9(4), 1971. p.16-18.

20 Vaish, L.P. Educational innovation at Rajasthan University. *University News*. 18(6), 1980. p.137-38.

C COMMITTEE/COMMISSION/REPORTS

01 Review Committee on Biochemistry in Indian Universities, 1959. New Delhi, University Grants Commission, 1963. p.70+ix. Chairman. Dr. B.C. Guha.

The review committee was appointed to examine the following main items: (a) The stage of development attained till now in training and research in biochemistry; (b) qualitative and quantitative appraisal of the researches in progress; (c) trends of research, its potentialities and steps to be taken for expansion of training and research facilities; (d) the syllabi and examination system at different levels and to suggest improvement and modernisation of syllabi; (e) ways of coordination between universities and nonuniversity teaching and research; and (f) improvement of facilities and amenities for the students and teaching staff.

02 Review Committee on Botany in Indian Universities, 1959, Report. New Delhi, University Grants Commission, 1963. 82p. Chairman : Prof. P. Maheshwari.

The committee was asked to examine specifically the stage of development in the field of botany in Indian universities; to make quantitative and qualitative appraisal the trends of research, its potentialities and steps to be taken for expansion of training and research facilities; to scrutinise the syllabi and examination system; and to suggest ways and means of coordination between universities and non-university institutions.

03 Review Committee for Mathematics in Indian Universities, 1959. Report. New Delhi, University Grants Commission, n.d. 98p. Chairman : Dr. B.R. Sath.

The committee looked into present state of development; qualitative and quantitative appraisal; trends of research and training; syllabi and examination at different levels; ways and means of coordination between universities and non-universities centres; and improvement of facilities for students and teaching personnel.

04 English Review Committee, 1960. Report. New Delhi, University Grants Commission, 1965. 56p. Chairman : Prof. G.C. Banerjee.

The committee was appointed to examine standards of teaching and methods of teaching english in colleges and universities. English in the first year of pre-university class and compulsory english in the intermediate and degree courses have also been discussed. The committee suggested that english may be a optional and honours subject for F.A. and M.A. and degrees. Research in english will mostly have to be confined to university teaching departments. Recommendations have been made (see page 56 of the report).

05 Review Committee for Chemistry in Indian University, 1960. Report. New Delhi, University Grants Commission, 1963. 107p. Chairman. Prof. T.R. Seshadri.

The chemistry review committee was appointed by the U.G.C. to examine the stage of development achieved so far; revision of syllabi and suggestions for the modification in present examination system; evaluation of the research works done so far and examination of the trends of research their potentialities and relationship to the general needs of the development programmes in the country; the action which may be taken for the development and expansion of training and research in certain special fields in chemistry; measures for improving the teaching personnel; and suggestion of ways and means of coordination between universities themselves and between universities and other centres of research such as the national laboratories.

06 Review Committee for Library Science in Indian Universities, 1961. Report. Delhi, University Grants Commission, 1965. Chairman : Dr. R.S. Ranganathan.

The committee was appointed to consider the question of improving the standard of teaching and research in the departments of library science in the universities. The different types of courses which should be offered by the universities, have been discussed. The entrance qualifications for the students for various courses have been presented. The committee has worked out agreed syllabus in each of the subjects for the different courses, including the relative place of theory and practice in each subject in the curriculum. The equivalence of diploma and Bachelor's degree course in library science have also been discussed. Co-operation between the department of library science and library have been discussed. Recommendations have also been made (see page 72 of the report).

07 Review Committee on Philosophy in Indian Universities, 1961. Report. New Delhi, University Grants Commission, 1966. 108p. Chairman : Prof. N.A. Nikam.

The committee was asked to define the objective of teaching and learning philosophy at the various levels of university education; to examine the standards of teaching and research in philosophy in Indian universities; to suggest measures for promoting its study; and to consider the problem of future growth of philosophy as an intellectual discipline. The committee has made certain valuable suggestions to make this subject more dynamic and attractive.

08 Review Committee on Psychology in Indian Universities, 1961. Report. New Delhi, University Grants Commission, 1962. Chairman: Dr. B. Kupuswamy.

The University Grants Commission appointed in March, 1961 a review committee on psychology in Indian universities. The committee held a number of meetings to discuss various issues relating to the objectives and contents of courses, admission requirements, standards of instruction and research and examination techniques in psychology.

The committee examined the existing facilities in the universities for teaching and research in psychology and allied subjects. It made several valuable suggestions and recommendations for improving the courses of study and for promoting research in this important field. For recommendations, see pages 31-37 of the report.

09 Review Committee on Sociology in Indian Universities, 1961. Report. New Delhi, University Grants Commission, 1966. p.72+vi. Chairman : Prof. M.N. Srinivas.

sociology in Indian universities and made recommendations with regard to the modernization and improvement of the course of study provided in this subject in our universities.

10 Committee on Education as an Elective Subject at the Undergraduate State, 1963. Report. New Delhi, University Grants Commission, 1966. 30p. Chairman : Prof. A.R. Wadia.

The University Grants Commission appointed a committee in December 1963 to introduce education as an elective subject for B.A./B.Sc. degree and to examine the question in various aspects. The committee suggested that the study of education as an elective subject at the undergraduate level might not be treated as an adequate preparation for teaching in high/higher secondary schools. It would be neither possible nor desirable to include a teacher-training programme in the undergraduate studies. The study of education as an elective subject might however, serve the following four purposes: (a) It may be a good independent and academic discipline which can promote cultural and liberal educational values; (b) it may get some students interested in teaching as a career. The course in education ought to promote the imaginative consideration of various general principles underlying a teacher's career; (c) it would be a useful subject for women candidates or for those who terminate their studies at the undergraduate level; and (d) education as an elective subject at the undergraduate level could also be introduced for those candidates who intended to take up a two-year master's degree in education or the desirability of education as an optional subject at the undergraduate level should be clearly identified. Reading and reference material, produced on a co-operative basis by the experts in various disciplines should be made available to the students.

11 Mathematics Reform Committee, 1964. Report. New Delhi, University Grants Commission, 1966. Chairman : D.C. Pavate.

This committee was appointed to examine the desirability of reviewing and revising the syllabus which knowledge is growing it these days. The existing facilities for teaching mathematics in the universities have been discussed. Proposals have also been made for examinations and preparing a syllabus in mathematics. The committee has made proposals for a syllabus in mathematics for pre-university, B.A. Part I, B.A., Parts II and III, and M.A. Parts I and II. Recommendations have also been made by the committee on page 22 of the report.

12 Committee on Physical Education, 1965. Report. New Delhi, University Grants Commission, 1968. Chairman : Dr. C.D. Deshmukh.

For removing inadequacies in and raising the standard of physical education, the University Grants Commission appointed a committee in December, 1965 to examine the present facilities for the same in Indian universities and colleges and to suggest how best such facilities can be improved upon and the quality of physical education can be bettered. The committee made general recommendations for the improvement of physical education in the universities and colleges. Recommendations are given at pages 20-24 of the report.

13 Review Committee on Geography in Indian Universities, 1965. Report. New Delhi, University Grants Commission, 1968. 143p. Chairman : Prof. S.P. Chatterjee.

The committee was appointed to report in detail about the stage of development achieved in teaching and research in the subject; and syllabi and courses of entry at various levels of university instruction and the trends of research, its potentialities and its relationship to general need and development of the country. The committee was also asked to suggest the measures to be undertaken for further development and extension of facilities for training and research and for encouraging specialization in specific fields.

The committee examined the existing facilities in the universities for teaching and research in geography and made several valuable suggestions and recommendations for the improvement of the courses of study and the promotion of research in this field. For recommendations, see pages 97-100 of the report.

14 Committee on the Status of Teaching of Sociology and Social Anthropology, 1974. Report. New Delhi, University Grants Commission. Part I. Recommendations, 1978. 48p. Part II. Regional Reports, 1979. 256p., Convener : Prof. M.S.A. Rao.

This report has been divided into two parts. Part I presents a summary of six regional reports and the recommendations while Part II gives the details of those reports covering all the states and the union territories of the country. The topics discussed in the regional reports are those related to, the organisation of teaching of sociology and social anthropology; courses; students; modes of teaching; evaluation; teachers; research and publications teaching of social anthropology in the departments of anthropology; and sociology and social anthropology in the institutions of professional courses.

15 Photochemistry – A Status Report, 1976. Delhi, University Grants Commission, 1982. 142p. Convener: Dr. M.V. George.

This report gives a detailed account of the trends in the development of different areas of research in photochemistry. The report also reveals that in India, Photochemistry has been a reglected area of research and hence, it says, special efforts be made to encourage its development. In this regard, the report has made certain recommendations. These relate to research and teaching activity; organisation of symposia, seminars and short-term courses; and the establishment of national and regional centres for photochemical research. The report has given a comprehensive bibliography on photochemistry, which includes more than 1200 references of books and articles.

16 Status of Linguistics in Indian Universities, 1977. Report. New Delhi, University Grants Commission, 1982. 46p. Convener : Dr. Bh. Krishnamurti.

This report gives an account of the performance of the departments of linguistics in as many as 14 universities in the country during the past two and a half decades. The factual informations presented in the report pertain to the enrolment for different courses; the strength of teaching and research staff; library holdings; the number of courses offered at M.A. level and the syllabi for M.A. linguistics. The report has made certain perceptive observations and a member of constructive suggestions on the development of linguistics in the country.

17 Status of Teaching and Research in the Discipline of Law, 1978. Report. Delhi, University Grants Commission, 1981. 69p. Convener : Prof. S.K. Agrawal.

This report, which begins with a brief historical background of the development of teaching and research in law, provides vital statistics about the departments of law in as many as 30 universities in the country. the informations relate to the different aspects of the discipline such as, teacher-student ratio; qualifications of full-time teachers; areas and topics of Ph.C research; and library acquisitions and expenditure. A number of recommendations have been given to improve the status of the discipline (See p.28-33 of the report).

18 Status Report on Anthropology, 1978. New Delhi, University Grants Commission, 1982. p.131+viii. Convenor : L.P. Vidyarthi.

This report was prepared to examine the organisational and academic aspects of the anthropology departments of the different universities and to provide guidelines for the development of anthropology in the future, particularly during the sixth five year plan. The report, which covers 18 universities, gives a fairly good account of the courses of study; the fieldwork facilities; eligibility criteria for admission; system of teaching and evaluation; research and teaching; and research project. The other topics referred to in the report are those related to faculty strength, infrastructure and equipment, and ancillary academic activities.

19 Political Science in India : State of the Discipline and Agenda for the Future, 1980. New Delhi, University Grants Commission, 1982. p.68+vi. Convener : Iqbal Narain.

This report recapitulates how political science in India, which began its life as an appendage of history, has come to have an independent identity of its own. The major focus of the report has been on the pattern of growth of the subject; research output; and syllabi and area of specialization.

Corporate academic activities, and the emergence of public administration as an autonomous sub-field of political science, are the other topics under discussion.

20 Report on the Status of Journalism & Communication Education in India, New Delhi, University Grants Commission, 1981. 124p. Chairman : Prof. K.E. Eapen.

This report presents vital statistics of the departments of journalism/communication in as many as 25 universities in the country. The aspects covered are those related to the nature of courses; intake capacity; media instruction, laboratory journalism; internship; staff; books and equipments; research; and master's course in journalism/communication. Besides, the role of University Grants Commission in the promotion of journalism/communication has been discussed at some length. The report makes certain significant observations and valuable suggestions with respect to the promotion of journalism/communication. It outlines a model syllabi for the Bachelor's and Master's courses in journalism/communication. The related issues, such as staffing pattern, the pattern of journalism education etc. have also been discussed in brief. (For details, see p.29-37 of the report).

21 Teaching and research in english, 1981. Report. New Delhi, University Grants Commission, 1981. 47p. Convenor : Prof. Ramesh Mohan.

This report on the status of teaching and research in english presents, the vital statistics of the postgraduate departments of english in as many as 44 universities in the country. The report makes certain very perceptive observations and constructive suggestions with respect to such problems as, the admissions to postgraduate departments of english; the need to subsidise the publication of textbooks and secondary material so that all students can be expected to acquire them; the useful academic liaison that can be established between the faculty in the post-graduate departments and the teachers of english at the under-graduate colleges affiliated to the university concerned; and the need to strengthen the tutorial component of postgraduate instruction. It also reviews the major break through these departments have made in the academic programme, they offer, which now include courses in American literature, Indian writing in english, commonwealth literature, world classics in translation, and applied linguistics. A fair assessment of the impact of the central institute of english and foreign languages on postgraduate courses in english, so that they become a little more learner-oriented than they are today, has been emphasized.

22 Status of Psychology in Indian Universities. New Delhi, University Grants Commission, 1982. p.34+vi. Convenor : Prof. R. Rath.

This report gives some of the salient features and orientations of teaching and research in psychology in Indian universities. It includes a brief history of development of the departments teaching the subject. It also contains references to all the important reports published so far regarding the status of research and teaching. Moreover, developmental trend in respect of enrolment of students; teacher-student ratio; and areas of specialization, etc., has been indicated with a view to present coherent picture in the Indian context. The report also carries certain valuable suggestions for the improvement of the status of the subject under consideration.

23 Status Report on Biological Sciences in Indian Universities. New Delhi, University Grants Commission, 1982. 54p. Convenor: Prof. A.K. Sharma.

The report outlines the status of research in plant and animal sciences, biochemistry, biophysics, molecular biology and marine biology. Environmental education is another area of research discussed in this report. The recommendations made in the report are primarily related to curriculum reform and training and research. This report not only provides an objective assessment of the areas of current research and important contributions made by Indian universities but also draws attention to the existing gaps and the need for promoting newly emerging areas in biological sciences, which have distinct relevance to the research and development efforts of the country.

24 Status Report on Economics Teaching in India, New Delhi, University Grants Commission, 1983. 20p. Convenor : Prof. H.K. Manmohan Singh.

This report was prepared to enable the U.G.C. committees to assess the needs of different departments to provide a database for assessing research proposals; and to help the commission in planning the development of economics on regional and national basis. It presents factual informations on departments of economics in as many as 33 universities in the country. There are 25 tables in this report which provide vital statistics with regard to the age of department; the courses offered; student enrolment; faculty strength; teacher-student ratio; library and computational facilities; research programmes; thrust areas; and major areas of specialization of teachers etc.

25 National Committee for Curriculum Development in Education : Post Graduate Level, 1986. Report. New Delhi, U.G.C., 1988.

University Grants Commission constituted Committee in 1986. The Terms of Reference of the Committee: U.G.C. guidelines are given below:

The committee will examine the existing curriculum in the respective subjects of different universities in the country in terms of quality as well as workload.

The committee will examine how the new curriculum would promote human resource development and identify areas which are crucial to make education meaningful in the task of national development.

The Committee will devise a model curriculum which will be relevant to the requirements of the country.

The Committee will suggest textual materials which would be required to follow the new curriculum.

The Committee will suggest ways and means for preparing textbooks, teaching aids, library as well as laboratory equipments in implementing the proposed curriculum.

It should also indicate how the teachers are to be trained in order to impart education according to the revised curriculum.

Recommendations of the committee:

For Finalisation of the Curriculum

- The UGC Curriculum Development Centre at the Department of Education, University of Kerala to continue functioning for another one year with a redrawn budget allocation and change in the manner of functioning.
- The present National committees to continue and to meet at least four times to complete the work on the present curriculum for the different specialisation papers.
- Six workshops to be organized to ten days duration to translate the curriculum for the specialisation papers into modules, with experts identified in terms of the particular expertise required.

For Implementation of the Curriculum

The curriculum prepared by the Curriculum Development Centre to be discussed and modifications made before it is accepted and implemented. To enable focused discussion in the curriculum the following suggestions are made:

- A National meeting of UGC officials, the curriculum committee members and twenty invited teacher educators from all over the country to discuss the curriculum.
- Regional Seminars, organised by UGC in collaboration with six departments of education at which teacher educators, administrators, research workers and other personnel in the field of teacher education, including those from undergraduate programme, to discuss and react to the curriculum.
- State level seminars organised by UGC and the University Department of Education at which concerned teaching faculty of Master's course in Education discuss and give their reactions to the curriculum.
- A National survey to be conducted on existing conditions in teaching departments.
- Arrangement of national level lectures on the curriculum to place the curriculum in a wider perspective.
- Publication of articles in the media by eminent educationists, on the existing conditions, indicating the need for change and presenting the possibilities of the new curriculum.
- Specific literature to be prepared and seminars to be organised on the modalities for use of modules in teaching.

Development of Materials to Support the Curriculum

- Creative workshops to be organised for preparation of materials to support curriculum such as basic books, technology software, reading lists etc.

Agencies and Bodies for the Implementation of the Curriculum

- A National Curriculum Development Centre to be established by the UGC.
- Six Regional Curriculum Development Centres need to be identified.
- Ten Teacher Training Institutions are to be established.
- Curriculum implementation cells to be established.
- A statutory body for National Curriculum Development in Higher Education is to be constituted.

Development of Curriculum as an Area of Inquiry

- Capabilities of Departments of Education need to be strengthened to contribute to curriculum studies.
- Publication of a *Journal of Curriculum Studies* and a *Curriculum Bulletin* with widespread circulation through a network of state, regional and national agencies.
- Research scholarships to be allotted especially for research in curriculum at the doctoral and post-doctoral levels. Research Associates and Research Assistants for curriculum research to be appointed in all University Departments of Education.
- Curriculum research to be included in the research agenda of national agencies.
- Experts in curriculum studies from foreign Universities be invited as visiting Professors in Departments of Education.

Action Required by U.G.C. on the Recommendations

For Finalisation of the Curriculum

- Sanction to be given to Curriculum Development Centre in the Department of Education to complete the work with the necessary change in functioning and with required financial assistance.
- Convene (a) National Meeting to discuss the curriculum, (b) Regional Seminars participating six Departments of Education to discuss and react to the Curriculum, (c) State Level Seminars inviting teaching faculty of Master's course in Education to discuss and give suggestions to the Curriculum.

For Implementation of the Curriculum

- Identify and establish
  - A National Curriculum Development Centre.
  - Six Regional Curriculum Development Centres.
  - Ten Teacher Training Institutions.
  - Curriculum Implementation Cells.
  - Curriculum Materials Units.
  - Departments of Curriculum Studies.
- Strengthen existing Departments of Education through *ad hoc* specific grants and services of experts in the area of Curriculum Development.
- Constitute a statutory body for Curriculum Development in Education.
- Organise creative workshops for preparation of materials to support curriculum.

14. DISTANCE EDUCATION

A BOOKS

01 Anand, Satyapal. *University without walls.* New Delhi, Vikas, 1979. 204p.

02 Association of Indian Universities. *Correspondence Education.* New Delhi, AIU, 1976. 154p.

03 ——. *Handbook of distance education, 1986.* New Delhi, AIU, 1986. 122p.

04 Borah, Swapna. *Distance education.* Delhi, Amar, 1987. 306p.

05 Chib, Sukhdev Singh. *Teaching by correspondence in India.* New Delhi, Light and Life, 1977. ix, 188p.

06 Khan, Inayat, ed. *Teaching at a distance.* Delhi, Amar, 1989. 167p.

07 Koul, B.N., Bakshish Singh and Ansari, M.M. *Studies in distance education.* New Delhi. Association of Indian University, 1988. 176p.

08 Madurai Kamaraj University. Department of Education. *Impact and performance of correspondence education programme of Madurai Kamaraj University.* Madurai, the author, 1983. 66p.

09 Parmaji, S. *Distance education.* New Delhi, Sterling, 1984. 160p.

10 Rao, K. Sudha, ed. *Open learning system.* New Delhi, Lancer, 1989. 148p.

11 Reddy, G. Ram, ed. *Open university the ivory towers thrown over.* New Delhi, Sterling, 1988. 270p.

12 Ruddar Datt. *Costing of correspondence education: Need for a rational policy* : Paper presented at AIU-ICSSR National Seminar of University and College Finance. New Delhi, 10-12 March, 1978.

B ARTICLES

01 Amrik Singh, Open university. *University News.* 11(8), 1973. p.4-6.

02 Asopa, Jai Narayan. Some aspects of post-graduate correspondence studies instituted by the university Rajasthan. *Prasar.* 3 (2 and 3), 1975. p.86-93.

03 Bakhshish Singh. Broad-basing the programmes of correspondence education in Indian universities. *Prasar.* (2 and 3), 1975. p.22-32.

04 Benjamin, B.N. Education by correspondence : A perspective *Education Quarterly.* 29(3), 1977. p.14-15.

05 Bhardwaj, O.P. Correspondence courses : Organisation and Administration. *University News,* 13(5), 1975. p.13-16.

06 Chaitanya, Z.I. Education through correspondence. *University News.* 17(17), 1979. p.454.

07 Chaudhari, Umrao Singh. Distance education and print media : Institutional strategies. *University News.* 26(27), 1988. p.4-5.

08 Chittibabu, S.V. Open university system at Madurai university. *Madurai University News Letter.* 1(1), 1977. pf students is provided for so as to reap the benefits of large-scale organisation (Paras 4, 16, 17 and 18). Courses in Indian universities. *Journal of Education.* 9(4), 1962. p.102-04.

11 Deshmukh, K.G. Model for an open university in Maharashtra. *University News.* 22(31), 1984. p.2-6.

12 ——. Open higher education innovations and technology. *University News.* 25(21), 1987. p.1-5.

13 Gopalakrishnan, N.S. Delhi university correspondence courses. *Educational Review.* 71(5), 1965. p.118-19.

14 Gunasekharan, K. Computers in distance education. *University News.* 25(33), 1987. p.1 and 6.

15 Gupta, M.L. Economics of correspondence education. *Education Quarterly.* 25(3), 1973. p.10-14.

16 Gupta, S.K. Distance education problems of coordination cooperation and functional autonomy. *Journal of Higher Education.* 7(3), 1982. p.237-42.

17 Guruge, Ananda W.P. Open university : Relevance to Indian context. *New Frontiers in Education.* 2(2), 1972. p.49-62.

18 Gurusuwamy, N. Education through open university. *University News.* 15(19), 1977. p.524-25.

19 Instituting correspondence courses and evening colleges in Indian universities. *Education and Psychology Review.* 1(2), 1961. p.51-53.

20 Joshi, K.L. Open university in India. *University News.* 11(2), 1973. p.4-7.

21 Kerala state open university : A back-grounder. *University News.* 25(31), 1987. p.11.

22 Kholodilin, A.N. On correspondence courses. *Journal of University Education*, 3(2), 1964. p.105-11.

23 Mahajani, G.S. Open University. *University News*. 9(7), 1971. p.17-18.

24 Malik, G.M. Open University. *University News*. 19(14), 1981. p.381-405.

25 Mukhopadhyay, M., Sujatha, K. Open learning system at the school level. *Journal of Educational Planning and Administration*. 2(3-4), 1988. p.99-105.

26 Narasaiah, P. and Mouli, C. Raja. An experiment in distance teaching: A case study of Andhra Pradesh Open University. *University News*. 28(4), 1990. p.3-6.

27 Pandey, K.P. Correspondence education on the Indian scene : A close-look. *Education Quarterly*. 25(3), 1973. p.6-9.

28 Pandey, Saroj. Changing scenario of education : Distance education. *University News*. 27(8), 1989. p.4-5 and 7.

29 Parashar, B.P. Distance education and free student choice. *University News*. 26(42), 1988. p.6-7.

30 Prasad, V.S. Openness of open university system. *University News*. 23(27), 1985. p.6-7.

31 Ram Behari. Correspondence education – Report of a conference. *University News*. 4(3), 1966. p.3-5.

32 Reddy, G. Ram. The Indira Gandhi National Open University. Its role in higher education. *Journal of Higher Education*. 11 (1 and 2), 1985-86. p.157-67.

33 Ruddar Datt. Correspondence courses : Some impressions. *Prasar*. 2(1), 1974. p.20-32.

34 ——. Financing of correspondence courses and the role of state. *Prasar*. 3 (2 and 3), 1975. p.67-76.

35 Safaya, Raghunath. Distance education. *University News*. 18(10), 1980. p.267 and 283.

36 Sahi, S.S. Distance education system and library service. *University News*. 25(11), 1987. p.6-8.

37 Satish Chandra. Correspondence education. *Prasar*, 3 (2 and 3), 1975. p.3-8.

38 Satyanarayana, P. Distance teaching universities. *University News*. 26(33), 1988. p.5-7.

39 Shah, Beena. Distance education : Taxonomy of courses, educational aims and teaching strategies. *University News*. 27(40), 1989. p.53-61.

40 Shahane, V.A. Open university not a replica of traditional set-up. *University News.* 16(16), 1978. p.1102.

41 Shukla, M.C. Higher education through correspondence. *University News.* 6(5), 1968. p.12-14.

42 Singh, R.K. Open university. *University News.* 14(11), 1976. p.4-5 and 8.

43 Vinayak, J.P. Open university is there need? *University Affairs.* Nov.-Dec., 1975, p.7-9.

44 Yadav, M.S. Correspondence education in Indian universities. *New Frontiers in Education.* 8(2), 1978. p.82-93.

45 Yadav, M.S. Higher education through correspondence : Some considerations for its remodelling. *New Frontiers in Education.* 8(2), 1978. p.82-93.

C COMMITTEES/COMMISSIONS/REPORTS

01 Expert Committee on correspondence courses and evening colleges, 1961. Report. Delhi, Ministry of Education, 1963. 18p. Chairman : D.S. Kothari.

In March, 1961, the Ministry of Education appointed Expert Committee to work out the pattern and relevant details of the scheme of correspondence courses in terms of the Central Advisory Board of Education Resolution passed at the Board's 28th meeting held at New Delhi on January 16th and 17th, 1961.

The Committee made the following recommendations:

(i) The committee recommends that correspondence leading to degree or equivalent qualifications should be administered by universities only (Para 7).

(ii) For the present, Correspondence Courses should be confined to a first university degree (Para 8).

(iii) For part of the course there should be personal contact between teacher and taught, "contact" classes being organised on a tutorial in preference to a lecture basis (Para 9).

(iv) To maintain educational standards, it is necessary to associate top-ranking scholars and teachers with the preparation of courses and the selection of textbooks. Some arrangements should be made to organise work by staff so as to ensure continuing improvement in the quality of work (Para 10).

(v) The Correspondence method is susceptible of use in both Science and the Humanities. However, for the present in view of organisational difficulties, the Committee recommends that the courses be started only in the faculties of Arts and Commerce. Science should be incorporated as early as possible (Paras 11 and 15).

(vi) For a first degree, correspondence courses should normally take longer than for a degree at a regular college, say, four years instead of the usual three. Outstanding students may, however, be able to compress this into a period of three years. Flexibility in all matters relating to the application of the system of varying needs is strongly recommended (Para 12).

(vii) Fees for students applying for these courses should be reasonably high in the first year but should be progressively lower in the second and third years and perhaps, if this is possible, be eliminated altogether in the fourth year (Para 13).

(viii) Two supplementary aids (a) Refresher Courses and (b) use of radio and television are recommended in order to raise standards in spoken language and to correct a too easy reliance on the written word (Para 14).

(ix) Correspondence courses should be run in the first instance by one University, *i.e.*, the University of Delhi, and the subjects to be included in the course as well as the details of administration should be as suggested by the Working Group (Para 15 and 18 and Appendix).

(x) It is important to ensure that the scheme is administered so as to achieve economy. This will be possible in virtue to the fact that items of expenditure normal at regular colleges can be eliminated under the Correspondence system, and also if an adequate number of students is provided for so as to reap the benefits of large-scale organisation (Paras 4, 16, 17 and 18).

15. DROPOUTS

A BOOKS

01 Deshmukh, A.G. and Kamat, A.R. Wastage and stagnation in college education. *In: Educational Studies and investigation,* Vol. I. New Delhi, NCERT, 1962.

02 Institute of Tribal and Rural Development and Arts and Commerce College, Surat. *Educational waste : A study in dropouts among scheduled tribe college students in Vyara, Surat,* The author, 1980. 66p.

03 Kamat, A.R and Deshmukh, A.G. *Wastage in college education : Two studies about students of the University of Poona.* Bombay, A.P.H., 1963. 202p.

B ARTICLES

01 Diraviam, K. Wastage in education. *New Frontiers in Education.* 3, (December), 1973. p.12-18.

02 Grewal, J.S. Educational rehabilitation of the college dropout. *Student Service Review.* 7(1), 1972. p.18-22.

03 How to avoid wastage in higher education? *Educational Review.* 69(7), 1963. p.157-58.

04 Kirpal, Vinay, Swamidasan, Nalini, Gupta, Amitabha and Gupta, Raj K. Wastage among scheduled caste and scheduled tribe students. *Journal of Higher Education.* 11 (1 and 2), 1985. p.111-16.

05 Pattanayak, D.P. Stagnation in higher education : A diagnosis. *Journal of University Education.* 5(1), 1966. p.1-5.

C RESEARCH STUDIES

01 Bose P.K and Mukherjee, S.P. Wastage and stagnation in collegiate education. Deptt. of Statistics. Calcutta University, 1977.

The main aim of the study was to assess the extent of failures in B.A. and B.Sc. Parts I and II examinations in Calcutta and mofussil colleges. To make a comparison over time possible, percentages of pass and honours candidates failing in Part I and Part II examinations in 1965 and 1968 were calculated and examined.

The findings of the study were: (i) Wastage and stagnation in collegiate education was rather high. (ii) The main reasons for this evil were: (a) lack of physical facilities, (b) dearth of competent teachers, and (c) inadequate attention to higher education in national plans and policies. (iii) The problem was more acute in the case of big affiliating and federal universities.

02 Kamat, I.R. and Deshmukh, A.G. Wastage in college education. Gokhale Institute of Politics and Economics, Poona, 1963.

The present investigation was an enquiry into some aspects, including wastage and stagnation, of higher education in India, aiming at: (i) estimating wastage and stagnation among students joining various types of facilities and colleges of Poona University, in part I and (ii) analysing the failures at pre-degree examination of the same university in the year 1961, in Part II of the study.

The part I of the study considered a three-year entry (1949-51) of freshers to the Ferguson College, Poona, and followed them until they took the first degree or left education without taking it. The sample consisted of 2080 students. The data, collected from (i) the admission forms, filled in by the students, (ii) the results of the Poona University examinations, and (iii) the register of leaving certificates of the college, were recorded on cards prepared for this purpose, and then put on punched cards for analysis. The part II of the study covered all candidates, about fourteen thousand, who appeared for the pre-degree examination of 1961, in arts, science and commerce throughout the area of the Poona University.

The findings of the part I of the study are (i) in the period 1949-51 the number of students in arts and science has increased each year; (ii) women students form forty per cent of students joining the arts class and they are much greater in number than those joining the science class; (iii) the number of married students is very small for both the sexes; (iv) the number of Marathi speaking students is not; (v) more than fifty per cent of men students are brahmins; (vi) the number of Marathi speaking students is not negligible; (vii) concerning guardian's occupation, preponderance of the professional classes, viz., doctors, pleaders, etc. is noted; (viii) the guardians of women students have on the average higher income; (ix) science students are on the average younger than arts students while women students are younger than men students; (x) urban students are on the average younger than the rural; (xi) average age of high income group is less than it counterpart; (xii) at least ten per cent of the students have no satisfactory accommodation; (xiii) the estimated wastage for science students of the Poona University is forty per cent approximately; (xiv) there is less stagnation among students from non-local schools than among those who come from local schools in the first stage, but the situation is reversed for the second stage and for the complete four year course where stagnation is worse among non-local students than among local students; (xv) from a regression analysis of examination marks it is found that although S.S.C. marks may appear reasonably to be a good indicator of the capacity of students to complete college education, it may not be a good indicator of the course of his academic development and performance in college. The findings of part II of the study reveal that (i) results at the pre-degree examination are as low as thirtyeight to forty per cent; (ii) external students constitute approximately twentyfive per cent of the total candidates in arts and ten per cent in commerce; (iii) Poona area is in a much better position to take advantage of the facility of the external examination and does in fact do so; (iv) the difference in effectiveness of the condonation rules as applied to science candidates on one hand and arts and commerce candidates on the other is quite substantial; (v) pre-degree science course seems to be more difficult to cope up with than pre-degree arts or commerce courses; (vi) pre-degree examination is not merely a continuation of the S.S.C., but stands at an altogether different level; (vii) women as a group show better performance than men in all centres and at all examinations; (viii) those who pass the S.S.C. examination in March have a far better performance than those who pass in October; (ix) March batches are the regular S.S.C. batches while the October batches consist mostly of repeaters; (x) the greater proportion of failures is due to failure in three or more subjects; (xi) a large majority of failures is decisive, not marginal; (xii) failures are mainly due to general lack of preparation or lack of general equipment of the science students and not so than to vagaries of the examination or to uneven standards of examination; (xiii) English accounts for an overwhelmingly big proportion (seventy per cent) of the singly subject failures, other subjects contributing significantly are geography, book-keeping and mathematics; (xiv) the Poona group is the best while the group of new centres is the worst according to performance; (xv) the better the performance in English at the S.S.C. the greater is the chance of passing in English at the pre-degree examination; (xvi) the contribution of the science subjects at the S.S.C. seems to be important for the pre-degree science course mostly as far as it contributes to the general equipment of the science students and not so much to their specific equipment in the particular subject; (xvii) a large number of candidates are in favour of writing in Marathi; and (xviii) those who write their answers in Marathi have an edge over those who write in English.

16. ECONOMIC ASPECTS

A BOOKS

01 Ansari, M.M. *Education and economic development.* New Delhi, Association of Indian University, 1987. 57p.

02 ——. *Research in economics of education – India.* New Delhi, The author, 1979. 66p.

03 Baljit Singh. *Economics of Indian education.* New Delhi, Meenakshi, 1983. 242p.

04 ——ed. *Education as investment.* Meerut, Meenakshi Prakashan, 1967. 236p.

05 Basu, Partha, Lahiri, K. and Datta, Amlan. *Report on the economics of education in some West Bengal Colleges.* Calcutta, World Press, 1974.

06 Crane, Robert I. Technical education and economic development in India. *In* C. Arnold Anderson and Mary Jean Bowman, eds. *Education and economic development.* London, Frank Case and Co., 1966.

07 Dholakia, B.H. *Sources of economic growth in India.* Baroda, Good Compansion, 1974.

08 Galbraith, J.K. *Economic development in perspective.* London, Harward University Press, 1962. Chapter 4; p.46-49.

09 Garg, V.P. *Cost analysis in higher education : A theoretical frame, empirical results.* Delhi, Metropolitan, 1985. 216p.

10 George, P.P. *Economics of higher education in Tamil Nadu.* Madras, Centre for Research on New International Economic order, n.d. 176p.

11 Gupta M.L. *Indian economy and higher education: with reference to correspondence education.* Jaipur, Aalekha, 1985. 147p.

12 Institute of Applied Manpower Research, New Delhi. *An analysis of the pattern of recurring expenditure and per student cost in the institutes of technology, 1968-69.* New Delhi, The author, 1972. 48p.

13 ——. *Pattern of expenditure and per student cost in Indian Institute of Technology*. New Delhi, The author, 1975. 76p.

14 Kamath, A.R. Unit institutional costs in higher education. *In* Kamath's *Unit cost in higher education – two studies in education.* Bombay, Asia Publishing, 1968.

15 Kothari, V.N. *Disparities in relative earning among different occupations*. Baroda, M.S. University of Baroda, 1970.

16 ——. *Factor cost of education in India*. Baroda, M.S. University of Baroda, 1965.

17 ——. Returns to education in India: Working paper of the seminar on education as investment organised by the Lucknow University. Lucknow, January 1966.

18 Nair, Bhaskaran. *Costs and returns of university education.* Trivandrum, CBH Publications, 1990. 160p.

19 Padmanabhan, C.B. *Economics of educational Planning in India.* New Delhi, Arya Book Depot, 1971.

20 Pandit, H.N., ed. *Measurement of cost productivity and efficiency of education.* New Delhi, National Council of Educational Research and Training, 1969. 434p.

21 Prahlad Kumar. *Study of private cost of education in Allahabad city.* Allahabad, University of Allahabad, 1978.

22 Rajaiah, B. *Economics of education.* Delhi, Mittal, 1987. 179p.

23 Sharma, G.D. *Economic Status*, New Delhi, National Institute of Educational Planning and Administration, 1984. 163p. (Research Studies, NCT-II).

24 Sharma, G.D. *Institutional costs of university education.* New Delhi, Association of Indian University, 1980. 105p.

25 ——. *Unit cost of college education : A case study of Hindu college.* New Delhi, Association of Indian Universities, 1978.

26 Singh, B., ed. *Education as investment.* Meerut, Meenakshi Prakashan, 1967.

B ARTICLES

01 Arun Kumar. Strife in higher education needed a national incomes policy. *Economics and Political Weekly*, 22(34), 1987. p.1445-1446.

02 Bajpai, A.D.N. Higher education and structural problems of Indian economy. *University News*. 27(23), 1989. p.7-8.

03 Bhandari, S.K.R. Cost of higher education : Methodology for measurement. *University News*. 17(7), 1979. p.182-85 and 198.

04 Brokar, V.V. and Kata, P.V. Cost structure of higher education in Marathwada. *Madras University Journal*. 9 (1), 1969.

05 Charles, K.J. and Panikar, P.G.K. Education and economic development: A case study of Kerala. *Development Digest*. January 1968.

06 Chaudhri, D.P. and Rao, Potluri. Private and social returns to higher education: A case study of Delhi graduates. *Economic and Political Weekly*. 5 (4) April 1970. p.605-608.

07 Chitnis, Suma, Investment in higher education: A reconsideration. *New Frontiers in Education*. 5 (4), 1975. p.23-46.

08 Chopra, S.L. Socio-economic background and educational opportunity in India. *Journal of Education and Psychology*. 27, 1970, p.365-69.

09 Datta, Bhabatosh. Indian universities and economic research. *Journal of University Education*. (1), 1962. p.33-42.

10 Debi, Sailabala. Cost structure of higher education: A case study of Orissa. *Journal of Higher Education*. 10 (1-2), 1984. p.57-71.

11 ——. Private rate of return to higher education in Orissa. *Indian Education Review*. 22 (3), 1987. p.63-77.

12 Dongre, G.S. Investment and returns in higher education. *Progress of Education*. 45 (3), 1970. p.207-211.

13 Education: The smell of money. *Economic and Political Weekly*. 6 June, 1981. p.998-999.

14 Goel, S.C. Education and economic growth in India. *Comparative Education*. 10, (October-December), 1974. p.18-26.

15 Heynemann, Stephen P. Investment in Indian education: Uneconomic? *World Development*. 8 (1980), p.145-163.

16 Israney, S.M. and Balachander, K.K. Economics of higher education: Concurrent trends and new priorities. *University News*. 24 (42), 1986. p.111-117.

17 Jha, L.K. Education and economic development. *Reserve Bank Bulletin*. (24), April, 1970.

18 King, A. Higher technical education and socio-economic development: Great Britain, West Germany and India. *Comparative Education*. 5, (December), 1969. p.263-81.

19 Krishnamurthy, V. Economics of higher education: A BITS experience. *University News*. 17 (10), 1979. p.267-70.

20 Mazumdar, Vina. The economic scene and its implications for higher education. *New Frontiers in Education.* 3 (1), 1973. p.11-20.

21 Mukherjee, K.C. Economic change and problems of education in India. *Educational Forum.* 33, (May), 1969. p.441-47.

22 Nair, D. Prabhakaran. Some economic aspects of higher education in Kerala. *Manpower Journal.* 22 (2), 1986. p.15-20.

23 Padmanabhan, C.B. Reforms in accounting in universities and colleges in India. *University News.* 19 (9), 1981. p.255-56.

24 Pandit, H.N. Economics of university of Delhi. *University News.* 12 (8), 1974. p.4-9.

25 Rahman, A. Scientists in India: The impact of economic policies and support in historical social perspective. *International Social Science Journal.* 22 (1), 1970. p.54-79.

26 Ramanathan, A. Cost benefit analysis in higher education: Some pitfalls. *University News.* 25 (41), 1987. p.4

27 Ray, M.S. Education and economic development. *AICC Economic Review.* 25 April, 1965.

28 Reddy, B. Shiva. Distribution of higher education subsidies: A case study of Panjab University. *Journal of Higher Education.* 8 (1), Monsoon, 1982. p.79-85.

29 Rethnam, V. Cost information and cost analysis in higher education. *New Frontiers in Education.* 7 (3), July-September, 1977. p.58-62.

30 Rizvi, F.H. Economics of higher education. *Education Quarterly.* 12 (48), Winter, 1960. p.347-52.

31 Sharma, G.D. Unit cost of college education: A case study of Hindu College of Delhi University. *University News.* 17 (8), April, 1979. p.212-17.

32 Tilak, Jandhyala B.G. Education and economic growth in India 1950-51 and 1969-70: An empirical investigation. *Indian Educational Review.* 10 (1), January, 1975. p.74-89.

D RESEARCH STUDIES

01 Datta, A., Economics of education in West Bengal colleges with special reference to size, techniques and location. Deptt. of Economics. Calcutta University, 1970.

The purposes of the study were (i) to estimate, separately, the contribution of student input and the college environment on student output, and (ii) to ascertain how far the quality of student output is determined by student input and how far by the college environment. Student output is the number of graduates of various qualifications. The number of students admitted to various courses of study is the input. The college environment is the collective name for the non-student resources like teachers, their qualifications, student-teacher ratios, floor area in relation to the number of students, library services and other more intangible things, such as the quality of management of the college and its tradition or reputation.

On the basis of stratified random sampling procedure, twentytwo colleges under the Calcutta University were selected for the study. Necessary data were collected on the basis of appropriate questionnaires and available reports. The marks obtained at the final examinations and the required number of classes for different courses of study were considered in combination while deciding upon a system of weights for different categories of graduates. This served as a measure of student output. The data on college environment were collected on the basis of the number of students enrolled (size of the college), floor area-student ratio, book-student ratio, student-teacher ratio, institutional cost per student and the age of the colleges. A number of regression equations were fitted to the sample data to discover the extent of correlation between the quality of student output on one hand, and the quality of student input and the college environment on the other.

The study revealed that (i) the quality of student input could closely determine the quality of student output; (ii) there was no significant influence of any of the factors of the college environment on the student output; (iii) costs declined with the increase in the size of the college; (iv) students from the highest income levels had, on the whole, markedly better examination results than poorer students; (v) 42.88 per cent of the sample students showed a preference for teaching research as a future career; and (vi) in most of the colleges in rural areas, majority of the students voted for teaching rather than for agriculture.

02 Garg. V.P., Cost analysis of the University of Panjab, 1950-51 to 1974-1975. Ph.D. Edu., Panjab University, 1981.

The major objectives of the study were: (i) to examine the trends of expenditure by objects and with respect to the functions of the university, (ii) to analyse the trends in the level, variation and subsidization of unit costs, (iii) to examine the applicability of cost-functions in relation to the optimum use of the resource-inputs, and (iv) to determine the level of private costs by types of courses.

It was a case study aiming at an *ex post facto* cost analysis of the economic and educational processes of internal organization of the Panjab University from the years 1950-51 to 1974-75 in general, and teaching departments and affiliated colleges in particular, which affect allocative efficiency of resource-inputs. This was realized through time and cross-sectional study of both institutional costs and private costs. The cost factor was examined by a systematic attempt which covered various aspects. For determining the private costs, a student's questionnaire was developed by the investigator. The sample consisted of 382 students, 279 from affiliated colleges and 103 from teaching departments. The sources of other data were the annual statistical surveys of the Ministry of Education, Government of India, the annual reports of the Panjab University, the Panjab University Calendar and the prospectus of affiliated colleges.

The major findings of the study were: (i) The level and composition of the university expenditure during these years showed an upward trend with recurrent expenditure increasing by 10.04 per cent and capital expenditure by 1.77 per cent per year. (ii) Till 1969 the general administration had the largest allocations in recurrent expenditure, followed by a shift in favour of teaching, municipal services, students' welfare, and general welfare functions of the university. (iii) The university expenditure was mainly affected by inflation, displacement and development. (iv) The cost-analysis of thirty teaching departments revealed that both recurrent and capital costs differed in terms of absolute level and their composition. Unit costs of laboratory-based departments were more than those of class-lecture-based departments. (v) The cost component of salaries was predominant in all departments. (vi) The level of capital costs was higher in the majority of the science departments and also in the departments of commerce and management, physical education, law, journalism and geography where investment in equipment and books was proportionately more as compared to the enrolment. (vii) The investigation of the dynamics of internal organization, in relation to enrolment, number of teachers and variations in unit costs showed that it was relatively consistent in the departments of botany, chemistry, zoology, chemical engineering, law and English whereas the departments of anthropology, bio-chemistry, education, history, political science and Sanskrit were relatively inconsistent in their internal organization. (viii) Some departments were making optimal use of their resources in terms of enrolment and teachers besides other factors. Some departments were found to be undersized, and some had more enrolment as compared to the number of the teaching staff. (ix) Subsidization of unit costs from public funds had increased over the years except for a few departments. (x) The rate of subsidization of maintenance expenditure of hostels per resident increased from Rs. 0.33 in 1966.67 to Rs. 84.44 in 1974-75. (xi) The levels of hostel expenses and of fee rates and other charges were higher in private colleges charging more than the prescribed limit. (xii) The economic status of the students from teaching departments was found to be better than that of the affiliated colleges. (xiii) Demand for higher education was more from the people belonging to administrative and professional services, farming and business, respectively.

03 George, P.P., Economics of higher education in Tamil Nadu, Ph.D. Eco., Maharaja Sayajirao University of Baroda, 1982.

The objectives, of the study were: (i) to evaluate the economic factors that influenced higher education, (ii) to find out the impact of economic factors on the choice of various courses by the students, and (iii) to determine the private and social costs of acquiring higher education.

The study was based on an analysis of data available on higher education in India, in general, and in Tamil Nadu, in particular. The undergraduates from different faculties were selected systematically from seventeen colleges. Data were collected through a questionnaire, from published materials, and from government, semi-government and private sources. Data were collected with respect to the growth of enrolment and educational expenditure on higher education from 1960-61 to 1975-76. The data were analyzed by percentages, correlation coefficient, factor cost, state's net domestic product, expenditure on education, benefit cost ratio, etc.

The major findings of the study were: (i) There was no correlation between the cost per pupil and the enrolment at primary and university general education stages. (ii) There had been an increase in Government's share of total expenditure on education at all stages except at the primary stage. (iii) Females, Scheduled Castes and Scheduled Tribes were still lagging behind at every stage of education as shown by the coefficient of equality. (iv) Considering the combined annual total expenditure of day scholars and hostel residents, the private expenditure-on professional education exceeded that of general education by 71 per cent and 49 per cent respectively. (v) The relative cost of higher education in Tamil Nadu with reference to the per capita expenditure on higher education and the per capita income of the State came to 8:1 (upper estimate) and 7:1 (lower estimate) for general education and 15:1 (upper estimate) and 14:1 (lower estimate) for professional education. (vi) The urban-based families benefited most from higher education.

04 Gogate, S.B., Unit Cost of Higher Education for Arts, Science and Commerce Colleges in Maharashtra (1973-74 to 1977-78), Indian Institute of Education, Pune, 1979.

The objective of the study was to find out the cost per student per year for education in the arts, commerce and science colleges in Maharashtra.

The state had 167 arts and commerce colleges, 67 arts and science and 99 arts, science and commerce colleges. There were all multi-faculty colleges. In addition, there were 31 commerce and 21 science colleges. In all, there were 385 colleges. Of these colleges, about 10 per cent were included in the sample. It was a stratified random sample. The information collected was for the years 1973-74, 1976-77 and 1977-78. A few colleges could not supply information for all the years. The sources for collecting data were primarily the records in the office of the Directorate of Higher Education.

The major observations and findings were: (i) Colleges, generally, received funds by way of fees, grants, donations, and receipts on miscellaneous items. Out of the fees, that received for obtaining eligibility certificate was credited to the university. Receipt on account of other fees was considered direct receipt of colleges by the Government. (ii) The sources for grants were the State Government and the UGC. (iii) The items of expenditure, generally, were salaries to the teaching and non-teaching staff, rent on the building, furniture, equipment, library, laboratory, gymkhana, and general maintenance. (iv) Till 31 March 1979, the grant-in-aid formula to colleges was deficit-oriented and was as follows:

Grant = 50% deficit + 5% or 10% admissible expenditure (for student strength of above 1,000 or less than 1,000), + up to 33.3% of dearness allowance provided the deficit was not covered by 50% + 5% or 10% of admissible expenditure. (v) The average cost per student in single-faculty science college was the maximum and that in the single-faculty commerce college was the minimum. (vi) Increase in the average cost per student from 1973-74 to 1977-78 had been about two times in all categories of colleges except single faculty commerce colleges where the increase had been one and a half times. (vii) Expenditure on staff emoluments and essential expenditure was 75 per cent of the total cost during the previous five years. (viii) By and large, colleges had to spend about 25 per cent on other items but as per government rules this expenditure should be limited to 12 to 18 per cent of the expenditure on salaries. (ix) Average cost per student in a college with a strength of less than 200 was Rs. 1009.21 in 1973-74 and Rs. 2169.66 in 1977-78. For a college with student strength of more than 2,000, it was Rs. 458.40 in 1973-74 and Rs. 791.64 during 1977-78. Larger colleges were more economical than smaller ones. (x) During 1973-74, the per student expenditure in a college with arts, science and commerce faculties was Rs. 486.35 and the same in 1977-78 was Rs. 1452.58. Corresponding figures for a science college were Rs. 1016.92 in 1973-74 and 1539.18 in 1977-78. For a commerce college, the figures were Rs. 373.07 during 1973-74 and Rs. 481.28 during 1977-78.

05 Panchamukhi, P.R., Economics of university finance. Deptt. of Economics, Bombay University, 1974. (ICSSR financed).

The project was an attempt to lay down the principles of economic of university finances with the Bombay University as a case in point. The specific objectives of the study were: (i) to define the objective function of the university in an operational sense; (ii) to analyse how the university attempted to attain its objective through raising and using resources; (iii) to inquire into the economic behaviour of the sources which contributed to the university; and (iv) to examine the resource-using activity as well as resource-getting activity of the university.

The study was a survey of university financed. The sources of data were the official records and published documents of different universities in general and Bombay University in particular. In analysing economics of university finances three principles were expounded, namely, the principles of raising resources, resosurce use, and financial soundness. On the whole, these three principles dealt with economic considerations that were kept in view in order to strengthen the financial basis of the university and make it function better. In respect of financial soundness of the university, autonomy, adequacy and built-in flexibility were the three criteria that had to be satisfied by the university before its financial position could be considered to be sound.

The following were some of the significant conclusions of the study: (i) Regarding the sources of finance the Bombay University needed to rationalize its attitude towards fee policy, endowments, extension services and publication. Raising tuition and examination fees, better efforts for more donations, more planned efforts at extension programme and rationalisation in pricing of university publications might prove to be more productive sources of revenue for, the university. (ii) The university could start more auxiliary enterprises of its own to increase its general fund. (iii) There was much ad hocism in the entire grant-in-aid policy to the university. While the state grants had, by and large, covered some of the revenue needs the UGC grants met partially the capital needs of the university. (iv) Income elasticity of expenditures was fairly high and it was rising over time. Maximum percentage share in expenditures was claimed by administration. (v) The financial position of the Bombay University could not be considered to be very satisfactory on the basis of the principles of financial soundness and in comparison with other universities. (vi) Increase in the basic infrastructure might prove to be a crucial factor in raising the functional efficiency of the university.

06 Kamat. A.R., Unit Institutional costs in higher education, Gokhale Institute of Politics and Economics, Poona, 1968.

The study was designed to estimate the recurring institutional expenditure per student per annum at the undergraduate and postgraduate stages in the University of Poona.

A data sheet giving the relevant information was prepared for each of the ten colleges selected from Poona. Nasik and Shrirampur. It listed the number of students in each class, the number of teachers, common expenditure classified under nine categories, and the divisible expenditure classified under three categories. The sheet also gave the division of divisible expenditure over relevant categories of student and finally recorded the component costs as well as the total cost per student per annum for different categories of students. The institutional costs borne by the University of Poona in its postgraduate departments were also found out in a similar way.

The study has revealed that the per pupil cost for the four-year period covering the pre-degree year and the three-year degree courses in commerce, arts and science are approximately Rs. 1200.00, Rs. 1500.00 and Rs. 1800.00 respectively. The higher costs in the science courses are, of course, due to the costs of laboratories and equipment. Somewhat lower costs in the commerce as compared to those in the arts courses are on account of the fact that commerce courses constitute a much more homogeneous group allowing fewer branches of specialisation. Per pupil cost in mofussil colleges is higher than in the colleges in Poona. The per pupil per annum cost of postgraduate instruction in the university departments is four or five times as high as that for undergraduate instruction in the colleges. The costs of technical education, such as, medicine and engineering at the undergraduate level are, again, four or five times as high as those of general education in arts and science.

07 Panchamukhi, P.R., Devaluation of education: A quantitative analysis. Unit in Economics of Education. Bombay University, 1974.

The basic objective of the study was to examine the implication of expansionism in education on devaluation of education. An attempt was made to quantify the degree and pattern of devaluation, especially in higher education.

To quantify the degree of devaluation of education, it was assumed that preferences and actions of employers pertaining to educated individuals for different jobs were revealed from the vacancy registers published in leading newspapers. So, from the *Times of India* details of job vacancies, such as job specification, educational requirements, experience desired, training needs, salary admissible, etc., were taken for three years, viz., 1954, 1964 and 1974 for 112, 379 and 319 jobs, respectively. Data for each year were grouped according to identical jobs. A comparison of these identical jobs was made with reference to above-stated job characteristics. To know which job categories experienced more devaluation, twenty-eight homogeneous job categories were compared at three points of time.

The main findings of the study were: (i) For all jobs taken together there was a low degree of overvaluation measured in terms of average years of schooling and experience during the period 1954-64. But there was clearly a marked devaluation for the same during 1964-74. (ii) Fewer job categories experienced devaluation for the same during 1954-64, but a maximum number of jobs revealed educational devaluation during 1964-74. (iii) There was a high degree of correlation between years of experience desired and years of schooling expected for each job. The coefficients of correlation and coefficients of regression increased over the years 1954-74 confirming the devaluation of education. (iv) It was difficult to identify which particular educational categories experienced more devaluation. However, on the additional information obtained from the vacancy register it was estimated that maximum devaluation was felt by the educational categories, which experienced more expansion, viz. arts, science and commerce graduates, engineering diploma-holders, etc. No categorical answer could be given to the question of exploitation of education unless estimates of indices of academic excellence for each type of education were drawn up.

08 Panchamukhi, P.R., Education and research in economics: A profile of the post-graduate students in economics of the Bombay University — 1930-1070. Deptt. of Economics, Bombay University, 1973.

The major objectives of the study were: (i) to design the trends in the facilities for postgraduate study and research in economics in the Bombay University; (ii) to study the socio-economic status of the students; and (iii) to study the effectiveness of the programme in terms of student achievement.

The main sources of data were the application forms of the students for admission to the department, budgets of the university, handbook of information of the department and other records of the university. Since all the records were not available for years before 1930 the study was restricted to the period 1930-31 to 1969-70.

The study revealed that (i) there had been a significant growth in the facilities for postgraduate study in economics during 1930-70; (ii) there had been a shift in students' preference from M.A. by thesis to M.A. by papers in recent years; (iii) though male students had greater representation, the number of female students were also fast increasing; (iv) while majority of students who offered papers were unmarried and were in the nineteen to twentyfour age group, majority of students who offered thesis were married and belonged to higher age group (v) a fairly high percentage of Ph.D. students was married and was in the age group of twentyfive years and above; (vi) students were largely from urban area; but in case of Ph.D. students, the percentage of rural area students was found to be increasing; (vii) in respect of demographic character, female students were more homogeneous than male; (viii) the course dropout rate for male was higher and increasing while that for female was slightly low and declining; (x) the dropout rates among M.A. by thesis and Ph.D. students were thirty-three and twentyfive per cent respectively; (xi) the Ph.D. productivity rate was very high, but it took five years on an average to complete; (xii) the overall pass percentage at M.A. examination was found to be fairly high but was found to show a declining tendency in the recent years; (xiii) the department's training enabled the students to improve their performance in graduate examination; and (xiv) the scholarship holders in general performed well but they dropped out also at a very significant level.

09 Panchamukhi, P.R., Operating Cost of Higher Education in the Bombay University, Centre of Advanced Study in Public Finance and Industrial Economics, Bombay University, 1965.

The objective of the study was to estimate the recurring cost of higher education of the Bombay University.

The major sources of the data for the study were the official publications of the university, namely, the budgets of the university, annual reports, etc. The modus *operandi* of the study was analysing the current account classified under following heads, namely, auxiliary enterprises and services, students aid expenditures, educational and general, administrative and general, instruction and research, the library account, plant operation and maintenance. The study did not include capital costs and opportunity costs of education. The per student cost on each of these heads had been calculated by dividing the total current expenditure (1963-64) by the total number of students and other members (staff) benefited and affected by the respective head. Further, in the study, the post-graduate departments of economics, chemical technology, applied psychology, sociology, civics and polities, management studies, statistics, law, Sanskrit, English and mathematics, and undergraduate arts and science colleges, undergraduate science colleges, undergraduate and postgraduate commerce colleges, engineering, medical, dental and training colleges were included.

The costs were calculated for the years 1962-63 and 1963-64.

The study revealed that (i) the expenditure per student on (a) academic and general administration was Rs. 17.16 (1962-63) and Rs. 18.26 (1963-64), (b) physical culture and student welfare was Rs. 2.61 (1962-63) and Rs. 2.77 (1963-64), (c) university press was Rs. 9.43 (1962-63) and

Rs. 10.20 (1963-64), (d) library (per reader) was Rs. 79.10 (1962-63) and Rs. 71.52 (1963-64), (e) Plant operation and maintenance was Rs. 2.80 (1962-63) and Rs. 2.69 (1963-64), and (f) instructions for hostel dwellers was Rs. 317.46 (1962-63); (ii) the recurring expenditure in science and technical education was higher than that in arts and social sciences; (iii) in the collegiate education, per student cost of commerce education was found to be nearly doubled in the course of ten years; (iv) for law, arts and science education the increase was marginal, for training college it had remained the same and it was slightly higher in case of engineering education; the costs grew two to three times more in case of medical and dental education; (v) the expenditure on personal emoluments to teaching and technical staff as a percentage of total recurring expenditure was found to vary between thirty per cent and sixty per cent for different subjects of postgraduate education; (vi) the instructional expenditure as percentage of total recurring expenditure was generally low (around thirty per cent) for commerce, law, arts and science subjects it was generally at forty per cent of fifty per cent; and (vii) the per student expenditure was found to vary inversely with the institutional size, namely, the number of students.

10 Ramanujam, M.S., Raghavan, K., Bolar, M., Nain, J.S., Srivastava, M.B. and Bhatt, P.R. Pattern of expenditure and per student cost in educational institutions in Jammu and Kashmir. Institute of Applied Manpower Research, 1979.

The aims of the study were: (i) to help the educational institutions at various levels in the State to appreciate their relative pattern of per student cost better and (ii) to analyse the determinants of cost structure through the estimation of long-run cost curve, with a view to facilitating future enrolment policies.

The per student cost estimated at various levels of education in this study referred to per student per annum recurring cost for the given level of education. Relevant data for the analysis pertaining to the year 1973-74 were collected from forty-three middle schools, fifty-two high/higher secondary schools, nine arts/science colleges including the Kashmir University, one teachers' training school, one teachers' training college, seven ITIs/craftsmen training institutes, one engineering polytechnic, one engineering degree college, one agricultural college and one medical college. Data were collected through a questionnaire designed for the purpose and through personal canvassing.

The findings were: (i) At the middle school level the average per student recurring cost was of the order of Rs. 232, of which 85.9 per cent was accounted for by salaries and allowances of the teaching staff and 8.7 per cent by salaries and allowances of the non-teaching staff. The expenditure on library and other operating cost and on scholarships was found to be very small in proportion. An analysis of the cost curve indicated that all the middle schools in the State were operating in increasing returns to scale phase. (ii) The per student cost estimated in respect of high/higher secondary level school education in the State was Rs. 270.80. Of this 83.2 per cent was accounted for by salaries and allowances of the teaching staff and 10.9 per cent by salaries and allowances of the non-teaching staff. The per student cost in high/higher secondary schools located in the rural areas was less than that in urban areas. As an analysis of the cost curve showed in all the schools, irrespective of the districts, increasing returns to the scale of operation were observed. (iii) At the undergraduate level in arts and science, the per student cost was Rs. 382 and Rs. 575, respectively. Further, the pattern of distribution of expenditure among various components at both arts and science courses was found to be more or less the same. When compared to undergraduate courses, the postgraduate courses in arts and science were found to be very expensive. The average per student cost for postgraduate courses in arts was found to be Rs. 2,624, while for science courses it was Rs. 5,314. (iv) At the teacher's training (certificate level), the per student cost was Rs. 2,075, of which 78.9 per cent was accounted for by scholarships. In contrast to teacher's training (certificate), the degree course was less expensive as the average cost was only Rs. 789. This was because in the case of the former more than three-fourths of the total expenditure was on scholarships alone while there was no expenditure on scholarships in the case of the latter. At the craftsmen training level, the per student cost was Rs. 792 of which 59.8 per cent was accounted for by salaries and allowances. The average per student cost at the ITI was Rs. 566. (v) The per student cost at the diploma level of engineering was Rs. 1,691, salaries and allowances of the teaching and non-teaching staff accounted for 85.2 per cent of the expenditure. (vi) At the degree level in engineering the per student cost was Rs. 4,716. On an average, 83.6 per cent of this expenditure was accounted for by salaries and allowances of the teaching and non-teaching staff. The expenditures on library and other operating cost and on scholarships were not very significant. (vii) The per student expenditure for the degree course in agriculture was Rs. 3,018 of which 88.5 per cent was accounted for by salaries and allowances alone.

11 Reddy, P.N., A study of social and private rates of return on higher education, Ph.D. Eco. Osmania University, 1981.

The investigation attempted to examine whether the policies in relation to allocation of resources to different levels and types of education were rational and efficient in terms of rate of return. The investigation posed four specific questions centred around social and private rates of return on (i) professional and non-professional graduates, (ii) professional graduates and postgraduates like doctors, engineers, agriculture graduates, and secondary school teachers, and (iii) different level of academic performance (first, second, and pass classes) among graduates and postgraduates. The hypotheses formulated were: (i) The rates of return were higher for postgraduates compared with graduates. (ii) The rates of return were different for graduates drawn from faculties of arts, science, and commerce, (iii) The rates of return were different for postgraduates drawn from arts, science and commerce faculties. (iv) Rates of return were higher for professional graduates representing doctors, engineers, agriculture graduates, and secondary school teachers as compared with non-professional categories of graduates and postgraduates. (v) The rates of return were different within the professional categories between doctors, engineers, agriculture graduates, and secondary school teachers. (vi) Rates of return of graduates and postgraduates were higher for higher levels of academic performance as between first classes as compared to second classes and pass classes.

The sample consisted of 2,080 employees, working in the offices and undertakings of the State, the Central Government, and the local bodies situated in Hyderabad and Secunderabad. An age-income profile of the respondents was constructed. Mean, percentage and correlation co-efficient were used to analyse the data.

The findings of the investigation were: (i) Investment in postgraduate non-professional education did not guarantee the expected financial success, (ii) Social and private rates of return for all postgraduates were found to be below 5 per cent, except those with first class. (iii) A variation in the trend in social and private rates of return for graduates of different faculties was found. (iv) Postgraduate education seemed to need special attention in terms of balancing the cost incurred and benefits accruing to individuals as well as to society. (v) The most favoured professional category of doctors and engineers was found to be distinguished from the not-so-favourable professional category of agriculture graduates and secondary school teachers. (vi) The superior students in terms of academic performance were found to be the highest beneficiaries.

12 Shah, A.B. and Inamdar, C.S., The unit cost of post-graduate education in the university of Poona: A case study, Indian Institute of Education. Pune, 1980.

The study sought to determine, in an approximate manner, the unit cost of higher education at the postgraduate level in the University of Poona. In the absence of balance-sheets and liabilities for the period from 1948-49 to 1977-78, interest charges on the total investment could not be calculated. Interest was calculated on the total non-recurring and capital receipts of the university during the period 1948-49 to 1977-78 (Rs. 58.617 million). The depreciation charges on buildings, library books, etc., were not taken into account. For the years 1973-74 to 1977-78 the actual expenditures were taken into account in the absence of audited statements. Only the major heads of recurring income and expenditure were considered. Under certain heads like examination, it was not possible to break up the expenditure into parts pertaining to undergraduate and postgraduate stages. While calculating the unit cost, the three Centres of Advanced Study in Sanskrit, Linguistics and Economics were not considered.

The major findings were: (i) The income and expenditure of the university had steadily gone up from its inception in 1948-49 to 1977-78. Since 1974-75 the university had a deficit budget. The accumulated deficit exceeded Rs. 10 million in 1979-80. (ii) The expenditure per student at the postgraduate level incurred by the university, exclusive of the expenditure on general administration and common facilities, had grown by nearly 50 per cent from Rs. 2,369 in 1973-74 to Rs. 3,462 in 1977-78. The cost per pupil was the highest in the science faculty and except for the year 1974-75, it was lowest in the humanities faculty. In 1977-78, costs per student in the humanities, social sciences, and natural sciences were Rs. 1,728, Rs. 2,757 and Rs. 3,462, respectively, without considering the non-departmental expenditure and interest charges on buildings, equipment, books, etc. If these charges were estimated and included, the cost of education of one M.A./M.Sc./LL.M./Ph.D. student was Rs. 6,033 per year in 1973-74 and Rs. 11, 056 per year in 1977-78. If the cost of conducting postgraduate examinations was added, the unit cost would go up a further amount of Rs. 225.

13 Shah, K.R. and Srikantiah, S., Education, earnings and income distribution: An inquiry in to equity issues involved in the government financing of higher education in India, Deptt. of Business and Economics, Maharaja Sayajirao University of Baroda, 1981 (ICSSR-financed).

The study attempted a scientific and critical analysis of the role of education as an equalizer and a tool for socio-economic change. The main objective of the study was to examine the syndrome of structure of subsidy and the equality of educational opportunities in the context of the Indian economy. Specific hypotheses tested were: (i) General public subsidy was less egalitarian under the prevailing economic, social, and political system and initial glaring inequalities. (ii) Specific subsidy helped reduce educational distance between generations and between socio-economic groups. (iii) The private demand for education was characterized by optimizing behaviour of maximizing economic welfare. (iv) The human capital and earnings were positively related. (v) The effect of family background on education was direct and substantial whereas that on earnings was indirect and small relative to the effect of education on earnings. (vi) Starting earnings were positively related to education. (vii) Present earnings were positively related to occupational rank showing, indirectly, the relation between education and earnings. (viii) Earnings and the nature of employment were positively related. (ix) Variations in earnings were explained more by the human capital than by mere education. (x) More equal distribution of income moved sympathetically with more equal distribution of schooling. (xi) Mere continuous expansion of education, altering the distribution of schooling of persons and the age structure of the labour force in favour of young persons, was capable of altering earnings distribution.

Necessary data were collected through survey from a 5 per cent sample of randomly selected graduates of the four benchmark years, 1961, 1965, 1970 and 1975 from the M.S. University of Baroda. The survey was conducted during the latter half of 1979. Of the sampled graduates spread throughout India, information could be collected form 294 graduates accounting for 56 per cent response. The data were mainly related to male earners classified as respondents, respondents' parents, and respondents' brothers and sisters. Cost calculations were based on private costs (investments) data collected through the field survey and the net of subsidies. The issue of intertemporal equity in educational opportunities was studied by employing the techniques of trend and ratio analysis to the tie series data covering the period 1960 to 1980. Size distribution of earnings of the labour force was assessed by analysing individual earning profiles involving the parameters of height (level), rate of growth (slope), and rate of change of growth (curvature). The technique of step-wise regression was followed to guage the significance of various determinants of earnings. Four widely known inequality measures, namely, Gini coefficient, skewness and dispersion, coefficient of variation, and variance of log of earnings and education, were employed to measure earnings inequality. The analysis was based mainly on the primary data collected through the field survey and partly on the secondary data.

The main conclusions of the study were: (i) Persons with low mean education, of older age, and preponderantly self-employed showed greater education and income inequalities. (ii) Persons with higher mean education, of younger age, and declining proportions of being self-employed showed less distribution of education and income. (iii) Tendency towards better size distribution of income was very slow and was not consistent. However, the financing of education had not furthered inequalities. (iv) The bridging of educational distance inter-temporally, the creation of efficient human capital stock, and better distribution of income were clear social benefits with far-reaching effects on the future course of the economy. (v) The emerging human capital stock was characterized by younger persons with more education and expected to have multiplier effect on future distribution pattern and earnings. (vi) With regard to the overall subsidy, the stratifier effect was much more pronounced than the equalizer effect. The specific subsidy, in contrast, did have the equalizer effect in the sense of higher per capita subsidy going to beneficiaries with low per capita income. (vii) Specific subsidy had reduced the educational distance between various classes and generations as revealed by relative enrolment ratio and relative participation rate which had improved for BC and ERC categories. (viii) Education and earnings were positively related only after a critical minimum education which was ten or more than ten years of schooling. (ix) The rates of growth of earnings were higher for persons with more schooling. The earnings were subject to diminishing marginal returns and the efficiency of the investment in education increased. (x) The results were in conformity with the wage competition model according to which diminished inequality of schooling was associated with diminished inequality of income.

14 Singh, H.K.M. and Singh, B.P., Unit cost of higher education. Dept. of Economics. Panjabi University, 1972. (A project sponsored by Planning Commission).

The study aimed at estimating the unit cost of higher education separately for science and nonscience students as well as combined, in one university, namely, Punjabi University.

The data on cost of education were collected from twentythree science and nonscience teaching departments offering master's degrees, undergraduate and postgraduate diplomas, and certificates. For the purpose of this study, cost of fortythree affiliated colleges and research department were excluded. Costs were calculated in terms of current costs including salaries, dearness allowance, house rent, provident fund, contingencies, etc., and capital cost. Both the current as well as the capital costs were calculated under direct and indirect cost. Indirect costs were further calculated under two heads — proportion of total joint cost for university departments and affiliated colleges, and costs involving solely the students of the university departments. Capital costs were worked out in the manner of depreciation allowed for under income tax regulations as given in *Income Tax Manual*, Vol. II, App. I. The division on science and nonscience categories was on the basis of the respective strength of each category to the total. The science students formed 29.2 per cent, 26.4 per cent, and 27.7 per cent of the total student population of the teaching departments of the university in the years 1969-70, 1970-71, and 1971-72 respectively for which the unit costs were calculated.

It was found that (i) students of teaching departments formed 4.45 per cent, 4.34 per cent, and 4.24 per cent of the total student population of the university for the years 1969-70, 1070-71, and 1971-72 respectively; (ii) the total current costs per science student were Rs. 3,162.58, Rs. 3,330.54, and Rs. 4,144.55 for the years 1969-70, 1970-71, and 1971-1972 respectively; (iii) capital costs per science student came to Rs. 813.23 (1969-70), Rs. 1,124.14 (1970-71), and Rs. 1,201.14 (1971-72); (iv) the current costs per nonscience student were estimated at Rs. 1,165.65 (1969-70), Rs. 1,357.36 (1970-71), and Rs. 1,745.73 (1971-72); (v) the capital costs per nonscience student were Rs. 188.40 (1969-70), Rs. 204.18 (1970-71), and Rs. 224.61 (1971-72); (vi) the unit costs per science student were worked out to be Rs. 3,975.81 (1969-70), Rs. 4,454.68 (1970-71), and Rs. 5,345.70 (1971-72); (vii) the unit costs per nonscience student came to Rs. 1,354.05 (1969-70), Rs. 1,561.54 (1970-71), and Rs. 1,970.35 (1971-72); and (viii) unit costs per student (science and nonscience combined) were worked out to be Rs. 2,119.36 (1969-70), Rs. 2,325.66 (1970-71), and Rs. 2,904.60 (1971-72) respectively.

15 Trivedi, M.D., An inquiry into the motivation for and cost of postgraduate education at Saurashtra University, Ph.D. Education. Saurashtra University, 1977.

Major objectives of the study were: (i) to evolve a hierarchical pattern of motivation factors — intrinsic and extrinsic — that prompted graduates to pursue postgraduate studies, (ii) to study private costs and recurrent institutional costs, (iii) to compare unit costs per student, by faculty, for the year 1972-73, and (iv) to present students' responses regarding fees, facilities and duration of postgraduate instruction at Saurashtra University.

As many as 1277 postgraduate students belonging to the faculties of arts, science, commerce, education and medicine of the Saurashtra University in the year 1972-73 formed the sample. A questionnaire and a data sheet were designed for collecting data on motivation and cost respectively. Multiple regression analysis of unit costs were carried out. Student's reactions were analysed.

The main findings of the study were as follows: (i) Majority of the students came from families with income of parents or guardians over Rs. 500 per month and the parents were mostly merchants, executives, doctors, engineers, teachers, or the like. (ii) About fiftytwo per cent of the students came from more-than-three children families and the rest came from smaller families. (iii) Regardless of faculty and sex, the intrinsic motivations were operative through an interest for advanced study and a desire to acquire deep knowledge of the subject of study. (iv) The extrinsic motivations were to enhance employability, to achieve greater success in a job, to obtain more economic gains, and to qualify for lecturership in a college. (v) In terms of mean private cost per annum, the faculties ranked in the order as medicine, science, education, arts and commerce. (vi) Total recurrent institutional costs per annum showed a gradual rise and became four-fold in 1972-73 in respect of the faculty of arts. They exhibited a galloping trend in the faculty of science, assuming in 1972-73 fifteen times the initial value. In faculties of commerce, education, and medicine, they assumed in 1972-73 respectively over twice, thrice and around twice their values in 1968-69.

17. EDUCATIONAL PSYCHOLOGY

A BOOKS

01 Ethirajula, T.K. *Analysis of factors entering into the academic achievement of student at the college level in different faculties.* Hyderabad, Osmania University, 1965.

02 Mitra, Shib K. *Problem of motivation in higher education.* New Delhi, NCERT, n.d 7p.

03 University Grants Commission. *Psychology of Indian Universities.* New Delhi, U.G.C., 1968, 71p.

B ARTICLES

01 Fernandes, H.J.X. Variables involved in prediction of college success. *Education and Psychology Review.* 7, July, 1967. p.150-165.

02 Trivedi, R.S. Teaching-learning process in higher education. *Journal of Educational Psychology.* 35 (3), 1977. p.115-117.

D RESEARCH STUDIES

01 Abraham, M., A sudy of certain psycho-social correlates of mental health status of university entrants of Kerala, Ph.D. Psychology, Kerala University, 1985.

The objective of the study was to explore the association between mental health status and psycho-social variables for total sample and subsamples. The main hypothesis was that each of the independent variables selected for study would exert a significant influence on the dependent variable (mental health status).

The sample for the study comprised 880 predegree students (454 males and 426 females) from colleges affiliated to the University of Kerala, selected on the basis of proportionate stratified sampling technique, with representation given to sex and age of subjects, area of residence and optional subjects selected for specialisation. The tools used were: Psychological Needs Inventory (M. Abraham and P. Koodapuzha, 1979); The Kerala Masculinity-Femininity Scale (A.S. Nair, 1978); The Kerala Introversion-Extraversion Scale (A.S. Nair, 1978); Students Adjustment Inventory (M. Abraham and R. Jacob, 1979); Students Activity Inventory (M. Avraham and R. Jacob, 1979); Family Integration Inventory (M.

Abraham and F. Fernandez 1978); Mental Health Status Scale (M. Abraham and B. Prasanna, 1981); and the Kerala University Test of Intelligence for University Entrants (A.S. Nair and Anandavalli Amma, 1972). The independent variables included (1) need for love and affection, (2) need for recognition and approval, (3) need for self-esteem, (4) need for security, (5) need for independence, (6) need for creative expression, (7) need for knowledge and new experience, (8) need for achievement, (9) need for delight, (10) need for adequacy, (11) need to be needed, (12) need to belong, (13) masculinity-femininity, (14) introversion-extraversion, (15) adjustment with opposite sex, (16) adjustment with authorities, (17) involvement in politics, (18) participation in extra curricular activities, (19) participation in social welfare activities, (20) family environment, (21) family relations, (22) family acceptance, (23) training for independence (within family), (24) freedom for action, and (25) mutual trust and approval (within family). The statistical techniques used were Pearson product-moment correlation, two tailed tests of significance for differences between means and factor analysis to compare factor structures of different groups.

The main findings were: 1. Twenty-three of twenty-five psycho-social variables except need for knowledge and new experience and involvement in politics, showed significant correlations with mental health status, but none of the values obtained were very high, showing that the influence was not considerable. The estimation of common variance confirmed this findings. 2. Twenty-two psychosocial variables discriminated between high and low mental health status groups (unselected group) and eighteen psycho-social variables discriminated between high and low mental health status groups equated for intelligence, age and sex. 3. The factor structure for the three groups — total sample, high mental health status group and low mental health status group, differed significantly from one another in terms of number of factors, the loadings and in terms of factors present in each structure.

02 Agrawal, M. A study of life stresses among university sudents, Ph.D. Psychology, Allahabad University, 1985.

The hypotheses were: (i) Evaluation of events in terms of distress and balance of affect, compared to change, would be more closely associated with measures of strain. (ii) Undesirable events would be more closely associated with strains than desirable ones. (iii) The self assessment of stress is expected to predict strains better than use of average scale values, (iv) Weighted stress scores compared to simple stress scores would be more highly correlated with measures of strain, (v) Subjects stress scores given due weightage would predict strains better than otherwise.

The sample consisted of 657 university students of graduate and postgraduate classes. A Scale of Stressful Experiences for Students (SSES) was developed by the investigator. The data were analysed with the help of correlation technique.

The findings were: (i) Simple stress score was a powerful predictor of strain, but the subjective assessment of events for the amount of distress they evoked (but not for change and balance of distress and relief) was more strongly correlated with the measure of strain. Weighted stress score based on ratings of independent group of judges was only as highly correlated with subjects symptom scores as the simple stress score. (ii) The events which occurred in one year prior to the study had consistently higher correlations than correlations of shorter periods within that year or the total life span excluding this one year. (iii) Life events did account for a significant proportion of variance in symptom scores but shared no variance in the number of times a subject sought medical help from a doctor. However, not all but only undesirable events could account for this variance. And from among undesirable occurrences, those which were threatening to the ego and related with the indisposition of the family members were more crucially linked with illness symptoms. Stresses emanating from interaction with family and study environment were also important contributors to strains. (iv) The occurrence of day-to-day problems had higher pathogenic significance than even major life events. (v) There was a trend for higher correlations on weighting for stress of recurrence but the differences between th two types of correlation were not significant. (vi) Stress scores were higher in case of males compared to females, muslims compared to hindus, rural students compared to urban students, students living in hostel, hired room or lodge compared to those staying in their own homes.

03 Badami, H.D., A scale for measuring attitudes of college students towards education. School of Philosophy, Psychology and Education, Gujarat University, 1973.

The major aim of the investigation was to construct a scale to measure the attitudes of college students towards various aspects of education — instruction, curriculum, teaching methods, teachers and examination procedures.

The Likert technique of developing an attitude scale was employed. Eighty-five items were collected from earlier studies, students' own expression concerning education and discussions with teachers. The items covered five areas mentioned earlier. On the basis of discussion with experts, the items were modified or rewritten. Five positive and five negative items for each of the five aspects of education were retained. For each item, the respondent was to give a choice of rating on a five-point scale, from 'strongly agree' to 'strongly disagree.' A sample of 100 respondents was randomly selected from three different colleges of arts, commerce and science. Item analysis was carried out by taking two extreme groups, namely, upper 25 per cent and lower 25 per cent. Critical ratios were calculated for each item. Eight items having the highest values for each aspect were selected. Reliability indices were as follows: (i) Test-retest reliability was 0.77 (N=40), (ii) Split-half reliability adjusted by Speerman-Brown formula was 0.85 (N=100).

04 Christian, J.A., A study of fear of failure, hope of success, achievement, motivation, anxiety and concern in the girl students of Sardar Patel University in relation to their socio-economic status and performance. Ph.D. Education, Sardar Patel University, 1977.

The objectives of the study were (i) to find out the level of the components of Need Achievement, Fear of Failure, Anxiety, Concern and Socio-Economic Status of the girl students of Sardar Patel University; (ii) to study the level of Need Achievement, Fear of Failure and Anxiety according to Performance, Age and streams of the subjects; (iii) to study the correlations of Need Achievement, Fear of Failure, Hope of Success, Anxiety, Concern, Performance and Socio-Economic Staus; and (iv) to study the effect of the various factors aforementioned on Need Achievement.

The sample consisted of 500 girl students of the Sardar Patel University. The tools used were the Pareek and Trivedi Socio-Economic Status Scale for rural sample, the Kuppuswamy's Socio-Economic Status Scale for urban sample, the McClelland's Thematic Apperception Test, the Birney's Thematic Apperception Test, the Badami's Self-Analysis, Scale, and the Cantril's Self-Anchoring Striving Scale.

The main findings of the study were: (i) the Need Achievement (n Ach) had no relation with age and anxiety; (ii) there was a significant positive correlation between n Ach and students' academic performance; (iii) there was a significant negative correlation between n Ach and fear of failure; (iv) there was greater hope of success feelings than fear of failure feelings in achievement situations; (v) there was a significant positive correlation between the fear of failure and hope of success; (vi) anxiety had no relation with age; (vii) there was a significant positive correlation between anxiety and hope of success, (viii) there were more personal fears than hopes; (ix) there was high concern for the nation's economic, social and political situations and international situations; (x) there was a significant negative correlation between performance and anxiety, and performance and hope of success; and (xi) there was a significant positive correlation between performance and fear of failure.

05 Farook Farzana, A study of the complexes and maladjustments of university youth by means of World-Association and cardiopneumopolygraph methods, Ph.D. Psychology. Aligarh Muslim University, 1974.

The main objective of the investigation was to study the complexes and maladjustment among university youths by using the techniques of word association and cardiopneumopolygraph.

The sample consisted of sixty highly adjusted and sixty highly maladjusted students selected from 1500 students of Aligarh Muslim University. The Personality Adjustment Inventory was administered to the above sample. The word association test was administered individually to the two matched groups. Of these students fortyseven were from the Faculty of Arts, fortynine from the faculty of Science and twentyfour from the professional courses. the word association test consisted of 100 stimulus words related to the following areas: (i) home and family; (ii) health and physical appearance; (iii) social, (iv) emotional; (v) financial; (vi) moral and religions; (vii) sex; and (viii) educational and vocational. Besides these, the Keller's Cardiopneumopolygraph was used. Statistical measures of central tendency and variability were used for analysing the data.

The investigation revealed that (i) no significant differences in maladjustments were found between the male and the female groups for, home and family, emotional, financial, moral and religious, and educational and vocational areas; but, in case of health and physical appearance, social and sex areas, the two groups differed significantly; (ii) the differences between the average reaction time scores of the adjusted and the maladjusted groups, both for critical and innocent words, were significant; (iii) in home and family area, the most frequent pattern of maladjustment was resentment and aggression against parents (more specifically against father) generally caused by the harsh, unsympathetic and strict disciplinarian attitude of fathers; (iv) in health and physical appearance area, maladjustment usually took the form of complex; (v) maladjustment in moral and religious area expressed itself in either of the two ways: (a) in the form of dissatisfaction and resentment against religion and morality, or (b) extreme religiosity and morality; and (vi) maladjustment related to educational and vocational area was usually expressed in the form of constant failures, dissatisfaction with studies, resentment against some teachers and these often led to strikes and other acts of indiscipline.

06 Harigopal, K., Self-disparity and personality factors among college students, Ph.D. Psychology, Andhra University, 1975.

The study attempted to find answers to the following questions: (i) What is the relationship between self-ideal-disparity (SID) and adjustment? (ii) What are the personality factors that significantly differentiates the high SID and low SID subjects? (iii) What are the typical personality profiles of high SID and low SID individuals?

The sample for the study consisted of 333 postgraduate students representative of arts and science faculties of Andhra and Osmania universities. The age range of these students was 19 to 34 years. There were 161 students from arts faculty and 171 from science faculty. The tools used in the study were: (i) The Osgood Semantic Differential Scales, (ii) essay to be written by subjects about what they thought about themselves, and (iii) The Cattell 16 P.F. Questionnaire.

The findings of the study were: (i) There was a significant relationship between SID and the personality factor of adjustment versus anxiety. (ii) The low SID subjects tended to have higher ego strength than the high SID subjects. The low SID subjects were emotionally more stable and mature than the high SID subjects. On the other hand, the high SID subjects because of low ego strength tended to be emotionally less stable, low in frustration tolerance, changeable and plastic, neurotically fatigued and of worrying disposition. (iii) SID was correlated linearly with ego strength. (iv) The low SID subjects tended to be high in character strength as measured by G factor. (v) SID was found to be related significantly in a negative direction to the personality factor—venturesome versus shy behaviour. (vi) SID was also negatively related with personality factor — shrewed versus artlessness. (vii) Guilt-responses as measured by the personality factor 'O' of 16 P.F. differentiated the high and low SID groups, with high SID groups scoring significantly higher than the low SID group. (viii) The low SID group was found to score significantly lower on factor O_2 indicating more of sociability and group dependence on their part than the high SID subjects. (ix) The self-concept control characterised the low SID group. (x) The low SID group tended to be more sedate, relaxed, composed and low in ergic tension as compared to high SD group. (xi) The low SID group presented the picture of socially outgoing, uninhibited individuals who were good in maintaining interpersonal contacts. The high SID subjects on the other hand were shy and inhibited in interpersonal contacts. (xii) The high SID group tended to be high in general emotionality and frustrated. The low SID group on the other hand was enterprising, decisive and having a resilent personality. (xiii) The high SID group scored higher on the factor of neuroticism then the low SID group. (xiv) The low SID group was found to be emotionally mature, stable and calm with adequate control over emotions and general behaviour. The high SID group on the other hand did not have control over emotions and was easily affected by the feelings that upset them.

07 Harmeet, K., A psychometric study of motivation of college and university students of Chandigarh, Ph.D. Psychology, Patna University, 1984.

The objective of the study was to test the following hypotheses: (i) the Indian students are higher on extraversion, social desirability, achievement motivation but lower on manifest anxiety and neuroticism. (ii) The female students are higher on neuroticism, anxiety, achievement motivation and realistic motivation in comparison to male students. (iii) On the whole male students score high on extraversion but low on neuroticism, manifest anxiety, achievement motivation and realistic motivation. (4) The science students are low on extraversion but high on neuroticism, anxiety, realistic motivation in comparison to arts students.

The sample of the study consisted of 773 students of Punjab University belonging to various categories as 163 university male arts group, fifty-three university male science group, forty-five university female science group, 160 university female arts group, fifty-two college male science group, fifty-one college male arts group, eighty-one college female science group, fifty-four college female arts group, fifty-four foreign male group and fifty-six foreign female group. These sample subjects were administered following tools: (i) The Eysenck Personality Inventory (1964). (ii) The Taylor Manifest Anxiety Scale (1953), (iii) The Lynn Achievement Motivation Test (1969), (iv) The Cattell 16 PF (1970), (v) The Spautz Realistic Employee Motivation Questionnaire.

The findings of the study were: (1) The Indian students in general scored lower on neuroticism and manifest anxiety than their foreign counterparts. (2) The foreign female students scored higher on neuroticism, achievement motivation and realistic motivation but lower on anxiety in comparison to foreign male students. (3) Indian male students scored higher on extraversion than female students. (4) Indian male students scored lower on neuroticism, manifest anxiety and achievement motivation than female students. (5) University male science group and college female science group were higher on extraversion in comparison to their counterparts in arts group. But university female science group and college male science group were lower on extraversion than their arts group counterparts. (6) Science students scored lower on neuroticism, anxiety and realistic motivation in comparison to arts students. (7) The cluster analysis of all the ten groups and all the eight variables showed that motivation of all the ten groups as different since no cluster was formed, however, there was clustering of different groups on different measures of motivation indicating some commonality as well as differences of motivational patterns in the students.

08 Hussain, M.O. A study of academic attainment in relation to level of aspiration and anxiety. Aligarh Muslim University, 1977.

The major aim of the investigation was to study the academic attainment of university students in relation to the level of aspiration and anxiety.

The sample comprised forty-five students of the undergraduate and pre-university classes of Aligarh Muslim University. Those students who fell within the top and bottom ten per cent of the distribution of scores on Mohsin's Intelligence Test were eliminated. The tools used were the L.A. Coding test by Ansari and Ansari and Sinha's Anxiety Scale. For measuring of academic achievement, the aggregate marks obtained by the students in their semester examinations, held after the administration of the other tests, were used. In order to study the effect of anxiety and level of aspiration and their interaction on academic performance a 3 X 3 factorial design of analysis of variance was employed.

The major findings of the investigation were: (i) The academic performance of the group with moderate anxiety was significantly better than that of both the high and the low anxiety groups. Anxiety bore a curvilinear relationship with academic achievement. (ii) The effect of the level of aspiration on the academic performance was also of the same nature as obtained in the case of anxiety. The academic performance of the group showing moderate goal discrepancy was better than that of the groups showing either higher or low goal discrepancy, implying a curvilinear relationship between the level of aspiration and academic performance. (iii) High anxiety had adverse effect on academic performance. Low anxiety also showed a lack of drive and motivation in the students. (iv) High and low aspiration showed unrealistic and defensive attitude resulting in low achievement. (v) Interaction between anxiety and aspiration did not exercise any significant effect on the academic performance.

09 Jain, K., Personality Studies of adolescent girls with specific reference to the students in the girls' colleges of Allahabad. Ph.D. Edu., Allahabad University, 1954.

The aim of the study was to explore and see the structure of the personality of the adolescent girls and to devise ways and means for its harmonious development.

One hundred girls in the age group 13 to 18 years studying in a girls' college in Allahabad were selected. The Rorschach Ink Blot Test and the Thematic Apperception Test were administered to these girls. Investigator's personal observations of behaviour in many and varied situations were also take into account.

The study revealed that an average adolescent girl had indulged in day dreaming about herself and there was more fantasy in her life than the capacity for abstract thought. She was an introvert type. She had a capacity of forming good emotional ties. She was perseverant and her reasoning was good. She had confidence in her own judgement. Socially she was well adjusted. She was ambivalent towards her mother. On the whole, sixtynine per cent of the total sample was found to be introvert type, eight per cent extrovert type and three percent ambivalent. There were seventynine per cent of girls in whom fantasy life was more than the amount of abstract thinking. Aggression widely prevailed among adolescent girls. Hero worship also existed among adolescent girls.

10 Jaiswal, K., A Study of anxiety, frustration and adjustment patterns of girl students at graduation level and their education implication, Ph.D. Education, Gorakhpur University, 1980.

The hypotheses tested in the study were: (i) There was difference in adjustment, frustration and educational attainment of girl students of high and lower anxiety level. (ii) There was difference in anxiety, adjustment and educational achievement of highly frustrated and least frustrated girl students. (iii) There was difference in anxiety, frustration and educational achievement of well-adjusted and maladjusted girl students. (iv) There was difference in anxiety, frustration and adjustment of married and unmarried girl students at the graduation level.

Five hundred girl students (464 of literary group and 36 of science group) were selected by the stratified random sampling technique from ten institutions of five districts of Eastern U.P. Statistical techniques used in the study were mean, standard deviation, percentile, correlate and critical ratio.

Important findings of the study were: (i) The educational achievement of low anxiety group of students was highest. (ii) There was no significant relationship between frustration level and educational achievement. (iii) There was a significant relationship between adjustment and anxiety, and frustration. However, there was no significant difference in the achievement of well-adjusted and maladjusted students. (iv) Science students had more anxiety and more adjustment ability. (v) There was no significant relationship between marital status of girl students, on the one hand, and anxiety, frustration and adjustment, on the other.

11 Jindal, C.R., A comparative study of some personality variables and affective reactions toward examinations of superior and failing college students, Ph.D. Education, Kurukshetra University, 1976.

The study had an objective to compare the superior and failing students on five personality variables, viz., (i) test anxiety, (ii) achievement orientation, (iii) intellectual achievement, (iv) socio-economic status, and (v) intelligence, along with affective reactions toward their final examination.

The sample of the study constituted 400 college students from the State of Haryana who either received fiftyfive per cent and more marks, or failed in their previous examinations. The tools used were: (i) the Mandler and Sarasoa Test Anxiety Scale, (ii) the Mahrabian Achievement Orientation Scale, (iii) the Grandall Intellectual Achievement Responsibility Scale, (iv) the Jalota General Mental Ability Test, and (v) the Jalota Socio-Economic Scale. The statistical techniques used were test and product-moment correlation.

The findings of the study were: (i) successful students were higher in achievement orientation and lower in test anxiety than failing students; (ii) successful students were more likely to attribute their success to their own. Than failing students; (iii) successful males were lower in test anxiety and higher in achievement orientation than failing males; (iv) successful females were higher in test anxiety and lower in achievement orientation than successful males; and (v) socio-economic status had a positive correlation with intelligence except in successful males and failing females.

12 Kumar, P., Cognitive styles of the postgraduates students in different streams of university education, Ph.D. Psy., DHSGVV, 1984.

The study was designed to ascertain the relationship of three cognitive style variables i.e. field dependence/independence, dogmatism and integrative complexity to curricular choices and achievement in four streams (sciences, social sciences, commerce and languages) of academic concentration.

The sample of the study consisted of 266 postgraduate students studying in the final years of different academic streams of the postgraduate departments of Sagar University. Of these, seventy-seven were from sciences, seventy-one from social sciences, forty-eight from languages and seventy from commerce. The data were collected by employing the Embedded Figures Test (EFT) which was a modification of figures selected from those used by Gottschaldt, Dogmatism Scale adapted in Hindi by Hasan and the Interpersonal Topical Inventory (ITI) developed by Tuckman. The product-moment coefficient of correlation, mean, t-values and ANOVA were used to analyse the data and draw conclusions.

The findings of the study were: (1) The students in science were significantly more field independent followed by commerce and social sciences. The subjects majoring in languages were most field dependent in comparison to other educational streams. The mean EFT scores of the students majoring in social sciences and commerce and social sciences and languages were not found significantly different. (2) Field dependence/independence dimension showed little relationship to overall examination performance. The results indicated that the subject's dependence/independence was not significantly related with performance in mathematics and science, while it was negatively and significantly related with performance in social science, languages and commerce. (3) No significant difference was observed in the degree of dogmatism held by subjects in various educational streams. This indicated that open or closed mindedness was not related to performance in major subjects. Out of four streams of education, significantly negative relationship was observed in social science majors which showed that students with a low degree of dogmatism performed better in the examinations using essay type tests. (4) Social science students were significantly more conceptually abstract than science students. Students of commerce were also more abstract than science students. Social science and commerce students did not differ in their level of integrative complexity. (5) Cognitively abstract students did better than cognitively concrete students in social sciences and commerce. (6) Students of social sciences and commerce were more cognitively abstract on the ITI measures than the science students and the students with cognitively abstract personality style did better than cognitively concrete students in commerce and social sciences. (7) The inter-relationship among three indices of cognitive style i.e. field dependence/field independence, dogmatism and integrative complexity was found insignificant except for the fact that highly dogmatic students were found field dependent and cognitively less differentiated or concrete in the area of interpersonal conceptual complexity. These three cognitive styles were therefore found to tap different aspects of personality proving their independent existence and relevance for curricular choice and achievement behaviour.

13 Malik, R.K., A study of self-disclosure, self-acceptance, and anxiety among college students, Ph.D. Psy., Agra University, 1978.

The objectives were (i) to investigate the degree of self-disclosure, self-acceptance and anxiety among college students, (ii) to investigate relationship between self-disclosure, self-acceptance and anxiety, (iii) to find out as to what factor had been largely related to self-disclosure, (iv) to trace the effect of educational level on self-disclosure and self-acceptance among college students, (v) to trace out the effect of sex on self-disclosure and self-acceptance among college students. The hypotheses were: (1) Self-disclosure and self-acceptance are measures of adjustment; hence they are positively related. (2) Self-disclosure has no significant relationship with anxiety. (3) Self-acceptance has no significant relationship with anxiety. (4) Sex has not significant relationship with self-disclosure as well as self-acceptance. (5) Education has no significant relationship with self-disclosure as well as self-acceptance.

The sample of 300 college students was selected from Agra University affiliated colleges by stratified random sampling technique. Of thee 200 were males and 100 females. They belonged to undergraduate as well as postgraduate classes. The self-disclosure was measured with the help of Green's Sentence Completion Blank while self-acceptance was measured with the help of Q-Sort Measuring Device also developed by Green. Sinha's Comprehensive Anxiety Test was used to measure anxiety of college students. The data were analysed with the help of correlation and chi-square techniques.

The findings were: (1) The self-disclosure and self-acceptance were positively correlated for undergraduate girls, postgraduate boys and postgraduate girls. These two variables were uncorrelated for undergraduate boys. (2) Self-disclosure had no significant relationship with anxiety, while self-acceptance had negative relationship with anxiety among college students. (3) Sex played significant role in self-disclosure. Girls tended to disclose more at both undergraduate and postgraduate levels. (4) Sex played important role in self-acceptance. Girls tended to be more self-accepting than boys at undergraduate level. (5) Education played significant role in self-disclosure only in boys. The undergraduate boys tended to be more self-disclosing than postgraduate boys. (6) Education played significant role in self-acceptance for both boys and girls at college level. The undergraduate girls tended to be more self-accepting than postgraduate boys.

14 Mathew, V.G., Personality patterns of college students specialising in different fields, Ph.D. Psy., Kerala University, 1971.

The aim of the present study was to find but whether there were significant differences in values, temperament and vocational interests among college students specialising in different fields (science, humanities, engineering, commerce, medicine, education, law, agriculture and veterinary). Only four groups (science, humanities, medicine and education) were considered in the case of women, as their numbers in the other groups were very small.

In the first phase of the study, three personality inventories were developed. AVL Study of Values and the Guilford-Zimmerman Temperament Survey were adapted to suit conditions present in Kerala. A new vocational interest inventory was developed along lines similar in certain respects to the Kuder Preference Record. The trial forms of the three tests were administered to about 370 college students and item analysis for internal consistency was undertaken. The reliability of scales was found by using the odd-even method. An attempt was made to validate tests by seeing how they differentiated certain groups and also by correlating with scores on other available tests. T score norms were found by using representative samples of students. The tests were administered to a minimum of 30 men from each of the nine groups and 30 women from each of the four groups. An analysis of variance was done for each of the 23 traits to see whether the nine groups of men differed in the traits concerned. A similar analysis was done for each scale in the case of women also. For men, F ratio was significant for all the six values, nine out of the ten traits of temperament and all the seven vocational interest scales. For women, F ration was significant for three value traits, two traits of temperament and all vocational interest scales. In the case of each scale, for men and women separately, the relative positions of the different groups of students were examined. Then in the case of each group of students, the personality pattern obtained on the 23 traits was delineated graphically and the results were discussed. Lastly, the differences between men and women in each scale were tested for significance in the case of the representative men and women student groups and for the four fields of study having both sexes. Many significant differences were obtained and they were in line with logical expectations.

The conclusion is that significant differences in values, temperament and vocational interests exist among college students specialising in different fields in Kerala.

15 Narinderbal, K., A study of certain personality and demographic correlates of sex role attitudes among college female students, Ph.D. Psy., Patna University, 1981.

The objectives of the study were (i) to find out differences between college girls having traditional sex role attitudes and those having self-oriented sex role attitudes on the variables-achievement motivation, ego strength, locus of control, conservatism/radicalism, anxiety, and attitude towards married working women, and (ii) to find out difference between self-oriented and 'other oriented' with respect to demographic variables, parents' education, parents occupation, socio-economic status, type of family structure and position in the family.

The sample of the study consisted of 498 TDC (Three-Year Degree Course), part II and III female students from the colleges of union territory of Chandigarh and Punjab state. Their age range was 16 to 22 years. They were administered the following tools: (i) The Fand's Inventory, (ii) The Qamar Hasan's Ego Strength Scale, (iii) The Sinha Anxiety Scale, (iv) Vasudeva Scale to measure attitude towards working married women, (v) The Singh Socio-Economic Status Scale, and (vi) a personal data sheet. These tools helped in measuring sex role attitude, achievement motivation, internal-external locus of control, ego strength, anxiety, conservation/radicalism, attitude towards married working women, socio-economic status, and demographic variables respectively.

The findings of the study were: (1) The more conservative the female students, the more they were traditional in sex role attitude. (2) The correlation between sex role attitude, and anxiety was significant. (3) The females scoring high on ego strength were high on non-traditional sex role attitudes. (4) The females having 'other oriented' sex role attitude tended to have negative attitude towards married women taking up jobs. (5) Subjects having high need for achievement were more self-oriented in sex role attitude. (6) The females with self-oriented attitudes tended to have mother with higher educational attainment. (7) Females having career mothers were more self oriented in their sex role attitude as compared to females whose mothers were housewives. (8) The relationship of father's education and occupation with sex role attitude of females was not significant. (9) Females belonging to joint family structure were more traditional or 'other oriented' in their sex role attitude. (10) The position of females in the family, that is, ordinal position had no impact on sex role attitude. (11) Socio-economic status of females and their sex role attitude were not significantly related. (12) The intention of females for higher education had nothing to do with their sex role attitudes. (13) Females who intended to become housewives were more 'other oriented' in their sex role attitude.

16 Nindrulehal, A study of certain personality and demographic correlates of sex role attitudes amongst college female students, Ph.D., Psy., Panjab University, 1981.

The major hypotheses of the study were: (i) There would be a positive correlation between self-oriented sex-role attitudes and radicalism, sex-role attitudes and internal locus of control, and with achievement motivation. (ii) There would be a negative correlation between other-oriented sex-role attitudes and attitude towards married women taking up jobs. (iii) There would be a significant difference between the sex-role attitudes of subjects having working mothers and subjects with non-working mothers. (iv) A significant relationship was there between subjects' sex-role attitudes and mothers' educational level. (v) Sex role attitudes would be significantly related to the socio-economic class.

The sample for the study comprised 498 T.D.C. Parts II and III female students between the age-range of 16 to 22, selected through stratified random sampling technique, from four women colleges (two of Chandigarh, one of Amritsar and one of Patiala). The study investigated the relationship between sex-role attitudes and certain personality and demographic variables. The tools used for collecting data were Fand's Sex-role Inventory, F.T.I. (French Test of Insight) developed by French, the Internal-External Control Inventory (Revised form of Liverant's Scale), Qamar Hasan's Ego-Strength Scale, Sinha's Anxiety Scale, Vasudeva's Conservatism/Radicalism, Scale, a scale to measure attitude towards working married women by Vasudeva, G.J. Singh's S.E.S. Scale, and a personal data sheet to measure sex-role attitudes, achievement motivation, internal-external locus of control, ego strength, anxiety, etc. Statistical techniques used for analaysing the data were coefficient of correlation, and analaysis of variance.

The main findings of the study were: (i) More conservative females tended to be more traditional in sex-role attitudes. (ii) The more other-oriented a woman was in her sex-role attitudes, the more anxious she was likely to be. (iii) More traditional attitudes in sex-role led to higher external locus of control. (iv) Females scoring high on ego-strength tended to be high on the non-traditional sex-role attitudes. (v) Those having the other-oriented sex-role attitudes tended to have negative attitude towards married women taking up jobs. (vi) Females high on need achievement were found to be more self-oriented in sex-role attitudes. (vii) Females having career mothers and mothers with higher educational attainment were significantly more self-oriented in their sex-role attitudes and *vice versa.* (viii) The relationship between father's education and occupation with sex-role attitudes was not found to be significant. (ix) Females belonging to joint family structure were found to be more traditional or other-oriented in their sex-role attitudes. (x) The position of females in the family had on impact on the sex-role attitudes. (xi) Significant relationship were not found between the SES of the females and their intentions for higher education and their sex-role attitudes. (xii) There was no impact of who decided for the education on the sex-role attitudes of the individual for whom the decision was made. (xiii) Females who intended to become housewives were more traditional or other-oriented in their attitudes on the sex-role. (xiv) The sex-role attitudes of females were closely related to their personality and environment.

17 Pal, S.K., and Saxena, P.C., The problems of over, under, and normal achieving college students, Deptt. of Edu., Allahabad University, 1970 (NCERT financed).

The investigation was undertaken with the purpose of empirically determining the extent, range and nature of problems of over, under the normal-achieving students and to know the degree to which these problems press upon the different groups of achievers to help or retard their academic performance. It also sought to probe into the study habits, self-concept, attitudes, interests and future vocational plans of overs, unders and normals. The hypotheses examined were: (i) the underachievers are troubled with larger number of problems as compared to overs and normals; (ii) the underachievers tend to indicate more problems in the areas of finance and adjustment to college work; (iii) the underachievers are concerned more with outdoor games as compared to others; (iv) the overachievers have better study habits; they devote more hours to study and possess positive attitudes towards school, peers, teachers and education; (v) problems of the under, over and normal-achieving students differ from curriculum to curriculum and (vi) the unders, overs and normals, from university and associated colleges are alike with respect to their problems, study habits, self-concept, study hours and attitudes.

The random sample consisted of 305 students from biology curriculum and 517 from mathematics curriculum of science faculties of Lucknow, Gorakh Pur. Allahabad universities and two affiliated colleges.

The three groups of over, under the normal achieving students were identified on the basis of the ability scores on the Joshi's Test of Mental Ability and the achievement scores (B.Sc. Part I marks). Those above average in ability and below average in achievement were regarded as the underachievers. The diagonally opposite categories represented the over-achievers. Those who had achievement commensurate with their mental ability were designated as normal achievers. Thus, 173 overachievers and 259 underachievers were identified. The rest were treated as normals. The three groups were matched for age, sex, caste, marital status, parental education, income and occupation. Personal data schedule, interview schedules for the under and over achievers and teachers, the Mooney's Problem Checklist (college form) and a Hindi Adaptation of the Brown and Holtzman's Survey of Study Habits and Attitudes were used.

The analysis revealed the following: (i) The underachievers had higher problem levels. They differed from curriculum to curriculum and were more interested in outdoor games. (ii) As regards the mathematics curriculum sample in universities, the underachievers showed more concern over finances, living conditions and employment than the others; they also had more problems in areas of adjustment to college work, the future vocational and educational plans, curriculum and teaching procedure as compared to the overachievers; they looked more for personal help from the teachers; they were also more inclined to be members of political parties; and study hours, attitudes and self-concept did not contribute to the underachievement of this group. (iii) As regards the biology curriculum sample, the three groups were alike in their problems. The underachievers identified numerically more problems in areas of finance, living conditions and employment and future vocational and educational plans; and study hours, study habits and self-concept did not influence underachievement. (iv) The underachievers showed more positive attitudes towards school, peers, teachers and studies. (v) The biology underachievers were less interested in botany and chemistry and their interests were in reading stories and playing outdoor games. (vi) As regards the mathematics and biology curricula in the associated colleges, there were few areas on which the under the overachievers from associated colleges had more problems as compared to the underachievers from the university. (vii) Their problems were concentrated in areas of health and physical development, finances living conditions and employment, social-psychological relations, home and family, morals and religion and the vocational and educational future. (viii) As regard the biology curriculum sample, the underachievers on associated colleges expressed more problems. (ix) The underachievers assigned underachievement to family's economic needs, defective college education overcrowding in classes, lack of motivation, parental disinterestedness and sociability. (x) Teachers thought underachievement was due to chance factors in examinations, weak background, nonacademic activities and financial difficulties. (xi) The overachievers in the mathematics curriculum of the three universities and fewer problems regarding finance, living conditions and employment, adjustment to college work, future vocational and educational plans, curriculum and teaching procedure as compared to the underachievers. (xii) The overachievers marked higher in problems of health and physical development and they possessed better study habits, study hours, attitudes towards school, teachers, peers and studies. (xiii) As compared to other groups, the biology overachievers of universities expressed numerically more problems in areas of social and recreational activities, home and family, adjustment to college work and curriculum and teaching procedure, and differed significantly from the other groups on the second and last areas; study did not help achievement; and more overachievers preferred teaching profession. (xiv) Comparing the overachievers of colleges and universities of the mathematics curriculum, the former appeared more concerned about health and physical development and differed significantly from the unders; and the overs from the associated colleges and better study habits and attitudes towards school, teachers, peers and studies. (xv) The overachievers in biology curriculum were more concerned with problems in the area of social and recreational activities, and differed significantly from the unders in health and physical development, but not as regards study habits, self-concept and attitudes towards school, teachers, studies and peers. (xvi) The overachievers attached importance to motivation and parental education. (xvii) The normal achievers of the mathematics curriculum of universities had problems in adjustment to college work; they put in more hours of study, had better study habits and possessed more positive attitudes towards studies, peers, school and teachers, but the self-concept made on difference; and their reading interest was high in detective stories and they participated more in social activities. In the biology curriculum, the normals put in less hours of work and possessed less positive attitude towards school, teachers, studies and peers, and they preferred professional colleges.

18 Pandey, L., *Leadership orientation among college students*, Ph.D. Psy., Magadh University, 1983.

The major objective of the study was to investigate the socio-psychological variables which were responsible for preferring a particular style of leadership. Twenthy-eight broad hypotheses were examined.

Field study approach was followed. Leadership Orientation Questionnaire was developed and Dore's Attitude towards Leadership Scale was adapted and used to measure dimensions of Leadership Orientation. Both Scales were standardised. Tripathi's Personal Preference Schedule and Sinha's Frustration Scale were also used. A sample of 673 college students (1st year to 4th year) of rural and urban areas with different socio-economic background was selected from Bhabua and Gaya by adopting incidental-purposive sampling technique.

The major findings were: (1) Age had no leadership orientation during college stage. Boys scored more on 'democratic and consideration oriented' and girls on 'responsibility oriented' leadership dimensions. (2) Lower SES students exhibited lower mean scores on democratic orientation than higher SES students. Higher caste and low socio-economic group students displayed lesser degree of democratic orientation than lower caste and higher and middle income group students respectively. (3) Atheists scored more on democratic and consideration oriented leadership dimension than theists. (4) Compared to rural, urban students scored higher on consideration oriented leadership dimension. (5) Highly leadership oriented students possessed higher degree of deference order, affiliation, intraception, succorance, dominance, abasement, nurturance, change, heterosexuality, impunitiveness, and impersistiveness as well as lower degree of achievement, exhibition, autonomy, endurance, aggression, extrapunitiveness, intropunitiveness, extrapersistiveness and intropersistiveness.

19 Parameswaran, E.G., Reddy, K.R. and Rao T.N., Aptitude of college students : A diagnostic study, Deptt. of Psy., Osmania University, 1968 (NCERT financed).

The objectives of the study were to find out (i) whether students in the science and engineering courses had the necessary aptitude; (ii) the extent to which the courses preferred by students agreed with the courses pursued by them; (iii) whether the actual courses pursued were in consonance with their aptitudes; (iv) whether students' educational and vocational preferences were related to their aptitudes and (v) and comparison between the performance of the Osmania University students with that of comparable American students.

The sample consisted of a group of engineering, arts, commerce and science students in the first year degree classes, young engineers working in engineering concerns, research scientists, research scholars and engineering and science students in the final year degree classes. The last four groups were included to find out the validity of the tests and the effects of the years spent in the course, on the test scrores. General intelligence and scientific and engineering aptitudes were measured by a combination of subtests from DAT and Engineering and Physical Science Aptitude Tests (EPSAT). Vocational interests were measured using a blank which was constructed on the basis of the Ministry of Labour and Employment's Vocational Interest checklist. An Educational Preference Schedule was constructed and administered to obtain information regarding student's aptitude for the course, other courses preferred and factors affecting the choice of a course. Means, standard deviations and percentiles were calculated for the different groups.

The comparisons revealed that (i) on the whole the first year engineering the science students were superior to the arts groups; (ii) the engineering group was significantly superior, indicating a higher degree of scholastic, scientific and engineering aptitudes; (iii) arts students performed very high on verbal and abstract reasoning; (iv) a few arts students' performance was superior to the average performance of the other two groups; (v) most of the students in the three groups, specially the engineering students, appeared to be interested in the subjects they were studying; (vi) more science students than arts students expressed a dislike for their subjects; (vii) on the whole, responses to vocational interests revealed patterns in line with courses of study for the engineering and science groups; (viii) a considerable degree of preference was expressed for jobs entirely unrelated to courses of study; and (ix) the American engineering students appeared considerably superior.

20 Patel, J.B., An investigation to study motives, concerns and fear of failure of ideationally conformist and deviant university students, Ph.D. Psy., Maharaja Sayajirao University of Baroda, 1982.

The specific objectives of the investigation were: (i) to develop a tool measuring conformity tendencies among university students, (ii) to study sex differences in ideational conformity among university students, (iii) to relate individual differences in ideational conformity to achievement motive, (iv) to relate individual differences in ideational conformity to affiliation motive, (v) to relate individual differences in ideational conformity to power motive, (vi) to study the concerns of ideationally conformist and deviant university students, and (vii) to relate individual differences in ideational conformity to the fear of failure.

The sample for the study consisted of 687 students including 356 males and 331 females studying in eight different faculties of the M.S. University of Baroda. For the measurement of conformity a situational types test was developed by the investigator. Test-retest reliability of the test was found to be 0.86. The motives of achievement, power, affiliation and the fear of failure were measured using Thematic Apperception Test of McClel-land as adapted by Prayag Mehta. Cantrill's Self-Anchoring Striving Scale was used to measure the concerns. The data were analysed by computing quartile deviations, product moment correlations, and t-ratio.

The major findings of the study were: (i) Students belonging to different faculties differed among themselves in respect of ideational conformity. (ii) Girls did not differ significantly from boys in their tendency to conform ideationally. (iii) Conformists and non-conformists did not differ significantly with respect to the need for achievement. (iv) Conformists and non-conformists differed significantly in their need for power and affiliation, and the fear of failure. Non-conformists scored higher on the need for affiliation and the fear of failure. (v) Conformity had significant negative correlation with the need for achievement and the need for power, and had significant positive correlation with the need for affiliation and the fear of failure. (vi) Conformists and non-conformists and similar concerns. They were more concerned about good married life, good jobs and good education.

21 Phutela, R.L., A study of some selected motivational factors in relation to academic achievement and socio-economic status among the college students in the states of Haryana and Punjab. Ph.D. Edu., Maharaja Sayajirao University of Baroda, 1976.

The major aim of the investigation was to study relationships among the selected motivational factors, keeping in view the factors causing variations in these relationships, i.e., sex, stream of course, socio-economic status and academic performance.

The sample consisted of students of fourteen colleges in all, from the States of Haryana and Punjab. Three colleges had semi-urban or rural background, six colleges had urban background and five colleges came from cities at district headquarters. The data were collected with the help of following tools: (i) the TAT test by Mehta (1969); (ii) the TAT test by Birney (1970); (iii) Questionnaires to assess Educational and Occupational Aspiration by Mathur (1969); (iv) Achievement Test by Patel (1971), and (v) the Kuppuswamy's Socio-Economic Status Scale, Form A, for urban students (1962). The data were analysed by employing the techniques of correlation, analysis of variance and t-test.

The findings concluded that need achievement and educational and vocational aspirations formed one group of the motivational variables, and fear of failure and achievement press formed another groups of the variables affecting academic achievement in their unique way. The former group was a significant predictor of academic achievement, while the latter group was not a significant determinant of it. The study of differences showed that the arts students had different motivational levels than the science students, more so, for the first group of motivational variables than the respect of second group of variables. These motivational levels were by the large independent of the differences in sex and academic achievement.

22 Ram, A.L., A study of cognitive complexity among college students as a function of their personality factors, Ph.D. Psy., Agra University, 1981.

The study aimed at investigating the relationship between cognitive complexity among the college students in five colleges affiliated to Agra University and certain background, personality factors and cognitive style.

Three major instruments were used in the study. To measure cognitive complexity Kelly's Role Construct Reportary Test was used. To measure personality factors the 16 PF Questionnaire, Form A (Hindi adaptation by Kapoor) was used. The sample of the investigation was 480 Agra University students enrolled in undergraduate and postgraduate classes. Out of these, 354 were males and 126 were females. The age range was 17 years to 26 years with the mean age of 22.5 years. After the pilot study, questionnaires and inventories were selected on the basis of feasibility of use in the final study. On the basis of median scores two groups were formed, namely, the high cognitive complexity (HCC) group and the low cognitive complexity (LCC) group. Correlation coefficients, chi-square test, t-test, analysis of variance, etc., were used to verify the hypotheses.

The major conclusions were: (i) Cognitive complexity was significantly related to and affected by some background variables like sex, discipline and college, cognitive style and various personality factors. (ii) There were differences in intercorrelation patterns between personality traits and cognitive complexity and cognitive style measures of the male and the female students in various disciplines. (iii) Inter-correlation pattern for the sampled respondents between eight background variables and cognitive complexity measures was different. Sex and discipline had significant positive correlation with cognitive complexity. (iv) The females had more cognitive complexity than the males. (v) The discipline of the respondents was a significant correlate of cognitive complexity. There were differences in the cognitive complexity levels among five different disciplines of students. The respondents of science and home science had more cognitive complex structure than those of the arts, agriculture and commerce. (vi) Among cognitive style categories of students, conceptual dominance and weak automization type of cognitive style had significant positive correlation with cognitive complexity. The students with conceptual dominance and weak automization groups of cognitive style were having more cognitively complex structure. (vii) Among sixteen different personality traits, shy vs. venturesome had a significant negative relationship with perceptual motor dominance and strong automization category of cognitive styles. They had weaker super-ego strength. (viii) Group dependent vs. self-sufficient had a significant positive relationship with cognitive complexity. The remaining personality factors had no significant relationship with cognitive complexity. (ix) There was significant difference between the cognitive complexity and cognitive style patterns of the male and the female students. (x) Students of different faculties had different types of cognitive styles; the arts, commerce, science discipline students had cognitive style of perceptual motor dominance type. Agriculture students had conceptual dominance cognitive style. (xi) There were significant differences between cognitive complexity and cognitive styles of different discipline students. The arts students significantly differed in relation to perceptual motor dominance vs. conceptual dominance and strong and weak automization type of cognitive style from the students of other disciplines. (xii) There seemed to be significant difference between the levels of cognitive complexity (high and low) and personality traits of reserved vs outgoing, sober vs happy-go-lucky, group dependent vs self-sufficient and relaxed vs tense. (xiii) The high cognitive complexity (HCC) and the low cognitive complexity (LCC) groups of female respondents were significantly different on the levels on cognitive complexity and personality factors, emotionally less stable vs emotionally stable, shy vs venturesome, forthright vs shrewd and conservative vs experimenting. (xiv) The mean differences between the scores of sixteen personality tests for factors reserved vs outgoing, expedient vs conscientious, conservative vs experimenting and indisciplined vs controlled of the male and the female respondents were significant. The remaining factors were not significant. (xv) Out of sixteen personality factors, eight, namely, reserved vs outgoing, less intelligent vs more intelligent, expedient vs conscientious, practical vs imaginative, placid vs apprehensive, conservative vs experimenting and relaxed vs tense, differed significantly with reference to the disciplines of the respondents. The remaining eight personality factors did not differ significantly. (xvi) Significant relationship between the college and the cognitive complexity level of the respondents was found. The college of the student was significant correlate of cognitive compledity. (xvii) The age of the students did not affect the cognitive complexity. (xviii) No difference existed between the undergraduates and the postgraduate students with regard to the high and low level of cognitive complexity. (xix) Urban and rural background and caste had no effect on the cognitive complexity of the students.

23 Salunke, R.B., A study of the home environment, socio-economic status and economic management in relation to the academic achievement of the first year college students of M.S. University, Baroda. Ph.D. Edu., Maharaja Sayajirao University of Baroda, 1979.

The main objectives of the investigation were: (i) to study home environment, educational climate in the home, emotional climate in the home, socio-economic status, economic management, with academic achievement of the first year college students of the M.S. University, Baroda, (ii) to find out the relationship of home environment, socio-economic status and economic management and academic achievement, and (iii) to find out the differences in home environment, socio-economic status and economic management of students of different faculties, sex and age.

The sample for the study consisted of 693 students of the first year from four faculties of the M.S. University of Baroda, viz., science, commerce, arts and home science. Data were collected by personally administering the questionnaire to the students. The questionnaire was in three sections – Section I was the socio-economic status scale which was a modified version of the original Kuppuswamy SES scale, Sections II and III were home environment questionnaire and economic management questionnaire, respectively, developed by the investigator. Data regarding academic achievement were obtained from the official records. Data were analysed employing the statistical techniques such as mean, standard deviation, t-test and coefficient of correlation.

The major findings of the study were: (i) The academic achievement of the students was related to their home environment. (ii) Educational climate and emotional climate were related with academic achievement. (iii) Educational facilities and emotional happiness in the home contributed positively to the academic achievement of the students. (iv) Socio-economic status was not related with academic achievement whereas economic management was related with academic achievement. (v) The socio-economic status, home environment and economic management of the students of different faculties differed. (vi) The students of home science and science faculties belonged to higher socio-economic status and the students of home science faculty were better in economic management. (vii) The male and the female students differed so far as their home environment was concerned but they did not differ with regard to their socio-economic status and economic management. (viii) Home environment and economic management had no relationship with different age groups whereas socio-economic status had relationship with age groups.

24 Sathappan, S., A study of the relationships of scientific productivity of college teachers to their professional attitudes, perceived organisational characteristics, manifest needs and anxiety, Ph.D. Psy., Karnataka University, 1984.

Differentiating the term productivity form creativity as performance judged in the context of organisational norms and expectations as done in the industrial context which gave the term productivity to science, it was suggested that the performance of scientists was to be 'rated in the normative manner against institutional expectations and yardsticks rather than as unique products'. Scientific productivity was then defined to include participation in research and discussion, production of research publications, participation in research competition and finally winning of awards. The study set the following hypotheses regarding relationship of productivity with other variables among college teachers: (1) The productive and non-productive groups differ significantly in their attitudes towards their profession. (2) The productive and non-productive groups differ significantly in their perceptions of organisational characteristics. (3) The productive and non-productive groups differ in their motivational need patterns particularly with reference to the following needs, achievement, order, autonomy, affiliation, dominance, change, endurance, aggression and level of anxiety. (4) These characteristics interact with each other and distinct clusters would emerge differentiating the two groups. (5) Difference can emerge among the different categories of teachers like medical, engineering, science, humanities, etc.

The sample consisted of 160 college teachers drawn from medical, engineering, science and arts faculties of various colleges in Madras city. Using a ten point scale of scientific productivity constructed for the purpose, the college teachers were classified as productive (n=63) and non-productive (n=97). A scale of attitude towards profession (with reliability coefficient of 0.498 and validity coefficient of 0.89) was developed. Indiresan's Organisational Atmosphere Scale, Edwards Personal Preference Scale, and IPAT Anxiety Scale were the other tools employed. The tools were administered individually to 160 subjects comprising the sample. They types of analysis employed included analysis of mean differences through t-tests, correlation analysis, multiple regression analysis and cluster analysis.

The major findings were: (1) In general and level of scientific productivity of college teachers appeared to be rather low. (2) The productive and non-productive groups did not differ on variables like professional attitudes and perceived organisational characteristics. They differed only in the need achievement with the former standing significantly higher. They did not differ on the level of anxiety. (3) Multiple regression analysis indicated that while need achievement was the only differentiating independent factor, the other variables in combination with need achievement appeared to be significantly related to scientific productivity. (4) The four subject groups had significant multiple regression coefficients with different clusters of factors.

25 Sathyagirirajan, S., Competency, personality, motivation and profession perception of college teachers, Ph.D. Edu., Madurai Kamaraj University, 1985.

The main objective of the study was to find out the extent of relationship between competency of college teachers and their personality, motivation and profession perception.

A Teacher Competency Rating Scale developed by the investigator based on Stanford Teacher Competency Appraisal and Teacher Rating Scale of San Jose College, a Self Actualising Person Inventory structured by the investigator, Cattell's 16PF Questionnaire, Tuckman Teacher Feedback Form and Patted's Teaching Profession Perception Scale were used to collect the required data from a stratified random sample of 300 college teachers in Madurai Kamaraj University area. Hypotheses regarding the relationship between the selected variables and difference between more competent and less competent college teachers with reference to the variables were formulated and examined. Regression analysis was done using the selected variables that correlated significantly with the criterion variable, namely, teacher competency.

The main findings were: (1) Teacher competency was significantly related to intelligence, emotional stability, conscientiousness, tendermindedness, trusted nature, placid nature, self-sufficiency and relaxedness factors of Cattell's 16PF Questionnaire. (2) It was significantly related to creativity, dynamism, organised demeanours and warmth and acceptance, self-actualisation and profession perception of teachers. (3) The more competent teachers significantly differed from the less competent teachers in all the above variables. (4) Those variables that correlated significantly with teacher competence, inter-correlated with one another significantly.

26 Sharan, M.B., A study of role conflict and its influence on role performance. Ph.D. Psy., Patna University, 1974.

The study was designed to understand role conception, role demands, personality and role performance of the college students. Some of the hypotheses tested were: (i) students' role conception would differ significantly from their parents' expectation; (ii) students' role conception would be similar to their friends' expectation, (iii) there would be positive correlation between parents' and teachers' expectations on students' role; (iv) students' role performance would be significantly lower than their role conception; (v) there would be one to one correspondence between self-concept and self satisfaction; (vi) the role performance of high role conflict group would be lower than that of low role conflict group; and (vii) the self-concept of high role conflict group would be lower than that of low role conflict group.

The study was designed on the line of role theory. Nine independent inventories, forms and schedules, namely, SRC Inventory, PESR Inventory, TESR, FESR, SRP Inventory, PIS, ISC Inventory, SC and SS Inventory were developed in order to measure different aspects of role performance in order to measure different a sample of 500 students (385 males and 115 females) of Bhagalpur University.

The important findings were: (i) male and female students differed significantly on five variables out of nine studied; (ii) the difference between students' role conception and parents' and teachers' expectations on students' role was not significant; (iii) there was a wide gap between students' role conception and their friends' expectations on students' role; (iv) there was positive correlation between teachers' and parents' expectations; (v) there was a wide gap between role conception and role performance of college students; (vi) there was a significant gap between ideal self concept and self concept of the college students; (vii) the relationship for one to one correspondence between self-concept and self-satisfaction was very high in both the samples of males and females; (viii) although the influence of role conflict depended upon the nature of role conflict, the conflicting expectations and definite influence upon their role performance, and (ix) the influence of perception of irregularities in society (as an index of role conflict) was not clear either upon personality or role performance of the students.

27 Sharma, S., Some personality characteristics of female college students of different socio-economic backgrounds, Ph.D. Psy., Patna University, 1975.

The present investigation attempted to study the relationship between socio-economic status and personality characteristics, values, and intelligence of female college students.

The sample for the study consisted of 300 randomly selected female students of Magadha Mahila College, Patna. The study used the Guilford Zimmerman Temperament Survey for measuring personality characteristics, the Allport-Vernon Scale for measuring values, and the Standard Progressive Matrices for measuring intelligence. A personal data blank was used, and a socio-economic scale was also constructed for data collection. The odd-even and test-retest reliabilities of the SES scale were found to be 0.94 and 0.97 respectively. Data were analysed by employing product moment correlation, t-test, and chi-square test.

The major findings of the study were as follows: (i) Significant and positive relationship was found between SES on one hand and ability, sociability and political valuation on the other. (ii) The relationship between SES, and thoughtfulness and emotional stability was found to be positive. (iii) Significant differences were found among different social classes in respect of expressed interest, cocurricular activities, expectations, importance attached to academic achievement, fatalistic ideas about success, and liking for the system of government. (iv) The social classes studied were not found to differ significantly in respect of leisure time activities, goal, self-concept of academic ability, cooperativeness and leadership role. (v) General activity, restraint, ascendence, objectivity, friendliness, personal relations, and different categories of values (theoretical, economic, aesthetic, social and religious) were not found to be related to SES.

28 Singh, G., A Study of the college environment and student's personality in medical education, Ph.D. Psy., Delhi University, 1975.

The objectives of the study were: (i) to find out the difference in the nature of perceived environment for learning in the medical colleges of all-India and regional characters; (ii) to find out the socio-economic background of the medical students and the patterns of change that might have taken place during the last few years; (iii) to study the changes in attitudes, values and achievement motivation of the medical students during the college years; (iv) to study the nature and change in anxiety and problems faced by the medical students during their academic life; and (v) to find out the nature of interaction between personality variables and college characteristics and to identify the predictive personality variables related to existing environment's in medical colleges.

The study included five medical colleges in three states of northern India. A random 'cross section' sample of 505 medical students and internee doctors was selected. The tools employed for the study were: (i) the CCQ scale; (ii) the Socio-Economic Status scale; (iii) the Allport — Vernon-Lindzey Study of Values; (iv) the McClelland's n-Achievement Test; (v) the Cattell's IPAT Anxiety Scale; and (vi) the Mooney Problem Checklist.

The significant findings of the investigation were: (i) the medical colleges of all-India character provided comparatively better learning environment than the colleges of regional character; (ii) the students of colleges of all-India character, in general, belonged to higher socio-economic background compared to their counterparts in regional colleges; (iii) medical students suffered from moderate degree of anxiety particularly of suspiciousness generated type; (iv) theoretical and social values were found to be the most dominant and religious values the least dominant in the prevailing value system; (v) a higher level of achievement motivation was found among the students of colleges of all-India character compared to students of regional colleges; (vi) high degrees of anxiety and worries about academic and nonacademic activities was a common characteristic of the medical students; and (vii) low proprietary characteristic of college environment tended to give rise to problems among medical students regarding social and psychological relations, personal and psychological relations, courtship, sex and marriage, home and family, adjustment to college work, and vocational and educational prospects in future.

29 Singh, R.S., Personality variables (traits and needs) and demographic correlates (sex, area and socio-economic states) of anxiety level among college students. Ph.D. Psy., Agra University, 1980.

The investigation attempted to analyse anxiety in relation to other traits and needs of the individuals as well as certain demographic factors. The objectives were: (i) to study the behavioural disposition which causes individual difference in the tendency to perceive a wide range of stimulus situations as dangerous or threatening and to respond to these with anxiety state reaction, and (ii) to study the relationship between anxiety and related antecedent demographic factors. The following hypotheses were formulated: (i) There will be consistent relationship, positive or negative, between anxiety and different psychogenic needs and the high, medium and low anxiety groups will show significant differences with respect to these needs (ii) There will be consistent personality traits. Furthermore, the high, medium and low anxiety groups will differ significantly with respect to these personality dimensions. (iii) There will be significant sex differences in anxiety and the direction of these differences will depend upon the interaction of sex with other demographic variables. (iv) Urban college students will be more conscious than rural college students and these differences will, at least in part, be determined by the interactions of area with other population variables. (v) There will be an inverse relationship between anxiety and socio-economic status and the relationship will depend upon the interaction SES with area and sex.

The study was conducted on two samples of 180 male college students from Gorakhpur (for personality correlates) and of 360 subjects for demographic variables. A 2×2×3 factorial design was used. The tools used were Comprehensive Anxiety Test (Sinha), 16 PF Questionnaire, Personal Preference Schedule (Tripathi), SES Scale, Forms A and B (Kulshrestha). The researcher used means, standard deviations, coefficient of correlation, Duncan's range test, analysis of variance and appropriate graphical methods to analyse the data.

The findings were: (i) Anxiety was positively related with ergic tension. (ii) The correlation between anxiety and ego-strength, as well as anxiety and temperamental threctia was negative. (iii) There was no relation between anxiety and intelligence. (iv) There was significant positive correlation between anxiety and need abasement and anxiety and nurturance. (v) There was negative relationship between anxiety and n-difference and anxiety and n-endurance. (vi) Anxiety has low negative correlation with need achievement. (vii) The correlation between anxiety and n-affiliation showed that the two were unrelated. (viii) None of the three demographic variables, i.e., sex, area, and SES, alone has any effect on anxiety. (ix) The interaction between sex and area played a significant role in the development of anxiety. (x) Socio-economic status differences resulted in difference in the anxiety level of the middle class and the lower class boys, the former having more anxieties.

30 Sinha, A.K. and Bhan, R.N. Mental health of university students. Deptt. of Phil., Kurukshetra University, 1978 (ICSSR financed).

The main objective of the research was to assess the mental health of university students and to find out its psycho-social dynamics.

The sample consisted of 259 male and 118 female students of Kurukshetra University and 293 male engineering students. The students were administered the Mas-low Security-Insecurity Inventory. On the basis of their scores, the students were divided into two groups; those who were below third decile were labelled as insecure and those who were above the seventh decile were taken as secure. These two extreme groups were administered the Thematic Apperception Test and the Crown and Crisp Middlesex Hospital Questionnaire. After the administration of the tests the sample subjects were interviewed through a structured interview schedule regarding the family background, socio-cultural background, inter-personal relations, mode of expenses, involvement in the problems of sex, interest in academic problems, aspiration level and vocational preferences and life view. The data so collected were analysed with the help of t-test.

The findings of the study were: (i) The engineering boys were significantly superior in mental health to the university boys. (ii) The boys and the girls of the university did not differ on emotional security.(iii) The Humanities and social science students also did not differ on emotional security. (iv) The natural science group was comparatively more emotionally secure than the humanities and social science group. However, the natural science group did not differ from the professional course group. (v) Emotionally insecure group suffered from neurotic symptoms and syndromes in a greater degree than the emotionally secure group. (vi) Those with secure emotional health ascribed positive characteristics to the central figure in the stories. (vii) The positive mode of the central figure as an important aspect of interpersonal situation was concomitant with emotionally secure mental health. (viii) Specific relationships used in the stories were independent of security-insecurity variable. (ix) The reactions of the central figure to superiors and subordinates were independent of emotional security-insecurity. (x) The withdrawal reaction characterized defence mechanism of insecure persons to defend themselves from disintegration when faced by stressful situation. (xi) Secure and insecure persons were equally distributed among planned and unplanned families. (xii) Emotional security-insecurity developed among siblings irrespective of their ordinal position. (xiii) Emotional insecurity was more prominent among children from the agricultural community. (xiv) Emotional security-insecurity was evenly spread among children from the business community and the service community. (xv) The democratic, permissive and rational home atmosphere assessed by the recognition and acceptance of opinion of the children was a potent factor behind emotional security. (xvi) Stressful situations and emotional insecurity were concomitant variables. (xvii) The favourable interactions with neighbourhood and frustrating interactions with neighbourhood were concomitant with secure and insecure emotional health, respectively. (xviii) Jealous and quarrelsome neighbourhood developed emotional insecurity among individuals. (xix) The two groups did not differ in their attitude towards their respective institutions, friends, the habit of spending on entertainment and seeing movies, the habit of smoking or using stimulant drugs, etc. (xx) The inseucre group had more sex problems and vagueness in making any unique contribution to their professions and their lives were less meaningful. (xxi) The two groups did not differ on sociability. (xxii) The secure subjects were significantly superior to the insecure persons regarding conceptual integration, ego-strength and aspiration level. (xxiii) Both the groups, secure and insecure, were equally cooperative in giving information about themselves to the interviewer.

31 Sinha, S. A study of personality and prejudice in university students. Ph.D. Psy., Patna University, 1966.

The purpose of this investigation was to study the relationship of anxiety, feeling of insecurity and intolerance of ambiguity with prejudice. It was hypothesised that certain personality traits, viz., anxiety, insecurity and intolerance of ambiguity are significantly related to prejudices. Differences in prejudices in respect of sex and educational levels for the same personality aspects were also studied.

A sample of 400 students from Patna University comprising 100 boy and 100 girl undergraduates, and 100 boy and 100 girl postgraduates was selected randomly. A prejudice scale used by the investigator for measuring anti-semitism was subjected to item analysis and a scale of 26 items was prepared for this study. The coefficients of reliability of the revised scale found by test-retest and split-half methods were .94 and .91 respectively. Other tools used were the Taylor Manifest Anxiety scale, the Maslow Security Insecurity Inventory and the Budner Tolerance Intolerance of Ambiguity Scale. Chi-square test and product-moment correlation techniques were used for analysing the data.

The study has revealed that (i) anxiety, sense of insecurity and intolerance of ambiguity have significant positive correlation with prejudices; (ii) there is no sex and grade (undergraduate and postgraduate) differences in prejudice scores in other personality variables, namely, anxiety, sense of insecurity and intolerance of ambiguity.

32 Sri Chandra. A psycho-social study of tension in college going Youth. Lucknow University, 1971 (ICSSR financed).

The study attempted to understand the psycho-social factors that accounted for the growing unrest, tension and frustration in the youth of the country. The hypotheses tested were: (i) tension would be due to unfavourable attitudes towards university authorities, police authorities, student-union leaders, political parties and government; (ii) discrepancy between achievement and aspiration levels would be higher among the group with high tension than among the group with low tension; (iii) tension would be due to lack of communication between students and teachers; (iv) tension would be higher among students with urban background than those coming from rural background; (v) tension would be higher among students from low and middle income groups than those from higher income groups; and (vi) tension would be higher among students from non-agricultural families than those from agricultural ones.

A specified number of colleges in the Lucknow district were randomly selected from urban and rural areas. A random sample of 803 students, in the age group of seventeen to twentyfour, was taken. A questionnaire, which was pre-tested on a sample of 200 students, was the main tool for investigation.

The findings indicated that the total sample of 803 students reflected almost an average amount of tension on its three indices, namely, level of adjustment, anxiety and insecurity. The medians in each of the three types of cases were found to be closely approaching the respective means. The two criterion groups, the low scorers (LS) and the high scores (HS) numbering 164 and 161 respectively, were compared on the different hypotheses which showed: (i) tension was higher among students from low and middle income groups than those from higher income groups; (ii) tension was higher among students with urban background than those coming from rural background; (iii) lack of clearcut ideas as to the choice of vocation was greater among the high than among the low tension group; (iv) tension in youth was due to lack of communication between teachers and students; (v) a significantly larger percentage of the students of the HS group, as compared to the LS group, felt that political parties took undue advantage of students and the government frequently exercised undue interference in the affairs of the students; (vi) lack of crystallization of either the traditional or modern values was greater among the high tension than among the low tension group; and (vii) discrepancy between achievement and aspiration level was higher among the group with high tension than among the group with low tension. The study concluded that a radical reconstruction of the educational system to meet the needs and aspirations of the students was urgently required.

33 Srivastava, R.K. and Saxena, V. Personality correlates of self-rated academic success and failure – a comparative study. Deptt. of Psy., P.P.N. College, Kanpur, 1979.

The major aim of the investigation was to study the personality characteristics of Indian students who rated themselves as academically successful and unsuccessful. The sample comprised 200 male students, of whom 110 were academically successful and 90 academically unsuccessful, from the graduate classes in arts of two degree colleges affiliated to Kanpur University. The research tool used was Cattell and Eber's Sixteen Personality Factor Questionnaire — Form A as adapted in Hindi by Kapoor. The criterion of academic success was based on the response to the question: Do you regard yourself as an academically successful student? The F-test was used to test the differences between the mean scores.

The major findings of the study were: (i) Students who had rated themselves as academically successful scored differently from those who had rated themselves as academically unsuccessful on two second order personality factors, namely, adjustment vs anxiety and introversion vs extraversion. (ii) The academically successful and unsuccessful students did not differ on two other second order factors — tenderminded emotionally vs alert poise and subduedness vs independence. (iii) Academically successful students were significantly lower on anxiety factor than unsuccessful students. (iv) Academically successful students were more extravert than academically unsuccessful students.

34 Srivastava, N.K., *A psychological study of the development of moral ideas among university students,* Ph.D. Psy., Kashi Vidyapeeth, Varanasi, 1981.

The main objectives of the investigation were: (i) to study the developmental trends of moral ideas among university students, (ii) to study the effects of education on moral development, (iii) to study the effect of age on moral development, and (iv) to study sex differences in moral development.

A sample of 566 students of Banaras Hindu University, 326 of Kashi Vidyapeeth and 350 of Sampurnanand Sanskrit University was drawn. The subjects were students of P.U.C., B.A. and M.A. classes of these universities. The age range of the students selected for the sample was 15 years to 28 years. The sex-wise break-up of the sample was 690 males and

552 females. The moral ideas of values of the subjects were measured with the help of two rating scales developed by the investigator, one consisting of 80 items for moral actions and other consisting of 80 items for moral actions and other consisting of 80 items for immoral actions. The data were analysed mainly on the basis of the t-test.

The main findings were: (i) For every increase on the educational ladder there was corresponding decrease in moral values. (ii) After the high school education, with the increase in age there was decrease in the magnitude of moral values. (iii) Female university students were significantly higher on morality score than their male counterparts.

35 Tripathi, S.L., Adjustment problems of under-graduates of Varanasi Division, Ph.D. Edu., Gorakhpur University, 1981.

The study was conducted to investigate into the adjustment problems of undergraduate students of Varanasi region, in relation to the socio-economic and intelligence levels of the adjusted male and female students. The objectives were: (i) to study the adjustment problems of undergraduates, (ii) to make a comparative study of the adjustment problems of male and female students belonging to different socio-economic, intelligence, locality, and adjustment levels, (iii) to determine the degree of relationship between intelligence, adjustment and socio-economic background of the students, and (iv) to study the response of highly adjusted, adjusted and maladjusted students regarding educational facilities like library, laboratories, book, etc. available at the college. The hypotheses were: (1) There is no difference in the adjustment scores of the students belonging to different groups in the main adjustment areas. (2) Intelligence and socio-economic levels have no relation with adjustment.

Tools used were (i) a Check-list for adjustment problem, (ii) Socio-economic Status Scale, (iii) an interview schedule (iv) Test of General Mental Ability by MC Joshi, (v) Vyaktitva Parikshan Prashnavali, and (vi) Adjustment Inventory by Saxena. The sample consisted of 400 students (310 boys and 19 girls) from Varanasi division in U.P. Percentage of responses to the various adjustment areas of the check list was calculated. Product-moment correlation was used to determine the correlation between adjustment, intelligence and socio-economic status of students. Critical ratio was calculated to check the significance of difference between the mean scores of various groups in the above test and inventories.

The following conclusions were drawn: (1) In all, 40% boys faced college environmental problems, 50% boys faced economic problems, 40% boys could not develop amicable relation with their classmates. (2) Problems of 53% girls were about spending leisure time, 47% were about lack of educational environment in the college. (3) About 53% urban and 42% rural students faced difficulty in their adjustment with the educational environment. (4) Girls were comparatively more adjusted to home area. Highly adjusted students secured better points on the intelligence test. Urban boys and girls were superior, in this respect to residents of rural areas. (5) Adjusted students had comparatively better socio-economic background. (6) Girls secured better points on the socio-economic status scale. (7) Intelligence and adjustment were mutually dependent. (8) Maladjusted students faced difficulty in maintaining domestic adjustment, economic crisis, educational environment, leisure time activities, etc. However, girls faced less difficulty in adjusting to the above situations. (9) The hypotheses were not supported by the obtained data.

36 Trivedi, R.S. and Patel, B.V., Comparative study of the performance and study habits of students reading in B.A. (English) and B.A.(Non-English) course of Sardar Patel University, Sardar Patel University, 1973. (SPU financed).

The objectives of the present study were: (i) to compare the achievement in common subjects of the students of B.A. (with English) and B.A. (without English); (ii) to find out the study habits of these students; and (iii) to compare the study habits of the students of B.A. (with English) and B.A. (without English).

The following tools were employed: (i) the B.V. Patel's Non-verbal Test of Intelligence; (ii) the Kuppuswamy's Socio-Economic Status Scale; and (iii) an attitude scale. These tools were administered to students of third year B.A. The sample included, 102 students who belonged to English and 138 who belonged to non-English groups.

The findings were: (i) the average performance of students of English stream was better and significant in comparison with the average performance of students of non-English stream; (ii) the standard of knowledge of students of non-English group was lower than the average standard of students of English group; (iii) the study habits of students of English stream were relatively better organised than the study habits of students of non-English stream; and (iv) students belonging to English stream had favourable attitude towards English than the students belonging to non-English stream.

37 Wadhwa, B.S., A study of attitudinal structure of university student dissidents within a social psychological framework, Ph.D. Edu., Kurukshetra University, 1982.

The objectives of the study were: (i) to develop a multidimensional attitude scale based on the factors central to the ideology of university student dissidents and a student questionnaire, (ii) to deal with the problem of classification of dissidents and non-dissidents, (iii) to investigate the factorial structure of attitudes on the basis of the data on student dissidents, (iv) to investigate the correlates of the factor scales and make a comparative study of dissidents and non-dissidents, (v) to determine the relationship between the attitude factor scales and the personality dimensions (neuroticism and extraversion), and (vi) to reveal the personality characteristics of certain extreme cases of dissidents and non-dissidents using Rorschach psychodiagnostics.

The sample consisted of 160 male students of various faculties of

Kurukshetra University of whom eighty had been identified as dissidents and eighty as non-dissidents. Two additional small samples of dissidents and non-dissidents from medical college (males) and Kurukshetra University (females) were also drawn for the purpose of comparison. The sample students were administered, through a snow-ball technique, a self-developed attitude scale about political participation and protest activities, a student questionnaire for participation in political activities, Maudsley Personality Inventory and the Rorschach Ink Blot Test.

The findings of the study were: (i) Six factors were identified in the students attitude scale for participation in political and protest activities, viz., democratic goals, religious beliefs, basic issues, tactics, radicalism and political functioning style. (ii) Dissidents and non-dissidents differed significantly on the radicalism scale. (iii) The dissidents of the medical college did not differ significantly from the dissidents of Kurukshetra University on participation in political and protest activities. (iv) Most of the dissidents were from homes having political background. (v) The comparison of the two dissident groups, viz., the dissidents whose parents were politically active and those whose parents were politically inactive, indicated that the two differed significantly on the radicalism scale. (vi) The dissidents had greater probability of taking interest in political news than the non-dissidents. (vii) The factors — democratic goals, religious beliefs, political functioning style — did not show any difference with respect to the variables of type, area, residence and subjects of the dissidents and non-dissidents. (viii) The rural dissidents scored significantly higher than the non-dissidents on the factor of basic issues. (ix) The science students scored significantly higher on the tactics scale than the humanities students. (x) The science student dissidents scored significantly higher than the humanities student dissidents on the tactics scale. (xi) The hosteler dissidents scored significantly higher than the hosteler non-dissidents on the tactics scale. (xii) The hosteler dissidents scored significantly higher than the hosteler non-dissidents on radicalism scale. (xiii) The dissidents and the non-dissidents differed significantly with respect to neuroticism and extraversion. (xiv) The university dissidents were more neurotic and extroverted than the medical college non-dissidents. (xv) The dissidents showed more hostility and inner anxiety than the non-dissidents. (xvi) The non-dissidents had high aspirational level, while the dissidents had aspirational level below their capacity as life circumstances did not permit complete achievement. (xvii) The non-dissidents were intellectually superior and had better organizational ability than the dissidents. (xviii) The dissidents had more control over impulsive expression of emotionality than the non-dissidents.

38 Wig, N.N. and Nagpal, R.N., A study of mental health in failing university students, postgraduate institute of medical education and research, Chandigarh, 1970. (ICMR financed).

The objectives of the study were: (i) to study the incidence and nature of emotional ill-health among the students who fail in the university examinations or dropout during the course of their study; (ii) to discover the different psycho-social factors associated with failure and dropping out; and (iii) to compare the findings in the successful and the unsuccessful students with a view to assessing the significance of emotional and psycho-social factors in determining their academic performance.

The study was completed in two parts. The sample consisted of 146 students failed in the annual examination of April-May 1967, from faculties of arts, science and commerce for part I. The sample for part II consisted of 1180 students of the above faculties. The tools administered on the above two samples were: (i) the Maudsley Personality Inventory; (ii) the Cornell Medical Index Health Questionnaire; (iii) a semi-structured questionnaire; (iv) interview on the model of psychiatric care taking; and (v) a structured questionnaire based on the findings of part I. The data were analysed with the help of t-test and chi-square.

The important findings were the following: (i) The scores of two groups were significantly different at 0.05 level on the physical distress (A-L) scale of the Cornell Medical Index Health Questionnaire. (ii) The two groups were significantly different on mental health score. The differences were marked in the areas, namely, school adjustment and college adjustment followed by the areas of social adjustment and neurotic traits in childhood. Parental deprivation, parental attitude and sexual adjustment were found to be non-contributing area. The successful students and the high achievers were significantly more represented in the lower age group. The students with better achievement in previous examination and with less incidence of failure did better at university examination. (iii) Among the high achievers there was significantly higher incidence of fathers with professional executive occupation and university/professional education. A high percentage of failing students listed their fathers as belonging to business occupations and having no formal education. In most of the cases the low achievers had fathers of agricultural background. (iv) The low and high achievers spent less time in extra curricular activities. No significant differences were found in the items on student satisfaction with teaching standard, adequacy of contacts with teachers, satisfaction with library, etc. Fifty per cent of the high achievers were satisfied with their preparation prior to examination as compared with only thirty-five per cent of the group which was later found to have failed. (vii) Only eight per cent of the failing students and twelve to eight per cent of third divisioners could predict their success correctly in contrast to seventy-four per cent of the second divisioners and fifty-eight per cent of the first divisioners. In the social relations, the failed students were more often reported as the extremes, either as social and mixing or as isolated and lonely.

Out similar forms from (a) five pairs of different forms, small plastic pieces of equilateral triangle, square, rectangle, rhombus and a cross, (b) six pairs of six forms — two similar right angled triangles added to (a); (viii) roughness discrimination test — to arrange in order of grade of roughness of five sand papers with graded roughness mounted on the pieces of sunmica and five small steel cylinders with graded roughness on sides, (ix) weight discrimination test — to arrange articles of same size but of different weight in order of heaviness — (a) to arrange five weights: 30

g, 24 g, 18 g, 12 g, and 6 g, and (b) to arrange seven weights: 30 g, 24 g, 18 g, 15 g, 12 g, and 6 g, (x) constructive ability test — to construct a steel rod out of smaller steel rods of given length with threads at one end and with holes or closed at the other end — (a) two rods of three inches each, (b) three rods of two inches each and (c) three rods of one inch each. The test was administered to 408 boys and girls of six to twentytwo years. The mean, SD and percentages for superior, average and below average levels at each group was found out. In certain cases composite mean scores of age groups eleven and twelve, thirteen and fourteen, fifteen and sixteen, seventeen and eighteen, and nineteen, twenty and twentyone have also been found out.

The index of measurement of efficiency, and the coefficient of reliability of different age groups ranged between 0.70 and 0.94 which is significantly high.

39 Xavier, G. Francis., A study of the attitudes of college students towards self-improvement, Ph.D. Edu., Karnataka University, 1987.

The study attempted to investigate into attitudes toward self-improvement which comprised physical, mental, emotional socio-economic, vocational and spiritual/moral aspects. Nine questions inquiring into differences in terms of attitudes toward self-improvement with respect to (i) sex, (ii) different religions, (iii) different age levels, (iv) different achievement levels, (v) different classes (educational) (vi) rural/urban status (vii) different parental occupations, (viii) parental educational levels and (ix) parental annual income among college students were raised and accordingly nine null hypotheses were formed.

An attitude scale touching the above aspects of self-improvement was specially constructed. The sample at this stage consisted of 215 persons who acted as judges for making value judgements following Thurstone's method of Equal Appearing Intervals. The final scale consisted of ten statements with score values ranging from 0 to 10 on each of the aspects of self-improvement. The main sample of the study consisted of 1051 college-going students from twentyeight institutions altogether. Construct validity of the scale was inferred from the mean scale scores obtained from a sample of 1051 college going students belonging to I, II, and III class levels of achievement. The validity coefficient was obtained to be 0.67 with Aaron's Attitude Scale on modernisation using forty-six students of University Agricultural Sciences, Bangalore as sample. Test-retest reliability was established to be 0.75 using a sample of thirty-six University Agricultural Sciences students. The analysis of variance was presented in two ways, viz., first with respect to each of the seven attributes of self-improvement comparing levels/types in each of nine variables of attitudes and next with respect to each variable of attitude comparing levels or types within each on all attributes of self-improvement. The correlational analysis was based on a table of correlations between variables and attributes of self-improvement. The step-wise regression analysis was used to explain attitudes by its determining variables. Finally a principal component analysis revealed dominant factors that contributed to self-improvement.

Major findings of the study were: (i) Female students secured higher scores on their attitudes toward self-improvement than male students. (ii) Religion had a marked influence on the attitudes of students toward self-improvement. (iii) Academic achievements positively correlated with attitudes toward self-improvement. (iv) The scores obtained by younger students (15-20) studying in PUC were higher than those of elder students pursuing degree, postgraduate and professional courses. (v) Urban students showed an edge over rural students in their attitudes toward self-improvement. (vi) Parental education had greater influence in developing positive attitudes toward self-improvement than occupation and annual income of parents. (vii) Students showed marked preference for vocational, physical and socio-economic improvements and negative preference for mental, moral and emotional improvements.

18. EDUCATIONAL SOCIOLOGY

A BOOKS

01 Cormack, Margaret L. *She who rides a peacock: Indian students and social change– a research analysis.* Bombay, Asia Publishing, 1961. 264 p.

02 Gandhi, Kishore. *Issues and choices in higher education:* A sociological analysis. Delhi, B.R. Publishing Corporation, 1977.

03 Shah, B.V. *Social change and college students of Gujarat.* Baroda, The Maharaja Sayajirao University, 1964. 231 p.

B ARTICLES

01 Adiseshiah, W.T.V. Social attitudes of College Students in India. *New Frontiers in Education.* 6(2) 1976. p. 1-10.

02 Chattopadhyaya, D.P. Social relevance University education. *Socialist India.* 12(20) 1976. p. 14-16.

03 Chitra, M.N. Higher education and society in Mysore under British Rule. *Sociological Bulletin.* 21 (Sept.), 1972. p. 91-102.

04 Chitra, Sivakumar. Social behaviour of students: A Women College in Mysore city. *Economic and Political Weekly.* 10(22), 1975. p. 859-866.

05 Das Gupta, Amiya. Role of higher educational institutions in the economic, social and cultural development of nations. *University Affairs.* 2(5), 1974. p. 3-10 and 16.

06 Devadas, Rajamal P. Community Social Sciences in Colleges. *Hindu.* 6, July, 1977. p. 8.

07 Gaudino, R.L. Indian University: A sociological study. *Journal of University Education* 2, March, 1964. p. 191-212.

08 Malik, Yogendra K. Marquette, Jesse F. Changing social values of college students in the Punjab. *Asian Survey.* (14), September 1974. p. 795-806.

09 Misra, P.K. University and society. *Man in India.* 53 (Oct.-Dec.), 1973. p. 333-346.

10 Nurul Hasan. Social responsibilities of the university system. *New Frontiers in Education.* 3(1), April, 1973. p. 106-111.

11 Parikh, G.D. University, Government and Society, the Indian experience. *Quest.* (88), 1974. p. 35-40.

12 Saxena, A.K. Study of social responsibility in NSS and non-NSS university students. *Journal of Education and Psychology.* 34(2), 1976. p. 111-114.

13 Sharma, S.L. University education and modernity orientation. *University News.* 15(18), 1977. p. 490-492.

14 Shukla, S. College as a Social System. *New Frontiers in Education.* 3 (3), 1976. p. 19-32.

15 ——. Social responsibility of the university teacher. *University Administration.* 3 (2), 1976. p. 21-27.

C COMMITTEES/COMMISSIONS/REPORTS

01 Socio-economic Survey of College Students of Aligarh, 1955-56. Report by Shanti S. Gupta. Aligarh, D.S. College, Aligarh, 1957. 42+16p.

This report, based on a survey of 1773 students from 9 colleges of Aligarh city, tries to explore the causes of falling academic standard and the growing indiscipline among the students. In this regard, the report makes a cross-sectional analysis of the factual informations regarding the professional and financial position of the guardians of the students; caste pattern of the students, their marital status and age structure; their plans for future profession; and their hobbies. The report also contains certain practical suggestions, based on the imperical analysis as well as authors's own teaching experience, with regard to the improvement of academic performance of the students and the sense of discipline.

D RESEARCH STUDIES

01 Agrawal, V. Value system and dimensions of university students of U.P., Ph.D., Lucknow University, 1959.

The present study was designed to explore the value systems and dimensions of students in U.P. The specific objectives were (i) to prepare a value scale for different faculties on the ways of life. (ii) to isolate and define the primary value variables from the conceptions of life, (iii) to find the individual differences on social, religious and theoretical values and (iv) to assess the agreement between different value systems and ways of life.

The data were collected from the students of six faculties, namely, arts, science, law, commerce, engineering and medicine of Lucknow and Roorkee Universities. On the lines of Charles Morris 'to explore the desired aspects of values' nine conceptions of good life were formulated. The main factors were: (1) social good, (2) liberation from worldly affairs, (3) enjoyment as the main aim of life, (4) contentment, tolerance and indifference, (5) healthy, vigorous life with some moral principles, (6) integration of action, enjoyment and contemplation, (7) fatalist view, (8) detached karma and (9) purification of self through restraint. A five point Likert type scale has been used for each way. Extractions of primary value variable have been done in arts faculty through Thurstone's centroid method of factor analysis. For value preference and social and religious values the significance has been tested by chi-square test. The independent variables were faculty, sex, income, place of residence and religion.

The major findings were : (i) the commonly liked ways of life are those having emphasis on self-restraint, moderation and integration of action, enjoyment and contemplation; (ii) the conceived values of an individual largely take into account the cultural pattern of the requirements of the social system; (iii) the value dimensions isolated by the factor analysis are : (a) to achieve the end or goal by any means, (b) self-restraint, (c) purity of thought, speech and action, (d) salvation through selfless actions; (iv) in religious values and temporal change, much emphasis is placed on human effort, and fate is also favoured suggesting the dependence and adherence to this culture; (v) in value preference, the value items preferred were qualities of friendship, worthy aim and aspiration; (vi) in case of social values (a) subjection to parental authority is not very rigid and it seems to be based on rational ground, (b) students are normally permissive towards sex and (c) students have a congenial outlook towards the outer world; and (vii) in synthetic approach value of 'closeness' permeates in interpersonal relationship among Indian students.

02 Annamma, A.K., Values aspirations and adjustment of college students in Kerala, Ph.D. Psy., Kerala University, 1984.

The main objective was to gain an understanding of the values, aspirations and adjustment of the college students in Kerala. The hypotheses were: (i) Sex, age, curriculum, religion, residential background, socio-economic status, family size and academic achievement are related to spiritualism and adjustment, (ii) Majority of students take a liberal stand with regard to husband-wife relationship, parent-child relationship and mixing of boys and girls, (iii) Majority of students believe in God and have an open minded approach to religion, (iv) Majority of students have high educational and vocational aspirations, but do not have clear plans relating to selecting a vocation or marriage and, (v) Majority of students do not have bad habits like smoking and drinking.

The sample for the study was made up of college students drawn from predegree college entrants (n = 300) and college leavers (final year degree, n = 1200) enrolled in 10 colleges. The sample was further stratified on the basis of sex and subjects of study. The tools used were Mathew Materialism Spiritualism Scale to measure an individual's materialism-spiritualism orientation, a questionnaire to measure aspiration with reference to education, vocation and marriage, prepared for the study, a problem checklist to study adjustment and a general data sheet which elicited information relating to values, aspirations, and adjustment, and also collected information about habits, practices and opinions. The problem check-list included educational health, home, financial, sexual, emotional and social problems. The data obtained were analysed applying two way analysis of variance techniques for testing the relationship of the seven areas of the problem checklist to materialism-spiritualism orientation and for testing the relationship with variables such as age, curriculum, religion, academic achievement, residential background, income, family size, father's educational and occupational level. The effect of sex was repeated for spiritualism scores as well Analysis based on percentages was done for the information obtained through the general data questionnaire.

The main findings were : 1. Majority of the college students were conformists, with a stable system of values, and without rebellious tendencies. 2. The younger college students were more spiritualism oriented as compared to the older group which was more materialism oriented. 3. Academic achievement, residential background and father's education and occupational status had no relationship to value orientation of college students. 4. Economic status was related to value orientation, with lower income group being more spiritualism oriented and higher income more materialism oriented. 5. Size of family was related to value orientation with students from large families being more spiritualism oriented and small size families more materialism oriented. 6. Majority of students did not have clear goals about education, occupation or marriage. 7. Male students exhibited higher aspiration than female students. 8. No discrepancies were seen between self and parental aspirations. 9. Marriage was not viewed as an immediate prospect. 10. Boys and girls approved intermingling, but girls were seen to prefer the customary type of marriage. 11. Female students were seen to be better adjusted than male students in all the areas studied. 12. College education was no seen to have any impact on value orientation and behaviour of the students.

03 Chattopadhyay K.P., Bose P.K., and Chatterji A. Undergraduate Students in Calcutta : How they live and work - A survey. Deptt. of Statistics, Calcutta University, 1959.

The major objective was to present a correct picture of the conditions under which undergraduate men students in Calcutta lived and worked.

The sample was drawn in a stratified random manner. All Calcutta colleges for imparting undergraduate courses were selected. The students were divided into two groups, first year and third year. The particular students of each college formed a stratum wherefrom the samples were chosen at random. A little over four per cent of total student population of boys only were studied. Although samples were drawn from girls' college also, only a limited number of cases could be investigated. The final sample size was 859, of whom 575 were first year and 284 third year students. The selected students were interviewed for information concerning self. The family information was collected from the head of the family as far as practicable.

The study revealed : 1. There was remarkable vitality of joint family and middle class traditions. Ninety per cent of the students lived with parents or relatives. Five per cent lived in hostels and five per cent in unrecognised messes where the monthly expenses were of the order of Rs. 50. A few only could afford to meet the cost of living away from the homes of relations. 2. In all, 13,000 students came from families where the per capita income was less than Rs. 30 per month, and 14,000 from families where the income lay between Rs. 30 and Rs. 50 per month. The former class lived below the subsistence level and the latter on the margin. 3. The poverty of students was reflected in food habits, incidence of illness and malnutrition from which about forty-three per cent of the student population suffered. The principal problem was that of poverty. The main factor was the limited means of the students who were largely drawn from middle class population which had been hit the hardest by the postwar conditions. 4. Living and working conditions of the majority of the undergraduate students in Calcutta was far from satisfactory.

04 Chilukala, G.K. Social attitude of Indian academic elite. Ph.D. Soc., Osmania University, 1981.

The study was based on the following assumptions: (i) It is possible to identify in a society a small number of groups that go by the name of elite groups. The ruling elite, the business elite, the religious elite and the academic elite are most common among such groups. (ii) These elite groups are responsible for upholding certain existing values and for introducing new values in their respective spheres. This phenomenon is reflected in their behaviour, speech and thought, influenced, as it is, by certain social needs and natural pressures within their society on the one hand and, on the other, by international standards of contemporary thought and action. (iii) A detailed, objective and in-depth study of these different elite groups provides interesting and instructive insights into the changing and non-changing foundations of our social structure.

The sample consisted of 570 college and university teachers engaged in research and academic pursuits. Data were collected through a structured questionnaire consisting of three sets of questions. A, B and C, each covering a broad area of attitudes and values. Part A covered value-orientation towards such matters as food habits, marriage, sex, wealth, health, etc., and Part B comprised questions on attitudes towards the government and its policies while Part C intended to elicit attitudinal information on labour unions, industrial management, public and private enterprise, individual income and landed property.

The study reported the following findings: (i) In the composition of the sampled elite, it was found that the members with an agricultural background were in a considerable majority followed by those with an urban background. The sons of businessmen, teachers, doctors and lawyers came next in that order. (ii) In terms of attitudes, there was a general approval of the government socialistic plans and policies because it was agreed that these policies were not richman-oriented but were intended for the welfare of the weaker sections. On the other hand, a general tone of dissatisfaction marked their attitude towards the implementation of these policies. A similar opinion was found on the educational policies of the government. Need for a drastic change in the system of education was emphasized and a ready adoption and absorption of these changes by the public was stressed. (iii) The foreign policy of the government was not totally supported though particular instances, such as refugee rehabilitation, won general approval. (iv) Administrative efficiency of the government related to the practical side of life was not held high. The government attitude to such enemies of the society as blackmarketeers was questioned. The government was held responsible for the problem of unemployment. (v) Respondents did not totally support the public enterprise for fear of fall in the efficiency standards while they favoured land-ceiling. Respondents were found to be against universal wage fixation and restriction on the individual's income. (vi) Almost all the respondents strongly deprecated the caste system as unhealthy and undesirable. As for marriage, they firmly recommended monogamy and strongly opposed caste restrictions. (vii) Religion and God occupied an important place in the attitude of respondents, but their religion was a religion free from fanaticism, coercion and cruelty. Most of them realized God through idol-worship while some were sceptical about the very existence of God. Many of them expressed great faith in religious functions, peaceful co-existence, hospitality and common good.

05 Gogate. S.B., Creating social awareness among college students, IIE, Pune, 1985.

The major objective was to initiate an action project to create social awareness among college students.

The project was initiated in five colleges in Pune City on an experimental basis during the year 1981-82. The coordinator of the project personally handled the project in all the colleges with the help of teacher and student representatives. Discussion on important topics of interest to youth, regular participation in some social activity around the college, visits to projects of social importance around the college and a three to four day annual camp were the activities employed as methods to create social awareness. During the years 1982-83, 1983-84 and 1984-85 the number of colleges voluntarily participating in the project was twenty-five, fifty, seventy-five respectively with around fifty students from each college. The function of the coordinator was to organize regional seminars for once in a year, and evaluate the programme of the year at the end of the academic year. A set of twelve booklets were prepared by the IIE in relation to this project. These booklets were useful for self-study and discussions in colleges.

The evaluation of the project yielded the following findings: 1. There was a small number of socially aware teachers in colleges. They were scattered. It was necessary to organize them in a group which could be influential in inculcating social awareness among students. 2. If properly motivated a small band of students could be raised in every college to do some fruitful social and developmental work around the college. 3. Unless the heads of colleges, the principals were willing to undertake the programme, no programme for which colleges had to raise small finance and had to incur some expenditure, would be successful. 4. Due to vacations, examinations, elections, sports and such other activities, college students found it difficult to participate in social activities, around the college regularly. 5. Teachers and students participated in the project without any additional benefits. 6. Coordination at regional or state level was necessary to make the project a success.

06 Govil, M. Changing social attitudes and behaviour patterns among the post-graduate students in Uttar Pradesh. Ph.D. Sociology, Agra University, 1967.

The study was conducted on 300 students of Lucknow University and College of Agra. The method adopted for selecting the sample was quota sampling method. The sample consisted of 29.6 per cent female and 70.4 per cent male students who hailed from different strata of society. The data on the problems of (a) marriage, (b) family, (c) status and role of women, (d) education and occupation and (e) students' behaviour and their participation in politics were gathered through an interview schedule.

The major observations on various aspects were: (i) the students show a marked desire of selecting the mates themselves, but also desire to finalise the marriage with the consent of the elders at home; (ii) greater stress is laid upon the individual qualities of bride and groom; (iii) underhand practice of dowry is still prevalent while denouncing this practice openly; (iv) average marriage age from boys and girls are 25/26 and 20/21 years respectively; (v) disintegration of the traditional family pattern is being brought about progressively on account of increasing industrialisation and urbanisation; (vi) women having higher education want to enjoy economic and social freedom; (vii) members of the younger generation grown up in a different atmosphere have less liking for joint family, but they do not want to cut the relationship with the family; (viii) professions considered suitable for women are those of teachers, physicians, surgeons, nurses, clerks, stenographers and administrators; (ix) women show keenness to participate in politics; (x) higher education is gaining popularity with the object of better job facilities; (xi) selection of a postgraduate course of study largely rests on the probability of its job potency; (xii) male students want to continue their studies till they get a job whereas female students want it to continue till they get married; (xiii) need of co-education at the postgraduate level is advocated for almost all courses; (xiv) sex segregation continues in co-educational institutions; (xv) most of the students depend for the financial assistance on their parents and when they start working, they like to help their parents; (xvi) most of the students do not like to follow the profession of their parents; (xii) teaching profession is liked most by males as well as females; and (xiii) political parties use students as a convenient tool for agitation.

07 Hassan, M.K. Social prejudice among college students – A sociological, study. Ph. D. Psy., Ranchi University, 1975.

The major objectives were: (i) to study the relationship of sociological variables like religious affiliation, caste-status and urban/rural origin with social prejudices (pertaining to religion, caste and sex), allied attitudes (religiousity and belief in caste system), religious information and social stereo-types (religion, caste and sex); (ii) study the relationships of personality variables, namely, anxiety and authoritarianism with social prejudices and allied attitudes; and (iii) to study the relative influence of sociological versus personality correlates of prejudice by examining the interrelationships of dimensions of prejudice and allied attitudes.

The study was conducted on a stratified random sample of 160 Hindu and 160 Muslim college students from Ranchi and Jamshedpur. Each group was sub-divided into equal subgroups based on upper and lower castes and urban and rural origin. The data were collected by using the Sinha's W.A. Self Analysis Form and a comprehensive questionnaire containing items on personal data, religious information, religious prejudice, caste prejudices, sex prejudices, religiously, belief in caste system, religious and caste stereotypes, sex stereotypes, and authoritarianism, selected from California F Scale Forms 40 and 45. The data were analysed by using t-test, chi-square and correlation.

The study revealed that (i) Muslim college students were more prejudiced than Hindu college students; the Muslim students had a higher degree of religiousity and stronger belief in the caste system than the Hindu students; (ii) the personality variables – anxiety and authoritarianism - were more closely related to prejudice than sociological variables (caste status, and urban/rural origin) except for religious affiliation having significant positive relationship with prejudice; (iii) the three sociological variables were interrelated and they were also significantly related to allied attitudes and personality variables; hence prejudice was an extension of personality; (iv) religiousity and prejudice had significant positive relationship; and (v) religious information and prejudice had significant negative relationship.

08 Hooda, S.S. Bombay collegian: A study in the social background. Ph. D. Soc., Bombay University, 1968.

The study intended to find out the social background of the students in Bombay colleges.

Seven colleges were chosen as representatives of almost all the colleges on the basis of stratified random sampling method. The number of students, thus selected, was 500 out of 37,000 students of four different classes and two different faculties. But only 400 students responded. The age of the sample ranged between 16+ and 38+ years. The tool of research was a questionnaire which included questions on the family, school, general aspects and on college and collegians. The families were categorised into four groups according to the educational levels of the parents and grand parents. A comparison of the Bombay collegians was made with model students as constructed by Ferdynand Zweig.

It was found that (i) about 24.6 per cent of the parents were sufficiently educated, 44.5 per cent were moderately educated, 25.5 per cent of the parents were just literate and 5.4 per cent illiterate; (ii) the higher the educational level, greater was the satisfaction the collegian enjoyed from the family; (iii) as many as 270 collegians had a home atmosphere where both the parents cooperate; (iv) for 330 students schooling began at the age between 5+ and 7 years; (v) 327 collegians never failed in the class; (vi) the medium of instruction was Gujarati for 137, Marathi for 113 and English for 100 students; (vii) 281 students attended co-educational institutions either at one level or at both the primary and secondary levels and seventy per cent stated to like co-educational institutions; (viii) mathematics, as an academic activity, was most liked by the collegians and excursion and picnic as the extracurricular activities; (ix) 'to be a doctor' was the ambition for a large number of students, followed by 'engineer', 'graduate' and 'lawyer'; (x) male teachers were liked much in comparison to female teachers; (xi) some of the students were not well adjusted with their family, (xii) the schools where they studied were not properly equipped with library, reading room and sports facilities; (xiii) in comparison to model students Bombay collegians lacked self confidence; (xiv) they were sociable but extending only to their own community members; (xv) they were anxious and worried about their own future; (xvi) they lacked optimism, will power, determination and character; (xvii) they were timid, conformist, with unrealistic aspirations, did not have political awareness and did not mix with opposite sex; (xviii) altruistic attitude was little present in most of the Bombay collegians; and (xix) they were quite careful about their dress, hair style and makeup.

09 Khopkar, A.D. A study of social commitment of postgraduate students of the University of Poona. Ph. D. Soc., Poona University, 1981.

The objectives of the study were: (i) to understand what was social commitment, (ii) to know the extent of social commitment among the educated youth in India, and (iii) to know the factors contributing to the development of social commitment or lack of it. Social commitment was *a priori* conceived in terms of emotional identification, social sensitivity, social awareness of the existing social problems, reasoning, on the lines of social responsibility, and participation in developmental activities.

The sample consisted of 423 postgraduate students belonging to the Poona University and studying in Poona city. They belonged to the faculties of arts, science and commerce. Information about the subjects' faculty, subject of specialization, age, sex, marital status, religion, caste, linguistic and regional background, rural-urban background, medium of instruction, academic record, and economic status, was obtained to analyse the data in terms of these factors. A questionnaire and a depth interview were used to collect data. Some questions of the questionnaire were open-ended. Some of the questions were based on the basic biographical information as of social commitment enumerated in the beginning. The depth interview was used with only thirty cases to probe into the factors that contributed to the development or lack of social commitment.

The findings of the study were: (i) Seventy per cent students belonged to the low, 20 per cent to the medium and 10 per cent to the high social commitment categories. (ii) Component-wise analysis showed that social awareness was found 13 per cent cases, participatory action in 21 per cent, reasoning along social responsibility in 23 per cent, social sensitivity in 63 per cent and emotional identification in 95 per cent. These findings led to the conclusion that a majority of students lacked social commitment. (iii) The faculty and the subject of specialization appeared as the most significant correlates of social commitment. Sex, caste, rural-urban background, economic status, academic record, regional background and medium of instruction were found to be significant correlates of one or the other correlates of social commitment. (iv) Depth interviews revealed that the following variables contributed to the development or lack of social commitment: family atmosphere, religion, reading habits, special experiences in life, influential personalities, membership of voluntary organizations, value attached to social service, ridicule by friends, generation gap, hiatus hypocrisy in the behaviour of elders/politicians/social workers, economic insecurity, feeling of hopelessness about a social change, non-academic atmosphere in educational institutions and hostels, and failure of the educational system in infusing the values of social commitment.

10 Kundu, N., Value pattern of college students and its relation to psycho-social variables. Ph. D. Psy., Calcutta University, 1982.

The major objectives were: (i) to trace whether uniformity in the relationship within different values really existed in a recognizable form in the college student population, and (ii) to find out whether there was any unique combination of the value pattern with the selected psycho-social variables.

The sample included 440 students, both male and female, of third year honours undergraduate and first year postgraduate arts and science departments of general courses of studies and only male students of fourth year engineering and medical courses. The sample was drawn from different colleges under Calcutta and Jadavpur universities. The departments from where the sample was drawn were selected randomly. Seven different tools, viz., Indian adopted form of Allport-Vernon-Lindzey Study of Value Scale, Kuppuswamy's Socio-Economic Status Scale (Urban) Form B. Catteil's Sixteen Personality Factor Test, Keer's Tulane Factors of Liberalism and Conservatism Attitude Value Profile, N.I.I.P. Group Test 70/23, an Occupational Aspiration Scale and an information schedule, were used to measure different variables, such as values, SES, attitudes, personality traits, intelligence, level of aspiration. Separate sets of analyses were done for different selections and the t-test was used to study the significance of the differences. Apart from judging the effects of various factors on the value pattern of college students, the relationship of the value to certain psycho-social variables was also found out by computing the product moment correlations. In determining the specific patterns of relationships between values and other psycho-social variables, the canonical correlations were computed taking the whole sample together.

The findings of the study were: (i) Recognizable value patterns were observable among college students, though the pattern was not a unique one. Two separate patterning modes were observed with slight overlapping between them. These two distinct sequences of values were (a) theoretical, economic, political, social, aesthetic and religious, and (b) theoretical, social, economic, political, aesthetic and religious. (ii) Different modes of relationships were found to exist between the value patterns of college students and the other selected psycho-social variables. These different modes of relationships had been depicted through the four significant canonical R's. (iii) There seemed to be a generalized trend toward the preference for theoretical value among the higher grade students' population indicating their true academic orientation and interest. (iv) A common trend of least preference for religious value seemed to be indicative of their more mature and realistic evaluative behaviour than the faith in supernatural power. (v) The profile analysis of sex variable failed to show significant difference in value patterns, though slight differences in the order of values were noted between the male and the female groups. (vi) Though the account of intergroup differences in value patterns was not under the purview of the study, the findings revealed that they existed between the groups. Apart from the resemblance of value patterns between different categories of students, the extent of maximization of each single value was found to vary from group to group.

11 Lal, M. A study of the problems, background factors and some personality factors of graduate students of Meerut University, Ph.D. Edu., Meerut University, 1979.

The objectives of the study were: (i) to study the level of intellectual potential of the graduate students of Meerut University, (ii) to study the socio-economic background factors of the graduate students, (iii) to study the values of these students, (iv) to study the nature of the problems of the graduate students of Meerut University, (v) to investigate the attitude of these students towards socio-political and economic problems, (vi) to investigate the academic motivation of these students, (vii) to study the expectations of these graduate students from their college and teachers, and (viii) to study their vocational aspirations.

A stratified sample consisting of 600 students was drawn from seven urban colleges (including one for women) and three rural colleges, representing the faculties of arts, science, agriculture and commerce. The tools used in the study included Cattle's Culture Fair Test, Agarwal's Students' Value Test and the Socio-Economic, Status (SES) Scale and a Schedule constructed by the researcher himself. The t-test and the chi-square were used for data analysis.

The findings were: (i) Higher education was easily available to the students of low intellectual calibre. (ii) The faculty of science with mathematics and biology generally attracted most intelligent graduate students. (iii) Nearly 60 per cent graduate students belonged to the rural areas. (iv) Larger percentage of the undergraduates were drawn from agricultural families. (v) An overwhelming majority of the students came from uneducated families. (vi) One-third of the college students belonged to the upper-income group and nearly half of the graduate students were drawn from the lower class. (vii) Only 17.33 per cent college students belonged to high SES and 70.00 per cent belonged to the middle SES. The rest of the students were from low SES. (viii) More than half of the students came from joint families. Nuclear families were found only in the industrial or urban areas. (ix) Ninety per cent students were unmarried. (x) Average age of the science students was lower than that of the students of other faculties. (xi) The students of high SES differed from others with respect to educational values and to some extent, personal values. (xii) The rural students were more religious and had higher humanistic values than the urban students while the reverse was true in the case of materialistic values. (xiii) Graduate students were facing financial hardships in various life situations. (xiv) The students of low SES had more financial hardships. (xv) Most of the students had shown their inability to express their ideas in English. (xvi) The majority of the students worried about employment and social evils. (xvii) Intelligent students were better adjusted in the society and school. (xviii) Most of the students felt that the society was heading towards materialism. (xix) Students were in favour of participation in politics and they were of the opinion that the voting-age should be reduced to eighteen years. (xx) The college should provide open playground, hostel accommodation and medical aid. (xxi) Students expected that teachers should possess a very high level of scholarship.

12 Munjal, B.M., A study of major sociological aspects of truancy among College-going male students of Indore City, Ph.D. Soc., Indore University, 1979.

The objectives of the study were: (i) to make an analysis of some of the major sociological aspects of truancy among the college-going male students of Indore city in order to ascertain the causes of truancy, (ii) to study the activities of the truants when they cut classes during the college hours, after the college hours and both times, and (iii) to have a deeper understanding of the above two aims, a faculty-wise statistical comparison was attempted.

In this study, the cross-sectional research design was employed by taking a group of 250 truants belonging to five faculties, namely, arts, commerce, science, engineering and medical, from nine different colleges, selected on the basis of ecological stratification, form of and courses of study. Also, a group of one hundred persons falling in the categories of the parents of the truants, the teaching community and university authorities was chosen. Data were collected by using an observation schedule and an interview schedule.

The findings were: (i) Truancy occurred more in the case of upper-caste respondents than in the case of lower caste. Among the upper caste, truancy incidences occurred more among Vaishas than among other castes. The majority of the truants happened to be from Hindu religion. (ii) Truancy occurred more in private educational institutions than in government institutions. (iii) The majority of the truants had either failed or got compartment in their last examination. (iv) Truancy occurred more in the case of the respondents who were accompanied by their friends from home to their institutions. (v) The truants had a feeling of shame and fear at the time of their first instance of truancy but they were not punished at the time of their first incidence of truancy. (vi) The main causes for truancy in the order of priority were friends and classmates, recreation, student leaders, teacher's behaviour, girl friends, dryness and boredom in study and refreshening. (vii) The literacy level of the family had no relation with truancy. The truancy incidences occurred more in the case of respondents belonging to higher income group. The respondents belonging to nuclear families were more prone to truancy than those belonging to joint families. In joint families the child was trained for more social responsibilities than in nuclear families. (viii) The habits of neighbourhood influenced the habits of truants to a great extent. (ix) Liking and disliking a particular subject caused truancy. (x) There was no direct relation between the age of truants and their reaction towards the discipline in their respective colleges. (xi) The more the distance between the residence and the college, the less were the incidences of truancy and the less the distance the more were the incidences of truancy. (xii) The discipline in a family had a positive relationship with the frequency of truancy. (xiii) The more the pocket money the more were the incidences of truancy. (xiv) Truancy occurred more in the case of teachers who were moderate and liberal rather than in the case of teachers who were strict. (xv) Incidences of truancy occurred more in the classes where the teachers used to give home work. (xvi) The habits of friends and associates also played an important factor in motivating the habit of truancy. (xvii) A system of earning while learning might prove worth while in minimizing the truancy habit. (xviii) The truants took part in multifarious activities. They participated not only in games and sports and literary activities, but also took part in organizational, recreational and domestic activities. (xix) Taking part in household activities was not a cause for truancy.

13 Ojha, R. S. Attitudes of college students towards certain social problems, Ph.D. Psy., Bihar University, 1968.

The major objectives of the present investigation were to find out (i) whether there were significant differences in the attitudes of the students towards college education, marriage, religion and war; (ii) whether economic status of the students' parents had a significant influence on the attitudes of the subjects; and (iii) whether such factors as educational level of the students' parents had a significant influence on the attitudes of the subjects under study.

In the first stage of the study a five point Likert type attitude scale was constructed. Out of initial 400 statements pertaining to certain aspects of college education, marriage, religion and war, only sixty statements were finally retained on the basis of item consistency and discriminatory power. The final form of the scale had spilt-half reliability of 0.85 after Speariman-Brown correction. This scale was then administered to a sample of 200 college students randomly selected from the different college of the University of Bihar. The age of the subjects ranged between eighteen and twentyfive. Besides this scale, a schedule was also prepared and used to assess economic status and educational level of the students and their parents.

The following were some of the major findings of the study: (i) It was found that students held favourable attitude towards college education. A majority of them stressed college role in helping for better job, providing vocational training, and creative thinking. They also stressed that coeducation should be there and English should be an optional subject. (ii) Majority of the students preferred healthy, younger and educated marriage partner and they liked love marriage and late marriage. (iii) Majority of the students held favourable attitude towards religious activities and unfavourable attitude towards war. (iv) The poorer section of the students favoured the goal of college education and the status of English as an optional subject, while the richer section held the opposite view. (v) The students of high and low socio-economic classes differed significantly with regard to their attitude towards marriage. Educated marriage partner and choice of the partner by themselves were favoured by richer section of the students. (vi) Students coming from low economic class had more favourable attitude towards religiousness and less favourable attitude towards war. (vii) Undergraduate students from illiterate families favoured the idea of vocational training as the goal of college education; postgraduate students from literate families did not hold this view, and they favoured sex education more than their peers from illiterate families. (viii) The students from literate and illiterate families alike were of opinion that war was inhuman.

14 Padhan, N., A study of the socio-economic background, academic performance and job-placement of university students, Ph.D. Edu., Maharaja Sayajirao University of Baroda, 1986.

The objectives of the study were (i) to study the cosmopolitan character of the university in horizontal, vertical and substantive firms, (ii) to study the academic performance of students in different courses with regard to socio-economic background of students, and (iii) to study the job-placement of students going out of the university after six months of the completion of courses.

The study was conducted on the students of the M.S. University of Baroda with the following samples : 2021 students for objective (i) 837 students for objective (ii) 413 students for objective (iii) The sample represented eleven faculties of the university. The tools used for the study were an information schedule, a questionnaire on academic life and future plan, and a questionnaire to follow up university students. Record surveys, personal administration of questionnaires and mailing the questionnaires were used for data collection purposes. The data were collected on the sample available for the year 1983-84. Different statistical techniques like ANOVA, t-test, were used for analysis of data.

The findings of the study were: (1) The student population of the M.S. University consisted of 77% Gujarati, 22% non-Gujarati and 1% of foreign students. (2) Students belonging to almost all parts of the country were admitted in different faculties. (3) The students belonging to SC and ST, non-Hindu, poor communities, rural areas and first generation learners were under-represented in the university. (4) The university had a good research and teaching atmosphere in almost all of its faculties. (5) The difference in academic performance of male and female, upper caste and SC and ST, Hindu and non-Hindu, hostelities and day scholars and the rural and urban students was found insignificant. (6) Only in the case of arts faculty, socio-economic background was found as a determinant of academic achievement. (7) Academic life of arts, science and commerce students affected academic achievement. (8) Out of the total student product, 53% were employed, 24% continued with further studies, 6% remained self-employed and 17% remained unemployed. (9) The employment position was higher among the products of engineering, medicine and home science facilities, whereas it was moderate among the products of fine arts, applied science, social work and education and psychology. (10) It was low in the case of arts, science, commerce and law graduates. (11) The future plans and demand in the job-market played major role in determining the employment of students of most of the faculties. (12) Out of the total employed alumni, 24% were underemployed; their percentages were more in the case of products of arts, commerce, law and social work. (13) Job perspectives of a course motivated the graduates to continue with further studies. (14) A large number of unemployed graduates had the plan for further studies provided they did not get jobs within a considerable period of time.

15 Rasool, G. and Suri, S.P., Statistical digest of the sociological features of the students of Jammu University, Deptt. of Edu., Jammu University, 1980 (UGC-financed).

The study was undertaken to investigate the socio-economic and cultural background of the students in the University of Jammu and its affiliated colleges. The major objectives of the study were: (i) to make a comparative study of the socio-cultural background of the undergraduate and the postgraduate students of the University of Jammu and its affiliated colleges, (ii) to collect information regarding the lodging facilities and the financial assistance they received from various agencies, (iii) to study the vocational preference of students, (iv) to study the views of the students on the participation in university/college activities, and (v) to study the pattern of their preferences for various games, hobbies, cultural activities and social problems.

A sample of 856 students consisting of 378 studying in postgraduate departments (148 male and 230 female) and 478 in affiliated colleges (225 male and 253 female) was selected using the technique of random sampling.

Data were collected on a questionnaire containing sixteen items covering different aspects of the socio-cultural background, prepared by the investigators. The collected data were analysed by using mean, standard deviation, critical ratio and Thurstone's Incomplete Rank Order.

The major findings were: (i) Girls in the affiliated colleges and in the university were in a better economic situation generally. The majority of the boys, on the contrary, came from the various strata of the middle class. (ii) The university students appeared to be having better cultural background. (iii) The majority of the university students (both sexes) resided within a radius of eight kilometres from the campus but a fair proportion of the college students resided at distant places from the institution. (iv) Only a small percentage of students got financial assistance from different agencies. (v) Boys appeared to be obsessed with the problem of employment. They generally started making efforts for a job at an early stage. (vi) The majority of the college and the university students expressed favourable opinion regarding students' participation in various curricular and non-curricular activities. (vii) The students preferred to join teaching, executive and military services. Clerical and nursing were less preferred occupations. (viii) Painting, games and sports were highly liked hobbies while hunting and keeping pet animals were the less preferred hobbies. (ix) Essay-writing and acting were the most-liked cultural activities.

16 Saxena, A.K. A study of hostility and alienation among university students, Deptt. of Psy., Gorakhpur University (ICSSR-financed).

The objectives of the study were: (i) to study the distribution of hostility trait in university students to know their pattern of hostility, (ii) to compare the hostility pattern of university students with a known aggressive group, (iii) to study the distribution of alienation problems, (iv) to study the differences between high and low hostile university students in frustration reactions, (v) to study the relationship between hostility and alienation response of university students, and (vi) to study the differences in alienation responses of high and low hostile university students.

The study of the problems of hostility and alienation was undertaken during the internal emergency in the country in 1975-77 and therefore emergency and post-emergency comparison was undertaken to see whether the emergency had any influence. Replication of the study was undertaken after the emergency in 1978. A Hindi version of projective test, Rosenzweig Picture Frustration Study (Pareek), Alienation Scale (Sinha and Sinha) and an inventory of trait hostility constructed by the investigator for the purpose along with Social Responsibility Scale (Harris) were used. On the basis of the hostility scale two extremes, high hostile (HH) and low hostile (LH) were selected which were similar in all aspects except hostility. Rural, urban location or socio-economic status was not considered as sharp differences did not exist between the two; as income data are usually unreliable income was not considered. The male students of Gorakhpur University in Gorakhpur in the age group 17-23 were selected for the study; it was a stratified random sample selected on the basis of the undergraduate and the postgraduate students attending regular courses in the arts, science and commerce faculties. The total sample comprised 500 students, half of whom were HH and the other half LH students. A group of prisoners was also selected for the purpose of comparison.

The study revealed: (i) Students, in general, were docile and low hostile; only a small section, 7 per cent, engineered the campus hostilities. (ii) The distribution of hostility trait was similar among the university youth and prisoners; it was difficult to locate a high hostile student or prisoner. (iii) Though the postgraduate arts students revealed a higher level of hostility and differences were not significant; the undergraduate arts students were significantly more hostile than their commerce and science counterparts though the difference between the latter group was not significant. (iv) As many as 23 per cent were highly alienated while only 14 per cent were low alienated. The undergraduate arts students revealed significantly low alienation while among the postgraduate students, there were no significant differences in the level of alienation. (v) There was a low negative relationship between social responsibility and alienation; it was not possible to differentiate the highly alienated students on the basis of social responsibility scores. (vi) Home involvement was a crucial determinant of alienation, the home residents experienced less alienation from the university campus. (vii) The high hostile students were more extragressive than the low hostile but the groups were equally introgressive. (viii) There was no relationship between the type of aggression and hostility. Regardless of hostility level differences group conformity ratings indicated that students largely conformed to their group patterns of behaviour. (ix) Low hostility and low alienation were related. Though high hostile students scored higher on alienation than low hostile students, the differences were not significant except in their perceptions of normalness and lack of morality. (x) The emergency and the post-emergency hostility pattern did not differ significantly. (xi) There were significant differences in the level of alienation in the two periods; the conditions during the emergency were conducive to low feeling of alienation. (xii) As regards differences in HH and LH students, though the differences were more sharp, the trends did not change during the emergency. (xiii) The HH and LH groups showed increasing awareness of campus alienation in the post-emergency period than during the emergency.

17 Seetharamu, A.S., Rural in-migrants to higher education, Institute for Social and Economic Change, Bangalore, 1982.

The study aimed at finding out: (i) the reason for the sudden fall in the student strength in Bangalore University, (ii) the factors responsible for the student migration from rural areas to Bangalore city for postgraduate education, (iii) the demographic, educational, social and economic backgrounds of these migrants, their aspirations, leadership behaviour and interpersonal relations while they pursued postgraduate studies, and (iv) the implications of these factors for university planning.

The sample for the study included all the 330 rural students admitted to the various postgraduate courses in Bangalore University in June 1978. When the data on enrolmet were collected in January 1980, it was observed that only 226 were on rolls, and out of them 174 responded. Data were collected by interview using a schedule.

The findings of the study were: (i) One out of every three students given admission to postgraduate courses in Bangalore University was from the rural area. Eighty-five per cent of the rural migrants were boys, hardly 15 per cent were girls. The rural migrants to higher education at Bangalore University were young and the majority of them had undergone a normal and smooth course of education. About 20 per cent of them were first generation learners and 53 per cent of them came from agricultural families. Two-thirds of the migrant students lived in hostels and 50 per cent got scholarships. With a few negligible exceptions all the rural students were Hindus. The majority of them were from nuclear and medium-sized families. (ii) A very low percentage of the rural students was represented on the various students bodies of the university. Hardly a few students associated themselves with cultural organizations in Bangalore city. (iii) A total number of 46 out of 174 students were not readily accepted by the urbanites when they joined the postgraduate course. According to the ruralites, the very fact that they were from a rural area was the reason for non-acceptance. Only three out of these forty-six reported strained relations when they were to leave the course. (iv) As many as 34 out of 174 rural students felt a sense of discrimination by teachers or heads of departments. The majority of ruralites had not developed close relations with any of their teachers: (v) As per the estimates from the obtained data it was observed that around a million rupees were transferred from rural areas to Bangalore city for every batch of students pursuing postgraduate education for a period of two years.

18 Shah, B., A sociological study of educational development of graduate students of Kumaun University with special reference of caste, Ph.D. Edu., Kumaun University, 1981.

The objectives of the study were: (i) to find out the relationship between various sociological characteristics pertaining to the graduates of Kumaun University, (ii) to know whether the differences in the sociological characteristics of the graduates of different castes account for any significant difference in their educational development, (iii) to identify the sociological characteristics that turn out to be the common and significant predictors of the educational development of subjects, and (iv) to study the effect of caste belongingness and educational development on the level of social adjustment, caste prejudices and social distance.

The sample of 1,050 graduate students was drawn randomly from students in graduate classes (B.A. II, B.Sc. II and B.Com. II) of the 1979-80 session from seven institutions of Kumaun University. A proportionate stratified random sample consisting of graduates of four castes (Brahmin, Kshatriya, Vaishya and other castes), with three categories of educational development (upward mobile graduates, irregular graduates and stagnate graduates) from three faculties (Arts, Science and Commerce) was chosen. Thus 4×3×3 factorial design with unequal cases in each cell was adopted. The tools administered were Social Characteristics Description Questionnaire, Social Distance Scale, Social Adjustment Inventory and the Indian Caste Prejudice Scale. Analysis of variance, chi-square test, percentages and t-test were used to analyse the data.

The important findings were: (i) The graduates of all castes were almost similar on the variables of curricular preferences, vocational aspiration of students, vocational mobility, determinants of courses of students, motivation for graduation and position among siblings. (ii) As regards family's educational background, father's vocational status and family reinforcement, the graduates of Brahmin and Vaishya castes were significantly higher than the graduates of Kshatriya and other castes. (iii) The economic condition of Vaishyas was the best, followed by that of Brahmins and Kshatriyas and then that of the other castes. (iv) During their academic life Vaishyas encountered few hurdles while Brahmins, Kshatriyas and other castes faced relatively more hurdles. (v) As compared to Vaishyas, a higher proportion of Brahmins, Kshatriyas and other castes was found in rural areas. (vi) Academic reinforcement was more prominent among the graduates of other castes; they were at an advanced age, significantly older than their higher castes counterparts. (vii) Cocurricular preferences of Kshatriyas were higher than those of others but were similar to those of Vaishyas. (viii) Educational development was affected more by different sociological variables than caste belongingness. (ix) Vocational aspirations of students, determinants of courses of studies and vocational mobility (in view of father's occupation) did not play a significant role in educational development. (x) Curricular preferences, age, vocational mobility (in view of traditional occupation), motivation for graduation and position among siblings were identified as weak predictors of educational development. (xi) Economic conditions, family educational background, father's vocational status, cocurricular preferences, family reinforcement, academic reinforcement, hurdles and social belongingness were factors affecting educational development. (xii) Although in respect of political, social and economic gain all the graduates were almost similar, on the variables of marriage and interpersonal relationship, education, employment and inhabitation and personal qualities the graduates of higher castes were more prejudiced. (xiii) As regards social distance, the graduates of other castes appeared more willing to retain intimate relations as well as friendly cooperation with the people of higher caste. (xiv) There were no caste differences as regards social adjustment. (xv) Higher education did not result in changing and fostering the attitudes of the Kumauni students toward different castes but the degree of educational development affected their caste perceptions.

19 Sharma, P., Leisure-time activities of college students of Delhi – A sociological study, Ph.D. Soc. Sc., Jawaharlal Nehru University, 1983.

The objectives of the study were: (i) to investigate the leisure-time activities of college students of Delhi University, and (ii) to explore the significance of the role of leisure in student life and its influence on their values.

Three colleges–one boys, one girls and one co-educational – were selected for the study. A sample of 514 student (301 boys and 213 girls) was drawn from these colleges by applying the multistage stratified systematic sampling technique to obtain a fairly representative sample of the student community. Observation and interview techniques were used throughout the first and second intervals of the field phase and the main part of the data were collected in the second interval by administering pre-coded and pre-tested questionnaire for the purpose of limiting the whole gamut of responses to specific alternatives provided for each set of questions. Percentages were worked out and chi-square test was used to determine the significance of the leisure-time activities of the students.

The major findings were: (1) A majority of students viewed leisure-time in terms of the time in which they were free to 'go as you please'. (2) The non-participation rate in college sponsored activities was as high as 75% to 87%. (3) Students' participation rate in legitimate leisure activities such as watching movies, going to cafe, playing games, reading and visiting was as high as 90% whereas the other legitimate activities such as relaxing with music, staying home or driving around were not popular. (4) The non-participation rate in different tabooed pleasures was as high as 40% to 96.1%. (5) By the large, the most popular legitimate leisure activities had equal influence on all students irrespective of variation of sex, institutional factors and socio-economic background. (6) The variables of sex (this includes not only male/female but the type of college as colleges basically reflect the sex-wise composition) exerted a significant influence on all types of leisure choices of students -- whether extracurricular, legitimate or tabooed to varying extents. (7) Among the institutional variables a course of study exerted a minor influence in the leisure choices of college-students. (8) The year of study significantly influenced students' participation in forbidden (tabooed) activities with the participation reaching its peak among the second year students as compared to the first and third year students. (9) The residence pattern exerted a strong influence on all types of leisure choices. (10) The type of family did influence students' cocurricular and tabooed choices, though it hardly exerted any influenced on their legitimate leisure choices. (11) Father's education, occupation and income exerted a significant influence on the students' extracurricular choices.

20 Sharma, R. Sub-culture of college students as a function of their adjustment, values, academic-motivation and attitudes, Ph.D. Edu., Meerut University, 1985.

The objectives were (i) to measure and compare different types of sub-cultures, (ii) to find out different types of sub-cultures of college students of different faculties, (iii) to find out how far the adjustment of students was related to their sub-cultures, (iv) to find out how far values were related to the sub-cultures of college students, (v) to find out how the academic motivation of college students was related to different types of sub-cultures, and (vi) to find out the extent to which different types of attitudes were related to each type of sub-culture.

The sample comprised 796 male students of five postgraduate colleges of Meerut University, from arts, science and commerce faculties. Personal Value Questionnaire developed by Sherry and Verma was used to measure values. Adjustment was measured with the help of Adjustment Inventory for College Students developed by Sinha and Singh. Academic Motivation Inventory for College Students, developed by Srivastava was used for measuring academic motivation. College Student sub-culture Questionnaire and College Student Attitude Scale were developed by the investigator. The split half reliability ranged from 0.63 to 0.71 and test-retest reliability from 0.68 to 0.77 for College Student Sub-culture Questionnaire. The test-retest reliability coefficients for College Students Attitude Scale ranged from 0.68 to 0.71. The data were analysed with the help of chi-square and analysis of variance followed by t-test.

The findings were: (1) College students possessed different types of sub-cultures. (2) Academic and vocational sub-cultural groups differed significantly. (3) The collegiate sub-culture was not found to be different from the vocational sub-culture. (4) The collegiate students differed from non-conformist students. (5) The students possessing vocational sub-culture differed from the non-conformist students. (6) The students of different faculties differed significantly as regards their types of sub-cultures. (7) The emotional, educational and total adjustment of students determined their academic sub-culture. Health, social and emotional dimensions of adjustments were significantly correlated with collegiate sub-culture. Social adjustment affected vocational sub-cultures. (8) Religious, aesthetic and knowledge values affected the academic sub-culture. Collegiate sub-culture was affected only by social value. Economic and hedonistic values affected the vocational sub-culture. Democratic power, family prestige, and health values were determinants of non-conformist sub-culture. (9) Academic motivation was found to be a significant factor in developing academic sub-culture of college students while it did not influence other sub-cultures. (10) Attitude of college students towards teachers and parents, discipline, religion and God were responsible in developing academic sub-culture. The collegiate sub-culture was affected by only the attitude towards college union. Vocational sub-culture was not affected by any type of attitude. The attitudes of non-conformist students towards different dimensions were negatively related.

21 Singh, Y., Academic role structure and modernization (A study of structural and cultural aspects of modernization among the university teachers), Deptt. of Soc., Rajasthan University, 1970 (ICSSR financed).

The purpose of the study was to analyse the various ramifications of tensions and equilibria which emerged in a university structure as a result of different types of integrations in the role structures of teachers in the context of modernisation which implied growth and development of roles on a progressive scale in societies.

The study was conducted on 248 male teachers of the teaching departments of Rajasthan University. The sample included professors, readers, senior lecturers and lecturers. The data were collected through a structured questionnaire in terms of a series of scales, which was developed for this study. It comprised items on modernisation, aspiration, morale, and commitment, and an open end question to elicit teacher cognitive association with modernisation. The reliability of the questionnaire was established. The data were analysed both qualitatively and quantitatively. Factor analysis was also utilised in analysing data.

The study revealed that (i) most of the teachers came from families having a tradition of professionalism; (ii) the mobility in respect of education seemed to be high between the generation of the self and fathers which was indicative of diversification of aspirations in the sphere of educational achievement; (iii) most of the teachers moved from lower middle class family status of middle class category; (iv) about 57.7 per cent of the families had high modernisation, which was again, more among the science teachers than among teachers of humanities and social sciences; (v) degree of modernisation was found to vary directly as commitment and inversely as aspiration; (vi) nearly 36.9 per cent teachers had role structures which were modern transitional, and fourteen per cent were purely modern which indicated a stage of transition in role structure towards modernisation; (vii) with the growth in the homogeneity in the structural context and modernisation process, the democratic values would also grow and authoritarianism would decline; and (viii) factor analysis of the modernisation scale revealed two factors, namely, 'Affective Neutrality' and 'Universalism-particularism'.

22 Srivastava, P. A comparative study of radicalism versus conservatism traits among adolescent boys and girls of intermediate colleges of Lucknow, Ph.D. Edu., Avadh University, 1981.

The main objective of the study was to find out how far the students in the intermediate colleges were radical or conservative in their attitude towards some vital personal, social and religious questions concerning the Indian society. It also tried to see if there were any differences among the radical and the conservative students as regards socio-economic backgrounds, sex and personality characteristics.

Data regarding radical and conservative attitudes were collected with the help of Duney's Radical-Conservative Attitude Scale. The sample consisted of 391 boys and 401 girls drawn from nine boys' and nine girls' institutions of Lucknow. Analysis of the scores on the attitude scale showed that among the boys 108 could be regarded as radical and 95 as conservative. Among the girls 100 were radical and 104 conservative. Out of these, 50 radical and 50 conservative boys, and 50 radical and 50 conservative girls were selected randomly. Data relating to socio-economic background and personality variables were collected with the help of a questionnaire and Cattell's HSPQ.

The main findings of the study were: (i) Girls were more radical than boys. (ii) More conservative boys and girls came from joint families. (iii) The majority of the radical boys and girls belonged to urban areas. (iv) The majority of the conservative boys and girls belonged to rural areas. (v) The majority of the radical boys and girls came from higher income groups. (vi) The radical boys were more warm-hearted, more intelligent and more self-sufficient than the conservative boys. (vii) The conservative boys were restless and excited. They were more reserved, less intelligent and less self-sufficient. (viii) The radical girls were more intelligent and had greater ego strength, dominance, surgency, and frustration. (ix) The conservative girls were more sober, more lax, more toughminded and less individualistic.

23 Thottam, George, *An evaluation of the system of mass communication education in Indian university with a view to propose a four-tier infrastructure*, Ph.P. Edu., Bombay University, 1983.

The objectives of the study were: (i) to assess the need for formal, university-based education in mass communication, (ii) to measure the response of the Indian mass media towards the academic programmes being offered by Indian universities, (iii) to assess the rate of growth of mass communication education in Indian universities, (iv) to evaluate the objectives, content and achievement level of these programmes, (v) to suggest methods for streamlining and improving the programmes, (vi) to propose a four-tier model which would serve as an infrastructure, and (vii) to suggest curricular models for each of the four levels, for reference or possible adoption.

The study employed descriptive research design and used analytical and comparative methods. The try out test was administered to a sample of six universities which conducted mass communication courses. The final data were collected from twenty-seven universities which conducted mass communication courses. Tools employed in this study were questionnaires for heads of departments, editors of newspapers, interview schedules for heads of departments, teachers, students, leading media professionals and communication educators. The data were analysed by using simple percentages.

Some of the major findings of the study were: (1) There was no infrastructure for mass communication education in India. (2) The universities were the best training grounds for mass communicators in India. (3) The non-university institutions involved in teaching and training in mass communication did not produce significant results. (4) The universities tended to include national needs in their goals and imparted more service ideals than private institutes. (5) The degree and diploma from universities enjoyed greater prestige and credibility in Indian society. (6) The universities could afford the high cost of mass communication and provide technical facilities which the private institutes with limited resources could not do. (7) There had been a rapid increase in the number of departments of journalism and mass communication since 1970. (8) There was need for the standardization of basic elements like the duration, curriculum content, minimum staff and physical facilities. (9) There was no inservice education to improve expertise and skills of the staff. (10) A majority of the teachers and heads of departments did not have the necessary academic qualifications or professional experience to teach mass communication effectively. (11) The departments did not have enough physical space for class rooms, offices, and libraries. (12) Although many departments taught mass communication research as a required course of their programme, departments of mass communication were not involved in any research activity. (13) The relationship between the media industry and the departments of mass communication was far from cordial. (14) The forty year history of journalism and mass communication education in India showed that there had been very little innovation.

24 Uniyal, M.P. and Shah, B., Study of caste-effect upon various academic areas at graduate level of Kumaun University, Deptt. of Edu., Kumaun University, 1979.

The basic questions which had been attempted in this project were: (i) Did the caste differences affect student enrolment trend, achievement, selection of the stream and courses of studies, attempts required to pass the examination and wastage and stagnation, etc.? (ii) Was there any hierarchy of different castes in different faculties on the basis of the above variables?

The sample of this longitudinal study consisted of the graduate students of the sessions 1973-74 to 1976-77 of Kumaun University. The year-wise students population of different castes (kshatriyas, vaishyas and other castes, consisting of scheduled castes, scheduled tribes and backward castes) along with their courses of studies, total marks and division obtained and attempts required to pass the first degree examination, etc., were noted from the University's annual examination registers. Other related information was also collected from the office of the registrar and colleges. The t-test, and chi-square test, were used as main statistical techniques.

The main findings of the study were: (i) The brahmins constituted the highest percentage of enrolment in all the faculties followed by kshatriyas, vaishyas and other castes. (ii) The other caste groups preferred the arts stream of science and commerce. (iii) The enrolment of male brahmin students in science tended to decline. It was the reverse in the case of the kshatriyas while the vaishyas and other castes showed irregular trends. (iv) In the case of arts faculty, the enrolment of the kshatriya and the other caste students was found to increase whereas the brahmin and the vaishya students showed a declining trend although the rate of decline in the case of the brahmin students was not of any significance. (v) In the commerce faculty, an irregular pattern of enrolment of the brahmin as well as the kshatriya students within a span of four sessions was observed, the vaishyas showed a regular rise while the other castes were at the explorative state. (vi) In regard to the girls' enrolment trend, in science stream a high degree of irregularity was found among all the castes. In the arts faculty, although the enrolment of the kshatriya and other caste females was tending to rise, yet the rate of increase was very slow in the case of kshatriyas. The female students of brahmin and other castes showed irregular trends of enrolment. (vii) Nearly 70 per cent of the total enrolment was in arts stream, on the other hand it consistently declined in the science stream whereas commerce was seen as gaining popularity. (viii) The caste was found highly effective in determining faculty preferences as well as subject preferences of the students. (ix) The highest preference of the brahmins for the science stream, of the vaishyas for the commerce stream, of the kshatriyas and other castes for the arts stream reflected the caste hierarchy in the selection of streams. (x) The subjects selected by the students as the courses of studies were found nearer to their traditional life-styles in the case of higher castes while the students of lower castes showed utilitarian preference; in fact, their preferences were more competition-oriented. (xi) The caste status was found to be singularly related to the academic achievement of the students. (xii) The vaishya and the kshatriya students were almost identical in mean total marks in all types of course. The brahmin students were nearer to the vaishya students in sceince courses but were nearer to the kshatriya students in commerce courses. (xiii) The students of other castes were found significantly below the traditionally privileged castes in respect to their academic success in all types of courses. (xiv) Above 90 per cent students belonging to the brahmin, kshatriya and vaishya castes had passed the arts and commerce graduate courses in one attempt. (xv) The wastage was high in the science stream as only about 85 per cent brahmin students, above 80 per cent kshatriya and vaishya students and about 60 per cent students of other castes passed the degree courses in one attempt. (xvi) Wastage and stagnation was comparatively high among the low caste students. (xvii) Not a single student among the other castes got a first division during the period under study. (xviii) The percentage of the brahmin students securing a first division was relatively high in all the faculties. (xix) The majority of the students of higher castes had passed the bachelor's degree in second division (xx) In the case of students of other castes, a majority obtained the bachelor's degree in arts and commerce courses with a third division while in the science stream they secured second division.

19. EDUCATIONAL TECHNOLOGY

A BOOKS

01 Association of Indian Universities. *Utilisation of Insat-1B for higher education*: Report of the task force. New Delhi, AIU, 1984. 68p.

02 Mukhopadhyay, M. *Educational technology in higher education.* New Delhi, NIEPA, 1978.

03 Natrajan, R. *Role of educational technology in higher education.* In Educational technology. Edited by M. Mukhopadhyay. 1990. p. 84-115.

04 Reddy, G. Ram. *New technologies in higher education.* In Educational technology. Edited by M. Mukhopadhyay. 1990. p. 69-75.

05 Shah, S.Y. ed. *New technologies in higher education.* New Delhi, AIU, 1986. 119p.

06 University Grants Commission. *Audio-visual aids in higher education.* U.G.C., 1969. 72p.

07 Vedanayagam, E.G. Teaching technology for college teachers. New Delhi, Sterling, 1988. 276p.

B ARTICLES

01 Gadbury, Adrian, Technological innovation: University roles. *University News.* 21 (18), 1983. p.598-602.

02 *INSAT-1B and higher education.* 14 (1), 1984. p.87-89.

03 *INSAT-1B and higher education.* 22 (5), 1984. p.1.

04 International conference on new technologies in higher education: A brief report. *University News.* 23 (46), 1985. p.9-10.

05 Joshi, D.C., Yadav, M.S., Mukhopadhyay, M. and Sanhana, S. Multi-media approach to collegiate instruction. *Journal of Higher Education.* 2 (1), 1976. p.118-120.

06 Kauagasabapathy, R. Management of change: A case study of Madurai Kamaraj University. *University News.* 25 (48), 1987. p.5-11.

07 Kapur, J.N. Technology of educational change: An experiment in Meerut University. *University News.* 7 (8), 1969. p.12-15.

08 New Technologies in higher education. *University News.* 22 (10), 1984. p.1-2.

09 Portia, D.R. Educational technology and higher education. *University News.* 15 (13), 1977. p.348-350.

10 Rais Ahmed. INSAT-1B and higher education. *University News.* 22 (10), 1984. p.3-4.

11 Rao, C.N.R. Technological revolution and education in India. *University News.* 9 (1), 1971. p.1-2 and 19.

12 Reddy, Usha Vyasulu. Television in higher education: The Indian experience. *Media in Higher Education.* 13 (2), 1988. p.165-176.

13 Shah, Beena. Computers in education: Teacher's role and teacher training programme. *University News.* 28 (8), 1990. p.1-6.

14 Shah, Beena. New technologies vs lecture tradition in higher education. *University News.* 26 (49), 1988. p.49-54.

15 Singh, R.K. Academic management of technical institutions. *University News.* 19 (7), 1981. p.189-191.

C COMMITTEE/COMMISSION/REPORTS

01 Committee on Audio-Visual Aids in Higher Education, 1967. Report. New Delhi, University Grants Commission, 1969. 72p. Chairman: Shri K.G. Saiyidian.

The committee was constituted to report on the present position of the use of audio-visual aids in higher education in India and to assess the possibilities of their development with particular reference to the institutions of higher education.

20. EMPLOYMENT

A BOOKS

01 Aisha Begum. *Problem of unemployment and need of changing the pattern of education in India*: Paper presented at workshop on alternative educational future, Policy Planning Unit, NCERT, New Delhi, 1977.

02 All India seminar on university employment information and guidance bureau, 2nd Bangalore, 1968. *Guidance services in colleges and universities*. Bangalore, Bangalore University and Directorate of Employment and Training, 1971.

03 *Andhra Pradesh utilization pattern of educated persons in Andhra Pradesh*. Hyderabad, Planing Department, 1968.

04 Bagga, Anjana. *Study of attitude of some cross-sections of post-graduate girls students towards employment of educated women*. Kurukshetra University, 1976.

05 Bhattacharya, A.K. *Problem of educated unemployment in India*. Meerut, Meenakshi Prakashan, 1982. 98p.

06 Blaug, M., Layard, P.R.G. and Woodhall, M. *Causes of graduate unemployment in India*. London, Penguin Press, 1969.

07 Borkar, V.V. and Kurulkar, R.P. *Employment experience of weaker caste graduate: Marathwada Region, India*. Paris, IIEP, 1987 (Occasional Paper No. 73).

08 Bose, P.K. *Graduate employment and higher education in West Bengal* by P.K. Bose, B.C. Sanyal and S.P. Mukherjee. New Delhi, Wiley Eastern, 1983. 289p.

09 Burgess, Tyrrel, Layard, Richard and Pant, Pitamber. *Manpower and educational development in India*. 1961-1986. Edinburgh, Oliver and Boyd, 1968.

10 Carnoy, Martin. *Higher education and graduate employment in India: A summary of three case studies*. Paris, IIEP, 1987.

11 Chowdhury, P.N. and Nandy, R.K. Scientific and technical personnel. In Amrik Sing and P.G. Altbach, eds. *The higher learning in India*. Delhi, Vikas, 1974. p.103-118.

12 Committee on Education and Total Employment. *Educated unemployment in India: Challenge and responses*. Delhi, Hindustan Publishing Corporation, 1972.

13 Dandekar, V.M. India. In Walter Adams, ed. *The brain drain*. New York, Macmillan, 1968. p.203-231.

14 Department of Science and Technology. *Science and technology doctorates*: An analysis of supply and employment characteristics. New Delhi, DST, 1985.

15 Dhar, T.N. *Education and employment in India — the policy news*. Calcutta, Minerva, 1975.

16 ——. *Politics of manpower planning: Graduate unemployment and the planning of higher education in India*. Calcutta, Minerva, 1974.

17 Directorate General of Employment and Training. *Employment Survey of alumni of Delhi University*. New Delhi, Ministry of Labour, 1962.

18 ——. *Pattern of Graduate employment*. New Delhi, Ministry of Labour, 1958.

19 ——. *Pattern of graduate employment*. New delhi, Ministry of Labour, 1963.

20 ——. *Report of the employment pattern of engineering graduates and diploma holders*. New Delhi, Ministry of Labour, 1971.

21 Directorate General of Rehabilitation and Employment. *Unemployment pattern among graduates*. New Delhi, Ministry of Labour, 1957.

22 Gujaral, Bureau of Economics and Statistics. *Study of utilisation pattern of educated persons in Gujarat*. Ahmedabad, Bureau of Economics and statics. 1967.

23 Gurbachan Singh. *Study of educated unemployeds in Kurukshetra district*. Kurukshetra, University of Kurukshetra, 1974.

24 Haryana. Planning Department. *Study of utilisation pattern of educated persons*. Chandigarh, Planning Department, 1966.

25 Ilachman, Warren F. *People in plenty-educated unemployment in India*. In Amrik Singh and philip G. Altbach, ed. *Higher learning in India*. Delhi, Vikas Publishing House, 1974.

26 Indian Institute of Management. *Educated unemployment in India*. Ahmedabad, IIM, 1968.

27 Institute of Applied Manpower Research, Delhi. *Demand and supply of engineering manpower (1961-75): Second report on engineering manpower survey*. New Delhi, the author, 1965.

28 Institute of Applied Manpower Research. *Engineering manpower analytical review of demand forecast methodology and provisional forecasts of growth.* New Delhi, IAMR, 1963.

29 ——. *A sectoral study of engineering manpower requirements.* New Delhi, IAMR, 1967.

30 ——. *Employment outlook for engineers: 1969-79.* New Delhi, IAMR, 1969.

31 ——. *Characteristics of unemployed engineers and scientists*: An analysis of live register cards of Delhi Employment Exchange, 1975.

32 Kerala, Planning Department. *A study of the utilisation pattern of educated persons in Kerala.* Trivandrum, Planning Department, 1969.

33 Maharashtra. Bureau of Economics and Statistics. *Pattern of utilisation of educated persons in Maharashtra.* Bombay Bureau of Economics and Statistics, 1966.

34 Majumdar, D.N. *Unemployment among the university educated.* Cambridge Mass.; centre for International Studies. Massachusetts Institute of Technology, 1967.

35 Ministry of Labour and Employment. *Report on the pattern of graduate employment.* Faridabad, Government of India Press, 1961.

36 Mukhopadhyay, S. *Unemployment, job search and the optimal waiting time.* New Delhi, Institute of Economic Growth, 1978.

37 Mysore, Directorate of Evaluation and Manpower. *Utilisation pattern of educated personnel.* Bangalore, Directorate of Evaluation of Manpower, 1969.

38 Nalla Gounden, A.M. *Education, employment and earning: A case study of post matriculation in India.* Madras, University of Madras, 1978.

39 Orissa, Education Department. *A study of the pattern of utilisation of educated persons in Orissa.* Bhubaneswar, Education Department, 1968.

40 Panchamukhi, P.R. *Employment and education policy: The Indian experience.* Bombay, University of Bombay, 1978.

41 ——. *Graduates and job market*: A quantitative study of universities in India. Paris, IIEP 1987. (Occasional Paper, No. 73).

42 Parmarji, S. *Education and Jobs.* New Delhi, Leela Devi, 1979.

43 Parvathamma, C.P. *Employment problems of university graduates.* New Delhi, Ashish Publishing House, 1989, 163p.

44 Rao, V.K.R.V. *University education and employment: A case study of Delhi graduates.* Bombay, Asia Publishing House, 1961. 45p.

45 Reddy, A.K.N. *The brain drain.* In Amrik Singh and P.G. Altbach, eds. *The higher learning in India.* Delhi, Vikas, 1974. p.373-394.

46 Saxena, J.P. *Educated unemployment in India: Problems and suggestions.* New Delhi, Commercial Publications, 1972.

47 Sanyal, B.C., Bose, P.K. and Mukherjee, S.P. *Graduate employment and higher education in West Bengal,* India. Paris, Unesco, 1983.

48 Shrimali, P.D. *Pattern of employment and earnings among graduates in Lucknow.* Lucknow, Labour Research Centre, 1967.

49 University of Calcutta. Department of Economics. *A study of the employment pattern of the post-graduate students of university of Calcutta,* May, 1972. New Delhi, Committee of unemployment, Ministry of Labour and Rehabilitation, 1975.

50 Varghese, N.V. *Higher education and employment in India: A review.* New Delhi, NIEPA, 1986. (Mimeo).

B ARTICLES

01 Adiseshiah, Malcolm S. Linking higher education and employment. *Bulletin Madras Development Series.* 17 (10), 1987. p.515-518.

02 Adisheshaiah, N.A. Unemployment of engineers in India. *Labour Development Abroad.* 15 (8), 1970. p.19-22.

03 Amrik Singh. Education, employment an plus two stage. *Mainstream.* 28.10.89 (Annual), 1989. p.45-46.

04 Apte, M.D. Education and unemployment in Kerala. *Economic and Political Weekly.* 10 (28), 1975. p.1041.

05 Bhutani, K.N. The Brain-drain – Some questions. *Indian Journal of Public Administration.* 15 (July-Sept.), 1969. p. 427-431.

06 Blaug, M. Educated unemployment in Asia: A contrast between India and the Philippines. *The Philippine Economic Journal.* 11 (1), 1972. p.33-35.

07 Bose, P.K. Graduate employment and higher education in West Bengal. *Journal of Higher Education.* 5 (3), Spring, 1980. p.281-299.

08 Chaudhari, D.P. and Rao, P. Private and Social returns to higher education: A case study of Delhi graduates. *Economic and Political Weekly.* 5 (15), 1970.

09 Chittibabu, S.V. Job-oriented courses in the field of higher education. *University News.* 13 (10), 1975. p.8-9.

10 Dhar, T.N. Enrolment and manpower: Target and policies. *Asian Survey*. 9 (Oct.), 1969. p.742-752.

11 Directorate General of Employment and Training. Survey of engineering graduates of University of Delhi, 64 batch. *Manpower Journal*. 2 (3), 1966. p.50-85.

12 Finance Department of Maharashtra. Utilization pattern of educated persons in Maharashtra during third plan. *Manpower Journal*. 3 (1), April-June, 1967. p.92-139.

13 Forrester, Duncan B. Initial occupational pattern of scheduled castes graduates in India. *New Frontiers in Education*. 5 (2), 1975. p. 49-65.

14 Gupta, S.P. University industry linkage. *University News*. 26 (25), 1988. p.5-6 and 17.

15 Hommes, Enno and Trivedi, N. The market for graduates: A field report. *Economic and Political Weekly*. 6, Dec., 1971. p.2486-2489.

16 Hone, Angus. Unemployed engineer. *Economic and Political Weekly*. 3 (13, April), 1968. p.616-618.

17 Ilchman, W.F. People in plenty: Educated unemployment in India. *Asian Survey*. 9 October, 1969. p.781-795.

18 Ilchman, Warren and Dhar, T.N. Student discontent and educated unemployment. *Economic and Political Weekly*. 5, July 1970. p.1259-1266.

19 Joshi, K.L. Education and employment in fifth plan. *University News*. 12 (2), 1974. p.22-24.

20 Merriam, Marshall F. Reversing the brain drain: A case study from India. *International Development Review*. 12 (Sept.), 1970. p.16-22.

21 Nanjundappa, D.M. Education, employment and development. *University News*. 19 (23), 1981. p.651-654 and 672.

22 Natarajan, V. Delinking degrees from Jobs. *University News*. 23 (7), 1985. p.2 and 6.

23 Pandit, H.N. Nature and dimensions of unemployed educated manpower in India, 1953-54. *Manpower Journal*. 1 (3 and 4), 1966. P.119-176.

24 ——. Supply and demand for secondary and higher educated manpower, 1960-61 to 1975-76. *Manpower Journal*. July-September, 1966p.

25 Pradhan, N. Educated unemployment: Causes and remedies. *University News*. 25 (24), 1987. p.9-11.

26 Ramakrishnan, A. Technical qualification: Gap between study and career. *University News*. 16 (20), 1978. p.1213.
27 Saxena, J.P. Unemployment among degree and diploma holders in engineering. *Artha Vijnana*. 19 (1), 1977. p.21-75.
28 Sen, Amitabha. Forging linkages between higher education and employment. *Manpower Journal*. 23 (3), 1987. p.1-13.
29 Sharma, G.D. and Masurkar, Mangla. Waiting period for unemployed graduates. *Eastern Economist*. 69 (24), 9 December, 1977. p.1131-35.
30 Sharma, Motilal. Education for optimizing vocational mobility. *University News*. 17 (3), 1979. p.1-3.
31 Sinha, Arun P. Demand characteristics of an educational market: Factors & forecast: A case study. *University Administration*. 3 (1), 1976. p.36-45.
32 Verma, M.C. Review of skilled manpower forecasts and changes in occupational structures in India. *International Journal of Educational Development*. 4 (3), 1984. p.173-221.

C COMMITTEES/COMMISSIONS/REPORTS

01 High Level Committee on Educational and Employment, 1982: Vol. II, Higher Education. Trivandrum, State Planning Board, 1984. Chairman: M.V. Pylee.

The Government of Kerala by G.O. Ms. 56/82/Plg. dated 4-10-1982 constituted six high level committees to assist the state planning board in discharging this function. One of these is the High Level Committee on Education and Employment. The Higher Level Committee on Education and Employment constituted five sub-groups in April 1983 and Higher Education is one of those subgroups.

After reviewing the development of higher education in the state, committee gave following recommendations:

Regarding qualitative improvement, committee recommended that only those with the required competence and aptitude should be admitted into the college. It is necessary to insist on the maintenance of correct attendance register. The university should reformulate their examination schedules. Adequate attention should be given in 7th plan for raising the level of infrasturctural facilities like buildings, laboratories and libraries. To construct large examination hall. Enforcement of rules prohibiting private tuition by college teachers. More attention to teaching by association of college teachers. The college teachers should be provided with incentives for their development. The university bodies should consider the need for changing the format of Degree certificates issued. The Academic Council of Universities should examine the feasibility of introducing the semester system for general courses. College student not be used as instruments by political parties.

The committee recommends common syllabus for pre-degree by all universities. A separate body for the conduct of predegree examination to be conducted. It necessary that the fee for college courses are raised.

The committee also recommends that norms to be framed for sanctioning new colleges and courses. Public accountability of money raised by colleges. It is better to scrap the whole procedure and make the Government responsible for selecting a suitable person as vice-chancellor. It is necessary to considerably enhance the facilities for vocational education after the secondary stage, restructuring of governing bodies of universities, establishment of an open university in the state, setting up of centres of excellence, Cochin university to be developed as an advanced centre for science and technology, advanced institute for physical education needed, some of the colleges in the states with a creditable record of performance may be identified and made into autonomous colleges. facilities for non-formal education to be increased.

D RESEARCH STUDIES

01 Chakrapani, C.H. Transactional paradigmatic study of unemployment as a stress or among unemployed graduates and postgraduates. Ph.D. Sociology, Andhra University, 1985.

The objectives of the study were: (i) to find out the relationship between age and stress, (ii) to find out the effect of education of parents on the stress among unemployed, (iii) to find out the difference between stress of graduates and postgraduates, (iv) to find out the relationship between stress indicators and health of the individual, and (v) to find out the difference between stress of individuals belonging to arts faculty and science faculty.

The sample for the study consisted of 312 unemployed persons out of which 212 were graduates and 100 postgraduates. All these individuals had been unemployed for at least one year. The data were collected with the help of following tools: (i) the General Stress Indicator Scale having dimensions like stress due to money matters, unemployment, criticism of family members criticism of relatives, criticism of friends, etc.; (ii) the Stress Indicator Response Scale. It was a battery of five scales concerned with emotionality, radicalism, hostility, behaviour adjustment, health, and the ego-strength. The scale had reliability ranging from 0.62 to 0.85. They had the factorial validity; (iii) the Unemployment Perceptions Scale having areas self-accountability, selective job performance, rational reaction, fairness of society, self-esteem and self-respect. The data were also collected about age, sex, marital status, caste, education, parental occupation, family size, number of close friends already employed, duration of unemployment, family as a source of help, extravagance, nonfamilial material support and religiosity. The data so collected were analysed with the help of analyse of variance, multiple regression and canonical correlation.

The findings of the study were: 1. Age was a positive contributor to stress. 2. Intermittent job experience was a predictor of stress. 3. The observed role of mother's education in promoting stress experience was the result of greater internalisation of work norms by educated mothers than uneducated mothers. 4. The respondent's unemployment anxiety was aggravated by his educated mother's anxiety. 5. The five stress indicator responses, viz., 'emotionality, radicalism, hostility, behaviour adjustment and health did not interrelate with one another. Emotionality was consistent in its association with behaviour. 6. Taking emotionality as an indirect stress indicator response, the regression analysis showed that self-esteem, selective job preference, and delinking of education from job contributed to lower emotionality among educated unemployed. 7. Postgraduates and respondents belonging to arts faculty and the artisam castes had reported high average radicalism scores. 8. Higher education and low caste status reinforced each other in causing high radicalism among the educated unemployed. 9. Ego-strength, family support, and fairness of society perception had been positively associated with radicalist tendencies. 10. None of the background factors such as age and sex, etc. except level of education was seen to affect the hostility dispositions. The graduates scored higher on hostility than postgraduates. 11. Neither background factors nor biographical and socio-economic factors affected behaviour adjustment. 12. None of the background factors accounted for variation in health response. 13. Perceptual and personality factors had a great role in stress responses. 14. The institutional factor of family support tended to cause a rational perception of unemployment among the respondents. 15. High religiosity contributed to a stronger ego and better behaviour adjustment as well as a balanced radical ideology. 16. Irrational unemployment perceptions caused variations in stress indicator response dimensions of hostility, emotionality and radicalism. 17. The educated unemployed had low stress experience, in general, with high behaviour adjustment and high health rating. Those who were getting good family support had strong ego. The institutions of caste, friendship, and education had specific and contingent effect on stress variation.

02 Parmaji, S. The relationship between general higher education and job-aspiration, job satisfaction and job-efficiency of non-professional job holders. Ph.D. Education, Maharaja Sayajirao University of Baroda, 1978.

The objectives of the study were to find out in what way (i) the general higher education and job aspirations were related, (ii) the general higher education and the clerical job satisfaction were related, (iii) the general higher education and the clerical efficiency were related, (iv) the pre-job aspirations and the clerical job satisfaction were related, (v) the pre-job aspirations and clerical efficiency were related, (vi) the clerical job satisfaction and clerical efficiency were related, (vii) the clerical efficiency was related to length of education and length of service, and (viii) the clerical job satisfaction was related to length of education and length of service.

The sample drawn on a stratified random basis consisted of 641 (571 males and 70 females) clerical workers having varying levels of educational attainments was drawn from the Life Insurance Corporation of India (L.I.C.) and the State Bank of Hyderabad. The data were collected with help of personal data blank, job aspirations inventory, job satisfaction questionnaire, which were constructed for the purpose, and job efficiency tool which was adopted from that of the L.I.C. Statistical techniques like mean, standard deviation and correlation were used in analysing the data.

The following were the results of the study: (i) Job aspirations escalated with the levels of education. (ii) Educated persons were generally less inclined towards occupations involving physical work. Whatever slight inclination they had towards such occupations was in the initial stages, and that inclination seemed to thin out with more education. (iii) Educated persons did not seem to have any inclination towards the non-salaried self-employing occupations either. Whatever little inclination was there during the early stages of education, tapered off into zero with the advancement of education. (iv) Only twelve per cent of clerical workers ever thought of becoming clerks at the various stages of attainment of their education. (v) The levels of education had a progressively negative association with the job satisfaction of the clerical workers. The negative association tended to intensify when the academic merit got added to the length of schooling. (vi) The length of schooling had a positive correlation with the measures of job efficiency. But when the academic merit was considered along with schooling, a clear trend was not obtained on the relationship between education and clerical efficiency. (vii) The relationship between the levels of pre-job aspirations and the levels of job satisfaction of the clerical workers was found to be negative. (viii) The relationship between the levels of pre-job aspirations and the levels of job efficiency of the clerical workers was not significant. (ix) The relationship between the measures of job satisfaction and the job efficiency of the clerical workers was not significant. (x) Length of service was a better predictor of clerical efficiency than the length of schooling (education). (xi) Education was a more potent predictor of clerical dis-satisfaction than the length of service.

03 Parvathamma, C.A. Sociological analysis of problems of employment of university graduates in Mysore. Deptt. of Post-graduate Studies and Research in Sociology, Mysore University, 1975. (Govt. of Mysore financed).

The major objectives of the present investigation were: (i) to find out the views of the students on the causes of unemployment in India and the role of formal education in relation to employment and unemployment; (ii) to find the differences of response, if any, between the professional and non-professional students; (iii) to study how the graduates' status was affected at home, and the status of the family was affected in the community; (iv) to study vocational interests of the students and the basis on which job preferences were made; and (v) to study the remedies the students offered for solving unemployment.

The investigation was a sociological survey and was exploratory in nature. In all, a sample of 2,617 students was selected at undergraduate and postgraduate levels from the faculties of arts, science, engineering, medicine and agriculture in the universities of Bangalore, Karnataka, and agriculture universities of the State. A questionnaire was administered to these students to gather information. Responses were coded, tabulated and examined.

The following were some of the significant findings of the study : (i) The general characteristics of the sample showed that there were more men students than women students. Science and technical courses had preponderance of men while arts subjects seemed to be favourites of women students. The sample was of predominantly Hindu, urban background, Kannada speaking, and single or unmarried college students. Brahmins were the largest single group followed by Lingayats and Okkaligas. (ii) Four-fifths of the respondents felt that education was necessary for employment. This view was held generally by the sons of white collared fathers. (iii) About ninety per cent of nonprofessional students, specially the girls, liked to continue for higher studies even if they failed to get a job. (iv) Students felt that overpopulation, lack of job oriented education, overcrowding of the universities, industrial under-development, and improper educational policies of the government were the causes of unemployment among the educated youth. (v) About seventyeight per cent favoured English as the common official language and fourteen per cent favoured Hindi. (vi) Only one-third non-professional and one-fifth professional students wanted Kannada as the medium of instruction. (vii) Opinion of the students was divided as to the use of Kannada in promoting job opportunities. (viii) About half of the students held that employment of both husband and wife created problems. (ix) Nearly half of the sample favoured government jobs, only a few favoured private concerns, and the remaining preferred independent professions. About sixtyfive per cent liked to go out of the State to do some work. (x) A majority of professional and nonprofessional students were willing to take up manual job. (xi) About half of the students did not mind being unemployed. A majority of the students were willing to take up jobs in the defence forces. (xii) A good percentage of students were willing to make arrangement for self employment. (xiii) Students felt that employment would bring them prestige and status. Without this they would be evaluated unfavourable by their families. They also felt that unemployment would cause increased unrest in general and would provide incentives to student unrest in particular.

04 Shah, M.V. A Study of unemployed graduates in Poona : Some sociological implications. Ph.D. Sociology, Poona University, 1978.

The objectives of the study were: (i) to shed light on some contributory factors, mainly sociological, to graduate unemployment, (ii) to study some sociological features of corruption in the recruitment of the jobs, (iii) to study the impact of unemployment on social relations as also its psychological consequences, (iv) to examine the problem of preferential employment (reservation of jobs) of job-seekers from the weaker sections of the society, (v) to analyse the views of the unemployed graduates and their socio-political significance, and (vi) to make a few suggestions on the basis of policy implications of the findings.

For the study, the unemployed graduate was defined as any graduate who had registered himself or herself at the central employment exchange at Poona and who, on the particular day of the visit by the researcher to interview him or her (between March 15, 1973 and September 25, 1973) was found to be normally resident in the Poona city and who was not having any paid job, in spite of his or her desire to have such a job, and who was not self-employed and who considered himself or herself to be involuntarily unemployed. The sample consisted of 163 respondents, 101 male and 62 female. They belonged to the faculties of arts (N=55), science (N=46), commerce (N=45), education (N=7), agriculture (N=6), and engineering (N=4). The tool used was a structured interview schedule which was pretested. The statistical analysis consisted of use of chi-square test.

The findings of the study were : (i) The system of higher education failed in achieving occupational socialization of students. (ii) Graduate unemployment in urban areas mostly affected the middle- and upper-income groups. (iii) There was very strong resistance to accept rural jobs on account of low compensation, inadequate amenities and insecurity on the jobs. (iv) The respondents, as a group, showed low geographical mobility. The mobility was dependent on the perception of local employment opportunity. Further, mobility appeared greater among the male, low income-per-family member respondents, and pass class graduates. The association between the length of unemployment and mobility was not significant. One of the most important reasons inhibiting mobility was attachment to the family. (v) The reluctance to accept non-desk job did not appear to be a significant contributory factor to unemployment. (vi) There was reluctance to accept low-paid jobs contributing to unemployment. (vii) By and large, psychological consequences of unemployment were significant but not severe. Similarly, the impact of unemployment on social relations of the respondents was also not grave. (viii) The majority of the respondents believed that corruption was common in employment practices. (ix) There was a sharp division among the respondents on the issue of the reservation of jobs for the scheduled castes and scheduled tribes.

05 Sinha, S.N. An investigation of some correlates of job orientation of university students. Deptt. of Psychology, Rajasthan University, 1971 (NCERT financed).

The major objectives of the study were: (i) to determine the extent to which the contemporary job orientation pattern prevailing among university students were based on students' awareness of job spectrum; (ii) to determine the degree to which students' job orientation was influenced by job availability and to estimate the discrepancy between idealised and actual requirements of jobs; (iii) to determine the extent to which students' job orientation was influenced by parental decisions or other superordinate decisions made by guardians, elderly family persons or teachers; and (iv) to ascertain whether job orientation and choices tended to be determined by such motivational categories of job stratification, such as esteem, fame, power leadership, prestige, social service, money, security, etc.

A random sample of 1,320 male and female students of first and third years of the three year degree course was taken. For data collection a questionnaire was developed.

The findings of the study were as follows : (i) The job orientation of students was considerably influenced by parental decisions and in some cases by friends and teachers also. (ii) The most preferred occupational category, among all the subjects of the sample was the professional and technical, while the administrative and sales job ranked second and third in order of preference. (iii) A considerable disparity was found between the values of the students and the jobs they sought. (iv) Most of the students were found to be vocationally immature in the sense that their job awareness was very low. (v) No correlation was found between awareness of job units and awareness of functions of the same units. (vi) A significant difference was found in the job preference and job awareness of the students. (vii) Marked discrepancies were found between the job availability and job preferences of students. (viii) No significant difference was found between the job awareness of science and arts students, but the job awareness of the commerce students was lower in comparison to that of science and arts students. (ix) The knowledge about jobs and their functions was possessed more by female students in comparison to male students.

21. ENROLMENT

A BOOKS

01 Kurulkar, R.P. *Enrolment and manpower*. Aurangabad, Marathwada University, 1967.

02 Sharma, G.D. *Enrolment in higher education: A trend analysis, 1961-75*. New Delhi, Association of Indian Universities, 1978. 115p.

B ARTICLES

01 Desai, Dhanwant M. Enrolment trend and behaviour in education in the Gujarat state. *Education and Psychology Review*. 7 (1), 1967. p.10-21.

02 Indian University Reform II. Higher education: Enrolments and programmes. *Minerva*. 5, (Winter), 1967. p.242-264.

03 Nurul Hasan, S. India restricting enrolments in higher education. *ACU Bulletin of Current Documentation*. (12) February, 1974. p.20-21.

04 Tripathi, O.D. and Singh, S. Higher education: Problem of enrolment. *University Administration*. 5 (1), 1978. p.22-29.

05 U.G.C. annual report for 1982-83 reveals increase in student enrolment in universities and college. *University News*. 22 (16), 1984. p.1-2.

D RESEARCH STUDIES

01 SHARMA, G.D., Enrolment in higher education — A trend analysis, AIU, 1977.

The objectives of the study were: (i) to examine the problem particularly in its locational or regional aspects, (ii) to trace the factors responsible for the declining trend, (iii) to examine the implications of such a trend, and (iv) to suggest possible measure to arrest the declining trend.

Data were collected from the UGC reports, Ministry of Education and Social Welfare, Government of India, and other secondary sources. Data were analysed quantitatively using regression analysis and trend analysis techniques. Besides, data were analysed qualitatively in terms of graphic presentations and description of facts.

The findings of the study were: 1. There have been declining rates of growth in enrolment in higher education during 1970-75. Negative rates of growth were observed in some faculties such as science, engineering and technology, arts, medicine and agriculture. However, there was higher rate of growth of enrolment from 1960 to 1970. 2. Inter-state variations were marked with regard to rates of growth of enrolment. 3. Among the factors considered, the expenditure on higher education was an important determining variable in the rate of growth in enrolment. 4. Government policy, new developments in education such as correspondence courses, permitting non-collegiates to appear for degree examinations and the new 10+2+3 system of education diverted students from regular colleges and thus affected the enrolment to some extent. 5. The declining trend in rate of growth affected the demand for educated people in the education industry. 6. Declining trends in the rate of growth of enrolment in the case of colleges in urban areas helped in the improvement of teacher student ratio. But in the case of colleges in rural areas with small enrolment further decline in the enrolment adversely affected the economic functioning of these colleges. 7. The faster rate of growth in the number of institutions of higher education and enrolment during 1950-70 had resulted in deterioration in the quality of higher education, establishment of a large number of colleges with small enrolment termed as under-populated colleges, and larger supply of graduate degree holders than the economy could absorb.

22. EVALUATION

A BOOKS

01 National Institute of educational Planning and Administration. *Evaluation of institutions of higher education: Planning and management dimensions*, New Delhi, NIEPA, 1989. 156p.

02 National Science Foundation. *Systems for measuring and reporting the resources and activities of colleges and universities*. New Delhi, NSF, 1967. 444p.

B ARTICLES

01 Amrik Singh. University and accountability. *Mainstream*. 28 (21), 1990. p.11-12.

02 Arun Kumar. Accountability and autonomy in higher education: Needed internal democracy. *Economic and Political Weekly*. 22 (44), 1987. p.1858-1861.

03 Banerji, R.C. Who should rate teachers? *Education Review*. 49 (1), 1973. p.249-53.

04 Baumgartal, Howard. Evaluation of management development efforts in the university setting: Problems, programmes and research model. *New Frontiers in Education*. 7 (1), 1977. p.36-60.

05 Bhatt, Anil and Shukul, H.C. Evaluation of teachers by students. *Journal of Higher Education*. 2 (3), 1977. p.415-418.

06 Bhatt, Mahesh. Accountability in education. *Educational Review*. 95 (11), 1989. p.1-3.

07 Chalam, K.S. Evaluation and accountability in higher education. *University News*. 28 (4), 1990. p.1-2 and 9.

08 ——. The concept of Accreditation and Assessment Council: Some observations. *University News*. 27 (17), 1989. p.4-5.

09 Dass, P.C. Sample study of evaluation of teachers by students. *Quest in Education*. 11 (3), 1977. p.222-232.

10 Evaluating evaluators. *University News*. 27 (36), 1989. p.6-9.

11 Francis, C.M. Teaching methods and evaluation techniques. *New Frontiers in Education*. 7 (4), 1977. p.1-18.

12 Gardner, Don E. Five evaluation frameworks: Implications for decision-making in higher education. *Journal of Higher Education.* 48 (5), 1977. p.571-593.

13 Hill, Walker H. Evaluation in university education. *Journal of University Education.* 3 (2), 1964. p.122-134.

14 Natrajan, V. Evaluating the structural unit of institution by multiple correlation. *New Frontiers in Education.* 7 (4), 1977. p.38-47.

15 Nigam, Raghuvir Sahay. Accountability of universities. *Education Review.* 80 (1), 1974. p.1-2.

16 Orpen Christopher. Evaluation and improvement of university teaching. *Journal of Higher Education.* 13 (1-3), 1987-88. p.47-62.

17 Panchamukhi, P.R. Devaluation of education: A quantitative analysis. *Journal of Higher Education.* 1 (1), 1975. p.15-30.

18 Parma, S.K. Examination or evaluation. *Educational India.* 41 (1), 1977. p.8-10 & 17.

19 Reddy, A. Venkata Rami. Internal assessment: A remedy worse than the disease. *Education Quarterly.* 28 (4), 1977. p.12-15.

20 Rice, Stephen L. Techniques of evaluating effective objectives. *Eastern Economist.* 67 (7), 1977. p.387-389.

21 Safaya, Raghunath. Macro-approach to evaluation. *Education Review.* 80 (6), 1974. p.121-123.

22 Samant, D.G. Implications of grades for university teachers. *Progress of Education.* 51 (12), July, 1977. p.218-220.

23 Saraswathi, L.S. Teacher evaluation by the taught. *Journal of Higher Education.* 1 (3), 1976. p.315-324.

24 Sharma, J.R. Assessment of teacher's work. *Education.* 34 (11), November, 1955. p.3-6.

25 Shastri, Diwakar, Accreditation and assessment council: Concepts and realities. *University News.* 27 (50), 1989. p.1-2.

26 Singh, K. Jagjit. Institutional accountability. *University News.* 27 (28), 1989. p.1-5.

27 Singh, Maharaja. Evaluation of research: Search for an objective criterion. *University News.* 27 (34), 1989. p.6-7.

28 Singh, M. Raghuram. Perspective view of educational evaluation. *Education Quarterly.* 26 (2), 1974. p.5-7.

29 Trivedi, Jyoti H. Understanding accreditation. *University News.* 28 (3), 1990. p.1-3.

30 U.G.C. annual report for 1982-83 reveals increase in student enrolment in universities and college. *University News.* 22 (16), 1984. p. 1-2.

23. EXAMINATION REFORM

A BOOKS

01 Amrik Singh. *Commonsense about examinations*. Delhi, Oxford University Press, 1984.

02 ——. Examinations: *Strategy of change*. In Amrik Singh and Altbach, eds. *The higher learning in India*. Delhi, Vikas, 1974. p. 291-311.

03 Amrik singh and Singha, H.S. *Management of examinations*. New Delhi, Association of Indian Universities, 1977. 264p.

04 Association of Indian Universities. *Management of examinations*. New Delhi, A.I.U., 1977. 254p.

05 ——. *Monograph on grading for universities*. New Delhi, A.I.U., 1977. 52p.

06 ——. *Monograph on internal assessment for universities*. New Delhi, A.I.U., 1977. 197p.

07 ——. *Monograph on test and item analysis for universities*. New Delhi, A.I.U., 1977. 256p.

08 ——. *Monograph on moderation of examination results*. New Delhi, A.I.U., 1981. 71p.

09 ——. Research Cell. *Monograph on question banking for universities*. New Delhi, A.I.U., 1977. 107p.

10 ——. *Monograph on test and item analysis for universities*. New Delhi, A.I.U., 1977. 256p.

11 ——. *Towards better questions (item writers cookbook)*. New Delhi, A.I.U., 1976. 126p.

12 ——. *Unfair means in university examinations : A study*. New Delhi, A.I.U., 1989. 157p.

13 Cieslak, E.C. et al. *Examinations of Indian higher education*. New Delhi, United States Information Service, 1959.

14 Datta, Asim Kumar. *Reform of the examination system of the small universities of West Bengal* : A study. Calcutta, Jadavpur University, 1970. 38p.

15 Inter University Board of India and Ceylon. *Examinations in higher education* : Report of a seminar held on Jan., 27-31, 1971, New Delhi. New Delhi, The author, 1971. 84p.

16 Joseph, D.T. Conduct of examinations. New Delhi, Association of Indian Universities, 1986. 108p.

17 Mishra, N.L. Organisation and Management of university examinations. Jaipur, National, 1988. 321p.

18 Natarajan, V. *Computer in examinations : Why and How*. New Delhi, A.I.U., 1982. 207p.

19 Natarajan, V. and Gunasekaran, K. *Scaling techniques, What, why and how*. New Delhi, Association of Indian Universities, 1986. 216p.

20 Natarajan, V. *Monograph on sample free item analysis for universities*. New Delhi, A.I.U., 1987. 171p.

21 National Council of Educational Research and Training, Department of Curriculum and Evaluation. *Report of the working group for developing comprehensive scheme of examination reform in university education, March 18-21, 1968*. 49p. (Mimeograph)

B ARTICLES

001 Alkara, Jacob. Internal assessment in higher education. *Education Quarterly*. 29 (3), 1977. p. 9-13.

002 Amrik Singh. Examinations : The strategy of change. *New Frontiers in Education*. 3 (2), 1973. p. 74-91.

003 ——. Mechanical aids in examinations. *University News*. 9 (4), 1971. p. 1.

004 Asrani, Shyam M. Wanted reforms in examination system. *Modern Review*. 137 (2), 1973. p. 131-133.

005 Asthana, B.C. Note on the examination research project at the Aligarh Muslim University. *Journal of Education and Psychology*. 14 (3), October, 1956. p. 149-53.

006 Bahuguna, S.D. Use of unfair means in examinations, Common Public View : A case study. *University News*. 10 (7), 1972. p. 16-18.

007 Banerji, Purabi. Examination reforms. Mainstream. 12 (45), 1974. p. 13-14.

008 Bureau, J.R. Failings of the exam. system. *University News*. 21 (22) 1983. p. 798-799.

009 Chari, M.S.V. Examination reform. *Educational India.* 38 (9), March, 1972. p. 307-308.

010 Dave, Ravindra and Hill, Walder. Educational and social dynamics of the examination system: A case study of India. *Comparative Education Review.* (18), February, 1974. p. 24-38.

011 Delhi University examination reform committee report. *University News.* 7 (4), 1969. p. 7-8.

012 Desai, D.M. Brief history of the movement for examination reform in Indian universities. *Education and Psychology Review.* 10 (3), July, 1970. p. 173-178.

013 ——. Examination reform in higher education in India. *Journal of Education and Psychology.* 29 (3), October, 1977. p. 181-92.

014 Deshpande, M.G. Few suggestions to the university and the S.S.C.E. Board. *Progress of Education.* 34 (7), February, 1960. p. 233-35.

015 Dongre, G.S. And these post-graduate examination too. *Progress of Education.* 35 (12), July, 1961. p. 398-402.

016 ——. Examination reform - A plan of action. *Progress of Education.* 48 (5), 1973. p. 148-151.

017 Duggal, S.L. System of internal assessment in education. *University News.* 6 (11), 1968. p. 14-18.

018 Examination reforms. *University News.* 15 (4), 1977. p. 79 and 94.

019 Examination reform: A plan of action. endorsed by the U.G.C. *New Frontiers in Education.* 3 (3), December, 1973. p. 98-113.

020 Examination reform: An opinion survey. *Educational India.* 30(10), April, 1964. p.333-38.

021 Examination reform in Indian universities. *Journal of Education and Psychology.* 15 (4), January, 1958. p. 187-89.

022 Examinations by universities. *Journal of Education.* 8 (1), September-November, 1960. p. 48-49.

023 Examinations reform in Mysore. *University News.* 3 (2), 1965. p. 1 and 17.

024 Fonseca, C. Danger to life and limb: Thoughts on examination reform. *New Frontiers in Education.* 3, December, 1973. p. 91-97.

025 Forrester, Jean. What makes a good examination paper? *Teaching.* 28 (1), September, 1955. p. 16-19.

026 Gayen, A.K. and Philip, P.J. Survey of examinations in Indian universities. *Indian Journal of Educational and Administrative Research.* 2, Winter, 1961. p. 1-118.

027 Goel, S.C. Examination reform : A new perspective. *Journal of Higher Education.* 2 (1), 1976. p. 48-58.

028 Grewal, J.S. Examination reform in an affiliating university. *University News.* 21 (9), 1983. p. 268-270.

029 Gunasekaran, K. A study of the reappearance cases of the Madras University. *University News.* 20 (13), 1982. p. 428-430.

030 Gupta, Arun Kumar. Open book examination in India : Some reflections. *Education Quarterly.* 25 (2), 1973. p. 6-9.

031 Gupta, S.C. Conversion of marks into grades : A comparative study. *University News.* 14 (10), 1976. p. 9-11.

032 Gurku, G.H. Examination reforms in Kashmir University. *University News.* 17 (20), 1979. p. 526.

033 Harper, A. Edwin. The problem of grading borderline marks. *University News.* 14 (8), 1976. p. 3-4.

034 Hill, Walker H. Internal assessment and external examinations. *Progress of Education.* 39 (2), September, 1964. p. 44-51.

035 IUB extraordinary meeting discusses examination reform. *University News.* 9 (11), 1971. p. 1.

036 Iyer, T.S.K.V. Examination reform: Innovation, teaching and learning. *Journal of Higher Education.* 2 (1), Monsoon, 1976. p. 83-94.

037 Jagdale, M.H. Examination reforms : A plan for action. *University News.* 15 (21). 1977. p.577-579.

038 Julka, Satya Pal. Examination reforms-I. *University Affairs.* May, 1976. p. 6-7.

039 Julka, Satya Pal. Examination reform-II, Grade System. *University Affair. June, 15 - July 15,* 1976. p. 5-7.

040 Julka, Satya Pal. Examination Reforms-III, Question banks. *University Affairs. July, 15 - Aug. 15, 1976.* p. 11-13 and 23.

041 Kahlon, A.S. Students evaluation and internal assessment. *University News.* 15 (3), 1977. p. 56-57.

042 Kannappan, D. Examination reforms in laboratories. *University News.* 27 (21), 1989. p. 7-9.

043 Khanna, Amar Nath. Examination reform. *Education.* 38 (4), April, 1959. p. 17-22.

044 Kothari Commission on examination reform. *Education and Psychology Review.* 6 (4), October, 1966. p. 163-65,

045 Mahajani, G.S. Examination reform. *University News.* 8 (5), 1970. p. 14-16.

046 Maharashtra ordinances, 1982. *University News.* 20 (11), 1982. p. 394-395.

047 Malik, Vimal. U.G.C. reforms of examinations: A critical review. *Education Quarterly*. 27 (4), January, 1976. p. 28-30.

048 Mathur, M.V. Examination reform. *Statesman*. Oct., 13, 1973. p. 13-14.

049 Mathur, R.K. Effectiveness of board and university examinations in India. *Bulletin of the Institute of Public Administration, Patna University*. 7 (1), 1962. p. 43-62.

050 Mathur, V.S. Examination business. *University News*. 15 (12), 1977. p. 325 and 337.

051 Mishra, N.L. Management of examination record. *University News*. 25 (18), 1987. p. 2-9.

052 Mishra, N.L. Student's service centre : A blue print. *University News*. 25 (7), 1987. p. 2-7.

053 Mishra, V.S. Proposals for examination reform. *Christian Education*. 52 (4), 1973. p. 8-21.

054 Mukherjee, Deb Narain. Urgent need for examination reform. *Education*. 27 (8), May, 1948. p. 47.

055 Nadkarni, Shirish M. No uniformity in Bombay Varsity assessment. *Opinion*. 21 July, 1970. p. 4-6.

056 Nair, K.R. Ramachandran. Open book examinations. *University News*. 18 (23), 1980. p. 653-654.

057 Nair, Srekumaran. New examinations system : A View from arts. *University News*. 7 (1), 1974. p. 11-12.

058 Natarajan, V. Design of internal assessment of universities. *University News*. 15 (10), 1977. p. 265-268.

059 ——. Examination reform : Programme and its outcomes. *University News*. 14 (1), 1976. p. 22-23 and 25.

060 ——. Grading of restructured examination. *University News*. 15 (8), 1977. p. 211-212.

061 ——. Grading system in university examinations. *University News*. 15 (11), 1977. p. 295-297.

062 ——. Question banks : At first degree level subjects for Madras University. *University News*. 14 (2), 1976. p. 9-11.

063 ——. Question banks : Their use in Indian examinations. *New Frontiers in Education*. 5 (3), 1975. p. 64-71.

064 ——. Question choice in examination. *University News*. 15 (20), 1977. p. 551-552 and 561.

065 ——. Restructuring of university examination. *University News*. 14 (11), 1976. p. 6-8.

066 ——. Scientific "Grace" in university examinations. *University News.* 17 (14), 1979. p. 379-380 and 383.

067 ——. Universities and national development : A status report and future projections in examination reforms. *University News.* 17 (12), 1979. p. 325-331.

068 Natarajan, V. and Arora, Asha. Re-evaluation : Some academic issues. *University News.* 20 (3), 1982. p. 154 and 156.

069 Natarajan, V. and Gunasekaran, K. Case for including objective type items in the university examinations. *University News.* 22 (33), 1984. p. 3-5.

070 Natarajan, V. and Ved Prakash. New approach for the construction of practical laboratory and field work examination. *New Frontiers in Education.* 8 (3), July-September, 1978. p. 56-64.

071 Nayudu, M.V. Examination reforms. *University News.* 12 (2), 1974. p. 19-21.

072 Patel, A.S. Case for reforming examination procedures : An experimental study. *Maharaja Sayajirao University of baroda Journal.* 17 April, 1968.

073 Prabhu, S.S. and Venkataramiah, H.V. Examination reform : Later grading system, some blind spots. *Journal of Higher Education.* 2 (1), 1976. p. 69-72.

074 Pathak, C.C. Examination reform and role of teachers' colleges. *Journal of Education and Psychology.* 27 (2), July, 1969. p. 217-22.

075 Punalekar, D.S. Examination reforms of the South Gujarat university. *University News.* 24 (10), 1986. p. 5-7.

076 ——. Reforming examination system. *University News.* 15 April. 1981. p. 217-219.

077 Rao, P. Kodanda. Teaching colleges vs. examining universities. *Education.* 8 (1), January, 1954. p. 29-32.

078 Rao, R.S.V. Examination reform. *Educational India.* 38 (7), January, 1972. p. 244.

079 Reddy, A. Venkata Rami. Internal Assessment : A remedy worse than the disease. *Education Quarterly.* 28 (4), January, 1977. p. 12-15.

080 Rippers, Victoria L. On the validity of university examinations : Some comments on the language of the debate. *University Quarterly.* 28 (2), 1974. p. 209-218.

081 Saraswati, L.S. Examinations reforms : An analysis of reforms suggested by UGC. *Education Quarterly.* 26 (1), 1974. p. 23-28.

082 Satish Chandra. Examination reform : A plan for action. *Statesman.* Oct., 13 1973. p. 10-12.

083 Shah, G.B. Examination reform : Some perceptions. *University News.* 20 (8), 1982. p. 267-268 and 272.

084 Shakare, M.L. and Ramaswami, T. Examinations of Union Public Service Commission *vis-a-vis* higher education of India. *Journal of Higher Education.* 7 (1), 1981. p. 45-50.

085 Shamsuddin. Examination reform. *Education Quarterly.* 26 (1), 1974. p. 29-33.

086 Sharma, J.N. Examination reform : UGC plan of action. *University News.* 15 (4), 1977. p. 1 and 94.

087 Sharma, J. Sakuntala. Sampling universes of questions for university examinations. *Educational Miscellany.* 6 (3-4), December, 1969 - March, 1970. p. 49-55.

088 Singh, M. Raghuram. Examination reform. *Naya Shikshak.* 18 (2), October-December, 1975. p. 29-37.

089 Singha, H.S. Declining ethics of examinations. *University News.* 12 (7), 1974. p. 3-6.

090 ——. Question banking in the universities. *University News.* 12 (5), 1974. p. 3-5.

091 Singhal, R.P. Reforming university examination system. *University News.* 23 (18), 1985. p. 2-6.

092 Srivastava, H.S. Some conceptual variations in examination reform. *Indian Education Review.* 12 (1), 1977. p. 1-10.

093 Sylvester, S.P. Examinations sans tension *University News.* 25 (7), 1987. p. 1 and 3.

094 Takwale, Ram. Examination reforms and restructuring of first degree programme. *University News.* 21 (8), 1983. p. 227-231.

095 Trivedi, Jyoti. Restructuring of undergraduate courses. *University News.* 21(11), 1983. p.345-346.

096 Trivedi, R.S. Towards examination reform. University News. 4 (5), 1966. p. 3-5.

097 Vasudev, T. Examination reforms and restructuring undergraduate courses. *University News.* 21 (13), 1983. p. 408-409.

098 Verma, D.P. The racket of representations. *University News.* 20 (13), 1982. p. 426-427.

099 ——. University examinations : Some sidelights. *University News.* 21 (16), 1983. p. 515-517.

100 Varma, M. Scope of research on examination. *Journal of Education and Psychology.* 9 (4), January, 1952. p. 207-12.

101 Visveswarayya, D. Examination reform. *Educational Review*. 65 (6), June, 1959. p. 131-37.

102 Wadia, A.R. Tangle of examination in our universities. *Journal of Education and Psychology*. 10 (2). July, 1952. p. 48-66.

103 What next in examination reform? *Teacher Education*. 2 (8-9), August-September, 1968. p. 54-58.

104 Workshop on computerisation and management of examinations : Report . *University News*. 23 (32), 1985. p. 1-8.

C COMMITTEES/COMMISSIONS/REPORTS

01 Committee on examination reforms, 1957. Report. New Delhi, University Grants Commission, 1962. 115p. Chairman: Shri S.R. Dongerkery.

The committee was constituted to study in detail the problems relating to examinations in Indian universities, and to suggest measures to bring about necessary improvements. This report, spread over seven chapters and 14 appendices, presents an exhaustive account of the existing system of examinations and educational problems of examination reform. The problem of marking, scaling, classification of students and medium of examination are the other aspects discussed in this report. The recommendations on examination reforms are presented in chapter 7 (see p. 39-45 of the report).

02 Committee on the Indian examination reform project, 1958. Report, Delhi, The Manager of Publications, 1959. Chairman: Shri B.C. Asthana.

The committee was appointed by the Government of India to visit the United States for the purpose of studying examination methods in American universities. The committee made recommendations on teaching methods as well as general recommendations which have been given in the report pages 63-70.

03 Committee on examination reform in central universities, 1966. Report. New Delhi, University Grants Commission, 1969. 29p. Chairman : Prof. F.C. Auluck.

The vice-chancellors of the central universities at their meeting, held on 1st December 1966, recommended the setting up of a committee to review the examination system of central universities and to suggest necessary changes in the techniques of measurement and evaluation with a view to ensuring greater reliability and validity. The committee made some general recommendations for the examination reforms. These are given on pages 26-29 of the report.

04 The Examination Reforms Committee, 1967. Report: The existing system of examinations and measures for improving upon it. Calcutta, University of Calcutta, 1967. 34p. Chairman : Bidhubhushan Malik.

The syndicate of the Calcutta University constituted a committee to investigate into the prevailing system of examinations and to suggest short-term remedial measures.

The committee recommended :

Lectures delivered in colleges should cover as much of the prescribed syllabus as possible. Boards of under-graduate studies should be consulted for ascertaining the heaviness or otherwise of the syllabus and for ensuring a judicious distribution of the total learning material for the degree course between Part-I and Part-II classes.

A question paper should provide double the number of questions to be answered. Questions should be couched in a simple unambiguous language and be distributed evenly over the entire syllabus. Where option is given to answer in Bengali, parallel questions in both English and Bengali or any other major Indian language should be set. Examiners should be appointed mostly from college teachers. The moderator should see that the paper contains a sufficient number of questions within the reach of an average student.

Separate papers of the same standard should be set for the collegiate and external candidates, the latter to be examined on separate dates. Wherever possible, examinees should be accommodated in their respective college buildings. Invigilators should be selected from among teachers.

Tutorial/seminar work should be obligatory for both pass and honours students. Students' performances in tutorial work should be considered for finalising results of college tests and should also be given some consideration in finalising results of University Examination. The number of teaching days in a college should be preferably 200. A lecture period should extend over 45 minutes or more. The weekly working load of teachers (excluding Principals and Heads of Departments) should be 18 hours or 24 periods of 45 minutes duration each.

A college should arrange for at least two periodical examinations in a year besides class examinations. Students should be sent up for a university examination on the basis of his/her performance in all the college tests considered together.

Regular reports of progress of study in each subject and of performances in periodical tests should be regularly secured from the Principals of colleges. If the percentage of successful examinees among candidates sent up by a college continues to remain below 30 for 3 consecutive years, appropriate steps should be adopted in respect of the college.

An Examination Research unit should be permanently attached to the office of the Controller of Examination.

05 Committee on Examination, 1970. Report. New Delhi, Central Advisory Board of Education, 1971.

During the last few years, malpractices and eruption of violence during the progress of an examination or after an examination have increased in the country. The Central Advisory Board of Education, at its 35th meeting held in 1970, expressed considerable concern about the conduct of public examinations held in different parts of the country and passed the following resolution: The Board requests the chairman to set up a committee on examination to examine the present situation and make recommendations to counteract malpractices and to give protection to invigilators and other concerned with examination. The chairman of the Central Advisory Board of Education appointed a committee in 1970. The committee has made recommendations under the headings, viz (a) legislation, (b) conduct of examinations, (c) the use of examination results, (d) the budgeting for education, (e) the research, and (f) novel ideas, etc. Recommendations are given on page 65 of the report.

06 Committee on Examination Reform, 1969. Report. Indore, University of Indore, 1969. 16 + x p. Chairman: K.L.Joshi.

The major reform recommended by the committee pertains to the introduction of semester system, particularly in the faculties of arts, science, commerce and home science. A detailed outline of the working of the semester system is the main focus of this report. The other problems of examination reform such as periodical tests and their types; the participation of the students in the organisation of tutorials, seminars and symposia; setting the questions papers, etc., have also been dealt with at some length.

07 Committee on Examination Reforms, 1966. Report. Calcutta, University of Calcutta, 1967. 34p. Chairman: Dr. Bidhubhushan Malik.

The committee was appointed to investigate into the prevailing system of examinations and to suggest short-term remedial measures. The report, based on an opinion survey of 365 persons, mostly the teachers of the affiliated colleges of the Calcutta University, makes a number of recommendations with a view to bring in desired changes in the system of examinations.

D RESSEARCH STUDIES

01 Association of Indian University. Unfair means in University examinations: A Study. Project team, V. Natarajan and Asha Arora. New Delhi, A.I.U., 1989.

This study attempts to gauge the magnitude of the malady in its various ramifications and to have fresh look at the functioning of the various components and stages of the conduct of university examinations and the system of punishment for use of unfair means in selected universities.

Data is collected through questionaires and interview. Data was collected in order to assess situation with respect to unfair means, details regarding examination centres, inspection team/flying squads and their functions, procedures and punishment of students engaged in unfair means etc. In all, responses from 35 Universities (20 Affiliating, 12 unitary and 3 Deemed) were obtained.

The findings are: there are unfair means at the pre-conduct stage involving essentially information and leakage of question papers; malpractices/unfair means and mass copying during the conduct stage; and unfair practices during the post-examination stage.

02 Bhat, R.N. Gunasekaran, K. and Shanmugham, M. A comparative study of the grade table and direct grading methods. Examination Reform Unit, Madras University, 1978.

The major objectives of the investigation were: (i) to study the consistency of grade distribution within the examination and between the examiners using the two methods of evaluation, (ii) to study the discrepancy in the distribution of grades under both the methods of evaluation, (iii) to study the consistency within the examiner in evaluating individual question/sections by using the two methods of evaluation, (iv) to study the extent of using the entire scale of evaluation, and (v) to study the opinions of the examiners about the two methods of evaluation.

The sample consisted of fifty answer scripts from among 397 scripts relating to the paper on Corporate Administration (including Company Law I) of the M.Com. examination of December 1976. Four examiners were selected from the list of examiners approved by the university for valuing papers in the subject. Each examiner had to value the scripts twice by each method with a time gap between each valuation. The same time gap between different valuations was attempted to be maintained for all the examiners. Each examiner, under each phase, was provided with a scheme of evaluation pertaining to the method (GTM/DGM), sheets for recording marks/grades and a copy of the question paper along with the answer scripts. A questionnaire was used to elicit opinions of the examiners regarding the practicability and suitability of the methods. Chi-square test was applied to test the association between the two sets of grades.

The major findings of the investigation were: (i) Three out of the four examiners were consistent within themselves in respect of grades under GTM. (ii) Each of the four examiners showed consistency within themselves in grading the scripts under DGM. (iii) The examiners were consistent between themselves when the scripts were ranked in order of merit under GTM as well as under DGM. (iv) There was no agreement between the examiners in respect of the distribution of grades by either method. (v) In general, there was more consistency in DGM evaluation than in GTM evaluation. (vi) Under GTM, the marks awarded by the four examiners ranged from zero to nine (maximum mark allotted to a question was twelve) but the grade points awarded under DGM ranged from zero to the maximum point. (vii) The examiners, in general, felt that objectivity in valuation was more in Direct Grading Method than in the Grade Table method of evaluation. DGM consumed more time than GTM. They further opined that DGM might be adopted in the university after taking care to remove certain administrative problems.

03 Bose, P.K., Roy, A. and Mukherjee, S.P. The existing system of examinations and measures for improving upon it. Department of statistics, Calcutta University, 1967.

The main aim of the study was to investigate the prevailing system of examinations and to suggest short-term remedial measures. An opinion survey was conducted during 1966-67. A questionnaire was circulated to teaching institutions and persons interested in education. The questionnaire included items on syllabus, the setting and moderation of question papers, conduct of examinations, admission to colleges, college tests, examination for external students, teaching in colleges, tutorial work, number of examinations and reports from colleges to the university. Opinions on all or some of the items were secured from 365 respondents comprising principals of affiliated colleges (N=48), teachers of affiliated colleges (N=266), teachers of Calcutta University (N=31) and other persons interested in education (N=20).

The finding of the study were : (i) On certain issues relating to the process of learning and evaluation there was a consensus of opinion among the respondents, while on certain others their opinions differed. (ii) The college teachers and the principals branded the existing syllabi as too heavy. Most principals and some college and university teachers wanted a change in the distribution of the total learning material between Part I and Part II. The existing syllabi in different subjects should be changed to ensure a smooth gradation from the syllabi in schools to the corresponding syllabi in university classes. (iii) A question paper should provide for double the number of questions to be answered and the questions should be distributed uniformly throughout the syllabus. (iv) The course material should be divided into groups and the question paper should be so set as to require the examinees to answer some questions from each group. Question papers should be moderated by the paper setters along with some other persons. (v) The university should undertake all the examinations in respect of collegiate education. Colleges should hold two of three periodical examinations in a year. Collegiate and external students should sit for the same examination. External candidates should be required to pass a test in some college in order to be eligible for appearing at the university examination. (vi) Opinions differed in respect of the method of teaching in colleges. (vii) The necessity for tutorial/seminar work was not accepted in the same spirit by all. (viii) Pass students should be required to pass Part I and Part II and Honours examinees be required to pass to their subsidiary subjects at these two examinations separately. (ix) Colleges should send reports of progress of study to the university once or twice a year. (x) Action should be taken against a college if the percentage of successful students sent by the college was poor for two or three consecutive years. (xi) An examination research unit should be permanently attached to the office of the Controller of Examinations.

04 Chauhan, D.S. A study of university examination. Pt. Jawaharlal Nehru College, Baroda, 1967.

The study made an analysis of answerbooks of a particular university examination at the graduate level. In the first part of the study an analysis was made to explain the causes of failure. In the second part, the content analysis of some important issues related to the level of performance of candidates were examined.

Two hundred and eightyfive answerbooks of one theory paper of the examination of the final year of a two year degree course held in March, 1963 formed the sample. The answerbooks were examined by the author himself, but the paper was set by a different examiner. Neither strict nor liberal marking was done. A rank order was determined for the different questions in the paper. The criteria adopted for ranking were simplicity, objectivity, clarity and exactness. On the negative side, vagueness and too technical language of the question were taken into account. The following statistics were calculated : correlation between the order of ranking and the selection of different questions, average marks secured by different categories of candidates in different questions, and degree of correlation between the nature of questions and the performance of candidates. For content analysis, a small sample of dozen cases was drawn on the basis of stratified random sampling method. The written answers of these twelve candidates were analysed from the view point of nature of answers, proportion of relevant and irrelevant matter, relationship between the length of answers and the marks secured, waste of space, language and some strange interpretations.

Some of the conclusions drawn were: (i) of the students who failed, large proportion failed not because of not knowing the subject matter, but because of some external factors like defective question paper, carelessness of examiners in evaluating answerbooks, evaluation by incapable examiners, etc; (ii) hardly 60 per cent of the total content presented by candidates was relevant and effective; (iii) expression of the candidates was generally poor; (iv) candidates generally made a wasteful use of paper; and (v) a gap between the medium of instruction–the medium of study and of expression, and the language in which the question paper was set for examination created many problems and contributed significantly to the failure in examinations.

05 Deo, P. Effects of revaluation on the results of candidates appearing at the university examinations. Deptt. of Education, Bombay University, 1980 (UGC financed).

The main objectives of the investigation were: (i) to study the extent of which the marks awarded to candidates in university examinations changed on account of revaluation, (ii) to study the extent to which the results of candidates changed on account of revaluation, (iii) to examine the nature of the changes in the results due to revaluation, (iv) to find out the difference between the original and the revalued marks of candidates, (v) to examine the nature and size of differences in the scores between the original and the revalued marks, (vi) to find out the size of correlations between the original marks, the revalued marks and differences scores, (vii) to study whether the marginal differences acceptable to some universities were effective in changing the final marks and results, (viii) to study whether the different rules of revaluation, adopted by various universities, affected the results of candidates, and (ix) to make suggestions for improving the process of revaluation.

The design was an *ex post facto* design. Multi-stage cluster sampling was done; all the universities, excluding agricultural universities and technological institutes, were sampled. A proforma was prepared for the purpose. Data were collected for different university examinations for original marks, revalued marks, original and final results, university rules for revaluation regarding fees and rules for minimum difference for accepting a change in the result. Data were collected through personal visits to the universities. Statistical techniques such as mean, standard deviation, t-test, percentage difference and product moment correlation were used. The analysis of data was done by forming the following categories of candidates: (i) failed and already passed, (ii) change and no change in marks, (iii) change and no change in results, and (iv) marks increased and decreased cases. Similarly, the nature of the reassessing examiner *vis-a-vis* the original examiner was classified in the following categories: (i) consistently liberal, (ii) consistently strict, (iii) maintaining the same standard, and (iv) haphazard.

The main findings of the study were: (i) More students from the arts faculty applied for revaluation than from other faculties and more candidates who had failed applied for revaluation than those who had passed. (ii) Changes in results in the case of failed candidates were larger than no changes in marks. (iii) The proportion of the cases of increased marks was larger than the cases where there was decrease in marks. (iv) The proportion of marks-increased cases in the failed group was larger than that of marks-increased cases in the already-passed group. (v) The proportion of no changes in results was larger than changes in results. (vi) There was significant difference between the means of the original and the revalued marks. (vii) The correlation between the original and the revalued marks was high. (viii) The correlation of difference scores with the original and the revalued marks was low and sometimes negative. (ix) Most changes of revaluation cases were due to the marginal difference which are applied by the universities. (x) The high correlation between the original and the revalued marks established the reliability of assessment of essay-type questions. (xi) Small differences between the original and the revalued marks also contributed to change in the results of candidates. (xii) Revaluation created many administrative, psychological and financial problems.

06 Gunasekaran, K. and Jayanthi, P. A study of the continuous internal assessment and the university examination marks of the undergraduate semester courses (1976-77 Batch). Examination Reform Unit, Madras University, 1980.

The major objectives of the study were: (i) to find out the correlation between the marks of continuous internal assessment (CIA) and the university examination (UE), (ii) to compare the marks of CIA and UE, (iii) to examine the distribution of marks in community social service (CSS), and (iv) to compare the distribution of divisions awarded in the non-semester and semester systems.

The study dealt with one paper from history, economics, philosophy, chemistry, botany, zoology and commerce. All the colleges offering these subjects were included in the study. Descriptive statistics and product moment coefficient of correlation were used for the analysis of the data.

The major findings of the study were: (i) The minimum, maximum and the average marks awarded by the colleges in the internal assessment differed considerably in all the subjects. (ii) In the university examinations also, the minimum, maximum and average marks varied considerably among the colleges. (iii) Discrimination between good and poor students was low in the internal assessment but the university examinations showed a good amount of dispersion with regard to the same set of students. (iv) Barring a few cases, the relationship between the marks of the internal assessment and the university examination was good. (v) The assessment in the community social service varied among colleges. In most cases the assessment was on the higher side. In many cases maximum marks were awarded uniformly to entire groups of students. (vi) The percentage of those passing and those getting higher classes had improved under the semester system as compared to the non-semester system. More students secured first and second divisions under the semester system.

07 Koul, L. Scaling of some significant innovations in examination system. School of Education, Himachal Pradesh University, 1979 (HPU financed).

The major objective of the study was to investigate the views of university teachers and students regarding the relative scale positions of significant innovations and to compare the two sets of ratings.

Two samples of 250 postgraduate students and 80 teachers were selected randomly from the various faculties of the Postgraduate Centre and Directorate of Correspondence Courses of Himachal Pradesh University. The tool consisted of a checklist developed by the author from a list of thirteen innovations. Each one of the thirteen innovations was combined in pairs with every other innovation and thereby seventy-eight pairs were formed. The pairs were arranged and enlisted in such a manner that every innovation in the twelve pairs in which it appeared, occupied the first and second positions equal number of times and the pairs in which it appeared were kept as far apart as possible in the checklist. Thurstone's paired comparison method was applied to determine the scale positions of the innovations for the samples of teachers and students separately.

The major findings of the study were: (i) There was a good deal of similarity in the scale positions of the innovations according to the views of the teachers and the students. (ii) Certain innovations like introducing the grade system of ranking, supplementing essay-type examination with objective-type examination, semester system and supplementing external examinations with periodic internal assessment, were in the top regions of the scales of the teachers and the students. Though individuals among the university teachers and students might differ in their views about the relative importance in innovations in the examination system, the collective opinion of both the groups was in favour of the grade system of ranking, internal assessment supplementing the external examinations, semester system and objective-type tests. (iii) The innovation, defining the scope of questions in simple and clear language, was also in the upper regions of both the scales. (iv) The teachers and the students differed regarding the scale position of the innovation, supplementing written examinations with oral tests. The teachers gave high importance to this innovation whereas the students gave low importance to oral tests. The university teachers were in agreement with the recommendation of the Education Commission (1964-66) but not the students. (v) Both the teachers and the students gave equal average importance to innovations such as orientation of paper-setters and evaluators and making evaluation instructions precise and clear. (vi) The innovations like open book examinations, use of computer and mechanical devices in preparing award rolls, scope for re-evaluation of answer books and spot evaluation of answer books, did not get importance from the teachers and the students.

08 Nair, J.R. A statistical analysis of the examination results of the South Indian universities. Kerala University, 1982 (U.G.C. financed).

The study aimed to analyse the compare the examination results of five South Indian universities -- Kerala, Calicut, Madras, Mysore and Tirupati. The S.S.L.C. Examination results of Kerala and Tamil Nadu, the pre-degree/pre-university examination results of Calicut, Kerala and Madras Universities and B.A. and B.Sc. examination results of all the five universities were compared.

The details of S.S.L.C. Examination were collected from the office of the Secretary of Government Examinations, of the pre-degree and pre-university examinations from the records of the concerned universities and of the B.A. and B.Sc. examinations from Form B (Statistics) of universities collected for the University Grants Commission. The analysis of variance technique was applied to measure the variance between years, and the technique of multiple comparison was applied for certain situations.

The main conclusion of the study were: (i) There was significant variation in the percentage of passes during the years under study, for all the examinations studied, but the extent of variation differed among the universities. An important reason identified for the variation was the standard and difficulty level of the questions. (ii) Sex differences in achievement were identified for all the five universities with women showing higher achievement. (iii) The interaction between the sex and the class or division showed a differential pattern indicating significant difference for certain examinations of particular universities only. (iv) The forward community students were significantly better in pass percentage than the backward community students in Kerala.

09 Nath B. University examination – an analytical study of the conduct of pre-university degree and master degree examinations of Gauhati University. Ph.D. Education, Gauhati University, 1980.

The main aim of the study was to present a systematic analysis of the prevailing system of essay-type examinations with special reference to the process of conduct and analysis of results. The major aspects of examinations, viz., the question paper, mode of evaluation, scaling of marks and their impact on examinations results, improvement of the design, structure and analysis of question papers in terms of difficulty values and discriminating powers of the terms, the problem of optional questions in a question paper, desirability and methods of introduction of internal assessment as a tool for continuous evaluation, predictive value of an examination and wastage and stagnation, were studied systematically.

The findings of the study were: (i) The quality of students admitted and the teacher-pupil ratio had a bearing on examination results. (ii) There were large variations in the percentage of attempts not only in different question items but also in a number of sub-questions of the selected question paper. (iii) In a majority of the subjects, the scores were higher in internal assessment. The assessments, both in internal and external examinations, were evenly distributed. Internal marks possessed some predictive values for external marks. There was a tendency towards overmarking in internal assessment. Internal assessment provided some incentives of students to do better in the external examination. The system of internal assessment should be introduced, after fulfilment of certain conditions, for making the examination more valid and for doing justice to students. (iv) The rate of wastage and stagnation varied from subject to subject. The overall rate of wastage was slightly higher among males than among females. But the rate of stagnation among females was significantly higher than among males. The highest and the lowest rates of wastage were in English and botany, respectively. There were year-to-year variations in the rates of wastage and stagnation. The major causes of wastage and stagnation were poor economic condition of parents, admission of poor quality students, absence of proper system of internal assessment and continuous evaluation, and general apathy of students towards their courses of studies. (v) The performance of students in M.A. previous and final examinations in all the subjects was closely related.

10 Rasool, G., Sarup R. and Sharma, N.R. A comparative study of internal and external awards at the postgraduate level in Jammu University, Jammu University, 1981.

The study primarily aimed at making a statistical analysis of the marks awarded by the external examiners and the marks awarded against the sessional work, i.e., internal assessment. The specific aims of the study were: (i) to examine the characteristics of the distribution of the scores awarded by the external and the internal examiners, (ii) to find out the degree of relationship between the external and the internal marks, and (iii) to find out the effect of the internal marks on the boosting of the overall result of students. The study was confined to 218 postgraduate students, both boys and girls, selected from thirteen postgraduate teaching departments of Jammu University.

The major findings of the study were: (i) The scores in most of the papers showed deviation from the normal distribution. They were either positively of negatively skewed with a slight kurtosis. (ii) The majority of the teachers preferred to maintain a low range in the marks of the internal assessment, that is, the gap between the lowest and the highest scores was narrow. The range of the external marks in the same papers was definitely more than that of the internal marks. (iii) Most of the coefficients of correlation appeared to be positive. This tendency indicated that there was some conformity in the scoring pattern of the internal and the external examiners. (iv) The internal assessment proved to be a booster of the final result of almost all the students. The marks awarded under the internal assessment helped the students in raising their aggregate percentage of marks. Though the internal assessment suffered from various drawbacks like the halo effect and error due to central tendency, etc., it appeared to be a blessing in disguise to students.

11 Reddy, A.V.R. Attitude of teachers of two institutions towards internal assessment – a comparative study. Department of Education, Sri Venkateswara University, 1979.

The investigation was designed to compare the views of the teachers of a university college where internal assessment (IA) was going to be introduced from the next academic year with those of the teachers of another university college where the system was being tried out for a few years.

The sample comprised 120 teachers equally distributed among the arts and science faculties in two university colleges in one of which (C1) IA was a practice for some years and in the other (C2) IA was to be introduced soon. Both the colleges were in the same university and had postgraduate courses. The sample included professors, readers and lecturers having at least two years of experience in the profession. The research tool was a Likert-type attitude scale developed by the investigator, consisting of forty items (nineteen positive and twenty-one negative). The scale had a split-half reliability of 0.96 (N=50). The t-test and chi-square were the statistical techniques used for data analysis.

The major findings of the investigation were: (i) All the subgroups of the teachers except those belonging to the arts faculty of college C1 were significantly favourable towards their system of internal assessment. (ii) The teachers of the college where internal assessment had not yet started did not differ in their attitude towards the system from those of the college where the system was in practice. (iii) The teachers of the arts faculty of college C1 did not differ significantly from their counterparts in college C2 as regards their attitude to the system of internal assessment. The same was true of the teachers of the science faculty. (iv) Many teachers preferred partial IA with an external examination at the end of the year. (v) Discussion with the students and the teachers of college C1 revealed that the students depended mostly on lecture notes. This was also seen when more than half of the teachers felt that the students did not learn the subject better in this system. (vi) The teachers of college C1 felt that high hopes about the system of IA were belied when the system was implemented in their college.

12 Shah, R.S. A survey and study of the internal evaluation system in the colleges of Saurashtra and evolving a plan for it. Ph.D. Education, Saurashtra University, 1972.

The objectives of the study were: (i) to find out which system of internal evaluation prevails in the colleges; (ii) to find out whether the same system prevails in the colleges of different faculties; (iii) to find out the scheme of distribution of marks allotted to the internal evaluation and whether the same scheme prevails in all the colleges; (iv) to find out what weightage different colleges give to different activities as regards marks allotted to tutorials; (v) to find out how the records of internal marking are maintained; (vi) to know the opinions of the principals, teachers and students on the system prevailing; (vii) to know the difficulties of the college offices, principals, and teachers, and students' experience; (viii) to know the reactions of principles, teachers and students and their suggestions for improving the prevailing system; (ix) to compare the assessment of the students in the university examination, college tests and tutorial work and to find out whether the difference between each of these variables is significant; (x) to evaluate the system of internal evaluation on the basis of the above study; (xi) to work out in the form of suggestion an improved scheme for internal evaluation; and (xii) to make suggestions as regards steps for a better evaluation of the students.

Out of thirty-four colleges of Saurashtra area, twenty-seven colleges were included in the study. The marks of the students appearing at the T.Y. B.A., T.Y. B.Com., TY B.Sc., and B.Ed. examinations of the university conducted in march/April 1967 and March/April 1968 were studied. The number of students studied in the year 1967 was 1970. The number of students studied in the year 1968 was 1768. In 1967, the students were 946, 374, 423 and 227 in T.Y. B.A., T.Y. B.Com., T.Y. C.Sc., and B.Ed., while in 1968 they were 891, 182, 366 and 329 respectively. A questionnaire, a suggestion sheet, an opinionnaire were used and interview technique was employed for the collection of data. The reports of the committees, seminars and meetings were studied. Changes introduced by the university in 1970-71 were also studied. The t-test was used for testing of mean differences. Coefficients of correlation were also calculated. The chi-square technique was also used and percentages were calculated.

The findings of the study are as follows: (i) The general pattern of internal evaluation is identical in arts, commerce and science colleges. Till 1969-70, the pattern was – for university examination 70 per cent, for internal evaluation 30 per cent out of which 20 per cent to college tests and 10 per cent to the tutorials were allotted. From June 1970, instead of 30 per cent, 20 per cent are allotted to the internal evaluation for college tests and 80 per cent of marks for the tutorials. (ii) In B.Ed. colleges, only 150 out of 850 marks were allotted to internal assessment till 1969-70, but from June 1970, semester examinations are introduced. In one year, out of 850 marks, 575 (275 – first semester, 100 – practical lessons, 100–practical work and 100–annual lessons) marks were for internal evaluation. Now out of 850 marks, 300 (200–lessons and 100–practical work) are with the college and both the semester examinations are held by the university.

There is a trend of decrease in the weightage given to the internal evaluation in arts, commerce, and science colleges, while there is a trend to give more weightage to it in the education colleges. (iii) The internal evaluation has increased the administrative and clerical work for the principals, teachers and college offices and has also increased the expenditure. (iv) The teachers and the principals are not in favour of the discontinuation of the internal evaluation. (v) The means of internal evaluation are reported to be significantly higher than that of the university examination marks. (vi) There is a significant positive correlation between internal assessment marks and the university examination marks but it is of moderate level. (vii) Except for colleges of education, means of college tests are found to be significantly higher than those of university examination marks. (viii) The means of the tutorial marks are found to be significantly higher than those of the university examination marks. (ix) The means of the tutorial marks are found to be significantly higher than those of the college test marks. (x) The correlation between the tutorial marks and the college test marks is not found to be significant.

13 Singh. S. A study of preparatory science examination results of the M.S. University of Baroda for the year 1974-75. Ph.D. Education. M.S. University of Baroda, 1978.

The aims of the investigation were: (i) to study the distribution of marks for normality, (ii) to study the main sources of variations involved in examination marks, (iii) to study the relationship between marks under each of the procedures of assessment and prediction of examination marks from the previous examination marks, and (iv) to study the abilities underlying the examination.

The sample was drawn from the students who appeared in the preparatory science examination conducted for the year 1974-75. In all, 1,054 students who were studying at the university campus, were included in the sample. Data were obtained by collecting the marks of S.S.C. examination from the students' admission. forms available at the office of the preparatory science unit. Preparatory Science (P.Sc.) marks were collected from the examination section of the university. The marks in all the papers were converted into percentage marks to bring them on the same scale. The marks were tested for normality by applying the chi-squared test. Variations in the marking were studied by applying the t-test. The relationship and prediction were studied by using product moment correlations and step-wise multivariate regression analysis, respectively. The principal component method of factor analysis was applied for identifying the factors.

The major findings of the investigation were: (i) The distribution of marks, when studied separately in theory, tutorial and practical examinations, was non-normal. The distribution of preparatory science aggregate percentage marks was approximately normal. (ii) In theory as well as in tutorials, the standard of marking of different papers in different subjects differed significantly at 1 per cent level. (iii) The relationships between tutorial marks in different subjects, theory marks in different subjects and practical marks in different subjects were significant at 1 per cent level. (iv) The marks in the S.S.C. examination had got high predictive value for predicting the performance in the preparatory science examination. The S.S.C. aggregate percentage marks were the single best predictor for predicting the success in the preparatory science examination. (v) The underlying abilities measured by tutorial and theory examinations, separately, were the same. (vi) The abilities identified under the preparatory science examination indicated that the examination was comprehensive in nature and measured many dimensions of achievement abilities. (vii) In theory as well as in tutorial examinations, the common factors were general scholastic, scientific verbal and scientific numerical, whereas in practical examination, there was only one common factor of general ability. When the marks of all the three assessments were added, one more factor, namely, problem-solving, was found. The marks in the S.S.C. examination indicated an independent common factor named as memorization.

14 Verma, L.K. Critical appraised of innovations for the improvement of examinations. Ph.D. Education. Kurukshetra University, 1981

The major objective of the study was to make experimental validations of some innovations implemented in the examination system of universities. These innovations included marking and grading, internal and external assessment, improvement of the essay-type question paper, open book vs. traditional examination, internal vs. external choice in questions, spot evaluation and revaluation.

Different procedures and sampling processes were followed to validate different innovations of the study. For marking vs. grading, fifty answer scripts of B.A. (history) were got evaluated on a five-point scale, seven-point scale and numerical scale of 101 points by five examiners. For internal and external assessment, internal and external assessment scores were collected for honours course of Utkal University, M.Ed. course of Jammu University, M.A. course of Sardar Patel and Bombay Universities, and M.B.A. course of Kurukshetra University. For the improvement of essay-type question paper, the question paper already set in the annual examination was reframed in simple, clear and precise language. It was administered to two groups of randomly selected fifty students. The answer scripts of the students of the two groups were evaluated by five examiners. In the case of open book vs. traditional examination, an objective-type test in chemistry was administered to pre-university students. They were also administered the Sinha Scientific Aptitude Test. The scores of the open book examination and the university examination were correlated separately with the criterion test and the significance of difference between the two correlations was tested. For internal vs. external choice in questions, a question paper with ten short answer type questions in two forms was administered to the students. In one form and students had choice for all the ten questions and in another form the questions were in paris. The answer books of the students were evaluated separately by three examiners. For spot evaluation, a self-prepared attitude scale was administered to 146 approved examiners of the universities in arts and science courses at the undergraduate level and the postgraduate level. These examiners had experience of on-the-spot evaluation. For revaluation, rules and regulations of eight universities of northern Indian were compared.

The findings of the study were: (i) Though there was no significant difference between the average assessment on five and seven-point scale, better discrimination was possible through the letter. (ii) The internal assessment scores highly correlated with the external assessment scores of the only two universities where the number of students was small. (iii) The inter-examiner reliability of the scores awarded by different examiners improved with the improvement of the question paper. (iv) The correlation coefficient between the scientific aptitude test and the essay-type test was low. (v) The scores of the students in internal choice questions had a significantly greater content validity than that of the scores in external choice questions. (vi) The arts and science examiners at the undergraduate level of an postgraduate level did not differ from each other on the different items of the spot evaluation attitude scale. (vii) There was no uniformity in the rules and regulations regarding revaluation in different universities; further, the different rules in a particular university might affect the same case differently.

24. FINANCE

A BOOKS

01 Amrik Singh and Sharma, *G.D. eds. University and college finance,* New Delhi, A.I.U., 1981. 246p.

02 Asian Institute of Educational Planning and Administration, New Delhi. *Report of the study on resource mobilisation for education.* New Delhi, The author, 1970. 67p.

03 Association of Indian Universities. *University finance: A statistical profile.* New Delhi, *The author*, 1978. 181p.

04 ——. *University finance: A statistical profile.* New Delhi, A.I.U., 1983. 446p.

05 Azad, J.L. *Financing of higher education in India.* New Delhi, *Sterling*, 1975. 236 p.

06 ——. *Financing of higher education in India: A critical study of the patterns, procedures and policies of the financing of higher education in India in the post-independence period.* New Delhi, Planning Commission, 1975. 321p.

07 ——. *Government support for higher education and research.* New Delhi, National Institute of Educational Planning and Administration, 1984. 202p.

08 ——. *Higher education in India: The deepening financial crisis.* New Delhi, *Radiant*, 1988. 257p.

09 ——. *State governments grants to colleges.* New Delhi, Association of Indian Universities, 1978.

10 Bakar, A. *Union and the states in education: A study in educational finance and planning.* New Delhi, Shad Sanchar, 1976. 258p.

11 Balvir Singh. *University finance: A case study of Delhi University*: Paper presented at AIU-ICSSR National seminar on university and college finances, New Delhi, 10-12 March, 1978.

12 Borkar, V.V. and Kate, P.V. *Cost structure of higher education in Marathwada University.* Aurangabad, Marathwada University, 1968.

13 Chalam, K.S. *Finances costs and productivity of higher education.* New Delhi, Inter India, 1986. 240p.

14 Education Commission. *Financing of education: Working paper of the seminar on education as investment organised by the Lucknow University*, Lucknow, January, 1966.

15 ——· *Notes on financing of education in India* by A.R. Prest. New Delhi, 1965. 27p. (Monograph-VIII. Task Force on Educational Finance)

16 Education Commission. *Two earlier studies in financing of education in India (1944 and 1950).* A summary and a brief critical appraisal of the relevant proposals of the Sargent Report, 1944 and the Kher Committee, 1950. New Delhi, 1965. 24p. (Task Force on Educational Finance, Monograph-1).

17 Garg, V.P. *Finances of the Panjab University: A trend analysis*: Paper presented at AIU-ICSSR, national seminar on university and college finances, New Delhi, 10-12 March, 1978.

18 Kamat, A.R. Financing of higher education: *A socio-political analysis of the basic issues: Paper presented at AIU-ICSSR national seminar on university and college finances.* New Delhi, 10-12 March, 1978.

19 Mathew, E.T. *University finances in India.* New Delhi, Sterling, 1980. 120p.

20 Mathur, Gautam. *Observations on U.G.C. grants procedures*: Paper presented at AIU-ICSSR national seminar on university and college finances, New Delhi, 10-12 March, 1978.

21 Merrett, S. *Rate of return to education: A critique.* Working paper of the seminar on education as investment organised by the Lucknow University, Lucknow, January, 1966.

22 Misra, Atmanand. *Education and finance.* Gwalior, Kailash Pustak Sadan, 1971. 335p.

23 ——· *Educational finance in India.* Bombay, Asia Publishing House, 1962. 616p.

24 ——· *Grants in aid of education in India.* Delhi, Macmillan India, 1973. 173p.

25 Mridula. *State funding of universities: A study of maintenance grants to universities.* New Delhi, A.I.U., 1985. 187p.

26 Mukherji, K. *Study of the finances of the Calcutta university.* Calcutta, Firma K.L.M., 1976.

27 Nair, P.R. and Pillai, N.P. *Study of the history and problems of educational finance in Kerala.* Trivandrum, University of Kerala, 1962. 115p.

28 Nanjundappa, D.M. *Working of university finance.* New Delhi, Sterling, 1976. 363p.

29 Nigam, M.S. *Rajasthan University Finance : A case study;* Paper presented at AIU-ICSSR National seminar on university and college finances, New Delhi, 10-12 March, 1978.

30 Padmanabhan, C.B. *Cost and financing of education in India: An aggregate study.* New Delhi, Asian Institute of Educational Planning and Administration, n.d. 83p.

31 ——. *Financial management in education.* New Delhi, Select Books, 1984. 236p.

32 ——. *Financing of education by local bodies and local planning.* New Delhi, National Institute of Educational Planning and Administration, 1983, 46 + 19p.

33 Panchamukhi, P.R. *Economics of university finances with special reference to the finance of Bombay university.* Bombay, University of Bombay, 1977.

34 ——. *Expansionism and financial crisis in higher education.* Bombay, University of Bombay, 1975.

35 Parikh, G.D. University finance problems and procedures. *In* Amrik Singh and Philip G. Altbach eds. *The higher learning in India.* Delhi, Vikas, 1974. p. 78-88.

36 Rahman, A. *Financing of scientific and technological research in India. In* Science and technology in economic development. Paris, UNESCO, 1970. p. 189-213.

37 Shah, A.B. (ed.) *Educational finance,* Bombay, Indian Committee for Cultural Freedom, 1966.

38 Sharma, G.D. *Resource allocation on education : An inter-temporal pattern analysis.* New Delhi, Association of Indian Universities, 1978.

39 Singh, B. *Resource constraints on national programmes of education in India.* Working paper of the seminar on education as investment organised by the Lucknow University, Lucknow, January, 1966.

40 Singh, Parmanand. *Financing of university education.* Delhi, B.R. Publishing, 1982. 236p.

41 Sobti, M.L. *Financial code for university systems.* New Delhi, Vikas, 1987. 424p.

B ARTICLES

01 Ansari, M.M. Financial health of universities: A diagnostic study. *University News*. 27 (1). 1989. p.1-14.

02 Ansari, M.M. Financial health of universities: A diagnostic study. *Journal of Higher Education*. 14(1-3), 1988-89. p.65-86.

03 ——. Resource allocation and financial accountability of universities. *University News*. 27 (40), 1989. p.17-21.

04 Azad, J.L. Academic and financial management of higher education. *University Administration*, 2(1-2), 1975. p.19-27.

05 ——. Academic and financial management of higher education. *University News*. 15 (21), 1977. p.344-347.

06 ——. Financing institutions of higher education in India: Need for a realistic fee policy. *Higher Education*. 5 (1), 1976. p.1-7.

07 ——. Resources for higher education: Problem and prospects. *University News*. 25 (50), 1987. p.12-18.

08 ——. Researches in educational finance: Problems and Perspectives. *University News*. 26 (24), 1988. p.5-11.

09 Balachander. K.K. Higher Education: Need for realistic grant policy. *Economic Times*, 18-12-86. p.5.

10 ——. Wanted: A new strategy for financing higher education-I. *University News*. 25 (29), p.3-9.

11 ——. Wanted: A new strategy for financing higher education-II. *University News*. 25 (30). p.9-15.

12 ——. Why public expenditure on higher education? *University News*. 26 (49), 1988. p.39-47.

13 Basargekar, S.K. Problems of the financial management of higher education. *University Administration*. 5 (2), 1978. p.32-52.

14 Bhandari, S.K.R. Financing of universities. *University News*. 19 (7), 1981. p.187-88

15 Bhatnagar, K.N. Management and financing of higher education. *University News*. 23 (6), 1985. p.2-4.

16 Bhatt, G.K. Profitability of private investment in higher education in Rajasthan. *Journal of Higher Education*. 8 (1), 1982. p.85-95.

17 Bhide, V.G. University of Poona. *University News*. 26 (23), 1988. p.1-12.

18 Blaug, M. The distributional effects of higher education subsidies. *Economics of Education Review*. 2(3), 1982. p.201-231.

19 Bniday, M.R. University procedure for providing grants to teaching departments. *University News*. 17(4), 1979. p.92-98.

20 Chitnis, Suma. Investment in higher education: A reconsideration *New Frontiers in Education.* 5(4), 1975. p.23-46.

21 Financing of universities. *University News.* 19 (5) 1981. p. 127-129.

22 Garg, V.P. Cost analysis of the university of Punjab. 1950-51 to 1974-75. *Indian Educational Review.* 17 (3), 1982. p. 85-103.

23 ——. Major trends in financing. *University News.* 12 (9), 1974. p. 12-15.

24 Ghosh, D.K. Financing of universities. *University News.* 15 July, 1981. p. 382-383 & 393.

25 Joshi, Navin Chandra. Investment in higher education. *University News.* 16 (14), 1978. p.1043-1044.

26 Kaptan, Sanjay Shankar. Reforming university budgeting. *University News.* 29 (9), 1990. p. 4-8 and 11.

27 Lakadwala, D.T. and Shah, K.R. Financing of universities in Gujarat. *Economic and Political Weekly.* 10 (20), 1975. p.795-801.

28 Lamba, P.S. Financing of agricultural universities. *University News.* 19 (10), 1981. p. 283-285 and 290.

29 Mathai, Samuel. Financing the autonomous college. *New Frontiers in Education.* 4 (2), 1974. p. 72-74.

30 Mathur, M.V. Universities and their finance. *University News.* 7 (7), 1989. p. 10-12.

31 Nayan, D.P. Financing of higher education. *University News.* 15 (4), 1977. p. 82-84.

32 Nigam, M.S. Study of the finances of the University of Rajasthan. *Journal of Higher Education.* 1 (3), 1976. p.400-402.

33 Padmanabhan, C.B. Budgetary situation of universities and its implications. *University News.* 14 (8), 1976. p. 5-6.

34 ——. Expenditure analysis in college management. *University News.* 18 (8), 1980. p. 198-201.

35 ——. Financial aspects of Indian educational administration with special reference to university education. *Education Quarterly.* 29 (1), April, 1977. p. 5-10.

36 ——. Financial management of universities and college in India. *New Frontiers in Education.* 10 (4), October-December, 1980. p. 59-64.

37 ——. Financial management of agricultural universities in India. *University News.* 18 (22), 1980. p. 627-629.

38 ——. Is financing Indian higher education equitable. *University News.* 23 (8), 1985. p. 25-27.

39 ——. Towards functional financial management in universities. *University News*. 22 (38), 1984. p. 2-6.

40 Panchamukhi, P.R. Economics of university finance: Basic principles and practice. *Indian Educational Review*. 15 (4), October, 1980. p. 117-119.

41 Parikh, G.D. Some aspects of university finance. *Quest*. (64), January-March, 1970. p. 34-40.

42 Puri, R.P. University finance and their accountability. *University News*. 7 (8), 1969. p. 16-18.

43 Ramanathan, A. Cost benefit analysis in higher education: Some pitfalls. *University News*. 25 (41), 1987. p. 4-7.

44 Saraf, S.N. Financial resources: Dimensions and dilemmas. *University News*. 23 (19), 1985. p.2-6.

45 Sharma, G.D. and Apte, M.D. Calling the tune without playing the piper. *Economic and Political Weekly*. 10 (12), 22 March, 1975. p. 508.

46 Singh, Bir. Financing the universities. *New Frontiers in Education*. 9 (4), October-December, 1979. p. 63-65.

47 Sivalingam, P. Financing of the new universities. *University News*. 19 (9), 1981. p. 251-254.

48 Tilak, Jandhyala B.G. Unit cost analysis of higher education in India. *Journal of Higher Education*. 5 (2), Autumn, 1979. p. 183-193.

49 Universities and the finance commission. *University News*. 21 (14), 1983. p. 443.

50 University finances, *University News*. 27 (40), 1989. p. 1-7.

51 Varghese, N.V. Resources for higher education in India. *Journal of Educational Planning and Administration*. 1 (3-4), 1987. p. 76-88.

52 Verma, D.P. University's Budget: A Brief analysis. *University News*. 22 (17), 1984. p. 2-10.

C COMMITTEES/COMMISSIONS/REPORTS

01 Committee on the ways and means of financing educational development in India, 1948. Report. Delhi, Manager of Publications, 1950. 78p. (Bureau of Education, Pamphlet No. 64) Chairman: B.G. Kher.

This committee was appointed to examine the existing financial resources and the programme for educational development for all provinces and states, and to make suggestions to ensure that educational development is not held up for want of funds.

02 Committee on revision of the basis of maintenance grants to non-government colleges affiliated to Delhi University, 1966. Report. New Delhi, University Grants Commission, 1967. 34p. Chairman: Dr. A.C. Joshi.

The committee was appointed to consider the proposal of Delhi University that owing to the steady increase in expenditure of the college, the basis of payment of maintenance grant to non-government colleges affiliated to it may be revised, and be made more-liberal in view of the limited resources of the colleges.

03 Committee on college finances: Grant-in-aid to affiliated colleges in the State of Gujarat, 1976. Report. Ahmedabad, Government of Gujarat, 1977. 60p. Chairman: Dr. Samuel Paul.

The committee was asked, (1) to examine the financial structure of the non-government colleges receiving grant-in-aid and to analyse the causes of their financial difficulties, in general and of the science colleges in particular; (2) to suggest norms for the viability of the existing colleges/faculties and measures for preventing establishment and growth of weak and non-viable colleges/faculties; (3) to examine and recommend financial and structural adjustment in the institutional set up of colleges following the introduction of 10+2+3 pattern of education in the state; (4) to suggest coordination of facilities, staff, equipment etc. for preventing duplication and effecting economy in expenditure of colleges; (5) to suggest measures through which the colleges can augment their financial resources and to stipulate the scale of financial assistance from government to enable them to progressively achieve a fair degree of self-sufficiency; and (6) to examine the impact of existing scheme for awarding financial assistance to the students belonging to Scheduled Tribes, Scheduled Castes and economically backward classes on college finances and to suggest measures to achieve their economic and optimum utilization. The recommendations of the committee have been presented in Chapter IX of the report (see p. 48-54).

D RESEARCH STUDIES

01 Azad, J.L. A critical study of the financing of higher education in India in the Post-Independence Period. Ph.D. Edu. Delhi University, 1972.

The study was undertaken: (i) to analyse the patterns of higher education finance — aggregative as well as institutional, (ii) to study the patterns and procedures of financing of higher education adopted by the central and the state governments, and (iii) to discuss certain basic policy issues relating to the subject under reference.

The study was mainly limited to higher education during 1947 to 1966. The data were obtained from various ministries of the Government of India and other concerned organisations as well as the state governments. A questionnaire, relating to the patterns and procedures of state grant-in-aid, including certain policy issues relating to financing of higher education, was sent to the vice-chancellors, principals of affiliated colleges and experts. In all, responses of 180 persons were analysed.

The major findings are as follows: (i) The annual rate of growth of expenditure over the years under study (at constant prices) is the highest (twelve per cent) in the case of higher education as compared to 9.1 per cent in the case of overall education and 3.4 per cent in the case of national income. (ii) Both as a percentage of national income and of the educational expenditure as a whole, the expenditure on higher education has indicated a much higher rate of growth. (iii) At constant prices, the increase in the per student expenditure is insignificant both in the case of education as well as higher education. (iv) If one considers the educational expenditure as a percentage of the national income, (converted into US dollars), India has exceeded only a few countries of Asia like Burma, Jordan, Pakistan and Vietnam. (v) In terms of per capita expenditure on education as proportion of the per capita net national product, there have been material changes in the position of states, over the years under study. It is, however, found that the differences among the states, with regard to 'effort' (as represented by the per capita expenditure on education as a proportion of the per capita net national product), have indicated a tendency to narrow down. It is also found that educational expenditure has been a social overhead and has an element of inevitability which must be incurred regardless of the states' financial capacity. The study has also revealed that the states which spent more on education also spent more on higher education. (vi) An analysis of the inter-institutional priorities revealed that the states have been making larger outlays on higher education than on other educational programmes. Further, the disparities amongst the states, as reflected in their proportionate expenditure on higher education, have narrowed down over the years. This is revealed by the decline in the coefficient of variation in respect of different states, over the years. (vii) The universities have been planning larger outlays on 'consumption', i.e., staff salaries, scholarships, and conduct of examinations than on 'investment' like buildings, equipment and libraries. (viii) The concentration of expenditure is more on universities than on colleges; further, the UGC has unduly spread its scope far too wide, with the result that its assistance has indicated a tendency to get diffused over a large number of items. (ix) The main sources of finance for higher education have been the central and the state governments; the fees are the second largest source of university finance. Their appropriate contribution has however been going down. Same is the case with endowments. Considered institutionwise, the bulk of central assistance (86.13 per cent) in 1963-64 was confined to universities, research institutions and professional colleges and the bulk of the state assistance was for professional colleges (41.9 per cent) followed by colleges for general education (33.9 per cent) and universities (21.5 per cent). (x) There has been no clear-cut demarcation between the central and the state governments in the matter of financing of institutions of higher education and the systems of financing by the government have not always been based on rationally devised criteria for providing requisite financial assistance; they seem to be the result of a policy of 'ad-hocism' born mainly out of the exigencies of the financial situation prevailing at the central and the state levels. (xi) There is a multiplicity of organisations concerned with the financial and academic management of higher education; the UGC, which is the main instrument of central government for the coordination and determination of standards, has an extremely truncated responsibility. (xii) The state governments' grants for various types of institutions of higher education are based on widely varying patterns and procedures — the system lacks specificity and dynamism and is largely attuned to a rigid institutional pattern which makes innovation and experimentation difficult, and the 'deficit' grant system, which is generally in vogue, dampens the enthusiasm of the private bodies to raise resources.

02 Azad, J.L., Government grants for higher education: A study of patterns procedures and policies, Planning Commission, New Delhi, 1975.

The objectives of the present study were: (i) to analyse the patterns, the procedures and the policies of financing of the institutions of higher education in India; (ii) to assess the adequacy or otherwise of the system of financial administration with a view to identifying its bottle necks; and (iii) to study certain basic issues of financial policy like purposes of central and state grants, fee policy, mechanism of student aid programme, respective responsibilities of the central and the state governments, etc.

The study was conducted in two stages. In the first stage, information about the patterns and procedures of grant-in-aid to institutions of higher education were collected from the state governments, tabulated and sent back for checking up and updating. In the second stage two questionnaires — one on patterns and procedures of state grant-in-aid and second on some policy issues on financing of institutions of higher education in India — were developed. The first questionnaire was mailed to 356 principals of affiliated colleges of arts, science, commerce, education, and engineering and technology representing ten per cent of the private colleges in each state with some weightage given to women's colleges. the second questionnaire was mailed to vice-chancellors of eightynine universities and to fiftyfour economists and educationists. However, the first questionnaire was responded by 144 college principals, while the second questionnaire was responded by twentyfive vice-chancellors and eleven experts only.

The study revealed that: (i) there were large variations in the type and quantum of state grants — the maintenance grants ranged between 33 $^1/_3$ and 100 per cent of the approved expenditure; (ii) the system of deficit grant and the concept of approved expenditure were disfavoured by the respondents; (iii) a majority of the respondents felt the need to streamline the UGC, extending its jurisdiction to include all types of higher education, establish regional centres or state UGCs; (iv) the establishment of an informal committee of vice-chancellors to advise the state government in formulation of grant-in-aid rules and annual allocation of grants was favoured; (v) the affiliation should, according to the respondents, be the concern of the university; (vi) the respondents felt that there was lack of coordination between the universities and the state governments in affiliating institutions and releasing grants; (vii) it was opined that the objectives of central and state grants were to equalise the spread of educational facilities, locate and help talent, and persuade private enterprise in education to help achieve nationally determined goals; (vii) it was felt by a majority of respondents that the central government should concentrate on qualitative improvement, and postgraduate education and research, while the responsibilities of the state governments should include undergraduate education, maintenance and development of collegiate institutions, encouragement of spread of education in backward areas and the development of the regional languages; (ix) half of the respondents thought it desirable to raise fees but only one-third supported it at this stage; (x) a large majority supported the idea of fixing standard fees with option to private institutions; (xi) private contribution was not much encouraged by the institutions — instead the proposal of enactment that private enterprise requiring technically trained manpower should contribute a portion of their profits for educational development was supported; and (xii) a combination of grant and loan to students to prosecute studies for higher education was favoured by respondents.

03 Begale, S.K., State budgetary allocation for higher education in Madhya Pradesh, University of Bhopal, 1979.

The State of Madhya Pradesh inspite of being gifted with natural and manpower resources presents a true picture of poverty amidst plenty. As major share of the benefits from mineral excavations goes to the central exchequer it leaves very little for the State Government. For instance in case of Panna Diamonds a meagre royalty of 5 per cent only is earned by the State. Thus the weak State exchequer faces employment problem of inhabitants specially in respect of middle and lower classes whereas a major industrial gain is shared by people from outside the State. What can be the reason for this anomaly? Does the State lack in technical personnel and technology or the institutions of Higher Education?

The data about contribution of the private institutions to Higher education which are large in numbers are collected by sample survey method and analysed.

The findings show that 37 per cent of the total budget provision of the Government is utilised on education and 1/4th of which is allocated to Higher Education. There are 10 Universities in Madhya Pradesh having 300 colleges including 140 non-Government institutions. Though Higher Education has adequate enrolment its standard is below the national level in spite of the percentage of passes being quite high. Consequently, the need of the society with regard to supply of skills and levels of education for future occupation is not wholly fulfilled. This state of affairs reveals the gap between investment on education and its returns and low income growth of the state in spite of hectic economic activities.

In the state out of every two individuals one lives below the subsistence level. Without improving the resources of the exchequer public expenditure cannot be increased and the infrasturctural facilities and incentives for capital formation cannot be provided according to needs. This paradox of weaker resources of budget, inter-sectoral competitions for allocation of funds and the public demand leaves very little for education.

The objectives of the study are not only confined to answering the questions raised above but to involve techniques and a system for preparing budget. The researcher is not to leave the old line Budget Method on the ground that the Britishers themselves had discarded it and had chosen new techniques suiting to their needs within the constitutional framework of their country, as new techniques are yet to be put to empirical tests in developing countries. This is the core coverage of this study.

The chapterization begins with the priority issue of education as an investment captioned as 'Impact of Higher Education on the Development of the Area'. Enough material on the subject has been published and discussed at the national and international levels covering mostly all aspects. In India, the issue has a different cultural and religious background where the philosophy of western materialism has been completely discarded for contentment with deep roots in Indian Sanskara and Gyana is the medium for solution in life. Thus knowledge for knowledge's sake is the consumption part of education but to bifurcate the two is difficult as independent parts will loose value. Secondly Higher Education which increases productivity, efficiency and fair standard of living of the people is thus purely an investment.

The old pattern of budget preparation needs a new turn to make it suitable to programmes and objectives for which the society fixes priority. As traditional method aims merely for controlling budget, it may not exceed the allocations, it ignores the achievements of the objectives laid down for the fulfilment of the policy framed for capital formation and economic regeneration activities.

04 Jha, D., *A study of the finances of the Patna University, Deptt. of Eco.*, Patna University, 1974 (ICSSR financed).

The major objectives of the investigation were: (i) to study the sources of income and their relative importance; (ii) to examine the steadiness and adequacy of the income; and (iii) to ascertain whether the university was under financial stresses and strains which adversely affected its operational efficiency. All these were with reference to Patna University.

The period 1952-53 to 1972-73 was selected for the purpose of inquiry. The sources of data were the annual budgets and audit reports, annual reports, minutes of the meetings of various bodies of the university, and the university handbooks and notifications. Besides, a questionnaire was also prepared and administered.

The study revealed that (i) the major sources of university finances were grants received from the state government and the UGC, and the fees and other charges realised from students; (ii) the grant from the state government increased from six per cent in 1947-48 to fiftythree per cent in

1952-53 and this further increased in recent years; (iii) income from examination fees was growing fast every year; (iv) when the university ceased to be an affiliating university after 1952 and became a teaching-cum-residential university the expenditure increased enormously; (v) development of new departments and modernisation of courses of study also entailed increase in expenditure; (vi) the rise in prices since 1962 had a very important influence on the university finances; (vii) the efforts to meet the revenue expenditure by diversion of funds from capital grants prevented the authorities to derive further capital grants which further added to the hardship of the university finances; (viii) from 1964-65, the university was running with increasing deficit budgets except in 1965-66 when there was a small surplus; (ix) during 1952 to 1974, due to large increase in enrolment at undergraduate and postgraduate levels, the university remained under constant pressure of increasing seats in all classes; and (x) the finance committee failed to function properly due to the absence of elaborate financial rules, lack of suitable conventions, and due to pressures exerted on them in the context of overall shortage of funds.

05 Kale, S.S., Financial accounting in the financial administration of private aided colleges and the institutions of higher education in Maharashtra State, Gokhale Institute of Politics and Economics, Poona, 1972. (Maharashtra Government Financed).

The investigation proposed to study broadly: (i) the objectives of keeping accounts; (ii) factors that influence and determine a particular pattern of the system of financial accounts and records keeping; (iii) broad outline and analysis of the existing system of financial account keeping; (iv) determinants of a satisfactory system of financial account keeping; (v) basis of accounting procedure; (vi) system of fund accounting and analysis of its suitability to the educational institution; (vii) operational development of the fund accounting system (the identification of distinct transactions and their segregation and grouping into functions); (viii) accounting records; and (ix) operating of funds accounts.

The study was restricted to all the private aided colleges or institutions of higher learning of the State of Maharashtra. Stratified random sample technique was employed for drawing out the sample. Two hundred and fifty institutions were selected for the purposes of collection of data relating to financial accounting. The sources of data were the records available from the colleges, universities and state government. The data were analysed by employing simple statistical measures indicating central tendency and dispersion. The study, thus, is a normative one.

The following were the findings of the study. The existing system had developed manifold confused and even conflicting objectives due to number of pressures. Moreover the existing system failed to operate as administrative and management tool as well as a planning technique. The educational system of financial accountancy differed from commercial system in its (a) nature and aims, (b) financial aims of education, (c) accumulation of assets and their structure in institutions of higher education, (d) attitude towards accumulation of capital and its treatment in the balance sheet, (e) treatment of inventories, (f) acquiring of capital and the nature of the liabilities emerging out of it and its reflection in financial accountancy, and (g) exemption from taxation. The system of financial accountancy in the institutions of higher education (a) based itself on the appreciation of institutional (educational) objectives, (b) operated as a safeguard to the funds, and (c) provided adequate information needed for institutional planning and programming, and administration and financial control.

06 Loganathan, V., State and higher education : Financing collegiate education with special reference to arts and science colleges in Tamil Nadu, Ph.D. Eco., Madras University, 1981.

The main aims of the study were: (i) to calculate the unit cost for pre-university, undergraduate and postgraduate students, (ii) to arrive at the amount of subsidy for students, and (iii) to examine the present system of financing from the efficiency and equity points of view.

The aided (private) arts and science colleges in Tamil Nadu (N=138 in 1976-77) offering pre-university, degree/postgraduate courses were considered for the study. A non-proportionate stratified random sample of thirty colleges was selected, the stratification being made on the basis of size. Required data were collected from the financial statements of the colleges, government publications, the schedules specially canvassed to be administered to students and from the data collected through the state sample of National Sample Survey. Only the direct expenditure was considered to calculate the unit cost, the capital costs and rent were not considered. The cost was computed on the basis of the old scales of pay and not on the revised UGC scales of pay. The average recurring cost per student consisted of the teachers' cost, general expenditure and special fees. The subsidy in the tuition fee structure was calculated for different levels of study by measuring the difference between recurrent cost and the fees levied at various levels. The net subsidy enjoyed by families under different income groups was also computed, by deducting the tax amount paid from the implicit subsidy.

The main findings of the study were: (i) The average recurrent cost for P.U.C. humanities was Rs. 546 and for sciences Rs. 738. For B.A.: English Rs. 2683, Tamil Rs. 4155; history Rs. 2188; economics Rs. 2294; philosophy Rs. 2560; co-operation Rs. 2771; business administration Rs. 3682. For B.Com.: Rs. 1536. For M.A.: history Rs. 1536, economics Rs. 1435; philosophy Rs. 1921; English Rs. 2275; Tamil Rs. 2517; social work Rs. 2711. For B.Sc.: mathematics Rs. 2735; physics Rs. 3519; chemistry Rs. 2972; zoology Rs. 3496; botany Rs. 3520; statistics Rs. 2068; home science Rs. 3066; rural development Rs. 4484. For M.Sc.: mathematics Rs. 3260; chemistry Rs. 3489; botany Rs. 10552; zoology Rs. 3603; statistics Rs. 5020; physics Rs. 5213. (ii) The average unit private costs without tuition and special fees were for P.U.C. Rs. 615; B.A. Rs. 2448; B.Sc. Rs. 1607; B.Com. Rs. 1291; M.A. Rs. 1416; M.Sc. Rs. 3449 and M.Com. Rs. 1105. (iii) Very few poor people used higher education facilities provided in aided colleges.

07 Mathew, E.T., A study of Kerala University finances, Deptt. of Eco., Kerala University, 1974 (ICSSR financed).

The major aims of the study were: (i) to find out the main sources of income in terms of their relative importance; (ii) to examine whether the income derived was steady and adequate, and (ii) to ascertain whether the university was subject to any financial stresses and strains which adversely affected its operational efficiency.

The period under study was 1947-48 to 1970-71, and within this period finances in 1970-71 were subjected to detailed study. The data were collected from the budget and audit reports, records of meetings of the various bodies of the university and the university handbooks and notifications. Analyses were done in terms of main trends in financing.

The study revealed that (i) the university derived revenues from university departments, grants from the state government, the UGC, the government of India and from other sources; (ii) the conducting of examination happened to be the single largest source and lately became a major concern for heavy outlay; (iii) till 1954-55, the state government was the main financier of the university, afterwards government of India came into picture and the UGC started financing from 1957-58; (iv) there had been a rapid expansion of expenditure in the university, frequent pay revision and fast expansion of number of employees being the suggested reasons; (v) more money was spent on examination than teaching and research; (vi) the expenditure in study and research in science departments was nearly the double of the funds spent in humanities; (vii) the overall expenditure of the university increased by seventeen per cent per year; (viii) the expenditure on general administration increased from seven per cent in 1947-48 to nineteen per cent in 1970-71; (ix) the teaching and research department ranked somewhat low on expenditure pattern of the university; (x) the budget estimates largely remained the same over the period 1970-71 to 1973-74; and (xi) in terms of finances, the university was entering a period of stringency.

08 Mukerji, K.M., Study of Calcutta University finances, Deptt. of Com., Calcutta University, 1974 (ICSSR financed).

The present investigation aimed at (i) studying the sources of finance of Calcutta University with relative importance on each source; (ii) examining the relationships between the state and the central authorities and the university regarding university finances; and (iii) ascertaining if the university had been under financial stresses and strains with the consequences thereof.

Methodologically, it was a descriptive and analytical survey. While the detailed study was restricted only to the year 1970-71 the total period of study was from 1947-48 to 1971-72. The data were collected from the budget and audit records, annual reports, minutes of the finance committee meetings and various notifications. Analysis of the data were done by categorising the receipts and payments under broad categories and subsequently breaking them down into subsidiary categories.

The study revealed that (i) the undergraduate examination fees by themselves, or the total examination fees, constituted the largest single source of receipt for the university; the next in order were grants from the state government, and individual small items like other fees, income from capital funds, etc.; (ii) the administrative expenditure remained stable around thirtythree per cent between 1948-49 and 1969-70, but the salaries of teachers after reaching a peak of 33.12 per cent in 1951-52 fell gradually to 18.76 per cent in 1969-70, and miscellaneous expenditures remained stable around eighteen per cent, though there were large fluctuations during the intervening years; (iii) the financial arrangements under which the university operated did not provided for any procedure by which a physical programme was considered and translated into financial terms; (iv) expenditure on academic aspects was often delayed due to redtapism; (v) there was found no departmental working plans with a reasonable synthesis between teaching, nonteaching and material inputs; (vi) the university did not have any formal legal support from the government in respect of financial liabilities although the institutional grant was becoming increasingly more important; and (vii) the trusts and endowments funds went a long way in the past to sustain the finances of the University of Calcutta.

09 Nanjundappa, D.M., A study of university finance, Deptt. of Eco., Karnataka University, 1975 (ICSSR financed).

The main objective of the investigation was to study the working of university finances with reference to (a) growth of revenue and behaviour of components of revenue; (b) growth of expenditure and behaviour of components of expenditure; (c) allocation of available funds among the different activities and disciplines; and (d) financial relations between the university and the UGC and that between the government and the university.

The finances of Karnataka University since its inception in 1949 to 1972-73 were studied. The data were collected from the university records.

The major findings were: (i) the total revenue increased from Rs. 1.45 lakhs (1949-50) to Rs. 177.85 lakhs (1972-73) showing an average annual growth of fortytwo per cent; (ii) the per capita revenue grew from Rs. 928 (1949-50) to Rs. 6910 (1959-60) and Rs. 2819 (1972-73); (iii) the state government financed up to fiftyfour per cent, the income from fees shared thirtyfive per cent and the UGC shared four to five per cent; (iv) there was a decline in the per capita grants indicating the comparative decline of university finances when compared to increased enrolement; (v) the total expenditure increased from Rs. 33,036 in 1949-50 to 2.23 crores of rupees in 1972-73; (vi) the change in the per capita expenditure was from Rs. 80.00 (1949-50) to Rs. 5401 (1958-59) and Rs. 3306 (1972-73); (vii) the rises in the per capita expenditure between 1949-50 and 1972-73 were from Rs. 261 to Rs. 275 in case of library, Re. 1 to Rs. 8 in student facilities, Rs. 46 to Rs. 70 in case of fellowships, Rs. 28 to Rs. 92 for hostels, Rs. 4 to Rs. 103 in case of examinations, Rs. 74 to Rs. 1500 for academic departments and Rs. 6 to Rs. 58 for administration; (viii) the cost of education of an individual amounted to Rs. 5372 of which net academic cost (public cost) came to Rs. 3242 and private cost to Rs. 2130; (ix) the physical facilities available during 1961-62 declined in the later years; (x) the establishment of UGC and its introduction of four tier pattern of grants was a boon and a life saver to the university — the larger share of UGC grants in approved schemes helped the university to reduce reliance on the state government; (xi) over the four plan periods the proportion of grants for teaching staff was only thirteen percent; and (xii) the economic-cum-functional classification showed that there was a non-optimal allocation of funds among the different items of expenditure indicating the utmost economy of expenditure to be imposed on general services.

10 Nigam, M.S., A study of the finance of the University of Rajasthan, Deptt. of Eco., Rajasthan University, 1974 (ICSSR financed).

The major objectives of the study were: (i) to find out the sources of income of the University of Rajasthan; (ii) to study the relative importance of these sources of income; (iii) to examine the steadiness and adequacy of the income; and (iv) to ascertain whether the university was subjected to financial stress that affected its operational efficiency and independence.

Out of the twentyfive years of its existence a slice of eleven years from 1960-61 to 1970-71 was selected for the study of finances. The data were collected from the following sources, namely, (i) published annual budgets of the university, (ii) annual reports of the university, (iii) minutes of the meetings of the various bodies of the university published from time to time and university handbooks and notifications. The financial position of the university was analysed in the context of autonomy, adequacy and flexibility.

The study revealed that (i) the different sources of finances were the fees from students, the grants received from the state government and the UGC; (ii) due to the phenomenal development of the university since 1962, there had been huge and recurring deficit in the budget of the university, the government grant was found to be inadequate; (iii) the method of ad hoc grants to cover deficit was found to be unsatisfactory; and (iv) the fixing of nonplan maintenance grant was a welcome measure, but the accompanying conditions curtailed the university autonomy of maneuvering of the fund to reallocate for their optimal use. It was opined that (a) a state level body in the pattern of UGC would help in settling the financial issues better; (b) within the university, selective allocation of funds to different departments would promote better settlement; and (c) the per capita material and educational facilities should be stabilised.

11 Ramachandran, A study of some problems of higher education in Kerala with special reference to the financing of education during the period 1957-75, Ph.D. Edu., Calicut University, 1981.

The major objectives of the study were: (i) to identify vital problem areas in higher education such as enrolment, expenditure, financing, and planning, (ii) to assess the total costs in higher education classified under relevant institutional categories, (iii) to compare costs for different aspects of higher education like salaries, laboratories, libraries, students amenities, and (iv) to compare investment of different agencies in higher education like the State Government, the UGC, etc.

This was a normative historical study. Necessary data were collected from primary sources like documents and reports of the State Government, universities, the UGC, and the Planning Commission. The secondary sources for data were mainly published books, research papers, reports of conferences and seminars on higher education.

The major findings of the study were: (i) There was a phenomenal growth of institutions of higher education in Kerala during the period under review. There was only one university in 1956 and the number increased to four, and the number of arts and science colleges increased from 46 to 128 by 1975-76. The establishment of colleges was done without much forethought and planning. The district-wise distribution of arts and science colleges and the population served by each college showed, in certain districts like Quilon, Palghat, Cannanore, and Calicut, the number of colleges were, on an average, less in relation to their population. (ii) More than 82 per cent arts and science colleges in the State were under private management. (iii) The average annual rate of growth of enrolment for general education courses was about 11.8 per cent during the period under study. (iv) Public expenditure on education has been growing very rapidly in the State of Kerala. A sum of Rs. 1,037 lakhs, about 31.5 per cent of the total revenue expenditure, was spent on general education in 1957-58, but the total expenditure increased to Rs. 13,226 lakhs by 1975-76, i.e. 37.3 per cent of the total expenditure of the State. Though the percentage of annual increase was not high, in absolute terms the increase was to the tune of 11.76 times. The index of growth during the period under review was 1275. The average annual expenditure on education during the period of study was about 34 per cent of the state's total budget. (v) Whereas the total public expenditure on general education was increasing year after year, the corresponding return to the revenue of the State Government was very low. The receipt under education was about 3.6 per cent of the total revenue receipts of the State in 1975-76, whereas total public expenditure on general education during this year was to the tune of Rs. 13,226 lakhs. (vi) The expenditure on university education showed phenomenal increase. When the total expenditure increased by 11.76 times the amount spent in 1957-58 the share of higher education increased by 28.61 times over the 1957-58 amount. The total expenditure was only Rs. 52.98 lakhs in 1957-58 but it increased to Rs. 1,568.79 lakhs by 1975-76 showing an increase to 29.61 times. The expenditure on higher education was only 6 per cent of the overall expenditure on education in 1957-58 but it constituted 11.9 per cent in 1975-76. (vii) The bulk of the public expenditure on higher education was spent for the development and maintenance of arts and science colleges in Kerala. The total direct expenditure on these colleges in 1957-58 was only Rs. 22.22 lakhs and formed about 41.9 per cent of the overall expenditure on higher education. An amount of Rs. 1,262.93 lakhs was the direct expenditure on arts and science colleges in 1975-76 and constituted 80.5 per cent of the total expenditure on higher education during that year. Thus expenditure on higher education showed tremendous growth both as a percentage of the total expenditure on higher education was well as in absolute terms.

12 Rizvi, F.H., Financing of higher education in less-developed countries, Aligarh Muslim University Press, 1960.

The major objective of the study was to investigate the question of financing educational facilities in less-dêveloped countries, with special reference to higher education. The following specific research questions were raised to investigate the problem: (i) Was there any method which could determine the optimal level of investment in the provision of educational services? (ii) What should be the proper role of the State in this sphere? (iii) Was there any special form of investment that could be considered desirable for less-developed countries with respect to higher education? (iv) What was the historical retrospect of educational finance in India? (v) In the light of the statistical data, was the size of the educational expenditure consistent with socio-economic policy of the country expressed through its official channels? (vi) Was the expenditure on universities and colleges in India, and its distribution between the different types of education, of a size and character that reflected optimum level of investment? If not, what were the main obstacles and what reforms could remove these obstacles and bring them adequate resources but without curtailing their autonomy or free choice of individuals? (vii) If the appraisal showed that the need for additional resources was imperative, who should acquire them and how?

The investigator had gathered materials from a large variety of sources, official and non-official, Indian and those of other nations and the international organisations ranging from purely educational to those relevant to economic theory.

The findings were: (i) The problem of resource allocation was real and almost universal and there was no universally acceptable formula that could serve as an easy, mechanical and fool-proof device for determining the size of the economic resources which tended to bring optimum investment in the provision of educational services. (ii) There was disagreement as to who or which institutions should perform the process of valuation. Different communities belonging to different political creed approached this problem differently and, consequently, their emphasis on the role of the State in this respect also showed radical differences. (iii) The lesson for less-developed countries was that State participation in education was necessary, particularly given the kinds of objectives commonly supported in such countries. However, State participation would have to be strictly on an individual rather than an institutional basis, if it was desired to encourage education which could be in tune with the economic and social needs of the country. (iv) In view of the acute economic backwardness, the right policy for less-developed countries would be to develop all types of education but to facilitate economic development and to banish disease, poverty, hunger, and ignorance, they should invest more in scientific and technical education. (v) Creation of new universities, expansion of arts and science colleges, professional, technical, and special education colleges and a substantial increase in enrolment were the highlights of the post-Independence era. However, the complexion of educational structure and its problems were more or less the same as they were in pre-Independence period. The only difference was that the outlook had become rather more expansionist, (vi) There had been a continuous rise in educational expenditure. Notable as this increase appeared to be, proportions of the outlays diverted to education and higher education of NDP (Net Domestic Product) were 2 per cent for general education and 0.37 per cent for higher education. Expenditure on higher education incurred by private bodies was 65.9 per cent, whereas on government-maintained institutions was 33.6 per cent. The public sector had larger share in the institutions imparting professional and technical education. Income from public funds and fees continued to be the mainstay of the higher education finance. The bulk of the public expenditure on education was incurred on primary education. Secondary education was given second priority. Higher education accounted for 11.4 per cent of the total public expenditure of education. (vii) The expenditure on higher education in India and its distribution between the different types of education was of a size and character that was well below the optimum level of investment. With reference to criteria of both the democratization of educational opportunities and higher education's effectiveness to serve as a sound and dynamic basis for the solution of the nation's socio-economic problems, there existed a vast disparity between the community's honest professions and a record of its actual achievements. This situation could be attributed to the low level of investment but primarily to the system of finance by which the already inadequate resources were actually made available to the institutions of higher education.

25. FUTURE

A BOOKS

01 Raza, Moonis & others. *Education and the future: An Indian perspective (A Unesco sponsored study)* New Delhi, National Institute of Educational Planning and Administration, 1983. 70 p.

02 Raza, Moonis. *Education and the futures : A vision.* New Delhi, NIEPA, 1983. 19 p.

B ARTICLES

01 Amrik Singh. Higher education in AD 2000. *Mainstream.* 28(18), 1990. p. 15-19.

02 Jan Mohamad. Higher education and its future. *University News.* 21 (16), 1983. p. 511-14.

26. LAW

A BOOKS

01 Agarwala, S.D. *Law of universities in U.P., Meerut*, Meenakshi Prakashan, 1981. I, xxxviii, 383, p.; 1035 p. 2 vols.

02 Kohlatkar, D.D. *Commentary on the university laws in India.* Indore, Lawyers Home, 1974.

03 Sharma, G.S., ed. *Educational planning: Its legal and constitutional implications for India.* Bombay, N.M. Tripathi, 1967.

B ARTICLES

01 Amrik, Singh. Justice in the universities. *The Times of India.* 15th July, 1989. p. 6.

02 ——. Parliament versus universities. *University News.* 20(22), 1982. p. 690-691.

03 Mathai, Samuel. University constitution. *University News.* 7, (3), 1969. p. 11-12.

04 Nayar, V.K. Sukumaran and Chander, N. Jose. Supreme Court and the private colleges. *University News.* 9(8), 1971. p. 15-19.

05 Pillay, K. Krishna. Highlights of the Kerala University Bill. *University Administration.* 1 (June-July), 1974. p. 41-55.

06 Tope, T.K. Constitutional provisions relating to education. *University News.* 27(5), 1989. p. 4-8.

07 ——. Universities and law courts. *University News.* 26 (15), 1988. p. 7-11.

08 ——. University and law courts. *University News.* 27(18), 1989. p. 2-3 and 5.

09 ——. Universities and law courts. *University News.* 27(33), 1989. p. 1-3.

10 ——. University and law courts. *University News.* 27(48), 1989. p. 7-11.

D RESEARCH STUDIES

01 Rao, K.S., Courts and University Education in India, Ph.D. Law, Osmania University, 1982.

The objectives of the study were (i) to indicate the trend of decisions of courts in the field of university education, (ii) to analyse difficulties and turbulations faced by the court in solving some of the disputes having purely academic flavour, and (iii) to study the restraint shown by the courts in interfering with educational matters.

The study employed case study approach where all the cases that had gone to the courts in India were studied keeping in view the various articles of the constitution and recommendations of education commissions. This was later on followed by analysis made in the light of certain principles evolved by courts like the principle of natural justice or hearing ultra-vires and principles of estoppel.

The findings of the study were: 1. The court had shown a great restraint and unwillingness to interfere with the internal autonomy or internal working of educational institutions and also the purely academic matters. 2. The question of issuing writ to educational institutions was complex as these bodies did not have a common pattern. 3. Apart from the writ remedies, the high court was empowered to issue directions and orders, as educational bodies discharged highly specialised nature of work based on their experience and understanding of the problem. 4. The courts had generally protected the minority interest and their right to establish and administer educational institutions. The minority institution was usually established by the minority community but it did not benefit only that community. 5. The Constitution gave the minorities right to enable them to maintain the individuality and distinct identity of their culture and language. 6. The study of plethora of cases on minority indicated that the state could certainly make regulating measures to promote efficiency and excellence of educational standards. It was entitled to regulate conditions of employment of teachers and health and hygiene of students. 7. The state provided grant-in-aid to the universities, and hence state could prescribe certain reasonable regulations. 8. An important aspect of university education was admission of students into educational institutions. The students had become legally and socially conscious to protect their right at the earliest opportunity. 9. The university and colleges had generally retained control over admission and exercised discretion in admitting students to a course. 10. The government usually laid down the policy of reservation and it was implemented by educational institutions. The universities were also entitled to prescribe certain reservations. 11. The important issues attracting the attention of courts had been reservation policy and criteria for determining backwardness. The courts had considered some objective conditions as relevant in adjudging backwardness. The accepted criteria by the courts had been caste, economic and social conditions. 12. The courts had been cautious regarding the examination and students discipline. They had treated these issues as purely internal matter of the universities. 13. The courts had accepted the need of treating student indiscipline cases on separate footing and generally had left the matter to university bodies.

27. MANAGEMENT

A BOOKS

01 Association of Indian Universities. *Internal management in universities: Status report series.* New Delhi, The author, 1980. 142 p.

02 Binod Kumar, (ed.) *Management of education in India: Problems and prospects.* Calcutta, Indian Institute of Management, 1976. 229 p.

03 Gupta, N.P. *Participation in decision making.* New Delhi, National Institute of Educational Planning and Administration, 1984. 41 p. (Research Studies. NCT-II).

04 Kiranmayi, Y.S. *Management of higher education in India.* New Delhi, Crown, 1989. 360 p.

05 Malik, S.C., (ed.) *Management and organization of Indian universities.* Simla, Indian Institute of Advanced Study, 1971. 283 p.

06 Matthai, Ravi J. *Exploratory study of decision making strategies and organizational health in a university: A research report.* Ahmedabad, Indian Institute of Management, 1976. 210 p.

07 Matthai, Ravi, Pareek, Udai and Rao, T.V., (eds.) *Institute building in education and research from stagnation to self-renewal.* New Delhi. All India Management Association, 1977, 174 p.

08 ——. *Management process in universities* by Ravi J. Matthai, Udai Pareek T. & Venkateswara Rao. Ahmedabad, Public Systems Groups, 1978. 20 p.

09 National Institute of Educational Planning and Administration. *Educational management in India: A diagnostic study.* New Delhi, The author, 1983. 131 p.

10 Subramaniam, M.K. Management of institutions of higher education: Norms and procedures. Ahmedabad, Indian Institute of Management, 1968, 16 p.

11 Verma, Yoginder, S. *University management and administration.* New Delhi, Deep and Deep, 1990. 308 p.

12 Varghese, Alexander V. *Higher education and management.* New Delhi, Ashish, 1989. 212 p.

B ARTICLES

01 Ali, Syed Hashim. Conflict management. *University News*. 25(43), 1987. p. 1-6.

02 Amrik Singh. Academics must have a say in decision-making. *University News*. 12(2), 1974. p. 26-27.

03 ——. Governance of universities. *University News*. 27(4), 1989. p. 1-2.

04 Bandyopadhyay, Swaraj. University Decision-making: In theory and practice. *University News*. 13(7), 1975. p. 4-6.

05 Bhagia, N.M. and Juneja, N. The role of the college principal. *EPA Bulletin*. 7(3-4), 1985. p. 62-72.

06 Bhattacharya, Swapan K. Developing unit structure in university organization : A study of alternative approach. *Journal of Higher Education*. 3(2), Autumn, 1979. p. 243-250.

07 ——. Managerial issues in university administration. *Bulletin Centre for Education Policy and Management*. July, 1976. p. 46-49.

08 Bhatawdekar, M.G. Students involvement in educational management. *University News*. 6(9), 1968. p. 10-11.

09 Chandi, P.T. Role of management in building up the college as an academic community. *New Frontiers in Education*. 6(2), 1976. p. 49-60.

10 Darji, D.R., Sharma, D.K. Decision-making and university management. *University News*. 22(12), 1984. p. 5-8.

11 Desai, D.M. Student participation in university decision-making process. *NIE Journal*. 4, March, 1970. p. 5-9.

12 Desai, Uday. Models of organisational governance and leadership role: The case of Indian universities. *Indian Journal of Public Administration*. 28(3), 1982. p. 651-664.

13 Gangrade, K.D. Student Participation in university management. *New Frontiers in Education*. 3, December, 1973. p. 62-65.

14 Gosh, D.K. Internal management of universities. *University News* 17(11), 1979. p. 302-304.

15 Gokak, V.K. Student participation in varsity affairs: A VC's view. *University News*. 7(6), 1969. p. 21-23.

16 Internal management of universities: Contributed by the University of Burdwan. *University News*. 17(12), 1979.

17 Iyear, T.S.K.V. Internal management of universities: BJTS experience. *University News*. 1 May, 1979.

18 Jain, M.C. The governor as chancellor. *University News*. 27(15), 1989. p. 1-5.

19 Joshi, Sneha. Towards successful educational management. *University News*. 27(33), 1989. p. 4-5. and 10.

20 Juneja, Nalini. College headship need a new definition. *New Frontiers in Education*. 17(1), 1987. p. 57-62.

21 Kanagasabapathy, R. Conflict the solution in management of colleges. *University News*. 26(20), 1980. p. 5-7.

22 ——. Management of Change : A case study of Madurai Kamaraj University. *University News*. 25(48), 1987. p. 5-11.

23 Kapatan, Sanjay. Management by objectives and university administration. *University News*. 26(42), 1988. p. 2-5.

24 ——. Modernizing university administration. *University News*. 27(13), 1989. p. 4-5 and 10.

25 Kaushal, R.K. Public relations in university management : Scope and limitations. *University News*. 25(24), 1987. p. 12.

26 Kiranmayi, Y.S. Restructuring organisational structure of universities in India. *University News*. 27(40), 1989. p. 23-38.

27 Kuriakose, P.T. Training of student leaders in colleges. *New Frontiers in Education*. 4(3), September, 1974. p. 79-85.

28 Maheshwari, K.L. Gaps in management education in Indian universities. *Indian Journal of Commerce*. 22, December, 1969. p.188-99.

29 Mohanty, Sunil Behari. Effective classroom management in higher education. *University News*. 27(49), 1989. p. 6-9.

30 Mukherjee, Subrata. Democratic experiment in Delhi University. *University News*. 15(21), 1977. p. 575-576 and 598.

31 Mukherjee, T.B. Internal management of Universities. *University News*. 17(5), March, 1979. p. 117-118.

32 Narayanaswamy, Srinivasa. Computerise varsity management. University News. 22(40), 1984. p. 1 cont. p. 7.

33 ——. Democratising the governance of universities and colleges. *University News*. 27(43), 1989. p. 1-3.

34 Nirmal Singh. Public relations in educational and research institutions. *University News*. 26(41), 1988. p. 4-7.

35 Pareek, Udai. Institution building : The frame-work for decision-making. *University Administration*. 2(1-2), 1975. p. 7-18.

36 Pavate, D.C. University management. *University News*. 11(10), 1973. p. 4-9.

37 Pillai, J.K. Leadership behaviour of college teachers. *Journal of Indian Education*. 3(5), January, 1978. p. 12-14.

38 Rao, M.R. and Raju, U.S. Management of the university department. *New Frontiers in Education*. 6(2), 1976. p. 19-31.

28. MANPOWER PLANNING

A BOOKS

01 Burgess, T, Layard, P.R.C. and Pant, P. *Manpower and educational development in India, 1961-86*. London, Oliver and Boyd, 1968. 89p.

02 Dhar, T.N. *Politics of manpower planning: Graduate unemployment and the planning of higher education in India*. Calcutta, Minerva, 1974.

03 Dhesi, Autar Singh. *Human capital formation and its utilisation*. New Delhi, Sterling, 1979. 291p.

04 Ginzberg, Eli. *Perspectives on Indian manpower, employment and income*. New Delhi, Ford Foundation, 1971.

05 Institute of Applied Manpower Research. *Engineering manpower analytical review of demand forecast methodology and provisional forecasts of growth*. New Delhi, IAMR, 1963.

06 ——. *Engineering manpower: A special study of engineering manpower requirements up to 1976*. New Delhi, The author, 1967. (Report No. 1).

07 ——. *A sectoral study of engineering manpower requirements*. New Delhi, IAMR, 1967.

08 Kidder, David. *Education and manpower planning in India*. Bombay, Progressive, 1973.

09 Rao, V.K.R.V. *Education and human resource development*. Bombay, Allied, 1966.

10 Veeraraghavan, J. *Manpower requirements*. In Amrik Singh and Philip G. Altbach, eds. *The higher learning in India*. Delhi, Vikas Publishing House, 1974. p. 91-102.

B ARTICLES

01 Aggarwal, S.P. and Kumar, S. Methods of estimating stock of educated manpower-illustrated with reference to graduate and above in arts, science and commerce. *Manpower Journal*. March,

education. In Bombay, the expansion had a basis of real demand, in Marathwada it was the created demand. (ii) The involvement of private managements extended into the academic and administrative areas. There was a great deal of variation in the patterns of involvement between Marathwada and Bombay. (iii) The principal had dual accountability, to the management and the university. How he conducted himself at both the levels — of the college and the university — was influenced by whether he was a member, a promoter, an employee or an adviser in relationship to the management. (iv) The patterns of involvement of private agencies varied between Bombay and Marathwada, not only because of the intra-organizational characteristics but also because of the differences in the ethos and culture of the larger community and structure. (v) The legal character and accountability of private managements needed clarification.

28. MANPOWER PLANNING

A BOOKS

01 Burgess, T, Layard, P.R.C. and Pant, P. *Manpower and educational development in India, 1961-86*. London, Oliver and Boyd, 1968. 89p.

02 Dhar, T.N. *Politics of manpower planning: Graduate unemployment and the planning of higher education in India*. Calcutta, Minerva, 1974.

03 Dhesi, Autar Singh. *Human capital formation and its utilisation*. New Delhi, Sterling, 1979. 291p.

04 Ginzberg, Eli. *Perspectives on Indian manpower, employment and income*. New Delhi, Ford Foundation, 1971.

05 Institute of Applied Manpower Research. *Engineering manpower analytical review of demand forecast methodology and provisional forecasts of growth*. New Delhi, IAMR, 1963.

06 ——. *Engineering manpower: A special study of engineering manpower requirements up to 1976*. New Delhi, The author, 1967. (Report No. 1).

07 ——. *A sectoral study of engineering manpower requirements*. New Delhi, IAMR, 1967.

08 Kidder, David. *Education and manpower planning in India*. Bombay, Progressive, 1973.

09 Rao, V.K.R.V. *Education and human resource development*. Bombay, Allied, 1966.

10 Veeraraghavan, J. *Manpower requirements*. In Amrik Singh and Philip G. Altbach, eds. *The higher learning in India*. Delhi, Vikas Publishing House, 1974. p. 91-102.

B ARTICLES

01 Aggarwal, S.P. and Kumar, S. Methods of estimating stock of educated manpower-illustrated with reference to graduate and above in arts, science and commerce. *Manpower Journal*. March,

1967. p. 9-46.

02 Amarjit Singh. Industry, growth and role of universities. *Journal of University Education*. 3 (2), 1964. p. 95-104.

03 Kennedy, Van. Commissions' conception of human resource development. *Asian Survey*. 9, October, 1969. p. 758-764.

04 Pathak, Mahesh and Patel, Arun. Supply of graduates from the Sardar Patel University during the fourth plan. *Artha-Vikas*. 6 (2), July, 1970. p. 11-12.

05 Tilak, V.R.K. Future manpower situation in India, 1961-76. *International Labour Review*. May, 1963. p. 435-47.

06 Ved Prakasha. Manpower planning and education in India. *New Frontiers in Education*. 1, December, 1971. p. 235-251.

07 Veena, D.R. Supply of manpower by educational levels in Gujarat: An analysis of extrapolation trend and transaction approach. *Manpower Journal*. 3 (2), December, 1976. p. 127-40.

08 Verma, M.C. Review of skilled manpower forecasts and changes in occupational structures in India. *International Journal of Educational Development*. 4 (3), 1984. p. 173-221.

29. NATIONAL DEVELOPMENT

A BOOKS

01 Association of Indian Universities. *Higher education and development*. New Delhi, The author, 1975. 166p.

02 Christian Literature Society. *Christian college and national development*. Madras, The author, 1967. 290p.

03 Kaul, J.N., (ed.) *Higher education, social change and national development*. Simla, Indian Institute of Advanced Study, 1975.

04 Kothari, D.S. *Higher education and national development*. New Delhi, U.G.C., 1972.

05 Raza, Moonis. *Education development and society*. New Delhi, Vikas, 1990. 226p.

06 *University research in science and technology in relationship to national development*. New Delhi, U.G.C., 1980.

B ARTICLES

01 Adiseshiah, Malcolm. Role of universities in international co-operation for development. *New Frontiers in Education*. 14 (2), 1984. p. 55-65.

02 Apparow, M.R. Role of higher education in the process of development and change. *University News*. 1 May, 1979. p. 238 and 241.

03 Atwal, A.S. Universities and national development: Linkage with environment. *University News*. 1 June, 1979. p. 300-302.

04 Bhalerao, C.N. Universities and their role in development. *University News*. 20 (16), 1982. p. 518-519.

05 Bhatia, S.C. Adult education, NPE, 1986 and the universities. *University News*. 25 (50), 1987. p. 57-63.

06 ——. National literacy mission and the universities. *University News*. 27 (4), 1989. p. 3-5.

07 Burman, B.K. Role of universities in rural development: The issues. *Social Change*. 12 (4), 1982. p. 40-44.

08 Chakravarty, S. Higher education and national development. *Indian Journal of Labour Economics.* 15 (1-2), April-July, 1972. p. 53-62.

09 Das Gupta, Amiya. Role of higher educational institutions in development. *University News.* 12 (12), 1974. p. 4-6.

10 Dore, R.P. Role of universities in national development. *University News.* 1 September, 1978. p. 1129-1133.

11 Dryhns, H.N. Education for national development. University *News.* 21 (11), 1983. p. 347-350.

12 Gerth, Donald R. Education and national development. *University News.* 27 (24), 1989. p. 4-7.

13 Ghanchi, D.A. National goals and higher education. *University News.* 27 (7), 1989. p. 1-4.

14 Hooja, G.B.K. National literacy mission and the universities. *University News.* 27 (38), 1989. p. 5-7.

15 Johnson, Harry G. Observations on the role of the university in development planning. *Minerva.* 12 January, 1974. p. 32-38.

16 Joshi, D.D. and Rajeshwar Prasad. Problems of higher education in the context of development in India. *Agra University Bulletin.* 7 (1-4), January-October, 1976. p. 167-72.

17 Joshi, Ram. Universities and national development: Linkage with environment: Educational innovation at Bombay University. *University News.* 17 (6), March, 1979. p. 145-147.

18 Madan, P.J. Universities and national development: Linkage with environment. *University News.* 17 (5), 1979. p. 121-123.

19 Mathew, P.I. Higher education in a developmental framework: Problems and prospects in India. *International Education.* 9 (Spring) 1980. p. 12-17.

20 Mishra, L. Role of the university system in NLM. *University News.* 26 (52). 1988. p. 1-5.

21 Parthasarthi, A. Universities and nation building. *Quest.* (52), Winter, 1967. p. 19-26.

22 Paul, R.C. Universities and national development. *University News.* 17 (5), 1979. p. 119-120 and 123.

23 ——. University research and national development in India. *Man and Development.* 2 (4), December, 1980. p. 105-119.

24 ——. University research and national development in India. *University News.* 18 (9), 9 May, 1980. p. 228-242.

25 Pichai, R.; Ramaraju, A.R. Role of students and national progress. *University News.* 13 (3), 19754. p. 4-5.

26 Pylee, M.V. Universities and national development. *University News.* 17 (7), April, 1979. p. 186-189.

27 Ramana, K.V. National literacy mission and the Andhra University. *University News.* 27 (49), 1989. p. 4-5.

28 Ross, Alec M. Education and national development. *India International Centre Quarterly.* 6 (4), 1979. p. 307-315.

29 Roy, Bunker, Universities and national development : Linkage with enrolment. *University News.* 17 (13), 1979. p. 358-359, 364.

30 Santanagopalan, S. Role of universities in environmental studies. *University News.* 15 (7), 1977. p. 172-173.

31 Satish Chandra. Role of universities in national development. *University News.* 15 (10), 1977. p. 271-273.

32 Shah, L.R. Universities and national development: Linkage with environment. *Education Quarterly.* 31 (2), 1979. p. 17-19.

33 ——. Universities and national development : Linkage with environment. *University News.* 17 (6), 1979. p. 148-149, 164.

34 Shah, Madhuri R. Universities and national development : Linkage with environment. *University News.* 17 (8), April, 1979. p. 207-208.

35 Sinha, R.S.N. Universities and National development : Linkage with environment. *University News.* 17 (13), 1979. p. 356-357.

36 Sudarsanam, R. Universities and national development : Linkage with environment. *University News.* 17 (12), 1979. p. 332-333.

37 Tope, T.K. Higher education for development. *University News.* 21 (4), 1983. p. 106-109.

38 Universities and national development : Contributed by the University of Burdwan. *University News.* 17 (10), 1979. p. 261-262, 270.

39 Yadav, M.S. University and national development: Linkage with the environment. *New Frontiers in Education.* 10 (4), October-December, 1980. p. 22-26.

30. NATIONAL INTEGRATION

A BOOKS

01 Braisted, Paul Judson. *Indian nationalism and the Christian colleges.* New York, Association Press, 1935.

02 Chib, S. *Language, universities and nationalism.* London, Oxford University Press, 1936.

03 Rao, V.K.R.V. *The role of the university in national integration: Convocation address.* Baroda, Maharaja Sayajirao University, 1966. 15p.

B ARTICLES

01 Ali, B. Sheik. National integration. *University News.* 27 (2), 1989. p. 1-4 and 7.

02 Mathur, V.S. Role of colleges in national integration. *University News.* 18 (15), 1988. p. 407-408 cont. 412.

03 Rao, V.K.R.V. National integration through education. *University News.* 7 (9), 1969. p. 9-12.

04 Sinha, H.P. Caste and minority interests in higher education in the context of national integration. *Man and Development.* 4 (3), 1982. p. 36-38.

05 Thiagarajan, K. University education and national integration. *Education Quarterly.* 81 (10), October, 1975. p. 188-90.

C COMMITTEES/COMMISSIONS/REPORTS

01 Committee on emotional integration, 1961. Report. New Delhi, Manager of Publications, 1962. 277p. Chairman: Dr. Sampurnanand.

This committee was appointed to study the role of education in strengthening and promoting the processes of emotional integration in national life and to advise on positive educational programmes etc. The main topics of discussion in this report, which is spread over fourteen chapters and thirtyfive appendices, are as follows: Philosophy of education, languages, script, school, university and adult education, youth programmes, teachers, curriculum, textbooks etc.

02 Committee on the Involvement of the universities and colleges in the promotion of National Integration, 1985. New Delhi, U.G.C., 1986. Chairman : M H. Beg.

The University Grants Commission appointed a committee to go into the question of involvement of universities and colleges in promoting national integration.

Committee recommended that a National Institute of National Integration should be set up on a priority basis as a central institution to help to promote and coordinate studies on programme of national integration. There should be a standing Advisory Committee at the UGC level to provide policy based directions and guidelines.

National integration can be promoted through teaching, research and studies on different aspects of national integration, training of teachers and decision-makers, extension type of activities on national integration and through documentation and dissemination of necessary knowledge and library collection besides appointment/exchange of teachers as also admission/ exchange of students on the national level. The UGC may suggest Model Status/ Ordinances for the guidance of the universities in this regard.

31. PLANNING

A BOOKS

01 Bharathidasan University. *Ten year plan perspective : A policy frame*. 31p.

02 Laska, John. *Planning and educational development in India*. New York, Teachers College Press. 1968.

03 Naik, J.P. *Educational planning in India*. Bombay, Allied Publishers, 1965.

04 Planning Commission. *First five year plan, 1951-1966*. New Delhi, Planning Commission, 1963. Higher education. p. 539-524 and p. 548-557.

05 ——. *Second five year plan, 1956-1961*. New Delhi, Planning Commission, 1961. Higher education. p. 511-512 and p. 517-518.

06 ——. *Third five year plan, 1961-1966*. New Delhi, Planning Commission, 1961. Higher education. p. 589-591.

07 ——. *Fourth five year plan, 1969-1974*. New Delhi, Planning Commission, 1969. Higher education. p. 359-360.

08 ——. *Fifth five year plan, 1974-1979*. New Delhi, Planning Commission, 1976. Higher education. p. 76.

09 ——. *Sixth five year plan, 1980-1985*. New Delhi, Planning Commission, 1981. Higher education. p. 357-358.

10 ——. *Seventh five year plan, 1985-90*. New Delhi, Planning Commission, 1985. University Education. II. p. 259-260.

11 ——. *Summary record of proceedings of the conferences of university planning forums held at Darjeeling*, New Delhi and Bhopal (May, 1958 to November, 1959). New Delhi, Planning Commission, 1961. 72p.

12 ——. *University planning forums: A review*. New Delhi, Planning Commission, 19058. 12p.

13 Premi. M.K. Educational Planning in India. New Delhi, Sterling, 1972.

14 Planning Commission. *University planning forums: Summary record of meetings April 1956-Sept., 1957.* New Delhi. Planning Commission, 1958. 110p.

15 Rajasthan. Directorate of College Education. *Planning forums in Rajasthan : A decade of working and progress 1968-77.* Jaipur, the author, n.d.

16 Raza, Moonis. *Educational planning: A long term perspective.* New Delhi. National Institute of Educational Planning and Administration, 1986. 488p.

17 U.G.C. Guidelines : *Seventh plan development proposals of colleges.* New Delhi, U.G.C., 1986. 34p.

18 U.G.C. Guidelines : *Seventh plan development proposals of universities.* New Delhi, U.G.C., 1986

B ARTICLES

01 Abraham, A.S. Plans afoot to demote India's rural colleges. *Times Higher Education Supplement.* 18 April, 1980. p. 6.

02 Approach to the development of higher education in the sixth plan. *Bulletin of Higher Education.* 5 (1-2), September, 1980. p. 1-20.

03 Bajaj, K.K. College development council : The planning role. *University News.* 27 (24), 1989. p. 1-3.

04 Bateille, Andre. Universities and government : The need for a reappraisal. *Times of India.* 18-1-88. p. 6.

05 Bhan, R.K. University education in the third five year plan. *Shiksha.* 15 (1), July, 1962. p. 75-83.

06 Biswas, S. and others. Linear programming model of obtaining optimal enrolment in various educational sectors: A return approach to educational planning. *Manpower Journal.* 10 (4) and 11 (1), January-June, 1975. p. 64-101.

07 College education in the fifth plan. *New Frontiers in Education.* 3 (1), April, 1973. p. 112-13.

08 Development of higher education in the sixth plan. *University News,.* 18 (24), 1980. p. 677-681.

09 ——. *University News.* 19 (2), 1981. p. 39-44.

10 Dhesi, Autar S. Some international aspects of educational planning. *Indian Educational Review.* 12 (3), July, 1977. p. 104-109.

11 Fifth five year plan on university education. *University Affairs.* August 2, 1973. p. 9-11 and 21.

12 Garg, V.P. Development of higher education : Issues related to its planning. *University News.* 26 (52), 1988. p. 6-8.

13 Guruge, Ananda W.P. Why second generation educational planning? *New Frontiers in Education.* 3 (2), 1973. p. 1-31.

14 Halstead, D. Kent. Statewide planning in higher education. Review by John D. Millett. *Journal of Higher Education.* 47 (1), 1976. p. 121-122.

15 Israney, S.M. Planning higher education in India. *University News.* 26 (41), 1988. p. 1-4.

16 Jan Mohammad. Institutional planning. *University News.* 21 (22), 1983. p. 794-795.

17 Jha, S.K. Planning university education. *University News.* 15 (2), 1977. p. 11-12.

18 Joshi, K.L. Some problems in planning of university education. *Journal of University Education.* 1 (1), 1962. p. 50-62.

19 Khan, Q.V. Statistics for educational planning. *Manpower Journal.* 4, October-December, 1968. p. 41-62

20 Lakdawala, D.T. New horizons in educational planning. *EPA Bulletin.* 1 (1), April, 1978. p. 9-19.

21 Leff, N.H. Note on the quantity-quality problem in educational planning. *Indian Economic Journal.* 15 (1), July-September, 1967. p. 67-74.

22 Mehrotra, S.N. Institutional planning at the college level. *New Frontiers in Education.* 2 (April-July), 1972. p. 68-77.

23 Menon, I.C. Some aspects of planning for higher education in India : Quantity versus quality. *New Frontiers in Education.* 4, January-March, 1974. p. 59-70.

24 Nanjudappa, D.M. Some critical issues in planning and management of higher education. *University News.* 21 (12), 1983. p. 371-377 and 383.

25 Narula, Manju. Issues in college planning and management. *University News.* 26 (21), 1980. p. 3-9.

26 Nayar, D.P. Basic concepts and techniques of education planning : An introduction. *Education Quarterly.* 29 (3), 1977. p. 1-5.

27 Padmanabhan, C.B. Educational Planning for economic development. *Indian Educational Review.* 3 (1), January, 19678. p. 199-203.

28 Priorities for higher education in the sixth five year plan. *New Frontiers in Education.* 8 (2), April-June, 1978. p. 107-110.

29 Safaya, Raghunath. Priorities in educational planning. *University News*. 18 (14), 1980. p. 379-381.

30 Saraf, S.N. Higher education and five year plans : policies, plans and perspectives-I, II and III. *University News*. 23 (3,4,5), 1985. p. 2-5, p. 2-6, p. 2-4.

31 Satish Chandra. Higher education in India – plans and prospects. *Journal of Higher Education*. 1 (1), 1975. p. 5-13.

32 Sen, S.N. Decentralisation? *University News*. 13 (8), 1975. p.1-11.

33 Shukla, R.S. Education in the fourth five year plan. *Progress in Education*. 45, October, 1970. p. 85-88.

34 Tilak, J.G.B. Approaches to educational planning and their applications in India. *Indian Economic Journal*. 24 (3), January-March, 1977. p. 263-94.

35 Tripathi, S.N.M. Planning of higher education in India. *University News*. 15 (18), 16 September, 1977. p. 488-489.

36 Venkataswami, T.S. Planning forums in social transformation. *Yojana*. 23 (6), April, 1979. p. 28-29.

37 Wood, Glynn. National planning and public demand in higher education : Case of Mysore. *New Frontiers in Education*. 2 (2), August, 1972. p. 63-79.

38 ——. Planning university reform: An Indian case study. *Comparative Education Review*. 16, June, 1972. p. 267-280.

39 ——. University of Mysore: A case study in decentralisation. *Economic and Political Weekly*. 6, (12) June, 1971. p. 1177-1182.

32. POLICY

A BOOKS

01 Association of Indian Universities. *New education policy : AIU recommendations on higher educations*. Delhi. AIU, 1986. 10p.

02 Ministry of Education and Social Welfare. *National policy on education*, 1968. New Delhi. The author. p. 7.

03 Ministry of Human Resource Development. *National policy on education - 1986*. New Delhi, The author, p. 14-15.

04 Ministry of Human Resource Development. *National policy on education : Programme of action*. New Delhi, The author, 1986. p. 39-47.

05 University Grants Commission. *Development of higher education in India : A policy frame*. New Delhi, U.G.C., 1978. 16p.

B ARTICLES

01 Adams, N.L. and Adams, D.M. Examination of some forces affecting English educational policies in India: 1780-1850 *History of Educational Quarterly*. 11, Summer, 1971. p. 157-73.

02 Adiseshiah, Malcolm S. Universities and national education policy. *Bulletin Madras Development Seminar Series*. 18 (4), 1988. p. 233-238.

03 ——. University to be a university. *University News*. 25 (50), 1987. p. 3-5 and 46.

04 AIU suggests basic changes in educational policy. *University News*. 15 (15), 1977. p. 403-417.

05 Ansari, M.M. Implementation of new schemes in higher education in India : A status report. A.C.U. *Bulletin of Current Documentation*. (90), 1989. p. 2-8.

06 Azad, J.L. Need for a realistic fee policy. *University News*. 14 (7), 1976. 10, 7-9.

07 Basu, Nighat. Adult education for rural women and national education policy. 1986. *University News*. 25 (18), 1987. p. 10-11.

08 Brahmananda, P.R. Current higher education policy: A critique. *University News.* 22 (29), 1984. p. 1-4.

09 Chaturvedi, R.N. Policy frame for the development of higher education. *University News.* 16 (9), May, 1978. p. 904-905.

10 Chittibabu, S.V. Job-oriented courses in the field of higher education. *University News.* 13 (10), October, 1975. p. 8-9.

11 Datt, Ruddar. Higher education and future educational policy. *Journal of Higher Education.* 3 (2), Autumn, 1977. p. 189-206.

12 Development of higher education in India : A policy frame of the U.G.C. *University News.* 16 (5), 1978. p. 792-799.

13 Ghanchi, D.A. New education policy : Strategic initiatives in higher education. *University News.* 26 (34), 1988. p. 1-4.

14 Hooja, G.B.K. New education policy : Making the system work. *University News.* 26 (49), Dec. 5, 1988. p. 33-38.

15 Kahane, Reuven. Education towards mediatory roles : An interpretation of the higher education policy in India in the 20th century. *Development and Change.* 7 July, 1977. p. 291-309.

16 Mathew, A. Role of the University Grants Commission in framing the policy of higher education. *Journal of Higher Education.* 9 (2), 1983. p. 177-195.

17 Mathur, V.S. Implications of the new pattern of education. *University News.* 15 (20), 1977. p. 553-555.

18 Monitoring and implementation of national policy on education. *University News.* 26 (28), 1988. p. 14-16.

19 Patel, S.P. New education policy and vocationalisation of education. *University News.* 25 (50), 1987. p. 47-52.

20 Rathuri, A.S. National educational policy and university autonomy. *University News.* 7 (12), 1969. p. 13-16.

21 Report of committee of members of Parliament on education, 1967, *University News.* 5 (8), 1967. p. 1-6.

22 Resolution on national policy on education. *University News.* 6 (8), 1968. p. I-III.

23 Salunkhe, D.K. Our universities need national policy. *University News.* 20 (14), 1982. p. 457-458.

24 Trivedi, K.D. Policy of rural higher education in India. *Naya Shikshak.* 12 (1), July-September, 1969. p. 92-105.

33. POLITICAL ISSUES

A BOOKS

01 Aiyer, S.P. *Students and politics in India. In* S.P. Aiyer, ed. *The politics of mass violence in India.* Bombay, Manaktalas, 1967. p. 94-103.

02 Altbach, P.G. *Student politics in Bombay.* London, Asia Publishing House, 1968. 218 p.

03 — (ed.) *Turmoil and transition: Higher education and student politics in India.* Bombay, Lalvani Publishing, 1968, 278 p.

04 Bureau of Social Science Research. *Political attitudes of Indian students.* Washington D.C., American University, 1955.

05 Dhar, Trilok N. *The politics of manpower planning: Graduate the unemployment and the planning of higher education in India.* Calcutta, Minerva, 1974.

06 Eakin, Terry Clay. *Students and politics: A comparative set from past survey research on political behaviour.* Bombay, Popular Prakashan, 1972. 222 p.

07 Franda, Marcus F. Perceived images of political authority among college graduates in Calcutta. *In* Richard L. Park, ed. *Urban Bengal.* East Lansing, Michigan, 1969. p. 87-116.

08 Ray, Anil Baran. *Students and politics in India: The role of caste, language and region in the Indian university.* New Delhi, Manohar, 1977. 232 p.

09 Rudolph, Llyod and Susanne, (eds.) *Education and politics in India, Studies in organisation, society, policy.* Cambridge, Harvard University Press, 1972.

10 Shinde, A.B. *Political consciousness among college students.* Bombay, Thacker, 1972.

11 Sirsikar, V.M. *Social and political attitudes of post-graduate students of the University of Poona, 1960-61.* Poona, University of Poona Press, 1963.

B ARTICLES

01 Abraham, A.S. Campus politics pose problems for Delhi. *Times Higher Education Supplement*. 9 December, 1977. p.6.

02 Aiyer, S.P. Politicisation of the Indian students. *New Frontiers in Education*. 2, August, 1972. p. 8-15.

03 Altbach, Philip G. Politics and the university. *Change*, 19(4), 1987. p. 56-59.

05 Amrik Singh. Emerging student power in India. *University News*. 12(6), 1974. p. 4-5.

06 ——. Parliament versus universities. *Times of India*. 20 October, 1982. p. 8.

07 ——. Politics in universities. *Round Table*. 1, 8 May, 1972. p. 2-12.

08 Andersen, Walter and Pant, Alok. Student politics at Allahabad University-I. *Economic and Political Weekly*. 5, 6 June, 1970. p. 910-916.

09 Das, Mamta; Rathor, Raka. Students attitude towards depoliticization of education. *University News*. 27(47), 1989. p. 4-7 and 13.

10 Oommen, T.K. Student politics in India : A case of Delhi University. *Asian Survey*. 14 September, 1974. p. 777-794.

11 Pandey, Rajendra. Student activism in British India. Journal of Higher Education. 11(1 and 2), 1985-86. p. 145-155.

12 Pereira, Nicolau Gracias. Students and politics. University *News*. 28(2), 1990. p. 4-5.

13 Politics and education. Editorial. *Educational Review*. 60(5), May, 1954. p. 98.

14 Rath, R. Attitudes of university students towards some politico-economic issues. *Indian Journal of Psychology*. 30, 1955. p. 43-54.

15 Ray, Anil Baran. De-politicising the Indian universities: A challenge to the Indian political system. *University Administration*. 3(2), 1976. p. 28-32.

16 Rudolph, Lloyd; Rudolph, Susanne Hocher; Ahmed Karuna. Student politics and national politics in India. *Economic and Political Weekly*. 6 (30, 31, 32), 1971. p. 1655-1688.

17 Shils, Edward. Government and universities I. *New Quest*. January-February, 1981. p. 5-13.

18 ——. Government and universities II. *New Quest*. March-April, 1981. p. 93-103.

19 ——. Government and universities III. *New Quest*. May-June, 1981. p. 152-161.

20 Singh, Shiv Mangal. Colleges college teachers and politics. *University News*. 10(1), 1972. p. 18-20.

21 Tiwari, S.C. and Kumar, V.K. Students attitudes towards political parties in an Indian university: A pre-fourth general election study. *Political Science Review*. (10), January-June, 1971. p. 124-134.

D RESEARCH STUDIES

01 Altbach, P.G., Student Politics in Bombay. Asia Publishing House, London, 1968.

The objectives of the study were: (i) to describe accurately and in detail student activity and aspects of student life and of society which might have bearing on student organisation and movements in Bombay, and (ii) to consider the much-discussed phenomenon of student indiscipline in its various manifestations, as well as the more permanent student political, social and cultural groups.

The study focused on a small area which could be considered to exemplify many of the problems and developments in the subcontinent as a whole. Therefore, the city of Bombay was selected for the study, as it was a relatively compact area which showed many characteristics of modern society. Besides being a key commercial centre and industrial city, its student population had taken an active part in the various campaigns of the nationalist period. While most of the data were collected by referring to various documents pertaining to the political and educational development of Bombay, a case study of communal student organisations along with necessary field-work and interviews was conducted.

The major findings were: (i) One of the major changes in the student movement had come with the divorce of student politics from national politics in India. While at one time students played an active, and at times important, part in the broader political arena of Bombay, they no longer took a direct interest in politics. Academic issues and grievances relating directly to inadequate academic programmes, economic insecurity or bad living conditions had not motivated the students in the direction of sustained unrest or political action. Thus, the pre-Independence trend was in the direction of student involvement in national issues and a substantial political awareness on the campus, the more recent period had been a reversal of this trend. (ii) Student organisations, especially those without official patronage and support, tended to be unstable and short-lived. In Bombay, Mass student movements were usually based on rather specific political or academic issues and lasted only as long as these issues remained vividly imprinted in the consciousness of the student population. Among the politically oriented organisations, value-oriented groups were better able to withstand organisational instability than those based on specific issues or short-term causes. Norm-oriented student organisations of a political or non-political nature were oriented towards specific issues which when settled or clearly defeated, left the group without a *raison d'etre*. Although both political and non-political student groups were similar in some of their characteristics, they did exhibit major differences as well. (iii) Student movements in Bombay had tended to be rather non-ideological in their approach to issues and events. Even those movements led by politically sophisticated, even sectarian, students had stressed issues and not ideologies. (iv) The left-wing student groups made lasting impact on the thinking of students of pre-independence generation. (v) During the struggle for Independence, much of the politically active student leadership came almost exclusively from the upper middle classes and from students with very high academic and social standing within their colleges. However, the situation had changed markedly. Students from upper classes and upper academic levels, in both natural sciences and liberal arts, avoided student politics. Much of the leadership had been taken over by students from the lower middle classes who had some experience with education and reasonably good command of English, but who were unfortunately less well-prepared than upper class students. Participation in student politics was no longer a mark of academic distinction, if anything, it had become the opposite. (vi) With the exception of the 1942 struggle, the direct impact of students on society in Bombay had been minimal. Students had on occasion aroused political protest among the public on particular issues, but they had failed to institute any changes. Student organisations had tried, usually in vain, to influence educational decisions. Yet, there had been some rewarding results of student agitations. Reappraisal of the examination system, free structure and other specific reforms had been instituted as a direct result of student agitation. With only a few exceptions, students had played only a peripheral role in the broader society. (vii) The activity of various political student organisations had varied greatly in different periods. During times of political awareness in the city as a whole, the political student groups were able to attract large number of students to meetings and other activities. Of much more importance during the post-1947 period had been the non-political organisations. Cultural and social student organisations had had a long history in Bombay and had maintained a consistently high level of activity through the years. While the college authorities had given much more support to such groups in recent years than in the past, they always had at least the tacit approval of educators and administrators. As a means of socialisation, particularly for the financially poorer students, the social and cultural associations had been more effective than the political groups.

02 Eakin, T.C., Selected aspects of political behaviour: An empirical study of a Bombay college student sample with comparative observations, Ph.D. Pol. Sc., Bombay University, 1970.

The objectives of the study were: (i) to study ideological orientations of college students, (ii) to enquire into the levels and consequences of political efficacy, political knowledge levels, feelings towards the democratic system and levels of political participation.

The students in the Bombay sample were drawn from the senior classes of two of the better arts and science colleges, one in the southern and the other in the northern part of the city. These colleges were chosen because of their better scholastic reputation and to provide a socio-economic and geographical dispersal. A sample of 280 students of senior classes was selected and tested in the academic year 1968-69. Two questionnaires were used to collect data; group interviews were conducted and eleven individual interviews were also conducted on those who had already been group interviewed.

The study revealed: (i) Students who were politically involved tended to come from politically involved homes. (ii) The activists had opportunities of participating in democratic decision-making in the home and school and were regular users of mass media. (iii) The activists were organisational members, were at least somewhat politically knowledgeable; and they supported the democratic system in larger numbers than the apolitical. The activists had political or politically related participation experiences when younger. (iv) Of the sample, 62 per cent had moderate ideological orientations while 14 per cent were further-left and 10 per cent further-right. (v) As many as 62 per cent had a high sense of political self-confidence while only 13 per cent had a low sense of political efficacy. (vi) As many as 77 per cent were members of at least one college group while 29 per cent were members of three or more groups; 16 per cent served as office-bearers while 30 per cent helped take group decisions. (vii) Political party involvement levels indicated 47 per cent supported a particular political party, 15 per cent were members of politically oriented groups and 28 per cent worked for a party candidate during the elections. (viii) Though 22 per cent opposed public protest demonstrations as a form of political behaviour, 4 per cent claimed they would start a demonstration to change an unjust college rule; 7 per cent had participated in college-centred demonstrations and 10 per cent in community-centred demonstrations.

03 Honap, L.S., Political socialisation of college girls in Poona, Ph.D. Pol. Sc., Poona University, 1981.

The broad purpose of the study was to explore the impact of socialising agents like family, school, college, peer groups and mass media on the political orientation of college girls. Specific hypotheses of the study were: (i) The higher the education of the family and the higher the extent of discussions, the higher would be the level of political knowledge, progressive political values, and liberal attitude. (ii) The higher the level of participation in extra-curricular activities in college, the higher would be the level of political knowledge, and progressive values, (iii) The higher the exposure to the mass media, the higher would be the level of political knowledge. (iv) The Marital status influenced the participatory attitudes more than political knowledge and political values. (v) Hindu girls would be more liberal in their attitude towards women's participation in politics and would be more progressive than non-Hindu girls. (vi) The higher the caste, the more liberal would be the political attitudes and progressive values. (vii) The higher the level of the economic class of the family, the higher would be the level of participation and liberal attitudes. (viii) The more the use of the regional language or the mother tongue (Marathi), the greater was the possibility of higher political knowledge.

The sample consisted of the final year girl students in arts, commerce and science colleges in Pune. In all, 482 (25 per cent) girls were included in the study. The tools of data-collection were a questionnaire and indepth interview of selected cases. The statistical technique used was chi-square.

The findings of the study were: (i) Family education influenced political values and attitudes more than political knowledge. (ii) Family discussions significantly influenced political knowledge and progressive values of the respondents. (iii) Participation in extra-curricular activities influenced political knowledge to a moderate extent and had positive influence on the progressive values of the respondents. (iv) Exposure to mass media developed political knowledge of the respondents. (v) The married respondents were more liberal in their attitudes than the unmarried ones. (vi) The Hindus were slightly less conservative and more progressive than the non-Hindus. They were also significantly higher on political knowledge. (vii) Brahmins and scheduled caste respondents were more liberal in their attitudes, but the latter were conservative about women's education and reservation of seats. Brahmins were higher on political knowledge. (viii) Higher economic status had no influence on actual participation but was associated with democratic or liberal attitudes. The middle class respondents scored higher on political knowledge than the others. (ix) The Marathi-speaking respondents had more political knowledge than the others. (x) The peer group did not influence political knowledge, political attitudes and values.

04 Khan, N.A., *Group affiliations and pressure politics in academic institutions*, Ph.D. Soc., Aligarh Muslim University, 1981.

The objective of the investigation was to assess the perception of freedom and restraints of the students and to study the genesis and the role of the pressure groups in academic institutions.

Data were collected from a representative sample of 300 Aligarh Muslim University students, using an interview schedule constructed by the investigator. The Kolmogorov Smirnov Test was used to find out the relationship between different variables. Some representative case histories were also prepared to supplement the results of the statistical analyses.

The major findings of the study were: (i) A considerable number of students wanted to enjoy greater freedom in the university in respect of teacher-taught relationship, students' hall administration, and students-university authorities relationship. (ii) Most of the students wanted to impose less overall restriction on their behaviour regarding academic pursuits, hall and general administration. (iii) Groups needed to be formed to achieve common goals and derive satisfaction from associating together. (iv) Most of the students believed that group affiliation provided certain privileges and benefits. (v) The students used different tactics to build up pressure and influence on the authorities to get their work done. These tactics included going in large groups taking the help of student leaders, and highlighting the weak points of the authorities.

05 Shinde, A.P., *Political consciousness among college students*, Bombay, Thacker, 1972.

The main objectives of the survey was to find out political consciousness among college students covering six aspects, namely, (i) reading habits, (ii) participation in discussions, meetings and political study circles, (iii) membership of parties and trade unions and involvement in their activities, (iv) interest in elections, (v) political attitudes and aspirations, and (vi) knowledge of national and international matters.

The selection of the sample was confined to the degree college in Kolhapur city and to the arts students of the post-graduate classes in Rajaram College. A systematic sample of 25 per cent of students from each class of each college was taken with a total sample size of 911 (761 males and 150 females). The sample adequately represented the rural as well as the urban population. To collect data, the students were administered a comprehensive questionnaire related to the occupation and education of their guardians, their reading habits, their participation in discussions, meetings and political study circles, their membership of parties, trade unions and students organisations and their involvement in their activities, their interest in elections and electioneering, their political aspirations and loyalties and their political knowledge of matters — national and international. The data were analysed by calculating percentages under various categories, namely, faculty, sex, caste and place of origin.

The findings were: (i) Almost all students (90.8 per cent males and 99.33 per cent females) read newspapers. A large number of students (72.54 per cent males and 59.63 per cent females) were primarily interested in political news. A large number of students read party newspapers whereas a considerable number of students read party literature and political literature. (ii) A majority of students (85.30 per cent males and 64.66 per cent females) discussed political subjects and associated themselves with political meetings organised by parties. However, a small number of students (13.93 per cent males and 3.33 per cent females) attended the study circles organised by political parties. Some students attended caste meetings also. (iii) There were a few students who were party members (16.55 per cent males and 4 per cent females). A majority of students (81.47 per cent males and 66.03 per cent females) had sympathy for parties. A sizeable number of students participated in party activities. A small number of students were members of trade unions; however, a majority of students had sympathy for trade unions. A meagre number of students were members of students' associations. (iv) Few students were voters at the general elections but a large number of them (52.83 per cent males and 14.63 per cent females) had canvassed in various elections. It was manifested that the number of students who canvassed for a party was significantly larger than the number of those who canvassed for an independent candidate. A considerable number of students (48.88 per cent males and 26 per cent females) had expressed their desire to contest elections. More than half of the students (53.79 per cent) had political ambitions. A large number of them (54.68 per cent males and 54.72 per cent females) aspired to be ministers. All the male and the female aspirants strove to achieve their political ambitions. (v) A majority of students had knowledge of national and international matters. Most of them stated that there was no emotional integration in India. A majority of students had categorically reported that democracy was suitable for India. Most of them had knowledge of political differences in western countries, communist nations and non-aligned states. (vi) Boys were more politically conscious than girls. (vii) The postgraduate students and the law students were more politically conscious than the students of other faculties but they were more passive in their political consciousness than the undergraduate students. (viii) The rural students were passively and actively more conscious than the urban students (ix) Both brahmins and Marathas were politically conscious but brahmins were not as much involved in active politics as the Marathas.

34. PRIVATE COLLEGES

A BOOKS

01 Naik, J.P. The role and problems of private enterprise in education. *In the Christian college and national development*, Madras, 1967.

02 Nirmal Singh, *Education Under Siege : A sociological study of private colleges*. New Delhi, Concept, 1983. 238p.

B ARTICLES

01 Adiseshaiah, Malcolm S. Why private colleges? *New Frontiers in Education*. 2, December, 1971. p. 21-26.

02 Amrik Singh. On private colleges.*University News*. 8 (9), 1970. p. 3.

03 Chacko, P.C. Kerala private colleges' crisis : The compromise and after. *New Frontiers in Education*. 2 (4), 1972. p. 90-94.

04 Nayar, V.K. Sukumaran; Chander, N. Jose. Supreme Court and the private colleges. *University News*. 9 (8), 1971. p. 15-19.

05 Dickinson, Richard. The private college as an agent for development and social justice. *New Frontiers in Education*. 4 (1), 1974. p. 28-35.

35. QUALITY AND QUANTITY

B ARTICLES

01 Chalapathi Rau, M. Quantity, not quality yet. *Link*. 10 August, 1980. p. 8.

02 Kumar, Prasanna. Higher education: quality vs. quantity. *Hindu*. 3 November, 1981. p. 23.

03 Menon, I.C. Some aspects of planning for higher education in India: Quantity versus quality. *New Frontiers in Education*. 4 (1), January-March, 1974. p. 59-70.

04 Misra, V.N. Higher education-quality and qualification. *University News*. 1 October, 1980. p. 539-540.

05 Mukerjee, S.N. Qualitative improvement of higher education. *Indian Education*. 7 (1-2), December, 1967-January, 1968. p. 14-31.

06 Pillai, Aludia, K. Quality improvement in higher education. *Hindu*. 2 January, 1979. p. 3.

07 Raychaudhuri, T. Quantity or quality : Our choice in higher education. *Journal of University Education*. 1 (3), March, 1963. p. 163-174.

36. REFORM

A BOOKS

01 Adiseshaiah, Malcolm S. *Remoulding Indian higher education*. New Delhi, Indian International Centre, 1982. 13p.

02 Aikara, Jacob, (ed.) *Innovations in higher education in India*. Pune, Dastane Ramchandra & Co., 1984. 107p.

03 Bordia, Anil. *Innovation in Indian higher education*. Paris. Unesco. 1976. 115p.

04 Murthy. V. Rama. *Restructuring the university*. New Delhi, Sterling, 1975. 90p.

B ARTICLES

01 Altbach, Philip G. Problems of university reform in India. *Comparative Education Review*. 16 (June), 1972. p. 251-261.

02 Altbach, Philip G. University reform. *New Frontiers in Education*. 5 (3), 1975. p. 1-14.

03 Bharati, Jai Prakash. Concept of a children university : An academic innovations. *University News*. 25 (45), 1987. p. 7-8.

04 Devanesen, Chandran D.S. Reform in university education. *Education Quarterly*. 21 (July), 1969. p. 17-19 and 22.

05 Fyzee, Asaf A.A. Reform in Indian universities. *Education Quarterly*. 12 (4-5), 1960. p. 92-96.

06 Indian University Reform I., Higher Education : Objectives and improvement. *Minerva*. 5 (Autumn), 1966. p. 47-81.

07 —— II. Higher education : Enrolments and programmes. *Minerva*. 5 (Winter), 1967. p. 242-264.

08 —— III. Higher education : The governance of Universities. *Minerva*. 5 (Spring), 1967. p. 391-412.

09 —— IV. *Science education and research*. 6 (Autumn), 1967. p. 48-80.

10 Jain, R.P. Failure of an innovation in a university : An investigation. *New Frontiers in Education*. 10 (4), 1980. p. 73-79.

11 John, V.V. Innovation and experiment in higher education. *Quest.* (88), May-June, 1974. p. 41-44.

12 Karve, D.D. On the improvement of the Indian universities. *Minerva.* 3 (Winter), 1965. p. 159-172.

13 Lakshmanna, C. Educational reforms: Myth and reality. *University Administration.* 5 (1), 1976. p. 1-7.

14 Mitra, C.R. Educational innovation in Britain and common interest with India. *New Frontiers in Education.* 3, December, 1973. p. 75-90.

15 Naik, J.P. Higher education in India: Some suggestions for reorganisation. *New Frontiers in Education.* 2 (2), 1972. p. 1-27.

16 Narul Hasan. Reform of higher education system necessary. *University News.* 13 (4), 1975. p. 4-6.

17 Prem Kirpal. Innovations in higher education. *Patriot.* 28 (August), 1984. p. 4.

18 Sharma, Ramesh Chandra. Educational innovation and change in India : Trends and bibliography. *University Administration.* 3 (1), 1976. p. 76-86.

19 Singha, H.S. How not to reform universities. *Economic and Political Weekly.* 8 (47), 1973. p. 2076-78.

20 Wood, Glynn. Planning university reform : An Indian case study. *Comparative Education Review.* 16 (June), 1972. p. 267-280.

D RESEARCH STUDIES

01 Kanagasabapathy, R., A study of management of Change in Madurai Kamaraj University, Ph.D. Edu., M.S. University of Baroda, 1986.

The objectives of the study were (i) to identify the various innovations that were introduced by the Madurai Kamaraj University into affiliated colleges during the last fifteen years and categorise them according to their nature and impact, (ii) to trace the travel paths of some selected innovations from the point of origin to the point of implementation, and (iii) to locate certain crucial points in the process of implementation of innovations by Madurai Kamaraj University into affiliated colleges with particular reference to planning, organising, staffing, leading and controlling. Twelve innovations that were introduced by Madurai Kamaraj University in its affiliated colleges during the period 1965 to 1980 were identified and to them three innovations, viz., grading system, semester system and cocurricular activities were chosen for the study.

Twelve of the eighty-one affiliated colleges were purposively selected as a sample of the study. Secretary of the college committee, principal, office manager, twenty randomly selected teachers, assistant professor of physical education and twenty randomly selected students constituted the sources of data from each college in the sample, besides, three Vice-Chancellors, four officers of the university, Director of Youth Welfare, Director of a Physical Education, Director of Adult Education and two members of the syndicate/academic council/senate were also treated as sources of information. The tools developed by the investigator for the study were (1) questionnaires for teachers, students and office managers/head clerks, and (2) interview schedules for Vice-Chancellor, convener of the syndicate sub-committee, officers of the university, secretaries of the college committees and principals of colleges. The data were processed in terms of percentages and frequency counts and analysed qualitatively.

The major findings of the study were : 1. An innovation could be institutionalised only if the user community found the need for the innovation. 2. A felt need was not a must in all cases of introducing innovations. 3. The university authorities not looking into the history of the innovation concerned was one reason for its discontinuance. 4. The university authorities not making any scientific calculation of their supportive and resistive forces came in the way of effective implementation of innovations. 5. Lack of participation on the part of the principals and other functionaries in the decision-making process came in the way of effective implementation of innovations. 6. Lack of familiarity with management by objectives on the part of the implementers and lack of seriousness with which objectives were taken by them, came in the way of effective implementation of innovations. 7. The effectiveness of strategies and tactics in implementation was different for different innovations. 8. Adequacy of the management information system varied from innovation to innovation. 9. Effective planning taking into account all management activities was essential for successful implementation of innovations.

02 Rao, P.M. A critical study of the implementation of some innovations in higher education in Andhra Pradesh in India, Ph.D. Edu., M.S. University of Baroda, 1980.

The main objective of the study was to know the factors affecting success or failure in the implementation of innovations in higher educational institutions. It was realised through an indepth study of the adopter system in terms of its date of establishment, strength of teachers and students, attitude of the people towards innovations, innovations implemented, the level of implementation, the resources needed for the implementation of innovations and the impact of innovations. The role of resource system was also studied to the extent of its floating innovations only.

Considering the purpose of the investigation case study was selected as the method to deal with the problem. Five universities, viz., Andhra University, Nagarjuna University, Osmania University, Kakatiya University and Sri Venkateswara University, and one autonomous post-graduate centre in Andhra Pradesh were selected sample. Three innovations from each institution were selected for the purpose of this study. In all, eighteen cases were studied. Data were obtained with the help of a case study proforma, a questionnaire, technique of interview, various records and participant observation. The data were analysed qualitatively.

The major findings of the study were: (i) Internal assessment in Andhra University and Sri Venkateswara University, the semester system in Andhra University and partially M. Phil. course in Osmania University failed mainly due to lack of proper orientation and dissemination of knowledge about the innovation. (ii) All the universities, which had discontinued the innovation were generally suffering from lack of proper understanding about the objectives of the innovation. (iii) Where the innovations were being implemented and continuing on temporary basis as in the case of Nagarjuna University, Kakatiya University and autonomous postgraduate centre, they were suffering generally from lack of resources. (iv) The unsuccessful functioning of the innovation of correspondence course in Osmania University was due to lack of infrastructure and adequate furniture. (v) Internal assessment was practised by all the six universities in the State, but Andhra University and Sri Venkateswara University had already discontinued the innovation. (vi) The factors commonly working for the successful functioning of the innovations were awareness of the people, communication facilities, decision-making procedure and general administration of the universities. (vii) In the case of the semester system, M. Phil. course and correspondence course, factors working for the successful functioning of the innovations were communication facilities, awareness of the people, library facilities and experienced teachers.

37. RESEARCH

A BOOKS

01 Association of Indian universities. *Universities and research.* New Delhi, AIU, 1980. 143p.

02 Buch, M.B. *Survey of research in education.* Baroda, M.S. University of Baroda, 1974. 618p.

03 ——, (ed.) *Second survey of research in education. 1972-1978.* Baroda, Society for Educational Research and Development, 1979. 614p.

04 ——, (ed.) *Third survey of research in education 1978-1983.* New Delhi N.C.E.R.T., 1987. 1148p.

05 Buch, M.B., Passi, B.K. and Padma, M.S. *Review of research in the M.S. University of Baroda, 1949-72.* Baroda, Centre of Advanced Study in Education, 1973. 68p. (Mimeograph)

06 Chandrakant, L.S. *Post-graduate engineering and research in India : Survey and outlook.* New Delhi, Ministry of Education, 1971.

07 Gopal, Mysore Hatti. *Science, universities and research in India.* Mysore, Geetha, 1976.

08 Holmes, W. Robert. *Research facilities in Bombay, Calcutta and Madras.* Delhi, Cambridge, 1968. 167p.

09 Rahman, A. Universities and scientific research, *In* Amrik Singh and Philip G. Altbach, (eds.) *The higher learning in the India.* Delhi, Vikas, 1974. p. 355-372.

10 Raza, Moonis and Sharma, G.D. *Research design.* New Delhi, National Institute of Educational Planning and Administration, 1984. ivp. (Research Studies for NCT-II).

11 Schonfield, Andrew. *Social science research in India.* New Delhi, Indian Council for Social Science Research, 1971.

12 University Grants Commission. *Development of higher education and research in the universities, 1980-85.* New Delhi, U.G.C., 1986. 86p.

13 ——. *Support for science research in the universities.* New Delhi, U.G.C., 1961. 10p.

B ARTICLES

01 Ahmed, Rais. University research and national development. *University News*. 18 (4), 1980. p. 87-88.

02 Chalam, K.S. The costs of university research : A case study of Andhra University. *University News*. 20(20), 1982. p.639-641.

03 Datta, Bhabatosh. State support to research in universities. *University News*. 18(6), 15 March, 1980. p.131-132.

04 Goel, B.S. Scientific research in India. *Quest*. (84), September-October, 1973. p.53-56.

05 Jayaswal, Sita Ram. Problems of research at the post-graduate level. *Education*. 45(3), March, 1966. p.5-8.

06 Joshi, Dinesh C. Researches in higher education. *University Administration*. 5(1), 1978. p.30-40.

07 Joshi, Ram, Research and Education: Linkage in universities. *University News*. 18(4), 1980. p.83-84.

08 Kapur, J.N. Some unethical practices in research programmes. *University News*. 25(51), 1987. p.1-3, 6.

09 Madan, P.J. Research and Education: Linkage in the universities. *University News*. 18(5), 1980. p.107-108.

10 Menon, I.C. Research in Indian universities. *New Frontiers in Education*. 4, July-September, 1974. p.61-78.

11 Moorthy, Rama M. Problems of Research work in colleges : A note. *University News*. 13(2), 1975. p.9.

12 Murthy, S.V. Higher education and scientific research, *University News*. 16(6), 1978. p.819 and 821.

13 Nayar, V.K. Sukumaran. Management of research in universities. *University News*. 15(6), 1980. p.85-86.

14 Rahman, A. Scientific research in Indian universities. *Journal of University Education*. 4(2), 1965. p.65-71.

15 Rajput, J.S. Implementation of research results in education. *University News* 21(5), 1983. p.1, 137.

16 Rangarajan, M.R. Role of research in higher education. *Educational Review*. 92(5-6), 1986. p.81-83.

17 Rao, C.N.R. Problems of research worker in India. *University News*. 7(1), 1969. p.14-15.

18 Rao, V. Bhaskara. Teaching and research in higher education: Some problems. *Journal of Higher Education*. 4(1), 1978. p.11-12.

19 Reddy, G. Ram. Management of research in universities. *University News*. 1 October, 1980. p.533-536.

20 Seshachar, B.R. Scientific research in the universities. *Indian Journal of Public Administration*. 15, July-September, 1969. p.544-553.
21 Singh, G.P. State support for science research in university. *University News*. 18(4), 1980. p.89.
22 Srinath, L.S. International co-operation of universities in research. *University News*. 26(24), 1988. p.1-4.
23 Swaminathan, M.S. The Nuclear Research laboratory at I.A.R.I.: An exercise in inter-constitutional and inter-disciplinary collaboration. *University News*. 10(2), 1972. p.13-14.
24 U.G.C.'s Policy and programme for improvement of research in the universities. *University News*. 22(48), 1984. p.1-4.
25 Venkataraman, Balu. Research orientation in science education. *New Frontiers in Education*. 2, December, 1972. p.80-89.
26 Venkatareddy, K. Value of academic research. *Hindu*. 26 October, 1981. p.19.
27 Vidyarathi, L.P. Research methodology in anthropology in Indian universities. *Social Science Information*. 13 (Aug.-Oct.), 1974. p.173-182.

D RESEARCH STUDIES

01 Buch, M.B., Passi, B.K., and Padma, M.S., Review of research in the M.S. University of Baroda (1949-1972), Centre of Advanced Study in education, M.S. University of Baroda, 19731. (MSU financed)

The objectives of the study were: (i) to take a stock of the existing position of research in the university; and (ii) to make suggestions for the improvement of the same.

The investigation had the characteristics of both historical and descriptive study. The data were collected from office records and also through interview schedules, from the Ph.D. students and members of staff of the different departments.

The results of the study were reported under three categories, namely, (i) research work done at the Ph.D. level; (ii) researches financed by the M.S. University; and (iii) researches financed by outside agencies. Under the first category the findings were: (i) during the period under review 976 research scholars were registered, of which 369 completed their work, 339 discontinued and the remaining were continuing; (ii) in facultywise analysis, the Faculty of Science (fifty per cent), Faculty of Arts (twenty-seven per cent) and Faculty of Education and Psychology (seventeen per cent) claimed approximately ninetyfive per cent of the Ph.D.s produced by the university as a whole; (iii) there was high incidence of wastage which came to nearly thirty-five per cent; (iv) the percentage of girl scholars was twenty-four, nine, and seven in the Faculties of Education and Psychology, Arts, and Science respectively and there was one girl scholar in the Faculty of Home Science; (v) on an average a scholar took 4.2 years to complete his Ph.D. degree; (vi) about twenty-seven per cent of the scholars (N = 263) received fellowships/scholarships for their research work; (vii) enrolment of Ph.D. scholars under professors, readers and lecturers was 593, 267 and 33 respectively. Under the second category it was revealed that (i) during this period the university spent Rs. 1.48 million on research projects; (ii) seventyfive per cent of the amount was utilised by Faculty of Science, Faculty of Arts and Faculty of Technology and Engineering; (iii) the university provided about 2.70 per cent for research in its budget estimates in 1956-57 and this percentage came down to 0.63 in 1972-73. Under the third category it was found that (i) there were thirtyfive different agencies which financed researches in the university; (ii) eight international, eighteen national, five State level and four private agencies from outside supported the researches in the university; (iii) the university started taking support from outside agencies since 1952-53; (iv) amongst the various agencies the national level agencies financed 165 projects, while international level, State level and private agencies financed fiftyfour, thirtysix and twelve projects respectively; (v) the percentage of financial contribution from international, national, State and private agencies was 69, 17.5, 12.7 and 0.8 respectively; and (vi) during the period under review, 267 projects were financed by the external agencies, and the Faculties of Arts, Science and Home Science claimed seventyone per cent of these projects.

02 Patel, V.B., and Shah, S.G., A survey of educational researches carried out at post-graduate level in the universities of Gujarat (1971-80), Deptt. of Edu., South Gujarat University, 1982 (SGU financed).

The major objectives of the study were (i) to abstract the dissertations undertaken at M.Ed. level in the universities of Gujarat during 1971-80, (ii) to prepare a list (yearwise and universitywise) of the dissertations undertaken at M.Ed. level in the universities of Gujarat during 1971-80, (iii) to assess the general errors found in the dissertations under study, (iv) to assess the strengths and limitations of the dissertations under study, and (v) to enlist the uncharted or least charted areas for further researches.

The study was confined to South Gujarat University, Sardar Patel University, Maharaja Sayajirao University, Gujarat University, Gujarat Vidyapith, Saurashtra University and Bhavnagar University. The dissertations submitted to these universities during the period under study were studied for preparing abstracts of the same. Personal visits to the universities were also made.

The major findings were: (1) In all 1459 dissertations were submitted to the universities under study. (2) The most preferred areas for research were administration of education, teacher training, teacher behaviour, teaching learning process, reading skills, and personality, adjustment, and pupils' behaviour. (3) Research designs most popular amongst researchers were survey and experimental. (4) Tools widely used by the researchers were questionnaires and psychological tests. (5) Major limitations of dissertations were neglect of case studies and action researches, defective questionnaires and loose style of writing, references and bibliography. (6) Some of the dissertations were found so good that they could have been submitted as Ph.D. theses.

03 Pillay, G.S., Nature of researches undertaken in social sciences and diffusion of findings, Deptt. of Education, Madurai Kamaraj University, 1986.

The objectives of the investigation were: (i) to estimate the projects taken up by the researchers of different disciplines of social sciences in Madurai Kamaraj University area and (ii) to study the nature of diffusion of research findings.

The sample included 450 teachers teaching post-graduate courses in social sciences either in the university or in the colleges with post-graduate courses in social sciences. The Institute of Correspondence Courses (ICC) also was included in the sample. Interview schedules and information proforma were the tools used for data collection.

The following findings were derived from the analysis of results: (1) The mean projects completed during the last five years by the faculty of university, ICC and colleges were 1.02, 0.44, and 0.36 respectively. (2) The mean projects progressing with the faculty of the university, ICC and colleges wee 0.98, 0.61, and 0.24 respectively. (3) The colleges differed very much with respect to the research projects completed. In some colleges, in certain post-graduate departments they had not taken any project at all. (4) Among the university departments, the faculty of education and that of Gandhian Thought had a mean completed project of two. It was followed by sociology, and management studies with a mean completed project of 1.25. The least was 0.25 for library and information science. (5) In the Institute of Correspondence Courses, the discipline of geography had the highest mean project of one, followed by history with a mean project of 0.75. (6) There was significant difference between the faculties of colleges, university and the ICC with respect to projects completed and projects going on in social sciences. (7) Nearly 55 per cent of research projects taken up were for getting degrees. (8) Faculties differed significantly in their purposes in taking up research projects. (9) For the college faculty the major purpose of taking up research project was the getting a M.Phil or Ph.D. But for the university faculty, it was not so. (10). There was significant difference in the project sponsored by the different agencies. UGC sponsored projects were significantly more than others. (11) The projects taken up by different faculty members varied significantly with respect to their cost. (12) There was no significant difference in the time taken for completing the projects by different faculties. (13) Very little joint efforts were made in attacking problems of social science research. (14) Research findings were not disseminated in all cases. (15) There was significant difference in the diffusion of research information among the faculties of colleges, university and ICC. (16) University faculties excelled the other groups in printing or cyclostyling the research reports and thus in disseminating the research findings. (17) Publishing of abstracts of the research reports was very popular among the university faculty, compared to their counterparts in ICC and colleges. (18) The different strategies of disseminations like submitting the report to the government, flashing the findings in newspapers, AIR, Doordarshan, and making use of the research findings for writing articles, etc. were practised to a very minimum level by the different faculty members under study. (19) With respect to the publication of books and articles other than research reports, the university faculty got significantly more mean publication of books and articles than the other two groups. (20) Heavy work load, lack of library facilities, lack of encouragement from management were found to be the main reasons for the college faculty for not coming forward to take up projects. (21) Lack of validity of findings, insignificant problems studied, outdated problems analysed, etc. were the reasons for not taking initiative for publishing the reports. (22) Though interested in disseminating the research information, the attempts of the funding agencies were not sufficient towards diffusion of research information to the users.

38. RURAL EDUCATION

A BOOKS

01 Barnabas, T. and Hulbe, S.K. University and the rural community. p. 86-100. *In* Airan. *Educational reform of India*. Ajmer, Sachin, 1979.

02 Gandhigram Rural Institute. *Linking extension with the university curriculum*. Edited by B.S. Nagarajan, R. Dhandapani and N. Narayanasamy. Tamil Nadu, Gandhigram Rural Institute, 1984. 115 p.

03 ——. *University at village doorsteps*. Tamil Nadu, The author, 1989. 27 p.

04 Mathai, Ravi J. *The rural University – The Jawaja experiment in educational innovation*. Bombay, Popular Prakashan, 1985. 360 p.

05 Morgan, A.E. *Rural university*. Sevagram, Hindustani Talimi Sangh, 1950.

06 Mukerji, S.N. *Higher education and rural India*. Baroda, Acharya Book Depot, 1956.

07 Seetharamu, A.S. *Study of responsiveness to development programmes from educational stimuli in rural areas*. Bangalore, Institute for Social and Economic Change, 1977.

08 University Education Commission. *Rural universities*. Chidambaram, Tamilnad Basic Education Society, 1951.

B ARTICLES

01 Bajaj, K.K. Communication and higher education: An interface for rural development. *University News*. 26(49), 1988. p. 17-20.

02 Deouskar, M. Non-formal education and rural development through higher education, *Indian Journal of Adult Education*. 44(4), 1983. p. 31-38.

03 Devendra Kumar. Bringing universities and the villages closer. *University News*. 25(27), 1987. p. 1-2.

04 Hiremath, R.C. Role of universities in integrated rural development. *University News.* 15(14), 1977. p. 380-383.

05 Pande, S.P. Role of agricultural universities in integrated rural development. *University News.* 15(2), 1977. p. 31 and 47.

06 Ramachandran, G. Concept and significance of a rural varsity. *University News.* 15(14), 1977. p. 382-383.

07 Rao, R.M. Mohan. Rural higher education for rural development. *Journal of Higher Education.* 14(1-3), 1988-89. p. 53-64.

08 Roy, Burman. Role of universities in rural development: The issues. *Social Change.* 12(4), 1982, p. 40-44.

09 Sundersing, John D. Madurai University and rural development. *Madurai University Newsletter.* 1(1), 1977. p. 17-21.

10 Swaminathan, M.S. Role in agricultural and rural development. *University News.* 13(5), 1975. p. 4-7.

11 Tripathi, Satyaendra. Role of BHU in rural development. *University News.* 20 (16), 1982. p.523 and 527

12 Vasudev, T. Role of universities in rural development: An Indian Perspective. *University News.* 22 (27), 1984. p.2-5.

C COMMITTEES/COMMISSIONS/REPORTS

01 Committee on higher education for rural areas: Rural Institutes, 1954. Report. New Delhi, Ministry of Education, 1954. 77 p. Charts. Chairman: K.D. Shrimali.

The committee was appointed to undertake a comprehensive survey and appraisal of promising ideas, institutions and experiments in the field of higher education in rural areas; to determine what specific projects and institutions should be encouraged to carry on experimental work in this field; to recommend a possible pattern for rural universities with particular reference to the aims, organisation and content of higher education in rural areas, its relationship to basic and secondary education; and other allied problems: to suggest ways and means of making education in the existing universities more useful and more closely related to rural needs and problems, so that a sound and reasonably uniform system of rural higher education suited to our needs and resources may be evolved for the whole country.

D RESEARCH STUDIES

01 Chatterji, A. Das. T.C. and Basu, P.K. The role of university students in village development work. Deptt. of Statistics, Calcutta University, 1956.

The main aims were: (i) to assess the possibilities of two schemes, viz.,

(a) the apprenticeship training in village development for selected university teachers and students and (b) social service camps organised by the colleges and sponsored by the university, which were implemented with a view to developing in teachers and students a realistic spirit of social service and an understanding of the problems of the village and villagers, and (ii) to highlight the social service work done by the students of the Calcutta University during the summer vacation, 1955.

The village development work carried out by the students was identified. A quantitative estimate of the work done was made. The nature and extent of work accomplished at the campus was ascertained. The workability of the schemes were studied.

The study revealed: (1) The main purposes of the schemes were fulfilled. The student workers had developed an attachment to the villagers. They had acquired a true picture of the conditions in villages, the problems of villagers and the knowledge of the methods to be adopted for inspiring them to help themselves. (2) The students had realised that in this work of national uplift everyone had his own part to play and the extension work was a continuous process, and had expressed their eagerness to be given further opportunities for participating in this national enterprise.

39. SCHEDULED CASTES AND SCHEDULED TRIBES

A BOOKS

01 Abbasayulu, Y.B. *Impact of higher education on scheduled castes and scheduled tribes and backward classes students within the Jurisdiction of Osmania University.* Osmania University, 1978.

02 Agra University. Department of Sociology. Institute of social sciences. *Educational problems of scheduled caste college students in U.P. West : Research report.* Agra, the Author, 1975 73p.

03 Aikara, Jacob. *Scheduled castes and higher education.* Poona, Dastance, 1980. 112p.

04 Banaras Hindu University, Varanasi. *The study of scheduled caste students of colleges in East U.P., 1973-74.* Varanasi, the Author, 1974. 424p.

05 Centre for Regional Development Studies, Surat. *Scheduled caste and tribe high school and college students in Bihar : A summary of findings.* Surat, the Author, 1975. 90p.

06 ——. *Scheduled caste high school and college students in Assam.* Surat, The Author, 1975.

07 ——. *Scheduled caste and tribe high school and college students in Kerala : A summary of findings.* Surat, the Author, 1975. 90p.

08 ——. *Scheduled caste and tribe high school and college students in Madhya Pradesh : A summary of findings.* Surat, the Author, 1975. 91p.

09 ——. *Scheduled caste and tribe high school and college students in Maharashtra : A summary of findings.* Surat, the Author, 1975. 94p.

10 ——. *Scheduled caste and scheduled tribe high school and college students in Orissa : A summary of findings.* Surat, the author, 1975. 93p.

11 ——. *Scheduled caste high school and college students in Punjab : A summary of findings.* Surat, the Author, 1975. 47p.

12 Centre for Regional Development Studies, Surat. *Scheduled caste and tribe high school and college students in Rajasthan : A summary of findings*, Surat, the Author, 1975. 93p.

13 ——. *Scheduled caste and tribe high school and college students in Tamil Nadu : A summary of findings*, Surat, the Author, 1975. 104p.

14 ——. *Scheduled caste high school and college students in U.P. : A summary of findings*, Surat, the Author, 1975. 47p.

15 ——. *Scheduled tribe school and college students in Assam.* Surat, the Author, 1975.

16 ——. *Scheduled tribe high school and college students in Manipur and Nagaland : A summary of findings.* Surat, the Author, 1975. 49p.

17 ——. *Scheduled caste high school and college students in Haryana : A summary of findings. 1975.* Surat, the Author, 1975. 44p.

18 Gangrade. *Educational problems of the scheduled castes in Haryana (college students and school students).* Delhi, Delhi School of Social Work, 1974. 159p.

19 Institute of Tribal and Rural Development & Research : Arts and Commerce College. Surat. *Impact of higher education on the tribal students of Vyara. College.* Surat, the Author, 1981. 151p.

20 Jodhpur University. *Educational progress and problems of scheduled castes and scheduled tribes college students in Rajasthan.* Jodhpur, the Author, 1974. 266+132p.

21 Kerala University. Department of Psychology. *Educational problems of the scheduled caste and scheduled tribe college students in Kerala.* Trivandrum, the Author, 1975. 377+25+4p.

22 Lal, Sheo Kumar and Nahar, Umed Raj. *Higher education : Scheduled castes and scheduled tribes.* Jodhpur, Jainsons, 1978. 345p.

23 Mysore University. Department of Post-Graduate Studies and Research in Sociology. *The study of scheduled castes and scheduled tribe college students in Karnataka.* Mysore, the Author n.d. 365p.

24 Nagpur University. Department of Sociology. *Educational problems of the scheduled caste and scheduled tribe secondary school and colleges students in Maharashtra.* Nagpur, the Author, 1975. 299+214p.

25 Panjab University. Department of Sociology. *Educational problems of scheduled caste students in the Punjab : College students.* Chandigarh, the author, 1974. 229p.

26 Parvathamma, C. *Study of scheduled caste and scheduled tribe college students in Karnataka.* Mysore, Mysore University, 1974.

27 Patole, N.K. (ed.) *Educational research in universities in Maharashtra : Platinum jubilee 1906-1981.* Pune, the Author, 1982. 204p.

28 Premi, Kusum K. *Higher education of scheduled castes and scheduled tribes : The problems and prospects.* Paper presented in the orientation programme for college principles organised by NIEPA, New Delhi, 1982. (Mimeographed).

29 Ramanathan, S. *Educational problems of scheduled castes and tribes in Tamil Nadu.* Madras, Madras Institute of Development Studies, 1973.

30 Rath, R. and Mishra, S.K. *Study of scheduled castes and scheduled tribes college students in Orissa.* Utkal University, Deptt. of Psychology, 1974.

31 Raza, Moonis and Premi Kusum. *Reservation in higher education for scheduled castes and scheduled tribes : A policy framework.* New Delhi, NIEPA, 1982.

32 Sachchidananda. *Education among the scheduled castes and scheduled tribes in Bihar : College students.* Patna, ANS. Institute of Social Studies, 1974.

33 Shah, B.V. and Thaker, J.D. *Educational problems of scheduled caste and scheduled tribe college students in Gujarat – 1973 : A research study.* Vidyanagar, Sardar Patel University, 1974. 41p.

34 Shah, Vimal, P. *Educational problems of S.C. and S.T. school and college students in India. (A statistical profile).* Surat a Centre for Regional Development Studies, 1975. Part I, II. 212p. 206p.

35 Shah, Vimal, P. and Patel Tara. *Who goes to college? Scheduled caste/tribe post-matric scholars in Gujarat.* Ahmedabad, Rachana Prakashan, 1977. 219p.

36 Surat. Centre for Regional Development Studies. *Scheduled caste and tribe high school and college students in Assam, a summary of findings.* Nanpura, the Author, 1975. 87p.

37 University Grants Commission. *Facilities to scheduled castes and scheduled tribes in universities and colleges,* 1982. 135p.

38 Utkal University. Department of Psychology. *The study of scheduled caste and scheduled tribe college students in Orissa.* 73+171+17p.

B ARTICLES

01 Adiseshiah, M.S. Scheduled castes and tribes in higher education in Tamil Nadu. *Journal of Higher Education*. 1(2), 1975. p.241-243.

02 Azad, J.L. Education of scheduled castes and scheduled tribes. *Journal of Indian Education*. 1(6), 1976. p.23-28.

03 Chhibbar, Yashpal. Study of students coming from disadvantaged sections of society. *Manpower Journal*. Vol. 6, October, 1970-March, 1971. p. 62-94.

04 Chitnis, Suma. Education of the scheduled castes. *Journal of Higher Education*. 1(2), 1975. p.167-178.

05 Dube, S.C. Educating weaker sections. *University News*. 19(15), 1981. p.413-415.

06 Karlekar, Malavika. Higher education and the scheduled castes. *Journal of Higher Education*. 1(2), 1975. p.172-187.

07 Kirpal, Viney. Higher education for the scheduled castes and scheduled tribes. *Economic and Political Weekly*. 13 (4 and 5), 1978. p.165-169.

08 Lal, Shiv Kumar. Scheduled caste college students in Rajasthan. *Journal of Higher Education*. 1(2), 1975. p.244-249.

09 Mehta, Pradeep. Education and assistance : A case study of government college, Sawai Madhopur. Rajasthan. *Journal of Higher Education*. 3(3), 1978. p.390-399.

10 Parthasarathy, G. Reservations for scheduled castes. *University News*. 11(12), 1973. p.13-14.

11 Premi, Kusum K. Educational equality and economic opportunities : A comparative study of scheduled castes and non-scheduled castes. *Journal of Higher Education*. 9(3), 1984. p.365-372.

12 ——. Educational opportunities for the scheduled castes : Role of protective discrimination in equalisation. *Economic and Political Weekly*. 10(45-46), 1974. p.1002-1010.

13 Rao, P. Kamalakar. Socio-economic background and academic achievement of the scheduled caste students in higher educational institutions, Andhra University, 1960-70. *The Journal of Social Transformation*. 3(2-3), 1979.

14 Rao, U. Amba. Higher education and occupational mobility among the scheduled caste youth. *Journal of Higher Education*. 1(3), 1976. p.305-314.

15 Sachchidananda. Scheduled caste students at college. *Journal of Social Research*. 18(2), 1975. p.108-125.

16 Satyanarayana, S.C. Educational problems of scheduled caste college students in Karnataka. *Journal of Higher Education.* 7(3), 1982. p.253.

17 Singh, D. Bright. A pilot study of scholarships awarded at university stage. *ICSSR Research Abstracts No. 5*, 1971.

18 Suri, Surinder. System of remedial education for underprivileged classes at university level. *New Frontiers in Education.* 9(2), April-June, 1972. p.1-33.

19 Uplaonkar, Ambarao T. Social background and occupational aspirations of college students: A case of scheduled castes *vis-a-vis* non-scheduled castes students in higher education. *Journal of Higher Education.* 8(1), 1982. p.63-73.

20 Uplaonkar, Ambarao. T. *Protective discrimination and the equality of opportunity. Journal of Higher Education.* 11 (1 and 2), 1985-86. p.117-126.

D RESEARCH STUDIES

01 Alkara, J. Scheduled castes and higher education – A study of college students in Bombay, Unit of Research in Sociology of Education, Tata Institute of Social Sciences, Bombay, 1980

The objective of the study were: (i) to find out the rate of stagnation and drop-out among scheduled caste (SC) students to investigate its reasons and post-drop-out situation, (ii) to understand the situation of SC college students, and (iii) to compare scheduled caste and non-scheduled caste college students, and scheduled caste students in different colleges.

In the sample for the study of the situation of the scheduled caste students, one college each from arts and science, commerce and law run by the government and by the organisations committed to the education of the weaker sections was selected. Besides, government college of medicine and engineering and two other private colleges were included in the sample. A questionnaire was mailed to all those scheduled caste students of the ten sample colleges who had met with stagnation or dropped out during the period of five years from 1968-69 to 1972-73, of which 52 per cent responded. The sample for studying the nature of educational problems of the scheduled caste was drawn through stratified random sampling where stratification was done on the basis of the performance of the students in the university examinations of the previous year.

The major findings were: (i) In comparison with the non-scheduled caste students, the scheduled caste students were found to be inferior in almost every aspect – in socio-economic and academic background and in performance and progress in studies. (ii) The students studying in the government colleges had a superior background and better performance record than those of private colleges. (iii) There had been a very high incidence of stagnation and drop-out among the scheduled caste students.

02 Chitnis, S., A Long Way to Go..., Report on a survey of scheduled caste high school and college students in fifteen states of India, Allied Publishers, Bombay, 1981.

The objectives of the study were to find out how the various types of facilities provided for promoting education among the scheduled caste and scheduled tribe children had been made use of and what kinds of problems were faced by these children in the process of education.

For conducting the study, ICSSR appointed a Coordinating Committee to work out a tentative programme and drew up a list of scholars likely to be interested in the project. The list sought to ensure coverage of all the regions of the country. The study was conducted in two phases. The first phase consisted of preparing a statistical profile of the scheduled caste/scheduled tribe population indicating demographic characteristics of the SCs/STs in the State, describing facilities available to them and indicating government and voluntary agencies working for their advancement. The second phase consisted of a field study on several aspects of the students' (high school and college) lives. The sample in each State was selected in three stages: districts, institutions and respondents. In the first stage, the district containing the capital city/largest metropolitan area was selected with certainty. The remaining districts were stratified on the basis of the number of SCs/STs and from each stratum of districts, two districts were randomly selected with probabilities proportional to the number of SC/ST students.

The major findings were: (i) The respondent scheduled caste students were unable to escape their low caste identity and their classmates' behaviour towards them was affected by this knowledge. (ii) They belonged to poor uneducated family, but at the same time were highly selected elite who had been able to overcome all the shortcomings in their backgrounds and were able to progress without failure to high school and college. (iii) The respondents had a poor exposure to mass media, a low level of politicisation, and an inclination to cling to protected positions and they rarely participated in extra-curricular activities. (iv) They showed an ability to overcome the handicap of the home background and had encouraging parents. (v) There were inter-sex, inter-caste and inter-State disparities in terms of educational advancement among scheduled castes. (vi) The study suggested that the problems of scheduled castes were very diversified ones. The study concluded that the scheduled castes had advanced a great deal, but they had yet a long way to go and, secondly, the policies and programmes for their welfare had benefited them greatly but they were nevertheless grossly inadequate.

03 George, E.I., Educational problems of the scheduled caste and scheduled tribe college students in Kerala, Deptt. of Psy., Kerala University, 1975 (ICSSR financed).

The major objectives were: (i) to study the factors that motivate the scheduled caste and scheduled tribe students to go to the college; (ii) to study the factors responsible for drop-out of scheduled caste and scheduled tribe students; and (iii) to study the facilities available to the scheduled caste and scheduled tribe students and their perception about the same.

The study was conducted on 250 scheduled caste and 100 scheduled tribe students selected from twenty-three institutions in six districts of Kerala on a stratified random basis having sex, age, grade, marital status and religion as the bases. The data were collected through two interview schedules and an information proforma.

The study revealed that (i) the reservation on the community basis needs to be changed to considerations like economic backwardness; (ii) the amount of scholarship was inadequate; (iii) the system of distribution of stipends was complicated; (iv) parents needed to be educated about the governmental programme in order to ensure proper utilisation of resources; (v) the students needed to be educated about the facilities existing and its purpose; (vi) the system of separate hostels for scheduled caste and scheduled tribe students was considered socially unhealthy as it widened the gaps with other higher caste students; (vii) a considerable number of scheduled caste and scheduled tribe students suffered from inferiority feeling and they needed to be protect through proper guidance; (viii) these students need vocational training in order to be self-dependent; (ix) the majority of the students of the present grow passed their school leaving examination at a higher age; (x) the scheduled caste and scheduled tribe students did not show high aspiration for technical professional jobs; (xi) there was no healthy relationship between the scheduled caste and tribe students and those who administered the programme; (xii) the distribution of scholarships was usually layed; and (xiii) a good number of teachers were found to be always with a helping hand which encourage the students.

04 Goyal, S.K., The study of scheduled caste students of colleges in east U.P., Deptt. of Soc., Banaras Hindu University, 1974. (ICSSR financed).

The study aimed at surveying the socio-economic background of SC college students in East Uttar Pradesh, and trying to see how it affected other aspects of life of the SC students, namely, their performance, their aspiration, their outlook in life, their ways of thinking and behaving, etc.

A sample of 230 students and sixtyfour teachers (including heads of institutions) were selected from sixteen colleges of Varanasi, Gorakhpur, Faizabad and Deoria districts of East Uttar Pradesh, on the basis of stratified random sampling. Questionnaires and interview schedules were used as tools for the study.

The study revealed the following: (i) U.P. had a high proportion of SC population. (ii) Literacy was very low as compared to the general population and it was still lower in the eastern districts of U.P. (iii) Literacy of the parents as well as the literacy of the younger generation of SC was low. (iv) Majority of them were from rural areas. (v) Majority of them opted for 'Arts' courses. (vi) The educational aspiration of the SC students was very high. (vii) They were found to be more local and ethnocentric and thus more homophilic in their friendship patterns. (viii) SC students with better education were receptive to the programmes for their upliftment.

05 Homchaudhuri, S., An analytical study of correlates of academic performance of college students (Tribal) of Mizoram, Ph.D. Edu., MS University of Baroda, 1980.

The investigation aimed at surveying the levels of self-concept, anxiety, family influence and socio-economic status and studying the relationship of these factors with academic performance. The effect of the above-mentioned variables on academic performance was also studied. It was also attempted to study the nature of perception of self, home, institution, studies, community and country of tribal students with high and low academic performance.

The sample for the study was drawn from all the five colleges of Mizoram. In all, 459 pre-university second year students were selected (349 boys and 110 girls). In order to collect the required data, students in each college were given the tests together in two sessions. To make the self-perception inquiry, Who Am I? and other five descriptive tools developed by the investigator were administered. Socio-economic status and family influence scales were also developed to measure the socio-economic status and students' perception of the influence of family along three dimensions, namely, democratic, lukewarm and authoritarian. To measure anxiety Sinha's Anxiety Scale was used. The data were computerised and means, standard deviations, correlations and t-ratios were computed and multiple regression analysis was carried out.

The major findings of the study were: (i) Self-concept emerged as the most significant correlate of academic performance. (ii) There was no significant difference between the girls and the boys with regard to self-concept. (iii) Socio-economic status also came out as a significant correlate of academic performance. (iv) Anxiety had low positive significant relationship with academic performance. (v) The high achievers were significantly more anxious than the low achievers. (vi) The high achievers found the emotional atmosphere of their homes to their liking. (vii) The low achievers found an absence of good environment at home. (viii) The high achievers showed quite a high level of expectation with regard to their performance in the examination. (ix) Their analysis of the performance was quite objective. (x) The low achievers showed an abnormally high level of expectation and great judgment discrepancy with regard to performance. (xi) A substantial proportion of high achievers did not like the manner in which the classes were taken; they thought the college should provide better teaching. (xii) Quite a sizeable proportion of the low achievers were critical of physical facilities and students' conduct. (xiii) The high achievers showed their liking for a number of values upheld in the community. (xiv) The low achievers showed their likes and dislikes for different aspects of community to a much less extent than the high achievers. (xv) The high achievers observed the marks of democracy in the life of the nation more deeply than the low achievers.

06 Gupta, Laxman Prakash. A study of personal characteristics and academic achievements of scheduled caste and backward class students of Meerut University, University of Meerut, 1978.

To study, evaluate, and differentiate the personality needs and self-concepts of the scheduled castes, backward classes, and non-scheduled caste students comparatively.

To study, evaluate, and differentiate the cognitive characteristics such as intelligence and also the level of academic achievement of the two groups, comparatively.

Population for the present research study conducted in 1977-78 has been defined as the total number of scheduled castes and backward class students of graduate and postgraduate classes of the six affiliated colleges of Meerut University. The research survey is confined to only male university students, sampling 544 of scheduled castes and backward classes and equal number of non-scheduled caste students for comparison of the two groups. The data for the study, were collected with the help of the scientific research tools measuring variables like ten personality needs, five aspects of self-concept, intelligence, and academic achievement, involved in the study. The research tools were: Raven's Progressive Matrices Test, Bhatnagar's Self-Concept Inventory, and Meenakshi Personality Inventory.

The findings are: The scheduled castes and backward classes, graduate and post-graduate students have significantly higher mean scores as compared to the non-scheduled castes students on need affiliation, N-Succourance, N-Abasement, N-Nurturance, N-Achievement, and N-Endurance. This means that the scheduled castes and backward class students, as compared to the non-scheduled caste students are more affiliative, more in need or feeling inferior, more nurturance, more achievement oriented, and more enduring.

The scheduled and backward class students harbour in their heart a lower level of Need-Autonomy, N-Dominance, and N-Aggression. This means they are less aggressive, less dominant, and less in need of autonomy as compared to their non-scheduled counterparts. These are the qualities of personality which are called for to push ahead in the modern complex and competitive society.

As regards the structure and organisation of the self-concept, the two groups of students are much different from one another. It is found that the scheduled castes and backward class students perceive themselves to be persons who feel comparatively more inadequate and inferior and who suffer more from feelings of emotional instability, in comparison of non-scheduled caste students.

So far intelligence is concerned the scheduled castes and backward class students, both graduates as well as post-graduates are found to be inferior in comparison to their non-scheduled caste counterparts. The difference between them is significant at 0.01 level.

The graduate and postgraduate students of scheduled Castes and backward classes are found to be poor academic achievers, as the mean academic achievement index of these students is significantly lower than that of the non-scheduled caste students. In view of lower level of intelligence, poor self-concepts characterising these scheduled caste students, poor academic achievement is not surprising. They have not yet come at par with the non-scheduled caste students. The study has, at least, reaffirmed the importance of personality characteristics and rich environment in academic-achievement. These findings have significant and critical implications. It may be that the various welfare schemes for scheduled castes and backward class students are required to be extended and intensified or the implementation of policies should be backed by practical actions and not simply paper benefits or lip sympathy. As such, revision of existing policies may be imperative.

07 Parvathamma, C., The study of scheduled caste and scheduled tribe college students in Karnataka. Department of Post-graduate Studies and Research in Sociology. Mysore University, 1974. (ICSSR financed).

The major aims of the study were: (i) to study the socio-economic background of the SC and ST college students of Karnataka, and (ii) to see how it affected their performance, their feeling of social distance, their opinion about governmental facilities and finally their educational aspirations.

The author had selected thirtythree colleges from the districts of Bangalore, Kolar, Mysore, Belgaum, Bijapur, Tumkur, Chitradurga and Dharwar of Karnataka State. In all 260 SC and 109 ST students of final B.A./B.Com. and B.Sc. classes were selected on random basis. Similarly, 113 college teachers were also selected to know their opinion about the SC/ST students studying under them. Questionnaires were administered and interviews were held to elicit opinion on the various aspects of the SC and ST students.

The study brought out the following facts: (i) SC/ST students remained in colleges more than the normal time required. (ii) Many of the C/ST student youths were still to come to education. (iii) A bulk of them lived in villages, whereas the colleges were in towns. So they mostly stayed at hostels or if possible, studied as day scholars if the college was within their reach. (iv) Hostels were crowded. (v) All the girls except one out of the fortynine under study, stayed with their parents. (vi) They felt that their teachers were sympathetic. (vii) They were also aware of the reservation of jobs for them. (viii) They were exposed to mass media. (ix) Some of them had experienced discrimination. (x) Some of them did have 'mixed' friendship — within and outside their community. (xi) In spite of their higher education the SC/ST students had to depend on their parents. (xii) Their opinion about their status was also 'mixed'; some felt that it had improved, while others did not agree to it. (xiii) They had some discontent about the amount and the disbursement of the scholarship. (xiv) There was no teacher from the ST on the college staff.

08 Pimpley, P.N., Educational problems of scheduled caste students in the Punjab : College students, Dept. of Soc., Panjab University, 1974 (ICSSR financed).

The study was undertaken to investigate the educational problems of the scheduled caste (SC) college students of Punjab. The author tried to see how their education affected their aspirations and performance, their life style, their social outlook, their attitude towards government assistance and finally their opinion about the status of SC, in general.

A sample of 233 SC students (219 male and fourteen female) was drawn from all the colleges in the five districts (Chandigarh, Jullunder, Hoshiarpur, Gurdaspur and Kapurthala) for the study. Questionnaire and depth interview were the research tools.

The major findings of the study were as follows: (i) The SC college students were mostly overaged; male students were over represented in the sample; about ninety per cent of them were unmarried and mainly Hindus rather than Sikhs. (ii) In most cases, their parents were illiterate and had meagre financial resources and the students had to spend a lot of time in domestic duties. (iii) Most of them could follow the class and wastage was not very high. (iv) Their educational as well as occupational aspirations were very high. (v) Exposure to mass media was quite high and national leaders and government servants were the most popular reference persons. (vi) Behaviour of other students towards them was determined by their status, yet many of them had non-SC friends. (vii) They had no experience of ill-treatment. (viii) Most of them considered endogamy and parental authority as most important. (ix) A large number of them felt that the government policy of providing facilities was useful but the programme was not administered satisfactorily. (x) They also felt that the status of SC had improved, but was still inferior.

09 Rangari, A.D., Comparative study of the scheduled caste and the non-scheduled caste college students of Aurangabad, Ph.D., Psy., Poona University, 1980.

The main objective of the study was to compare the scheduled caste and the non-scheduled caste college students on self-concept, interpersonal relationships, personality adjustment, intelligence and academic achievement. While comparing these groups, comparisons on account of sex and rural-urban background were also made. The specific hypotheses of the study were, therefore, stated in terms of the five variables compared on caste, sex and rural-urban background. All these considerations led to fifteen hypotheses.

The sample consisted of scheduled caste and non-scheduled caste boys and girls randomly selected from the student population of the seven colleges in Aurangabad town. The total sample of 1,197 students consisted of 676 scheduled caste and 521 non-scheduled caste students. There was adequate representation of both the sexes and rural-urban students in both the groups. The tools used for data-collection were a structured proforma for personal information, Self-Concept Inventory of Jogawar, the FIRO-B

Test of Schutz, Personality Adjustment Inventory of Palsane, Non-Verbal Test of Intelligence of Nafde, Structured Proforma for Academic Achievement, Socio-Economic Status Scale (Urban) of Kuppuswamy and SES Scale (Rural) of Pareek and Trivedi. Chi-square test and t-test were used in statistical analysis for comparisons.

The findings of the study were: (i) The non-scheduled caste (NSC) college students as a total group tended to have higher scores on perceived self-social self and ideal self than their scheduled caste (SC) counterparts. Sex differences were not significant for perceived self and ideal self but were significant for social self. Rural-urban differences were mostly not significant on any aspect of the self-concept. (ii) There was no significant difference between the total involvement score of the NSC and the SC students. Sex differences were significant among the SC students and the students from rural background. Men showed greater involvement than women. The rural-urban differences were less marked than the sex differences. The marginal differences which existed favoured the rural group. (iii) Significant differences existed on the different sub-variables of adjustment. By and large, the NSC students showed better adjustment in different areas than the SC students; the females were better than the males and the urban were better than the rural. (iv) On intelligence, the NSC students did better than the SC and the urban than the rural. Sex differences were not noticeable. (v) On educational achievement, the NSC students did better than the SC students. Among the SC students women did better than men while among the NSC students men did better than women. The students from the urban background did better than those from the rural. (vi) The socio-economic status was used as a control variable and it was found that when this was controlled the differences between the SC and the NSC students either disappeared or their magnitude was reduced.

10 Rath, R. and Misra, S.K., The study of scheduled caste and scheduled tribe college students in Orissa, Deptt. of Psy., Utkal University, 1974. (ICSSR financed).

The major objectives of the study were: (i) to assess the types and extent of educational problems of scheduled caste and scheduled tribe college students; (ii) to make an objective evaluation of government policies for the education of scheduled caste and scheduled tribe students; and (iii) to suggest measures to achieve better and quicker results with their implications to the present policy and method of implementation.

A multistage random sampling technique was used at three levels — district, institution and students. The scheduled caste sample was selected from five districts and scheduled tribe from four districts, but both included Puri, the capital district. In all, 247 scheduled caste, 171 scheduled tribe students, twenty-one heads and seventynine readers or lecturers, selected from twenty institutions having scheduled caste students and fifteen having scheduled tribe students, formed the sample of respondents. The questionnaires and interview were the main tools.

The study revealed that (i) the majority of the scheduled caste college students were Hindu, unmarried, males, poor, and first generation of people having collegiate education; (ii) stagnation and drop-out phenomena were also there; (iii) ninetythree per cent of the students were from rural areas, thirtyeight per cent lived in hostels and they mostly opted for arts courses; (iv) the scheduled caste college students were self-dependent in taking decisions about marriage and future career; (v) ninetysix per cent of the students favoured the government programmes meant for their benefit; (vi) they did not feel neglected either by the teachers, or by the students of other communities; (vii) among the scheduled tribe students, majority were unmarried; (viii) the scheduled tribe students included Hindus (twentyeight per cent) and Christians (twentynine per cent), and the rest belonged to other tribal religions; (ix) the scheduled tribe students usually had a poor economic and educational background; (x) about seventyfive per cent of them lived in hostels and were in good terms with students from other communities; (xi) ninetyfour per cent felt that the scholarship amount was inadequate; many considered the educational facilities as inadequate and not useful; (xii) scheduled tribe students understood their teachers less than the scheduled caste and they felt neglected; (xiii) some scheduled tribe students believed that there was some kind of discrimination against them; (xiv) eightyone per cent did not want to go back to their family profession; (xv) only two to five per cent of teachers belonged to scheduled caste or scheduled tribes; (xvi) some of the teachers considered these students as equally intelligent, poor achievement as being due to poverty; and (xvii) most of the principals felt that scheduled caste and scheduled tribe students did not create any problem for them.

11 Sachchidananda, Education among the scheduled castes and scheduled tribes in Bihar (College Students), A.N.S. Institute of Social Studies, Patna, 1974. (ICSSR financed).

The major objectives of the study were: (i) to assess the status of the scheduled caste students in the colleges, (ii) to compare the scheduled caste and scheduled tribe students, wherever possible, with other classes of students, and (iii) to identify the kinds of discrimination and types of difficulties and obstacles that they faced.

The present study was a sociological survey. By the method of stratified random sampling, selection of the sample was done at three levels, viz., district, institutions, and students and teachers. As many as 225 scheduled caste college students were sampled from the districts of Patna, Monghyr, Muzaffarpur, Singhbhum and Shahabad, and 243 scheduled tribe college students were selected from the districts of Patna, Ranchi, Singhbhum, Santal Pargana and Bhagalpur. The students were selected from twenty colleges in the groups of five scheduled caste/scheduled tribe districts. These were second and third year students of B.A., B.Sc. and B.Com. courses, and their ages were fifteen year and beyond. In addition to this, another sample of 144 teachers of the selected colleges were drawn for giving their views on the academic and other aspects of the sampled students. Questionnaire and interview were the tools used for collection of data. In analysing the data, responses were coded and tabulated.

The following were some of major findings of the study: (i) Girl college students were twenty-five per cent among the scheduled tribe, and only 0.4 per cent among the scheduled caste. (ii) Nearly thirty per cent of the scheduled caste college students were married. (iii) Three-fourths of the students in both communities went in for arts courses. Science claimed only seventeen per cent. (iv) At college level the students were not much burdened by household duties and responsibilities. (v) In general, the teachers had helpful attitude towards them. (vi) Most of the students had high academic and occupational aspirations. (vii) Most of them were exposed to mass media of communication. (viii) Bulk of the students were politicised. (ix) They had friends mostly from their own caste or tribe. (x) Very few had experienced discrimination. (xi) Most of them were aware of the reservation of government jobs for them. (xii) A large number of students felt that their status had improved but not as much as that of the caste Hindus. (xiii) By and large male and female students did not differ in the choice of their courses of study. (xiv) Educational aspiration of both male and female students was nearly the same as also their pattern of social interaction. (xv) Most of the teachers regarded their scheduled caste and scheduled tribe students as inferior, the reason being the absence of conducive atmosphere at home.

12 Shah, B.V. and Thaker, J.D., Educational problems of scheduled caste and scheduled tribe college students in Gujarat. Deptt. of Sociology, Sardar Patel University, 1974. (ICSSR financed).

The study was undertaken to investigate the demographic characteristics and the socio-economic background of the scheduled caste (SC) and scheduled tribe (ST) college students of Gujarat and see how their education affected their aspirations and performance, life style, participation in cocurricular activities, social outlook, attitude towards the government facilities and concessions, and feeling and outlook on the status of SC and ST.

The study was conducted on a sample of 205 SC and 195 ST students of second and third year B.A./B.Sc./B.Com. from nineteen colleges from seven districts of Gujarat, where SC and ST population was numerically significant. The sample was drawn on the basis of multi-stage stratified random sampling. Ninetysix teachers and thirty-two principals were also included in the study in order to know their opinion about their SC and ST students. Questionnaires and interview schedules were used as research tools.

The major findings of the study were as follows: (i) With the entry of SC/ST students at the college level our education system had to cater to the needs of different socio-economic groups with widely differing abilities, aspirations and facilities. (ii) The governmental assistance for education to the SC/ST groups created inequalities of utilisation between different SC/ST groups within the State. (iii) As the SC/ST students were largely the first generation educated, motivated not by self or their family but by the governmental encouragement, they were likely to lack strong motivation, ability, good study habits, good performance, etc., required for study. (iv) The SC/ST college students being exposed to a new type of social, economic and political environment, felt shy of exposing themselves more to mass media and modernising their attitudes and behaviour, and participated less in the politicisation process; they showed ambivalent attitudes in several areas and sought shelter in their traditional group ties by sharing rooms with members of their own caste/tribe or groups and showing high homophyly in their friendship pattern. (v) As these students came up, sheltered under the governmental umbrella, for education as well as for jobs, the non SC/ST groups developed a negative attitude towards them. As a result the final assimilation of SC/ST groups in the main stream of Indian social life began to face obstacles.

13 Shah, V.P. and Patel I., Who goes to college? — A study of scheduled caste/tribe, post-matric scholars in Gujarat, Deptt. of Soc., Gujarat University, 1977.

The specific objectives of the study were: (i) to examine the types of courses, year of study and academic background of the scheduled caste/tribe post-matric scholars, (ii) to study the differential utilisation of government assistance by various scheduled castes/tribes *vis-a-vis* their population, (iii) to examine the socio-economic characteristics of the scheduled caste/tribe post-matric scholars, (iv) to analyse rural-urban differences in the distribution of the scheduled caste/tribe post-matric scholars, and (v) to study the relationship between differential utilisation of government assistance for higher education by the scheduled castes/tribes and their contextual characteristics.

The study was based on an analysis of information available from fresh/renewal application forms filled in by the scheduled caste/tribe students who were awarded post-matric scholarships in the years 1967-68 and 1971-71. In all, the application forms of 3,630 or 82.51 per cent of the scheduled caste post-matric scholars and 1,428 or 92.36 per cent of the scheduled tribe post-matric scholars in 1967-68 could be retrieved. Similarly, the application forms of 7,487 scheduled caste and 3,390 scheduled tribe post-matric scholars in 1971-72 could be retrieved from the office of the Directorate of Social Welfare, Gujarat. An attempt was made to examine the various aspects of the study, separately for males and females. The data were analysed in a comparative manner so as to discern differences between the different categories of the scheduled caste/tribe post-matric scholars and also to find out changes, if any, over the five-year period. Also, an attempt was made to consider the data separately for different sub-castes/tribes. In addition to frequency and percentage analysis, the study used such statistical techniques as coefficients of equality, measures of central tendency and dispersion, and correlational analysis.

The major findings of the study were: (i) Only about 1 per cent of the scheduled caste/tribe post-matric scholars were enrolled for certificate courses offered by vocational/technical schools. There was a downward trend in the proportion of scheduled caste/tribe post-matric scholars enrolled for diploma courses. (ii) Among those enrolled for diploma courses, the largest proportion was enrolled for basic training (P.T.C.) course. Next to the P.T.C. course, the scheduled caste male scholars were enrolled for diploma courses in engineering (polytechnic), *lok-sikshan* and education, while the scheduled tribe male scholars were enrolled for diploma courses in *samaj-shastra, vyayam*, engineering (polytechnic) and agriculture. (iii) Among the scheduled caste/tribe post-matric scholars enrolled for degree courses, about one-half of the males and about three-fourths of the females were enrolled in arts colleges. (iv) There was a considerable decrease in the percentage of the scheduled caste/tribe males as well as females enrolled in science colleges and a considerable increase in the percentage of those enrolled in commerce colleges. (v) There was a decrease in the percentage as well as the absolute number of the scheduled caste/tribe males scholars enrolled in engineering colleges. (vi) The percentages of the scheduled caste/tribe male scholars enrolled in ayurvedic and medical colleges remained stable at about 1 per cent and 3 per cent, respectively. (vii) There was a considerable increase in the number of post-graduate students among the scheduled castes and the scheduled tribes, but the number of the females among them remained rather insignificant. (viii) During the five-year period, there was a modest increase in mean years of post-matric study by the scheduled castes and tribes. However, the figures were greater for the scheduled castes than for the scheduled tribes, and also for the males than for the females. (ix) A little over one-half of the scheduled caste/tribe scholars had got second class at the SSC examination, about one-third of them had been placed in pass class, and about 7 to 12 per cent had secured first class or first class with distinction. The level of academic performance of the males was higher than that of the females. (x) About 5 to 10 per cent of the scheduled caste post-matric scholars had failed once or more during their course of study, while about 3 to 7 per cent of the scheduled tribe scholars had failed once or more during their course of study. (xi) Out of a total of sixty-eight scheduled castes in Gujarat, there was not a single post-matric scholar from as many as twenty-eight scheduled castes. About 95 per cent of the scholars belonged to only six categories, namely, vankar/maru vankar, chamar, mahyavanshi, rohi, samgar, nalia, garoda and bhangi. (xii) Out of a total of sixty-seven scheduled tribes in Gujarat, twenty-three tribes had no representation at all among the post-matric scholars; about 85 per cent of the scholars belonged to only five tribes, namely, dhodia, chaudhari, bhil, dungri garasia and gamit/gavit. (xiii) Fathers/guardians of only about one-fifth of the scheduled caste scholars worked in white-collar occupations, about a third of them worked in middle-level occupations and a little less than one-half of them worked in low-level occupations. (xiv) Fathers/guardians of only about one-twelfth of the scheduled tribe scholars worked in white-collar occupations, about one-half of them worked in middle-level occupations, and about one-third worked in low-level occupations. (xv) About one-tenth of the scheduled caste post-matric scholars and about 2 per cent of the scheduled tribe scholars were gainfully employed. (xvi) The urban-based scheduled castes were probably benefiting more than the rural/forest-based scheduled tribes. (xvii) The income of the family was closely related to the father's/guardian's occupation and the employment of the scholars themselves. In general, the scholars came from families with only modest income. However, the mean family income of scheduled caste scholars was greater than that of the scheduled tribe ones. (xviii) Parents/guardians of only about 40 per cent of the scholars owned a house. Land holdings of the scheduled tribe scholars were in general less than those of the scheduled caste ones. (xix) The proportion of the scheduled caste/tribe post-matric scholars from urban areas was a little less than double the proportion of their population residing in urban areas. (xx) About one-half of the scheduled caste post-matric scholars came from Ahmedabad and Mehsana districts. Another one-fourth of them came from Kaira, Baroda, Surat and Bulsar districts. (xxi) About two-thirds to three-fourths of the scheduled tribe post-matric scholars came from Surat and Bulsar districts, another one-fifth to one-third of them came from Sabarkantha, the Panchmahals and Broach districts. (xxii) About two-thirds of the scheduled caste and 53.4 per cent of the scheduled tribe scholars in 1967-68 were studying in the districts of their permanent residence. These figures rose to 75.0 per cent and 58.1 per cent, respectively in 1971-72.

14 Sharma, J.P. A study of scheduled caste students in Patna University, Ph.D. Edu., Patna, Patna University, 1982.

The purposes of the study were: (i) to identify social, economic, educational and political problems of the scheduled caste students studying in Patna University, and (ii) to study their relationship with teachers and students of upper caste.

The sample of the study consisted of 130 scheduled caste students studying in the faculties of arts, science, commerce, law, engineering and education of Patna University. The subjects, randomly chosen, belonged to chamar, dushadh, rajak (dhobi), pasi, dome, bhuiya, bhangi, and kunjara subcastes. An interview schedule was developed covering areas like age, courses undertaken, subjects chosen, religion, habitation, marital status, age at the time of marriage, family income, education of parents, parental occupation, lodging, distance of daily travelling for attending classes, locality of lodging, facilities at home, treatment of authorities, years spent in each class, reasons for the choice of courses, perception about the course content, scholarship facilities, attitude towards classroom teaching, teachers' willingness to help, satisfaction or dissatisfaction with examination results and reasons thereof, preparation for examination, favour by teachers to upper caste students, friendship pattern, reservation policy and hostel life. A total number of 130 students were interviewed, by the investigator, over a period of nearly one year.

The main findings of the study were: (i) There was disparity between scheduled castes and other castes in respect of age, habitation, facilities, per capita income, parental education, study facilities, choice of subjects, rate of stagnation, adjustment to the climate in the hostel and in the institution, and level of academic achievement. (ii) The members of the scheduled castes felt neglected and alienated in the university system. (iii) Immediate measures should be taken to develop confidence among the scheduled caste students and also for developing in them a sense of belongingness to the university system.

15 Solanki, S. A study of the problems of tribal students going for higher education, Tribal Research and Training Centre, Gujarat, Vidyapith, Ahmedabad, 1976.

The main objectives of the study were: (i) to find out the particular tribes from which students came for higher education and also the particular branches they joined, (ii) to find out the socio-economic and educational background of the parents of the tribal students who came for higher education, (iii) to find out the various difficulties faced by them during their primary and secondary schooling, (iv) to find out the difficulties faced by the students in getting scholarship, and (v) to assess their attitude towards the hostel life, studies and social adjustment.

A detailed questionnaire was prepared covering various aspects of the life of the tribal students. The questionnaire was sent to 536 tribal students who had been awarded scholarship during the year 1964-65. Of these, 321 students responded to the questionnaire forming the basis of the the present study. Apart from this, information was collected from the Backward Class Welfare Department.

The major findings of the study were: (i) Out of the twenty-eight tribes in Gujarat State, children from only fifteen tribes had gone for higher education. Eighty per cent of these came from dhodia, bhil and chandari tribes. (ii) Most of the students joined arts, while very few joined medical, engineering and agriculture. (iii) Forty-five per cent of the students came from families with educated parents. The majority of them hailed from joint families. (iv) For more than half of the drop-outs at the college level, the annual income of their parents was less than Rs. 1200. (v) One-fourth of the students were in such a condition that they had to either earn while learning, or get a scholarship, or borrow money from their relatives and friends in order to complete their education. (vi) Many of them faced financial problems during their primary and secondary education for procuring clothes, food, books, etc. (vii) More than two-thirds of the students faced difficulties in getting admission to college or hostel, paying the first term fees, paying the mess charges, etc. (viii) A large number of students complained of not getting the scholarship on time. A considerable number of them received the scholarship late in the year. (ix) Most of the students complained that the scholarship amount they received was not adequate. (x) Even when the Backward Class Department released the scholarship, the concerned college considerably delayed the payment to the students. (xi) All the students agreed that they could not have gone for higher education if special facilities were not provided to them by the government and suggested that the practice should continue. (xii) Most of them expressed their liking for hostel life. They said that they did not mind staying with SC students in SC hostels. (xiii) They had friends from non-tribal as well as SC groups and did not find any problem of social adjustment.

40. SEMESTER SYSTEM

A BOOKS

01 Association of Indian Universities. *Monograph on semester system for universities.* New Delhi, A.I.U., 1979. 360 p.

02 Devdas, R.P. *Semester pattern for the undergraduate courses.* Madras, University of Madras, 1976.

03 Patil, V.T. *Semester system: Substance and problems.* New Delhi, Sterling, 1984. 76 p.

04 University Grants Commission. *Principles and mechanics of the semester system.* New Delhi, U.G.C., 1971. 38 p.

B ARTICLES

01 Akhtar, Parveen. Semester to serve students. *University News.* 22(26), 1984. p. 6-7.

02 Desai, D.M. The semester systems for higher education in India. *Education and Psychology Review.* 10 (April) 1970. p. 60-69.

03 Nagaratnam, S. Semester system - An appraisal. *University News.* 18(17), 1980. p. 469 and 477.

04 Patel, A.S. Need to revitalise teaching and evaluation at university level: A case for semester system. *Education and Psychology Review.* 9 (October), 1969. p. 162-174.

05 Rais Ahmed. Semester systems as means of improving university education. *University News.* 8(10), 1970. p. 14-16.

06 Siddiqi, Zakia A. Semester system : An appraisal. *Educational Review.* 83(4), April, 1977. p. 68-69.

07 Yadav, M.S. and Mukhopadhyay M. College teaching in semester system. *Educational Quarterly.* 28(1), 1976. p. 14-17.

08 Yelikar, D.S. Semester System: A bird's eye view. *University News.* 9(2), 1971. p. 16-18.

D RESEARCH STUDIES

01 Akhtar, P.R. A critical study of the semester systems in selected universities in India. Ph.D. Edu., Maharaja Sayajirao University of Baroda, 1980.

The objective of the study was to investigate the semester system in selected universities in India with particular reference to (i) purposes of introducing the semester system, (ii) flexibility and freedom in the formulation of courses, (iii) the methods of teaching adopted by teachers on account of the academic freedom provided to them, (iv) evaluation, (v) the opinion of teachers and students with regard to academic improvement and study habits, (vi) the difficulties faced by teachers and students, and (vii) the attitudes of teachers and students towards the semester system.

The sample was drawn randomly from ten selected universities of India. In all, 583 students and 363 teachers were included in the sample. Data were collected with the help of two questionnaires developed by the investigator in order to study the purposes of the semester system and to study the opinion of teachers and students about the semester system. Their attitude was measured with the help of an attitude scale. Unstructured interviews also were held to substantiate the responses given on the questionnaires. The data obtained were analysed by computing the percentages of responses on the questionnaires, calculating coefficient of correlation by rank difference method and using t-test for comparisons.

The major findings of the study were: (i) The university authorities took initiative in introducing the semester system with the help of experts. Teachers also were involved in such decision-making. (ii) The semester system was implemented to assess the day-to-day performance of students, to provide flexibility and freedom in teaching and evaluation and to provide freedom in framing the courses and to give opportunity to brighter and weaker students to make progress. (iii) Teachers' opinion was that they enjoyed flexibility and freedom in the formulation of courses. (iv) In most of the teachers' and students' opinion, students preferred courses under the semester system because it divided the workload and made provision to improve the grades through continuous assessment. (v) On the question that the semester system kept the students busy throughout the year, the opinion of the teachers and the students was divided. (vi) About 30 per cent of the teachers and 50 per cent of the students did not prefer the courses under the semester system whereas others preferred. (vii) A large number of teachers felt that the semester system gave them freedom to use alternative methods of teaching, but still the lecture method dominated the scene. (viii) A large number of students (60 to 65 per cent) from the undergraduate and post-graduate classes felt that the present method was satisfactory as lecture, discussion, team teaching programmed learning, quizes and field work, etc., were used by the teachers. (ix) Out of the ten universities selected nine assessed the students through continuous internal assessment. Along with internal assessment, external examination, grade and marks system prevailed in the universities. (x) Internal assessment increased the cordial relationship with the students and encouraged innovations in teaching methods. (xi) Teachers felt that the semester system helped in the academic improvement of the students as it made them study systematically all through the year. (xii) Students devoted more time for studies. (xiii) A section of teachers faced difficulty due to a few reasons. Inadequate teaching time, increased clerical work, pressure of increased evaluation of home assignments and more of holidays brought difficulty to the teachers.

02 Pillai, J.K., and Mohan, S., Working of the semester system — A review, Deptt. of Education, Madurai Kamaraj University, 1986.

The objectives of the inquiry were (i) to find out the views of students and teachers regarding the semester system, teaching-learning techniques, evaluation procedures and the functioning of the system, and (ii) to study parents' opinion about the system as a whole.

The sample comprised eighty-three colleges of which forty colleges responded. In addition, the sample included 1260 teachers, 1225 students and 110 parents or citizens. A Semester Review Questionnaire developed by the investigators was the main tool used. The analysis consisted mainly in converting the frequency of responses into percentage.

The major findings were: (1) About sixty-nine per cent of teachers agreed that the courses of study were designed as self-contained units. (2) Seventy per cent of the men teachers and eighty-one per cent of women teachers were of the opinion that the semester system had geared the students to a tight schedule. (3) About seventy-five per cent of teachers said that ninety working days were ensured per semester. A large percentage suggested that uniform dates should be fixed for opening of colleges. (4) About sixty per cent of teachers reported that adequate lecture hours were available to complete the course units. (5) More than eight per cent of teachers agreed that the courses were effectively planned, schedules notified and followed closely. (6) Teachers used lectures, discussions, assignments and seminars as major instructional strategies. They used continuous assessment and assignments to help the students to learn systematically. They felt that ratio of 75 : 25 for external and internal assessment was adequate. They opined in favour of non-detention policy. (7) A majority of the teachers were keen to ensure uniformity in awarding internal marks among the colleges and various subjects by converting raw scores into standard scores. (8) The students (sixty-five per cent) felt that the courses of study were well-designed as self-contained units, and they geared them to a tight work schedule. (9) Seventy per cent of students reported that there was effective planning of courses, schedules were notified in advance and followed closely. (10) About fifty per cent of the students felt that teachers provided discussion, assignments and seminars more frequently than fieldwork, project work, guided reading and debates. (11) Sixty-five per cent of the students felt that they were involved in the learning process, learnt more systematically, assumed definite responsibility for their progress, got periodical feedback from the results of sessional tests to improve their learning and the semester system left little time to involve in frivolous activities. (12) Students wanted the class size to be not more than forty. They were satisfied with the existing ration of external and internal assessment. They, however, were not in favour of too many tests. About forty per cent of students doubted the reliability of external assessment and suspected subjectivity in internal assessment. (13) On the whole, ninety per cent of students felt that the semester system was a good system. (14) Almost all parents favoured continuing the semester system. According to them, the system resulted into regular work by their wards and periodical tests and feed back resulted into morale boosting and better learning.

03 Roshiah, R.F., A Critical Study of the perceptions of college communities about the desirability and feasibility of introducing semester system in their colleges in the city of Madras, Ph.D. Edu., Maharaja Sayajirao University of Baroda, 1980

The major objectives of the study were: (i) to find out the components of the semester system perceived by the teachers of affiliated colleges, autonomous institutions and university departments as feasible and desirable, (ii) to determine the influence of sex, age, teaching experience and qualifications on teachers' perceptions of the desirability and feasibility of introducing the semester system, (iii) to find out differences in the perceptions of college teachers and college administrators of the semester system, (iv) to find out whether teachers in the various faculties like arts, science, commerce, medicine and education differed in their perceptions of the semester system, and (v) to find out whether factors like institutional climate, leadership behaviour, teachers' morale, and teachers' dogmatism influenced teachers' perceptions of the semester system.

Five hundred teachers selected at random from the affiliated colleges, autonomous institutions and university departments of the Madras University formed the sample. Tools used in the study were a Semester System Perception Description Questionnaire, a questionnaire on institutional climate, Teacher Morale Inventory (Baroda version), Leadership Behaviour Description Questionnaire and an adapted version of Milton Rokeach's Dogmatism Scale. Product moment correlation, t-test and factor analysis were the statistical techniques used for the analysis of data.

The major findings of the study were: (i) The teachers of autonomous institutions perceived the semester system more favourably than the teachers of affiliated colleges and university departments. (ii) The teachers of university departments perceived the semester system more favourably than the teachers of affiliated colleges. (iii) The college teachers perceived the semester system as a desirable proposition rather than a feasible one for adoption in their colleges. (iv) The faculties of engineering, medicine, technology and veterinary science perceived the adoption of semester system more favourably than the faculties of education, law, science, arts and commerce. (v) Top educational administrators perceived the semester system both desirable and feasible for adoption by colleges and their perceptions were more favourable than those of other categories of educational administrators and teachers. The heads of departments came next in this respect and they, too, considered it to be equally desirable and feasible. The principals of colleges and professors perceived the semester system as desirable but not feasible. The lecturers, demonstrators and tutors considered the semester system as neither desirable nor feasible. (vi) Age, sex, academic qualifications and teaching experience influenced teachers' perceptions and teaching experience influenced teachers' perceptions of the semester system. The teachers in the age range 31 to 50 years were more favourable to the semester system than the younger and the older teachers. The professional degree-holders were more favourable to the semester system. The male teachers were more favourably inclined to the feasibility of the semester system than the female teachers. The teachers with 11 to 20 years of teaching experience showed a more favourable inclination to the semester system than other teachers with more or less teaching experience, (vii) The institutional climate showed no relationship with the teachers' perception of the semester system. (viii) Leadership behaviour and teachers' dogmatism were not related to their perceptions of the semester system. (ix) Factor analysis helped to identify eight factors in the perceptions of the college teaching communities.

04 Somaiah, M. *A study of the attitude of teachers and students towards semester system of education*. IIM, Bangalore, 1980.

The main objectives of the study were: (i) to find out the positive and negative attitudes of teachers and students of the post-graduate level of Bangalore and Mysore Universities towards the semester system of education, (ii) to find out the differential attitude of students grouped on the basis of the levels of higher education, family size and income, (iii) to find out the differential attitude of teachers working in different levels of institutions and with different specialisations, and (iv) to find out the possible reasons for favourable and unfavourable attitudes of teachers and students towards the semester system.

An attitude scale having twenty-six Likert-type items, selected on the basis of the initial responses of 50 students and 10 teachers, was mailed to 500 students and 150 teachers of the postgraduate departments of the Bangalore and Mysore Universities. The returns from 280 students (56 per cent) and 118 teachers (79 per cent) formed the final sample of the study. Percentage analysis and chi-square techniques were employed as statistical procedures.

The main findings of the study were: (i) There was no consensus either among teachers or among students for favouring or disfavouring the semester system. (ii) The system was favoured by both teachers and students on certain positive aspects. The system was found to be useful by them on account of the fact that it helped to divide the curriculum into smaller units, that the short duration made learning and teaching more regular and that it kept the students busy throughout the year. (iii) It was not favoured by them because the students were not oriented to studying under this system, they found it difficult to adjust themselves; it needed a lot of planning and there was delay in admission and the starting of classes. (iv) Both the teachers (96 per cent) and the students (94 per cent) tended to agree that the system could be successfully implemented with a smaller teacher-pupil ration of 1:30. The teachers and the students suggested that the orientation programmes should be conducted for teachers to work under the system. (v) Both the teachers and the students (80 and 85 per cent, respectively) favoured the system since it reduced the stress and strain on the mind of the students. But the students felt that the system reduced the opportunities for co-curricular activities to which about 45 per cent teachers agreed. A majority of the students (78 per cent) and the teachers (75 per cent) tended to favour the system as it helped to reduce the uncertainty of one's success by expanding the scope of evaluation based on the performance throughout the semester. (vi) The chi-square test revealed no significant difference in the attitude of the teachers of institutions for women and of those working in co-educational institutions. (vii) There was no difference in the attitudes of teachers and students of women's institutions, the disciplines of physical sciences and social sciences. There was a significant difference in the attitude of teachers and students of general education institutions and professional institutions. (viii) The students coming from different income groups and from different family sizes differed in their attitude towards the semester system of education.

41. STAFF DEVELOPMENT

A BOOKS

01 Naqvi, K.A., Chopra, K. and Kapur, Aasha. *Mobility and inbreading*. New Delhi, National Institute of Educational Planning and Administration, 1984. 128 p. (Research Studies. NCT - II).

02 Raza, Moonis and Fernades, Morjorie. *Professional and career development*. New Delhi, National Institute of Educational Planning Administration, 1984. 126 p. (Research Studies, NCT - II)

03 Shukla, S. Higher education and the teaching of teachers. *In* Amrik Singh and P.G. Altbach, (eds.) *The higher learning in India*. Delhi, Vikas, 1974. p. 409-418.

04 Chitnis, Suma and Altbach, Philip G., (eds.) The Indian academic profession. New Delhi, Macmillan, 1979.

B ARTICLES

01 Aggarwal, Bishan Swarup. In-service education. *Educational India*. 40(2), 1973. p. 73-79.

02 Amrik Singh. Academic staff colleges, *University News*. 25 (50), 1987. p.25 and 31.

03 Anjni Kumar. AIU and training of university administrators. *University News*. 27(24), 1989. p. 8.

04 Atma Ram. Faculty development and education. *University News*. 20(8), 1982. p. 269 and 272.

05 Baruah, H.K. In-service programmes for new faculty members. *University News*. 15(11), 1977. p. 299-300.

06 Bayti, Jamnalal. Role of management in in-service teacher education. *Educational Review*. 95(11), 1989. p. 198.

07 Chalam, K.S. Academic staff orientation scheme : Some crucial issues. *University News*. 25(50), 1987. p. 26-31.

08 Chaudhari, U.S. Professional competence of college teachers. *University News*. 27(45), 1989. p. 6-7.

09 Das, Mamata. Need for restructuring teacher education. *University News*. 27(12), 1989. p. 6-8.

10 Dwarakinath, R. and Rao, B.V. Venkata. Teacher productivity and academic standards. *University News*. 18(11), 1980.

11 George, Mathew. Academic staff orientation programme: A model. *University News*. 25(50), 1987. p. 22-24.

12 Guidelines in the implementation of faculty improvement programme pertaining to teachers in affiliated colleges. *Journal of Higher Education*. 15(24), 1977. p. 651-652.

13 Jacob, George. Orientation of college teachers. *University News*. 9 (12), 1971. p. 19-20.

14 Joshi, D.C. In-service education of teachers: Plea for new approaches. *Teacher Education*. 10 (4), 1976. p.17-21.

15 Joshi, Sucha. Professional Preparation of university teachers. *University News*. 25(50), 1987. p. 33-35.

16 Krishnamurthy, S. Professional education of college teachers. *Educational Review*. 76(11), 1970.

17 Mahajan, J.M. College teachers and professional preparation. *Educational India*. 34(2), 1967. p. 51-53.

18 Madan Mohan and Hill, Ronald E. Model for in-service education of teachers. *Educational Technology*. 15(2), 1975. p. 41-43.

19 Mahajan, J.M. College teachers and professional preparation. *Educational India*. 34(2), 1967. p. 51-53.

20 Nigam, Reghuvir Sahay. Training a college teacher. *Educational Review*. 76(8), 1970. p. 184-185.

21 Patted, G.M. Professional preparation of college teachers in modern democracies. *Journal of Higher Education*. 3(1), Monsoon, 1977. p. 123-127.

22 Pillai, N.P. Recommendations of the education commission on teacher education. *Journal of Education and Psychology*. 27, July, 1969. p. 125-128.

23 Puri, R.P. Training of university administration. *Eastern Economics*. 55, 21 August, 1970. p. 313-21.

24 Recommendations of Asian conference on teacher education. *University News*. 9(8), 1971. p. 8.

25 Seminar on higher education, 1977. In-service education programme in methodology of teaching for fresh and newly appointed lecturers of the M.S. University of Baroda. *University Administration*. 3(2), 1976. p. 37-45.

26 Should the university and college teachers be trained: A symposium. *Education Quarterly*. 15(57), 1963. p.20-26.

27 Sriniwasan, R. Professionalizing college faculty. *University News*. 28(8), 1989. p. 11-12.

28 Uday Shanker. Integrated course for teachers training. *University News*. 7(2), 1969. p. 16-17.

C COMMITTEES/COMMISSIONS/REPORTS

01 General Inspection Commission for the Training Colleges, 1963. Report. Madras, University of Madras, 1964. Chairman : A.N. Tampi.

By a resolution of the syndicate, the university of Madras appointed a commission to conduct a local enquiry at the colleges and submit a report on the present condition of the colleges in regard to the courses of study taught in the colleges, the number of students, accommodation provided, equipment and teaching facilities available etc. and also suggest such improvements as may be necessary with a view to improving the standard and efficiency of instruction in each Department of the College.

Commission recommended the Constitution of State Council for Teacher Education with representatives of the university government and the schools. The commission recommends the integration of training colleges with the schools around. The Master of Education course has to be recognised. Some select colleges may be converted into comprehensive colleges of education. Research ought to receive greater attention in training colleges. Extension service programmes are to be undertaken by every training college. The quality of staff in training colleges needs improvement. The salary scales of training college teachers should in no case be lower than these of arts and science college teachers. There should be a stricter selection of trainees.

The commission also made recommendation about accommodation equipment, library, practice teaching, evaluation guide teachers, model school, practical work, fee, method of instruction and curriculum.

The commission recommended that the degree awarded should be B.Ed. and not B.T. M.Ed. course should be thoroughly revised department of education should be organised in the university and facilities should be available in the department for research leading to the Ph.D. degree.

42. STATISTICS

A BOOKS

01 Ministry of Education. *Education in universities in India: A statistical survey, 1947-48*. New Delhi, Manager of Publications, 1950.

02 Mridula. *Educational statistics at a glance*. New Delhi. AIU, 1987. 193p.

03 Rajasthan, Directorate of College Education. *Higher education in Rajasthan at a glance, educational statistics. 1977-78*. Jaipur, the Author, 1978. 58p.

04 University Grants Commission. *India pocket book on university education, 1972*. 3rd ed. New Delhi, the Author, 1972. 261p.

05 ——. *Statistics in Indian universities*. New Delhi, U.G.C., 1970. 140p.

06 ——. *University Development in India: Basic facts and Figures, 1957-58*. New Delhi, UG.C.

43. STUDENTS

A BOOKS

01 Khusro, A.M. *Survey of living conditions of students of the University of Delhi*. Bombay, Asia Publishing House, 1967.

02 Oomen, T.K. *Students unions in India*. New Delhi, Visva Yuvak Kendra, 1971.

03 United States Educational Foundation in India, Delhi. *Student services manual: A guidebook for college/university teachers, counsellors and administrators*. New Delhi, the Author, 1965. 106p.

04 Weitz, Henry, *Organisation of student services in Indian colleges and universities*. New Delhi, U.S. Educational Foundation in India, 1971.

B ARTICLES

01 Amrik Singh. On student services, *University News*. 6 (5), 1968. p.3.

02 ——. Youth activity in the universities. *University News*. 15 (6), 1977. p.139-140.

03 Balan, K.R. Meaningful guidance to students. *University News*. 17 (17), 1979. p.455.

04 Bhatawadeka, M.G. Vital need for students services in universities. *University News*. 6 (4), 1968. p.8 and 23.

05 Bhatti, Surjit Singh. Students problems — An analysis by a student. *University News*. 6 (5), 1968. p.16-17.

06 Ghanchi, Dawoodbhai A. Students services programme for higher education. *University News*. 26 (15), 1988. p.1-7.

07 Joshi, Sneha and Desai, Nikhil. Students unions in universities. *University News*. 27 (41), 1989. p.1-4.

08 Mahadevau, Udaya, Guidance services in colleges. *University News*. 27 (50), 1989. p.8-10.

09 Mehta, Prayag, Some perceived needs and problems of university youth. *Journal of Education and Psychology*. 28, July, 1970. p.4-16.

10 Natarajan, R. Management of student activities in higher education. *Journal of Higher Education*. 12 (1 and 2), 1986-87. p.57-68.

11 Oommen, T.K. Nature and types of student voluntary associations at Delhi University. *New Frontiers in Education*. 2 (August), 1972. p.15-24.

12 ——. Role of student voluntary organisations in Indian universities. *New Frontiers in Education*. 1 (May), 1971. p.5-11.

13 Roy, D.M. Survey of living conditions of Meerut college students. *Agra University Journal of Research*. 5 (Jan.), 1957.

14 Sen, Satyendra Nath. Calcutta University and its student problem. *Science and Culture*. 25, May, 1969. p.189-192.

15 Shaffer, Robert H. Contribution of student personnel services to the improvement of teacher education. *Journal of Education and Psychology*. 27, July, 1969. p.176-183.

16 Sharma, I.R. Questions that baffle the youth. *University News*. 10 (8), 1972. p.20-24.

17 Sharma, J.D. Youth activities in universities. *University News*. 15 (8), 1977. p.207-208, 230.

18 Singh, Surya Nath. Needs and problems of university students living in 'digs'. *University News*. 16 (19), 1978. p.1210-1212.

19 Tulsyan, S.L. An exploratory study of students reactions in colleges and universities. *University News*. 20(19), 1982. p.614-615.

C COMMITTEES/COMMISSIONS/REPORTS

01 Student welfare in Indian universities. Report of the national seminar organised by World University Service (India) in colloboration with the National Education Commission, Government of India (Delhi, August 30-September 2, 1965) Delhi, The Author, 1966. 164p.

The focus of the papers contained in this report is on the problems of students' welfare in universities in general, and those related to students' health; individual aid; lodging and living; and educational facilities in particular. The report also carries a number of recommendations made in this regard by various participants of the seminar.

02 Committees on Students Welfare and Allied Matters, 1965. Report. New Delhi, University Grants Commission, 1967. Chairman: Dr. T. Sen.

The committee was constituted to suggest ways and means to improve the morale of and the discipline among the students in the universities and colleges. The committee suggested that education should be connected with employment, so as to bridge the gulf that separates a student's education for eventual employment. Steps should be taken to prevent political parties from interfering in the internal affairs of the universities and colleges. The committee has also made other suggestions for maintaining discipline among students.

D RESEARCH STUDIES

01 Amarsingh. Normative study of physical fitness of Panjab University men students, Ph.D. Phy. Edu., Panjab University, 1986.

The objectives of the study were: (i) to develop a test battery for measuring physical fitness of men students, (ii) to establish norms for the physical fitness of men students belonging to Panjab University, (iii) to establish norms for different age group of men students belonging to Panjab University, (iv) to establish norms for rural and urban men students belonging to Panjab University.

A sample of 4,000 students was randomly selected from forty different colleges affiliated to Panjab University. Their age ranged from 17 to 22 years. Physical fitness of the sample subjects was measured with the help of the Fleishman Physical Fitness Test Battery. The battery included tests such as — extent flexibility, dynamic flexibility, shuttle run, cricket ball throw, pull ups, leg-lifts, cable jump, standing broad jump, dodge run, 600 meter run-walk.

The study concluded: (1) Fleishman Physical Fitness Test Battery was found to be quite workable tool to measure physical fitness of men students of Panjab University. (2) Percentile and T-Scale norms were established for age groups 17 years through 22 years separately for each of the test items of Fleishman Physical Fitness Test Battery. These included extent flexibility, dynamic flexibility, cricket ball throw, shuttle urn, pull ups, leg-lifts, cable jump, standing broad jump, dodge run and 600 meter run-walk. (3) Physical fitness improved linearly according to age, with subjects falling in the age group of 20 years and 21 years having exhibited superiority over the other age groups taken in the study. (4) The students belonging to the rural areas were significantly superior in their performance on different items of Fleishman's Physical Fitness Test Battery, when compared age-wise to the students from urban areas.

02 Badami, H.D. A survey of use of leisure time among the pre-university college students. University School of Psychology, Education and Philosophy, Gujarat University, 1969 (UGC financed).

The survey was undertaken with the following specific objectives: (i) to study various types of leisure time activities among the college students; (ii) to study sex differences in the use of leisure time among the students; and (iii) to enlighten the community and various educational agencies about the need for effective use of leisure time of college students and to provide them guidance for worthy use of leisure.

The sample consisted of 327 male and 131 female students drawn from twelve colleges. Questionnaire was the main tool employed for data collection. The data were analysed with the help of t-test and chil-square test.

The findings revealed the following: (i) A majority of the group spent their leisure time in extrareading, tours/picnics, while very few spent in photography. Except extra reading, significantly more males spent their leisure time in tours/picnics, games/sports, and gossiping. (ii) A majority of the group was found to have interest in reading novels, short stories, and detective stories and very few were found to have interest in reading poems, essays, letters, diaries and criticism; practically no one was found to have interest in books on industrial and commercial arts, science and travels. Significantly more males than females had expressed interest in novels, detective stories, and biographies; comparatively more females were interested in reading poems. (iii) There was a significant difference between the level of interest expressed by both the groups — males and females. (iv) About seven students out of ten had expressed preference for social and detective movies; and few had shown interest for documentary, historical, and thrillers; significantly more males than females had shown interest in mythological, scientific, and documentary movies.

03 Bandyopadhyay, B. Physical fitness and respiratory functions in urban and rural male college students with reference to their energy balance, Ph.D. Physiology, Calcutta University, 1982.

The study dealt with anthropometric status, body fat, energy metabolic status, physical fitness and respiratory functions of college students and inter-relations between some of these factors. The differences due to domicile and habitual physical activity in both the groups of urban and rural college students were also examined.

The sample consisted of 705 male college students in the age group 16 to 24.5 years, stature 144 to 190 cm and body weight 32 to 90 kg classified into four groups, urban nonathletes (n=193), urban athletes (n=160), rural nonathletes (n=188) and rural athletes (n=164). The subjects were randomly selected from healthy male college students of several districts of eastern India. The data were collected by studying the subjects in their respective places (and not in a laboratory condition). The tools used wee harvard Step Test (for physical fitness), Dry Gasmeter (for respiratory functions), Skinfold Thickness Measurement at various sites (for body fat), Scholander Micrometer Gas Analyser (for energy expenditure) and an oral questionnaire (for nutritional status). In addition the thermal loads on the subjects were assessed by determining heat stress indices, using whirling psychrometer, Kata cooling thermometer and a globe thermometer. The statistical tools used were t-test, percentiles, product-moment correlation and regression coefficient.

The major finding were: (1) The body heights of the students of urban nonathletes (UN), urban athletes (UA) and rural athletes (RA) were same, whereas the students of rural nonathlete (RN) group were significantly shorter. (2) RAs had higher body weight than RNs but there was no difference in body weight between UAs and UNs. (3) Urban group had better nutritional status than the rural group, but the RA was in negative caloric balance, whereas other three groups were in positive caloric balance. (4) The daily energy intake of RNs was lower than that of UNs but on the contrary the daily energy expenditure of RNs was higher than that of UNs. (5) Body fat was highest in UN, then came in order RN, UA and RA; the caloric balance in the four groups was also in the same sequence. (6) In relation to the physical fitness and respiratory function, athletic students were better than nonathletic students urban and rural taken together; but there was no difference between UN and RN or UA and RA. (7) Habitual physical activity greatly altered the physiological status of the subjects as evident from the better health status of the athletic students, both urban and rural, but the difference in physiological status between the urban and rural students was negligible.

04 Chirackal, G.S.J. Study of student services in selected colleges in Madras. Deptt. of Social Work, Loyola College, Madras, 1970. (NCERT financed).

The objectives of the study were: (i) to find out the state of student personnel services in the arts and science colleges of Madras city; (ii) to study the effect of student personnel services on the academic performance, interpersonnal relations, discipline and personality development of students; (iii) to examine how far the recommendation of the Education Commission (1964-66) on student welfare services had been implemented in the colleges; (iv) to explore better ways of eliciting student participation in student services; and (v) to suggest, if necessary, better ways of organising student personnel services in colleges.

Fourteen colleges out of sixteen were selected for the study. Interview, observation and study of documents were used as tools for collection of information from students and members of staff of the colleges.

The findings were: (i) Out of fourteen colleges only six colleges conducted orientation programme and the programmes were better organised in women's colleges than in the men's colleges; (ii) the orientation programme had a positive effect on the academic performance, interpersonal relations, discipline and personality development of students; (iii) nine colleges had dispensaries attached to the hostels and only one college had a full time doctor, (iv) out of the 29,615 college students 4977 were residing in college hostels, (v) in the case of majority of male students who stayed in the hostels, residing in hostels had no positive effect on their studies but in the case of female students the residence in the hostel had positive effect on their academic performance; (vi) four colleges had 'day-scholars centres'; (vii) five colleges had guidance and student counsellors except in the case of one college where a full time counsellor was appointed; (viii) in all colleges students' unions were functioning; (ix) in all colleges, except two, the relationships between the principals and the unions were harmonious; (x) financial aid helped a number of deserving students to complete their higher education and secure university degrees, (xi) many Harijan students, who had no desire for counselling centres which were served by part time higher education, enrolled themselves in the college and the hostels just to get residential scholarships, and (xii) in some case rich students received scholarships which were meant for poor Harijan students.

05 Chitnis, S. *Drugs on the college campus, unit for research in the sociology of education*, Tata Institute of Social Sciences, Bombay, 1974.

The objective of the study was to make a realistic estimate of the incidence of drugs among college students in Bombay. Two art and science colleges of Bombay, often quoted in connection with the use of drugs by students, were selected for the study. The study was conducted in two parts. The first part consisted of a broad survey and the second part consisted of some case studies. While the survey provided a rough idea of the overall drug situation in the college scene, the case studies offered a close look at the students who used drugs.

The major findings of the study were: (i) Both the survey and the case study suggested that curiosity and boredom seemed to be the major factors that had prompted the students interviewed to try drugs. The influence of the peer group, the desire to belong with the hep crowd, and the desire of heighten sensations of colour and sound were some of the other factors mentioned frequently. (ii) A few students said that they turned to drugs to escape from the harsh realities of their lives. (iii) That drugs were harmful and the belief that it was unbalanced persons who needed drugs, were major factors that restrained students from the use of drugs. Fear of addiction and of hurting parents, and the influence of friends were other important factors. (iv) The peer group seemed to be at least as important in inhibiting the use of drugs as it was in promoting experimentation with drugs. (v) The majority of the drug-takers came from upper class homes. (vi) The majority of the students never tried drugs. (vii) The use of drug was largely confined to marijuana, which was non-addictive and relatively harmless. (viii) As many as 57.2 per cent of those who had tried drugs had used them barely once or twice or not at all during the course of two months prior to being interviewed, 17.6 per cent tried more than ten times, and 7.7 per cent used them more than 30 times during this period. (ix) The continued use facilitated experimentation with a wide range of drugs and increased the chances of graduation to the more dangerous ones.

06 Grewal, C.S., A Study of physical fitness, attitude towards physical activity and adjustment among university students across socio-economic levels, Ph.D. Phy. Edu., Panjab University, 1986.

The objectives of the study were. (i) to determine difference in three socio-economic groups in relation to physical fitness, attitude towards physical activity and adjustment, and (ii) to find out relationship between physical fitness, attitude towards physical activity, and adjustment.

The sample for the study consisted of 549 subjects studying at undergraduate level. They were selected from ten colleges affiliated to Panjab University, Chandigarh. The data for physical fitness were collected through AAHPER Youth Fitness Test comprising of pull ups, sit ups, shuttle run, standing long jump, 50 yard run and 600 yard run. The other tools used for collecting data were: (i) The Bhullar Physical Activity Attitude Scale (1976) and (ii) The Bell Adjustment Inventory (1937).

The findings of the study were: (1) The subjects of three socio-economic levels, i.e., high, middle and low differed on the variables of physical fitness, attitude towards physical activity and adjustment. (2) The middle socio-economic group was superior in physical fitness to other two groups. This group also had positive attitude towards physical activity than high and low socio-economic groups. (3) The socio-economic level groups differed in various components of physical fitness as measured by AAHPER Youth Fitness Test. (4) The middle socio-economic group was better adjusted to the variable of adjustment over the low socio-economic group. (5) There was a significant difference between home adjustment of middle socio-economic group and high socio-economic group. But there was not difference in home adjustment of high SES group and low SES group. (6) There was no significant difference in middle and low socio-economic level groups with respect to attitude towards physical activity. (7) There was a significant relationship between attitude towards physical activity and adjustment in case all the socio-economic groups. (8) There was no significant relationship between physical fitness and attitude towards physical activity in any of the three socio-economic groups. (9) All the socio-economic groups showed that there was no relationship between physical fitness and adjustment.

07 Gajjar, J.J. A critical study of perceptions of M.S. university community towards student personnel service. Ph.D. Edu., Maharaja Sayajirao University of Baroda, 1974.

The study was undertaken with a view to surveying and reviewing the student personnel services provided at the M.S. University campus and to finding out how far the university students, teachers and administrators were aware of it and to what extent their advantage was being taken. It also aimed at measuring and comparing the perceptions about these services among the various segments of the university community.

Using the stratified random sampling technique a sample of 982 students, eightythree teachers and fortyone administrators was drawn. This sample included 694 men and 288 women. Of the total sample of the students 105 were post-graduates, 625 were undergraduates and remaining 252 were preparatory students. The sample of teachers included eight professors, fourteen readers and sixtyone lecturers. Among the administrators were included thirtythree senate members and eight syndicate members. The data were collected mainly through specially prepared questionnaires and were supplemented in certain cases by non-structured interviews. The questionnaire consisted of six sections for students, ten sections for teachers, and nine sections for administrators; some sections were common to all while some were common to teachers and administrators and one section was specially meant for administrators.

Major findings of the study were: (i) the M.S. University community was not fully aware of all the twenty-one student personnel service available on its campus, (awareness for a given service ranged from a maximum of eightythree per cent to a minimum of two per cent); (ii) considerable difficulties were experienced by new entrants; (iii) the university community was not sufficiently clear about the impact of personnel services on students; (iv) among the students, variables like length of stay at the university, residential states, sex and economic level were related to the knowledge and use of services; (v) variables like age, urban-rural background and caste status were not related to the frequency and types of difficulties experienced at the time of entry; (vi) reactions of administrators, though, on the whole, favourable, were usually focused on the financial aspects; (vii) students as well as teachers felt that though adequate provision for student personnel services was not a complete answer to student unrest, it could play a significant role in preventing some undesirable occurrences and in reducing the intensity of some others; (viii) teachers who had either studied at or visited the U.S.A. perceived more clearly the importance and impact of these services than those who did not get such an opportunity; (ix) majority of administrators (teachers as well as non-teachers) had some confusion between the physical facilities and personnel services; (x) only about ten per cent of the administrators felt that the university should make efforts on its own to get finances for student services; (xi) teachers who had better personal contacts with the students and/or who were active members of the committees pertaining to students' affairs were more clear about the needs of the students and the role of personnel services in helping the students in various ways; (xii) the university was moving, though slowly but steadily, towards the fuller recognition of importance and subsequent implementation of student personnel services.

08 ICMR, Evaluation of internship programme at Department of Medicine, Medical College, Rohtak, New Delhi, 1972.

The investigation aimed at studying, how far the internship programme for medical students was successful, after evaluating different aspects of the programme.

The sample of the study consisted of 263 interns from the medical colleges at Agra, Amritsar, Chandigarh, Ludhiana, New Delhi, Patiala and Rohtak. Interview was the main tool used for collecting data. A proforma had been prepared for four categories of respondents, viz., (a) those interns who had started with this training programme in their respective medical colleges, (b) those who had just finished their internship, (c) senior professional teachers of various medical colleges where such a training was being imparted, and (d) doctors working in primary health centres, and medical practitioners. In each case, the respondents had been asked to reflect their reaction to the existing pattern of internship.

The main findings of the study were as follows: (i) Data indicated that those who had undergone this type of training evinced different and varied reactions towards it. (ii) It was found that there were certain types of deficiencies and irregularities in the training programme, which were responsible for failing to make it functionally significant from the point of view of the interns. This trend further revealed that the interns lacked clarity on their functional role in the system of this type of training.

09 ICMR, Follow-up of students admitted to St. John's Medical College, Bangalore, New Delhi, 1974

The present study aimed at a follow-up of students at different stages of MBBS course.

The follow-up study of medical students admitted to St. John's Medical College, Bangalore, was carried out on the basis of the students' performance in the pre-university course (PUC) and the entrance examination as well as their performance on some psychological tests.

The findings of the study indicated that the predictive validity of psychological tests was significantly high in forecasting academic success and training wastage. As compared to psychological tests the validity of PUC was significantly low in predicting academic success. The validity of entrance examination came in between that of psychological tests and PUC. The coefficients of multiple correlation and regression analysis revealed that the combination of psychological tests and entrance examination had significant precision of prediction at each and every stage of MBBS course.

10 ICMR, Socio-economic survey of Indian medical students, New Delhi, 1972

The objective of the study was to survey certain demographic and socio-economic aspects of the medical students in the country.

The survey was conducted at various centres in the country. The students in these colleges formed the sample of the study.

The highlights of the information obtained from this study were as follows: (i) Most students were from urban areas and were unmarried. (ii) Approximately two-thirds of the students came from families of the low income group. (iii) Guardians of most students belonged to technical professions or administrative services, very few being agriculturists. (iv) Thirteen per cent of the guardians were reported to have incurred debts for supporting their wards. (v) Most students had chosen this career out of their own liking. (vi) A little less than half of the students had expressed dissatisfaction with regard to the present curriculum. (vii) Regarding the methods of assessment, majority of the preclinical students appeared to be satisfied with the methods but more than half of the clinical students were dissatisfied. (viii) Majority of the students had expressed a need for more opportunities for practical work during the internship training.

11 John, P. and Abraham, M. A study of under-achievement among college students with a view of formulating a guidance profile, Deptt. of Edu., Kerala University, 1981 (UGC-financed).

The main objectives of the study were: (i) to identify the non-intellective variables which differentiate achieving and under-achieving college students, and (ii) to prepare a profile of the under-achievers to help in drawing up guidance programmes for raising the level of achievement of under-achieving college students.

The variables, studied were regularity of habits, optimism-pessimism, anxiety (freedom from), rigidity-flexibility, perception of reality, mastery of environment, sociopathic tendency (freedom from), emotional maturity, goal perception, delayed gratification, self-effort vs fatalism, attitude towards college, attitude towards optional subjects, attitude towards teachers, attitude towards academic work and attitude towards parental authority. The first eight variables were measured by available rating scales while separate scales were prepared for the remaining variables. The total sample for the study was 868 college students, of whom 616 were pre-degree students and 254 degree students. The number of boys in the sample was 455 and of girls 413. The achievers and under-achievers were classified by applying regression techniques by which 224 under-achievers and 644 achievers were identified. Achievers and under-achievers were compared for each of the variables by testing the significance of the differences between the means. Percentage differences between relevant subgroups were also tested.

The seven variables which differentiated significantly between achievers and non-achievers were: (i) Optimism-pessimism, (ii) Goal perception, (iii) Delayed gratification, (iv) Self-effort vs Fatalism, (v) Attitude towards optional subjects, (vi) Attitude towards teachers, and (vii) Attitude towards academic work.

12 Karandikar, S.P., Problems and conditions of students in the Poona University area. Ph.D. Edu., Poona University, 1975.

The major objective of the study was to identify the problems of degree course students in the Poona University area and suggest probable solutions.

The study was conducted on a stratified random sample of 2276 (about ten per cent of the population) arts, science and commerce students of forty colleges in the area of Poona University. The distribution of students was 894 in arts, 688 in science and 694 in commerce. The data were collected through a questionnaire administered to the sample; only 1545 were available for use. Fiftysix teachers were also interviewed to supplement the data. The various aspects covered in the study were students' socio-economic background, living conditions, facilities for studies, study habits, participation in cocurricular activities, leisure time activities, health habits, friendship, relationship with parents, relationship with teachers, expectations, aspirations, special problems of women students and insight of teachers into the problems of students.

The study revealed that: (i) students came from varied socio-economic background and a large proportion from rural areas; (ii) while rural and urban students did not differ in overall life aspiration, the former group showed clear preference for teaching profession and the latter for other occupations; (iii) rural and urban students were comparable in achievement, but the rural students were somewhat better in sports and games and other nonacademic activities than the urban students; (iv) the popular notions that the students cram guides, do not respect teachers, are indifferent to studies, are interested in agitation and are not ready to move out for job, were proved unfounded; (v) students expected efficiency and affection from college teachers; (vi) the generation gap between parents and students were not prominent as most of the students had no feeling of rejection for their illiterate and poor parents; (vii) deficient economic conditions was responsible for many of the problems; (viii) the women students represented highly selective families and they preferred to manage both home and job after graduation; and (ix) the teachers educated in the pre-independence era were not aware of the problems of students and seemed to be complacent of the present conditions of the colleges.

13 Krishnan, P.A., An analysis of the problems of college women students and their relation to intelligence and achievement, Madras University, 1977

The enquiry attempted to study the problems of college women students and their relation to intelligence and achievement. The hypotheses examined were: (i) The problems of women students would vary from the pre-university class to the graduate classes. (ii) Highly intelligent students would have less problems than less intelligent students. (iii) High-achievers would have less number of problems than low-achievers.

The sample comprised 300 students selected on a random basis from a college. The tools used were Raven's Standard Progressive Matrices and a modified version of Mooney Problem Check List.

The major findings were: (i) The low-intelligence group had significantly more problems than the high-intelligence group for all classes except the pre-university class where the high-intelligence group had more problems than the low-intelligence group. (ii) A significant difference existed between high-achievers and low-achievers in respect of problems faced by them. Low-achievers had more problems than high achievers in all classes except the pre-university class where high-achievers had more problems.

14 Kurrien, J., University and college hostels, unit for research in the sociology of education, Tata Institute of Social Sciences, Bombay, 1979 (UGC-financed).

The objectives of the study were to investigate the living conditions of students in university and college hostels. The study focused on (i) the provision of facilities in hostels and their utilisation, (ii) the profile of the students who lived in hostels based on their academic and socio-economic background, (iii) the staffing of hostels with special emphasis on the role of the warden.

Of the 2,933 hostels in the country, 827 hostels (28 per cent) responded to the mailed questionnaires.

The major findings: (i) There was a minority of hostels which catered to almost every physical need of the residents. There was a smaller group in which the physical facilities were grossly inadequate. The vast majority of the hostels fell between these two extremes. (ii) Provision of adequate facilities was important but not a sufficient condition for ensuring suitable living conditions. Provision of facilities needed to be complemented by adequate administration, supervision and an appropriate corporate hostel life. (iii) Most hostels did not adhere to the UGC norms for residential accommodation. (iv) In all the aspects of hostel amenities adequate attention was not paid to maintenance. (v) Hostels seemed to promote most of the objectives of residential living. (vi) A small number of hostels had an all-India character. (vii) In the vast majority of hostels, the residents developed an appreciable degree of mutual tolerance and community feeling.

15 Lal, V.B., Student union elections: A study of methods and finance, Ph.D. Edu., Avadh University, 1981.

The study aimed at tracing the historical development of student unions in colleges in India and the present practices of student union elections and the sources of their finances.

Two questionnaires were developed for the study, one for the student leaders and the other for vice-chancellors, principals, deputy directors of education, police officers, political leaders, librarians, administrators and parents.

The main findings were: (i) During the student union elections financial support was provided by political parties, many of which had their youth wings which were concerned with the organisation of student unions in educational institutions. (ii) Students got financial assistance from businessmen also. (iii) The student union elections led to the development of groupism among students. (iv) Caste considerations also played their role in the student union elections. (v) Students with academic bent of mind were less interested in union elections. (vi) The activities of student unions led to the spread of indiscipline in college. (vii) Student leaders were more concerned with their personal matters than with the general welfare of students.

16 Mishra, A.N., A study of the hostel-life of university students of Haryana, Ph.D., Edu., Kurukshetra University, 1987.

The objectives of the study were (i) to survey the various physical facilities available to the hostellers in the three universities of Haryana, (ii) to survey the opinion of the hostellers regarding various facilities available to them, (iii) to attempt inter-university comparisons on the opinions of the hostellers, (iv) to attempt comparisons of opinions regarding various facilities as expressed by rural and urban hostellers, (v) to survey and compare the general habits of the hostellers (H) and non-hostellers (NH) in the three universities, (vi) to compare the general habits of urban and rural hostellers in the three universities, (vii) to identify the additional facilities desired by the hostellers of the three universities, (viii) to select problems in some selected areas as experienced by the hostellers of the three universities, (ix) to survey the influence of hostel-life as perceived by the hostellers, (x) to attempt comparisons on the five different dimensions of emotional maturity and total emotional maturity based on (a) inter-university differences, (b) rural and urban differences, (c) H and NH differences, and (xi) to attempt comparisons on the five different dimensions on AICS and total adjustment on inter-university differences, rural and urban differences and H and NH differences.

The tools used were General Information Sheet (GIS), Observation Schedule-I (OS-I), Observation Schedule-II (OS-II), Emotional Maturity Scale (EMS) by Yashvir Singh and Mahesh Bhargav and Adjustment Inventory for College Students (AICS) by A.K.P. Sinha and R.P. Singh. Of the five tools, first three tools were prepared by the researcher himself and the last two tools were standardised tools. A purposive sampling method was employed to select sample from all the three universities of Haryana — Kurukshetra University, Kurukshetra (KUK), Haryana Agricultural University, Hissar (HAU), and Maharashi Dayanand University, Rohtak (MDU). The sample consisted of 600 male students — 100 hostellers and 100 non-hostellers from each of the three universities. Only those hostellers were selected who had been living in the university hostels continuously for four years or more and such non-hostellers were selected who had never been in a hostel.

The main findings were: (1) In KUK, a majority of the hostellers coming from urban area did not consider most of the facilities favourably while hostellers from the rural area found the facilities as adequate. (2) Almost all the physical facilities were considered as 'good' by both the groups of urban and rural hostellers of HAU. (3) Both the groups of urban and rural hostellers of MDU expressed dissatisfaction with almost all the facilities provided to them in their hostels. (4) Hostellers belonging to urban areas in KUK, were found to possess more undesirable habits than rural based hostellers but a reverse trend was observed both in HAU and MDU. (5) More than 50% of the hostellers and non-hostellers of KUK had habits like 'visiting religious places' and 'becoming regular in studies'. However, both the groups reported to have had habits of visiting prostitutes (H = 7%, NH = 6%), masturbation (H = 34%, NH = 25%), smoking (both groups 29%), drinking (H = 27%, NH = 22%), and copying in the examinations (both groups 14%). The percentage differences of extravagant (H = 28%, NH = 13%), homosexual (H = 15%, NH = 7%) and eve-teasing (H = 25%, NH = 12%) were found significant meaning thereby that the hostellers (H) of KUK possessed more bad habits than the non-hostellers (NH). Almost a similar trend was found in MDU as well. But the non-hostellers of HAU were found dominating on both good and bad habits except on 'masturbation' (H = 56%, NH = 29%). (6) In all the three universities the residents have demanded for better quality of food, permission to use electric appliances and guest room provision. (7) A good number of hostellers (74%) of KUK and 72% residents of HAU felt that they learnt courtesy/manners and received social/academic guidance in the hostels. Similarly 65% of KUK, 68% of HAU and 65% of MDU residents reported that their shyness was removed during their stay in the hostels. (8) The hostels generally did not provide residential accommodation for the wardens or any teacher except for the tutors. Generally undergraduate students have not been accommodated. (9) About 8% of the residents of KUK prepared food in their rooms without seeking any permission. Similarly, the residents of KUK (40%), HAU (60%) and MDU (24%) prepared tea in their rooms. (10). As many as 56-60% of the residents were found to have hung or pasted pictures of pin-up girls in their rooms. (11) Residents had the habit of smoking – 24% in KUK, 28% in HAU, 30% in MDU while they used wine - 8% in KUK, 10% each in HAU and MDU. (12) The students of HAU were more emotionally instable than the students of KUK. (13) The non-hostellers of HAU seemed to be lacking social adaptability as compared to the hostellers. (14) The HAU non-hosteller group was higher on personality disintegration as compared to the HAU hostellers group while the position was reverse in the case of KUK and MDU. (15) Hostellers exhibited higher level of tendencies, like parasitic dependence on others, lacking objective interest and being unreliable as compared to non-hostellers. (16) Hostellers, on the whole, were emotionally more mature as compared to the non-hostellers. (17) Hostellers exhibited a better home adjustment and health adjustment than the non-hostellers. (18) Students of KUK have the highest level of social adjustment followed by MDU and HAU. Hostellers are found to be better socially adjusted than the non-hostellers. (19) KUK had the highest level of emotional adjustment followed by MDU and HAU. KUK topped in terms of educational adjustment of the students. (20) Urban hostellers were found to possess lower level of adjustment than the rural hostellers.

17 Raghavulu, C.V., Reddy, V.E. and Rao, R.M. The study of the problems of the Andhra University students. Deptt. of Sociology, Andhra University, 1967.

The main objective of the study was to examine the attitude and behaviour patterns of students, their interaction with the education system, and then relate these, wherever, possible, to the issues of indiscipline and unrest.

The investigation was an exploratory survey. Post-graduate students were selected for this study on the basis of stratified random sampling method. The sample consisted of eightysix students selected randomly from the departments of the Andhra University after these departments were initially categorised into three groups, namely, natural and physical sciences, social sciences, and humanities. Interviews and questionnaire were the main tools of collecting data. About one-fourth of the sample students were interviewed to gather data of the participants in activities of indiscipline. Besides, a select group of students who had been playing major role in campus activities were interviewed. Over and above the questionnaire and interview techniques of data collection, two check lists were used to know the pattern of utilisation of time by students and their attitude towards the present system of examination.

The major findings of the study were as follows: (i) Teacher-student communication had a vital bearing on the student morale. (ii) Students were not fully satisfied with the class lectures. (iii) In many instances of unrest, there was no relation between the immediate grievance and the amount of anger and violence let loose. (iv) Nearly half of the students joined the post-graduate class unwillingly in want of a suitable job, and they had no sense of commitment to the educational process. (v) It was found that the employment opportunities were the lowest in the social sciences; consequently, the leaders in activities of unrest mainly came from this area, although the extent of non-availability of employment opportunities could not always be correlated to the degree of indiscipline. (vi) Leaders of student unrest were very often characterised by rich family background, influential connections, excellence in extra-curricular activities and strong affiliation with political parties. (vii) A large majority of the students felt that their grievance got a better hearing from the authorities when represented by groups rather than by a single or few individuals. (viii) The students did not have faith in the existing cultural frame of the society since the normative values governing the behaviour of members of the society were not followed by the leaders. A large majority of the students felt that the standards of public conduct had been deteriorating, more so, in case of political leadership at various levels. (ix) A majority of the students did not have any serious commitment to the educational process. The examination system, the standards of teaching and the extent of teacher-student communication were decisive factors that shaped the students' attitude towards the pattern of utilisation of time.

18 Sayeed, S.M., Politicisation of the student leaders – A study of the leaders of the Lucknow University Union from 1948 to 1970, Deptt. of Pol. Sc., Lucknow University, 1973 (Lucknow University Financed).

The study attempted to investigate: (i) whether the student leaders were drawn from politicised families and whether the participation or non-participation of their parents had any bearing upon the emergence of student leadership; (ii) why did the student leaders get interested in politics and what motivated them to take part in unionism; (iii) whether the student leaders had really a natural inclination towards politics or they emerged as tudent leaders incidentally; (iv) what was the political standing of the student leaders when they entered the university and what were the forces which stimulated them to take part in active politics at the university stage; (v) what factors contributed to their emergence as student leaders and enabled them to capture the union office.

The sample consisted of twenty-six persons who were holding the offices of the president and secretary of the Lucknow University Union during the period 1948 to 1970. Information from the respondents was collected through personal interviews on the basis of a schedule prepared in accordance with the objectives of the study. Descriptive statistical techniques were employed to analyse the data.

The findings were: (i) The majority of the student leaders were drawn from impoliticised families. Student politics was not an end but a means to help the attainment of independence. Most of them took no interest in student politics during the college life. The majority of the student leaders entered union politics incidentally and they had never planned to be leaders in the student world. (ii) Most of the student leaders confessed that they hardly thought of entering union politics before reaching the university. The student leaders belonging to the first decade from 1947, unanimously contended that the merit of the student used to be primary condition for his success in politics. They attached secondary importance to the role of the youth organisation and the professionals in getting the student's prominence in politics. (iii) Almost all the respondents who held the offices after 1957 declared that leadership had little to do with the capacity of the students as the leaders were manufactured by the professionals. (iv) Student leaders wee of the view that it was the professionals who recruit union members, impart and political training and convert them into leaders. The respondents were of the view that the success of a student would depend upon the factors other than his own merit. Student politics became a costly affair and it would be beyond the limit of a poor student to take part in unions. (v) The student leaders were undergoing a change since 1957. The professionals assumed the role of the king makers in student politics. Most of them were found to have affiliation to one or another political party. They had every opportunity to be in touch with the prominent leaders of the political parties and in most of the crucial occasions they acted according to the directions of their party leaders.

19 Shah, A.B., Karandikar, S., Kulkarni, V.M., Palsane, M.N. and Patankar S.A. Problems of students of higher education in the Maharashtra State (in Marathi). Student Welfare Association, Pune, 1981.

Twenty-five different investigators studied different aspects of the students' problems in the colleges and universities in the State of Maharashtra. The various aspects studied were the problems of junior college students, post-graduate students, handicapped students, women students, students in professional courses, students in hostels, external students, problems related to extracurricular activities, sex and emotional adjustment, students' welfare programmes in the universities, student-teacher relations, students movements, curriculum, health and so on. The common objective for all the investigators was to identify the various problems, to study how they affected the student life and adjustment, how it had arisen and how it could be prevented and remedied.

Respondents for the above investigation were students, teachers, principals and other administrators and social workers. Factual information on the above aspects was collected through personal interviews, group discussions and in some cases through questionnaires. Content analysis of the available literature was also undertaken. The collected information was presented as descriptive and interpretative reports.

The report revealed a large number of students' problems in their specific contexts. The results and their interpretations provided a mine of hypotheses for more specific studies with more sophisticated sampling designs, research tools, and technique of analysis. The study brought to light a highly significant fact that students and teachers, in general, lacked awareness of the problems and their detailed analysis as well as enthusiasm to seriously undertake their study.

20 Shah, B.C. and Others, A study of guidance needs to the graduate and graduating students of arts and home science colleges of the SNDT Women's University in Bombay, SNDT, 1977

The major objectives of the enquiry were: (i) to study the educational and vocational aspirations of the students of graduate and post-graduate classes of Arts and Home Science Colleges of the SNDT, Women's University of Bombay, (ii) to study the relationship between the educational and vocational aspirations of the students, (iii) to survey their guidance needs, (iv) to locate the needs of students in relation to their entry into the world of work, (v) to know about the leisure time activities of students, and (vi) to study the experiences, of students who were employed and of those who had tried to seek employment. The tool used was a questionnaire consisting of thirty-seven items covering eight different aspects of the enquiry.

The major findings of the enquiry were: (i) Most of the students were engaged for marriage and consequently did not have any educational aspirations. Those who expressed a desire to study for personal development, selected academic subjects and professional courses also. (ii) The purpose of future educational pursuit had not crystallized in the case of most of the students. (iii) The intention to earn was higher in the case of students of the arts faculty. (iv) Teaching and clerical work were the chief careers aspired for by the arts and the home science students. (v) In the arts faculty, the highest percentage of students who desired to study further had offered Gujarati, followed by Hindi, sociology and economics. In the home science faculty the highest percentage of students who wanted to study further had offered textiles and clothing followed by foods and nutrition, child development and general home science. (vi) In the arts faculty, the highest percentage of students aspiring to work had offered economics and similar students in home science faculty had offered textiles and clothing. (vii) The main areas where the students needed assistance were: (a) choice of courses and further studies and specialisation, (b) occupational information, (c) assessment of their potentialities, and (d) information regarding sources of financial assistance. (viii) The main leisure-time activities of students were fancy work, reading and household activities. It was concluded that the exposure of the students to the world of work was very limited.

21 Shah, R.P., A survey of the problems and guidance expectations of the students of Gujarat Vidyapith, Gujarat Vidyapith, 1973.

The purpose of the study was to find out the guidance needs of the students and to plan out suitable guidance programme.

A questionnaire was prepared after making a preliminary tryout with forty pupils of standards X and XI studying in one of the secondary schools in Ahmedabad. The questionnaire for the preliminary tryout was prepared by an all India committee on educational and vocational guidance. The preliminary tryout was conducted with high school pupils in order to obtain reactions regarding their guidance expectations and thus to modify the questionnaire accordingly. The final form of the questionnaire was administered to a sample of 450 college students.

The major findings were: (i) provision for measuring special abilities of the students was felt necessary; (ii) a system of loan library could be established; (iii) it was necessary to have the guidance and counselling programme for the first and the third year students; (iv) an information centre was needed for disseminating the information about vocational training; (v) self-study materials were required to be made available for the students in Gujarati for providing self guidance; and (vi) students expressed concern regarding changes in examination system.

22 Singh, B., A study of personality traits of student leaders and non-leaders of selected Indian universities and their expressed opinion towards leadership traits, Ph.D. Edu., Banaras Hindu University, 1974.

The study was undertaken with the following objectives: (i) to find out the difference between personality traits of leaders and nonleaders and to prepare personality profiles; (ii) to find out the difference between the intelligence of these two groups; (iii) to find out the difference between the expressed opinion towards leadership traits of leaders and nonleaders; (iv) to make a comparative study of their academic achievement; (v) to determine the extent of relationship between the socio-economic status and student leadership; (vi) to find out the relation between ordinal position and student leadership, and (vii) to find out the relation between the political consciousness and student leadership.

The present empirical study consisted of 200 student leaders and 500 nonleaders. The sample was drawn from six selected universities of U.P., viz, BHU, Kashi Vidyapith, Varanaseya Sanskrit University and the universities of Allahabad, Lucknow and Gorakhpur. The incidental-cum-purposive sampling technique based on normative survey was adopted in case of both the groups – leaders and nonleaders. The tools used were: (i) the Indian Adaptation of the 16 PF Test by Jalota and Kapoor, (ii) the 16 PF Test (Factor B – intelligence) and the Joshi Group Test of General Mental Ability, (iii) Leadership Trait Investory developed by the investigator, and (iv) General Information Sheet developed by the investigator. The statistical techniques used were: critical ratio, chi-square, t-values, product moment correlation, and cluster analysis.

The main findings of the study were as follows: (i) The student leaders in comparison with the nonleaders were more warm and sociable, emotionally mature and stable, dominant, having stronger character or superego strength, tended to be more adventurous, tough and realistic, practical, sophisticated and polished, confident, secure, cheerful and self-composed. (ii) Both the leaders and nonleaders were more or less similar in their general mental ability. (iii) The leaders appeared to have higher self-image towards leadership while the nonleaders appeared to disagree with the leader's self-rating. (iv) The nonleaders were found to be better achievers than the leaders. They were more regular in the class and also secured higher percentage of marks at the examinations than the leaders. (v) The leaders in comparison with the non-leaders belonged to higher income groups and better educated families. (vi) The ordinal position had no significant relationship with student leadership. (vii) The leaders were found to be politically more conscious, participating in various occasional student movements, going to jail for students' causes, having a desire to become a leader in future and so on.

23 Singh, D.B., A pilot study of scholarships awarded at university stage, Madurai University, 1971. (ICSSR financed).

The aims of the study were: (i) to assess the economic and social costs of scholarships; (ii) to examine the extent to which the award of scholarships has secured its purpose; and (iii) to ascertain the real cost of scholarships.

For this pilot study the Thiagarajan Arts College, Madurai was selected. Out of 1,115 scholarship holders (of 1969-70), 103 were randomly selected and fifty scholarship holders, who had completed their studies, were also selected. For the collection of data three schedules were adopted: (i) to interview the scholarship holders; (ii) to interview the principal and the lecturers concerned; and (iii) to study the family budgets of a few selected scholarship holders and to elicit information from their academic records in the college.

The main findings were: (i) eleven types of scholarships were available, but the majority of students received their scholarships (80 out of 103) from the Harijan Welfare Department; (ii) the scholarships were given, on the whole, to deserving candidates; (iii) there were some cases of overlapping spatially between scholarships and fee concessions; (iv) the amount received on the average as scholarship by a college student was adequate, or perhaps more than adequate, to meet his educational expenditure; (v) academic performance of scholarship holders was satisfactory as it was found that out of the fifty ex-students who were scholarship holders fortyfive came out successful; (vi) it was reported that the payment of scholarships was prompt and regular; and (vii) excepting in a few cases, the amount paid as scholarship was utilise properly.

24 Singh, S.N., Needs and problems of university students living in Digs, Fac. of Edu., Banaras Hindu University, 1978 (BHU-financed)

The objectives of the investigation were: (i) to explore the family background, residential conditions and financial, academic, social and general problem of university students living in *digs*, and (ii) to find out the needs and professional aspirations of these students.

The study was undertaken with a normative survey design. The sample consisted of 1,000 students studying in different departments (viz., arts, social sciences, science, commerce, law, education, oriental learning, fine arts and agriculture) of Banaras Hindu University and residing in unapproved lodges built by profiteers in slum areas. The sample did not include students from the faculties of medicine and technology as none of them were living in *digs*. The religious break-up of the sample was 950 Hindus of different castes and 50 Muslims. Data were collected with the help of a questionnaire consisting of eighty items and through interviews. Only percentages were calculated for presenting the results.

The major findings were: (i) Students living in *digs* belonged to low and lower middle class families. Nearly 55 per cent of them were upper caste Hindus and the parents of 70 per cent students were either illiterate or had education only up to the primary stage. All of them came from poor families which had to support, on an average, ten members within an income of Rs. 3000 per annum. (ii) The living conditions and physical facilities available to these students were far from satisfactory. More than 60 per cent students in the *digs* had not electricity facility and used kerosene oil lamps. Nearly 70 per cent of such students did not have bathroom and latrine facilities. They either cooked their meals or took them in a shabby common mess. (iii) More than 70 per cent of the students belonged to lower socio-economic strata and managed their expenses within Rs. 100 per month. These students spent less on books, stationery and food than on clothes and cosmetics. (iv) Only 5 per cent students had all the textbooks. Their average annual expenditure on books and stationery was Rs. 120. The study centres established by Banaras Hindu University for city students were used only by 40 per cent of such students because of their distances from the *digs*. The greatest disturbance to the academic pursuit to these students was their neighbourhood as it was inhabited or visited by criminals, drunkards, and quarrelling and shouting people. (v) The social life in the *digs* was far from satisfactory. More than 10 per cent students had formed undesirable habits through contact with their neighbours, 4 per cent of them suffered from venereal diseases, 5 per cent had learnt gambling, stealing, and taking narcotics and liquor. They believed in religion, God, fate, etc. The percentage of atheists and agnostics was less than 5. They wanted educated wives but preferred the purdah system. (vi) These students were depressed by their poverty and their level of aspiration was very low. They were convinced that they had no future. Only 7 per cent wanted to go back to agriculture, 3 per cent aspired for higher jobs, the rest of them felt that if they got some clerical jobs it would be a boon for them. Only 20 per cent wanted to pursue higher studies, the rest of them were willing to leave them as soon as they got jobs. They preferred white-collar jobs with less salary to jobs which required manual labour but were more paying. About 90 per cent of them did not expect a first class in examinations, they just wanted to pass. Nearly 60 per cent feared that things were going to get worse for them with the passage of time.

44. STUDENTS UNREST

A BOOKS

01 Aikara, Jacob. *Ideological orientation of student activism.* Poona, Dastane Ramchandra, 1977.

02 Asthana, H.S. and Chitnis, Suma. *Disturbed campus. In* M.S., Gore, I.P. Desai and S. Chitnis, (eds.) Papers in the sociology of education in India. New Delhi, National Council of Educational Research and Training, 1967. p. 311-334.

03 Chandra, Prabadh. *Student movement in India.* Lahore, All India Students' Federation, 1939.

04 Cormack, Margarete. *She who rides a peacock: Indian students and social change.* Bombay, Asia Publishing House, 1961. 264 p.

05 Damle, Y.B. *College Youth in Poona.* Poona, Deccan College, 1966.

06 Datta, B.N. *Youth unrest : Causes and cures.* Bombay, India Publishing House, 1969. 64 p.

07 DiBona, Joseph. *Change and conflict in the Indian university.* Bombay, Lalvani, 1972.

08 Gautam, G.S. *Crisis in temples of learning.* New Delhi, S. Chand, 1972.

09 Institute of Constitutional and Parliamentary Studies. *Student Unrest: Problems and perspectives.* New Delhi, The author, 1966.

10 Kabir, Humayun. *Student unrest: Causes and cure.* Calcutta, Orient Book Co., 1958.

11 Kakar, S. and Chowdhry, *K. Conflict and choice: Indian youth in a changing society.* Bombay, Somaiya, 1970.

12 Lakshminarayana, H.D. *College youth : Challenge and response.* Delhi, Mittal, 1985. 95 p.

13 Mansukhani, G.S. *Student power in India.* New Delhi, Oxford, 1975. 110 p.

14 Mehta, Prayag, (ed.) *Indian Youth: Emerging problems and issues.* Bombay, Somaiya, 1971.

15 Nelson, John Peter. *Student unrest in India : A topology and a socio-structural analysis.* Munchen, Weltforum Verlag, 1973.

16 Patel, A.S. *Report of the symposium on student unrest and indiscipline.* Baroda, Cantre of Advanced Study in Education, 1967. 165 p.

17 Reddy, M. Muni. *Student movement in India.* Lucknow, K.S.R. Acharya, 1947.

18 Ross, Aileen. *Student unrest in India.* Montreal, McGill-Queen's University Press, 1970.

19 Sarkar, Chanchal. *Unquiet campus.* New Delhi, The Statesman, 1960.

20 Satyasundaram, I. *Student unrest in India.* Madras, Machilipatnam, 1976.

21 Shah, A.B. Student discipline. *In* S.P. Aiyer, (ed.) *Politics of mass violence in India.* Bombay, Manaktalas, 1967. p. 104-111.

22 Shinde, A.B. *Political consciousness among college students.* Bombay, Thacker, 1972.

23 Shrinivas Rao, K. *University discipline and law : A sociolegal analysis.* Hyderabad, Osmania University, 1978.

24 Singh, Amar Kumar. Academic politics and student unrest: The case of Ranchi university. *In* P.G. Altbach, (ed.) *Turmoil and transition.* Bombay, Lalvani, 1969. p. 204-240.

25 Singhal, Sushila. *Academic leadership and student unrest.* New Delhi, Newman Group of Publishers, 1977.

26 Singhvi, L.M. (ed.) *Youth unrest: Conflict of generations.* Delhi, National Publishing House, 1972.

27 Sinha, M.P. and Gangrade, K.D. *Inter-generational conflict in India.* Bombay, Nachiketa, 1971.

28 Srivastava, Harish Chandra. *Genesis of campus violence in Banaras Hindu University, Varanasi.* Allahabad, Indian International Publications, 1974. 106 p.

29 *Student unrest : Problems and perspectives.* New Delhi, Institute of Constitutional and Parliamentary Studies, 1966.

30 University Grants Commission. *Report on the problems of student indiscipline in Indian universities.* New Delhi, U.G.C., 1960.

31 Vidyarthi, L.P. *Student unrest in Chota Nagpur,* 1969-70. Calcutta, Punthi Pustak, 1976. 408 p.

32 Vishwa Yuvak Kendra. *Dynamics of student agitation.* Bombay, Somaiya, 1973.

B ARTICLES

01 Altbach, Philip, Transformation of the Indian student movement. *Asian Survey*, 6, August, 1966. p. 448-460

02 Anand, Adrash. Student movement in Kashmir. *Youth and Communism*. 2, December, 1959. p. 33-34.

03 Anderson, Walter and Pant, Alok. Student politics at Allahabad University-II. *Economic and Political Weekly*. 5, 13 June, 1970. p. 941-948.

04 Bajaj, K.K. Sixty second constitutional amendment and student activism. *University News*. 27(13), 1989. p. 1-3.

05 Balachandran, P.K. Anatomy of a crisis. *Seminar*. (166), June 1973. p. 23-28.

06 Chitra, M.N. A student strike in Mysore - A sociological analysis. *Journal of University Education*. 4 (March), 1966. p. 149-161.

07 Casual attention to studies leads to indiscipline. *University News*. 5(11), 1967. p. 9.

08 Das, B.C. Educated youth. *University News*. 12(10), 1974. p. 9-11.

09 DiBona, J. Indiscipline and student leadership in an Indian university. *Comparative Education Review*. 10, June, 1966. p. 306-319.

10 ——. Righteous cause in Indian student protest. *Malaysian Journal of Education*. 6, June, 1969. p. 82-92.

11 Dongerkery, S.R. Problem of student indiscipline. *Journal of University Education*. 1(2), December, 1962. p. 112-122.

12 Fonseca, C. Student power in Gujarat. *New Frontiers Education*. 4(2), 1974. p. 88-94.

13 Gandi, Rajnikant S. Conflict and cohesion in an Indian student community. *Human Organisation*. 29, Summer, 1970. p. 95-102.

14 Gangrade, K.D. Inter-generational conflict: A sociological study of Indian Youth. *Asian Studies*. 10, October, 1970. p. 924-936.

15 George, E.I. and Matthew, V. George. View of college students on student indiscipline. *Indian Journal of Social Work*. 30, July, 1969. p. 133-139.

16 Ghanchi, D.A. The student at risk. *University News*. 27(31), 1989. p. 1-5.

17 Ghosh, Sadlan Kumar. Student revolution in India. *Quest*. 70, May-June, 1971. p. 51-54.

18 Goetz, Ignacio. Reflections on unrest in the universities. *New Frontiers in Education*. 4, October-December, 1974. p. 18-26.

19 Goswami, D.H. Student unrest and universities. *University News.* 13(7), 1975. p. 7-8.

20 Jayaram, N. Sadhus no longer: Recent trends in Indian student activism. *Higher Education.* 8 (Nov.), 1979. p. 683-699.

21 Jha, Akhileshwar. Roots of campus malaise-I: Failure of palliative measures. *Times of India.* 6 April, 1982. p. 6.

22 —. Roots of campus malaise-II. *Times of India.* 7 April, 1982. p. 6.

23 Jindal, S.K. Student activism in Indian Universities: Priority areas of research. *Journal of Educational Research and Extension.* 25(4), 1989. p. 225-231.

24 John, V.V. India's lost generation, *Quest.* 3, December, 1957. p. 29-41.

25 —. Student unrest. *Quest.* (61), April-June, 1969. p. 63-66.

26 Joshi, A.C. On student unrest - Part I & II. *University News,* Vol. 5(2), 1967. p. 3-5 5(3), 1967. p. 3-5.

27 Kakar, S. and K. Chowdhry. Student leader and the strike. *Quest.* (61), April-June, 1969. p. 54-62.

28 Mahajani, G.S. Phenomenon of student unrest. *University News.* 5(9), 1967. p. 3-4.

29 Nagia, Bhupendra Kumar. Youth unrest in contemporary Indian university. *Journal of Higher Education.* 8(3), Spring, 1983. p. 289-298.

30 Natarajan, R. Management of student activities in higher education. *Journal of Higher Education.* 12(1-3), 1986-87. p. 57-68.

31 Parker, Clyde A. Student indiscipline in Indian universities. *University Administration.* 3(1), 1976. p. 16-35.

32 Parker, Clyde, A. and others. Student protest and administrative response in Indian universities. *University Administration.* (1), June-July, 1974. p. 23-40.

33 Sarkar, Chanchal. Variety of student discontents. *Round Table.* 59, April, 1969. p. 173-178.

34 Sayeed, S.M. Student Revolt in India: A study of student agitations in the university of Lucknow. *Indian Journal of Social Research.* 14, Dec. 1973. p. 179-193.

35 Schlesinger, Benjamin. Student unrest in Indian universities. *Comparative Education Review.* 6, February, 1963. p. 218-223.

36 Shah, B.V. Students unrest: A sociological hypothesis. Sociological Bulletin. March, 1968. p. 53-64.

37 Shamsuddin. Student indiscipline. *NIE Journal.* 6, November, 1971. p. 21-24.

38 Sharma, Motilal. Undercurrents of campus disquiet. *University News.* 16(4), p. 768-769 and 771.

39 Sharma, R.R. Behavioural deviation among students. *University News.* 27(1), 1989. p. 1-4.

40 Sheikh Imtiaz Ali. Problems of student discipline. *University News.* 23(13), 1985. p. 3-4 and 14.

41 Sinha, Durganand. Dimensions of students agitation in India. *Journal of Social Economic Studies* 3 (Sept.,) 1975. p. 193-211.

42 Sohal, T.S. and Gupta, Mohand Prakash. Students' motives behind strikes. *Indian Education Review.* 5, July, 1970. p. 97-106.

43 Srivastava, Ravishankar. Roots of discontent, Symposium on the causes of unrest on the campus. *Seminar.* (176), April, 1974. p. 14-18.

44 Student agitational approach in universities. *University News.* 21 (18), 1983. p.291-292.

45 Student unrest: An analysis. *University News.* 4(11), 1966. p. 3-4.

46 Student unrest: Convocation address by P.C. Chunder at University of Jabalpur, February, 1978. *University News.* 16(5), 1978. p. 800-802.

47 Student unrest - the other side. *University News.* 4(11), 1966. p. 1-2.

48 Tiwari, S.C. and Kumar, V.K. Students' attitudes toward political parties in an Indiand university : A pre-fourth general election study. *Political Science Review.* 10 (Jan. - June), 1971. p. 124-134.

49 Venkatar, Angaiya M. Student agitation. *Educationed India.* 35 (April), 1969. p. 335-342.

50 Verma, Pavan. Problem: Symposium on the unrest on the campus. *Seminar*, (176), April, 1974. p. 10-13.

C COMMITTEES/COMMISSIONS/REPORTS

01 Committee on students indiscipline in Indian universities, 1959. Report. New Delhi, University Grants Commission, 1960. 25 p. Chairman: Dewan Anand Kumar.

The main recommendations made by the committee include, (i) students should be admitted to colleges and universities on merit basis; (ii) to raise the minimum age of entry from 16 to 17; (iii) no college should be allowed to have more than 1,000 students; and (iv) university and colleges should take appropriate steps to bring about increasingly close touch between teachers and students.

02 Commission of Enquiry on Orissa Students' Agitation in 1964. Report by justice S.B. Burman. Cuttuck, Home Department, Government of Orissa, 1967. I: 699 p., II: 325 p.

Beginning with the problem of disquietude in modern youth, this report discusses in detail the background, the cause, the nature and the extent of students' unrest in Orissa. A comprehensive account of the individual incidents of alleged excess is also included in the first volume. The role of different groups such as press, political parties and the other organisations and individuals, the loss, damage or injury to person or property are the major topics dealt with in the second volume. The other topics of discussion are those related to the code of conduct and certain measures to be adopted for such situations in future.

03 Committee of inquiry on orissa students' disquietude, 1967. Report. Cuttuck, Education Department, Government of Orissa, 1969. Chairman: Biswonath Das.

This committee was appointed to enquire into the problem of students unrest in Orissa in 1967. In this regard, the committee was asked to deal with the following aspects. (a) To examine the problems of the students in general; (b) to identify the reasons of causes of the students disquietude in the state; (c) to recommend measures (both temporary and permanent) and priorities thereof, consistent with the conditions obtaining in the state to remove the causes of such disquitude and examine the recommendations made by the Indian Education Commission, Barman Commission and such other bodies on this subject; and (d) to suggest a code of conduct for individuals and organisations concerned.

D RESEARCH STUDIES

01 Chaturvedi, G.K., A case study of student agitation, Banaras Hindu University, Ph.D. Edu., Banaras Hindu University, 1981.

The main objectives of the study were: (i) to investigate the causes of agitation in Banaras Hindu University (BHU) during the post-Independence period, (ii) to cross-examine the reports of enquiry committee set up from time to time, (iii) to find out the socio-economic conditions of the students of BHU, and (iv) to find out remedial measures for the agitational activities of the students.

The investigation was limited to the preparation of case studies of six major agitations launched in 1958, 1965, 1968, 1971, 1972 and 1978. Data were collected through documentary evidences and eminent eye-witnesses or those who were concerned with the specific agitations of this university. The tools used were an interview schedule and two questionnaires for finding out the causes of agitation and the involvement of political parties in them. Incidental purposive sampling technique had been employed. Interviews were conducted with thirty-five individuals and the questionnaires were administered to 200 students, 100 teachers, 50 guardians and 40 administrators. All the subjects were directly or indirectly involved in the agitations. For analysing the data obtained through various tools, percentages, analysis of variance, t-test and chi-square test were used.

The findings of the study were: (i) The causes of the agitations might be classified into four broad categories, viz., political, socio-economic, administrative and academic. (ii) Political factionalism among students was due to teachers and political parties who had their vested interest. (iii) Regionalism, communalism-cum-religious sentiments, casteism and vested interest of the authorities were the main causes of these agitations. (iv) Excessive government control also came in the way of smooth functioning of the university and increased the interference of power group politicians. (v) More than 60 per cent students of the university came from families having a monthly income of less than Rs. 600. So the majority of students faced acute economic problems and felt insecure. The poverty-ridden parents also did not find time to guide them. This resulted in a mental conflict which prompted the students to become agitators rather than academic learners. (vi) The majority of the students (54 per cent) in this university came from rural areas and belonged to the first generation learner group. The gap between the rural background and the academic life of the university often gave rise to conflict which generally culminated in aggressive behaviour. (vii) The administrative causes were related to lack of proper facilities to the poor students and lack of attention towards the problems of sincere students. (viii) Due to administrative weakness several substandard students succeeded in seeking admission to various courses and polluted the academic environment of the university by exciting the fellow students for agitational activities. (ix) Hackneyed and traditional teaching methods, teachers not interested in academic pursuits, and overcrowding in classrooms were the academic causes of agitations.

02 Dasgupta, S. and others. The great gherao of 1969: A case study of campus violence and protest methods. Gandhian Institute of studies. Varanasi, 1972. (ICSSR financed).

The important aims of the study were: (i) to find out the *modus operandi* of the gheraos at Calcutta University in 1969, their genesis, objectives and functions; and (ii) to find out the roles of students leaders, university authorities, state government, central government, political parties, students fronts and the non-involved students in the unrest.

The data were collected from the documents, newspapers, social case records of actual events and case studies of (a) six students leaders, (b) teachers' politics in the university and (c) the students' fronts. Student leaders, teachers, administrators, political party leaders and uncommitted students were interviewed.

The significant findings were: (i) the movement was not a cross generation conflict and it was not a generation gap problem; (ii) it was a conflict of programmes and ideologies between different political and factional groups; (iii) it was not a creation of separate youth culture; (iv) the aim of students' fronts was not to create student power, but to aid their respective political parties; (v) the student movement was not an attempt to gain an identification; (vi) there was no intra-group unity; (vii) the movement was not an expression of dissatisfaction in the infra-structure of education system; (viii) the movement was a battle for power between rival groups of students to put up their own political party at the seat of the government; (ix) the battle was more of a psychological warfare rather than the physical one; and (x) no group intended to initiate violence but tried to make the other group to initiate violence.

03 Gupta, I., Obedience to authority amongst university students: An experimental study, Ph.D. Psy., Delhi University, 1983.

The objectives of the study were (i) to analyse the causes of obedience/disobedience behaviour amongst students of University of Delhi, (ii) to find answer to the following questions: (a) Is there a significant difference in the mean level of shock administered and percentage of fully obedient subjects in different experimental conditions? If yes, what factors account for these differences: (b) Is there any sex difference in obedience behaviour? (c) Is sex of the victim an important factor in evoking difference in obedience behaviour? (d) Do subjects experience any tension during the course of the experiment? (r) Do subjects relinquish personal responsibility? (f) Do subjects' predictions underestimate the actual shock level? (g) Are there differences between predictions of self and others? (h) Does normative information have any effect upon subjects predictions? (i) What specific factors account for the obtained obedience/disobedience behaviour?

The study was undertaken to judge the validity of Milgram's analysis of the factors of obedience and disobedience to the authority. Employing Milgram's obedience paradigm the study was planned in two phases. The phase I study was designed to examine the role of forces that acted upon an individual in an obedience situation, specially, the role of age, sex, group pressure, pain cues, status and frame of reference, and individual's obedience behaviour. The sample for this phase consisted of 140 subjects, 120 undergraduates and twenty graduates. The study was conducted on the pretext of a scientific inquiry in which the subjects were asked to act severally against the other person (a confederate) by giving him shocks under the commands of teacher authority. The measures recorded for each subject were the level of maximum shock administered, the level of maximum tension reported, level of subjects estimate, the maximum pain felt by the victim, attribution of responsibility to the experimenter, teacher, and reasons for obedience and disobedience behaviour observation made by the experimenter. The analysis of data was done with the help of analysis of variance. The second phase of the study was designed to investigate the predictions of the subjects about their obedience behaviour to the commands of the authority and to see the effect of the factors of sex and normative information on their self and other's predictions. The normative information was provided by presenting the break off of the subjects in the voice feedback condition. The sample consisted of forty-eight subjects, twenty-four males and twenty-four females; each subject was required to predict the maximum shock level for self, other males, and for other females, under conditions of normative information and non-normative information. The data were treated with analysis of variance and t-test.

The findings of the study were: 1, There was a definite sex difference. Male subjects were more obedient than female subjects. Female subjects were more obedient while working against male victims than the female victims, and there was higher obedience to male authority than to female authority. 2. In the absence of pain cues from the victim, the obedience behaviour increased in 'remote condition'. 3. There was an increase in obedience with age. Graduate subjects in 'voice feedback condition' obeyed to a higher level than undergraduates in the simple condition. 4. The behaviour of the defying peers accounted for lower obedience in 'group pressure condition'. 5. The status of the victims was an important factor in 'authority as victim condition'. 6. The level of obedience decreased with increases in status of the victims. 7. The prior knowledge of consequences of the act given to the subject enhanced obedience behaviour in 'induced frame of reference condition'. 8. Females and defiants reported higher level of tension and pain as compared to males and obedients. 9. 'Scientific purpose' and 'forced by authority' were the two main reasons reported for obedience behaviour. 10. The reasons reported for disobedience were 'unreasonable severity of punishment', 'forced by authority' and 'conducted the experiment', 'administered shocks on command, for attribution to the self' and 'incapable to learn', 'attribution to the learner'. 11. Females and defiants relinquished more personal responsibility than males and obedients. 12. Higher obedience behaviour was predicted by males both for self and others, and also higher obedience behaviour was predicted for males than for females. 13. The predicted obedience behaviour was higher under normative information condition than under non-normative information condition. 14. Self-predictions were significantly lower than others' predictions in no-norms condition, but not so in norms condition. 15. Self-predictions of the males were higher than those of females. 16. The subjects in the prediction group underestimated their obedience behaviour as compared to experimental group; female underestimated more than males.

04 Khan, S.R., A psycho-social study of tension in the college-going youth, Ph.D. Psy., Aligarh Muslim University, 1980.

The study was undertaken to investigate the psycho-social causes of tension in the college-going youth. The hypotheses stated were: (i) Uncertainty concerning employment opportunities was likely to be more among the high tension group of youth than among the low tension group. (ii) The high tension group was likely to be more vacillating in regard to the choice of traditional versus modern values. (iii) Tension in the young student community is associated with unfavourable attitude towards government, university authority, student leaders, political parties, police and parents and guardians. (iv) Tension among the young students was likely to be associated with inadequate communication between teachers and students. (v) Tension was likely to be greater among young students who hailed from urban areas than among those who resided in rural areas. (vi) Economic conditions could be a relevant variable as far as tension among the youth (students) was concerned. (vii) The patterns of responses on Cantril's Self-anchoring Questionnaire may reflect passivism or unrealistic level of aspiration on the part of the tense youth.

The sample of 704 students falling in the age group 18 to 22 years was selected from intermediate and B.A. first year classes of the colleges situated in Aligarh and Bulandshahar. The Sinha Anxiety Scale, Security-Insecurity Inventory and Cattell's Q4 dimension of ergic tension were taken as the measures of different components of tension. In order to identify the two required groups, namely, the high tension and the low tension of relaxed, the composite of scores on these three scales was used as the measure of tension. The modified version of the questionnaire developed by Chandra was used to collect data related to motivational aspect, aims and goals, values regarding family traditions and customs, intercaste and inter-communal marriages, attitudes and communication with the teacher. The level of the aspiration was measured by administering Cantril's Self-anchoring Questionnaire (Ladder Scale). The data were analysed by computing chi-square and critical ratios.

The findings were: (i) Uncertainty concerning the possibility of employment was significantly more among the youth having high tension than among the low tension youth. (ii) The high tension group was significantly more vacillating in regard to the choice of traditional versus modern values. (iii) Tension in the student community was associated with unfavourable attitude towards government, university authorities, student leaders, political parties, police and parents and guardians. (iv) Tension among the young student was associated with inadequate communication between teachers and students. (v) Tension was more among young students who hailed from urban areas than among those who resided in rural areas. (vi) There was no difference in tension between the high income group and the middle income group, and the high income group with the low income group but there was significant difference between the middle and the low income groups. (vii) There was more discrepancy, both positive and negative, in the aspiration and previous level of attainment in the case of the high tension group. The high tension group also showed the patterns of ratings which indicated sense of despair and fear of failure. In contrast, the low tension group seemed to be hopeful about a brighter future.

05 Majumdar, T., Academic leadership and student unrest — A pilot study, Zakir Husain Centre for Educational Studies, Jawaharlal Nehru University, 1974 (ICSSR financed).

The main purpose of the study was to evolve an explanation of the student unrest in the colleges and departments of the University of Delhi in 1972-73.

The sample of the study included (i) academic leaders (N=116) — formal (N=67) and informal (N=49), of which 47 were students and 69 were teachers; (ii) a group of 73 college and university teachers selected at random; and (iii) a group of 274 students selected randomly. Tools employed were: (a) the Teacher-Student Study Questionnaire; (b) the Interpersonal Communication Form; (c) the Allport-Lindzey-Vernon Value Scale; (d) the Sentence Completion Test; (e) interviews; (f) records available from the offices of the Proctor, teachers' associations and students' union; (g) newspapers records; and (h) anecdotes.

The main results of the study were : (i) The events of the year 1972-73 in the University of Delhi did not indicated a generalised pattern of unrest either in terms of campus/off campus or pure arts and arts and science colleges. (ii) About 55.56 per cent teachers did not spend adequate time on preparation for teaching. Their attitude towards students was of indifference and negative in case they supported the authorities. (iii) The existing academic programmes failed to gratify students' psychological needs at three levels, namely, cognitive, affective and conative and helped in fomenting student unrest. (iv) Although the relationship between intellectual climate and student unrest was significant, the overall organisational climate also affected student unrest. (v) Students indulged in violence and vandalism prematurely and under conditions of perceived psychological threats. (vi) The police and governmental interference affected the organisational climate, attitudes of teachers and students negatively, and encouraged the neglect of codes of conduct. (vii) Nearly 56.93 per cent of students listed economic insecurity as one of the important sources of students' frustrations. (viii) Political interest in Indian colleges and university campus was natural and real one. (ix) Student agitations represented complex, multidimensional and dynamic social behaviour of student groups. (x) Formal leadership was perceived more favourable in times of unrest. (xi) A substantial percentage of students and teachers perceived informal leadership as playing double roles or redundant.

06 Manaral, J.B.S., A study of indisciplined behaviour in Kumaun and Garhwal University Students as related to creativity and personality, Ph.D. Edu., Kumaun University, 1985.

The investigation was designed to study the indisciplined behaviour among Kumaun and Garhwal University students as related to creativity and personality of students.

The sample for the study consisted of 556 students from the faculties of arts, science, commerce, law and education in the universities of Kumaun and Garhwal. Of these, 353 were male and 203 were female students. Group Test of Intelligence for Adults by Tandon was used for measurement of intelligence. Personality Inventory by Yashvir Singh and Harimohan was used for assessment of personality. Verbal Test of Creativity by Baqer Mehdi was used for assessment of creativity and Anushasan Heenta Mapani (A Scale for Assessment of Indiscipline) was devised by the investigator for measurement of indisciplined behaviour.

The main findings of the study were: 1. There was negative correlation between the level of intelligence and the tendency to create indiscipline. 2.

The various measures of creativity i.e., fluency, flexibility and originality correlated negatively with the tendency to create indiscipline. 3. In general, tendency for creating indiscipline had positive relationship with extroversion for the sample as a whole. 4. In library situation introversion had positive relationship with the tendency to create indiscipline. 5. In the Kumaun University hostels introversion had positive relationship with the tendency to create indiscipline.

07 Sarkar, S.N., Student unrest in Bihar sactors underlying it, Ph.D. Psy., Ranchi University, 1965.

The major objective of the present investigation was to draw out all possible environmental factors supposed to be responsible for student unrest and then to survey opinions of teachers, administrators (academic), students and their guardians in terms of their agreement or disagreement on the factors identified.

The present study was an opinion survey. Questionnaire, interview, observation and information data sheet were the tools used in the study. At the preliminary stage, 104 opinion items were collected thorough interview, open ended questionnaire and survey of available literature. After screening, only thirtysix items were retained, which were then formed into a Likert type five point scale and tried out. After tryout the final questionnaire had thirtyfive items. The test-retest reliability of this scale was found to be high enough. After tryout stage a few hypotheses were reformulated pertaining to the different causal factors of student unrest. The final sample of the study consisted of 400 respondents including 100 college/university teachers, 100 academic administrators, 100 guardians of college/university students and 100 college/university students of which fifty were from professional and fifty from nonprofessional institutions of Bihar. In order to substantiate the findings of the opinion survey of different subsamples, student personal information data sheet was applied to a group of eighteen indisciplined and eighteen disciplined students. Observation and reports obtained from authorities or interviews also served as important sources of data for the study. In statistical analysis of the data mean, standard deviation, and correlation coefficient *(r)* were computed and chi-square test and t-test were applied in testing the hypotheses.

The following were some of the major findings of the study: (i) There was appreciable difference of opinions about relative importance of some factors causing student unrest. (ii) The respondents rated high those statements that were objectively most salient for them. (iii) In most of the items students of professional and nonprofessional colleges did not differ significantly. (iv) The absence of a full-fledged and properly organised system of coeducation was one of the contributory factors leading to unrest among college students. (v) The socio-economic and academic factors were considered by the sample as more important than the administrative factors in contributing to the development of student unrest in the state of Bihar; of course, the administrative factors were also held partially responsible.

08 Singh, Narendra Pratap. Frustration amongst youth (A study of the colleges of Faizabad Division), Ph.D. Edu., Avadh University, 1986.

The objectives of the present study were (i) to study the nature and extent of frustration among college youth, (ii) to study the level of frustration among college youth in relation to various socio-economic levels, (iii) to study the degree of sense of responsibility among the college students of arts, science and commerce streams, (iv) to compare the mean responsibility scores of the students of high and low frustration groups, (v) to see the relationship between scores of frustration and socio-economic status with the sense of responsibility, and (vi) to test the hypotheses of frustration in relation to socio-economic status and the sense of responsibility.

The research was a survey type study. The sample of the study consisted of 400 male students selected by employing stratified random sampling technique in session 1984-85 from Part one classes of B.A. (300), B.Sc. (70), and B.Com. (30) of six affiliated colleges of Avadh University situated in urban areas. Tools of the study were Nairashya Mapa (frustration test) by Chauhan and Tiwari (1972); Scale of Sense of Responsibility by Pandey and Upadhya; and a Personal Information Sheet prepared by the investigator himself. The collected data were tabulated and analysed using suitable statistical techniques.

The findings of the study were: 1. The average frustration scores of students of all the three academic streams were found to be high. Most of the students appeared to be lying above the central point of the scale. 2. The highest mean frustration score was of students of arts group and the lowest was for science group. The differences in mean frustration scores between arts and science groups was significant. 3. All the three academic groups had average SES but the students of science group were in better position. 4. Students belonging to low SES were comparatively more frustrated. 5. The distribution of scores on the test of sense of responsibility was normal. It was highest for science group and lowest for arts group, and the difference was significant at .01 level. 6. The mean aggression score of science group was lowest while it was highest for arts group. 7. The tendency of showing resignation behaviour was greater in arts group than in science group. 8. The youths of commerce group were found more regressive than rest of the groups. It was lowest for science group. 9. As for fixative tendency in behaviour concerns the youths of science group were found to possess high potential. 10. High degree of responsibility was noted among youths of low frustration group, but the picture deviated for commerce group. 11. A negative but significant correlation came to exist between frustration and the sense of responsibility scores. 12. SES and the individual's sense of responsibility were positively but insignificantly correlated with each other. 13. Negative but highly significant correlation between the SES scores and the level of frustration was found.

09 Sinha, S., Valuational generation gap in the view of students and their parents on student unrest, Ph.D. Psy., Agra University, 1981.

The main objectives of the study were: (i) to understand the dynamics of the student unrest from the point of view of students themselves, (ii) to understand the dynamics of the student unrest from the point of view of the parents of the same students and to tap their optimism and pessimism through imagination about the best and the worst educational, economic, political, religio-social and familial set-ups and their hopes and fears about them, (iii) to compare the two frames of references held by the students and the parents in order to study the points of difference and to measure the width of gap between the two generations, (iv) to measure the value-orientation and value patterns of the students and their parents, (v) to compare the hierarchy of values held by the two generations and to study the gap between the two, and (vi) to study the impact of the gap in values of the two generations with special reference to the prevailing student unrest.

The investigation was on a sample of 300 students from the colleges in Agra, studying in five faculties (arts, science, law, commerce and agriculture). The parents of the same students were also contacted for obtaining their views on the student unrest and their values; thus, there were 600 informants. The Personal Value Questionnaire (PVQ) was used to measure value-orientation and patterns of values for the students and their parents. To measure the aspects of the students unrest and other related educational problems, the researcher prepared a tool based on the Self-Anchoring Scale (Cantril) and the method of multi-dimensional ratings, extended by Rossi and Inkeles, known as QEU. Both the PVQ and QEU scores pointed out the generation gap in the respective areas. For statistical analysis t-test, chi-square test, correlations and Kendall's coefficient of concordance were used in the study.

The findings of the study were: (i) The generation gap was apparent in value patterns. Value-orientation gap was not statistically significant. (ii) There was growing dissatisfaction among students and their parents about the existing system of education in the country with reference to syllabi, teaching methods, the evaluation method, the examination system, the aims of education, the teacher-taught relationship and the standard of educational performances. It was observed that the situation was declining day-after-day and was becoming more and more serious. (iii) students were treated apathetically by teachers, district authorities and social and political leaders. The unrest among students seemed to be the natural outcome of the impoverished conditions, apathetic treatment, denial of facilities and, above all, lack of attention towards planning a better future for them. The behaviour of elders was also not exemplary and worth imitating. (iv) The picture of an ideal education (from the students' point of view) necessitated the need for developing a better and civilised person, the need for earning a livelihood, the need for the strengthening of character, the need for acquiring greater knowledge and the need for promoting world brotherhood and patriotic feeling. From the parents' point of view, the picture was similar but with a slightly altered order. (v) The students and their parents believed in democratic methods of introducing change. The role of parents, teachers, the principal of the college was helpful to the students whereas the role of educational authorities (Registrar and the Vice-Chancellor) and the district authorities was neutral and just. But the role of the police administration and of political leaders was not helpful to the educational set-up, resulting in more disturbances.

10 Tripathi, O.D., A study of student activism in a university, Ph.D. Edu., Maharaja Sayajirao University, 1981.

The major objectives of the investigation were: (i) to study the trend of participation in political and protest-type activities among the students of Banaras Hindu University (BHU) with respect to faculties and both the sexes, and (ii) to study the intensity of the student activism among the students of BHU with respect to personal, sociological, institutional, political and perceptual variables.

The sample consisted of 520 male and female students of undergraduate and post-graduate classes of arts, social science, science, technology and law faculties selected by using the purposive sampling technique. The research tools used were Activism Scale, a questionnaire and an interview schedule. The activism Scale was developed by the author with the reliability coefficient of 0.96 through split-half method. The statistical techniques used were analysis of variance and t-test.

The major findings were: (i) Seventy-six per cent male and 69 per cent female students took interest in politics and 42 per cent male and 50 per cent female students favoured participation in active politics. (ii) Fifty-two per cent male students and 30 per cent female students took part in active politics. The law and the social science students took lead in this respect. (iii) Fifty-one per cent boys and 47 per cent girls had some sort of association with political parties. (iv) Sixty-nine per cent students associated with political parties belonged to kurmis-koiris and 29 per cent belonged to kayasthas-vaishyas. (v) The association of the male students with youth organisations was low (only 10 per cent). (vi) About 88 per cent students pursued protest-type methods effectively for realising students' demands. (vii) The usual demands for which protest-type methods were pursued effectively were: postponement of examination, union election, admissions, residential facilities and opposing police entry into the examination hall. (viii) Fifty-eight per cent male students and 26 per cent female students had participated in public protest-type activities in varying degrees. (ix) Twenty-six per cent male students and 7 per cent female students had already participated in student movements in their schools. (x) Sex influenced significantly the intensity of the student activism (boys more than girls) but age did not influence the intensity of activism. Caste did not influence the degree of activism in either sex. (xi) The intensity of the student activism did not differ in the case of boys whether their residence was home or hostel, but the girls staying in hostels indicated a greater intensity of activism than their female counterparts staying with parents. (xii) The marital status of the students did not influence their degree of activism. (xiii) The rural male students showed a greater intensity of activism than the urban male students but such a trend was not seen in the case of females. (xiv) The male students from eastern U.P. and Bihar showed a higher intensity of activism than the male students from other States. (xv) The parents' socio-economic status was not associated with the student activism in the case of male students. (xvi) The students with a weak economic background tended to show more interest in the issues covering socio-political and union matters. (xvii) In the case of female students, parents' socio-economic status was positively related to the student activism; girls from high socio-economic status were high activists. (xviii) The male students from agricultural families were high activists than the students from the service class families. (xix) Educational commitment had a negative relationship with student activism in the case of male students but there was no relationship in the case of female students. (xx) The male students of the law faculty showed a greater intensity of activism than the students from other faculties. (xxi) The female science students tended to be high activists as compared to the art and the social science students. (xxii) Students' perception of guardians' political activities appeared to be positively related to the student activism in the case of students of both sexes. (xxiii) The male students associated with political parties like Janata, Congress (I). The students associated with the communist parties showed greater intensity of activism than those associated with other parties.

11 Upadhyaya, R., Student unrest — A study of the degree colleges of Eastern Uttar Pradesh, Ph.D. Edu., Banaras Hindu University, 1975.

The objectives of the study were: (i) to examine the intensity of the various causes of student unrest; and (ii) to suggest remedies to check student unrest as given by the four groups, viz., the students, teachers, parents, and administrators.

The sample of the study consisted of degree colleges from seven districts and affiliated to the universities of Allahabad and Gorakhpur. As many as 400 students, 100 teachers, guardians and fifty administrators were the respondents. The main tool for the investigation was the questionnaire, which was standardised for the purpose.

The study revealed that the following were the most important causes for student unrest: (i) inadequate teacher-taught contacts; (ii) defective method of teaching; (iii) education system being divorced from Indian conditions and needs; (iv) authorities indifferent to problems of students; (vi) future of students being uncertain even after completing the education up to degree course; (vi) inadequate parent-teacher contacts; (vii) recognition being given to indisciplined rather than serious and studious students. (viii) direct or indirect support of political parties for candidates at the time of union elections; (ix) abuse of student unions; and (x) secret association of teachers with students for the sake of personal gains and selfish motives. The respondents also suggested many remedial measures. Some of them were: (i) to motivate students and teachers to confine their activities to college affairs only; (ii) to set up finance committees to control the college union budget; (iii) to examine and check the teacher's role in helping the students by unfair means; (iv) to appoint and promote teachers on the basis of qualifications and efficiency; (v) to develop proper skills among students to make them self-sufficient; (vi) to organise parent-teacher conferences; (vii) to send progress reports of students to their parents regularly; (viii) to debar the indisciplined students from the membership of various college committees; (ix) to encourage teachers to visit students' homes and to contact their parents; (x) to set up a welfare committee consisting of the representatives of students, teachers, principal and the managing committee to look into the problems of students; (xi) to lay emphasis on extra-curricular activities in the college; (xii) to improve the management of the hostels; (xiii) to introduce mother tongue as the medium of instruction; (xiv) to change the teaching methods, to emphasise discussion method and to assign more home work; and (xv) to develop the feelings of nationalism and social service through the curriculum.

12 Vidyarthi, L.P., Student unrest in Chhota Nagpur (1969-70), Deptt. of Anthrop., Ranchi University, 1972. (UGC financed).

The major aim of the present study was to identify the factors which were of crucial significance in causing and promoting students' unrest.

The investigation was a social anthropological survey. Sampling was stratified and random. A total of 422 students from eight colleges and institutes of higher learning at Ranchi formed the main stratum of the sample. Two colleges, one at Chaibasa and the other at Daltonganj, were studied intensively as systems. In addition to studying the attitude of the students towards social, moral, professional, religious and political issues, certain student leaders were interviewed at depth, and the functioning of their unions also was studied at length. Besides interview, questionnaire was the other tool of research used. Over and above studying the community of students, opinion about student unrest was sought from sixtyfive guardians, fiftynine teachers (including principals of the colleges and heads of university departments) and fortyeight civil servants and police officers, by means of questionnaires developed by the investigator himself.

The following were some of the major findings of the study: (i) Although the students deviated from certain norms of traditional culture, by and large they adhered to it. (ii) Most of the students gave a wide berth to political matters, disfavoured Naxalite activities and were appreciative of governmental interest in student welfare. (iii) Attitude of the students spoke of their awareness and optimism about future career. It was interesting to note that a majority would like to take up the profession of a teacher. (iv) The students did not get help from their teachers in academic and personal problems. (v) Most of the students felt that college/university authorities were inactive in serving the cause of the students. (vi) In general, the students' link with their union was very loose, but, by and large, they did not like that outside agencies should interfere in their own union affairs. (vii) The guardians opined that political parties made the students restive. They did not approve of agitational methods of the university students, and wanted stricter control over their wards by the teachers, at the same time more intimate teacher-pupil relationship. (viii) The teachers located the causes of student unrest in interference and instigation by political elements both in teacher and student communities, tactless handling of police and magistracy, and in overall frustration of the young generation due to economic and political conditions prevailing in the country. (ix) According to the majority of the administrators instigation by the political leaders, mismanagement of the affairs of examination and evaluation, and resentment and grievance against authorities were the most potent causes of student unrest. The general impression of the administrators regarding the student unrest were (a) that only few students engineered disturbances and their militant attitude threatened other students to join them; (b) that the strikes and disturbances were launched on the genuine grievances of the students, which were not redressed in time; and (c) in strikes the students were provoked and misguided by outside elements including the political bosses. (d) In the background region of Chhota Nagpur, student unrest was caused generally by disintegration of academic values and sinister influence of the politically motivated students.

The study provided the historical background of education in India as well as Mauritius, and an appraisal of existing pattern of education in Mauritius. Following the description of variety of educational patterns in different States of India, and study revealed that the prevailing pattern of education in Mauritius comprised seven years of primary education followed by five years of secondary education and two years of higher secondary education, or by a seven year technical education. The higher secondary education was followed by three year university education leading to a diploma. However, the proposed model envisaged three years of foundation education followed by eight years of general education at junior stage and four years at senior stage. The university education or in-service training for three years would start after this senior stage. Professional education also should start simultaneously after the junior stage of general education. The university education in Mauritius started only in 1968. In 1968-69, there were only 869 students enrolled in the school of agriculture, school of administration and school of industrial technology. The number of participants in seminars and school term courses was 428. The university administration was carried out under the authority of provisional council by the academic board or the provisional senate, the boards of schools of agriculture, administration and industrial technology, student affairs committee, etc. An alternative form was proposed in the thesis and in the new structure great emphasis was placed on the starting of a department of education. Regarding the aims of education, the author accepted the line of the Education Commission (1964-66) of India where education was visualised to be related to productivity, strengthening social and national integration, hastening the process of modernisation and striving to build character by cultivating social, moral and spiritual values.

13 Wangu, R.S., Socio-psychological correlates of disciplined-indisciplined behaviour among university students, Ph.D. Edu., Panjab University, 1980.

The major hypotheses of the study were: (i) the values were significantly related to the disciplined-indisciplined behaviour tendencies in university students, (ii) personality characteristics, some factors in the environment, and socio-economic status formed significant correlates of the tendency to indulge in disciplined and indisciplined acts by the students, (iii) the disciplined and the indisciplined students differed from each other in terms of values, personality characteristics, perception of environmental press, and socio-economic status, (iv) the tendency to create disciplined and indisciplined behaviour varied with sex, and from one faculty to the other, (v) the variables of values, personality characteristics, environmental press, and socio-economic status clustered together in different factors underlying the disciplined-indisciplined behaviour, and (vi) the faculty-to-faculty differences existed in respect of different constellations of variables explaining the common factor variance in different factors.

The study was completed in two phases. Six hundred and ninety-eight students and 58 teachers of the Panjab University formed the sample for the first phase in which the Discipline-Indiscipline (D-I) Scale and Socio-Economic Status (SES) Inquiry Form were standardised. The final sample in the second phase comprised 352 students. The statistics used in the first phase for the standardisation of D-I scale were median, interquartile range, point-biserial coefficient of correlation, product moment coefficient of correlation and the technique of factor analysis. In the second phase descriptive statistics such as mean, median, standard deviation, skewness, and kurtosis were calculated. Product moment coefficient of correlation, factor analysis, and t-ratios were also used.

The major findings of the study were: (i) Values, personality characteristics, environmental factors and SES correlated significantly with different measures of disciplined and indisciplined behaviour, for different groups of students. (ii) Disciplined and indisciplined students differed from each other in terms of values, personality characteristics, and SES but not in the perception of environmental press. (iii) The sex of the student affected the disciplined or otherwise behaviour. (iv) All the four variables mentioned above clustered together in creating disciplined or otherwise behaviour. (v) The faculty-to-faculty differences were significant in the behaviour pattern of the students. (vi) In general, the lower level of intelligence, lack of acceptance of group moral standards, insecurity, independent mindedness, lack of botheration, apprehensiveness, low frustration tolerance and higher level of assertiveness were associated with indisciplined behaviour. Some of these were more dominant in girls and others in boys and the same held true for different faculties.

45. TEACHER EVALUATION

A BOOKS

01 *Task Force on Performance Appraisal of Teachers,* U.G.C. Report: Considered and adopted by the commission in its meeting held on Nov. 4, 1988. New Delhi, U.G.C., 1988. 17p.

B ARTICLES

01 Amrik Singh. Incompetent teachers. The case for periodic assessment. *University News.* 14 (2), 1976. p.4 and 21.

02 Banerji, R.C. Who should rate teachers? *Education Review.* 49 (1), 1973. p.249-53.

03 Bansal, G.D. Evaluation of teacher. *Seminar.* (196), 1975. p.64-67.

04 Bhatt, Anil and Shukul, H.C. Evaluation of teacher by students. *Journal of Higher Education.* 2 (3), 1977. p.413-418.

05 Chanda, S.M. Assessing teacher's ability. *University News.* 20 (11), 1982. p.371.

06 Dass, P.C. Sample study of evaluation of teachers by students. *Quest in Education.* 11 (3), 1977. p.222-232.

07 Kapoor, A.D. Integrated assessment of a teacher performance. *Seminar.* (196), 1975. p.47-52.

08 Lamba, S.S. Research vs teaching: Some insights with reference to teacher evaluation. *Seminar.* (196), 1975. p.38-43.

09 Portia, D.R. Criteria for evaluating teacher's efficiency in the universities. *University News.* 19 (16), 1981. p.499 and 467.

10 Rao, P.V. Faculty evaluation programme as an aid to self-criticism and self-development of teacher. *Seminar.* (196), 1975. p. 1-7.

11 Samant, D.G. Implications of grades for university teachers. *Progress of Education.* 51 (12), July, 1977. p.218-220.

12 Saraswathi, L.S. Teacher evaluation by the taught. *Journal of Higher Education.* 1 (3), 1976. p.315-324.

13 Sharma, J.R. Assessment of teacher's work. *Education.* 34 (11), November, 1955. p.3-6.

14 Sood, Nandita. Teacher evaluation. *Seminar.* (196), 1975. p.12-17.

D RESEARCH STUDIES

01 Kulshrestha, N.K. An approach to the appraisal of the performance of college teachers in Rajasthan Educational Service, The HCM State Institute of Public Administration, Jaipur, 1977.

The study attempted to suggest an approach to the formats of annual performance appraisal of college teachers of Rajasthan Education Service. The investigator adopted a systems approach to appraisal. Instead of appraising the college teachers, the performance of a college unit was appraised.

The important conclusions of the study were: (i) The key areas of college where performance could fbe judged were academic performance—teaching and research, curricular and extra-curricular activity and extension services. Extension services represented an area of social change. (ii) The points to be taken into consideration in appraising teaching performance were quantity and quality of teaching, contribution to library and teaching insights which reflect the effort expanded. (iii) While appraising academic growth of a college teacher, the following factors might be incorporated in the departmental formats: (a) the number of books reviewed, (b) the number of papers/articles published with the names of journals, (c) the number of articles published after acquiring Ph.D., (d) whether he had been awarded Ph.D./was doing Ph.D. If he had been awarded Ph.D., whether the thesis was published, (e) how the publication of Ph.D. thesis had been financed — personal/ICSSR grant/publisher, (f) the papers read and contributed in seminars, (g) seminars, workshops, summer schools directed (for senior persons only), (h) seminars attempted at his own cost, (i) membership of professional societies, etc. (iv) In appraising the potential of college teachers, the departmental format might incorporate the following points: (a) attitude adopted toward the principal during crisis in the college, (b) his specific contribution by way of suggestion as a faculty member or incharge or a member of committee formed, (c) any innovative idea given which might increase efficiency or economise college administration, (d) any practicable suggestion given for furtherance of research and modification in RES rules, (e) in the case of a new college, his contributions to its growth and development, (f) his specific contribution to social service — NSS and national calamities, and (g) his assistance in building the image of the institution. (v) In appraising the college principals, the following areas need to be incorporated in the proforma: (a) management of growth of the institution in terms of population, (b) faculty development and research, (c) innovation in administration in administrative procedures, information systems, and conduct of examination, (d) management of crisis, (e) college environment as reflected by academic, extra-curricular and extension activities and discipline, (f) stability in organisation as reflected by better human relationships in the college, (g) building the image of the institutions, (h) proper communication system and grievance procedure, and (i) organising ability in the case of a new college.

02 Ramanamma, A. and Bambawala, U. Academic role performance and modernisation, Deptt. of Soc., Poona University, 1979.

The major aims of the study were: (i) to assess whether the university teacher was modern in his approach to the university as a system, (ii) to assess his self-image, and (iii) to know how far his performance was in keeping with the needs of his role. The emphasis was on the measurement of the levels of modernisation through aspiration, commitment and authoritarianism among the teachers.

The study followed an intensive pattern of inquiry. Academicians' education and academic commitments were the independent variables and the quality of academic role performance and the modernisation of university teachers were the dependent variables. The sample comprised 155 teachers selected on quota sampling basis out of the 300 teachers of the departments of Poona University in the faculty of arts, social sciences, science and law. The research tool was a questionnaire substantiated with a personal interview. It covered three areas, namely, bio-data, teaching commitment and ideas of modernity. Factor analysis was the statistical technique used for data analysis.

The major findings were: (i) There was a great disparity between the socio-economic background of the men and women teachers in Poona University. Such a disparity did not exist in the case of the enrolment of the student community. A clear bias in favour of employing men in faculty positions was seen. (ii) A greater number of teachers were married, in the age group of 31-45 years, and they belonged to higher castes. They come from homes where a climate for higher education prevailed. It was found that the social structure of the academic profession was relatively closed in favour of traditionally better-placed groups. (iii) Conflicting values of ingroup feeling and westernisation were evident. However, in spite of high ingroup feeling, the teachers showed remarkably high percentage of westernisation. (iv) The factor analysis of modernization scale yielded some important dimensions for teaching like political affiliation and westernisation. The presence of a high ingroup feeling could be due to the psycho-cultural contingency. Commitment and to some degree the levels of aspiration entered the academic role structure as significant variables in the context of modernisation. Aspiration was determined mainly by academic self-image and prevailing conditions. (v) One-third of the teachers did not have a doctoral degree. A great many of them were in the profession for more than eight years and were well-acquainted with their role performance. (vi) Art teachers had radication syndrome whereas science teachers showed stoicism. (vii) A majority of the teachers adhered to the syllabus and about half of the teachers did not encourage discussions in the classroom. Sixty-two per cent teachers spent a limited time for preparing lectures, sixty-six per cent read only textbooks, fifty-eight per cent regularly read newspapers, indicating the lack of modern trends amongst the teachers. Seventy-two per cent had contributed papers to various journals. (viii) Twenty-five per cent teachers felt that their salary was high and twenty per cent felt that it was low. Recognition in the profession was very high in the case of the majority of the teachers and yet they expressed some dissatisfaction. It was also found that a considerable number of teachers had selected teaching as a second choice and about twenty per cent wanted to make a change for better remunerative jobs. A majority of the teachers preferred their children accepting jobs other than teaching, as the first choice. Nearly fifty per cent aspired for migrating to foreign countries. (ix) The factor analysis did not point out one single important factor accounting for modernisation. A concensus of values helped towards modernisation.

03 Umadevi, S. Organisational goal, organisational climate and faculty performance assessment — A case study of Andhra University, Ph.D. Soc., Andhra University, 1983.

The objectives of the study were: (i) to study the organisational climate and measure it as per the faculty performance, and (ii) to find out relationship between faculty performance and two climates measured by indirect and alternative ways.

The sample for the study consisted of eighty teachers of various categories, viz., professors (N=20), readers (N=20) and lecturers (N=40). The data were collected with the help of a questionnaire consisting of three parts. The part one was related to background information of the university faculty and indicators of academic performance, the second part consisted of items designed to measure perceived importance and perceived attainment of university goals and part three comprised small set of items designed to measure the climate phenomenon directly.

The findings of the study were: (1) There was consensus over the goals of providing extension courses for part-time students and providing consultancy and guidance. (2) The faculties perceived skill goals even more important than the teaching and research goals. The faculty perceived that university goals were rational, realistic and highly professional. Further there was no significant difference in the perception of goals among the three faculty categories. (3) Regarding attainment of university goals, it was found that perceived attainment had never come close to perceived importance for any of the research and teaching goals. A consistent goal failure was reported and this was more prominent in research goals than in teaching goals. (4) With regard to extension and other social functions it was found that there were considerable goal gaps. Their consistant goal failures, faculty thought, led to low climate of the university organisation. (5) The important factors to reckon with in the analysis of university organisation were identified as university management on one hand and the student community on the other. (6) There was no relationship between the age of the faculty members and perception about university climate. (7) The climate evaluation of arts faculty teachers was significantly different and lower than that of science and technology group. (8) The goal attainment failure in Andhra University was high and wide spread in the areas related to research and promotions. (9) The performance profile of the university faculty revealed that there were significant differences in readers and lecturers with respect to journal-article publications. But these differences were not significant between arts and science groups. Further engineering group had the lowest performance with respect to journal-article publication. (10) Age of the faculty members was found to be the promoter of academic output, academic attainment, and academic affiliation and organisations. (11) The multiple correlation revealed that it was the age of the respondent and not the global university climate which determined the performance of the faculty members. (12) The climate factor of the university had less to do with faculty performance and more to do with faculty satisfaction.

46. TEACHER ROLE AND RESPONSIBILITY

A BOOKS

01 Ahmed, Shakti R. and Luthra, S.N. *Work ethos*. New Delhi, National Institute of Educational Planning and Administration, 1984. 180p. (Research Studies. NCT-II).

02 Chitnis, S. Teachers in higher education. In Amrik Singh and P.G. Altbach, (eds.) *The higher learning in India*. Delhi, Vikas, 1974. p. 237-48.

03 Dongerkery, S.R. *Role of the university teacher in a changing society*. Ahmedabad, Harold Laski Institute of Political Science. 1962.

04 Dube, S.C. and Swarup, Hemlata. *Professional values*. New Delhi, National Institute of Educational Planning and Administration, 1984. 52 + xxi p. (Research Studies, NCT-II).

05 John, V.V. *Orbiting professor*. Bombay, Pearl Publication, 1970.

06 National Seminar on Sociology of the Teaching Profession in India, 1968. *Sociology of the teaching profession in India*. New Delhi, National Council of Educational Research and Training, 1970.

07 Shils, E. Influence and withdrawal : The intellectuals in Indian political development. In. Dwaine Marvick, (ed.) *Political decision-makers*. New York, Free Press, 1961. p. 29-56.

08 Sinha, D.N. *Social status*. New Delhi, National Institute of Educational Planning and Administration, 1984. 56p. (Research Studies. NCT-II).

09 *Task Force on Code of Professional Ethics for University and College Teachers*, 1988. Report. New Delhi, U.G.C., 1989. 6p.

10 University Grants Commission. *Role and responsibility of teachers*. New Delhi, U.G.C., 1981. 59p.

B ARTICLES

01 Amrik Singh. On being a teacher. *Mainstream.* 23 (22), 1985. p. 43-45.

02 Chaudhari, U.S. Professional competence of college teachers. *University News*, 27 (45), 1989. p. 6-7.

03 Desai, B.H. Teachers in higher education. University News. 25 (16), 1987. p.6-8.

04 Filella, J. College professor. *Quest.* (71), July-August, 1971. p. 63-67.

05 Gilbert, I. Indian academic profession: The origins of a tradition of subordination. *Minerva.* 10, July 1972. p. 384-411.

06 Jagjit Singh, K. Code of professional ethics for teachers. *University News.* 25 (50), 1987. p. 17-21.

07 Joseph, K.J. Changing role of the teachers. *New Frontiers in Education.* 1, August 1971. p. 173-76.

08 Krishnamurthy, S. Professional ethics for college teachers. *Educational Review.* 77, January 1971. p. 2-5.

09 Mahajan, J.M. College teachers and professional preparations. *Progress in Education.* 44, July 1970. p. 422-25.

10 Reddy, G. Ram. Value orientation in education. *University News.* 25 (41), 1987. p. 1-3.

11 Shils, E. Academic profession in India. *Minerva.* 7, Spring 1969. p. 345-72.

12 ——. Culture of the Indian intellectuals. *Quest.* (24), January-March 1960. p. 41-53.

13 Shukla, S. College as social system. *New Frontiers in Education.* 3, December 1973. p. 19-32.

14 ——. Social responsibility of the university teacher. *Educational Trends.* 2 (2), 1987. p. 8-13.

15 Trivedi, Anirudh P. Teacher as preacher : Role of academicians in world peace. *University News.* 25 (10), 1987. p. 6-10.

16 Verma, Yoginder Singh. University teacher in the contemporary society. *University News.* 27 (2), 1989. p. 5-7.

D RESEARCH STUDIES

01 Bisht, Uma, A study of interpersonal trust among undergraduate students and teachers of Kumaon Region. Ph.D. Edu., Lucknow University, 1986.

The study was designed to determine the interpersonal trust of undergraduate students and teachers of Kumaon region.

The sample for the study consisted of 720 undergraduate students and 120 teachers drawn from four colleges of Kumaon region. A Likert type scale was constructed by the investigator to measure interpersonal trust of undergraduate students and teachers. The questionnaire consisted of twenty-two negative and twenty-six positive items.

The main findings of the study were: (1) Male interpersonal trust was higher than that of the females. (2) The interpersonal trust of science undergraduate girls was significantly lower than that of the boys. (3) There was no significant difference in the interpersonal trust among arts boys and girls. (4) The interpersonal trust scores of arts students were significantly higher than those of the science students. (5) There was no significant difference in interpersonal trust among affiliated and constituent college students. (6) There was no significant difference in interpersonal trust among affiliated college teachers and constituent college teachers. (7) There was no significant difference in interpersonal trust among science teachers in affiliated and constituent colleges.

02 Chitnis, S. The teacher-role in the college system. Ph.D. Soc., Tata Institute of Social Sciences, 1973.

The objectives of the study were : (i) to identify the influences that the university or the college as a system, within which the teacher functions, had upon the teacher's role; (ii) to develop a profile of college teachers in terms of their attributes, attitudes, performances and outlook on education; and (iii) to develop a college profile in terms of its sponsorship, aims, programmes, management, administration and the composition of student population.

The major assumption of the study was that the difference in the college profile would differentiate the teacher's role. The data regarding the attributes and attitudes of the teachers were collected through intensive interviews, based on interview schedule and an information schedule. The sample of the study was 171 teachers out of 195 full time teachers, belonging to three non-professional colleges, namely, Elphinstone, St. Xavier's and Ruia, affiliated to the Bombay University. Relevant records and documents of the university and the colleges were screened to find out other aspects of the data. Chi-square test was used to find out the significance of inter college differences of teacher attributes, attitudes and activities.

Some of the findings were : (i) Majority of college teachers were male and majority of them were below forty years. (ii) Hindu community formed the biggest group and fiftyseven to fiftynine per cent were Brahmins. In St. Xavier's College, Christians (thirtyfive per cent) were also in good number. (iii) Marathi speaking people formed the largest group of teachers while the Gujarati speaking people followed next. (iv) The teachers in St. Xavier's had an edge over others in the matter of academic qualifications. (v) The interaction between the teachers and students was extremely limited. In the classroom, lecture method was followed and the interaction in the form of questions and answers or discussion was negligible. (vi) Teaching was mostly examination centred at Ruia, while it was not so in Elphinstone. (vii) Most of the teachers had a workload of twelve to twenty-one hours a week. (viii) Variation due to programmes differentiated the college teachers with respect to their qualifications, academic activities and general outlook on education. (ix) The aims and objectives of the college influenced the patterns of teaching. (x) Management influenced the recruitment policies; hence the age, sex, qualifications were determined accordingly. (xi) Student population influenced the self-image of the teachers, interaction between teachers and students, and style or character of teaching. (xiii) College culture influenced the choice of medium of instruction, academic climate and teacher morale.

03 Jaleel, S.S. and Pillay, G.S., Bureaucratism of college teachers and their attitude towards teaching profession. Deptt. of Edu., Madurai Kamaraj University, 1979.

The major objectives of the inquiry were : (i) to analyse the attitude of college teachers towards teaching with respect to age and professional experience. (ii) to analyse the bureaucratism of college teachers with respect to age and professional experience, and (iii) to find the relationship between the attitude of college teachers towards teaching and their bureaucratism.

The tools used were Gordon's Work Environment Preference Schedule (WEPS) consisting of twenty-four items relating to self-subordination, unpersonalisation, rule conformity and traditionalism, and Ahluwalia's Teacher Attitude Inventory. The sample comprised twenty-seven college teachers from twenty-one different colleges. Descriptive statistics and product moment coefficient of correlation were used for data analysis.

The major findings of the inquiry were : (i) Nearly two-thirds of the college teachers in the sample were highly bureaucratic. (ii) The age and experience of college teachers appeared to have definite positive relationship with their attitude towards the teaching profession. As teachers grew in age and experience their attitude towards the teaching profession grew more favourable. (iii) Bureaucratism was negatively correlated with age and experience. (iv) Bureaucratism as an aspect of personality was related to the attitude of college teachers towards the teaching profession. (v) The teachers who had developed sound attitude towards the teaching profession were relatively more traditional and impersonal.

04 Khanna, K., Academic role structure and modernisation – A sociological study of the teachers of the university of Jodhpur, Ph.D. Soc., Jodhpur University, 1980.

The study attempted to understand the various facets of the life of the university teachers in the context of their social background, career pattern, role enactment and role set. It also attempted to explore the extent to which the teachers of the University of Jodhpur were able to internalise the norms of modernity and manifest these norms in their actual behaviour.

The study was empirical in nature. The sample consisted of 395 teachers of the University of Jodhpur. Among these, eighteen were professors, fifty-five were readers and three hundred and twenty-two were lecturers. Of these teachers, three hundred and forty were males and fifty-five were females. Data were collected with the help of an interview schedule. It contained both open and closed questions. The interview schedule was pre-tested on twenty teachers. Chi-square, percentage, and critical ratio were used to analyse the data.

The findings were : (i) A vast majority of the teachers were Hindus and most of the teachers were young. An overwhelming majority of the teachers were from upper and middle castes. (ii) The representation of the rural element in the teaching profession was very low. Most of the teachers were born and brought up in urban environment. (iii) In terms of region, the teachers from Rajasthan were found to be in a majority, specially in lower rank. However, most of the teachers, holding senior positions, were from outside Rajasthan. (iv) The mother tongue of a majority of the teachers was Hindi. In addition to their mother tongue, on an average, they had acquaintance with at least two to three languages. (v) Only a little more than one-fifth of the teachers, most of them from higher ranks, had visited foreign countries. A little less than a half of the teachers possessed a doctoral or post-doctoral degree. (vi) Almost nine out of every ten teachers were married. A majority of them belonged to nuclear families. (vii) The university provided residential quarters to a small number of teachers. Most of the teachers lived in rented houses. (viii) The average monthly income of the University teachers, both from salary and other sources, was Rs. 1259.58 only. (ix) A little less than a half of the respondents decided to become teachers after completing their education. A majority of the teachers of the faculties of science and engineering thought of choosing teaching career after completing education, whereas a majority of the teachers of the general faculties decided this during their student life in the university. (x) A vast majority of the respondents attributed their recruitment to their competence. However, some of the teachers felt that other factors such as political pressure and personal influence also played a role in the recruitment. (xi) Dedication to the profession, academic excellence, integrity and character were found to be the special qualities that the teachers felt the university teachers should possess. (xii) The teachers took little interest in active participation in academic activities. (xiii) Compared to their respective counterparts, the teachers of the professor rank and the teachers of male sex published more research papers and attended and addressed more conferences and seminars. The professors devoted more time for study and research than the readers and the lecturers. The male teachers devoted almost double the time to these activities as compared to the time devoted by the female teachers.

05 Sinha, B.N. A survey of the problems and attitudes of university teachers in Bihar. Ph.D. Psy., Ranchi University, 1969.

This research was conducted to study the problems and attitudes of the university teachers in Bihar as well as to examine how their problems and attitudes were related to some specified factors.

A sample of arts and science teachers, one hundred each, was chosen from all the five universities of Bihar. The selection of teachers was done on a random basis from the total number of teachers working in five universities of Bihar. Most of the teachers were interviewed by the investigator himself on an interview schedule which was prepared on the basis of a pilot research.

The survey indicated that a little less than half (48.5 per cent) of the teachers had selected the profession of their own choice. Almost half of them came to it without liking. Those who had joined the profession on their own had expected to receive opportunities for further studies and research (70.4 per cent) and had thought the teaching profession to be independent, ideal, honest and peaceful (65.8 per cent). One hundred and twenty-seven teachers out of 200 were disillusioned in their expectation for the reasons of (a) absence of comfort and dignity because of lack of academic and other facilities (67 out of 127) and (b) absence of recognition of merit due to favouritism and casteism (54 out of 127). The sources of dissatisfaction among the teachers, identified through the survey, were: (a) lack of interest and encouragement on the part of the authorities (thirtyfour per cent), (b) favouritism in the universities (twentyseven per cent), and (c) lack of respect for university teachers by the society (sixtysix per cent). Seventyfour per cent teachers had not done any research. Fortyseven per cent reported 'lack of time' as an obstacle to research. Teachers had little contact with the students due to large size of the class and lack of permanent rooms. This was found to a great factor responsible for student indiscipline. Teachers were in favour of Hindi at undergraduate level (eightyeight per cent) and English at the post-graduate level (seventyfive per cent), as the medium of instruction. Though only nine per cent of the teachers wanted to teach by dictation method, they believed that a large percentage of their students (fiftyfive per cent) preferred it. Only three per cent of the students wanted to be taught by lecture method. Only fiftyeight per cent of the teachers wanted to remain in the profession even if they had an alternative.

The average income of the university teachers of the sample was Rs. 413 - p.m. Twenty-three per cent considered the financial position as 'bad'. At the time of survey, fortyfive per cent of teachers were under debt ranging from Rs. 500 to Rs. 8000. Thirteen per cent teachers had wives who were graduates. Fiftytwo per cent had wives whose educational level was less than matriculation. Wives of thirty per cent teachers did not take any interest in the education of their children. Thirtythree per cent were undecided about the possibilities of happiness in marrying a known girl friend or an unknown girl selected by parents. Fortysix per cent believed that it made little difference whether one married through friendship or through negotiation. A majority of them supported emancipation of women. Majority expressed unfavourable attitude towards religion. In their overall attitude towards society, the teachers displayed a very deep sense of alienation. Seventy per cent of them believed that honesty and hard work in contemporary Indian society do not pay. Seventyfive per cent felt that it was difficult to find a person who could be taken with confidence. The survey did not find any significant difference betweer conditions. Problems and attitudes of teachers of residential nonresidential universities. The survey also did not bring out difference between the teachers of arts and science faculties. Signifi association was however, found between two variables, namely, age a urban origin. Younger teachers had more modern attitudes than the old teachers. A greater number of the former were less religious, mor favourable of love marriage and emancipation of women. Older teachers experienced greater financial strain but lesser degree of academic difficulties than younger teachers. Teachers with urban origin had more modern attitudes than those of rural origin. They were less religious, less family-oriented, not in favour of arranged marriages, and were more liberal to women than the teachers of rural origin.

06 Verma, B.K., Politics of pressure group in higher education in Bihar: A study of the role of the Federation of University (Service) Teachers' Associations of Bihar, Ph.D. Pol. Sc., Bhagalpur University, 1985.

The study proposed mainly to analyse the role of the Federation of University (Service) Teachers' Associations of Bihar (FUSTAB) as a pressure group in the field of higher education, its contribution and relevance.

An in-depth, descriptive-analytical study was made. Both primary and secondary sources were used. Office bearers of FUSTAB were interviewed through an interview schedule. FUSTAB's role from 1971 till 1980 was studied.

Some of the major findings were: (1). In spite of some limitations the achievements of FUSTAB had been quite considerable, particularly about betterment of service conditions of teachers, revision and implementation of pay scales, promotion of teachers, providing medical benefits, work for temporary medical benefits, work for temporary teachers and demonstrators, etc. (2). The strategy and tactics adopted by FUSTAB to achieve its objectives had been quite reasonable. (3). As a pressure group in higher education in Bihar, FUSTAB's working had a positive approach for its qualitative improvement. (4). Its contribution had been substantial in higher learning. The role FUSTAB had, so far, positively contributed to higher education in Bihar. But its effort as a pressure group towards influencing and giving desired directions to state government's educational policies regarding universities had little effect. (5). Most of its demands relating to autonomy and internal democracy of the universities had very limited impact on government. (6). Existence of factions ion FUSTAB affected its functioning to some extent.

47. TEACHER SERVICE CONDITIONS

A BOOKS

01 Amrik Singh. *Recruitment; Base and procedure: Research study.* New Delhi, National Institute of Educational Planning and Administration, 1984, ivp. (Research studies, NCT II).

02 Calcutta University. *Ordinances relating to the terms and conditions of services of officers and employees of the university.* Calcutta, the Author, 1969. 26p.

03 Gos University. *Ordinance relating to conduct of interview by a selection committee in making recommendation for appointment of professor, reader, lecturer, librarian and principals of colleges and institutions maintained by the university*, 1984.

04 Pylee, M.V. *Grievances and their redressal: Research study.* New Delhi, National Institute of Educational Planning and Administration, 1984. 78p. (Research study, NCT II).

05 Sharma, G.D. *Economic status: Research study.* New Delhi, National Institute of Educational Planning and Administration, 1984. 163p. (Research study, NCT II).

06 Sinha, B.N. *University teachers and their problems.* New Delhi, Puja Publication, 1982, 135p.

07 University Grants Commission. *Central universities retirement benefit rules, 1967.* New Delhi, U.G.C., 1979. 54p.

08 University Grants Commission. *Central universities rules, 1967.* Contain general provident fund-cum-pension-cum-gratuity rules and contributory provident fund-cum-gratuity rule for the central universities and Indian Institute of Science, Bangalore, corrected up to 31st December, 1977. New Delhi, U.G.C. 1978. 89+ivp.

B ARTICLES

01 A fair deal for teachers. Editorial. *Educational India.* 32 (10), 1966. p.355-56.

02 Amrik Singh. The teachers strike and after: Emerging trends and issues. *Economic and Political Weekly*. 23 (29), 1988. p.1484-1486.

03 Arun Kumar. Strike in higher education needed a national incomes policy. *Economic and Political Weekly*. 22 (34), 1987. p.1442-1446.

04 Atma Ram. College teachers: Their problems and solutions. *Education Review*. 73 (7), July 1967. p.162-65.

05 AIU for reconsideration of sen's recommendations. *University News*. 15 (14), 1977. p.379 and 390.

06 Bhardwaj, Krishna. Unrest in higher education: The broader issues. *Economic and Political Weekly*. 22 (42-43), 1987. p.1801-1804.

07 Burdwan University Problems: Resolution passed by the convention of teachers. *Journal of Education*. 8 (3), March-May 1961. p.113-115.

08 College teacher's payscale and U.G.C. recommendations. Editorial. *Education*. 45 (5), 1966. p.1-3.

09 Fair deal for teachers. *Educational India*. 32 (10), April 1966. p.355-356.

10 Flather, Paul. Lecturers angry as strike is called off. *Times Higher Education Supplement*. 18-9-1987. p.9.

11 Gurbir Singh. College teachers strike. *Economic and Political Weekly*. 22 (38), 1987. p.1588.

12 Goel, Suresh. Selection procedures for faculty positions in universities. *University News*. 16 (15), 1 August 1979. p.403-404.

13 Hooja, G.B.K. Teachers strike. *University News*. 25 (35), 1987. p.1 and 14.

14 Parmar, S.L. On frustration of teachers. *New Frontiers in Education*. 1, May 1971. p.18-23.

15 Parthasarthy, R. and Sharieff, I.A. Counselling skills for college teachers. *University News*. 25 (25), 1987. p.7.

16 Puri, R.P. The faculty recruitment-I. *University News*. 14 (2), 1976. p.5-8.

17 ——. Management of committees: Professional file-II. *University News*. 14 (4), 1976. p.5-9.

18 ——. Appointment of the faculty: Professional file-III. *University News*. 14 (5), 1976. p.5-10.

19 Raghavachari, V.P. Pay scales and national policy on education. *Educational India*. 34 (11-12), 1968. p.377-378.

20 Rajeshwar, P. Welfare of school and college teachers in India. *Agra University Journal of research*. July 1968. p.15-28.

aza, Moonis and Fernandes, Marjorie. Functions of teachers in higher education. *Journal of Higher Education.* 13 (1-3), 1987-88. p.3-27.

22 Sarkar, Tanika; Sarkar, Sumit and Datta, Pradip Kumar. Teachers' strike: The DUTA experience. *Economic and Political Weekly.* 22 (42-43), 1987. p.1791.

23 Singh, R.P. Teachers in higher education: A review of their problems and status. *Education Quarterly.* 37 (1), 1985. p.4-11.

24 Sufferings and struggle of West Bengal college teachers. *Journal of Education.* 11 (4), January-December 1964. p.219-224.

25 Susan Ram. Plight of teachers of private colleges. *Economic and Political Weekly.* 23, September 1978. p.1619-1621.

26 Teachers' salaries in colleges. *Progress of Education.* 25 (7), February, 1951. p.213-214.

27 Umakantha, N. Post-graduate teachers in varsities: Appointments and promotions. *University News.* 13 (8), 1975. p.4-9.

28 Uniform norms for work load of college teachers. *The Hindu.* 19-7-89. p.3.

29 University Grants Commission. Approved scheme: New pay scales for college teachers. *Journal of Education.* 7 (1), 1959. p.20-41.

30 Yash Pal. An open letter to fellow academics and friends of academia. *University News.* 25 (40), 1987. p.7-9 and 13.

C COMMITTEES/COMMISSIONS/REPORTS

01 Committee on Governance of Universities and Colleges, 1969. Report. New Delhi, University Grants Commission, 1973. Part II: Teachers: Conditions of service, emoluments, responsibility and other matters relating to university and college teachers. 20p. Chairman: S.N. Sen.

The committee considered the issues relating to the following; the need to attract the best talents; the need to improve the functions and professional competence of teachers, pay scales and their rationale; university teachers, college teacher; evaluation of teachers; principals of colleges; tutors and demonstrators; basis of fixation of pay; scale of pay of library staff and physical instructor; the need for a national wage policy; recruitment of teachers in affiliated colleges; conditions of service; and code of conduct.

02 Committee on Revision of Pay Scales of teachers in Universiti colleges, 1983. Report. New Delhi, University Grants Comm. 1986. Chairman: R.C. Mehrotra.

The University Grants Commission constituted a committee on Dec., 1983 with the following terms of reference:

To examine the present structure of emoluments and conditions o service of university and college teachers, taking into account the total packet of benefits (such as superannuation/medical/housing etc.)

To make recommendations on the above having regard to the necessity of attracting and retaining talented persons in the teaching profession and providing professional advancement opportunities to teachers of universities and colleges.

The committee has made recommendations on emolument and conditions of service of university and college teachers. The committee has also made recommendations on other benefits such as superannuation/medical/housing etc. Committee has given serious consideration to the problems of attracting and retaining talented persons in the teaching profession and providing them with professional/career advancement opportunities. The committee has given considerable thought to the problem of accountability and has made detailed recommendations in this direction as a integral part of service conditions.

48. TEACHING

A BOOKS

01 Andhra Pradesh. Education Department. *Teaching methods in higher education* by M.V. Rajgopal; Hyderabad, State Council of Educational Research and Training, 1975. 26p.

02 Shah, A.B., (ed.) *Modernisation of university teaching: Teaching of natural and social science*. Bombay, Machiketon, 1969. 196p.

03 Sharma, G.D. and Ahmed, Shakti R. *Methodologies of teaching in colleges*. Delhi, NIEPA, 1986. 217p.

04 University Grants Commission. *Hand book of teaching facilities in higher education, 1984-85*. New Delhi, UGC, 1987. 131p.

05 University Grants Commission. *Handbook of teaching facilities in higher education, 1985-86*. New Delhi, UGC, 1988. 214p.

06 University Grants Commission. *UGC guidelines regarding the minimum number of actual teaching days. Programme of examination reform and work load for teachers in university colleges*. New Delhi, UGC, 1989. 9p.

07 Upasain, N.K. *Effective college teaching : Foundations and strategies*. Bombay, S.N.D.T. Women's University, 1980.

B ARTICLES

01 Airan, J.W. Teaching of natural sciences. *Journal of University Education*. 3 (3), 1965. p. 193-206.

02 Balasuriya, C.P. Teaching of political science in Indian universities: Some observations. *Political Science Review*. 90, July-December, 1970. p. 337-46.

03 Bhat, M.N. College teaching. *Progress of Education*. 37 (7), February, 1957. p. 247.

04 Francis, C.M. Teaching methods and evaluation techniques. *New Frontiers in Education*. 7 (4), 1977. p. 1-18.

05 Filella, J. College teaching in India: An academic fun... a personal relationship or coating for examinations. *Journal of Higher Education.* 3 (3), Spring, 1978. p. 321-331.

06 Gabriel, J. and Pillai, J.K. An alternative teaching experience. New Frontiers in Education. 2 (4), 1981. p. 42.

07 Heredia, Rudolf. Some dilemmas in college teaching. *New Frontiers in Education.* 16 (3), 1986. p. 30-33.

08 Jacob, P. Improvement of teaching learning in colleges. *New Frontiers in Education.* 5 (August), 1975. p. 55-63.

09 Joshi, Navin Chandra. In higher education the neglected aspect of good teaching. *Education Quarterly.* January, 1980. p. 8-10.

10 Kappuswamy, G.; Natarajan, R. Lecture method : Strategy for improvement. *Journal of Higher Education.* 14 (1-3), 1988-89. p. 87-99.

11 Krishnamurti, B.H. Medium of instruction in higher education: Regional language vis-a-vis English – the Indian dilemma. *University News.* 26 (28), 1988. p. 1-5.

12 Kuppuswamy, G. and Natarajan, R. Lecture method : Strategy for improvement. *Journal of Higher Education.* 14 (1-3), 1988-89. p. 87-99.

13 Mahajan, G.S. Practicable pattern of the tutorial system. *University News.* 5 (7), 1967. p. 3-4.

14 Mathias, T.A. Change in college teaching. *New Frontiers in Education.* 7 (3), July-September, 1977. p. 63-72.

15 Mehrotra, R.N. No-directive techniques in Indian educational institutions. *Teacher Education.* 4 (4), 1976. p. 32-34.

16 Mohanty, Sunil Behari. Effective teaching in colleges. *University News.* 27 (40), 1989. p. 43-51.

17 Mukherjee, L. Are the standards of teaching in our universities really deteriorating. *Progress of Education.* 28 (3), October, 1953. p. 66-71.

18 Murty, S. Krishna. Is college teaching a profession? *Educational Review.* 76 (9), September, 1970. p. 197-199.

19 Nair, K.R. Ramchandran. Team Teaching. *University News.* 21 (12), 1983. p. 378-379.

20 Natarajan, V. and Malhar, P.K. Conventional methods of teaching in universities. *New Frontiers in Education.* 14 (1), 1984. p. 64-70.

21 Orpen, Christopher. Evaluation and improvement of university teaching. *Journal of Higher Education.* 13 (1-3), 1987-88. p. 47-62.

22 Paul, R.C. Contemporary teaching methods and technologies in higher education. *University News*. 21 (20), 1983. p. 659-661.

23 Prabhu-Ajgaonkar, S.G. Education and teaching in universities. *University News*. 36, October, 1969. p. 8-10.

24 Rajagopal, M.V. Tutorial system in collegiate teaching. *Educational India*. 36, October, 1969. p. 111-15.

25 Ravishankar, S. Modern technology for effective and useful teaching. *University News*. 22 (46), 1984. p. 26-27.

26 Sharma, Motilal. Developing university advisory teaching service. *University News*. 17 (15), 1979. p. 404-406 & 415.

27 Sharma, M.N. Research and teaching in higher education. *University News*. 16 (10), 1978. p. 932.

28 Sharma, Omprakash. On the art of lecturing. *Journal of University Education*. 4 (1), September, 1965. p. 27-30.

29 Sheffield, Edward F. Approaches, mostly elsewhere to the improvement of teaching in higher education. *Improving College and University Teaching*. 21 (1), 1973. p. 5-9.

30 Srivastava, A.P. Improving reading activity in colleges. *University News*. 17 (2), 1979. p. 40-41.

31 Subramaniam, V. Rationalising communication strategy in college classes. *Journal of Higher Education*. 5 (3), Spring, 1980. p. 335-342.

32 Teaching staff in colleges and universities, and standards of teaching. *Educational India*. 16 (9), March, 1950. p. 259-64.

33 Umakantha, N. Post-graduate teachers in varsities : Appointments and Promotions. *University News*. 13 (8), 1975. p. 4-9.

34 Work load of teachers : A study. *University News*. 16 (5), 1978. p. 791 and 815.

35 Yadav, M.S. and Mukhopadhyay, M. College teaching in semester system. *Education Quarterly*. 28 (1), 1976. p. 14-17.

D RESEARCH STUDIES

01 Pattenshetti, M.M. Effectiveness of self-instructional microteaching course in improving college teaching. University of Karnataka, 1986.

The major purpose of the present investigation is to devise self-instructional microteaching course for improving college teaching and to evaluate its effectiveness.

The specific objectives of the study are :

1. to identify basic lecturing skills and the corresponding instructional behaviours;
2. to prepare lecture rating scale;

3. to prepare self-instructional microteaching course (SIMC) materials;
4. to provide in-service training to the college teachers through self-instructional microteaching course;
5. to evaluate the effectiveness of the self-instructional microteaching course materials in improving college teaching;
6. to construct a rating scale to study the reactions of participant lecturers to the SIMC;
7. to study the reactions of participants lecturers to the SIMC.

Scope: (i) The self-instructional microteaching course was confined to the following four basic lecturing skills: (a) Orientation skill, (b) Skill of explaining, (c) Skill of stimulus variation, and (d) Skill of achieving closure. (ii) The self-instructional microteaching course materials was prepared with examples drawn from History, Political Science, and Sociology subjects only. (iii) The study was confined to in-service college lecturers teaching History, Political Science, and Sociology subjects working in degree colleges of Davangere and Harihar (Karnataka State) during the year 1981-82.

Findings are:

1. The self-instructional microteaching course is effective in improving teaching competence of college teachers in terms of the following lecturing skills taken together – (a) orientation skill; (b) skill of explaining; (c) skill of stimulus variations; and, (d) skill of achieving closure.
2. The self-instructional microteaching course is effective in improving the orientation skill of college teachers, studied and practised.
3. The self-instructional microteaching course is effective in improving the skill of explaining of college teachers, studied and practised.
4. The self-instructional microteaching course is effective in improving the skill of stimulus variation of college teachers, studied and practised.
5. The self-instructional microteaching course is effective in improving the skill of achieving closure of college teachers, studied and practised.
6. College teachers sustain teaching competence in terms of the four skills taken together, strengthened by the self-instructional microteaching course even two months after the training.
7. College teachers sustain the orientation skill strengthened by the self-instructional microteaching course even two months after the training.
8. College teachers sustain the skill of explaining strengthened by the self-instructional microteaching course even two months after the training.
9. College teachers sustain the skill of stimulus variation strengthened by the self-instructional microteaching course even two months after the training.
10. College teachers sustain the skill of achieving closure strengthened by the self-instructional microteaching course even two months after the training.
11. Majority of participant lecturers favoured the self-instructional

microteaching course for the improvement of teaching competence.

12. For the further strengthening of the self-instructional microteaching course, all the participant lecturers suggested that video cassette and video tape recorder be used at the time of experiment.

The following are the major by-products of the study: (i) Dharwad Lecture Rating Scale; (ii) Self-instructional microteaching course materials; and (iii) Scale to assess the reactions of participant lecturers to the SIMC.

02 Joshi, D.C., Joshi, S.D., Joshi, S.M., and Patankar, S.D., A study of the classroom climate and methods of teaching adopted by Indian Universities. Maharaja Sayajirao University of Baroda, 1984. (UGC financed).

The objectives of the inquiry were (i) to study classroom climate in the faculties of science, arts and home science of Indian universities, (ii) to study the attitudes of university and college teachers towards teaching methods, class-room process and communication patterns and (iii) to find out the general patterns of teaching adopted by the college university teachers.

In order to collect data, two tools, viz., Attitude towards Classroom Teaching (ACLT) Scale of Likert type and Students' Perception of Classroom Climate (SPCC) questionnaire were constructed by the investigators. The sample of the study consisted of 1094 degree class students of eleven universities of India. The teachers sample included sixteen home science teachers, nineteen science teachers and fifty-five arts teachers of the affiliated colleges and faculties of above universities. The data were analysed on the basis of percentages. The responses on the open ended items in the SPCC questionnaire were analysed qualitatively.

The major findings of the study were : (1) There was sufficient democratic climate in the classrooms in the colleges and faculties under study. Most of the students had cohesive feelings, master image of their teachers and sense of achievement. Most of them accepted the positive authority of their teachers. There was a good amount of mutual trust between the students and the teachers. However, in the case of science faculty a significant number of students expressed less impressive image of classrooms. (2) Majority of the teachers used both teacher-centred and student-centred techniques in their teaching. They were aware of various communication patterns and favoured their practices. The teachers favoured periodic reinforcement through periodic evaluations. They showed their concern for academic and professional growth of students. They had expressed higher degree of commitment to the professional values. (3) Further studies were needed for identifying the underlying factors that resulted in making science classes less democratic.

03 Patankar, S.D., A study of instruction at the post-graduate level in the M.S. University of Baroda, Ph.D. Edu., Maharaja Sayajirao University of Baroda, 1984.

The objectives of the inquiry were (i) to study and compare opinions of students and teachers of post-graduate classes regarding objectives of various teaching techniques like lectures, seminars, tutorials, practicals, field trips and assignments, (ii) to survey the opinions of students and teachers regarding the utilisation of these techniques in the actual instructional process, (iii) to study the perceptions of students and teachers regarding the effective utilisation of these techniques, (iv) to study the constraints faced by students and teachers in the instructional setting, and (v) to collect views of teachers regarding pedagogic training for teachers, evaluation system and utilisation of vacations for academic purposes.

This was a descriptive survey. The tools used were questionnaires and interviews The data were qualitatively analysed. The sample consisted of 465 students and eighty-seven teachers of the first and second year of the Master's degree courses in eight faculties of the university. Out of eighty-seven teachers, seventy-five were respondents to the questionnaire and twelve were interviewed.

The major findings of the study were: (1) About ninety-five per cent students and 100 per cent teachers accepted the knowledge objective of lecture technique whereas 74.62 per cent students and 93.33 per cent teachers accepted that lectures could promote critical thinking. Only 65.80 per cent students and seventy-two per cent teachers felt that lectures could promote attitudinal change. (2) About 91.50 per cent students and 93.30 per cent teachers agreed that seminars could promote critical thinking. About 89.80 per cent students and 93.3 per cent teachers could develop ability to pose arguments. Seminars could develop higher order cognitive skills and certain communication skills according to 82.12 per cent students and 81.33 per cent teachers. (3) About 84.7 per cent students considered tutorials as helping students to overcome certain communication inhibitions; 77.92 per cent students felt that tutorials developed critical and independent thinking. 71.90 per cent students found tutorials suitable to develop rapport with teachers. About eighty-nine per cent teachers considered establishing rapport as the main purpose of tutorials. (4) Regarding practicals, students (87.91 per cent) opined that their value lay in their ability to develop certain mechanical skills of handling apparatus and equipment whereas about eighty-nine per cent teachers considered the main purpose of practicals was to develop ability to test and validate theories. (5) About seventy-five per cent teachers and students felt that the main purpose of field trips was to stimulate interest in the subject and build up group morale. (6) With regard to the assignment method, students considered that the most important outcome was enrichment in participation in group discussions, followed by developing good study habits and critical thinking. Teachers stated that assignments were most apt for developing study habits, secondly for developing critical thinking and lastly for enriching participation in group discussions. (7) Students tended to be more pragmatic in their views than teachers who tended to become more idealistic with regard to all teaching techniques. (8) A large majority of students were satisfied with lectures. Supplying handouts was not a regular practice but providing bibliography seemed to be done more regularly. In faculties of Home Science and Social Work, lectures were more often accompanied by written assignments.

Seventy-six per cent teachers used group discussion technique through the use of relevant bibliography. Teachers felt that students' participation in group discussion was confined to clarifying the issues. (9) A majority of students considered 40-60 students per class as desirable for a lecture and 15-30 for a seminar and a group discussion session. Students preferred a lecture or a seminar session to have a duration of 40-60 minutes. (10) Tutorials were not conducted in many faculties of the university. (11) Fifty-two per cent teachers seemed to be satisfied with facilities to arrange practicals. More students (74.71 per cent) than teachers (58.66 per cent) felt that practicals were linked with the theory. (12) A majority of students and teachers agreed that lectures could be made more effective if they were linked with discussion and question-answer session. (13) Both students and teachers felt the absence of departmental libraries as the biggest constraint for effective learning.
The teachers felt that the university library was not up to data whereas students felt that xeroxing facilities were lacking. Teachers seemed to be using few teaching aids during lectures. The main reason for the non-use of teaching aids was the non-availability of suitable aids. (14) Teachers felt a need for some sort of pedagogic orientation for university teaching. They preferred freedom to arrange tests for internal examinations. Twenty-seven per cent teachers found the traditional pattern of evaluation constraining them from adopting student centred teaching. Thirty-seven per cent teachers felt that students should not be evaluated by those who taught them. (15) Teachers did not favour any programme that encroached upon their vacation time. They felt that during vacation, students could best use library.

The major educational implication of this study is a need for the authorities of the university to plan out a programme of pedagogic orientation of the university teachers so that effective techniques of instruction and evaluation could be confidently used by teachers.

04 Pattanshetti, M.M., Effectiveness of self-instructional microteaching course in improving college teaching, Ph.D. Edu., Karnataka University, 1985.

The objectives of the study were (i) to prepare self-instructional microteaching course (SIMC) materials, (ii) to evaluate the effectiveness of the SIMC materials in improving college teaching, and (iii) to study the reactions of participant lectures to the SIMC. It was hypothesised: (1) SIMC is effective in improving lecturing competence of college teachers in terms of the following lecturing skills taken together — (a) orientation skill, (b) skill of explaining, (c) skill of stimulus variation, and (d) skill of achieving closure and each skill independently, (2) College teachers sustain lecturing competence in terms of the four skills taken together and each skill independently, strengthened by the SIMC even two months after the training.

Ten social science college teachers participated in the experiment. The Dharwad Lecture Rating Scale (DLRS) was prepared using scientific procedure. It consisted of nineteen instructional behaviours (covering four skills) to be rated on a 5-point scale. Its inter-rater reliability was found to be 0.76 (N=20) and convergent validity 0.74 (N=20). Another rating scale was also prepared with a view to collecting reactions of participant lecturers to the SIMC. It had thirty-six statements representing positive and negative reactions to the course as a whole and to the different aspects of the course. Single group pretest and post-test design was used. The SIMC material was prepared mainly in the form of four handbooks — one on each skill. Each participant was provided with four handbooks and an audio-cassette containing model explanations and model micro-lectures. Participants completed activities in forty-five days at the rate of two hours a day. The effectiveness of the course was tested by comparing pre-treatment scores with immediate post-treatment scores and immediate post-treatment scores with delayed post-treatment scores using t-test. Reactions of participants to the SIMC were analysed in terms of percentages.

The findings of the study were: (1) The SIMC was effective in improving lecturing competence of college teachers in terms of the four lecturing skills taken together and each skill independently. (2) College teachers sustained lecturing competence in terms of the four lecturing skills taken together and each skill independently, strengthened by the SIMC even two months after the training. (3) The participant lecturers held favourable attitude towards SIMC.

05 Patted, G.M., Lecture pattern of college teaching — A study in college teaching, Deptt. of Education, Karnataka University, 1984. (UGC financed).

The objectives of the study were (i) to find out the average duration of time out of one hour of lecturing period used by college teachers for the seven major components of lecturing process — informations processing, soliciting, responding, reacting, giving directions, pausing, and providing scope for student participation, (ii) to identify specific behaviours under each major component of lecturing process for which college teachers showed preference in their lectures, and (iii) to compute certain indices with a view to understanding the nature and quality of college teaching in general.

An equivalent category observation system for describing and analysing college teaching in terms of twenty behaviours was developed. The inter-rater reliability of the system was found to be consistently above 0.80. Three hundred forty-eight college teachers teaching humanities and social sciences in forty colleges situated in the jurisdiction of the Karnataka University constituted the sample for the study. Each teacher was observed twice for thirty minutes duration. The observer listened carefully to the teacher or student talk, decided the category/code number that best represented the three second segment of teacher/student behaviour and recorded in the observation sheet. The category-wise frequencies relating to teacher and student classroom verbal behaviour were added up for all the teachers and they constituted raw data for analysis and computation of indices.

The findings of the study were: (1) Out of a lecturing period of one hour's duration, college teachers used fifty-six minutes and three seconds in information processing, thirty seconds in soliciting, twenty-five seconds in responding to student queries, nine seconds in reacting to student answers or ideas, fifty-one seconds in giving directions to students, one minute and eleven seconds in the use of pause and fifty-one seconds for giving scope to student participation. (2) College teachers showed a preference for restricted and factual types of information processing, questioning and responding to student queries, routine type of reacting to student ideas/answers and giving directions to students. (3) They used 'pausing' with and without a purpose, and provided very less scope for student participation. 4. They predominantly exhibited direct teaching behaviour.

College teachers need orientation and training in respect of the lecturing skills of (1) expanded and evaluative information processing, (2) expanded and evaluative questioning, (3) reacting to student ideas at the rationalised level, (4) giving extended directions, and (5) encouraging student participation.

06 Pandian, C., Learning styles and teaching strategies in higher education, Ph.D. Edu., Madras University, 1983.

The study conceptualised a causal relationship between learner characteristic, their cognitive styles, learning styles, and their preference to teaching strategies. The objectives of the study were to identify (i) learning styles of college students and their preferred teaching strategies, and (ii) association between learning styles and predictive variables like type of college, sex, subject of study, personality traits, locus of control and English language ability.

Science and arts students (numbering 1200) from six out of twenty three city colleges, were selected using multiple random sampling technique. The tools used were Grasha Reichamann Student Learning Style Scale to identify learning style, Cattell's 16 Personality Factor Questionnaire, James External/Internal Locus of Control Scale, English Proficiency Test (standardised at the Central Institute of English and Foreign Languages, Hyderabad), Teaching Method Ranking List, and personal data information sheet. The analysis was done by using chi-square test to establish relationship between learning style and other variables, principal component analysis to identify teaching strategies, multiple discriminant function analysis, profile analysis for analysing the profiles of learning style and path analysis to test the validity of the path model.

The major findings were: 1. College students differed in their learning styles and in their preference to teaching strategies. 2. Four teaching strategies evolved for each of the seven learning styles. 3. Except their 'subject of study' all other variables were related to their learning styles. 4. Irrespective of students' learning styles, their preference for teaching methods formed three clusters. 5. The learner characteristics and cognitive styles were found to influence directly and also through learning style, their preferences for teaching strategies.

07 Pillai, J.K., Instruction and evaluation at the post-graduate level in Madurai Kamaraj University — An experiment, Deptt. of Education, Madurai Kamaraj University, 1984 (UGC financed).

The objectives of the study were: (i) to make a study of the teaching methods and evaluation procedures at the post-graduate level in Madurai Kamaraj University Colleges, and (ii) to investigate whether some micro-laboratory sessions could be held to convince the teachers to redefine the purpose of post-graduate education, of the need to vary methods to match their objectives and adopt new teaching — evaluation techniques to enhance student learning.

The experiment was conducted in three phases using 'single-group' design. In the first phase, objectives of higher education were analysed in terms of abilities to be developed among students. Elements of instruction and evaluation were analysed through observation. In the second phase, teachers were introduced to broad principles of self-instructional materials and laboratory sessions. They were encouraged to self-assess, peer rate each other and be evaluated by their students. In the third phase, self-learning modules were developed on skills of teaching and were distributed to teachers for self-study. The sample comprised seventeen teachers from the disciplines of Tamil, English, economics, history and sociology. These teachers had not undergone any pedagogic orientation and had less than five years of teaching experience. The tools consisted of an observation schedule, students impression proforma and self-instructional modules.

The major conclusions drawn from the study were: 1. Dominance of examination made the students concentrate on narrow range of lower objectives (recall). The students resorted to memory because of language difficulty. 2. The project work helped the students in fostering enquiry approach. 3. University teachers realised that at post-graduate level, students needed to be helped to be verbally articulate, to write coherently, to think critically to think independently and work confidently on their own. 4. Teachers realised the need to improve the process of teaching-learning-evaluation. 5. The teachers showed readiness to try out new techniques and methods in spite of various constraints. 6. Teachers opened out their classes to their colleague and researchers for observation, assessment and feedback. 7. Teachers, students and observers agreed upon teaching behaviours which needed improvement. 8. Teachers were convinced about securing students' involvement and participation in the learning process. 9. Teachers introduced improvement in the lecturing, questioning and evaluation techniques. They found that student-centred small group discussions were desirable exercises and students learnt more through interaction with peers.

08 Prasada Rao, Y.F.W., Factors that make a lecture effective at the college level, Ph.D. Edu., Maharaja Sayajirao University of Baroda, 1984.

The objectives of the study were to find out (i) the factors that made a lecture effective in teaching arts, commerce and science subjects according to the teachers and students of arts, commerce and science faculties respectively, (ii) the dimensions of various factors that made a lecture effective in teaching arts, commerce and science subjects according to the teachers and students of arts, commerce and science faculties respectively, and (iii) the factors and dimensions of various factors in common that made lecture effective in teaching arts, commerce and science subjects according to the teachers and students of arts, commerce and science faculties.

The study employed survey method of research. The tools used were (i) the Factor Categorisation Schedule and (ii) the Dimension Categorisation Schedule, both developed by the investigator. The sample consisted of 366 teachers and 442 students of both sexes belonging to the arts, commerce and science faculties, randomly selected from various colleges of Andhra Pradesh. Analysis was based on the percentage of preference for the various factors and dimensions.

The major conclusions were: 1. The most important factors which made a lecture effective in teaching arts, commerce and science subjects, according to the teachers and students, were (i) teachers' preparation, (ii) securing students' attention, (iii) explaining subject matter clearly, and (iv) describing subject matter in detail. 2. The personal factors involved in an effective lecture according to all the teachers and students were (i) ability on the part of the teacher to speak clearly, (ii) using simple language, and (iii) treating all students with equal friendliness. 3. Teachers and students expected an introduction to a lecture to be brief and related to the previous topic. 4. Teachers and students believed that the use of questions was the best means of securing students' attention. 5. Students had a strong desire to express personal ideas and expected a free atmosphere in the classroom. 6. Students of all three faculties and teachers of science faculty believed in creating cooperative and competitive situation in the classroom. 7. Teachers and students of the three faculties did not seem to prefer the teacher presenting handouts at the beginning of the lecture. 8. Students and teachers of arts and commerce faculties did not like the use of teaching aids in the classroom.

The study implies that there should be proper orientation programmes for college teachers on how to make their lecture effective and also on how to augment it by the use of teaching aids, demonstrations, etc.

09 Sachdev, P., A critical study of teaching in higher education in Bombay with special reference to Physics, Ph.D. Edu., Bombay University, 1986.

The major objectives of the study were (i) to identify the teaching styles of teachers as described by themselves and to compare these with the way they were perceived by their students, (ii) to study teaching in higher education in Bombay, (iii) to evaluate teachers on seven criteria as perceived by students, viz., (a) commitment to teaching, (b) commitment to discipline, (c) presentation of content, (d) student directedness, (e) academic climate in the class, (f) classroom procedure, and (g) personal attributes, (iii) to prepare a profile of teachers with each style with a view to describing their relative ratings on the seven subscales, (iv) to describe the college teachers with respect to attitudes to professional training, job satisfaction and research orientation, (v) to describe students on the basis of their self-ratings, performance at college tests and reac. independent study and assignments. The main hypothesis of the stu 1. There is no significant difference in mean ratings on the seven su. by the students of teachers who possess the different styles of teachin

The study employed descriptive research design by using survey. observations. The population considered was the students who optec physics at the B.Sc. level, the lecturers who taught physics at the degr level, the heads of departments of physics and the principals of t. colleges. Pre-pilot test was administered in one college and pilot test was administered in six colleges which were randomly selected and multistage cluster sampling technique was used. In the pilot study questionnaires were administered to fifty-seven teachers of which only thirty-two questionnaires were returned and 284 students belonging to the I, II and III year of the degree level filled in the questionnaire. The final sample included ten colleges which were distributed over the four geographical zones of Greater Bombay, offering physics as one of the options at the degree level. The method of incidental sampling was used for the selection of the final sample. The final sample consisted of 424 students, fifty-six lecturers, nine principals and one vice-principal from ten colleges out of twenty-eight randomly selected in Greater Bombay. The tools used in the final study were as follows which were all prepared by the investigator: (i) the Faculty Questionnaire, (ii) the Student Questionnaire, (iii) the Rating Scale for Curriculum, (iv) the Rating Scale for Instruction, (v) Interview Schedule for heads of department, and (vi) Interview Schedule for principals of colleges. The data were analysed by using descriptive and inferential statistics.

The major findings and conclusions of the study were: 1. Students were fairly one in the way they perceived their teachers' instruction. 2. Many of the girls did not decide about continuing further in an occupation related to physics. 3. Students of third year and of first year rated their curricula significantly higher than students of the second year. 4. Students with a lower level of qualification rated their curricula higher than those with a higher qualification level. 5. Students of different years perceived different methods as being effective in helping them to learn physics. Students from all years perceived the small group methods as being effective for theory work and only second to practical work. 6. Students who joined physics for different reasons varied in their perception of the least effective method of instruction. 7. The majority of all students perceived their difficulties to be teacher centred. 8. Majority of the students felt that their teachers should be evaluated. 9. Majority of the students preferred the discovery-oriented style the most, and the control oriented style the least. Girls preferred a content oriented style over a sympathy oriented one. Reverse was the performance of boys. 10. Students with a higher qualification level preferred the discovery oriented style first. Students with a lower qualification level preferred the content or the sympathy oriented styles first. 11. Teachers perceptions of the evaluation systems were consistent. 12. Male teachers had significantly more publications to their credit than female teachers. 13. Male teachers attitude to the profession was relatively more negative when compared with that of female teachers. 14. The role of the college of general education in the system of higher education was not well-defined.

49. UNIVERSITY GRANTS COMMISSION

A BOOKS

01 Mathai, Samuel. University Grants Commission. *In* Amrik Singh and Philip G. Altbach, eds. *The higher learning in India.* Delhi, Vikas, 1974. p.25-37.

02 Sharma, G.D., *U.G.C. : A critique.* Paper presented at AIU-ICSSR seminar on university and college finances, New Delhi, 10-12 March, 1978.

03 University Grants Commission. *Annual report.* 1953. New Delhi, the Author.

B ARTICLES

01 Amrik Singh. Education Tangle : UGC vs states. The *Hindustan Times.* 14-9-87. p.11.

02 ——. Foundation and role of U.G.C. *Journal of Higher Education.* 7(1-2), 1981.

03 ——. The Indian University Grants Commission. *Higher Education.* (13), 1984. p.517-33.

04 ——. Reconstituted U.G.C. *Economic and Political Weekly.* 5, 15 (August), 1970.

05 Bhatacharyya, Nirmal C. Union University Grants Commission and State University Grants Commission. *Journal of Education.* 4(3 & 4), 1956-57. p.117-122.

06 Dongerkery, S.R. Role of the University Grants Commission in the development of Indian universities. *New Frontiers in Education.* 3(2), 1973.

07 John, V.V. Renaming the U.G.C. : A prelude to adventure. *University News.* 15(18), 1977. p.487 and 489.

08 ——. University Grants Commission. *University News.* 9(9), 1971. p.15-16.

09 Joshi, K.L. U.G.C. and the review committee. *University News.* 15(22), 1977. p.603-605.

10 Mathai, S. University Grants Commission: A retrospect. *Journal of University Education.* 3(3), 1965. p.175-80.

11 Nigam, N.A. University Grants Commission: A preliminary analysis. *Public Affairs.* 15, (July), 1971. p.154-162.

12 Narayan, S. Problems of university education and the activities of the University Grants Commission. *Science and Culture.* 39(1), 1973. p.23-34.

13 Rama Rao, D. University Grants Commission, its objectives and achievements: A review. *Public Affairs.* 15, (January), 1971. p.7-16 and (February) 1971. p.38-47.

14 Satish Chandra. The University Grants Commission and its role. *Journal of Higher Education.* 10(1-2), 1984. p.3-8.

15 Sen, S.N. Role of UGC in university system. *University News.* 14(7), 1976. p.3-5.

16 Sharma, D.C. University Grants Commission. *Indian Education.* 4(2), 1965. p.6-9.

17 Sinha, B.M. U.G.C., objectives and functioning. *Hindustan Times.* 6, April, 1982. p.7 and 22.

18 Varadacharyulu, N.C. Making the UGC more effective. *University News.* 27(3), 1989. p.1-2.

C COMMITTEES/COMMISSIONS/REPORTS

01 Review Committee on the University Grants Commission, 1974. Report. New Delhi, Ministry of Education and Social Welfare, 1977. 165p. Chairman: Dr. V.S. Jha.

The committee was asked to review the functioning of the University Grants Commission, with particular reference to coordination and determination of standards of higher education, and to make recommendations conducive to more effective discharge of its responsibilities. The other topics discussed in detail are those related to grants; research, planning and evaluation; organisation and structure; and constitutional and legal aspects. The recommendations have been presented at the end of the report.

50. WOMEN EDUCATION

A BOOKS

01 Ahmed, K. Women's higher education: Recruitment and relevance. *In* Amrik Singh and P.G. Altbach, eds. *The higher learning in India*. Delhi, Vikas, 1974. p.180-201.

02 National Institute of Educational Planning and Administration. *Women's education in India : The regional dimension.* New Delhi, the Author, 1983. 1v.

03 Sharma, Savitri. *Women students in India: Status and personality.* New Delhi, Concept, 1979. 171p.

B ARTICLES

01 Ahmad, Karuna. Equity and women's higher education. *Journal of Higher Education.* 5(1), 1979. p.33-49.

02 Desai, Neera. Pattern of higher education of women and role of a women's university. *Journal of Higher Education.* 3(1), Mansoon, 1977. p.5-20.

03 Gupta, Promila. Pioneer in women's education. *University News.* 7(3), 1969. p.18-19.

04 Israney, S.M. Institutional barriers to women students in Indian higher education. *University News.* 27(32), 1989. p.10-13.

05 John, Pushpita. New approaches to higher education for women. *Education Quarterly.* 34(4), 1982. p.28-30.

06 Mazumdar, Vina. Higher education of women in India. *Journal of Higher Education.* 1(2), 1975. p.155-165.

07 Murugkar, Lata. Development goals and women's higher education. *Journal of Higher Education.* 8(3), Spring, 1983. p.321-326.

08 Nair, K.R. Ramachandran Women's education and women's colleges. *University News.* 19(6), 1981. p.159-160.

09 Nigam, Reghuvir Sahay. Universities and female education. *Educational India.* 36(7), 1970. p.233-34.

10 Sat Vir Singh. Women's education in India: A statistical

presentation. *Indian Education*. (4), 1975. p.34-38.

11 Shah, Madhuri. Deal is still unfair. *New Frontiers in Education*. 1978. p.57-59.

12 Shastri, Diwakar. Women's universities or universities for wom Mission of women's institutions in higher education. *Univers. News*. 27(23), 1989. p.3-5.

13 Suryakumari, A. Women's studies and the Mother Ter sa Women's University. *University News*. 25(32), 1987. p.7-9.

14 Trivedi, Jyoti H. Future images of women's universities. *University News*. 27(32), 1989. p.5-9.

15 Venkataraman, Leela. Change of attitude towards education of women. *Education Quarterly*. 27(2), 1975. p.13-15.

16 Wasi, Muriel. Case for co-educational colleges vs. women's colleges. *New Frontiers in Education*. 8(1), 1978. p.42-46.

17 Women Education Commission on higher education. *University News*. 15(6), 1977. p.144-145.

C COMMITTEES/COMMISSIONS/REPORTS

01 Rajalakshmi, R.S. Study of the social, economic and political aspects of the growth of higher education of women in the Madras presidency, 1921-1947. Ph.D. Jawaharlal Nehru University, 1985.

The main objective of the study is to examine the growth and development of higher education of women in the Madras Presidency during 1921-1947.

This work is based on a variety of sources-primary and secondary. The primary sources include contemporary newspapers, magazine, periodicals, memoirs, autobiographies, speeches and writing of social reformers, annual reports of public instruction and quinquennial review of the progress of education, census reports, administrative reports, original government orders, reports of committees and commissions and relevant papers in the state and central archieves.

Study revealed that there was a tremendous expansion of higher education of women in Madras Presidency during 1921-1947. In terms of number of institutions the period had witnessed 18 per cent increase. Christian missionaries played an important role in the development of women's education. 57.47 per cent of arts colleges (women) and 80 per cent of professional colleges (women) were started by the missionaries. Government endeavour in this field was very limited, viz., 28.7 per cent of the arts colleges for women and 20 per cent of the professional colleges for women.

The examination of the economic aspects revealed that in the beginning 'high officials' along took interest in imparting higher education to their daughters. Expenditure of higher education of women as a component of expenditure on overall education in the Presidency constituted less that one per cent throughout the period.

The comparative performance of females and males showed that pass percentage of women were higher than man.

An examination of the social aspect revealed that during this period higher education of girls in Brahmin community had shown signs of improvement as the growth rate stood 14.07 per cent. It was also noted that the educated women of the province played a major role in starting Rescue Homes and Training Centre for the less privileged women. It has also been found that the political history of the Madras Presidency lasting impressions were made by the educated women of the province.

D RESEARCH STUDIES

01 Desai, N. *Socio-economic background of married women students of the university and their educational problems*. 1969. (NCERT and SNDT financed).

The study aimed at inquiring into the problems of married women performing their student role. The specific objectives of the investigation were to study: (i) the socio-economic background of the married women students; (ii) the way in which the married women students were performing their two roles; (iii) the issues emerging out of the performance of the two roles; (iv) the nature of adjustment made by the three parties, e.g., the educand, the family and the educational institution; and (v) the awareness of the role tensions of the married women students. It was hypothesised that the role conflict is inherent.

The sample consisted of 372 married women students of SNDT and Bombay Universities. The questionnaire was the main tool to collect data. Opinions from their husbands, mothers-in-law, father-in-law and administrators of educational institutions were gathered through interviewing a sample of thirtyseven members.

The findings of the study revealed that (i) sixtyone per cent respondents had started their higher education after marriage; (ii) the restrictive impact of the marriage was found in the case of sixtyeight per cent students who had to become external students after marriage; (iii) some respondents reported inadequacy of time to pursue studies; (iv) the students predominantly belonged to upper castes and there was total absence of scheduled caste students; (v) the respondents belonged to either middle or upper income groups; (vi) forty per cent of the students belonged to teachers training colleges; (vii) the academic performance of the married women students was good as 56.37 per cent never failed and 29.27 per cent secured more than fifty per cent marks; (viii) economic need was found to be the predominant factor in the case of the respondents whose husbands belonged to managerial or professional positions; (ix) a good number of the students were found to be well-adjusted to their two roles while many of them exhibited a feeling ranging from acute strain to acceptance of challenge; (x) majority of husbands had the consent for their wives' educational pursuits and a few of them were willing to share the family tasks; (xi) the administrators expressed that the married students were irregular in their studies but they were sympathetic towards their problems

(xii) certain basic changes were occurring in Indian social structure with regard to husband-wife relationships; and (xiii) a new image of married woman, who wished to develop her personality, was emerging and there was the growing indifference to the criticisms against married women's role as a student.

02 Chitnis, S., Traditional stereotypes and roles of women – A report on a study on "co-education" and "professional education" as factors influencing the attitudes and outlook of college girls in Bombay City, Tata Institute of Social Sciences, 1975.

The objectives of this study were: (i) to examine the extent to which college women accepted traditional stereotypes and customary roles and to understand the extent of independence available to them; and (ii) to examine the impact of co-education and professional education on these features.

The study was confined to the city of Bombay and it covered 1,005 students residing in the hostels of nine colleges and the university. As many as 250 students were interviewed and approximately twenty-five per cent students of each hostel were interviewed.

The findings were: (i) a large majority of the respondents (more than eighty per cent) agreed fully or at least partially with the notion that women were naturally passive, submissive, patient, tradition-bound and a fairly large number (fiftysix per cent) also believed that women were more disciplined than men; (ii) women were better than men in cooking, household work and child care; (iii) personal freedom was available to some women but it was limited even in the case of college women living on their own in hostels in a metropolitan city; (iv) the majority of the respondents did not favour free mixing between the sexes because the boys expected physical intimacy in course of social interaction; (v) the 'non-coeds', rather than ''co-eds' favoured free mixing between boys and girls; (vi) comparisons between the students of professional degrees and students of general degrees indicated that the former were more liberal than the latter about mixing with the opposite sex; (vii) the findings supported the expectations that the students of professional courses were more independent and were oriented to change than the non-professionals; (viii) lower middle class and upper class homes were more favourably inclined towards education of girls than the middle class homes; (ix) a low level of education of the parents might not function as a constraint to the higher education of girls from lower middle class and upper class homes but it seemed to function as a constraint to higher education of girls of middle class families; (x) orthodoxy of the parents did not seem to be an obstacle to the higher education of girls, but orthodoxy combined with poor education and a middle class economic status appeared to function as a constraint; (xi) girls from the lower class homes did not enjoy approval for mixing with the other sex, girls from middle class families enjoyed the freedom only if their parents were educated and liberal, but the upper class girls seemed to be in a position to mix freely with boys.

03 Mehta, P., Attitude and choices of college girls in Rajasthan. Deptt. of Psy., Udaipur University, 1974, (ICSSR financed).

The major aim of the study was to measure the attitudes and choice of college girls of Rajasthan.

The sample of 375 girls was selected from the local government college and the Home Science Department of Udaipur University. The data were collected through questionnaires.

The outcomes of the study were: (i) almost all the girls came from middle or lower middle class families; (ii) majority of students had selected the subjects of their own choice and the arts students were independent in this decision-making process; (iii) the girls of highly educated mothers showed better perception regarding the relationship with opposite sex; (iv) majority of respondents believed that women in India had been traditionally submissive and passive and there was a need to change with time; (v) a great number of girls of educated mothers showed dissatisfaction with the present status of women; (vi) majority of girls thought that it was difficult for women to break the traditional customs and conventions; (vii) home science students showed highest degree of confidence with regard to chalking out a career and science students had more confidence than the arts students in this respect; (viii) the science and arts girls tended to show greater career orientation than the home science girls and this was influenced by two significant factors, namely, mother's education and coeducation; (ix) girls of more educated mothers were more inclined towards a career than the girls of less educated mothers; (x) a majority of girls of educated mothers, in comparison to the girls of less educated mothers, perceived on difference in decision making on account of sex difference and they felt that girls could take a decision in a similar way as boys could; (xi) eight out of ten students felt that discipline came naturally to the girls and they could handle responsible jobs with competence.

AUTHOR INDEX

REGIONAL INDEX

The Regional Index has been compiled as a guide for the reader, who is interested in locating all the references to a particular State within the bibliography. For each entry the page number, which appears in bold type, is followed by the relevant entry numbers.

UNIVERSITY INDEX

The University Index has been compiled as a guide for the reader, who is interested in locating all the reference to a particular University within the bibliography. For each entry the page number, which appears in bold type, is followed by the relevant entry number.